PEARSON ALWAYS LEARNING

Compiled and edited by
James M. Glasgow, MBA • Julie A. Pirsch, PhD

Competitive Effectiveness Integrating Management and Marketing

Fourth Custom Edition for The Villanova School of Business
School/Course Affiliation: Villanova University

Taken from:
Marketing: Defined, Explained, Applied, Second Edition
by Michael Levens

Marketing: An Introduction, Eleventh Edition
by Gary Armstrong and Philip Kotler

Marketing: Real People, Real Choices, Seventh Edition
by Michael R. Solomon, Greg W. Marshall, and Elnora W. Stuart

Modern Management: Concepts and Skills, Twelfth Edition
by Samuel C. Certo and S. Trevis Certo

Fundamentals of Management: Essential Concepts and Applications, Eighth Edition
by Stephen P. Robbins, David A. DeCenzo, and Mary Coulter

Developing Management Skills, Eighth Edition
by David A. Whetten and Kim S. Cameron

Fundamentals of Management: Essential Concepts and Applications, Sixth Edition
by Stephen P. Robbins, David A. DeCenzo, with contributions from Henry Moon

Social Media Marketing
by Tracy L. Tuten and Michael R. Solomon

Cover Art: Courtesy of Villanova University

Taken from:

Marketing: Defined, Explained, Applied,
Second Edition
by Michael Levens
Copyright © 2012, 2010, by Pearson Education, Inc.
Published by Prentice Hall
Upper Saddle River, NJ 07458

Marketing: An Introduction, Eleventh Edition
by Gary Armstrong and Philip Kotler
Copyright © 2012, 2010 by Pearson Education, Inc.
Published by Prentice Hall

Marketing: Real People, Real Choices,
Seventh Edition
by Michael R. Solomon, Greg W. Marshall,
and Elnora W. Stuart
Copyright © 2012, 2009, 2008, 2006, 2003 by
Pearson Education, Inc.
Published by Prentice Hall

Modern Management: Concepts and Skills,
Twelfth Edition
by Samuel C. Certo and S. Trevis Certo
Copyright © 2012, 2009, 2006, 2003, 2000 by
Pearson Education, Inc.
Published by Prentice Hall

Fundamentals of Management: Essential Concepts and Applications, Eighth Edition
by Stephen P. Robbins, David A. DeCenzo,
and Mary Coulter
Copyright © 2013, 2011, 2008, 2005, 2004 by
Pearson Education, Inc.
Published by Prentice Hall

Developing Management Skills, Eighth Edition
by David A. Whetten and Kim S. Cameron
Copyright © 2011, 2007, 2005, 2002, 1998 by
Pearson Education, Inc.
Published by Prentice Hall

Fundamentals of Management: Essential Concepts and Applications, Sixth Edition
by Stephen P. Robbins, David A. DeCenzo, with
contributions from Henry Moon
Copyright © 2008, 2005, 2004, 1998, 1995 by
Pearson Education, Inc.
Published by Prentice Hall

Social Media Marketing
by Tracy L. Tuten and Michael R. Solomon
Copyright © 2013, by Pearson Education, Inc.
Published by Prentice Hall

Pearson Learning Solutions, 501 Boylston Street, Suite 900, Boston, MA 02116
A Pearson Education Company
www.pearsoned.com

Printed in the United States of America

2 3 4 5 6 7 8 9 10 VOUD 18 17 16 15 14

000200010271870311

RM/MB

ISBN 10: 1-269-72969-1
ISBN 13: 978-1-269-72969-7

Brief Contents

Contents

CHAPTER 2 Developing Teams and Teamwork 18

CHAPTER 3 Team Leadership and Membership Roles 33

CHAPTER 4 Fundamentals of Organizing 41

CHAPTER 16 Branding 208

CHAPTER 17 Communication 221

CHAPTER 18 Approaches to Leadership 233

CHAPTER 22 Personal Selling 328

CHAPTER 23 Direct, Interactive, and Social Media Marketing 339

CHAPTER

1

Decision Process[1]

Decision-making is typically described as choosing among alternatives, but this view is overly simplistic. Why? Decision-making is a process rather than the simple act of choosing among alternatives. Figure 1.1 illustrates the decision-making process as a set of six steps that begins with identifying a problem or opportunity; it moves through selecting an alternative that can achieve the goal and concludes with evaluating the decision's effectiveness.

This process is as applicable to your decision about what you're going to buy, or do this weekend, or how you solve your team's project problems, as it is to the decisions executives make as they shape any organization's future.

Step 1: Define the Decision Problem

The decision-making process begins with the identification of a problem (step 1) or, more specifically, a discrepancy between an existing and a desired state of affairs.[2] Identification of the correct problem or opportunity to be addressed is important. The person who mistakenly solves the wrong problem perfectly is just as likely to perform poorly as the person who fails to identify the right problem and does nothing. Problem identification is neither a simple nor an unimportant part of the decision-making process.[3]

Let's develop an example illustrating this point to use throughout this section. For the sake of simplicity, we'll use an example most of us can relate to: the decision to buy a car.

FIGURE 1.1

The Decision-Making Process

The process is applicable to both individual and group decisions.

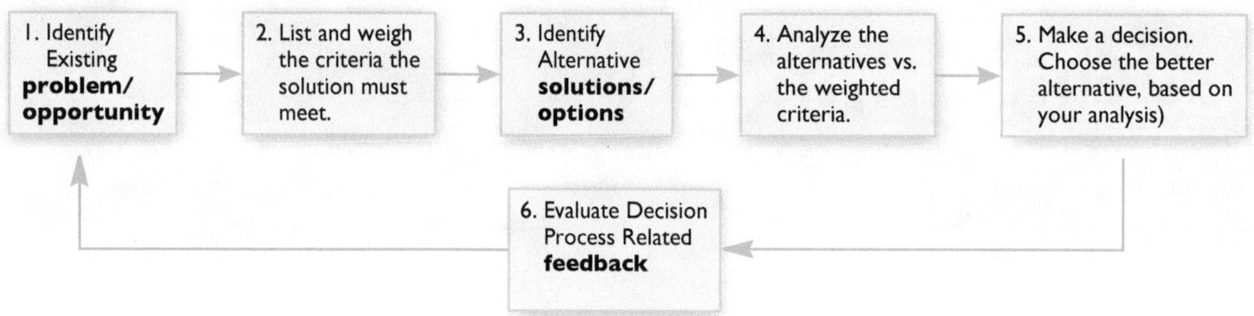

The steps involved in buying a vehicle provide a good example of the decision-making process, which applies to both individual and group decisions. For this young woman, the process starts with a problem: She needs a car to drive to her job. Then she identifies decision criteria (price, color, size, and performance); assigns priorities to the criteria; develops, analyzes, and selects alternatives; and implements the decision. In the last step of the decision-making process she evaluates the effectiveness of her decision.

Liz relies on her car to transport her to and from work. She spent nearly $2,000 on auto repairs over the past few years, and now the car has a blown engine. It is not economical to repair the car. Furthermore, convenient public transportation is not available.

So now we have a problem that results from the disparity between Liz's need to have a car that works and the fact that her current one doesn't. To properly identify the problem Liz needs to compare her current situation to some standard, which can be past performance, previously set goals, or a desired situation. In our car-buying example, the standard is previous performance—a car that runs and would be a reliable source of transportation.

Step 2: Identify Decision Criteria and Their Relative Importance

Once a problem is identified and needs attention, the decision criteria that will be important in solving the problem must be determined.

In our car-buying example, Liz assesses the factors that are relevant in her decision, which might include criteria such as **price, model** (two-door or four-door), size (compact, or intermediate), **manufacturer** (French, Japanese, South Korean, German, American), **safety** (navigation system, side-impact protection), and **repair records.**

FIGURE 1.2

Important Criteria and Weights in Liz's Car-Buying Decision

Criterion	Weight
Price (8,000 <> 10,000)	10
Model 4 door	8
Repairs Required	8
Operating cost (25 mpg minimum)	6
Safety Features	5
Color	2
Manufacturer	1
TOTAL Points	40

These criteria reflect what she thinks is relevant to her decision. Every decision maker has criteria—whether explicitly stated or not—that guide his or her choices. Note that in this step in the decision-making process, it is important to identify the factors that are important to a successful solution.

In decision-making situations, the criteria are normally not all equally important.[4] It's necessary, therefore, to allocate weights to the items listed in step 2 in order to give them their relative priority in the decision (step 3). A simple approach is to give the most important criterion a weight of 10 and then assign weights to the rest against that standard. Thus, in contrast to a criterion that you assigned a weight of 5, the highest-rated factor would be twice as important.

The idea is to identify your preferences, or needs, and assign priorities to the relevant criteria which will influence your decision. You indicate their degree of importance by assigning a weight to each of the criteria. Figure 1.2 lists the criteria and weights that Liz developed for her vehicle replacement decision. Price is the most important criterion in her decision, with performance and handling having lower weights.

Step 3: Identify Alternatives

Now Liz looks at sites on the Internet (Kelly Blue Book, Edmunds, and Consumers' Report) to compare prices, service records, and read reviews by people who actually drive the different models. Based on that research she identified three possible used cars that appeared to meet her criteria: Kia Optima, Honda Civic, and Ford Fusion.

Step 4: Analysis of Alternatives

Liz then visited the Internet and physical sites of different dealers to look at and to test drive the cars. She prepared a spreadsheet to help her compare the criterion and make her decision.

Important Criteria and Weights in Liz's Car-Buying Decision

Criterion	Weight	Honda Civic	Ford Fusion	Kia Optima
Price (8,000 <> 10,000)	10			
Model 4 door	8			
Repairs Required	8			
Operating cost (25 mpg minimum)	6			
Safety Features	5			
Color	2			
Manufacturer	1			
TOTAL				

Liz would fill in the columns for each of the cars based on how well each met her criteria. Hypothetically, if the mpg of the Civic was 30, the Fusion was 25, and the optima was 20, then she would record the following on her grid, based on the comparison or ratio of the car's mpg to her criteria of 25 mpg:

Criteria	Weight	Honda Civic	Ford Fusion	Kia Optima
Operating cost (25 mpg minimum)	6	1.25 × 6 = 7.5	1 × 6 = 6	.8 × 6 = 4.8

And for each of the criteria Liz would assign a number reflecting how well each car met her decision standards. After completing her due diligence the criteria comparison could look like the following:

Criterion	Weight	Honda Civic	Ford Fusion	Kia Optima
Price (8,000 <> 10,000)	10	9	11	10
Model 4 door	8	8	8	8
Safety Features	5	7	5	4
Repairs Required	8	9	8	7
Operating cost (25 mpg minimum)	6	7.5	6	4.8
Color	2	2	2	2
Manufacturer	1	1	1	1
TOTAL Points	40	43.5	41	36.8

Step 5: Select the Alternative and Implement Decision

Based on the information that Liz acquired, she would probably choose the Honda Civic and buy the car. Liz has made an informed, rational decision based on facts and assessed the "value" of each option compared to her criteria. That does not mean she made a perfect decision. It does mean that her decision process was thoughtful and disciplined so that her choice was based on objective, rational criteria, not a subjective whim.

Step 6: Evaluation of Decision Effectiveness

At some reasonable point in time after the decision is implemented assess if your choice is as good as you thought it would be in meeting the goal. If not, revisit the process to determine if all of the steps were addressed, were the criteria relevant and complete, and were the criteria assigned the correct weights?

If the decision is effective, in the long term, Liz can replicate the process the next time she needs to make a significant decision. If the decision turns out to be ineffective, she can review her actions and criteria for each step to possibly identify what went wrong. Then, adjust the process.

By evaluating past decision processes you will improve decision-making skills and simply become more effective and efficient when making all types of decisions.

Decision Rules

When establishing the decision process we need to also identify the rules for choosing which alternative to select. In Liz's case she could have set a minimum of 40 point as the threshold for an acceptable alternative to be selected. Decision rules simply provide a consistent structure to our process of selecting between or among alternatives.

Examples of common decision rules for groups/teams:

- Simple Majority (51%)
- Super Majority (Majority (60%-70%)
- Highest number of votes (could be significantly less than majority so is not encouraged for important decisions that require team support)

Although everyone in an organization makes decisions, decision-making is particularly important to anyone managing a function, department, or organization. As Figure 1.3 shows, it's part of all four managerial functions. In fact, that's why we say that decision-making is the essence of management.

FIGURE 1.3

Decisions Managers May Make

PLANNING

- What are the organization's long-term objectives?
- What strategies will best achieve those objectives?
- What should the organization's short-term objectives be?
- How difficult should individual goals be?

ORGANIZING

- How many employees should I have report directly to me?
- How much centralization should there be in the organization?
- How should jobs be designed?
- When should the organization implement a different structure?

LEADING

- How do I handle employees who appear to be low in motivation?
- What is the most effective leadership style in a given situation?
- How will a specific change affect worker productivity?
- When is the right time to stimulate conflict?

CONTROLLING

- What activities in the organization need to be controlled?
- How should those activities be controlled?
- When is a performance deviation significant?
- What type of management information system should the organization have?

When we make decisions not only do we use our own particular style, we may use "rules of thumb" or **heuristics** to simplify our decision-making process.[5] Rules of thumb can be useful because they help make sense of complex, uncertain, and ambiguous information. Even though we may use rules of thumb, that doesn't mean those rules are reliable. Why? Because they may lead to errors and biases in processing and evaluating information.

Figure 1.4 identifies seven common decision errors and biases that we make. Let's look briefly at each.[6]

- **Anchoring Effect.** When decision makers fixate on initial information as a starting point and then, once set, fail to adequately adjust for subsequent information.
- **Selective Perception.** Decision makers selectively organize and interpret events based on their biased perceptions. Decision maker sees only the information they want to see.
- **Availability Bias.** Occurs when decision makers tend to remember events that are the most recent and vivid in their memory. It distorts their ability to recall events in an objective manner.
- **Confirmation Bias.** Decision makers who seek out information that reaffirms past choices and discounts information that contradicts past judgments.
- **Overconfidence Bias.** When decision makers tend to think they know more than they do or hold unrealistic positive views of themselves and their performance.
- **Escalation of Commitment.** An increased commitment to a previous decision despite evidence that it may have been wrong.
- **Groupthink.** Occurs when groups fail to appraise alternatives or minority views objectively. It jeopardizes the ability of the group to make a quality decision.

FIGURE 1.4

Common Decision-Making Errors and Biases

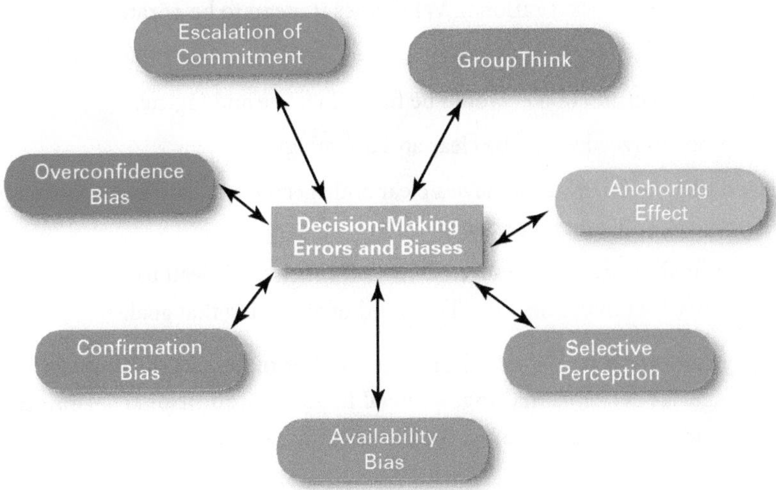

We can avoid the negative effects of these decision errors and biases by being aware of them and then not using them! Beyond that, we also should pay attention to "how" we make decisions and try to identify the heuristics we typically use and critically evaluate how appropriate those are.

Decisions are not always time-consuming or complex. The decision process is often not evident to an outside observer. Every day of the year you make a decision about what to eat for dinner. It's no big deal. You've made the decision thousands of times before. It's a pretty simple, routine decision and can usually be handled quickly. It's the type of decision you almost forget *is* a decision.

Business people make dozens of these routine decisions every day. For example, they determine which employee will work what shift next week, what information should be included in a report, or how to resolve a customer's complaint. Keep in mind that even though a decision seems easy or has been faced by a person a number of times before, it still is a decision.

The Rational Model of Decision-Making

When Hewlett-Packard (HP) acquired Compaq, the company did no research on how customers viewed Compaq products until "months after then-CEO Carly Fiorina publicly announced the deal and privately warned her top management team that she didn't want to hear any dissent pertaining to the acquisition."[7] By the time HP discovered that customers perceived Compaq products as inferior—just the opposite of what customers felt about HP products—it was too late. HP's performance suffered and Fiorina lost her job.

We assume that most decision-making will be **rational.** That is, decision makers will make logical and consistent choices to maximize value.[8] After all, we have all sorts of tools and techniques to help us be rational decision makers. But as the HP example illustrates, people aren't always rational. What does it mean to be a "rational" decision maker?

- A rational decision maker would be fully objective and logical.
- The problem faced would be clear and unambiguous
- The decision maker would have a clear and specific goal and know all possible alternatives and consequences.
- Finally, making decisions rationally would consistently lead to selecting the alternative that maximizes the likelihood of achieving that goal.

These assumptions apply to any decision—personal or managerial. However, for rational, managerial decision-making, we need to add one additional assumption—decisions are made in the best interests of the organization.

What Is Bounded Rationality?

All people, managers included, are expected to act rationally when making decisions. We understand that "effective" decision makers do certain things and exhibit good decision-making behaviors as they identify problems, consider alternatives, gather information, and act decisively but prudently. When they do so, they show others that they're competent and that their decisions are the result of intelligent deliberation.

However, a more realistic approach to describing how most people make decisions is the concept of **bounded rationality,** *which says that we make decisions rationally, but are limited (bounded) by our ability to process information.*[9] Because we can't possibly analyze all information on all alternatives, we tend to **satisfice,** rather than maximize. That is, we accept solutions that are "good enough." We're being rational within the limits (bounds) of our ability to process information. Let's look at an example.

Suppose that you're a finance major and upon graduation you want a job, preferably as a personal financial planner, with a minimum salary of $45,000 and within a hundred miles of your hometown. You accept a job offer as a business credit analyst—not exactly a personal financial planner but still in the finance field—at a bank 50 miles from home at a starting salary of $39,000. If you had done a more comprehensive job search, you would have discovered a job in personal financial planning at a trust company only 25 miles from your hometown and starting at a salary of $43,000.

You weren't a perfectly rational decision maker because you didn't maximize your decision by searching all possible alternatives and then choosing the best. But because the first job offer was satisfactory (or "good enough"), you behaved in a bounded rationality manner by accepting it.

How do we know when to accept a "satisficed" decision and when to push for a "fully rational" decision, which identifies and examines all alternatives? How do we determine how much effort to put into a given decision? Certainly we could fall victim to "Analysis Paralysis" if we tried to identify every potential alternative.

"**Analysis Paralysis**" refers to over-analyzing (or over-thinking) a situation so that a decision or action is severely delayed or never taken, in effect paralyzing the process of deciding. A decision can become over-complicated, with too many detailed options, so that a choice is never made, rather than choose a "reasonable alternative" and change if a major problem arises.

What Types of Decisions and Decision-Making Conditions Do People Face?

Laura Ipsen is a senior vice president and general manager at Smart Grid, a business unit of Cisco Systems, which is working on helping utility companies find ways to build open, interconnected systems. She describes her job as "like having to put together a 1,000-piece puzzle, but with no box top with the picture of what it looks like and with some pieces missing."[10] Decision-making in that type of environment is quite different from decision-making done by a manager of a local Gap outlet store who needs to determine which products to display in which section of the store, or which employees to assign to the tasks of stocking or selling, or customer service.

How Do Problems Differ?

Structured Problems-Programmed Decisions: Some problems are straightforward. The goal of the decision maker is clear, the problem familiar, and information about the problem easily defined and complete. Examples might include a supplier who is late with an important delivery, a customer who wants to return an Internet purchase, an experienced TV news team that has to respond to an expected event, or a university that must help a student who is applying for financial aid. Such situations are called **structured problems.** They align closely with the assumptions underlying perfect rationality.

Unstructured Problems-Non-Programmed Decisions: Many situations faced by decision makers, however, are **unstructured problems.** They are new or unusual. Information about such problems is ambiguous or incomplete. Examples of unstructured problems include the decision to enter a new market segment, to hire an architect, for the first time, to design a new office park, a decision to merge two organizations, or an inexperienced TV news team that has to respond to an unexpected and fast-breaking event. For instance, when Andrew Mason founded his online coupon start-up Groupon, he faced a situation best described as an unstructured problem.[11]

How Do We Make Programmed Decisions?

Just as problems can be divided into two categories, so, too, can decisions. Programmed, or routine, decision-making is the most efficient way to handle structured problems.

An auto mechanic damages a customer's rim while changing a tire. What does the manager do? Because the company probably has a standardized method for handling this type of problem, it is considered a **programmed decision.** For example, the manager may replace the rim at the company's expense. Decisions are programmed to the extent that they are repetitive and routine and to the extent that a specific approach has been worked out for handling them. Because the problem is well structured, the manager does not have to go to the trouble and expense of an involved decision process.

Programmed decision-making is relatively simple and tends to rely heavily on previous solutions. The develop-the-alternatives stage in the decision-making process is either nonexistent or given little attention. Why? Because once the structured problem is defined, its solution is usually self-evident or at least reduced to only a few alternatives that are familiar and that have proved successful in the past. Which toothpaste do you decide to buy? How extensive is that decision process?

In many cases, programmed decision-making becomes decision making by precedent. People simply do what they and others have done previously in the same situation. The damaged rim does not require the manager to identify and weight decision criteria or develop a long list of possible solutions. Rather, the manager falls back on a systematic procedure, rule, or policy.

PROCEDURES A **procedure** is a series of interrelated sequential steps that a manager can use when responding to a well-structured problem. The only real difficulty is identifying the problem. Once the problem is clear, so is the procedure. For instance, a purchasing manager receives a request from computing services for licensing arrangements to install 250 copies of Norton Antivirus Software. The purchasing manager knows that a definite procedure is in place for handling this decision. Has the requisition been properly filled out and approved? If not, he can send the requisition back with a note explaining what is deficient. If the request is complete, the approximate costs are estimated. If the total exceeds $8,500, three bids must be obtained. If the total is $8,500 or less, only one vendor need be identified and the order placed. The decision-making process is merely the execution of a simple series of sequential steps.

RULES A **rule** is an explicit statement that tells a person what he or she ought—or ought not—to do. Rules are used frequently by organizations that confront structured problems because they're simple to follow and ensure consistency. In the preceding example, the $8,500 cutoff rule simplifies the purchasing manager's decision about when to use multiple bids.

POLICIES A third guide for making programmed decisions is a **policy.** It provides guidelines to channel a manager's thinking in a specific direction. The statement that "we promote from within, whenever possible" is an example of a policy. In contrast to a rule, a policy establishes parameters for the decision maker rather than specifically stating what should or should not be done. It's at this point that one's ethical standards will come into play. As an analogy, think of the Ten Commandments as rules and the U.S. Constitution as policy. The latter requires judgment and interpretation; the former do not.

How Do Nonprogrammed Decisions Differ from Programmed Decisions?

When problems are unstructured, decision makers must rely on nonprogrammed decision-making in order to develop unique solutions.

Examples of **nonprogrammed decisions** include deciding whether to acquire another organization, deciding which global markets offer the most potential, or deciding whether to sell off, or perhaps buy, an under-performing division. Such decisions are unique and nonrecurring. When we confront an unstructured problem, no cut-and-dried solution is available. A custom-made, nonprogrammed response is required.

The creation of a new organizational strategy is a nonprogrammed decision. This decision is different from previous organizational decisions because the issue is new; a different set of environmental factors exists, and other conditions have changed. For example, Amazon.com's Jeff Bezos's strategy to "get big fast" helped the company grow tremendously. But this strategy came at a cost of perennial financial losses. To turn a profit, Bezos made decisions regarding "sorting orders, anticipating demand, more efficient shipping, foreign partnerships, and opening a marketplace allowing other sellers to sell their books at Amazon." As a result, for the first time in company history, Amazon became profitable.

How Are Problems, Types of Decisions, and Organizational Level Integrated?

Figure 1.5 describes the relationship among types of problems, types of decisions, and level in the organization. Structured problems are responded to with programmed decision-making. Unstructured problems require nonprogrammed decision-making. Lower-level managers essentially confront familiar and repetitive problems; therefore, they most typically rely on programmed decisions such as standard operating procedures. However, the problems confronting managers are likely to become less structured as they move up the organizational hierarchy. Why? Because lower-level managers handle the routine decisions themselves and pass upward only decisions that

FIGURE 1.5

Types of Problems, Types of Decisions, and Organizational Level

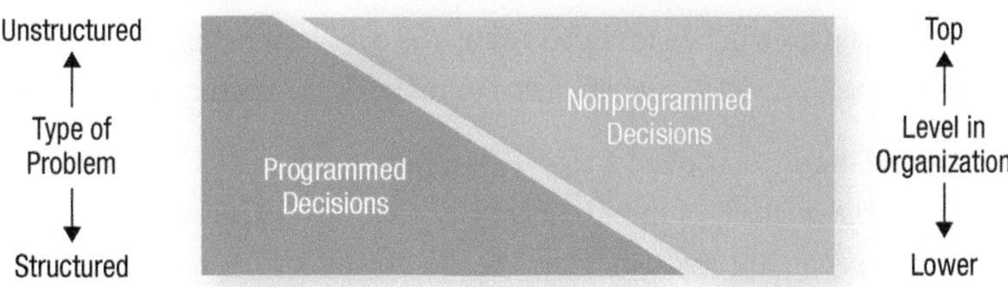

they find unique or difficult. Similarly, managers pass down routine decisions to their employees in order to spend their time on more problematic issues.

Few decisions in the real world are either fully programmed or fully nonprogrammed. Most decisions fall somewhere in between. Few programmed decisions eliminate individual judgment completely. At the other extreme, even the most unusual situation requiring a nonprogrammed decision often can be helped by programmed decision-making procedures. The more nonprogrammed decision-making a person is required to do, the greater the judgment needed. Because sound judgment is an uncommon quality, it costs more to acquire the services of people who possess it.

What Decision-Making Conditions Do We Face?

When making decisions, we may face three different conditions: certainty, risk, and uncertainty. Let's look at the characteristics of each.

The ideal situation for making decisions is one of **certainty,** which is a situation in which a person can make accurate decisions because the outcome of every alternative is known. For example, when a state treasurer decides where to deposit excess state funds, he/she knows exactly the interest rate being offered by each bank and the amount that will be earned on the funds. He/she is certain about the outcomes of each alternative. As you might expect, most decisions aren't like this.

A far more common situation is one of **risk,** conditions in which the decision maker is able to estimate the likelihood of certain outcomes. Under risk, the decider has historical data from past experiences or secondary information that lets them assign probabilities to different alternatives.

What happens if you face a decision where you're not certain about the outcomes and can't even make reasonable probability estimates for all of the options? We call this condition **uncertainty.** Everyone faces decision-making situations of uncertainty. Under these conditions, the choice of alternative is influenced by the limited amount of available information and by the psychological orientation of the decision maker.

How Do Groups Make Decisions?

Many decisions in organizations, especially important decisions that have far-reaching effects on organizational activities and personnel, are typically made in groups. It's a rare organization that doesn't at some time use committees, task forces, review panels, work teams, or similar groups as vehicles for making decisions. Why? In many cases, these groups represent the people who will be most affected by the decisions being made. Because of their expertise, these people are often best qualified to make decisions that affect them.

Studies tell us that managers spend a significant portion of their time in meetings. Undoubtedly, a large portion of that time is involved with defining problems, arriving at solutions to those problems, and determining the means for implementing the solutions. It's possible, in fact, for groups to be assigned any of the six steps in the decision-making process.

What Are the Advantages of Group Decision-Making?

Individual and group decisions have their own set of strengths. Neither is ideal for all situations. Let's begin by reviewing the advantages that group decisions have over individual decisions.

- Group decisions provide more complete information than do individual ones.[12] There is often truth to the saying that two heads are better than one. A group will bring a diversity of experiences and perspectives to the decision process that an individual acting alone cannot.[13]
- Groups also generate more alternatives. Because groups have a greater quantity and diversity of information, they can identify more alternatives than can an individual. Quantity and diversity of information are greatest when group members represent different specialties.
- Furthermore, group decision making increases acceptance of a solution.[14] Many decisions fail after the final choice has been made because people do not accept the solution. However, if the people who will be affected by a certain solution, and who will help implement it, participate in the decision they will be more likely to accept the decision and encourage others to accept it.

A group decision process increases legitimacy. The group decision-making process is consistent with democratic ideals; therefore, decisions made by groups may be perceived as more legitimate than decisions made by a single person or only a few people. The fact that the decision maker(s) has complete power and has not consulted others can create a perception that a decision was made autocratically and arbitrarily.

What Are the Disadvantages of Group Decision-Making?

If groups are so good, how did the phrase "a camel is a racehorse put together by a committee" become so popular? The answer, of course, is that group decisions are not without their drawbacks.

- First, they're *time-consuming.* It takes time to assemble a group. In addition, the interaction that takes place once the group is in place is frequently inefficient. Groups almost always take more time to reach a solution than an individual would take to make the decision alone.
- Groups may also be subject to *minority domination.* Members of a group are rarely perfectly equal.[15] They may differ in rank in the organization, experience, knowledge about the problem, influence on other members, verbal skills, assertiveness, and the like. This imbalance creates the opportunity for one or more members to dominate others in the group. A minority that dominates a group frequently has an undue influence on the final decision.
- Another problem focuses on the *pressures to conform* in groups. For instance, have you ever been in a situation in which several people were sitting around discussing a particular item and you had something to say that ran contrary to the consensus views of the group, but you remained silent? Were you surprised

groupthink
Group members withhold deviant, minority, or unpopular views in order to give the appearance of agreement.

to learn later that others shared your views and also had remained silent? What you experienced is what Irving Janis called **groupthink.**[16] In this form of conformity, group members withhold deviant, minority, or unpopular views in order to give the appearance of agreement. As a result, groupthink undermines critical thinking in the group and eventually harms the quality of the final decision.

Groupthink affects a group's ability to appraise alternatives objectively and may jeopardize the arrival at a quality decision. Because of pressures for conformity, groups often deter individuals from critically appraising unusual, minority, or unpopular views. Consequently, an individual's mental efficiency, reality testing, and moral judgment deteriorate.

How does groupthink occur? The following are examples of situations in which groupthink is evident:

- Group members rationalize any resistance to the assumptions they have made.
- Members apply direct pressures on those who express doubts about any of the group's shared views or who question the validity of arguments favored by the majority.
- Those members who have doubts or hold differing points of view seek to avoid deviating from what appears to be group consensus.
- An illusion of unanimity is pervasive. If someone does not speak, it is assumed that he or she is in full accord.

But groupthink can be minimized if the group is cohesive, fosters open discussion, and has an impartial leader/facilitator who seeks input from all members.[17]

When Are Group Decisions Most Effective?

Whether groups are more effective than individuals depends on the criteria you use for defining effectiveness, such as accuracy, speed, creativity, and acceptance.

- Group decisions tend to be more accurate. On average, groups tend to make better decisions than individuals, although groupthink may occur.[18]
- If decision effectiveness is defined in terms of speed, individuals are superior. With few exceptions, group decision-making consumes more work hours than individual decision-making. In deciding whether to use groups to make a decision primary consideration must be given to assessing whether increases in effectiveness are more than enough to offset the losses in efficiency.
- If creativity is important, groups tend to be more effective than individuals.
- If effectiveness means the degree of acceptance the final solution achieves, the nod again goes to the group.

The effectiveness of group decision making is also influenced by the size of the group—the larger the group, the greater the opportunity for heterogeneous representation. On the other hand, a larger group requires more coordination and more time to allow all members to contribute. This factor means that groups probably should not be too large: A minimum of five to a maximum of about fifteen members is best.

How Can You Improve Group Decision-Making?

Three ways of making group decisions more creative are brainstorming, the nominal group technique, and electronic meetings.

WHAT IS BRAINSTORMING? **Brainstorming** is a relatively simple idea-generating process that specifically encourages any and all alternatives while withholding any criticism of those alternatives.[19] In a typical brainstorming session, a half-dozen to a dozen people sit around a table. Of course, technology is changing where that "table" is.

- The group leader states the problem in a clear manner that is understood by all participants.
- Members then "freewheel" as many suggestions as they can in a given time.
- No criticism is allowed
- All the alternatives are recorded for later discussion and analysis.[20]

Brainstorming is merely a process for generating ideas. The nominal group technique, helps groups generate ideas and to arrive at a preferred solution.[21]

How Does Nominal Technique Work?

Nominal group technique (NGT) is a structured method for group brainstorming that encourages contributions from everyone. When a group meets, it's often the case that people who shout loudest, or those with higher status in the organization, get their ideas heard more than others. So when it comes to gaining consensus on important decisions or priorities, how do you make sure you get true consensus and a fair decision for the group?

The benefit of this technique is that the group discusses all issues before making a decision and each group member has a chance to contribute their ideas. The process begins with each participant proposing his or her ideas. Once all ideas are posted for all to consider, the ideas are ranked on a scale from 1 to 10. Then the better supported ideas can be discussed and developed further.

When to Use Nominal Group Technique

- When some group members are much more vocal than others.
- When some group members think better in silence.
- When there is concern about some members not participating.
- When the group does not easily generate quantities of ideas.
- When all or some group members are new to the team.
- When the issue is controversial or there is heated conflict.

The Nominal Technique in Action

1. Select a group facilitator. (The remaining steps assume you are the group leader.)
2. Present the objectives to all the group participants. Typically the objective is to identify issues or projects that are most important to the group.
3. Encourage group members to ask questions and to seek clarification about the process.
4. Give participants time to consider which issues are the most important.
5. Ask each participant to write down his or her responses on paper.
6. Record the group's responses on a master list, for the group to view.
7. After all responses have been assembled on one list, review the responses as a group, combining similar ideas, and eliminating duplicates.
8. Ask participants to pick their top priorities, say 4 to 6, depending on the number of issues that the group needs to agree on.
9. Ask each participant to rank the issues in order of importance.
10. Collect the group members' rankings and combine to form a joint response; This is the group's consensus on important issues.

EXAMPLE

At its yearly meeting, the Wilmington PTO planning committee must reach agreement on which school projects to support for the coming year. With limited time and money, the committee has to choose just 6 projects.

To establish its priorities, the PTO uses the Nominal Group Technique process. This means that the committee members nominate and rank their top 6 projects. After comparing responses and eliminating any duplicates, the group has 8 projects to consider. The most popular project is assigned a "5"; the least popular a "1." The grid on the next page shows the top 6 projects that the planning committee submitted and each member's ranking of the projects. The last column shows how the group voted on all the projects, with the "Outdoor Awareness" program gathering the most votes.

By using this numbered ranking system, the planning committee's consensus can easily be found by adding up the scores of the 6 PTO members. The project with the highest score is the group's top priority.

PTO Project	Bill	Linda	Anne	Tom	Teresa	Sam	"Score"	Group Priorities
Family support program	5			5	4	1	15	3
Reading program	4	3	4	3	3	4	21	4
Community outreach				4		2	6	1
Spring auction	2	1	2	2	2	2	11	
Outdoor awareness	4	5	2	5	4	2	22	5 (top priority)
Companion animal project	4		3	3	3		13	2

>> END EXAMPLE

Conclusion

Today's world is complex. It revolves around making decisions, often challenging ones, with incomplete or inadequate information, and under time constraints . . . Knowing how to make more thoughtful decisions, the approaches we use can use to make different types of decisions, and the biases that groups and individuals are subject to will produce better decisions, only if we decide to use that information.

CHAPTER

2

Developing Teams and Teamwork

The intent of this chapter is to identify proven techniques and skills that will help you be an effective team member, function more effectively in team settings, and to foster effective team processes. One important reason for this emphasis on teams is that participation in teams is fun for most people. There is something inherently attractive about being engaged in teamwork.

The Advantages of Teams[1]

Whether one is a manager, a subordinate, a student, or a homemaker, it is almost impossible to avoid being a member of a team. Some form of teamwork permeates most people's daily lives. Most of us are members of discussion groups, friendship groups, neighborhood groups, sports teams, or families in which tasks are accomplished and interpersonal interaction occurs. Teams are simply groups of people who are interdependent in the tasks they perform, affect one another's behavior through interaction, and see themselves as a unique entity.

What we discuss in this chapter is applicable to team activity in most kinds of settings. The principles of effective team performance, team leadership, and team participation we address here, are virtually the same across all kinds of teams. Our focus is on helping you develop skills that are relevant in all kinds of team situations, whether as a team leader or a team member.

Developing team skills is important because of the tremendous explosion in the use of teams in work organizations over the last decade. For example, 79 percent of *Fortune* 1000 companies reported that they used self-managing work teams, and

91 percent reported that employee work groups were being utilized (Lawler, 1998; Lawler, Mohrman, & Ledford, 1995).

More than two-thirds of college students participate in an organized team, and almost no one can graduate from a business school anymore without participating in a team project or a group activity. Teams are ubiquitous in both work life and at school. Possessing the ability to lead and manage teams and teamwork is a commonplace requirement in most organizations. In one survey, the most desired skill of new employees was found to be the ability to work in a team (Wellins, Byham, & Wilson, 1991).

In September 2011, a survey of was conducted of 3,100 recent graduates (representing all majors) of **Villanova's School of Business**. The responding students (n=447) had been in the workforce for periods of one to six years at the time of the survey. Ninety percent of the respondents reported that they worked in business teams after graduation. Those students who were in the workforce for one or more years after graduation reported their engagement in business teams to be above 90 percent, while those who had been in the work force for less than one year reported that 64 percent of them were engaged with business teams (Arvanites, Glasgow, 2012). The inference is that regardless of a business student's area of study, the vast majority of them will work in business teams. Therefore, learning how to be a better team member is a valuable skill.

Team Development

Regardless of whether you perform the role of team leader or team member, in order to function effectively in a team it is important that you understand that all teams progress through stages of development. These stages reflect the changing dynamics within the team, the shifting relationships among team members, and the modification of effective leader behaviors. In this section we outline the four major stages that teams pass through from early stages of development—when a team is still struggling to become a coherent entity—to a more mature stage of development when the team has become a highly effective, smoothly functioning unit. The skill we want you to develop is to be able to diagnose the stage of your team's development so that you will know what kinds of behaviors will most effectively enhance your team's performance.

Evidence of predictable patterns of team development has been available since the early part of last century (Dewey, 1933; Freud, 1921). Research shows that teams tend to develop through four separate, sequential stages. These stages were first labeled by Tuckman (1965) as **forming, norming, storming,** and **performing.**

Table 2.1 summarizes the four main stages of team development. In order for teams to be effective and for team members to benefit most from team membership, teams must progress through the first three stages of development to achieve Stage 4. In each separate stage, unique challenges and issues predominate, and it is by successfully diagnosing and managing these issues and challenges that a team matures and becomes more effective. For each of the four stages, we first identify major team member questions, then we identify the behaviors that occur during that stage, finally we address the tasks and actions that help the team effectively transcend that stage of development.

TABLE 2.1
FOUR STAGES OF TEAM DEVELOPMENT

STAGE	EXPLANATION
Forming	The team is faced with the need to become acquainted with its members, its purpose, and its boundaries. Relationships must be formed and trust established. Clarity of direction is needed from team leaders.
Norming	The team is faced with creating cohesion and unity, differentiating roles, identifying expectations for members, and enhancing commitment. Providing supportive feedback and fostering commitment to a vision are needed from team leaders.
Storming	The team is faced with disagreements, counterdependence, and the need to manage conflict. Challenges include violations of team norms and expectations and overcoming groupthink. Focusing on process improvement, recognizing team achievement, and fostering win/win relationships are needed from team leaders.
Performing	The team is faced with the need for continuous improvement, innovation, speed, and capitalizing on core competencies. Sponsoring team members' new ideas, orchestrating their implementation, and fostering extraordinary performance are needed from the team leaders.

The Forming Stage

When team members first come together, they are much like an audience at the outset of a concert. They are not a team but an aggregation of individuals sharing a common setting. Something must happen for them to feel that they are a cohesive unit. When you meet with a group of people for the first time, for example, chances are that you do not feel integrated with the group right away. In such a setting, several questions are probably on your mind.

TEAM QUESTIONS DURING FORMING

- Who are these other people?
- What is expected of me?
- Who is going to lead?
- What is supposed to happen?

The questions uppermost in the minds of participants in a new team have to do with establishing a sense of security and direction, getting oriented, and becoming comfortable with the new situation. Sometimes, new team members can articulate these questions, while at other times they are little more than general feelings of discomfort or disconnectedness. Uncertainty and ambiguity tend to predominate as individuals seek some type of understanding and structure. Because there is no shared history with the team, there is no unity among members. Thus, there are four typical interpersonal relationships that dominate this stage.

TYPICAL BEHAVIORS DURING FORMING

- Silence
- Self-consciousness
- Dependence
- Superficiality

Even though some individuals may enter a team situation with great enthusiasm and anticipation, they are usually hesitant to demonstrate their emotions to others until they begin to feel at ease. Moreover, without knowing the rules and boundaries, it feels risky to speak out or to even ask questions. Seldom are new members willing to actively query a leader when a team first meets together, even though uncertainty prevails. When questions are asked of team members, rarely does someone jump at the chance to give an answer. When answers are given, they are likely to be brief. Little interaction occurs among team members themselves, most communication is targeted at the team leader or person in charge and each individual is generally thinking more of himself or herself than of the team. Interactions tend to be formal and guarded. Congruent behaviors are masked in the interest of self-protection.

Individuals cannot begin to feel like a team until they become familiar with the rules and boundaries of their setting. They don't know whom to trust, who will take initiative, what constitutes normal behavior, or what kinds of interactions are appropriate. They are not yet a real team but only a collection of individuals. Therefore, the task of the team in this stage is focused on developing the team itself. Helping team members become comfortable with one another takes precedence over task accomplishment. A team faces the following kinds of task issues in its first stage of development.

TEAM TASKS DURING FORMING

- Orienting members and getting questions answered
- Establishing trust
- Establishing relationships with the leader(s)
- Establishing roles, clarity of purpose, norms, procedures, and expectations

This stage may be brief, but it is not a time to rely on free and open discussion and consensus decision making to accomplish an outcome. Direction, clarity, and structure are needed instead. The first task is to ensure that all team members know one another and that their questions are answered. Because relatively little participation may occur during this stage, the temptation may be to rush ahead or to short-circuit introductions and instructions. However, teams tend to flounder later if the challenges of this stage are not adequately managed.

The Norming Stage

Once team members have become oriented, achieved clarity about the team's goals, and accepted their place in the team, the main challenge of the team is to create a cohesive unit or a "sense of team." Norms, rules, and expectations are established in the Forming Stage, but an underlying team culture and informal relationships among members must also be developed.

The need to move the team from a group of individuals sharing a common goal to a highly cohesive unit is the motivation that leads the team to a new stage of development—the norming stage. The more team members interact with one another, the more they develop common behaviors and perspectives. They experience a certain amount of pressure to conform to the expectations of other team members, so the team begins to develop a character and culture of its own. We all have experienced strong peer pressure, the clearest example of the dynamics in this stage of team development. A new cohesive team culture affects the amount of work done by the team, its style of communicating, approaches to problem solving, and even team member dress.

The major focus of team members, in other words, shifts from overcoming uncertainty and establishing standards in the forming stage to developing a unified group. Below are typical questions in team members' minds during this stage.

TEAM QUESTIONS DURING NORMING

- What are the true norms and values of the team?
- How can I best get along with everyone else?
- How can I show my support to others?
- How can I fit in?

During the norming stage, team members become contented with team membership and begin to value the team's goals more than their own personal goals. Individual needs are met through the team's accomplishments. Members of the team, rather than the leader or a single person, start to take responsibility for solving problems, confronting and correcting mistakes, and ensuring success. Agreement and a willingness to go along characterize the climate of the team. Individuals experience feelings of loyalty to the team, and the interpersonal relationships that most characterize team members are discussed below.

TYPICAL BEHAVIORS DURING NORMING

- Cooperativeness
- Conformity to norms, standards and expectations
- Heightened interpersonal attraction
- Ignoring disagreements

This norming stage is a time when effective teams encourage relationship-building roles in addition to task completion. Participation by all team members is encouraged, and the team takes responsibility for ensuring the tasks are met during this stage.

TEAM TASKS DURING NORMING

- Maintain unity and cohesion
- Facilitate participation and empowerment
- Show support to team members
- Provide feedback on team and team member performance

The Storming Stage

Playing different roles often causes team members to develop different perspectives and to develop ideas that challenge the leadership and direction of the team. Virtually every effective team goes through stages in which team members question the legitimacy of the team's direction, the leader, the roles of other team members, the opinions or decisions of others, and the task objectives.

Up to now, the team was largely characterized by harmony and consensus. Individual differences were suppressed in order to create a sense of team. However, such a condition will not last forever without team members becoming uncomfortable about losing their individual identity, subjugating their feelings, or stifling differing perspectives. The team's long-term success, therefore, will depend on how well it manages the storming stage of development. Below are typical questions that arise in team members' minds during this stage.

TEAM QUESTIONS DURING STORMING

- How will we handle dissension?
- How can we make decisions amidst disagreement?
- How will we communicate negative information?

An old Middle Eastern proverb states: "All sunshine makes a desert." Similarly, team development implies that some struggles must occur, some discomfort must be experienced, and some obstacles must be overcome for the team to prosper. The team must learn to deal with adversity—especially that produced by its own members. Tendencies toward groupthink must be attacked head-on. **If team members are more interested in keeping peace than in solving problems and accomplishing tasks, the team will never become effective.** No one wants to remain in a team that will not allow for individuality and uniqueness and that wants to maintain harmony more than it wants to accomplish its goals. Consequently, harmony is sometimes sacrificed as the team attacks problems and accomplishes objectives.

Of course, team members do not cease to care about one another, and they remain committed to the team and its success. But they do begin to take sides on issues, to find that they are more compatible with some team members than others, and to align themselves with certain points of view. This leads to the following typical behaviors, discussed below.

TYPICAL BEHAVIORS WHEN STORMING

- Coalitions or cliques being formed
- Competition among team members
- Disagreement with the leader and members
- Challenging others' points of view

This testing of norms and boundaries is sometimes merely an expression of a need for individuality, while in other instances it is a product of strong feelings that the team can be improved. The main task issues to be addressed by the team in this stage include the following tasks.

TEAM TASKS DURING STORMING

- Managing conflict
- Legitimizing productive expressions of individuality
- Turning counter-dependence into interdependence
- Fostering consensus-building processes

Conflict, coalition formation, and counter-dependence create conditions that may lead to the norms and values of the team being questioned. Rather than being stifled or resisted, however, effective teams encourage members to turn those challenges into constructive suggestions for improvement. It is important for team members to feel that they can legitimately express their personal uniqueness and idiosyncrasies, so long as they are not destructive to the overall team.

It is clear from research on teams that when they face difficult or complex problems, teams are more effective if membership is heterogeneous than if all team members act, believe, and see things the same way (Campion, Medsker, & Higgs, 1993; Hackman, 2003). Diversity is productive in fostering creativity, individuality, and solutions to difficult problems (Cox, 1994). It has been said that, "teams make complex problems simple." The trouble is, "teams also make simple problems complex," so diversity and heterogeneity are not universally appropriate. The first two stages of team development, in fact, are purposeful in minimizing diversity and heterogeneity. In this stage, however, maintaining flexibility in the team implies that tolerance for individuality is acceptable and that changes and improvements are promoted.

STORMING REMEDIES In the storming stage of development, tensions arise between forces pushing the team toward cohesion and forces pushing it toward differentiation. At the same time strong bonds of team unity have been fostered, individuals begin differentiating themselves from one another and adopting unique roles in the team. They become complementary. This complementarity of roles may actually foster team cohesion and productivity rather than conflict, however, if the team displays the following BEHAVIORS.

- Reinforces team commitment with recognition of team-level performance
- Maintains visibility of vision and superordinate goals
- Turns students into teachers by having team members teach the group's values and visions to each other

The Performing Stage

The performing stage of development represents highly effective and efficient team functioning. Because the team has worked through the issues embedded in each of the previous stages of development, it is able to work at a high level of performance. The team has overcome issues of skepticism, uncertainty, non-engagement, dependence, and self-centeredness typical of the first, or forming stage of development. It has developed a clear mission, personal commitment to the team, a high degree of loyalty and morale, and has overcome tendencies toward groupthink that can occur in the norming stage. It has fostered differentiation and variety while also overcoming tendencies toward counter dependence, conflict, polarization, and disharmony typical of the storming stage. It now has the potential to develop the attributes of a high-performing team.

These attributes are those that produce the benefits (e.g., productivity improvements, quality achievements, speed, and cost reductions). By and large, teams produce the dramatic successes in organizations reported in the best-practice literature only if they reach the performing stage of development.

The team in the performing stage is not, of course, free of challenges. The common issues that tend to dominate members of high-performing teams are as follows.

TEAM QUESTIONS DURING PERFORMING

- How can we help our members thrive?
- How can we foster continuous improvement and creativity?
- How can we build on our core competencies?
- How can we maintain a high level of energy in the team?

Team members' questions in this stage change from being static to being dynamic. They shift in focus from merely accomplishing objectives to fostering change and improvement and achieving extraordinarily positive performance. Continuous improvement replaces accomplishment as an objective. Up to this point, the team has been trying to manage and resolve issues that lead to three key outcomes: (1) accomplishing tasks or objectives, (2) coordinating and integrating team members' roles, and (3) assuring the personal well-being of all team members. It can now turn its attention to achieving a level of performance above the ordinary. The interpersonal relationships of team members are characterized by the following behaviors.

TYPICAL BEHAVIORS DURING PERFORMING

- High mutual trust
- Unconditional commitment to the team
- Mutual training and development
- Entrepreneurship

Team members in this stage exhibit an enhanced sense of shared responsibility and concern for one another as they carry out their work. Their relationships are not limited merely to accomplishing a task together, but also extend to ensuring that each team member is learning, developing, and flourishing. Coaching and assisting one another is common.

In addition to multifaceted relationships and unconditional commitment to one another, high- performing team members also take responsibility individually for continuously improving the team and its processes. Experimentation, trial-and-error learning, freewheeling discussions of new possibilities, and personal responsibility by everyone for upgrading performance is typical. The team adopts a set of behaviors that help to foster and perpetuate this stage of development.

TEAM TASKS DURING PERFORMING

- Capitalizing on core competence
- Fostering innovation and continuous improvement
- Enhancing flourishing relationships
- Encouraging positive deviance

The most effective teams in this stage develop the capacity to consistently perform beyond the norm. They achieve outcomes that are extraordinary. They extend the boundaries of what is possible.

Teams in this fourth stage of development are not all outstanding, of course, and unfortunately, are quite rare, yet their power and influence on team members is transformational. Once a person experiences this kind of excellence, team performance stuck in the first three stages of development will never be satisfactory again. Some of the prescriptions for achieving these levels of extraordinary success are highlighted in the text as we discuss skills involved in leading teams and in being an effective member of teams.

The Five Bad Habits All Teams Should Avoid

Patrick Lencioni, president of the management consulting firm, The Table Group, has written about the Five Dysfunctions of a Team in his 2002 book of the same name. He developed these principles after coaching thousands of CEOs and Fortune 500 management teams.

The five bad habits are the following:

1. Lack of trust.
2. Aversion to conflict.
3. Absence of commitment.
4. Avoiding team accountability
5. Disregarding the team's objectives.

1. Lack of Trust

According to Lencioni, a lack of trust is the most severe dysfunction a team can exhibit. Without trust, productive work and growth are impossible. Team members spend too much energy protecting themselves rather than focusing on the work and goals of the team.

By contrast, when team members trust each other, they're willing to be open with the group. They trust that no one will attack them so they use their energy for the work at hand.

Team members exhibit a lack of trust when they behave in the following ways:

- Hold grudges.
- Don't ask for help, or don't give constructive feedback.
- Hide mistakes, problems, or weaknesses.
- Avoid spending time with other team members.

HOW TO DEVELOP TRUST It takes time for a team to build trust. This means keeping your word, being honest, and being a good role model. Each team member, leaders included, needs to demonstrate that they are willing to work in a constructive manner.

To assist in gaining trust, teammates need to open up. Tell peers your background, some stories about your achievements, and, most importantly, admit to some imperfection. If you show your own vulnerability, it will help others open up as well.

It might be difficult to convince people you don't know to trust you. Teammates may have experienced broken trust in the past. Or the team might be new, with no past relationships to build on.

Teams can start building trust by getting to know one another. Have everyone sit around a table and, one by one, each person should answer a few personal questions. Your team members could talk about where they grew up, their hobbies, their goals, or the challenges they faced in school.

2. Aversion to Conflict

Conflict can be useful if it happens with a solid sense of trust on both sides. With this type of conflict, people challenge each other's ideas, and even better ideas result. Productive conflict does not mean personal attacks or destructive fighting.

Team members who fear conflict spend too much energy being nice to everyone, and hold back their real opinions. This means that they may fail to share negative information, and thus the team loses opportunities to confront difficult truths.

Signs that your team is avoiding conflict include the following:

- Everyone agrees with everyone else, or avoids tough issues during meetings.
- Team members talk about other people behind their backs.

HOW TO EMBRACE CONFLICT

- Discuss that conflict is good for a team, that it stimulates new ideas and views. Conflict is productive when it's not personal. Encourage all team members to challenge one another's ideas if they disagree, to offer alternatives, to discuss the rationale supporting different ideas or views, and to engage in healthy, spirited debate.
- Engage everyone in meetings by asking questions, not making pronouncements.

3. Absence of Commitment

Teams that lack commitment delay making decisions and thus miss opportunities. People sometimes want to gather more data before making a decision.

Lack of commitment can also relate to an aversion to conflict: without honest debate about a course of action, people may feel that they haven't been heard. When this happens, they may not support a decision that isn't theirs, no matter how feasible it is.

Teams can suffer from a lack of commitment if they display the following behaviors:

- Don't support decisions that the team or organization makes.
- Miss opportunities for success by spending too much time analyzing data and options.
- Repeatedly discuss options but don't take firm action.

HOW TO OVERCOME A LACK OF COMMITMENT When you need to get support for a decision, involve everyone in the process. People won't always agree on the best way to proceed, but at least make sure that each person has a chance to voice an opinion, including the less vocal members of the team.

To encourage commitment, people make their decisions in a reasonable amount of time, even when facts are uncertain. It's also good to recognize the consequences of delayed decisions, and encourage team members to use their initiative to move things forward.

4. Avoiding Team Accountability

People who avoid team accountability don't challenge one another about mistakes that could hurt the entire group. They don't pressure team members to improve, nor do they question others' ideas or actions, or hold each other to high standards. More than this, they don't fill-in or compensate for weaker team members, meaning that the team can miss its goals.

Team members who avoid accountability may behave in the following manner:

- Resent each other because of differing workloads or standards of performance.
- Rely on the team leader to notice mistakes, provide feedback, and manage performance.
- Avoid discussions with colleagues about performance and behaviors.
- Allow the team to fail without making any effort to avert the problem.

HOW TO OVERCOME LACK OF ACCOUNTABILITY Make sure that everyone takes responsibility for their own work and actions. Develop and use a team charter with clear position descriptions so people know their roles and responsibilities within the team, as well as the team's objectives. This makes it clear who is responsible for what, and ensures that people know what's expected of them.

Encourage team members to be constructive with each other, providing feedback on work, behavior, and achievements. This is very important whether people are performing very well, badly, or just not taking responsibility for their work.

5. Disregarding the Team's Objectives

This happens when people work toward objectives that don't actually help team members accomplish their goals. For instance, some team members might want to work on a social issue rather than work to help the team succeed.

Your team may have issues with this sort of dysfunction if members exhibit the following behaviors:

- Focus on their own goals instead of those of the team.
- Fail to pull together to succeed.

HOW TO OVERCOME INATTENTION TO TEAM OBJECTIVES Make sure that team members focus on the real goals of the team. Mission statements and team charters help highlight your team's goals in a clear and obvious way. Once everyone knows what the team is working toward, it's harder for people to ignore the goals.

Team Charters[3]

One tool that effectively guides teams through their developmental stages is the Team Charter. It is a document that defines the purpose of the team and how it will function. Team Charters are "roadmaps" that the team creates to ensure all members are clear on where the team is headed, and how they plan to get there. Team Charter identifies the processes and rules that all members of the team agree to follow.

The precise format of team charters varies from team to team. Much of the value of the charter is derived from the team discussions and decisions regarding their processes and rules they all agree to follow. Two sources for team charter templates and suggestions are the web sites for Mindtools.com and Teamhelper.com

A key to success is to thoughtfully create a team charter and have each person on the team sign it affirming their agreement to its contents. Refer to the contents of the charter periodically to verify that the principles it contains are realistic and implemented. *Much of the value of the Charter comes from the team thinking through and agreeing to the various elements.*

Adapt the following elements to your team's situation.

1. Context
2. Mission and Objectives
3. Composition and Roles
4. Authority and Boundaries
5. Resources and Support
6. Operations
7. Negotiation and Agreement

1. Context

This is the introduction to the charter. It sets out why the team was formed, the problem it's trying to solve, how this problem fits in with the broader objectives of the organization, and the consequences of the problem going unchecked.

- What problem is being addressed?
- What result or delivery is expected?
- Why is this important?

2. Mission and Objectives

This section is at the heart of the Charter. By defining a mission, the team knows what it has to achieve. Without a clear mission, individuals can too easily pursue their own agendas independently of, and sometimes irrespective of, the overarching goal.

The next stage is to take the mission, and turn it into measurable goals and objectives. These are the critical targets and milestones that will keep the team on track.

When writing goals and objectives, consider using the **SMART** framework (SMART usually stands for Specific, Measurable, Attainable, Relevant, and Time-bound). The key here is to make sure each objective can be measured, so that success can be monitored.

3. Composition and Roles

Look to your mission and objectives to determine what roles are needed on the team to make sure its goals can be accomplished. Look at what each person will do to support the team in its mission. While this may seem like overkill at the very beginning of team formation, it will help you

- Match team members to roles.
- Spot gaps in skills and abilities that are necessary for the team to reach its goals.

The best way to go about this is to list each team member and define the roles and responsibilities of each.

- Who will be the team leader?
- Who is the liaison between the team and the other stakeholders?
- Who is responsible for what duties and outcomes?

4. Authority and Empowerment

With the roles defined, you now need to look at what team members can and can't do to achieve the mission:

- How much time should team members allocate to the team mission, and what priority do team activities have relative to other ongoing activities?
- How should team members resolve any conflicts between their other responsibilities, interests and the team mission?
- What can the team do, what can it not do, and what does it need prior approval to do?

5. Resources and Support Available

This section lists the resources available to the team to accomplish its goals. This includes budgeted time, equipment, and people on the team as well as those in supportive roles (coach, librarian, etc.).

6. Operations

This section outlines how the team will operate on a day-to-day basis. This can be as detailed or as minimal as the situation warrants. It may be comprehensive and detailed for a long-duration team, or limited to a few bullet points in a team that is expected to have a short life.

EXAMPLE **TEAM MEETINGS**

- The team will meet every Monday afternoon from 2:00PM to 3:30PM for the duration of the project.
- Each member is expected to present a short status report for the aspect of the project they are working on.
- If a member is unable to attend, a notification must be sent to the team leader and someone else designated to report on the status and communicate further expectations.
- A summary of each meeting will be prepared by Jim and emailed to all members by the morning following the meeting.

>> END EXAMPLE

---

7. Negotiation and Agreement

A good Team Charter emerges naturally through a process of negotiation. The team's CE client establishes the Context and Mission. Objectives, composition, roles, boundaries and resources ideally emerge through negotiations with the client, the team, and other stakeholders.

We're using the word "negotiation" here, although it may not seem to be that way! Three things are key to success here:

- Discussion within the team to ensure that the mission and team charter are credible.
- Negotiation between the supervising faculty and the team to ensure that the mission is achievable, and sufficient resources are deployed.

Ultimately, the team needs to believe that the mission is achievable, and commit to it.

Approval

Last, but not least, comes approval. This is where all members of the team sign off on the Charter and commit to the principles it contains and the roles and responsibilities detailed.

This is an important gesture that communicates full commitment to the mission and objectives. It also helps to create accountability to one another and to the organization.

Key Points

By negotiating a Team Charter at the outset of a project, you set up team projects for success. You ensure that everyone understands why the project needs to be carried out, knows what the objectives and measures of success are and knows who is doing what, with what resources.

More than this, by negotiating the Charter assertively, all parties can shape the project so that it stands a good chance of success. Then can then commit wholeheartedly to the project's success.

Negotiating a Team Charter can also be useful as a way of minimizing the odds of developing a dysfunctional team. Objectives can be confirmed, goals structured and agreed, roles aligned, and resources can be recommitted. Finally, after fair negotiation, people can be asked to commit to the Team Charter, and can be managed appropriately.

Conclusion[4]

All of us are members of multiple teams—at work, at home, and in the community. Teams are becoming increasingly prevalent in the workplace and in the classroom because they have been shown to be powerful tools to improve the performance of individuals and organizations. Consequently, it is important to become proficient in leading and participating in teams.

CHAPTER 3

Team Leadership and Membership Roles[1]

In highly effective teams, members' behavior is interdependent, and personal goals are subservient to the accomplishment of the team goal. A commitment to and desire for team membership is present. Even though individuals may be formally designated as a team, if they act so as to bring exclusive credit to themselves, to accomplish their own objectives instead of the team's objective, or to maintain independence from others, they are not truly a team, regardless of the name of the group. A key challenge, then, is to find ways to create the elements of a highly effective team—interdependence, efficiency, magnetism, shared responsibility, positive energy, mutual encouragement, and trust—when individuals may have had no prior commitment to one another or to a common task.

One important factor in creating effective teams, of course, is the role of the leader(s). Many teams will have multiple formal leaders, so the following applies to all leaders on a team. As pointed out by Hackman (2003), however, it is not the style of the leader that makes a difference. Multiple leadership styles can be effective, and no one style has particular advantages over others. Rather, it is the skills and capabilities of the leader, or the tools and techniques put into practice that account for effective versus ineffective team performance. We highlight two especially critical aspects of team leadership here as they have emerged in the scholarly literature as critical factors in leading almost any kind of team (Edmonson, 1999; Hackman,

1990). The first is developing credibility and influence among team members. The second is establishing a motivating vision and goals for the team.

Developing Credibility

Effective leaders have the respect and commitment of team members. That is, they develop credibility (Kouzes & Posner, 1987). Establishing credibility and the capacity to influence team members are the first key challenges faced by leaders of teams. Except in rare circumstances (e.g., in a crisis), leading a team by command or direct control is much less effective than leading through influence and indirect control (Druskat & Wheeler, 2000; Hackman, 1987). Consequently, we focus on ways that you can be effective by working *with* team members rather than working *on* team members. Giving directions, articulating goals, or trying to motivate team members are all wasted efforts if you have not established credibility and respect.

There are ways to enhance a manager's influence and trust, which are components of credibility. We highlight behaviors you can use to help establish leadership credibility in a team. Team members, of course, will not follow a person whom they don't trust, who is hypocritical or dishonest, or whose motives appear to be for their personal benefit instead of the welfare of the team. Once credibility has been established, then goals for the team can be articulated and the team can move toward high performance.

Team leaders build credibility with their team members by displaying the following attributes:

1. **Trust** means that you consistently do what you say, you behave accordingly to the team's values, and you are believable in what you say.
2. **Be clear and consistent** about what they want to achieve without being dogmatic or stubborn. That helps produce confidence on the part of others. Being wishy-washy or inconsistent in your viewpoints inhibits credibility.
3. **Create positive energy** by being optimistic and complimentary. Most teams do not perform effectively when there is a climate of criticism, cynicism, or negativity. Needlessly criticizing team members, others outside the team or even being critical of the circumstances in which the team finds itself are usually not effective ways to help a team perform well. Teams perform better when positive energy, optimism, compliments, celebrations of success, and recognition of progress dominate the culture.
4. **Manage agreement and disagreement.** When team members tend to disagree with, or hold conflicting views, use two-sided arguments. That is, present both sides of the case and then demonstrate how one point of view is superior to the contrary perspective.
5. **Share information.** Credible team leaders are knowledgeable about the preferences and talents that reside in the team and about the tasks facing the

team. Building credibility means coming to understand the perspectives of team members as well as a sense of their talents and resources. Coming to know your team members well is crucial for successful leadership. One way to do this is to use the principle of "frequent checking." This merely involves asking questions and checking with team members regularly to determine levels of agreement, obstacles, dissatisfactions, needs, and interpersonal or team issues.

6. **Encourage others** means to help others develop courage—to tackle uncertainty, to achieve beyond their current performance, to disrupt the status quo. Encouraging team members not only involves compliments and supportive statements, it also involves coaching and assistance. Effective encouragement, then, is more than cheerleading. It involves giving both positively reinforcing comments and helpful advice or direction.

In summary, being an effective leader of a team requires the ability to develop credibility (trust) among team members and keeping the team focused on goal attainment, while enjoying the journey. These are obviously not the only skills that effective team leaders possess. However, without these two core capabilities it is unlikely that a team leader will be successful.

Team Membership

Most of the time, most of us will not serve as the leader of the teams in which we participate. Whereas you will want to prepare for the leadership roles you will play in the future, the vast majority of the time you will be an active member of a team, working for the common good of the group, rather than the person in charge. You will be valuable to your team because of the contributions you make in non-leadership roles. You can be as effective as a member of a team as you can be as the team's leader in having an affect on its performance.

The main skills associated with effective team membership are the ability to perform task and relationship roles and providing helpful feedback to others. Once again, these skills are not complicated, but they have been found to be highly effective in helping team members foster team success (Parker, 1996).

Advantageous Roles

Work teams face two main challenges: (1) accomplishing the task that has been assigned; and (2) building unity and collaboration among the team members. As a member of a team you can enhance or inhibit those two challenges as much as can the team leader. All of us have experienced teams that just seemed to click, that were able to get results quickly and effectively, and were fun to be in. Those dynamics don't happen by chance but depend on certain key roles played by team members.

A great deal of research has been done on the power of group pressure and the influence of team members on one another. The classic Solomon Asch experiments (1951) were among the first to highlight the influence of team members on one another. The Asch experiments showed, for example, that when other team members verbalized agreement with a statement that was obviously false—say, "The federal government controls the stock market"—the person being observed also tended to verbalize agreement with the obviously false statement. Team members' behavior dramatically influenced the behaviors of other team members. Most teams don't operate on the basis of blatant pressure tactics, of course, but team performance can be markedly enhanced by having team members play certain roles that facilitate task accomplishment as well as group cohesion.

Two main types of roles exist that enhance team performance: **task-facilitating roles** and **relationship-building roles** (Schein, 1976). It is difficult for team members to emphasize both types of roles equally, and most people tend to contribute in one area more than the other. That is, some team members tend to be more task-focused whereas others tend to be more relationship-focused.

There are multiple tools which help to identify the inclination that team members have towards task or relationship roles. Task-facilitating roles are those that help the team accomplish its outcomes or objectives. Relationship-building roles are those that emphasize the interpersonal aspects of the team.

Task-Facilitating Roles

- **Directing.** Identifying ways to proceed or alternatives to pursue and clarifying goals and objectives.
- **Inquiring.** Asking questions, analyzing knowledge gaps, requesting opinions, beliefs, and perspectives.
- **Communicating.** Providing data, offering facts and judgments, and highlighting conclusions.
- **Elaborating.** Building on the ideas expressed by others; providing examples and illustrations.
- **Monitoring.** Checking on progress, developing measures of success and helping to maintain accountability for results.

Performing task-facilitating roles helps the team work more efficiently and effectively in achieving its objectives. Without having at least one team member displaying task-facilitating behaviors, teams tend to take longer to achieve their objectives and have difficulty staying focused. In your role as a team member, you will find it useful to sometimes play the role of task facilitator. Sometimes keeping the team "on task" is the most important thing you can do. These roles are especially important when: progress toward goal accomplishment is slow, when the team is being deflected from its task, when time pressures exist, when the assignment is complex or ambiguous and it is not clear how to proceed, or when no one else is helping the team move toward task accomplishment.

One doesn't have to be a taskmaster to be an effective facilitator of outcomes. In fact, just recognizing that the team is in need of task facilitation is a big part of being an effective team member. In most effective teams, you will find several members performing these task-facilitation roles.

Relationship-Facilitating Roles

In addition to task accomplishment, high-performing teams also require a certain amount of interpersonal cohesion and collaboration. Relationship-building roles are those that emphasize the interpersonal aspects of the team. They focus on assisting team members to feel good about one another, enjoy the team's work, and maintain a tension-free climate. These roles become especially important when disagreement is prevalent, tension is high, or team members are not contributing to the team's performance. The following identifies the most common relationship-building roles:

- **Supporting.** Praising the ideas of others, showing friendliness, and pointing out others' contributions.
- **Harmonizing.** Mediating differences between others, and finding a common ground in disputes and conflicting points of view.
- **Tension relieving.** Using jokes and humor to reduce tension and put others at ease.
- **Confronting.** Challenging unproductive or disruptive behaviors; helping to ensure proper behavior in the team.
- **Developing.** Assisting others to learn, grow, and achieve; orienting and coaching members of the team.

The chemistry of the group just seems to improve when interpersonal aspects are addressed. It becomes easier to work and more enjoyable to be a team member. A certain amount of magnetism and positive energy exist and members tend to take more responsibility, collaborate more readily, and try harder to find consensual outcomes. These are the results that are generated by performing relationship-building roles. They are not designed to deflect attention away from the task, but they assist the team in working more effectively together.

Without both task-facilitating and relationship-building roles, teams struggle to perform effectively. Some members must ensure that the team accomplishes its tasks, while others must ensure that members remain bonded together interpersonally. These are usually not the same individuals, and at certain points in time, different roles may become more dominant than others. The key is to have a balance between task-oriented roles and relationship-building roles displayed in the team. The downfall of many teams is that they become one-dimensional—for example, they emphasize task accomplishment exclusively—and do not give equal attention to both types of roles.

Of course, each role can also have a downside if performed ineffectively or in inappropriate circumstances. For example, *elaborating* may be disruptive if the team is trying to reach a quick decision; *tension relieving* may be annoying if the team is trying to be serious.

However, it is likely that some team members will display other unproductive roles rather than inappropriately utilize task or relationship roles.

Blocking Behaviors

Unproductive behaviors inhibit the team or its members from achieving what they could have achieved, and they destroy morale and cohesion. They are called **blocking behaviors.** We point out a few of them here because, as you analyze the teams to which you belong, you may recognize these blocking behaviors and then will be able to confront them:

- **Dominating.** Excessive talking, interrupting, or cutting others off.
- **Stalling.** Not allowing the group to reach a decision or finalize a task by sidetracking the discussion, being unwilling to agree, repeating old arguments, and so on.
- **Passivity.** Not being willing to engage in the team's task. Staying on the fringe or refusing to interact with other team members. Expecting others to do the team's work.
- **Faultfinding.** Being unwilling to see the merits of others' ideas or criticizing others excessively.
- **Premature decision-making.** Making decisions before problems, goals and criteria are clearly defined, research is completed, information is shared, or alternatives are assessed.
- **Presenting opinions as facts.** Failing to examine the positive and concerning aspects of proposals and labeling personal opinions as truth.

Each of these blocking behaviors has the potential to inhibit a team from efficiently and effectively accomplishing its task by crushing morale, destroying consensus, creating conflict, hampering progress, and making ill-informed decisions. Effective team members recognize when blocking behaviors are displayed, confront and isolate dysfunctional members, and provide feedback to those who are inhibiting effective team performance. Knowing the most effective ways in which that feedback can be delivered is the second key skill of team members.

Roles on Competitive Effectiveness Teams

Teams in Competitive Effectiveness class at Villanova's School of Business are comprised of approximately 10 students and so utilize a simple organizational structure to work on their projects. It is a flat design that may have only two or three levels. For the most part, students tend to work as a large team with a core leadership team that includes one overall project manager. The advantages are efficiency (proper use of resources) and flexibility.

A role is a set of behavioral expectations associated with a position on a team. We are familiar with role designations on sports teams: Center, Guard, Offensive, Defensive, etc. So on CE project teams we have roles for Leader, HR, manager, Research Director, Editor, and so forth.

CE Position Descriptions (Partial Examples)

- **Project Manager**
  - Leads the planning and control activities of the team
  - Ensures team is meeting deadlines
  - Organizes team assignments
  - Team liaison with Professors and Client

- **Management/Marketing Paper Directors**
  - Develops, with the team, the writing, editing, processes for the papers.
  - Ensures attainment of quality expectations for all written assignments.
  - Plans and audits work so it is allocated evenly within the team.
- **Editor(s)**
  - Reviews and edits all written assignments (marketing or management).
  - Provides feedback and direction on issues of grammar, organization, sentence structure, continuity, etc.
- **HR Director**
  - Conducts multiple (3–4) Team Climate Surveys to assess team perceptions of team effectiveness/efficiency, role quality, leadership, processes, etc.
  - Analyzes results and reports findings to the team.
  - Discusses, with team, methods for improving the CE experience.
- **Research Director(s)**
  - Communicates market research requirements and processes to the team.
  - Ensures all citations follow the approved format and are included in the bibliography of papers and presentation.
  - Liaisons with librarian and marketing professor regarding market research.

The selection and staffing process of a team is effective when the following five conditions are met:

1. There are enough people to do the job, *but not so many that people get bogged down.*
2. All members understand and support the mission and objectives of the team.
3. Members thoughtfully determine which functions are needed on the team to make sure its goals can be accomplished.
4. Responsibilities of each function and the criteria the position holder must meet are clearly defined.
5. Members evaluate the skills, interests, and experiences of each person and determine how each person can best support the team in its mission.

Pitfalls that exist in staffing a team are noted below:

First: Overlapping Responsibility, or **Role Ambiguity,** refers to a situation in which more than one individual is responsible for the same activity. Generally speaking, only one person should be responsible for completing any one activity. When two or more employees are unclear about who should do a job because of overlapping responsibility, it usually leads to conflict and poor working relationships.[2] Often the job does not get done because each employee assumes the other will do it.

Second: Role Conflict, or when an individual is responsible for conflicting outcomes or competing demands of responsibilities needs to be avoided. Envision the individual on a team who is responsible for enhancing relationships and fostering a cohesive environment, and is also responsible for team discipline and exacting fines from those who fall short of their goals.

Third: Role Overload occurs when too much is expected from an individual and they become overwhelmed. Sometimes that occurs when a person is selected for a role for which they do not have the talent or drive to perform. Think of the person who has poor self-discipline or lacks conscientiousness who is selected the leader of a team or any other managerial role. It can also occur when individuals "step up" to cover for those who are not doing their share of the work. All of the stress, lack of sleep, etc. now falls on the shoulders of the person who "stepped up" and is attempting to do too much. In both situations the attainment of objectives is probably sub-par.

Fourth: Role Underload occurs when an individual's responsibilities are too minimal, unchallenging, and too little is expected of them. They are simply underutilized.

Fifth: A **Responsibility Gap** exists when certain tasks are not included in the responsibility area of any individual organization member. In this situation, nobody within the organization is obligated to perform certain necessary activities.[3]

Organizations should avoid creating job activities for accomplishing tasks that do not enhance goal attainment. Organization members should be obligated to perform those activities that lead to goal attainment.

Though teams initially develop structures and role descriptions that are perceived to be effective and efficient it is prudent to periodically assess the responsibilities so that the roles do not suffer from any of the noted pitfalls.

Conclusion[4]

In this chapter we highlighted additional behaviors that can be used to help establish leadership credibility in a team. Team members, of course, will not follow a person whom they don't trust, who is hypocritical or dishonest, or whose motives appear to be personal aggrandizement instead of the welfare of the team. Once credibility has been established, then goals for the team can be articulated and the team can move toward high performance.

CHAPTER 4

Fundamentals of Organizing[1]

Organizing is the process of establishing orderly uses for resources within the organization or team.

Orderly use of team resources emphasizes the attainment of organizational objectives, assists in making objectives clear and in clarifying which resources will be used to attain them.[2] A primary focus of organizing is determining what tasks individual team members will do and how their individual efforts should best be coordinated to attain the stated objectives.[3]

Below are guidelines for developing effective organizations (Figure 4.1).

The Importance of Organizing

The organizing function is extremely important because it is the primary mechanism organizations use to achieve plans.[4] Organizing creates and maintains relationships between all organizational resources by indicating which resources are to be used for specified activities and when, where, and how they are to be used. A thorough organizing effort helps avoid or minimize costly weaknesses, such as excessive responsibilities (Role Overload, duplication of effort (Role Ambiguity), and idle organizational resources (Role Underload).

EXAMPLE **THE ORGANIZING PROCESS**

The management of a restaurant can serve as an illustration of how the six steps of the organizing process works.

The **first step** the restaurant manager would take to initiate the organizing process would be to reflect on the restaurant's plans and objectives. Planning involves

FIGURE 4.1

The Six Main Steps of the Organizing Process

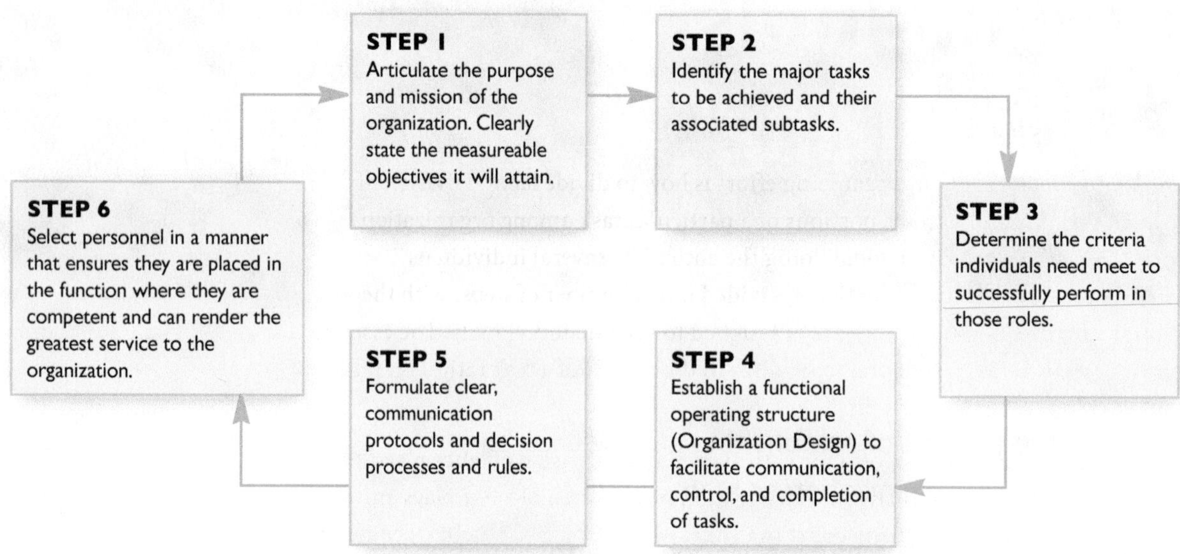

determining how the restaurant will attain its objectives, and organizing involves determining how the restaurant's resources will be used to achieve the plans. The restaurant manager must start to organize by understanding the plan and objectives.

The **second step** of the organizing process focuses on tasks to be performed within the organization. Designate the major tasks or jobs to be done within the restaurant. Two such tasks are serving customers and cooking food. Then the tasks must then be divided into subtasks. For example, the restaurateur might note that serving customers includes the subtasks of taking orders, cooking food, and clearing tables.

The **third step** is to identify the types of skills and talents that will enable the achievement of the tasks and subtasks. What are the functional skills and personal characteristics that cooks, servers, table clearers must possess to be successful? Specific job descriptions are written, which detail the essential responsibilities of each position.

The **fourth step** is determining the functional structure. How many people are needed to take orders, cook, and clear the tables? What will be the details of the relationships among these individuals? The size of tables and how they are to be set are other factors to be considered.

In the **fifth step** the communication and decision processes are identified. How, when, why will the different functions communicate, who "reports to whom", how will decisions be made and how will disputes be resolved?

In the **sixth step,** after all of the organizing details are complete, the staff is hired based on the skills criteria established during step 3. Now, the restaurant is ready for business.

Later, evaluating the results of the implemented organizing strategy, the manager of the restaurant gathers feedback on how well the organizational design is working. This feedback should furnish information that can be used to improve the existing organization. For example, the manager finds that a particular type of table is not large enough and that two cooks are needed, not one if the restaurant is to attain its goals.

>> END EXAMPLE

Classical Organizing Theory

The following sections discuss two components of classical organizing theory: division of labor, and structure.

Division of Labor

A primary consideration of any organizing effort is how to divide labor. Division of labor is the assignment of various portions of a particular task among organizational members.[5] Rather than one individual doing the entire job, several individuals perform different parts of it. Production is divided into a number of steps, with the responsibility for completing various steps assigned to specific individuals. The essence of division of labor is that individuals specialize in doing part of a task rather than the entire task.[6]

Although most associate division of labor with automobiles, division of labor plays an important role in a variety of businesses. For example, division of labor plays an important role in the manufacturing of art in China. At some manufacturing facilities, several artists help to paint copies of the same picture. When individuals finish painting their particular sections, they pass the painting on to other members to finish their own sections.[7] This approach allows Chinese galleries such as the JiYiYuang Gallery to sell paintings for lower prices.

It is clear, then, that the division of labor influences a variety of organizations. The following sections discuss the advantages and disadvantages of division of labor, the relationship between division of labor and coordination.

ADVANTAGES AND DISADVANTAGES OF DIVISION OF LABOR Several explanations have been offered for the usefulness of division of labor.

- First, when workers specialize in a particular task, their skill at performing that task tends to increase.
- Second, workers who have one job and one place in which to do it do not lose valuable time changing tools or locations.
- Third, when workers concentrate on performing only one job, they naturally try to make the job easier and more efficient.
- Lastly, division of labor creates a situation in which workers need only to know how to perform their part of the work task rather than the entire process. The task therefore, does not become too burdensome.

Arguments have also been presented against the use of division of labor.[8] Essentially, these arguments contend that division of labor focuses solely on efficiency and economic benefit and overlooks the human variable in organizations. Work that is extremely specialized tends to be boring and therefore will eventually cause production rates to go down as workers become resentful of being treated like machines. Clearly, there needs to be a reasonable balance between specialization and human motivation.

DIVISION OF LABOR AND COORDINATION In a division-of-labor situation, the importance of effective coordination of the different individuals doing portions of the task is obvious. Mooney has defined **coordination** as "the orderly arrangement of group effort to provide unity of action in the pursuit of a common purpose." In essence, coordination is a means for achieving any and all organizational objectives.[9] It involves encouraging the completion of individual portions of a task in a synchronized order that is appropriate for the overall task.

Groups cannot maintain their productivity without coordination.[10] Part of the synchronized order of assembling an automobile, for example, is that seats are installed only after the floor has been installed; adhering to this order of installation is an example of coordination.

FOLLETT'S GUIDELINES ON COORDINATION Mary Parker Follett provided valuable advice on how managers can establish and maintain coordination within the organization.

- First, Follett said that coordination can be attained with the least difficulty through direct horizontal relationships and personal communications. In other words, when a coordination problem arises, peer discussion may be the best way to resolve it.
- Second, Follett suggested that coordination be a discussion topic throughout the planning process. In essence, organization should plan how the various factors of the team will work together to coordinate their efforts.
- Third, maintaining coordination is a continuing process and should be treated as such. We cannot assume that because coordination existed in a team yesterday that it will be coordinated tomorrow. The development and implementation of effective process controls is important to ensure the plan is implemented as it was envisioned.

Structure

In any organizing effort, managers must choose an appropriate structure. Structure refers to the designated relationships among resources of the management system. Its purpose is to facilitate the use of each resource, individually and collectively, as the organization attempts to attain its objectives.[11]

The two basic types of structure within organizations are formal and informal structures.

- **Formal structure** is defined as the defined relationships among organizational resources; a formal structure is represented primarily by the roles and titles noted in the organization chart.
- **Informal structure** is defined as the patterns of relationships that develop because of the informal activities of organization members. It evolves naturally and tends to be molded by individual norms and values and social relationships. Essentially, an organization's informal structure is the system or network of interpersonal relationships that exists within, but is not usually identical to, the organization's formal structure.[12]

Organizational structure is represented primarily by means of a graphic illustration called an **organization chart.** Traditionally, an organization chart is constructed in pyramid form, with individuals toward the top of the pyramid having more authority and responsibility than those toward the bottom.[13] The relative positioning of individuals within boxes on the chart indicates broad working relationships, and lines between boxes designate formal lines of communication between individuals.

In addition to specifying formal relationships within the firm, an organization chart can also communicate to outsiders the complexity of the organization. Structure involves two primary dimensions: the vertical dimension and the horizontal dimension. The following sections discuss each dimension in detail.[14]

VERTICAL DIMENSION Refers to the extent to which an organization uses vertical levels to separate job responsibilities. Vertical dimensioning is directly related to the concept of the chain of command. Every organization is built on the premise that the individual at the top possesses the most authority and that other individuals' authority is scaled downward according to their relative position on the organization chart. The lower a person's position on the organization chart, then, the less authority that person possesses.[15]

HORIZONTAL DIMENSION (Span of Control) It is important to consider the influence of span of management—the number of individuals a manager supervises. The more individuals a manager directly supervises, the greater the span of management. The span of management has a significant effect on how well managers carry out their responsibilities.

The central concern of span of management control is to determine how many individuals a manager can supervise effectively.[16] To use the organization's human resources effectively, managers should directly supervise as many individuals as they can best guide toward achievement of the organization's goals. If they are supervising too few people, they are wasting a portion of their productive capacity. If they are supervising too many, they are losing part of their effectiveness.

DESIGNING SPAN OF MANAGEMENT CONTROL As reported by Harold Koontz, several important situational factors influence the appropriateness of the size of an individual's span of management:[17]

- **Similarity of functions**—the degree to which activities performed by supervised individuals are similar or dissimilar. As the similarity of subordinates' activities increases, the span of management appropriate for the situation widens. The converse is also generally true.
- **Geographic continuity**—the degree to which subordinates are physically separated. In general, the closer subordinates are physically, the more of them the manager can supervise effectively.

These employees at a Bangalore, India call center all perform essentially the same customer-service function, which means of the span of management for their department's supervisor can be relatively wide.

TABLE 4.1
MAJOR FACTORS THAT INFLUENCE THE SPAN OF MANAGEMENT

FACTOR	FACTOR HAS TENDENCY TO INCREASE SPAN OF MANAGEMENT WHEN—	FACTOR HAS TENDENCY TO DECREASE SPAN OF MANAGEMENT WHEN—
1. Similarity of functions	1. Subordinates have similar functions	1. Subordinates have different functions
2. Geographic contiguity	2. Subordinates are physically close	2. Subordinates are physically distant
3. Complexity of functions	3. Subordinates have simple tasks	3. Subordinates have complex tasks
4. Coordination	4. Work of subordinates needs little coordination	4. Work of subordinates needs much coordination
5. Planning	5. Manager spends little time planning	5. Manager spends much time planning

- **Complexity of functions**—the degree to which workers' activities are difficult and involved. The more difficult and involved the activities are, the more difficult it is to manage a large number of individuals effectively. This is particularly true for research and development departments, which typically include numbers of engineers and scientists.[18]
- **Coordination**—the amount of time managers must spend synchronizing the activities of their subordinates with the activities of other workers. The greater the amount of time that must be spent on such coordination, the smaller the span of management should be.
- **Planning**—the amount of time managers must spend developing management system objectives and plans and integrating them with the activities of their subordinates. The more time managers must spend on planning activities—whether those activities are repetitive and routine or infrequent but complex—the fewer individuals they can manage effectively.[19]

Table 4.1 summarizes the factors that tend to increase and decrease the span of management.

HEIGHT/WIDTH OF ORGANIZATION CHART Span of management control directly influences the height of an organization chart. Normally, the greater the height of the organization chart, the smaller the span of management. The wider the width of the chart, the greater the span of management.[20] Organization charts with little height are usually referred to as flat, while those with much height are usually referred to as tall.[21]

Figure 4.2 is a simple example of the relationship between organization chart height and width, and the span of management. Organization chart A has a span of management of six, and organization chart B has a span of management of two. As a result, chart A is flatter than chart B. Note that both charts have the same number of individuals at the lowest level. The larger span of management in A is reduced in B merely by adding an intermediary level to B's organization chart.

FIGURE 4.2

Relationship Between Organization Chart Height and Span of Management

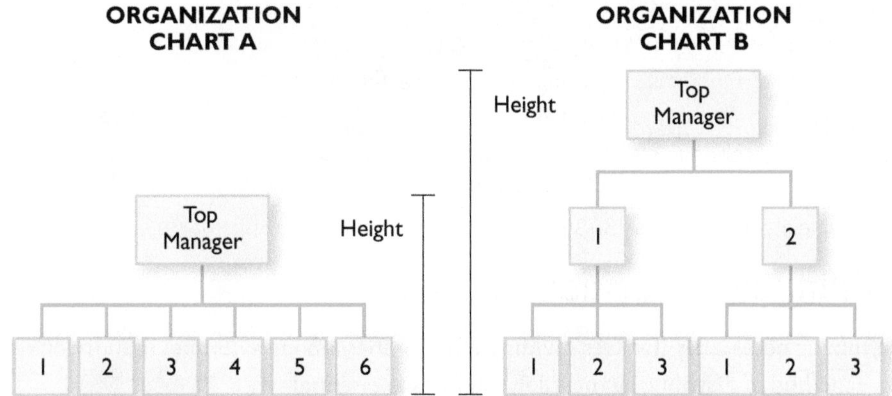

Responsibility

Responsibility is the obligation to perform assigned activities. It is the commitment and obligation to handle a job to the best of one's ability. The source of responsibility lies within the individual who accepts a job and agrees to carry out a series of duties or activities or to see that someone else carries them out.[22] The act of accepting the job means that the person is obligated to see that job activities are successfully completed.

Even though a manager may delegate a task to another employee, the manager still remains responsible for the completion of the task. In other words, responsibility is, in a sense, shared by both the manager and the employee.

The Job Description

An individual's job activities within an organization are usually summarized in a formal statement called a **job description**—a list of specific activities that must be performed by whoever holds the position. Unclear or ambiguous job descriptions can confuse employees and may facilitate their under-performance or to lose interest in their jobs. On the other hand, a clear job description can help employees become successful by focusing their efforts on the issues that are important for their position. When properly designed, job descriptions communicate job content to employees, establish performance expectations that employees must attain/maintain, and act as a guide that employees must follow to help the organization reach its objectives.

Job activities are clearly identified to enhance the accomplishment of organizational objectives. A sound organizing strategy delineates specific job activities for every individual in the organization.

FIGURE 4.3

Sequences of Activities for the Functional Similarity Method of Dividing Job Activities

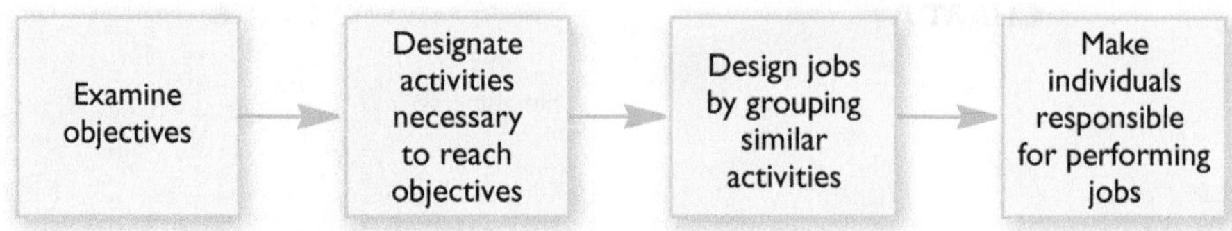

Dividing Job Activities

Organizing necessarily involves dividing job activities among a number of individuals. Some method of distributing these job activities is essential.

CREATING POSITIONS IN AN ORGANIZATION Organizations should take four basic interrelated steps to divide job activities in the following sequence:

1. Examine organizational objectives
2. Designate appropriate activities that must be performed to reach those objectives
3. Design specific jobs by grouping similar activities—write job descriptions
4. Make specific individuals responsible for performing those jobs

Figure 4.3 illustrates this sequence of activities.

Each member of a train crew performs separate yet complimentary tasks, minimizing overlapping responsibilities.

Conclusion

The absence of clear, goal-related, non-overlapping responsibilities undermines organizational efficiency and effectiveness.[23] When job responsibilities are distributed inappropriately, the organization will have both responsibility gaps and overlapping responsibilities.

CHAPTER 5

The Meaning of Marketing[1]

Marketing Concept Explained

Marketing, as stated earlier, involves the creation of value that results in effective customer relationships. **Customer relationships** are created when businesses and consumers interact through a sales transaction of a product or service and continue that relationship based on ongoing interaction between the business and the customer. The management of customer relationships, commonly referred to as customer relationship management (CRM) involves those elements of business strategy that enable meaningful, personalized communication between businesses and customers. CRM is composed of activities that are used to establish, develop, and maintain customer relationships. For example, customer-generated reviews can create a feedback mechanism and reinforce a strong relationship between businesses and customers. The understanding and interaction with customers becomes increasingly important as customers have greater access to information about different choices. By implementing CRM, a business is committing to understanding customer lifetime value. **Customer lifetime value** includes the projected sales revenue and profitability that a customer could provide to a firm. If customer relationships serve as the foundation for marketing activities, then a business is practicing the **marketing concept.**

Marketing Concept Applied

Although generally considered a contemporary idea, the marketing concept has been used for many years, in practice, if not in name, by businesses trying to distinguish themselves from their competition by focusing on the customer. L.L.Bean founded its business in 1912 by referring to the customer as ". . . the most important person ever in this office—in person or by mail." L.L.Bean developed a marketing philosophy based on customer service and marketed a guarantee to provide ". . . perfect satisfaction in every way."[2] Currently, many businesses, as well as churches, schools, and state and local tourism entities, practice the marketing concept by focusing on fulfilling the expectations of their customers.

PHOTO: Missouri Tourism Commission

EXAMPLE **MARKETING CONCEPT**

Missouri began an advertising campaign in 2008 with its central message: "Close to home. Far from ordinary." This message is designed to attract visitors from nearby states. The idea is that visitors will drive to Missouri and experience the wide range of activities available. The message concentrates on the actual experience of travel and not simply the destination. Practicing the marketing concept, this advertising has targeted specific groups of individuals, including families, young women, and baby boomers. By targeting certain groups, Missouri can create tailored messages that in turn create additional value that surpasses the value that might be obtained by communicating a broader message to the entire population.

Contrast Missouri's advertising campaign to the Las Vegas advertising campaign. Look at the two ads, and you can see that they appeal to different groups. After Las Vegas moved away from previous advertising as a family destination, the "what happens here, stays here" advertising campaign clearly establishes Las Vegas as an adults-only playground. The campaign focuses on the core benefit of a wide range of adult activities and targets those who place value on those activities. Las Vegas's advertising campaign even inspired the 2008 movie *What Happens in Vegas*.[3]

>> END EXAMPLE

Evolution of Marketing: Early Years Until 1950

Sales and marketing activities have existed in varying forms throughout time, from ancient civilizations through the modern era. Traditionally, the marketing emphasis was placed on the production of crafts, agricultural products, and other goods for sale through local markets. Over time, distinctive marks and designs such as cattle brands were associated with these products to distinguish one seller from another.

The early years of American marketing included advertisements that were placed in newly created media, such as newspapers and magazines, as well as the formation of the first advertising agency in the United States. In 1704 the *Boston News-Letter* published the first newspaper advertisement offering items for sale. The advertisement was for real estate on Oyster Bay, Long Island.[4] The first American magazine ads were published in Benjamin Franklin's *General Magazine* in 1742.[5] The first advertising agency was opened in Philadelphia in 1843.[6]

Sales opportunities in the United States expanded rapidly after the Revolutionary War as individuals moved across the country selling products such as clocks and books.[7] These sales roles evolved to salespeople managing orders for newly formed manufacturing companies of the nineteenth century.[8]

Through the early part of the twentieth century, both marketing and sales activities were designed to support production. Products were often created, and then customers were sought. The production orientation reflects a business focus on efficient production and distribution with little emphasis on any marketing strategy. This period existed roughly from the mid-1800s until the 1920s. With the advent of the Great Depression in the late 1920s and early 1930s, and the resulting increase in product inventory, the sales function became a primary activity and was considered synonymous with marketing. A **sales orientation** reflects a business focus on advertising and personal selling to create demand and move product inventory. This period lasted from the 1930s until the 1950s.

Evolution of Marketing: 1950–Present

From the 1950s into the 1980s, companies generally focused on the needs and wants of customers more than they did in prior years. A **consumer orientation** reflects a business focus on satisfying unmet consumer needs and wants. Also in the 1980s, businesses began to consider not only consumer but also suppliers as sources of value-based relationships. A relationship orientation reflects a business focus on creating value-added relationship with both suppliers and consumers. A value-added relationship is much more than buying and selling. The idea of value-added relationships involves business practices that support long-term relationships. These relationships may incur short-term costs, such as additional customer support and enhanced after-sales service, but are intended to reinforce the value of the product or service, relative to the competition.

EXAMPLE **EVOLUTION OF MARKETING: 1950–PRESENT**

Kelly Services, operating in 37 countries and territories and providing employment to over 750,000 employees annually, provides business services, such as temporary staffing services and outsourcing solutions, and consumer services, such as temporary and full-time job placement. Kelly's marketing efforts are targeted both to employers and to workers who are unemployed or looking to change careers. Kelly's "work to live, not live to work" advertising is targeted primarily toward workers and creates value for them by identifying with an individual's desire to balance work and home life. Kelly's communication to employers is designed to address specific needs in automotive, contact center, education, electronic assembly, engineering, finance and accounting, health care, information technology, legal, light industrial, marketing, office, scientific, and security clearance. Kelly's consulting and outsourcing activity uses the advertising message "If it's outside your scope, it's probably within ours." Value is created for business clients by offering expertise in specific employment fields.

>> END EXAMPLE

PHOTO: ©2008 Kelly Services, Inc.

Evolution of Marketing: Social Responsibility

During the last decade, there has been an increased focus on social responsibility, ethics, and accountability in business. The overriding idea is that a person (or business) can make

PHOTO: PepsiCo Inc.

money by focusing on socially responsible marketing activities and by high ethical standards. Social responsibility is the idea that businesses consider society as a whole as one of their stakeholders and that businesses make decisions that take into account the well being of society. For example, organizations such as the American Marketing Association (AMA) developed standards for ethical behavior for marketers.

A major issue that organizations must consider when practicing socially responsible marketing involves how products affect the global environment. Everything from the pollution generated by producing the products, forms of packaging used and their potential for recycling, and the amount of energy used to consume products must be considered. Some organizations adopt operating standards that govern their socially responsible marketing practices, while others choose to financially support causes that benefit society. Many accomplish both by developing green marketing products and supporting cause-marketing activities. Socially responsible marketing can be both altruistic and profitable. A recent study by Cone LLC found that two-thirds of Americans claim that they consider a company's business practices when making purchase decisions.[9]

EXAMPLE **EVOLUTION OF MARKETING: SOCIAL RESPONSIBILITY**

Pepsi, a PepsiCo brand sold in 200 countries, made a major decision in 2010 by electing not to run its traditional Super Bowl advertisement and, instead, launched a $20 million social responsibility campaign. The Pepsi Refresh Project was designed to provide millions of dollars to fund ideas that will "refresh" the world. Pepsi launched an advertising campaign using television, online sources including Facebook, Twitter, and YouTube; radio; print; and outdoor billboards inviting people, businesses, and nonprofits to submit ideas that would have a positive impact on the world; these ideas were eligible within six categories: Health, Arts & Culture, Food & Shelter, The Planet, Neighborhoods, and Education. Each month, visitors to its Wed site voted on the ideas. At the end of the month, finalists were selected to receive grant money—up to $1.3 million. Pepsi's objective was to create more two-way communication and to establish deeper relationships with its customers than can typically be achieved through more traditional advertising campaigns.[10]

>> END EXAMPLE

Marketing Functions Explained

Noted management guru Peter Drucker identified the critical role that marketing performs for business: "Because the purpose of business is to create a customer, the business enterprise has two—and only two—basic functions: marketing and innovation."[11] The process of creating value through uniqueness occurs well before and well after the selling process. **Marketing functions** can be grouped into three general categories with functions from each category occurring throughout the marketing process. The three categories are the following:

- Exchange functions
- Physical functions
- Facilitating functions

Exchange functions are activities that promote and enable transfer of ownership. Examples of exchange functions include buying, selling, and pricing, as well as advertising, sales promotion, and public relations. **Physical functions** are activities that enable the flow of goods from manufacturer to consumer. Examples of physical functions include assembling, transporting and handling, warehousing, processing and packaging, standardizing, and grading. **Facilitating functions** are activities that assist in the execution of exchange and physical functions. Examples of facilitating functions include financing and risk-taking, marketing information and research, as well as the promise of service.

Internal Marketing Participants

There are many different marketing stakeholders. Those stakeholders within a business or with direct oversight include the following:

- Marketing department
- Other business departments
- Business leadership/board of directors

The marketing department performs a primary role in managing marketing functions, including activities such as establishing a product or service portfolio, determining pricing, establishing distribution channels, and creating promotions. These elements compose the most common representation of the marketing mix, referred to as the **4 Ps** (Product, Price, Place, and Promotion). The marketing mix is a collection of marketing variables that are managed to achieve the desired sales performance in a target market. In addition, functions such as defining the brand and creating a CRM process are all activities performed by the marketing department.

Other business departments, such as finance, use marketing information and contribute to marketing activities in a variety of ways, including securing financing for expanded manufacturing or by providing cost information to marketing to assist in understanding the profitability of marketing decisions. Persons in positions of business leadership, such as the president or chief operating officer, and the board of directors also consume marketing information and make decisions to support or limit marketing activities through resource allocation.

External Marketing Participants

There are a number of marketing stakeholders that operate outside a business, yet have tremendous influence on marketing activities. They include the following:

- Investors
- Consumers/Customers

- Advertising/PR agency
- Information providers/marketing research companies
- Government
- Partners
- Competitors

Investors can influence marketing ideas through letters to management and through attending shareholder meetings. Recent investor actions have included proposals to practice more socially responsible marketing.

Consumers and customers influence marketing through purchase decisions and feedback on survey questions. Advertising and public relations companies assist businesses in understanding consumers and customers, as well as in presenting products and services in the most favorable perspective through the creation of media content. Information providers and marketing research companies collect a wide range of consumer and market information for marketing departments. Whether studying the success of advertising or the product desires of consumers, the collection of information is critical to marketing decisions.

The government primarily influences marketing through legislation or regulation. Partners, other businesses or organizations that already work with or may work with a particular business, influence marketing choices by presenting opportunities to reach more consumers or to share in the cost of marketing activities. Competitors also influence marketing actions by their advertising investment and product launches. Thus, there are many marketing stakeholders, and their collective efforts will ultimately define the level of success a business will realize in their marketing practices.

PHOTO: Courtesy of Gongos Research, Inc.

EXAMPLE **EXTERNAL MARKETING PARTICIPANTS**

When people think of marketing research, they tend to think of receiving phone calls during dinner and being stopped at shopping malls to complete surveys. In fact, the marketing research field is far more complex. Gongos Research is a custom marketing company that has enjoyed rapid growth through the use of technology and innovation such as iCommunities and metaCommunities. These are private online communities of individuals who have chosen to become active in the communities' social aspects (such as creating their own discussion groups) and business aspects (such as completing surveys), and are compensated for their involvement. Gongos Research assists a wide range of businesses in many different business sectors, including financial services, automotive, PowerPoints, and consumer products.

>> END EXAMPLE

Applied Marketing Functions

In practice, some businesses view marketing from a limited perspective by considering it synonymous to sales or advertising. Other businesses understand that marketing performs a broad range of functions, ranging from securing products to servicing products after a sale, and that the marketing ability is connected to all other business functions. Successful businesses generally consider marketing departments as the link between customers and businesses. Marketing departments are in a unique position to identify and communicate customer requirements to other departments within an organization, such as finance, accounting, manufacturing, and business planning.

FIGURE 5.1

Four Major Components of Marketing Planning

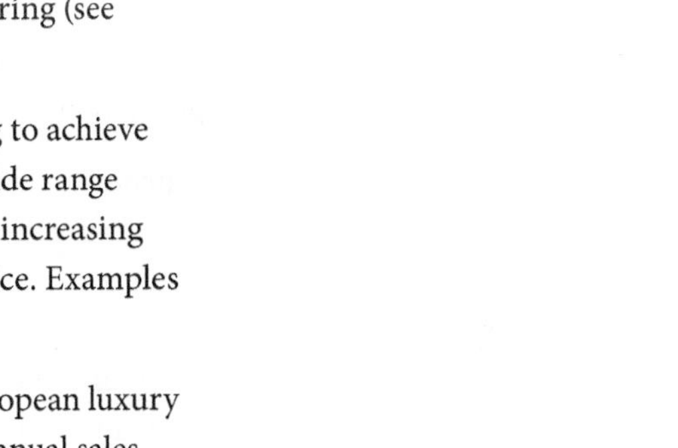

Marketing Planning Explained

Strategic planning identifies the overall direction of a business. Individual functions within a business must develop plans to support the business strategy. Marketing planning connects businesses to the environments in which they function, in particular to the consumers of the business's products and services. The ability for marketing planning to address changes in the environment is an essential business function.

There are four major components of marketing planning: marketing objectives, marketing audit, marketing strategies, and allocating resources and monitoring (see Figure 5.1).

A marketing objective is something that a marketing function is attempting to achieve in support of a strategic business plan. A marketing function can select a wide range of possible objectives, including building awareness of a product or service, increasing sales, increasing market share, and reducing resistance to a product or service. Examples of marketing objectives include the following:

- Increase sales of high-end navigation systems among owners of European luxury cars by 10% in one year. This can be measured through analyzing annual sales data.
- Increase market share of a specific brand of office furniture within the business market by 5% in six months. This can be measured through industry data published by an office furniture trade association.
- Create awareness of a new wetsuit line among high school swimmers. This can be measured through a questionnaire given to high school swimmers.

EXAMPLE **MARKETING PLANNING**

Speedo launched the LZR Racer swimsuit, a full-body suit, in 2008, several months in advance of the Beijing Olympics. After 25 world records were broken in the 1976 Olympics when goggles were first allowed, initial demand for the new swimsuit by athletes of all levels skyrocketed. Speedo's marketing objective was to use the Olympics to launch the new product. Speedo collaborated with NASA to help design the suit that dramatically reduces drag in the water. Even though the suit noticeably improved swimming times, some swimming organizations have banned full-body

PHOTO: Schmid Christopher/Shutterstock

suits for competitions because the suits are considered unfair performance-enhancing gear. Speedo responded to concerns by launching the LZR Race Elite in 2010, in compliance with all FINA (International Swimming Federation) requirements and rules governing collegiate, high school, and club swimming in the United States.[12]

>> END EXAMPLE

After marketing objectives are established, the next step is the marketing audit. A **marketing audit** is the comprehensive review and assessment of a business's marketing environment. An important part of the marketing process is that a business understands the external and internal forces that can influence its success.

Once the marketing audit has been completed, the marketing function is responsible for developing marketing strategies. A **marketing strategy** is a statement of how a business intends to achieve its marketing objectives.[13] A marketing strategy includes two critical functions:

- Select a target market.
- Create an appropriate marketing mix for the target market.

A **target market** is a group of consumers that a business determines is the most viable for its products or services. Consumer wants, needs, and business resources and strategies all contribute to the selection of a target market. In some cases, several targets are selected. A marketing mix is a group of marketing variables that a business controls with the intent of implementing a marketing strategy directed at a specific target market. The most common variables of the marketing mix include product, place, pricing, and promotion.

A **product strategy** identifies the product and service portfolio, including packaging, branding, and warranty for its target market. An automobile manufacturer creates a product strategy when it decides to offer consumers a choice of a diesel or hybrid engine in a new vehicle. This strategy helps meet growing consumer demands for a wider choice of engine types. A **place strategy** identifies where, how, and when products and services are made available to target consumers. A newspaper publisher develops a place strategy when it decides to offer customers newspapers in newsprint and online. A pricing strategy identifies what a business will charge for its products or services. A company creates a **pricing strategy** with its clothing brand when that company decides to charge more for products sold in its retail stores than for the same products sold through the company website. A **promotion strategy** identifies how a business communicates product or service benefits and value to its target market. A perfume manufacturer develops a promotion strategy when that manufacturer decides to advertise a new brand of perfume both in-store and on television.

Following the development of marketing strategies, the next step is allocating resources and monitoring performance. People and money both must be assigned to support implementation of marketing strategies. The monitoring process is essential to determine if the target market is responding to marketing strategies. Proper monitoring requires identifying performance measures so that actual performance can be compared to expected performance. Performance measures can include different variables, for example, customer satisfaction, average value of customer orders, and level of advertising recall.

The result of marketing planning is the creation of a marketing plan. A marketing plan is a document that includes an assessment of the marketing situation, marketing objectives, marketing strategy, and marketing initiatives.

Marketing Planning Applied

In practice, marketing planning is subject to the same challenges as business planning, including a potential lack of focus on business objectives, a lack of involvement of all aspects of the marketing activity in the planning process, and the failure to track performance against objectives. The structure and culture of marketing activity has much to do with managing these potential challenges. Clear roles and responsibilities regarding planning responsibility and the level of understanding of a business's environment contribute significantly to successful marketing planning.

SWOT analysis is a tool that helps identify business strengths, weaknesses, opportunities, and threats. A SWOT analysis can assist in the marketing, planning process particularly with marketing audit.

Strengths and weaknesses are based on internal characteristics, and opportunities and threats are external. Strengths and opportunities can be considered potential advantages, but weaknesses and threats are problems to be addressed. Strategically, weaknesses must be examined to search for opportunities. Strengths should be managed against potential threats. The Five Forces of Competitive Position Model can also assist in completing a marketing audit.

Marketing performance must be evaluated relative to objectives, as well as against the overall financial investment in the marketing activity. Increasingly, marketing is being asked to justify its contribution to business performance through identifying a return on marketing investment. Marketing planning should be designed to identify the relative contributions of each aspect of the marketing activity, including advertising and promotions, toward achieving overall objectives. **Return on marketing investment (ROMI)** is the impact on business performance resulting from executing specific marketing activities. Funding can then be allocated to the most efficient investment option.

EXAMPLE **MARKETING PLANNING, SWOT**

Studying the Jeep SWOT analysis leads to questions about the appropriateness of the portfolio and the potential for new market segments that might be viable. Price sensitivity among consumers, as well as shopping patterns and promotional opportunities that leverage brand strength, should also be considered.

>> END EXAMPLE

PHOTO: Andresr/Shutterstock

Customer Value Explained

The number of products that are available to potential buyers has increased significantly in recent decades. Products are offered with a variety of features, at different levels of quality, and at various prices. With so many different options, how do buyers determine which products to purchase? At the most basic level, buyers make a purchase decision based on the value they perceive a product will deliver. Buyers accomplish this by weighing the difference between the expected benefits gained from owning the product and the expected costs of the product. This can be shown with the following formula:

Customer Perceived Value = Expected Benefits – Expected Costs

Because buyers have different perceptions as to the benefits a products delivers, as well as different interpretations of its costs, the perceived value that a product delivered will vary. In most cases, buyers select the product they believe will offer them the greatest value. Some buyers will therefore select a high-quality, high-priced product loaded with features, while others will opt for a product that has a minimal number of features, but offers a low price.

Customer Value Applied

Products deliver benefits to a customer in many different forms. The most basic and visible benefits of products—which are referred to as functional benefits—relate to the specific attributes of the product. For example, the functional benefits of a digital camera are based on the number of mega-pixels, the size of the screen, and the magnification of the zoom offered by the camera. Additional benefits, referred to as psychological benefits, are created primarily through a company's branding efforts. These benefits include emotional benefits, self-expression benefits, and social benefits.

On the cost side, the cost of a product often includes much more than the purchase price. For example, there can be additional costs that should be taken into consideration, such as the costs of using, maintaining, and disposing of a product. For example, in addition to its higher purchase price, the total cost of owning an SUV is much higher than that of owning a smaller, more fuel-efficient automobile. These additional costs, such as operating costs (due to lower fuel efficiency) and higher disposal costs (due to lower resale values), have resulted in many buyers lowering the perceived value for SUVs and an increase in the sales of smaller vehicles that are less expensive to operate. In the first quarter of 2008, as gasoline prices were rising toward $4 per gallon, the demand for trucks and SUVs decreased by 28%.[14] The trade-off between benefits and costs is shown in Figure 5.2.

To better understand the concept of customer value, the **value map** shown in Figure 5.3 examines the trade-offs customers make between costs and benefits (performance in

FIGURE 5.2

Customer Perceived Value

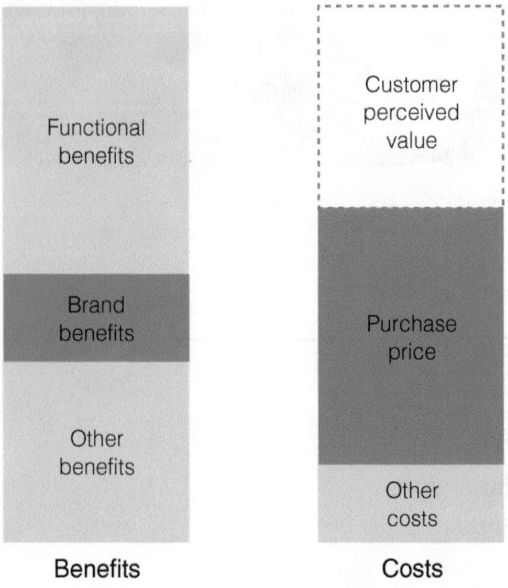

FIGURE 5.3

Price-Performance Value Map

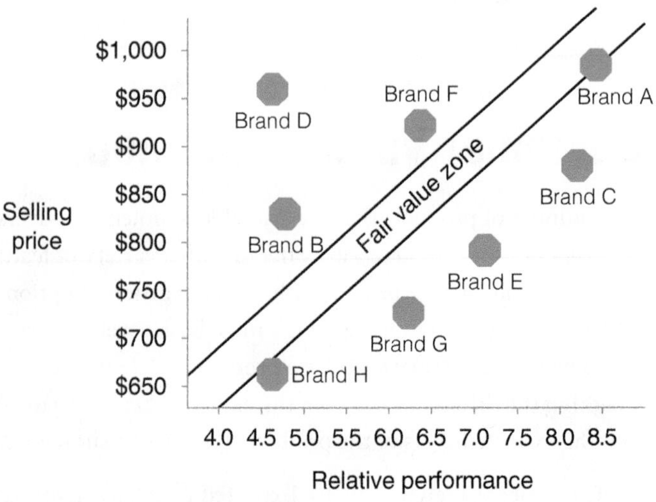

this example) when making a purchase decision. Products that fall within the **fair value zone** are perceived to deliver benefits equal to the products' total cost. Products below, or to the right of, the zone are perceived to have greater benefits than their associated costs, Products above, or to the left of, the zone are perceived by buyers to deliver fewer benefits than what the products costs.

iTunes, first launched by Apple in 2001, is a free application for the PC or Mac that organizes and plays your digital video and music stored on a computer. It syncs media with a variety of Apple products, including the iPad, iPhone, iPod, iBook, and Apple TV. Additionally, iTunes can connect to the iTunes Store through the Internet to gain access to 13 million songs as well as movies, TV shows, audiobooks, podcasts, and applications. The iTunes Store was created in 2003 to provide value to customers through a virtual store where people can purchase and download digital music on demand. In 2009, Apple adjusted its uniform $0.99 download per song pricing to a three-tier pricing model to better reflect customer demand. The new pricing tiers were established as $0.69, $0.99, and $1.29. The most expensive songs are those deemed to create the greatest value to customers, such as top songs by the most popular artists. Business through the iTunes Store has grown significantly from 4 billion downloads in 2008, to surpassing 10 billion downloads in 2010.[15]

Managers use a value map to track and manage the perceived value customers assign to their brands, as well as to competitors' brands. The value map shown in Figure 5.3 highlights a market with eight competitors, each of which has various levels of performance and price. Brands B, D, and F all fall to the left of the fair value zone, which indicates low customer perceived value. The low perceptions by customers will translate into low market share for these brands. Brands C, E, and G, are rated by customers as having high customer perceived value. Brands A and H are rated has having performance benefits equal to their selling price. In this example, brand C is priced around $200 higher than brand H. Is brand C worth the added cost? One could make the case that because brand C has a much higher performance rating, the additional $200 is acceptable.

Companies can alter the customer perceived value in one of three ways: increase the perceived benefits, decrease the perceived cost, or create a combination of the two. For example, perceived benefits can be increased by adding new features to a product while either maintaining the current price of increasing the price only slightly. Perceived costs can be altered through a price reduction or by improving a product's efficiency. An example of the latter would be an automobile manufacturer improving the gas mileage of one of its models. Improved fuel efficiency lowers the overall operating expenses, thereby reducing the perceived cost of the vehicle. Even if the perceived benefits remain the same, the reduction in overall costs results in an increase in the perceived value.

Customer Satisfaction Explained

When customers have contact with a company, or an interaction with a product, they formulate an evaluation of their experience. This evaluation is based on the expectations they had before the experience. Customers' evaluation, or their level of satisfaction, will fall within one of three categories: The experience will either be positive, neutral, or negative. A negative feeling, or dissatisfaction, is the result when the product's performance does not live up to expectations. A neutral outcome occurs when a product's performances matches expectations. In this situation, a buyer has reached the baseline level of satisfaction. If expectations are exceeded, then a positive experience has occurred, leaving the buyer highly satisfied. This high level of satisfaction is referred to as delighted. The varying levels of satisfaction, and likely outcomes associated with each, are shown in Figure 5.4.

The initial level of satisfaction is normally determined at the time a product is purchased. However for some products the level of satisfaction may change over time.

FIGURE 5.4

Outcomes of Varying Degrees of Satisfaction

Negative	Neutral	Positive
• Dissatisfied • Defect	• Satisfied • Switchable	• Delighted • Loyal

For example, the purchase and consumption of a new flavor of soft drink will result in an initial level of satisfaction. In most cases, customers will make up their minds as to whether they would purchase that brand again in the first few sips. It is unlikely that a week after trying the new flavor that a person would alter his or her level of satisfaction without having a new experience with the product. This may not be the case for other types of products. Take the purchase of an ink-jet printer as an example. At first, the buyer may experience a high level of satisfaction due to a low purchase price and an acceptable quality of the pages being printed. However, over time the level of satisfaction may diminish as the customer seeks to replace the ink cartridge and finds the price to be much higher than expected. Where once there was initial delight, dissatisfaction takes over. For products where long-term ownership is expected, the company's product and customer service quality play an important role in customer satisfaction.

Customer Satisfaction Applied

Creating satisfied customers requires that a company manage the expectations customers have with the brand. While a company can generate higher initial sales volume by inflating claims of a product's superiority, if these claims are not delivered, customers will experience higher levels of dissatisfaction and are more likely to switch to a competing brand. As such, companies strive to manage expectations in an effort to not "overpromise and underdeliver." Even customers who have a neutral experience—that is, their experience matches expectations—are susceptible to switching to a competing offering. It is only customers who are delighted by their experience that can be counted on to remain loyal to the brand.

Companies with highly satisfied or delighted customers generate significant benefits for themselves in the following forms:[16]

- **Loyalty**—Customers who are satisfied are likely to continue to purchase the same brands, or do business with the same service provider.
- **Product champions**—Satisfied customers cannot wait to share their experiences with anyone who listens.
- **Reduced costs**—The costs benefits of having satisfied customers is found in multiple areas from lower warranty expenses (satisfied customers have fewer problems, hence lower warranty expenses) to few phone calls to customer service representatives.
- **Larger share of wallet**—Satisfied customers are more likely to purchase other products from a company to which they are loyal.

These benefits in turn lead to greater profitability for the company, as well as an increase in revenue due to satisfied customers purchasing other products from the company. Satisfied customers may also become product advocates by referring the brand to their friends and colleagues. This word-of-mouth, or viral, advertising carries much greater weight with potential buyers than any advertising campaign could develop.

Measuring Customer Satisfaction

Because of its importance for long-term growth, companies make an effort to measure the satisfaction levels of their customers. The measurement of satisfaction can take the form of surveys where customers are asked to rate their level of satisfaction on a scale of 1 to 10. These types of surveys traditionally ask respondents questions such as the following: How satisfied are you with the product or service? Do you intend to purchase the product in the future? Would you recommend the product to a friend? Capturing ratings for customer satisfaction provides managers with insights into how well the company is performing in the marketplace. However, the data alone are of little use unless they are compared against the company's previous ratings or against the satisfaction ratings competitors have earned.

Independent rating organizations such as J.D. Power and Associates and the American Customer Satisfaction Index (ASCI) are also involved in the assessment of customer satisfaction. The ACSI conducts more than 65,000 customer interviews annually and links customer expectations, perceived quality, and perceived value to develop an overall ACSI score. Measures are taken across a wide variety of consumer and business-to-business product categories, allowing managers to see their customers' level of satisfaction in relation to industry averages and specific competitors.

EXAMPLE **CUSTOMER SATISFACTION**

According to the American Customer Satisfaction Index, Southwest Airlines customers are the most satisfied of the major air carrier customers in the United States. Southwest accomplishes this by consistently delivering superior customer service and customer value through its low prices, which in turn leads to high levels of customer satisfaction. In 2009, Southwest Airlines was awarded Best Customer Service in the Reader's Choice Awards by Smarter Travel and was named the top U.S. airline on the University of Michigan's American Customer Satisfaction Index. Customers know exactly what to expect from Southwest: low fares, open seating, and limited amenities (you get a bag of peanuts and a soft drink). Southwest Airlines has shown a profit for 37 consecutive years, a record that has been unmatched in the airline industry.[17]

>> END EXAMPLE

Customer Loyalty

Customer loyalty is the degree to which a customer will select a particular brand when a purchase from that product category is being considered. Customer loyalty can also be described as a buyer's feeling of attachment to a particular product, brand, or company. Buyers exhibit varying degrees of loyalty toward the brands they purchase. Some buyers have high levels of loyalty to a particular brand and will purchase only that brand. Other buyers may split their loyalty among two or three brands in a category. Still others may hold loyalty to no brand and select perhaps the lowest priced product when a purchase decision must be made. It is the first group of customers, those who are

PHOTO: Yuri Arcurs/Shutterstock

loyal to a specific brand, which organizations strive to create and expand by delivering high levels of customer satisfaction. Companies also seek to ensure that highly loyal customers remain loyal. At the same time, companies try to move those customers who are only somewhat loyal into a state of high loyalty. To accomplish this, companies seek to ensure continued relationships with select groups of customers.

While it can be assumed that loyal customers will continue to purchase a specific brand, this does not mean they are the most profitable customers. Nor is it the case that the heavy users (customers who purchase in higher quantity) of a product are the most profitable. For example, heavy users may stock up on a product because of special deals or price promotions. In business-to-business markets, large volume buyers may also require additional company resources, such as higher levels of customer service or special product specifications. These additional resources result in higher costs and, thus, lower profitability. To determine which customers are profitable and which are not, an in-depth customer profitability analysis should be conducted. A profitability analysis of customers involves assigning actual marketing costs to customers, based on the actual costs that are required to perform various marketing activities, such as sales calls and product shipping. Looking at customers in this light allows the company to determine the overall value, in terms of profitability, that a customer generates for a company.

The Value of a Customer

It is important to note that not all customers are created equal. According to the Pareto Principle, or what is commonly referred to as the 80/20 rules, 80% of a company's profits are generated by 20% of its customers. Another 60% of customers generate the remaining profits for a company. This leaves an additional 20% of customers who generate a loss for the company. This observation has led many companies to offer tiered levels of service. With the most profitable customers receiving high levels of customer service and unprofitable customers receiving minimal levels of service. For example, credit card companies ensure a "live" customer service representative answers a highly valued card holder's phone call in a matter of second; a phone call from a card holder that generates lower profits is generally routed through an automated phone system.

Customer Lifetime Value

Customer lifetime value (CLV) is the present value of all profits expected to be earned in the future from a customer. To determine the value of a customer, companies utilize metrics such as customer lifetime value. The befit of using CLV can be seen in a simple example using a typical AT&T cell phone customer who pays $75 per month for service. The average customer generates $1,800 in revenue for AT&T over the life of a contract. If AT&T earns 20% profit on revenue from cell service, then the customer generates a total profit of $360 during the two-year contract period. At the most basic level, this $360 in profit can be viewed as the lifetime value of that customer. If the cost to recruit and retain the customer is less than $360, then this would be a profitable customer for AT&T.

Customer lifetime value goes much deeper than the preceding example demonstrates. Companies must also take into account the fact that revenue collected in the future is worth less than if that revenue were collected up front. To account for this, companies use what is known as a discount rate, which averages between 10% and 15%. The concept behind the discount rate is also referred to as the time value of money.

To calculate customer lifetime value, a company must know five pieces of information:

1. Customer average purchases per year
2. Profit margin earned on those purchases
3. Costs to service the customer
4. Customer retention rate (percentage of customers who remain customers)
5. The firm's discount rate

Customers represent different levels of value in terms of the amount of profits they generate for an organization. Because of the high expense and effort required, companies use metrics such as CLV to determine which customers should receive the focus of the company's relationship marketing efforts. Perhaps equally important, knowing a customer's lifetime value also allows a company to know with which customer to not seek to build relationships. For example, some companies have opted to "fire" unprofitable customers. Take the 2007 case of Sprint, which identified and terminated the contracts of cover 1,000 customers who repeatedly contacted the company's customer service department an average of 40 times per month, some even after the original complaint was resolved. This move generated a great deal of negative publicity for Sprint, but other cell phone providers acknowledged that they had also cancelled customer contract for similar reasons.[18]

Customers can add value to a company in addition to their lifetime value, because many highly satisfied customers may become champions for the products they buy. These loyal customers will go out of their way to refer a brand to anyone who will listen.[19] Research conducted by Purdue's Center for Customer Driven Quality shows that 87% of consumers follow the opinion of their friends and family.[20]

Customer Retention

Companies are continuously seeking to attract new customers to increase sales and profits. For many companies, attracting new customers is necessary to replace customers who defect to competing products, or who leave the market entirely. This is especially the case for those organizations that achieve low customer satisfaction scores, or even an entire industry, such as cellular phone service providers. Replacing lost customers is critical to growing a company's sales and profits, or to maintain current sales levels in those firms with high defection rates. However, companies that work to retain current customers are reaching higher levels of profitability. A majority of a company's marketing efforts are often geared toward recruiting new customers, but, in addition, today's savvy businesses are turning their attention to retaining current customers.

PHOTO: Galyna Andrushko/Shutterstock

EXAMPLE **CUSTOMER RETENTION**

Searching for ways to connect with its "healthy, active, outdoor, aspirational" target customers, Nature Valley, a large heath-oriented General Mill's cereal bar brand, called on consumers to post stories about their favorite nature activities, such as hiking and kayaking. The brand's Web site was redesigned in hopes of making the site a clearinghouse for information appealing to outdoor enthusiasts. Nature Valley also promoted a contest on YouTube where consumers posted videos highlighting their favorite place. The overall winner of the contest won two trips, one to Antarctica and the other to the North Poll. A total of 127 videos were submitted; they were viewed a total of 250,000 times. The Web site and contest gave Nature Valley the means to build a relationship with a core customer group and to retain this group of customers.[21]

>> END EXAMPLE

Relationship Marketing Explained

In the past, companies would determine the value of customers based on their most recent purchase. Previous purchases or future purchases were of lesser concern. This transaction-based view gave way to the relationship-based view of an exchange with the emergence of the marketing concept. Today's successful companies have sought to focus their marketing efforts on building long-term, mutually beneficial relationships with profitable or potentially profitable customers. The primary goal for developing customer relationships is to increase customer loyalty and retention. In thinking about long-term customer relationships, companies understand that customer profitability may be limited or even at a loss at the beginning of a relationship, but over time, profits increase. Relationship marketing is especially important, given the following data:[22]

- A company can lose up to 50% of its customers over a five-year period.
- It costs 5-7 times more to recruit new customers than it does to retain existing customers.
- Even small increases in customer retention rates can have a profound impact on a company's profit.

According to Michael Porter, a world-renowned strategy guru, a business can differentiate itself from competitors based on the following: (1) the core product or service, (2) price, and (3) the total relationship and customer experience. Companies are finding that the first two are difficult in today's competitive environment and are focusing on the importance of developing strong customer relationships. Relationship marketing, or one-to-one marketing, requires that an organization be committed to the development of a customer relationship.

Relationship Marketing Applied

Developing relationships with customers requires a complete, committed effort on the part of the organization. This is because a relationship requires the delivery of superior customer value that results from high product quality and exemplary customer service. Building relationships with customers is not a short-term undertaking; it requires a long-term plan and strong commitment from the organization, as well as the proper investment. It is important to understand that customers have different reasons for wanting to establish a relationship with a company. Customers may enter into a relationship because of the added value they receive, to reduce anxiety throughout the purchase/repurchase process, or to achieve a sense of belonging.

EXAMPLE **RELATIONSHIP MARKETING**

Seeking to establish a community with loyal customers, Patron Spirits launched an online social networking Web site. The Patron Social Club provides tequila aficionados with a central gather place for Patron (Spanish for "the good boss") enthusiasts. The site is interactive and open to members only. With the help of a worldwide, integrated marketing campaign, the brand is meeting the desires of its top customers. The information the company has gained from hosting the site has led to members receiving Super Bowl XLII. The addition of the Web site and the marketing campaign have raised awareness of the brand 61% from the previous year and increased cased sales by 45%.[23]

PHOTO: Grant Terry/Shutterstock

>> END EXAMPLE

Customer Relationship Management Explained

Customer relationship management (CRM) seeks to ensure that every effort an organization undertakes has as its purpose the development and maintenance of a profitable customer relationship. The practice of CRM requires internal and external processes. External processes are those that connect the company with its customer, while internal processes involve the management of information acquired from customers. A breakdown in either process will result in the CRM experience not meeting the expectations of either the company or the customer.

Customer Relationship Management Applied

Perhaps the most critical element of practicing CRM is in the information such a system can provide the organization. Companies should not only collect information regarding their customers, such as demographics and usage patterns, but also seek to gain information to help assess the customers' needs. The information that a company collects is stored in a customer database, which is an organized collection of information about a customer. The information in this database must be constantly updated and should be designed for ease of use.

There are four steps in the development of one-to-one relationships with customers:[24]

1. Identify and gather as much detail as possible about your customers.
2. Differentiate customers based on their needs and the levels of value they bring to your company.
3. Talk to your customers and find ways of improving cost efficiencies as well as the customer interaction experience.
4. Customize your products or services for each customer segment.

Customer Identification

For any companies, such as those in the business-to-business (B2B) market, taking the first step of identifying and collecting information about customers is relatively simple. However, the effort in the consumer market is much more challenging. In the B2B market, firms know who their customers are because of previous purchases. For example, ArcelorMittal, the world's largest steel manufacturer, can easily pull up a customer list from a previous order and begin building the necessary information needed for its CRM systems. However, in the consumer market, companies must make great effort to even identify their customers. Imagine the difficulty that Proctor & Gamble (P&G) has determining which consumers purchase Tide detergent or Crest toothpaste. Although some of this information may be available from supermarkets that have implemented a loyalty program, issues abound when sharing information among firms.

In the process of identifying customers and collecting pertinent information, companies should seek to err on the side of having too much information, rather than too little. Information that should be collected includes the standard names and contact information, as well as other data that may be specific to your brand, company, or industry. For example, a consumer products company may benefit from knowing whether a customer is married, has children (along with their ages), or the type of job he or she holds. This information may allow the company to promote other products the company produces. Companies should also focus on ways to determine a customer's needs, for example, how the product is perceived, what features the customer finds valuable, and how the product is used. Perhaps the most critical piece of information that should be collected, either directly from the customer or from other sources, involves a customer's purchase history. This information will allow the company to perform a customer profitability analysis that, along with the other information mentioned, will be valuable in the next step of the process.

Customer Differentiation

The ability to differentiate customers based on the value they bring to the company in the form of profits and based on the customers' needs gives the company the means to find groups of customers who share similar characteristics. The information collected in Step 1 (customer identification) allows the company to identify its top customers in terms of sales and profitability. The differentiation step allows a company to detect customers whose purchases have been significantly fewer this quarter than they were last quarter. This might indicate that the customer has become less satisfied with the products. The company then might contact the customer to prevent the loss of this customer to a competitor. Companies that do not utilize a CRM system may not find out about a dissatisfied customer until it is too late.

Customization

The first three steps, when implemented properly, can provide the company with increased revenue, decreased costs, and ultimately higher profitability. However, the fourth step may be the source of the greatest benefits to the organization. Taking the information learned and using this information to deliver what customers actually need generates enormous goodwill and loyalty. Customers see the value in continuing the relationship, and their degree of loyalty increases. Companies are better able to craft marketing messages through personalized direct-mail pieces, which leads to higher success rates for such advertising programs.

Loyalty Programs

Some brands lend themselves well to developing loyal customers based on the quality, customer service, or even price of the product. However, some product categories find that building repeat business requires the development of reward or loyalty programs. These types of efforts are found in many product categories and among retailers. They represent an attempt to entire customers to repurchase from the company in exchange for various rewards. Companies also benefit from loyalty programs by collecting information about customers, including contact information and a customer's spending habits. This type of information may even be the most beneficial part of a loyalty program. The various types of programs that are used include frequent flyer miles (airlines), cash back (credit cards), discounts on select products (supermarkets), and discounts on purchases (department stores), just to name a few. According to Jupiter Research, more than 75% of consumers are enrolled in at least one loyalty program. Consumer product manufacturers are also using various programs to build some degree of loyalty among their customers. Coca-Cola offers its customers free merchandise for the continued purchase of their beverages (see Mycokerewards.com). Retailers such as Nordstrom and Best Buy have implemented programs to encourage customer loyalty.

EXAMPLE **LOYALTY PROGRAMS**

In an effort to increase customer value, and thus build loyalty, online music retailer eMusic.com launched *A+R Access + Rewards* in early 2010. The program offers subscribers the chance to win concert tickets, discounts on accessories, and chances to meet musicians. Developing loyalty is critical for a firm like eMusic, which has access to significantly fewer songs than its largest competitor iTunes.[25]

>> END EXAMPLE

PHOTO: HYEPSTOCK/Shutterstock

Technology

Implementing and utilizing a customer relationship management system requires a major investment in computer systems, including specialized software that allows for in-depth analysis of the information that is collected. Dedicated employees are also needed to manage the flow of information from customers to managers. Although a CRM system can provide managers with an instantaneous view of customers, these systems can be expensive. Over $15 billion was spent on CRM programs in 2007 and that amount is forecasted to expand to 422 billion in 2012.[26]

Formal CRM systems can be too expensive for small firms, but those companies can still realize the same benefits by using other, less expensive, methods such as basic databases created in Excel. Much greater effort is needed to generate the same level of information as systems costing millions, but companies may see greater returns because they might place of higher value on the information they receive. It is important to remember that no matter how much a company invests in its CRM program, if customer information is not maintained, the benefits will be minimal. A well-maintained database offers companies the potential to uncover market opportunities through the use of **data mining.** This statistical technique has been used successfully in direct marketing to uncover individuals or groups of individuals who are most likely to respond to an offer and the types of offers that will elicit a response. Data mining has helped reduce costs by eliminating duplicate customer entries. Retailers have also benefited from data mining techniques that identify local buying patterns, thus allowing them to tailor the types of merchandise carried by individual stores.

Special precautions must be taken with the sensitive information contained in databases because customers have great concern regarding privacy and security issues. There have been numerous incidents of customer information being compromised through security breaches or lost laptops. The expenses incurred because of lost of stolen customer information can reach into the millions, not counting the losses associated with the negative publicity. It is estimated that a company can incur a cost between $30 and $300 for every customer record that is compromised. A security breach at retailer T.J.Mazz in 2007, where over 45 million customer credit card and debit card numbers were stolen by computer hackers, cost the company more than $250 million.

Conclusion

A company's marketing efforts should be focused on developing profitable and loyal customers. Building customer loyalty is the result of delivering value to the customer in excess of their expectations. Exceeding expectations creates feelings of satisfaction with the brand or company. Higher levels of satisfaction (or delight) cause customers to continue to purchase the brand. Customer loyalty can be enhanced through the use of relationship marketing, where the focus is on the individual customer, not only at a single point in time, but over the lifetime of the relationship. However, not all customers are worth of the effort and expense required to build a long-term relationship. It is only through in-depth analysis of customer lifetime value that a company can decide with which customers to build a relationship and which customers to fire.

TABLE 5.1
CAREERS IN MARKETING

MARKETING FIELD	WHERE CAN I WORK?	WHAT ENTRY-LEVEL POSITION CAN I GET?	WHAT COURSE WORK DO I NEED?
Advertising	**Advertising agency:** Media, research, and creative departments; account work **Large corporation:** Advertising department: brand/product management **Media:** Magazine, newspaper, radio, and television selling; management consulting; marketing research	Account coordinator (traffic department); assistant account executive; assistant media buyer; research assistant; assistant brand manager	Undergraduate business degree
Brand Management	**Any size corporation:** Coordinate the activities of specialists in production, sales, advertising, promotion, R&D, marketing research, purchasing, distribution, package development, and finance	Associate brand manager	M.B.A. preferred, but a few companies recruit undergraduates. Expect a sales training program in the field from one to four months and in-house classes and seminars.
Business-to-Business Marketing	**Any size corporation:** Only a few companies recruit on campus, so be prepared to search out job opportunities on your own, as well as interview on campus.	Sales representative; market research administrator; product manager; pricing administrator; product administrator; assistant marketing manager; sales administrator; assistant sales manager; sales service administrator	Undergraduate business degree. A broad background of subjects is generally better than concentrating on just one area. A technical degree may be important or even required in high-technology areas. Courses in industrial marketing and marketing strategy are very helpful.
Direct–Response Marketing	**Any size corporation:** Marketing-oriented firms, including those offering consumer goods, industrial products, financial institutions, and other types of service establishments. Entrepreneurs seeking to enter business for themselves.	Direct-response marketing is expanding rapidly and includes direct mail; print and broadcast media, telephone marketing, catalogues, in-home presentations, and door-to-door marketing. Seek counsel from officers and directors of the Direct Marketing Association and the Direct Selling Association.	Undergraduate business degree. Supplemental work in communications, psychology, and/or computer systems recommended.
Supply-Channel Management	**Any size corporation, including transportation corporations:** The analysis, planning, and control of activities concerned with the procurement and distribution of goods. The activities include transportation, warehousing, forecasting, order processing, inventory control, production planning, site selection, and customer service.	Physical distribution manager; supply chain manager; inventory-control manager; traffic manager; distribution-center manager; distribution-planning analyst; customer service manager; transportation marketing and operations manager	Undergraduate business degree and M.B.A. Broad background in the core functional areas of business, with particular emphasis in distribution related topics such as logistics, transportation, purchasing, and negotiation.
International Marketing	**Large corporations:** Marketing Department at corporate headquarters	Domestic sales position with an international firm may be the best first step toward international opportunities.	M.B.A. A broad background in marketing is recommended, with some emphasis on sales management and market research.

TABLE 5.1
CAREERS IN MARKETING *(CONTINUED)*

MARKETING FIELD	WHERE CAN I WORK?	WHAT ENTRY-LEVEL POSITION CAN I GET?	WHAT COURSE WORK DO I NEED?
Marketing Models and Systems Analysis	**Large corporations:** Consult with managers who are having difficulty with marketing problems.	Undergraduate: Few positions available unless you have prior work experience. Graduate: market analyst, market research specialist, and management scientist.	M.B.A. Preparation in statistics, mathematics, and the behavioral sciences.
Marketing Research	**Any size corporation:** Provide management with information about consumers, the marketing environment, and the competition	Assistant market analyst or assistant product analyst level.	M.B.A. or an M.S. in Marketing Research although prior experience and training may improve an undergraduate's chances.
New Product Planning	**Any size corporation:** Marketing of consumer products, consumer industries, advertising agencies, consulting firms, public agencies, medical agencies, retailing management	Assistant manager or director of product planning or new product development.	M.B.A.
Retail Management	**Retail corporations**	Assistant buyer positions; department manager positions	Undergraduate business degree
Sales and Sales Management	**Profit and nonprofit organizations:** Financial, insurance, consulting, and government	Trade sales representative who sells to a wholesaler or retailer; missionary sales representative in manufacturing who sells to retailers or decision makers (e.g., pharmaceutical representative); technical sales representative who sells to specified accounts within a designated geographic area.	Undergraduate business degree; M.B.A.; *Helpful courses:* consumer behavior, psychology, sociology, economics, anthropology, cost accounting, computer science, statistical analysis, communications, drama, creative writing. Language courses, if you're interested in international marketing; engineering or physical science courses if you're interested in technical selling.
Services Marketing	**Any size corporation:** Banking and financial service institutions, health care organizations, leisure-oriented businesses, and in various other service settings.	Assistant brand manager; assistant sales manager	Undergraduate business degree; M.B.A.; Additional course work in management policy, research, advertising and promotion, quantitative analysis, consumer behavior, and the behavioral sciences should prove useful.

Source: This information was based on an excellent compilation prepared by the marketing faculty of the Marshall School of Business, University of Southern California at **http://www.marshall.usc.edu/marketing/resources/resources-overview.htm** (accessed June 11, 2010). For average salaries broken down by job type and state consult the *Aquent/AMA Survey of Marketing Professionals* at **http://www.marketingsalaries.com/aquent/Home.form** or commercial websites such as **payscale.com** and **rileyguide.com.**

Product and Service Strategies[1]

CHAPTER 6

Products and Services Explained

In the United States, tens of thousands of new products are introduced every year: shampoos, video games, soups, T-shirts, credit cards, and home security systems, to name just a few. Every product is defined by a set of attributes that include its features, functions, benefits, and uses. For example, the Dyson DC07 vacuum cleaner has a brush control (a feature) that deactivates its brushes at the touch of a button (a function). This feature helps protect delicate rugs (a benefit) when vacuuming carpets and other floor surfaces (a product use). The following are other examples of product attributes: product design (including visual appearance and ease of use), brand name, level of quality and dependability, logos or identifiers, packaging, and warranty.

The basic purpose of a **product** is to deliver benefits to consumers. Benefits define a product's utility, or what that product does for a customer. When choosing between two or more products, consumers evaluate the attributes and benefits of each. They select the product that offers them the maximum set of benefits.

products
Items consumed for personal or business use.

The term "product" is often used as an umbrella term to refer to both goods and services. According to the *Central Intelligence Agency World Factbook,* **services** produced by private industry accounted for 76.9% of the U.S. gross domestic product in 2009.[2] Products can be thought of as falling on a continuum, from pure goods (for example, a hairbrush) to pure services (for example, a haircut). Most products are neither purely goods nor purely services, but a blend of both. Products that appear on the surface to be pure goods usually contain services, like the lifetime warranty on a Craftsman hammer. And services are often associated with goods, such as souvenir T-shirts at a Coldplay concert.

services
Activities that deliver benefits to consumers or businesses.

Four ways in which services differ from physical goods are as follows:

- **Intangibility**—A service cannot be perceived by the five senses before it is purchased and delivered.
- **Inseparability**—A service cannot be separated from whomever is providing the service. It must be bought, and then produced and used simultaneously.

- **Variability**—Service quality is sometimes inconsistent because it depends on factors that are difficult to control. For instance, the skill of the people providing the service can vary.
- **Perishability**—A service cannot be stored for later use. Once it is actually produced, it must be immediately consumed, or its value perishes forever.[3]

The ways that services differ from products create challenges and opportunities. While it can be difficult to easily demonstrate benefits in advance of a service, in some cases it is possible to customize a service to create even greater benefits to a particular customer. This is generally not possible with a product.

Products and Services Applied

All parts of the marketing mix are important, but a sound product strategy is essential. It is through the sale and use of products or services that benefits are delivered to customers. Product strategy refers to all decisions that have an impact on a firm's product offerings, while service strategy refers to decisions about a company's services. Successful companies spend a large amount of time and effort on product management because it presents a great opportunity to grow sales, improve margins, and increase customer satisfaction. How should products be developed? What attributes and benefits should they have? Will they need to fit into a larger portfolio (or collection) of other products? What marketing strategies should be employed based on product type? The answers to questions such as these compose a product strategy.

Levels of Product

Marketers recognize that consumers buy products for a variety of reasons and distinguish between various levels of a product (also called layers). At the most basic level, all sodas quench thirst. Beverage brands such as Pepsi or Mountain Dew add a level of differentiation to their products through unique combinations of color, flavor, sweetness, carbonation, packaging, and brand image. Products can be viewed on three levels:[5]

- **Core benefits**—The fundamental product benefits that the customer is buying. For instance, people buy cars to have a means of transportation.
- **Actual product**—The combination of tangible and intangible attributes that delivers the core benefits. Each automobile has a particular combination of attributes, such as horsepower and fuel economy that determine its acceleration and cost of ownership. For some owners, the vehicle brand may also be a status symbol, for example, BMW or Lexus, and provide emotional rewards in addition to functional ones.
- **Augmented product**—Additional services or benefits that enhance the ownership of the actual product. For example, new vehicle purchases can also secure financing or extended warranties.

As an example of sustained innovation, Nintendo's Wii is the best-selling console in the world. Launched in 2006, Nintendo designers added a revolutionary level of physical interaction between players and games. The core features included wireless motion-sensitive remote controllers and built-in Wi-Fi capability. The simplicity of the Wii and its playability make it popular with all age groups. Residents at senior centers compete in nationwide Wii bowling tournaments. Nintendo launched the Wii Fit in 2008, Wii Fit Plus in 2009, and created a wide range of downloadable Wii games for 2010. These new offerings have helped the Nintendo Wii retain its dominant market position.[4]

PHOTO: Alamy Images

Looking beyond the core level of a product may create an opportunity to compensate for a product deficiency or to add a product benefit. Consider the case of Kia automobiles. To address concerns about its quality among U.S. consumers, Kia augmented its product by offering a 10-year/100,000-mile power train warranty. When all products in a category have similar core benefits, the appeal of one can also be enhanced by differentiating it at the actual or augmented level.

EXAMPLE **LEVELS OF A PRODUCT**

Dell manufactures computers for the home and office. One of its most popular items is the laptop computer, used by many college students studying at home or away at school.

PHOTO: ArchMan/Shutterstock

- At the core product level, a Dell laptop computer allows its user to manage information, enjoy personal entertainment, and connect to the Internet.
- Dimensions of the actual product include its color, screen size, weight, memory capacity, processor, software, and video card. The Dell brand image may also represent good value and quality to the laptop's owner.
- At the level of the augmented product, Dell offers financing, warranties, tech support, and customer service for every laptop that it sells.

>> END EXAMPLE

Product Classifications

Marketers classify products based on customer behavior, as shown in Table 6.1. Depending on the classification, there are clear implications for shopping behavior, and thus marketing strategy. Consumer products are products that directly fulfill the desires of consumers and are not intended to assist in the manufacture of other products. **Convenience products,** such as potato chips or chewing gum, are bought frequently with little or no advanced planning. They usually have low prices and are widely distributed, so people can buy them easily when the mood strikes. For example, candy is usually prominently displayed near cash registers to motivate impulse purchases. Brand loyalty for convenience products is low, so manufacturers try to build awareness and preference through advertising and other forms of promotion, such as coupons.

Shopping products are more complex and are bought less frequently than convenience products. Consumers will spend more time cross-comparing product features and benefits—for example, product quality, brand name, and special features—before purchasing shopping products. Blue jeans or airline flights are examples of shopping products. Their prices are higher than convenience products and they are distributed through fewer locations, because customers are willing to make a greater effort to find them. Along with advertising, personal selling at point-of-sale plays a major role in promoting shopping products because salespeople are able to carefully explain product attributes and benefits.

Specialty products have unique characteristics, like highly prized brand names or one-of-a-kind features. Luxury cars, high-end designer clothes, and gourmet chocolates

TABLE 6.1
CONSUMER PRODUCT CLASSIFICATION

MARKETING IMPLICATIONS	CONVENIENCE PRODUCTS	SHOPPING PRODUCTS	SPECIALTY PRODUCTS	UNSOUGHT PRODUCTS
Purchase frequency	Frequent	Less frequent	Infrequent	Infrequent
Amount of comparison and shopping effort	Minimal	Moderate	High	Minimal
Brand loyalty	Low	Higher	High	Low
Price	Low	Higher	High	Low to high
Distribution	Widespread	Fewer outlets	Few outlets	Low to high
Promotion	Mass promotion (for example, advertising, sampling) by manufacturer	Advertising and personal selling by manufacturer and retailer	Targeted promotion by manufacturer and retailer	Heavy advertising and personal selling by manufacturer and retailer
Examples	Chewing gum, potato chips, magazines	Blue jeans, TV sets, sofas	Luxury cars, deluxe vacations, fine crystal	Funerals, life insurance, retirement plans

are some examples. Specialty products are purchased infrequently, and consumers are willing to expend more effort, search more locations, and spend more time to find exactly what they want. Because customers are willing to exert extra resources and effort, these items usually carry high prices and are distributed in far fewer locations. Promotional activities are highly targeted to particular audiences or lifestyles because mass communication would be far too inefficient.

Unsought products, such as life insurance or funeral planning, are items consumers often do not like to think about purchasing. People are generally unaware of brand names or specific product benefits. Purchases are made infrequently, often with a minimum amount of shopping effort. Price and distribution strategy will vary, based on the type of product sold. Life insurance is relatively low priced and easily available, but funeral services are fairly expensive and available at only a few locations. Heavy promotion and personal selling are common marketing strategies, because consumers will not actively seek out these products and marketing messages must be aggressively taken to them.[6]

Industrial products sold to businesses and governments, like factory equipment or legal services, may also be classified. Types of products consumed by the business-to-business market are the following:

- **Equipment**—Factory buildings or copy machines are classified as equipment, and their marketing strategy frequently involves personal selling and product customization.
- **MRO products**—Items used for the maintenance, repair, and operation of a business are called MRO products. Because they are purchased frequently, prices for MRO products are kept as affordable as possible. Screws, nails, and washers are all MRO products.

- **Raw materials**—Raw materials include products such as lumber, wheat, or cotton. Offering lower prices and superior customer service are two common strategies for marketing raw materials.
- **Processed materials and services**—Firms also purchase processed materials and services, like fabric for clothing or copy-machine repair services.
- **Components**—These are finished products that organizations use to fabricate their own products. For example, liquid crystal displays are components in the manufacture of cell phones and computer monitors.[7]

EXAMPLE **PRODUCT CLASSIFICATIONS**

PHOTO: Pablo Eder/Shutterstock

Wrigley's chewing gum is perhaps the ultimate convenience product. The marketing strategy for Wrigley gum is an almost textbook example for how to market convenience products. Chewing gum is purchased frequently, so every Wrigley product package is small and lightweight, making it easy to purchase and carry. On average, consumers spend 16 seconds shopping for confections such as candy or gum. Because consumers often buy on impulse with little or no product search, intensive distribution for these items is critical. Wrigley is committed to building strong relationships with its retailer partners, which helps to keep its products on shelves in locations as diverse as grocery stores, convenience stores, gas stations, drug stores, mass merchandisers, and wholesale clubs. Prices for Wrigley gum products are always affordable and competitive, so they are easily attainable for customers. Regarding promotion strategy, Wrigley follows the precept laid down by its founder William Wrigley Jr.: "Tell 'em quick, and tell 'em often." The company consistently invests in advertising and other promotional activities to support its brands. Traditional print and TV ads are combined with new media to reach on-the-go, tech-savvy consumers. By strengthening the equity of its brands, Wrigley is able to create primary demand for its gum and avoid excessive discounting.[8]

>> END EXAMPLE

New Product Development

For companies to remain vital, they must develop a steady stream of new products. Unfortunately, the failure rate for new products in the packaged goods sector is as high as 80%.[9] To improve these odds, a new product development process incorporates insight into a firm's customers and its environment. The steps involved in new product development follow and are illustrated in Figure 6.1:[10]

- **Idea generation**—Formulate an idea for a new product or service.
- **Idea screening**—Review the idea to ensure that it meets customer wants and company goals.
- **Concept development**—Concretely define the features and benefits of the new product.
- **Marketing strategy**—Create a marketing strategy for the product's introduction.
- **Business analysis**—Validate that the new product will meet all sales and profit objectives.

FIGURE 6.1

Product Development Stages

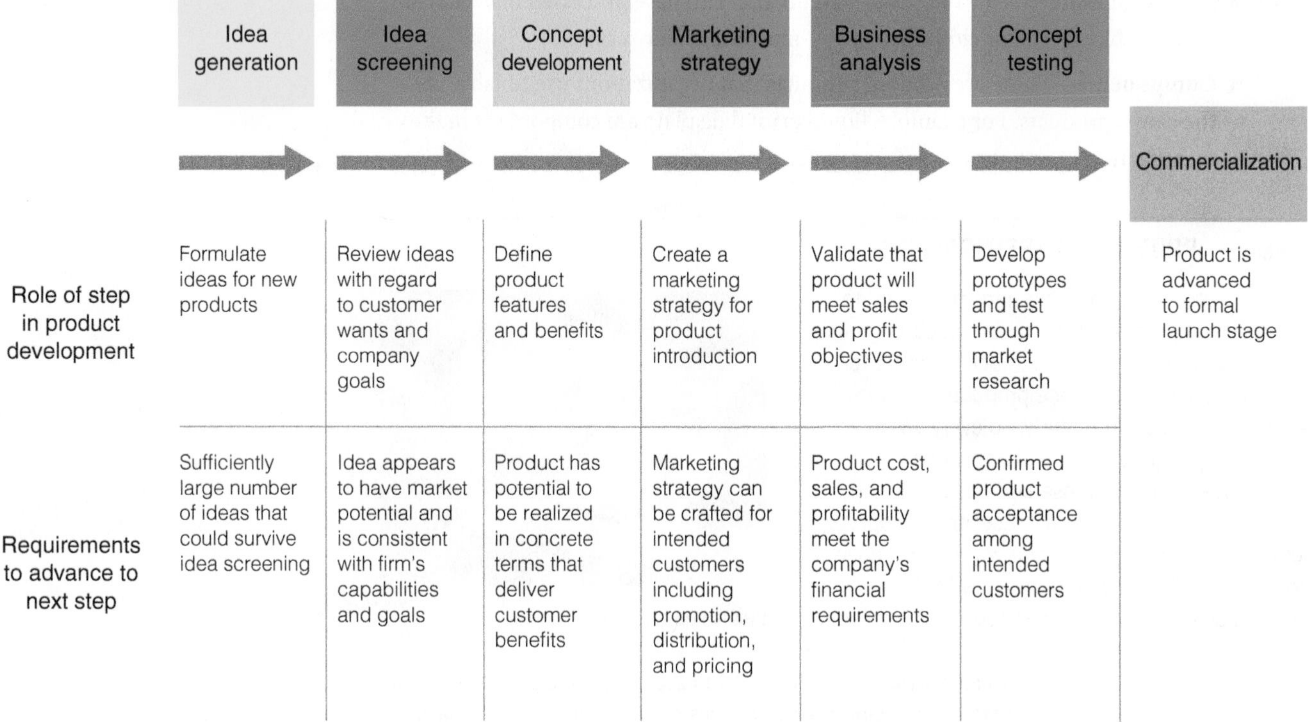

- **Concept testing**—Develop prototypes of the product for test marketing.
- **Commercialization**—Launch the new product in the marketplace.

Product concepts must pass through each stage of the process to move on to the next. At each step, ideas that fail to make the grade are weeded out. As a result, companies strive to generate a large number of ideas up front, knowing that only a few of those ideas will survive to commercialization. During the concept-development step, focus groups or other qualitative research techniques are often used to refine product ideas based on customer feedback. Before commercialization, a company may also invest in test marketing, during which actual products are introduced into select geographic areas. Test markets involve full-scale launch activities, including advertising, pricing, sampling, and distribution. Although costly, test markets help firms avoid more costly mistakes and can suggest ideas for product improvements.

EXAMPLE **NEW PRODUCT DEVELOPMENT**

To broaden the appeal for their brand, marketers at Yoplait were looking to introduce a new product. At that time, yogurt was available in three styles: sundae-style (with fruit on the bottom), Swiss-style (with fruit mixed in), and plain. To uncover a new opportunity, Yoplait followed a classic product development process:[11]

- **Idea Generation**—According to market research, consumers liked Yoplait's flavor, but its smooth consistency led some to reject the brand. The Yoplait marketing team, along with its advertising agency, generated 26 new product ideas to address this problem.

- **Idea Screening**—To pass through the screening stage, new product ideas had to meet specific sales volume objectives. Only 7 out of the original 26 ideas met those criteria.
- **Concept Development**—The most promising idea was a new custard-style yogurt. The product needed to be firm and thick, yet smooth and creamy. Yoplait refined the product concept by experimenting with combinations of fat, fruit, color, and texture.
- **Marketing Strategy**—Yoplait marketers were faced with several product strategy options:
  - Should the new product be positioned as a snack, meal substitute, or dessert?
  - Should it use the traditional conical Yoplait package?
  - Would a 4-oz or 6-oz serving be more appealing?
  - What should be the fat level (full or low)?

PHOTO: David Davis/Shutterstock

- **Business Analysis**—Yoplait marketers needed to ensure the new products would meet business requirements. The overall financial impact of the new portfolio was reviewed.
- **Concept Testing (Product development)**—Hundreds of prototypes were developed in search of the right combination of fruit, color, feel, and other attributes. Marketers sampled batches and used their judgment to narrow down the number of product concepts.
- **Concept Testing (Test marketing)**—Seven product concepts were tested in a mini-market test in Eau Claire/LaCrosse, Wisconsin. Each concept used a different positioning and mix of package, size, and fat level. The "winning" alternative was positioned as a full-fat snack in a traditional 6-oz Yoplait package. Market test results suggested that the new product would add 36% incremental volume to the Yoplait line with a low risk of cannibalization.
- **Commericalization**—Based on favorable concept test results. Yoplait custard style yogurt was launched nationwide in six flavors.

Yoplait custard style yogurt is now available in a dozen flavors, such as Key Lime Pie and Peaches 'N Cream.

>> END EXAMPLE

Product-Development Steps—Roles and Requirements

There is no single, best way to encourage innovation and new ideas. Some firms establish new product teams that are multidisciplinary groups (including representatives from marketing, finance, manufacturing, and other departments) that meet on a regular basis to discuss new product ideas. Other companies maintain formal R&D (research and development) groups responsible for presenting new product concepts to brand managers.

Some new product ideas are discontinuous innovations that change our everyday lives in dramatic ways. Personal computers and portable phones are some examples. But innovations are not only revolutionary, breakthrough ideas. According to Peter Fisk, there are typically three kinds of new product ideas:[12]

- **Cosmetic change**—The most basic type of innovation, involving some evolutionary change to an existing product or service. New versions of existing automotive nameplates (such as Toyota Camry or Ford Escape) are introduced every few years, although they are rarely total product redesigns.
- **Context change**—When an existing product or service is taken into a new context or market. The context for the Bacardi Breezer was repositioned from a big bottle in the supermarket to a cool club drink.
- **Concept change**—This is an advanced innovation that changes everything. IKEA rethought home decoration and do-it-yourself shopping, and brought affordable Scandinavian design to the masses.

Ideas for new products come from almost anywhere. Mistakes can even be a source of innovation. In the 1970s, a researcher at 3M was trying to find a strong adhesive. His experiments led to an adhesive that was the opposite of strong; in fact, it was so weak that after sticking to a surface it could be easily removed. Years later, 3M came to understand the hidden potential in this discovery, and the product known as 3M Post-it Notes was born.

Another source of product innovation is packaging. One aspect is packaging design, which delights consumers by making products more attractive and easy to use. In 2006, CARGO Cosmetics won a DuPont Award for packaging for its ColorCards single-use portable eye shadows. Each ColorCard is the size of a credit card and employs a patented printing process that deposits a thin layer of eye shadow onto a 12-point decorated board. Marketers are also searching for ways to incorporate recyclable and environmentally safe ingredients into packages. The wedge-shaped Tetra Pak is designed to heat sauces in microwave ovens and is made with over 70% renewable materials.[13]

Product and Service Quality

Consumers will pay for a product (or service) only if it has an adequate level of quality at a fair price. But quality is in the eye of the beholder, and no two people define quality in exactly the same way. Quality is most frequently defined as the customer's overall reaction to the attributes of a product or service. For example, consider a trip to the dentist. For one patient, a quick visit with minimal discomfort is a "quality" experience, while another person will be satisfied only if their dentist also has an engaging, personable manner.

A product quality strategy, therefore, specifies a level of performance for each product attribute relative to the target market's perception of quality and value. Not every product needs to have superior performance on every attribute. In fact, few customers will pay for products that offer "the best of everything." Higher quality usually means higher costs, due to better engineering, superior materials, or a more highly trained workforce. A quality product for many people is one that excels on those few dimensions that are important to them, and is merely adequate on others. In this instance, they will give up some benefits for a lower price.

To implement a product and service quality strategy, marketers set performance level targets for attributes in alignment with customer wants and needs. Then, every activity of the firm, from research and development to customer service, is aligned to deliver those objectives. QFD (quality function deployment) is a method some companies use to translate customer needs into product and quality requirements. Process tools like Six Sigma use statistical analysis to continually reduce manufacturing defects. Firms compliant with ISO 9000 and ISO 9001 standards follow a strict set of rules governing internal processes from record keeping to annual reviews. A well-thought-out and well-executed product quality strategy will reduce costs, improve customer satisfaction, reduce customer defection, increase sales, and improve profitability.

Product Design

Although often overlooked, product design is a critical element of product strategy and has the potential to add differentiation and value. The term **product style** refers to the visual appearance of a product, but **product design** is a broader term that includes a product's style, its tactile appeal, and its usability. Consider two products with identical core benefits. The well-designed product is more pleasurable to look at, feels better in your hands, and is easier to use. The page you are currently reading was designed by graphic artists to make it legible and easy to understand.

Good design evokes positive feelings in the customer and is a source of strategic advantage. The OXO brand specializes in ergonomically designed tools for household tasks such as cooking, repairing, and gardening. Each OXO tool is designed to be visually appealing and comfortable to hold. Services as well as goods may be well designed. Online marketers often apply experience design principles to improve their services. Amazon.com has redesigned the online buying experience by offering a "1-Click" feature that stores personal credit card information so returning customers can make quicker, easier purchases with a single mouse click.

EXAMPLE **PRODUCT DESIGN**

How can design be used to make an everyday product, such as a prescription bottle, more useful and attractive? After her grandmother accidentally took her grandfather's medication, designer Deborah Adler looked for a better way to design medicine bottles. Her ideas became the inspiration for the ClearRx prescription bottles offered exclusively through Target stores.

Every ClearRx bottle has numerous features to improve the way medicine is used and stored:[14]

- An easy-to-read label with large type
- A color-coded ID ring with a color for each family member
- A top label with the name of the drug clearly printed for easy identification in case the bottle is stored in a drawer
- A slide-in information card with important patient and drug information
- An oral syringe to make measuring liquid doses easier
- Free flavoring for liquid medicine, with flavors such as watermelon or bubble gum
- A free magnifier to make label reading easier

PHOTO: Elena Ray/Shutterstock

>> END EXAMPLE

Product Portfolio Explained

product portfolio (also called a product mix)
A collection of all products and services offered by a company.

Most companies sell more than one kind of product or service. If a product is successful, a firm usually introduces additional variations on the basic product, or additional new products, into its **product portfolio.** When a firm targets multiple customer segments, it may also need to offer a range of products tailored for each target group.

A company's product portfolio includes all of the brands, subbrands, and varieties of products or services that it offers. The number of products in a portfolio can add up quickly, so managing them might become overwhelming. A product that is popular today could go out of fashion tomorrow. The strategic challenge is to keep the firm's product portfolio fresh and relevant in the marketplace.

Product Portfolio Applied

Portfolio management comprises all of the decisions, or strategic wagers, a company makes regarding its portfolio of current and future products. Managing the product portfolio is an important component of the marketing strategy because company resources are finite. Even the most successful firms have limits on the amount of time and money they can devote to any one product. Resource-investment decisions are made based on which products the company believes have greater, or lesser, potential in the marketplace. The company must choose which products to keep within, remove from, or add to the portfolio. Because the success or failure of any particular product is uncertain, the resulting set of investment decisions adds up to a firm's collective wagers, or "bets," on the future performance of the portfolio.

When discussing product portfolios, several terms are used. A **product line** is a group of closely related products. Table 6.2 is an example of Sony's U.S. product lines in the spring of 2010.

Some organizations employ a **full-line product strategy** by offering a wide range of product lines within a product portfolio. Procter & Gamble sells a variety of household products in categories such as oral care, cleaning products, and childcare. Other companies pursue a **limited-line product strategy** and focus on one or a few product lines. The product portfolio is managed along three dimensions:[15]

- **Product mix width** refers to the number of product lines a company offers.
- **Product mix length** is the total number of products offered.
- **Product mix depth** is the number of versions of products within a line.

These terms are helpful when thinking about ways to expand or contract a portfolio. A firm may decide to change the width of its product mix by adding or eliminating a product line. **Line extensions** are additions to an existing product line and are one way to increase the depth of a product line. Developed as a stand-alone product, the popular Swiffer cleaning brush has inspired a series of line extensions, including Swiffer SweeperVac, Swiffer WetJet, Swiffer Dusters, and Swiffer CarpetFlick. Another way to increase the depth of a line is to stretch it upward (or downward) by introducing products of superior (or lesser) quality or price. **Line expansions** occur when entirely new lines are added to a product mix. For example, Pepsi added the Naked Juice health-drink line to its beverage portfolio by acquiring the brand's parent company in 2007.

TABLE 6.2
SONY U.S. PRODUCT PORTFOLIO, SPRING 2010

	PRODUCT CATEGORY					
	COMPUTERS	CAMERAS AND CAMCORDERS	TV AND HOME ENTERTAINMENT	MP3 AND PORTABLE ELECTRONICS	MOVIES AND MUSIC	GAMES
PRODUCT LINES	VAIO notebooks	Cyber-shot digital cameras	Televisions	Walkman Video MP3 players	DVD movies	PlayStation systems
	VAIO desktops	Digital SLR cameras	Home theater systems	Reader Digital Book	Blu-ray Disc movies	PlayStation 3
	Digital Home	Handycam camcorders	Blu-ray Disc	Sony Ericsson	UMD videos for PSP	PlayStation Portable (PSP)
	Disc burners	Digital picture frames	DVD players	Mobile phones	Music	
	Personal Internet Viewer	Photo printers	Home Entertainment Servers (HES)	GPS navigation		
	Accessories	Photo services	Home audio components	Portable DVD and CD players		
	Software and media		Mini stereo systems	Bluetooth devices Radios and boom boxes Headphones Voice recorders iPod accessories		

EXAMPLE **PRODUCT PORTFOLIO**

The Hershey Company is the largest market of chocolate and sugar confectionery products in North America. Although it is most famous for its Hershey bars and Kisses, the Hershey Company maintains a product mix of great width, length, and depth. Reese's, Almond Joy, Mounds, are just a sampling of its chocolate and confectionery brands. The Hershey premium product lines include Cacao Reserve chocolate bars, Joseph Schmidt handcrafted chocolate gifts, and Dagoba organic chocolate products. Ice Breakers mints and Bubble Yum gum are some of Hershey's refreshment product lines.[16]

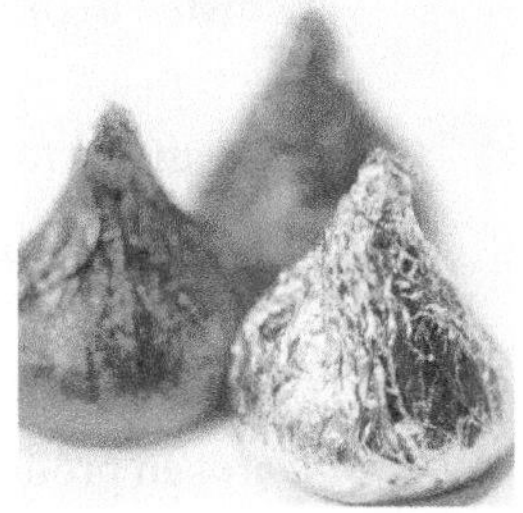

PHOTO: Joseph/Shutterstock

>> END EXAMPLE

When adding products to a portfolio, marketers should pay attention to the possibility of cannibalization, which occurs when a new product takes market share from an established product. Cannibalization is not necessarily to be avoided, but it has the potential to ruin a business if a new, less profitable product is an attractive substitute for an older, more profitable entry. It could even become necessary when an aging product needs to be replaced by a newer, fresher alternative due to changes in consumer tastes or technological innovation. In the late 1990s, Charles Schwab recognized a potential opportunity in the emerging online stock-trading business. It deliberately cannibalized its own traditional brokerage business by instituting a common price for both online and offline stock trades. By cannibalizing itself, within six months $51 billion in assets poured into Charles Schwab and the firm captured 42% of the online stock-trading market.[17]

Product Life Cycle Explained

product life cycle (PLC)
A model that describes the evolution of a product's sales and profits throughout its lifetime. The stages of the product life cycle are as follows: Introduction, Growth, Maturity, and Decline.

The popularity of a product evolves over time, growing and fading as consumer tastes change or as a newer, more desirable product is introduced in that product's place. The **product life cycle (PLC),** illustrated in Figure 6.2, assumes that products follow a common pattern of evolution through a series of life stages. The PLC is based on an analogy taken from the realm of biology, where organisms evolve in a predicable pattern. Although only a model, or picture, of how the real world operates, the PLC can still be valuable because it contains implications for marketing strategy at each stage of evolution. The four stages of the PLC are as follows:

- **Introduction stage**—During this stage, a new product is introduced to the marketplace. Sales volume increases as potential customers gain awareness of the product.
  - Highly innovative tablet PCs (like Apple's iPad) will continue to be in the introduction stage for the near future as new products come to market with even more exciting features.
- **Growth stage**—Many products fail during the introductory phase of the PLC. Those gaining acceptance in the marketplace progress to the growth stage, where sales increase rapidly. For marketers, this is an exciting time, because the new product also becomes very profitable.
  - Plasma or LCD widescreen TV sets are currently in the growth stage of the PLC, with a greater range of brands and models on sale as demand for these items continues to grow.
- **Maturity stage—**At some point, markets become saturated. Customers are sated with products and all of their variations. At this point, the product has graduated to the maturity stage, where sales growth peaks and eventually flattens. Although a few first-time buyers are coming to market, most product sales are replacements for previous purchases.
  - For many years, the DVD player has been in the maturity stage of the PLC. Prices are now so affordable that DVD players are within the budget of the majority of U.S. consumers. Many purchases are sales made to replace older or broken products.

FIGURE 6.2

Product Life Cycle

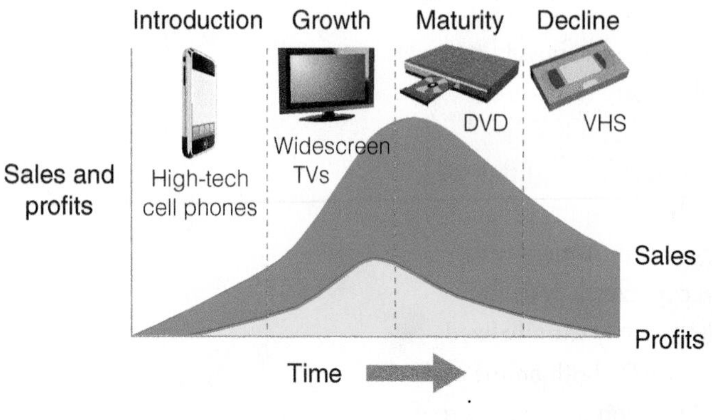

- **Decline stage**—Every product eventually reaches a decline stage where sales and profits fall. A product may go into decline for many reasons, including technological obsolescence, an erosion of brand equity, increased competition, and changes in customer preferences. One product may fade away slowly and gracefully, while another vanishes abruptly.
  - In the mass consumer market, VHS players are in decline due to technological advances like DVD players, laptops with video capability, and TiVo. Previously easy

to purchase and rent, VHS tapes and players are now difficult to find as manufacturers scale back models and production.

The PLC is not fixed, unchangeable, and true for each and every marketing situation. The PLC is a model for how products generally behave, based on past experience. Each product is unique; it has its own set of customers, benefits, competitors, brand names, and other attributes. Any of these could shorten, lengthen, or change the shape of an individual product's life cycle.

Product Life Cycle Applied

The PLC is a useful tool for marketers because it provides a clear, predictable framework for sales and profit levels over time. Marketers may take advantage of general rules or strategies that have been devised for each stage of the PLC. Although accurately estimating sales volume or profit at each stage can be difficult, and products may follow different life-cycle patterns, the PLC remains a useful source of ideas for marketing strategies throughout a product's lifetime.

Product Life Cycle and Marketing Strategies

The PLC model assumes that sales build through successive stages of the life cycle until a product reaches maturity, and that each stage has different implications for marketing mix strategy (product, pricing, placement, and promotion), as shown in Table 6.3. In contrast, profits are low (or negative) in the introduction stage, rise to a peak during growth, and then begin to decline over time, until they are essentially eliminated.

During introduction, the goal is to gain acceptance for the new product in the marketplace so companies will invest heavily in promotion and distribution. Prices may be high or low, depending on whether the firm has chosen to pursue a **penetration strategy** (holding price low to gain share) or a **skimming strategy** (keeping price high to maximize return).

Upon reaching the growth stage, the emphasis shifts to capitalizing on an expanding market opportunity. Competitors are attracted to the new profit opportunity and introduce their own variations of the successful product. Pioneer firms respond by attempting to build preference for their brands or by adding features to the basic product. Defending a high-market-share position during the growth stage can be expensive. Although investments in new product development or brand advertising may forfeit short-term profits, they can also leave a firm well positioned to compete in the maturity stage.

As sales growth slows during the maturity stage, competitors struggle over a more finite pool of available customers. Downward pressure is exerted on profits as most firms are forced to invest in marketing incentives and/or to reduce prices. This is usually the longest stage because some products may remain in maturity for decades.

TABLE 6.3

Stages of the Product Life Cycle

MARKETING IMPLICATIONS	INTRODUCTION	GROWTH	MATURITY	DECLINE
Sales	Low	Growing	Peak—Sales curve flattens out	Declining
Profit	Low or even negative	Rising	Falling	Low and eventually negative
Marketing goals	Build awareness for product category; encourage trial	Take advantage of growing demand; build brand preference	Maximize market share and profit	Eliminate product or reduce investment
Product	Basic	Add features and product line extensions	Diversify to attract new customers and extend life cycle	Reduce costs and slow-selling versions
Price	May be high or low	Lower	Low to meet competition	Low
Distribution	Selective, with few outlets	More outlets	Maximize number of outlets	Phase out unprofitable outlets
Promotion	Heavy expenditure to build targeted awareness	Mass communications to build general awareness	Mass communications to build brand preference	Reduce to minimum level

Recognizing the challenges of the maturity stage, companies take steps to extend its duration as long as possible.

During the decline stage, some firms choose to simply pull out of the market, thus **divesting** themselves of a product. The declining product could be discontinued or sold outright to another firm. Others prefer licensing the brand name or product design to another company, allowing the original owners to maintain a degree of profitability without significant expense. LEGO licenses its brand name to the Clic Time Company, which manufactures clocks and watches using LEGO's distinctive colors and product design. **Harvesting** is a third option in which a firm continues to sell a product while gradually reducing, and eventually eliminating, all of its marketing investment.

Duration of the Product Life Cycle

Innovations take time to spread through the marketplace. Not every business or consumer is equally willing to try new things. Diffusion of innovations refers to the speed with which consumers and businesses adopt a particular product. Marketers segment populations into five groups with various degrees of openness toward innovations (see Figure 6.3):

- **Innovators** (2.5% of population): The innovators are the most willing to adopt innovations. They are open-minded, adventurous, and tend to be younger, better educated, and more financially secure. They try new things just because they like having something new and unusual.
- **Early adopters** (13.5% of population): Early adopters are more socially aware than innovators and consider the prestige or social implications of being seen using a new product. They are media savvy, and more mainstream groups look to early adopters for cues as to what is the "next big thing."
- **Early majority** (34% of population): Members of the early majority do not want to be the first or the last to try a new product. Instead, they wait to see what excites the early adopters, and only then do they begin to buy a product. Once the early majority adopts a product, it is no longer a cutting-edge item, but has become part of the mainstream.
- **Late majority** (34% of population): Older and more conservative than other groups, the late majority will not adopt a product they consider to be too risky. They will purchase something only if they consider it to be a necessity or when they are under some form of social pressure.
- **Laggards** (16% of population): Laggards are heavily bound by tradition and are the last to adopt an innovation. By the time laggards take up a product, it may already have been rendered obsolete by another innovation.

FIGURE 6.3

Innovation Segments

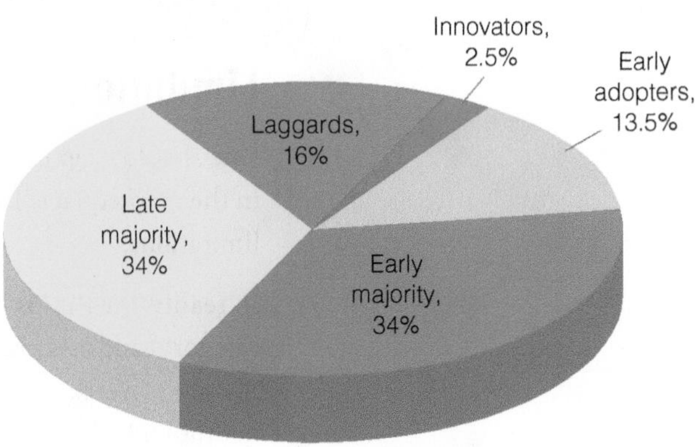

When launching a new product, marketers will focus their efforts on innovators and early adopters to get the diffusion process rolling. Depending on how readily these groups adopt the new product, the PLC may be quite short or very long.[18]

Although the average human lifetime is approximately 78 years, the estimated life cycle for a product or service is only 13 years.[19] Not every PLC is this short, however, because some products may be long lived. Colt pistols, Stetson hats, Vaseline emollient, and Pepsi-Cola have endured for more than 100 years.

Marketers can extend a product's life span by doing the following:

- Promoting the product to new customers or markets
- Finding new uses or applications for the product
- Repositioning the product or brand
- Adding product features or benefits
- Offering new packages or sizes
- Introducing low-cost product variations and/or reducing price

Graphical representations of the PLC usually depict all four of its stages as roughly equal in duration. In reality, some stages might be longer or shorter than others. For example, when a product is a fad, it rapidly gains and then loses popularity in the marketplace, resulting in a PLC with a tall, narrow shape. The PLC graph for a style of product has a more wave-like appearance, as its popularity rises or falls over time. For instance, consider women's hemlines. Ankle-length skirts (or miniskirts) may be fashionable for a while, lose their appeal, and then become stylish again years later.

Limitation of the Product Life Cycle

One should keep in mind that the PLC is a model, or theory, about how products behave in the marketplace. Like most models or approximations of the real world, the PLC has limitations.

In reality, the PLC is most applicable to classes of products (like the Blu-ray player category) and less predictive of behavior for individual products or brands (like Sony Blu-ray players). The PLC works best in modeling categories of product innovations, and not individual products. Determining the life stage for a class or category of products is fairly straightforward, because the sales and profits for all brands can be rolled up into a single metric. However, identifying the life stage for a particular brand can be more difficult. Although the overall product category may continue to hold appeal for consumers, not all brands may be equally preferred. Therefore, each one may perform differently.

It may also be difficult for marketers to identify the exact stage of their products in the life cycle because PLC curves come in many different shapes, for example, fads and styles. Your product's profit curve is rising, but does this mean it is progressing within the growth stage, or has it reached its peak of maturity? A "normal" life-cycle curve shows profits rising over a reasonable period of time, but in the case of a fad, sales and profits peak very quickly.

Perhaps the biggest controversy surrounding the PLC is that some say it stifles original marketing thought. If you believe a product is in decline, and you follow the suggestions of the PLC model completely, you will cut back R&D investment and promotion. Although the product may have had the potential to be resurrected, this disinvestment may simply force it into decline, as needed resources are pulled away. The PLC can serve as inspiration for marketing strategy, but it should never be the final word about what actions to take in each and every marketing situation.

Conclusion

It is through the creation and management of products and services that a company delivers value to its customers. Portfolio management and new product development are two methods companies employ to keep their assortment of products and services relevant and vital. The product life cycle model suggests ways to improve performance at each stage in a product's life. Carefully formulated product and service strategies, when aligned with the marketing plan, will pave the way for the remaining elements of the marketing mix.

CHAPTER 7

External Environment[1]

Marketing Environment Explained

Businesses strive to create value that leads to productive customer relationships. Many factors influence value creation and the nature of customer relationships, including factors that are internal to the business and factors that are external to the business. The **internal environment** of a business involves all those activities, including marketing, that occur within the organizational functions in a business. **Internal marketing** is the implementation of marketing practices within an organization to communicate organizational policies and practices to employees and internal stakeholders. The topics of internal marketing efforts are the business's resources, including human and financial capital, as well as intangible assets, such as brands or patents. These factors represent many of the elements that can influence changes within a business.

marketing environment
A set of forces, some controllable and some uncontrollable, that influence the ability of a business to create value and attract and serve customers.

The **external environment** of a business involves all activities, such as supplier and customer actions that occur outside the organizational functions of a business. **External marketing** is the implementation of marketing practices directed outside the business to create value and to form productive customer relationships. External marketing influences the external environment in distinct areas, including the microenvironment and the macroenvironment, which can either enhance or diminish the ability of a business to create value for its customers.

Marketing Environment Applied

In practice, businesses typically concentrate their efforts on developing strategies that assist in managing the microenvironment. The increasing sophistication of methods to gather marketing research information, from checkout scanner data to purchase transaction databases, allows for quicker responses to changes in the microenvironment. More companies are realizing the importance of internal marketing to employees and internal stakeholders. Such internal marketing communicates the values and expectations of the business and creates business proponents in the marketplace when the employees interact with others. Many companies are also engaged in lobbying the U.S. government and governments of other countries to influence the macroenvironment. Businesses, however, typically do not directly influence the macroenvironment.

Microenvironment

The microenvironment includes those forces close to a company, yet outside its internal environment that influence the ability of a business to serve its customers.[2] The microenvironment comprises entities such as customers, suppliers, competitors, and other businesses that assist or influence a business's ability to sell, distribute, promote, and develop products or services. A tool that helps determine where power exists in the microenvironment of a business is Porter's Five Forces of Competitive Position Model.[3] The Porter analysis can assist a business with understanding the potential for new product development, the attractiveness of a particular market segment, or the potential to reduce costs of supply or distribution, among many other applications.

The central concept of the Five Forces of Competitive Position Model is that five forces determine the power in a business's microenvironment. Those forces are the following:

- Threat of new entrants
- Bargaining power of suppliers
- Bargaining power of customers
- Threat of substitute products
- Competitive rivalry within an industry

The threat of new entrants can influence a business's level of power in an industry by the existing barriers to entry. Strong barriers to entry, such as intellectual property or economies of scale, provide a company power to resist new entrants.

Suppliers can assert power if they are the only one or one of a few businesses that can provide a particular product or service. Buyers (or customers) can also exert power on a business through the number and nature of buyers. The more buyers that are available, the less important an individual buyer is to a business. The fewer buyers that are available, the more power they can project. In some cases, one buyer, such as Walmart, is so large that it constitutes a significant percentage of total purchases from a business.

The threat of substitutes can reduce the power of a business if many substitutes exist for a particular product or service. If a product exists that is tied to another product, such as certain technical computer software, there is less threat from substitutes.

The nature of the rivalry among existing industry competitors influences the balance of power in the industry. Any change in status, whether it be the quantity and size

The Health Care and Education Reconciliation Act was signed into law by President Barack Obama on March 30, 2010. Building on its predecessor, the Patient Protection and Affordable Care Act, the health care initiative affected both consumers and businesses in a variety of ways. Coverage is expanded over several years to 32 million Americans who were uninsured at the time of the bill signing. Some other elements of the law include the creation of state-based health care exchanges for the uninsured and self-employed, families with income under a particular level are subsidized, Medicare prescription drug assistance is provided, Medicaid coverage is expanded, insurance companies are forbidden from denying coverage to certain groups of individuals such as children and individuals with pre-existing conditions, and most individuals are mandated to purchase insurance. The implications are extensive. Demand for medical services and hospitals will most likely increase. The HMO industry will most likely be negatively impacted through increased competition and governmental mandates. Individuals may also have new or different choices as the law is implemented. There will be a variety of exchanges of information, and marketing activities, among the government, individuals, insurance companies, health care providers, and many other entities impacted by this law.[4]

PHOTO: Pincasso/Shutterstock

of competing businesses, their portfolio, or their financial position, will influence the power any one business can exert on the industry.

EXAMPLE **MICROENVIRONMENT**

PHOTO: Dundanim/Shutterstock

OnStar, a subsidiary of General Motors (GM) that provides subscription-based communication, tracking, diagnostic, navigation, emergency response, and other convenience services, is available on most GM vehicles and a few non-GM models. The product, referred to as telematics, is a combination of telecommunications and informatics/computer science. It consists of a mobile phone, onboard computer, sensors, and a Global Positioning System beacon. The product is available at no charge for a specific duration when an eligible new vehicle is purchased. After an initial period the service is subscription-based priced at approximately $200 annually. While unique to certain vehicles, many of the OnStar services have substitute products available. A mobile telephone could be considered a substitute for the OnStar hands-free calling service, a roadside service such as the American Automobile Association could be considered a substitute for OnStar's roadside assistance, and a portable navigation system could be considered a substitute for OnStar's Turn-by-Turn Navigation. The value that customers attribute to substitute products, including considerations such as switching costs, ease of use, and capability, influences the value that the customers attribute to the bundle of OnStar services.[5]

>> END EXAMPLE

Macroenvironment

The macroenvironment includes societal forces that are essentially uncontrollable and influence the microenvironment of a business. Part of the external environment of a business, the macroenvironment contains the following variety of sub-environments:

- Economic
- Social and cultural
- Competitive
- Legal
- Political
- Technological

EXAMPLE **MACROENVIRONMENT**

PHOTO: Jack Cronkhite/Shutterstock

A legislative change can create challenges for some businesses, and opportunities for others. As a result of a 2010 law requiring newly manufactured diesel-fueled trucks to meet new environmental emission standards, a New Jersey–based motor oil and fluid manufacturer and supplier, Prime Lube, looked to Europe, which has been dealing with similar standards since early 2000, for potential partners. Prime Lube became one of the first U.S. distributors of the German product BlueSky Diesel Exhaust Fluid, and began manufacturing it in the United States in July 2010. BlueSky is injected into the catalytic converter of a truck in a mist form where it interacts with nitrous oxide, the black soot that is released from most diesel exhaust systems, and converts it to water and carbon dioxide. The result is close to zero emissions. Prime Lube took advantage of a change in the macroenvironment to secure a new product that solves challenges for its customers before its competitors could do so.[6]

>> END EXAMPLE

ECONOMIC ENVIRONMENT As mentioned, one of the components of the macroenvironment is the economic environment. The **economic environment** includes factors that influence consumer purchase ability and buying behavior. Inflation rates, income levels, and unemployment levels all contribute to the economic environment. Inflation is an increase in the price of a collection of goods that represents the overall economy. As inflation increases, prices of items such as gasoline, food, and health services generally rise, and, if average income does not keep pace, products and services can become too expensive for consumers. The result is that demand generally decreases either voluntarily or involuntarily. **Income levels** are average consumer earnings used to approximate national earnings. Changes in income inversely relate to changes in demand. **Unemployment levels** are the number of unemployed persons divided by the aggregate labor force. Increases in unemployment reduce the ability of individuals to purchase products and services.

SOCIAL AND CULTURAL ENVIRONMENT The social and cultural environment includes factors that relate marketing to the needs and wants of society and culture. Changes in various types of demographics contribute to the social and cultural environment. Demographics are characteristics of human population that are used to identify markets. These characteristics include elements such as age, race, and household structure. As consumers age, levels of income generally increase and life stages change. The result is differing product and service demands. Businesses must carefully track changes such as age to make sure their portfolio continues to provide value to a market of relevant size. The United States is becoming an increasingly diverse market. As population segments such as Hispanics, Asian Americans, and African Americans increase, product and service requirements and different advertising methods change to reach diverse audiences. Household structure is also changing. There are more single-family households because people wait to marry later in life or not at all. The quantities and types of products and services produced need to reflect these realities.

EXAMPLE **ECONOMIC ENVIRONMENT**

The American Recovery and Reinvestment Act (ARRA) of 2009 included a number of either new or expanded tax benefits on expenditures to reduce energy use or create new energy sources. ARRA provided for a uniform credit of 30% of the cost of qualifying improvements up to $1,500. Expiring on December 31, 2010, the law sharply increased demand, during a very difficult economic time, for a wide range of

PHOTO: Christina Richards/ Shutterstock

products such as insulation, energy-efficient exterior windows and doors, and energy-efficient heating and air conditioning systems as well as contractor services.[7]

>> END EXAMPLE

COMPETITIVE ENVIRONMENT The competitive environment includes factors that relate to the nature, quantity, and potential actions of current and potential competitors. Changes in the context of competitors contribute to the competitive environment. If a business operates with a small number of competitors, there are fewer requirements to react to a competitive action and more time to make strategic decisions. In a competitive market, however, many more factors can impede a business from taking the actions that it wants to take. For example, if maintaining margins on products is important to generate money to fund important new product development, then a competitor's aggressive move to reduce price could hurt that business strategy. Maintaining margins would take second place to a need to respond to maintain market position.

EXAMPLE **COMPETITIVE ENVIRONMENT**

The 1972 launch of Pong, a video game that looked like video table tennis, is credited as greatly expanding the video game market. Pong first appeared in arcades, but Atari launched a home version in 1974. Atari's home version was a console-based game system that used cartridges and was wildly successful. In the early 1980s, competition from PC manufacturers and other video game manufacturers began eroding Atari's market share. A lack of product investment and oversupply of inventory, among other factors, caused a dramatic decline in Atari's fortunes. Atari struggles to this day. In contrast, Nintendo entered the U.S. market in the early 1980s with its proprietary console, the Nintendo Entertainment System. Nintendo had to convince resellers to stock its product in light of Atari's problems. Nintendo reduced the risks of resellers by agreeing to take back products that did not sell. Nintendo carefully controlled its inventory and focused on building quality products. It built a strong market presence and used that presence to influence resellers to stock a higher share of its products than those of competitors. Nintendo enjoyed great success with this strategy and continues that success today with its Wii system, among other products.

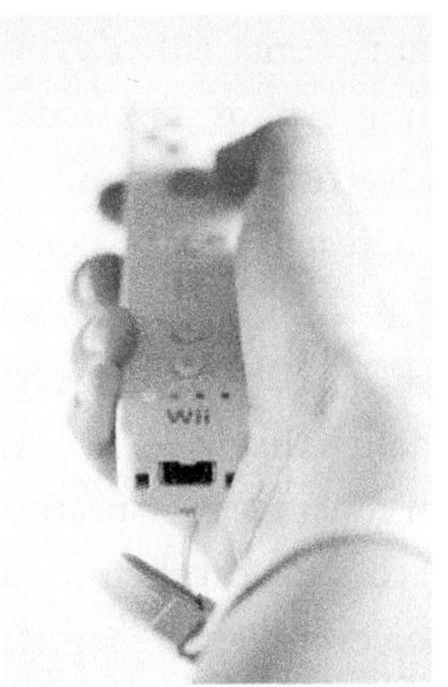

PHOTO: ST Images/Alamy Images

>> END EXAMPLE

LEGAL ENVIRONMENT The legal environment includes factors that provide rules and penalties for violations, and is designed to protect society and consumers from unfair business practices and to protect businesses from unfair competitive practices. Changes in legislation and regulations contribute to the legal environment. There are many different categories of legislation, including trade practices (fair trade), business competition, product safety, environmental protection, consumer privacy, fair pricing, packaging, and advertising disclosure and restrictions. Regulatory agencies include the Federal Communications Commission (FCC), an agency responsible for regulating interstate and international communications by television, satellite, cable, radio, and wire; the U.S. Consumer Product Safety Commission (USCPSC), an agency responsible for protecting consumers from unreasonable risks of serious injury from over 15,000 types of consumer products; and the Food and Drug Administration (FDA), an agency within the Department of Health and Human Services that has nine different centers, ranging from radiological health to food safety. In addition to national governmental legislation and regulations, there are also state and local legal requirements. The legal environment can become even more complicated as businesses increase global activities and must deal with foreign governments' legal environments that are different from those within the United States.

POLITICAL ENVIRONMENT The political environment includes factors that select national leadership, create laws, and provide a process for discourse on a wide range of issues. Changes in form of government and scope and type of social movements contribute to the political environment. A federal system of government, where a central government performs specific duties such as national defense and state and local governments have limited autonomy, is practiced in the United States. However, some countries, such as North Korea, are dictatorships. The government in those countries control everything, including commercial practices. The implications for businesses are significant, because investment may be restricted when high levels of risk exist. Social movements, either a new political party or cause, can also create trends such as interest in "green" or "fair trade" products. Whether protesting in cities or funding advocacy advertisements, these causes can have tremendous influence on consumer attitudes and interest in products or services.

TECHNOLOGICAL ENVIRONMENT The technological environment includes factors that influence marketing based on scientific actions and innovation. Changes in consumer perspectives on scientific activities and new discoveries contribute to the technological environment. Policies on cloning, stem cell research, or other controversial topics influence marketing opportunities. Funding is either made available or is restricted based on consumer perspectives that are often translated into legal framework. New discoveries, such as fiber-optic cable and hybrid vehicle propulsion systems, create marketing opportunities where businesses can take advantage of creating value in a way that competitors cannot. Consumption patterns could change based on the significance of the product or service.

PHOTO: Rena Schild/Shutterstock

EXAMPLE **TECHNOLOGICAL ENVIRONMENT**

Even existing technology, when utilized in a different context, can create unique customer value. Domino's Pizza Tracker allows customers to follow the progress of their pizza from order through delivery via a Web interface. The interactive tool uses a customer phone number to identify status as the pizza passes through five distinct stages: Order Placed, Prep, Bake, Quality Check, and Out for Delivery. Advancing mobile technology will create further opportunities for Domino's and other pizza companies as well as companies involved with manufacturing and suppliers of other products and services.[8]

>> END EXAMPLE

Consumer Markets Explained

Both macroenvironments and microenvironments influence, through factors such as demand and supply, consumers and businesses as they make purchase decisions. U.S. consumer buying power exceeds $10 trillion.[9] Over one-third of that buying power comes from the California, Texas, New York, and Florida consumer markets.[10] **Consumer markets** exist with respect to the product or service being marketed and can be considered as broad as the population of an entire country for certain food products, or as small as the limited number of people who can afford to be space tourists. **Consumer products** are products that directly fulfill the desires of consumers and are not intended to assist in the manufacture of other products.[11] Consumers make purchase decisions in consumer markets by assessing the utility of the products and services offered. A **consumer's surplus** occurs when a consumer purchases a product or service at a price less than the utility of the product or service.[12] This surplus reflects a marketer's missed opportunity to charge more for products or services and reflects an advantage to consumers. However, a significant disparity between purchase price and perceived utility may cause consumers to question what might be wrong with the product or service to warrant such a discount. Ultimately, marketing links production and consumption in the consumer market.

consumer markets
The end users of the product or service who include individuals and households that are potential or actual buyers of products and services.[13]

Consumer Markets Applied

In practice, purchase decisions in consumer markets are influenced heavily by the marketing and promotion of brands. Brands are used to convey value to consumers and conveying this value is accomplished through a wide range of marketing activities, including advertising and sales promotion. Marketing can be used to influence perceptions of utility and present one brand of product or service as different from another. Certain consumer markets, such as the market for shampoo and other personal care products, are saturated with brands, while others, such as the market for ultra luxury yachts, are served by few brands. Regardless of the number of competitors, each brand strives to be unique, as opposed to its competition, while remaining relevant to its consumer market.

Conclusion

Building on the concept of marketing and the marketing function, the marketing environment was introduced, as were consumer and business markets. The marketing environment is a set of forces, some controllable and some uncontrollable, which influence a business's ability to create value and attract and serve customers. Many factors influence value creation and the nature of customer relationships in the marketing environment. Some of those influential factors are internal to the business, while others are external. The internal environment of a business involves all activities, including marketing, that occur within the organizational functions in a business. The external environment of a business involves all activities that occur outside the organizational functions of a business. The external environment can be divided into the microenvironment and the macroenvironment. The central concept of the Five Forces of Competitive Position Model is that five forces determine the power in a business's microenvironment. The macroenvironment includes societal forces that are essentially uncontrollable and influence the microenvironment of a business. Consumer markets include individuals and households that are potential or actual buyers of products and services that assist in further production only indirectly or incidentally, if at all.

CHAPTER 8

Running Effective Meetings[1]

There are good meetings and there are bad meetings. Bad meetings drone on forever, you never seem to get to the point, and you leave wondering why you were even present. Effective ones leave you energized and feeling that you've really accomplished something.

So what makes a meeting effective?

Effective meetings have three characteristics:

- They achieve the meeting's objective.
- They take up a minimum amount of time.
- They leave participants feeling that a sensible process has been followed.

If you structure your meeting planning, preparation, execution, and follow up around these three basic criteria, the result will be an effective meeting.

The Meeting's Objective

An effective meeting serves a useful purpose. This means that in it, you achieve a desired outcome. For a meeting to meet this outcome, or objective, you have to be clear about what it is.

Too often, people call a meeting to discuss something without really considering what a good outcome would be.

- Do you want a decision?
- Do you want to generate ideas?

- Are you getting status reports?
- Are you communicating something?
- Are you making plans?

Any of these, and a myriad of others, is an example of a meeting objective. Before you do any meeting planning, you need to focus your objective. To help you determine what your meeting objective is, complete this sentence:

At the close of the meeting, I want the group to . . .

With the end result clearly defined, you can then plan the contents of the meeting, and determine who needs to be present.

Use Time Wisely

Time is a precious resource, and no one wants their time wasted. With the amount of time we all spend in meetings, you owe it to yourself and your team to streamline the meeting as much as possible. What's more, time wasted in a meeting is time wasted for everybody attending. For example, if a critical person is 15 minutes late in an eight person meeting, that person has cost the organization two hours of inefficient/ineffective activity.

Use an Agenda

To ensure you cover only what needs to be covered and you stick to relevant activities, you need to create an agenda. To prepare an agenda, consider the following factors:

- **Results**—What do you need to accomplish at the meeting?
- **Sequence**—In what order will you cover the topics? Schedule the most important topics first.
- **Timing**—How much time will you spend on each topic?
- **Date and Time**—When will the meeting take place?
- **Place**—Where will the meeting take place?

With an idea of what needs to be covered and for how long, you can then look at the information that should be prepared beforehand. What do the participants need to know in order to make the most of the meeting time? And, what roles are they expected to perform in the meeting, so that they can do the right preparation?

Start the meeting on time, do not spend time recapping for latecomers and finish on time.

Meeting Minutes

The minutes will be forwarded to all participants within a day or two after the meeting is concluded. They are a record of what was accomplished and who is responsible for what as the team moves forward. This is a very crucial part of effective meetings.

You need a written record of what transpired, along with a list of actions that named individuals have agreed to perform. Make sure someone is assigned to take notes during the meeting, perhaps rotate that responsibility.

Meeting Management

A Short Guide for Meeting Facilitators and Participants[2]

Becoming a skillful planner and conductor of meetings is a prerequisite for organizational effectiveness. There are several reasons this skill is a crucial one:

- One reason is because so much time is spent in meetings. As you move up the hierarchy of an organization meeting demands increase substantially. The more senior the manager is, the more meetings he or she attends.
- A second reason is meetings are a significant cost. About 15 percent of most companies' personnel budget is spent on meeting matters. With flatter organizations and an emphasis on teams and teamwork, the number of meetings has grown exponentially.
- A third reason is that meetings are the place where most decisions are actually made, or reviewed. Hence, the matter of decision quality—the amount of useful results from the meeting—becomes crucial for the health of the organization.
- A fourth reason relates to the concept of whole life, as opposed to work life. Skills that are useful at work are also useful and important away from work. Many people spend a substantial portion of their time in network-oriented meetings. For example, any community volunteer work; church activity; or participation in art councils, youth programs, and civic associations requires a lot of meetings.

Because meetings are such a pervasive activity both in and out of work settings, being a skillful meeting participant has important rewards beyond those associated with team building. Teams, if properly managed, can make higher-quality decisions than individuals. The phrase "if properly managed" is the key. If not properly managed, meetings become the supreme organizational and civic time waster. They can actually set the organization back by making rotten decisions and wasting time.

The Five *Ps* of Effective Meetings[3]

Effective meeting managers know the five steps in preparing for and conducting meetings: (1) purpose, (2) participants, (3) plan, (4) participation, and (5) perspective.

1. Purpose

Purpose refers to the reason for which a meeting is held.

There are three functions a meeting frequently performs—to share information, to make decisions, and to brainstorm. Of these three, only the second two count as viable reasons for actually holding a meeting. When information can be adequately conveyed by a memo or phone call and when there is no advantage to holding a meeting, no meeting should be called. In short, if there are no decisions to be made, no brainstorming needed, or reasons for a face-to-face get together, cancel the meeting.

A meeting should be held when one or more of the following needs apply:

- **Information sharing—idea generation.** When all needed information is not held by any single person, when ideas will be stimulated by getting people together, and when it is not clear what information is needed or available.
- **Plan development and commitment building.** When individuals need to become committed to a course of action and when they are involved in its planning and implementation.
- **Discussion and feedback.** When the real issue is not the dissemination of information, but gauging the reaction and allowing for "ventilation," then a meeting is very helpful. When many people must receive the same message in the same way, e-mail is better.
- **Problem solving.** Groups outperform the best individuals in accomplishing complex tasks and making high-quality complex decisions. Therefore, meetings should be called to manage complex problems and discuss the options for decisions.

2. Participants

The second *P*, **participants,** refers to the individuals invited to attend a meeting.

In conducting an effective meeting, it is important to determine the *size, composition,* and *skills* of the participants. Meetings can fail because too many or too few participants attend or because the wrong mix of people is present.

If a meeting is too large, discussion may be superficial and diffuse; few people will be able to participate. If a meeting is too small, not enough information will be shared and problems will not be adequately solved.

Meeting composition refers to three main dimensions:

- Cooperation–Competition
- Task–Process
- Skills

Groups whose members are **cooperative,** are working toward a common goal and who adopt a cooperative stance toward one another perform more effectively and produce higher levels of member satisfaction than groups whose members are striving to fulfill individual needs or are pursuing competing goals.

On the **task-process** dimension, meetings are more effective if they have participants who generate a balance of both task and process.

- Task-oriented participants are "all business." They have little tolerance for joking or for discussions of feelings and friendships. The task is accomplished efficiently, but satisfaction may be low.
- Process-oriented participants emphasize *esprit de corps* and engagement. They are sensitive to participants' feelings and satisfaction. They may sacrifice some degree of accomplishment in favor of members' enjoyment. (This usually turns out to be a bad choice; the greatest enjoyment comes from accomplishment.)

If there is a lot of process focus, you can emphasize task. If there is an "all task" mind-set, then add a bit of process.

Skills address the competencies participants bring to the meeting. We can think of three *general* skill sets that should be present in the meeting *at the same time.*

- **Problem or goal identifiers:** participants who have some sense of the problem under discussion.
- **Solution providers:** participants who are creative and imaginative, who are willing and able to generate and evaluate ideas and proposals.
- **Decision-makers:** participants who use objective, fact/research based criteria and information to make thoughtful decisions.

If all these three skill sets are in the same room at the same time, and the process is a good one, the likelihood of a high-quality decision (timely, creative, and participative) is great.

3. Planning

The third *P,* **planning,** refers to preparation of the meeting agenda.

Unfortunately, participants often come to the meeting unprepared, may be unaware of critical information, may be unclear about their specific roles, and may be unsure about how to possibly achieve the objective. Conversely, the meeting planner may try to cram too much into a single meeting, schedule too many presentations, handle too many documents, or cover too much business.

It is important to publish an agenda of topics to be discussed and any supporting documents at least one day in advance of the meeting to ensure that all have the opportunity to come prepared.

4. Participation

The fourth *P,* **participation,** refers to the actual process of meetings and the methods used to ensure meetings involve everyone present.

ESTABLISH DISCUSSION PROCESS RULES Establishing a structure and clarifying the discussion process for the meeting at the outset helps keep the meeting on track.

One effective and efficient discussion process is the lateral process in which all members of the meeting discuss the positive or negative aspects of a proposal in concert. That is, rather than continually changing focus by discussing a positive aspect, then a negative aspect, then another positive aspect, etc., the entire team discusses the positives first and then the negatives. This keeps the discussion on track, is very efficient, and keeps all members focused on the topic.

Additional ways to promote discussion among meeting participants include the following:

- Ask open-ended questions rather than questions that can be answered with a "yes" or a "no."
- Make eye contact with those to whom you are talking and summarize their points when they finish their statements.
- Ask group members for their reactions to points made by other meeting participants.

CLARIFY DECISION RULES Decision rules are norms the team established for making various decisions. Reinforce them at the beginning of the meeting. The more common decision rules are simple and super majorities. Clarify if the votes will be by voice or paper, public or private.

ENCOURAGE AND ESTABLISH PARTICIPATION Engagement in a meeting should be equitable among participants, which does not mean everyone must make exactly the same number of comments. Those with more information or those with vested interests in the topic will naturally participate more.

However, it is important to control the person who likes to dominate the discussion, as well as encourage those who may have something to contribute but may not be inclined to share it. The role of each participant, including the meeting leader is to facilitate the discussion, not dominate it.

Assigning a particular topic of discussion to various people is a great way to increase participation and interest. On the agenda, indicate who will lead the discussion or presentation of each item.

SUMMARIZE ACCOMPLISHMENTS AND OBJECTIVES Close the meeting by summarizing the decisions reached, tasks assigned, progress accomplished, key points discussed, and what was learned in the meeting. Review action items that will be reported on at the next meeting. Help meeting participants feel a sense of accomplishment for having spent their time in the meeting. This may be a good time to anticipate the next meeting by identifying when the minutes from this meeting and the next meeting's agenda will be distributed and what preparation will be required.

5. Perspective

The last *P* is **perspective.** Perspective directs us to view the meetings from a distance. It means evaluating each meeting and, every so often, the decisions of and process of the meeting series.

At the end of each meeting, for example, you can use KSS methodology to do a quick and simple assessment. Pass out a piece of paper to each participant. Ask each participant to respond under each of the three letters—*K, S,* and *S.*

- ***K* means "keep"**—What went well about this meeting that we should keep or expand.
- ***S* means "stop"**—What about this meeting is nonproductive and should be stopped or phased out.
- ***S* means "start"**—What about this meeting is not happening and should be started. You may get the usual irreverent responses (for example, "better doughnuts"), but if you look for serious patterns of feedback, you can constantly improve the meeting series. The next week, give the participants the results (in summary form) and let them know how their feedback is employed to improve their meetings.

Suggestions for Group Members

So far in this discussion of effective meeting management, we have focused on the role of the meeting facilitator—the person who calls, plans, and serves as the meeting's "conductor." This role is key to the success of any group activity. However, meeting participants also bear responsibility for the meeting's effectiveness.

It is important for each participant to appreciate the effect of her or his contribution, both in shaping the short-term outcomes of meetings and affecting long-term opportunities. The success of the meeting is the responsibility of everyone.

Following are several pointers for contributing to the effectiveness of meeting from a participant's perspective.

- Take time to prepare for the meeting, and gain a clear understanding of the items on the agenda.
- Respect other group members by arriving on time and leaving personal agendas at the door. (Arriving Early = Being on time)
- Listen to other group members, be supportive of them, and clarify and build upon points made by others.
- Encourage participation by all members.

Conclusion

Meetings are a pervasive part of organizational life, especially for managers. Few important initiatives are forged without extensive and intensive group efforts. However, meetings are one of the most maligned aspects of organizational membership. To avoid poorly managed meetings a Five-*P*'s approach: purpose, participants, plan, process, and perspective was explained.

CHAPTER 9

Planning and Control

Primacy of Planning[1]

FIGURE 9.1

Planning as the Foundation for Organizing, Influencing, and Controlling

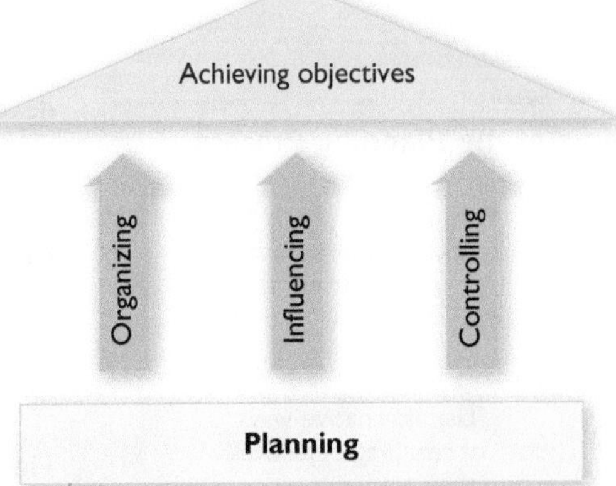

Planning is the primary management function-the only one that precedes and is the basis for the organizing, influencing, and controlling functions of managers. Only after plans are developed can you determine how best to structure the organization, place people in roles, and establish organizational controls. Planning, organizing, influencing, and controlling are interrelated. Planning is the foundation function and the first one to be performed. Organizing, influencing, and controlling are all based on the results of planning. Figure 9.1 shows this interrelationship.

Steps in the Planning Process

The planning process consists of the following seven steps. It is important to note, though, that the planning process is dynamic; in other words, effective planners will continuously revisit the planning process to assess the effectiveness and efficiency of the plan and its execution.

1. **State organizational objectives**—Because planning focuses on how to achieve the organizational objectives, a clear statement of those objectives is necessary before planning can begin. In essence, objectives stipulate those areas in which organizational planning must occur.[2]
2. **List alternative ways of reaching objectives**—Once organizational objectives have been clearly stated, the next step is to list viable alternative means for reaching those objectives.
3. **Develop premises on which to base each alternative**—To a large extent, the feasibility of using any one alternative to reach organizational objectives is determined by the premises, or assumptions, on which the alternative is

based. For example, two alternative ways an organization could address the objective of increasing profit might be to do the following:

(a) increase the sale of products presently being produced; and (b) produce and sell a completely new product. Alternative (a) is based on the premise that the organization can gain a larger share of the existing market by attracting new users or increasing consumption by current users. Alternative (b) is based on the premise that a new product would capture a significant portion of a new market, or perhaps the existing market. The viability of options is dependent on the capabilities of the firm and the competitive environment (S.W.O.T.).

4. **Choose the best alternative for reaching objectives**—An evaluation of alternatives must include an evaluation of the premises on which the alternatives are based. Identify the criteria the approach must meet or its restrictions. If any of the premises are unreasonable or unfeasible they should be excluded from further consideration. This elimination process helps identify which alternative(s) would better accomplish organizational objectives.
5. **Develop plans to pursue the chosen alternative**—After an alternative has been chosen, begin to develop strategic (long-range) and/or tactical (short-range) plans.[3]
6. **Put the plans into action**—Once plans that furnish the organization with both long-range direction and short-range tactics have been developed, they must be implemented.
7. **Evaluate**—Does the execution of the plan put the organization on track to achieve the objectives? Does it actually achieve the objectives? Controls enable to auditing of progress vs. the plan. If performance is lagging behind planned achievement or not successful, then the viability of the goal, the plan, and the execution of the plan are reassessed and appropriate corrective action taken.

Figure 9.2 shows the sequencing of the seven steps of the planning process.

FIGURE 9.2

Elements of the Planning Process

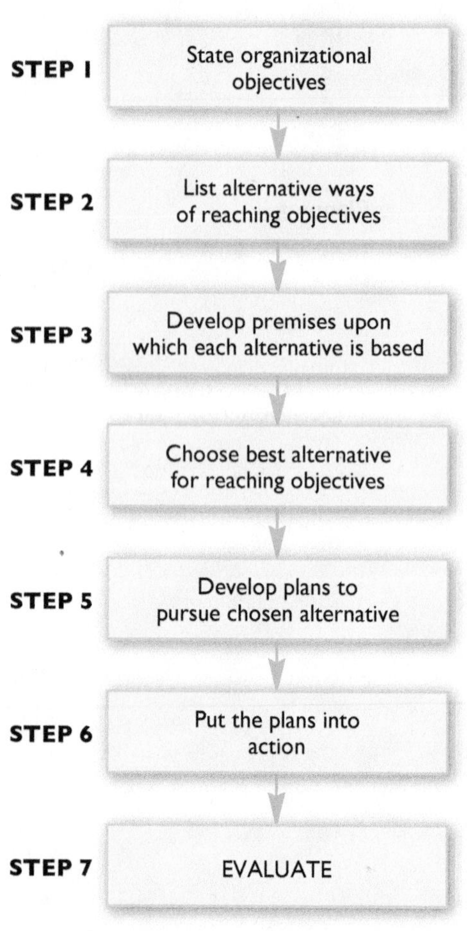

Implementation

Effective implementation is the key to a successful planning process. If plans cannot be transformed into appropriate action, they are not of value.

Developing a Hierarchy of Objectives

In practice, the overarching organizational objective must be broken down into subordinate objectives so that individuals at different levels and sections of the organization know what they must do to help reach the overall organizational objective.[4] An organizational objective is attained only after the subordinate objectives have been reached.

The overall organizational objective and the subordinate objectives assigned to the various people or units of the organization are referred to as a hierarchy of objectives. Figure 9.3 presents a sample hierarchy of objectives for a medium-sized company.

Conflicting Objectives: exists when subordinate objectives are established to achieve contrary goals or not directly aimed at accomplishing the overall organizational objective. This is possible within the company whose hierarchy of objectives is depicted in Figure 9.3. The first subordinate objective for the finance and accounting department clashes with the second subordinate objective for the supervisors. This conflict could occur if supervisors needed new equipment to maintain production and the finance and accounting department couldn't approve the loan without the company's borrowing surpassing 50 percent of company assets and violating one of their objectives. In such a situation, in which established subordinate objectives are aimed in different directions, the managers would need to choose which objective would better contribute to obtaining overall organizational goals and should therefore take precedence.

It is important to check for and address conflicting objectives by developing a thorough understanding of how various parts of the organization relate to one another and by ensuring that subordinate objectives properly reflect and do not conflict these relations.

FIGURE 9.3

Hierarchy of Objectives for a Medium-Sized Organization

TOP MANAGEMENT
1. Represent stockholders' interests—net profits of 10% or more
2. Provide service to consumers—provide reliable products
3. Maintain growth of assets and sales—double each decade
4. Provide continuity of employment for company, personnel—no involuntary layoffs
5. Develop favorable image with public

PRODUCTION DEPARTMENT
1. Keep cost of goods no more than 50% of sales
2. Increase productivity of labor by 3% per year
3. Maintain rejects at less than 2%
4. Maintain inventory at 6 months of sales
5. Keep production rate stable with no more than 20% variability from yearly average

SUPERVISORS
1. Handle employee grievances within 24 hours
2. Maintain production to standard or above
3. Keep scrappage to 2% of materials usage

SALES DEPARTMENT
1. Introduce new products so that over a 10-year period, 70% will be new
2. Maintain a market share of 15%
3. Seek new market areas so that sales will grow at a 15% annual rate
4. Maintain advertising costs at 4% of sales

DISTRICT SALES MANAGER
1. Meet weekly sales quotas
2. Visit each large customer once each month
3. Provide sales representatives with immediate follow-up support

FINANCE AND ACCOUNTING DEPARTMENT
1. Borrowing should not exceed 50% of assets
2. Maximize tax write-offs
3. Provide monthly statements to operating departments by 10th of following month
4. Pay dividends at rate of 50% of net earnings

OFFICE MANAGERS
1. Maintain cycle billing within 3 days of target date
2. Prepare special reports within 1 week of request

Guidelines for Establishing Quality Objectives

The quality of goal statement, like that of all humanly developed commodities, can vary drastically. Here are some general guidelines to increase the quality of objectives:[5]

1. **Let the people responsible for attaining the objectives have a voice in setting them**—Often the people responsible for attaining the objectives know their job situation better than managers do and can therefore help make the objectives more realistic. People will also be better motivated to achieve objectives that they have had a say in establishing.
2. **State objectives as specifically as possible**—Precise statements minimize confusion and ensure that all have explicit directions for what they should do.[6] Research shows that when objectives are not specific, the productivity of individuals attempting to reach those objectives tends to fluctuate significantly over time.
3. **Relate objectives to specific actions whenever possible**—In this way, personnel do not have to infer or guess what they should do to accomplish their goals.
4. **Pinpoint expected results**—Clarify what success looks like, how will it be determined whether an objective has been reached and the quality of that attainment?
5. **Set goals high enough that people will have to strive to meet them, but not so high that they will give up trying to meet them**—Research shows that establishing goals that are too easy or too difficult result in underperformance or frustration.
6. **Set a time frame, a completion date for when goals are expected to be achieved**—People need a time frame for accomplishing their objectives. They then can pace themselves accordingly.
7. **State objectives clearly and simply**—The written or spoken word must be understood and not impede clearly communicating a goal to organization members.

FIGURE 9.4

The Effect of Goals on Performance

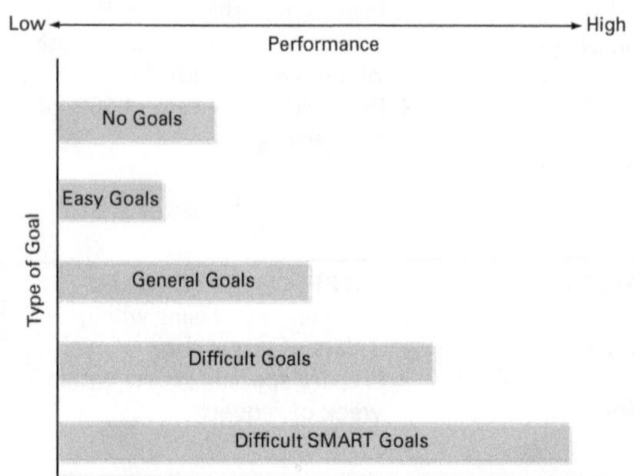

Source: University of Michigan, "Positive Organizational Scholarship" by Kim Cameron.

Establish SMART Goals

It is important to identify goals that the team can achieve and levels of performance to which team members can aspire. The goals that characterize high-performing teams are called **SMART goals.** Setting challenging, but attainable goals enhances team performance.

Figure 9.4 shows that when people are given *no goals* ("Here is your task ("go sell"), their performance tends to be low, even though most people will perform at a minimum level even when they are not certain of the standard that they should achieve.

However, being provided with an *easy goal* ("The average number of sales calls is 10 per day, but you are expected to make 4.") leads to even lower performance. People tend to work toward the standard that has been established, and when it is easy, they slack off. Identifying *difficult, but attainable goals* ("The average is 10 per day, but you should shoot for 12.") produces far higher levels of performance.

SMART goals possess five characteristics. The acronym SMART identifies these attributes:

- **S**pecific—The goal is clear, and precise targets and standards are identified.
- **M**easurable—The goal can be assessed and quantified. The extent to which the goal has been achieved is obvious.
- **A**ligned/**A**ttainable—The goal is supportive of and consistent with the goals of the broader organization. People are not pursuing their own objectives independent of their team.
- **R**ealistic—While being difficult and causing performance to stretch, the goal is not foolhardy or a fantasy.
- **T**ime-bound—An end point is identified or a completion date established so that goal achievement is not open-ended.

Consider the difference between goal statements such as "We will be the best in our industry," compared to a goal statement that is SMART: "We will achieve a 5 percent improvement in the on-time delivery of our products by the end of the quarter." The latter provides a more motivating goal in that it is specific, measurable, aligned with key outcomes, realistic, and time-bound. It gives people something they can easily understand and shoot for. It is important to keep in mind, however, that articulating motivating goals and identifying the methods to achieve them are different. The former specifies the target. The latter specifies the means for achieving the target. The former is crucial to successful team leadership. The latter is often lethal.

What Is Control?[7]

Control is the management function that involves monitoring activities to ensure that they are being accomplished as planned and correcting any significant deviations. Managers cannot really know whether their units are performing properly until they have evaluated what activities have been done and have compared the actual performance with the desired standard.

control
The process of monitoring activities to ensure that they are being accomplished as planned and correcting any significant deviations.

An effective control system ensures that activities are completed in ways that lead to the attainment of the organization's goals. The effectiveness of a control system is determined by how well it facilitates goal achievement. The more it helps managers achieve their organization's goals, the better the control system.

Generally three different approaches to designing control systems are used: market, bureaucratic, and clan controls, which are summarized in Figure 9.5.

Market control emphasizes the use of external market mechanisms. Controls are built around such criteria as price competition or market share. Organizations using a market control approach usually have clearly specified and distinct products and services and considerable competition. Under these conditions, the various divisions of the organization are typically turned into profit centers and evaluated by the percentage of total corporate profits each generates. For instance, at Matsushita, each of the various divisions that produce such products as videos, home appliances, and industrial

market control
An approach to control that emphasizes the use of external market mechanisms such as price competition and market share.

FIGURE 9.5

Characteristics of Three Approaches to Designing Control Systems

TYPE OF CONTROL SYSTEM	CHARACTERISTICS
Market	Uses external market mechanisms, such as price competition and relative market share, to establish standards used in system. Typically used by organizations with clearly specified and distinct products or services that face considerable marketplace competition.
Bureaucratic	Emphasizes organizational authority. Relies on administrative and hierarchical mechanisms, such as rules, regulations, procedures, policies, standardization of activities, well-defined job descriptions, and budgets to ensure that employees exhibit appropriate behaviors and meet performance standards.
Clan	Regulates employee behavior by the shared values, norms, traditions, rituals, beliefs, and other aspects of the organization's culture. Often used by organizations in which teams are common and technology is changing rapidly.

equipment is evaluated according to its contribution to the company's total profits. Using these measures, managers make decisions about future resource allocations, strategic changes, and other work activities that may need attention.

bureaucratic control
An approach to control that emphasizes authority and relies on administrative rules, regulations, procedures, and policies.

A second approach to control systems is **bureaucratic control,** a control approach that emphasizes authority and relies on administrative rules, regulations, procedures, and policies. This type of control depends on standardization of activities, well-defined job descriptions to direct work behavior, and other administrative mechanisms—such as budgets—to ensure that organizational members exhibit appropriate work behaviors and meet established performance standards. At BP Amoco, managers of various divisions are allowed considerable autonomy and freedom to run their units as they see fit. Yet they are expected to stick closely to their budgets and stay within corporate guidelines.

Zhung Yu, chief executive of Broad Air Conditioning in Chang Shai, China, discusses the company's ethical standards and his expectations regarding appropriate work behavior with new employees. By sharing his company's ethical and other cultural values, Yu applies the clan approach to designing control systems.
PHOTO: AP Photo/Lauren Greenfield/VII

Clan control is an approach to designing control systems in which employee behaviors are regulated by the shared values, applied norms, traditions, rituals, beliefs, and other aspects of the organization's culture. In contrast to bureaucratic control, which is based on strict hierarchical mechanisms, clan control depends on the individual and the group (the clan) to identify the truly valued and expected work-related behaviors and performance measures, which are important to the group.

It is important to recognize that most organizations do not totally rely on just one of these three approaches to design an appropriate control system. Instead, an organization typically chooses to emphasize either bureaucratic or clan control and then add some market control measures. The key, however, in any of the approaches is to design and use appropriate control systems that help the organization to effectively and efficiently reach its goals.

The Importance of Control

Planning can be done; an organizational structure can be created to efficiently facilitate the achievement of objectives; and people can be directed and motivated. Still, an organization has no assurance that activities are going to occur as planned and that the goals are, in fact, going to be attained. Control is the final link in the functional chain of management. *However, the value of the control function lies predominantly in its relation to planning and delegating activities.*

Simply stating objectives and establishing a plan is no guarantee that the necessary actions are accomplished. Effective management requires follow up to ensure that the actions others are supposed to take and the objectives they are supposed to achieve are, in fact, being taken and achieved in a timely manner.

The Control Process

The control process consists of three separate and distinct steps: (1) measuring actual performance, (2) comparing actual performance against a standard, and (3) taking managerial action to correct deviations or inadequate standards (see Figure 9.6).

FIGURE 9.6

The Control Process

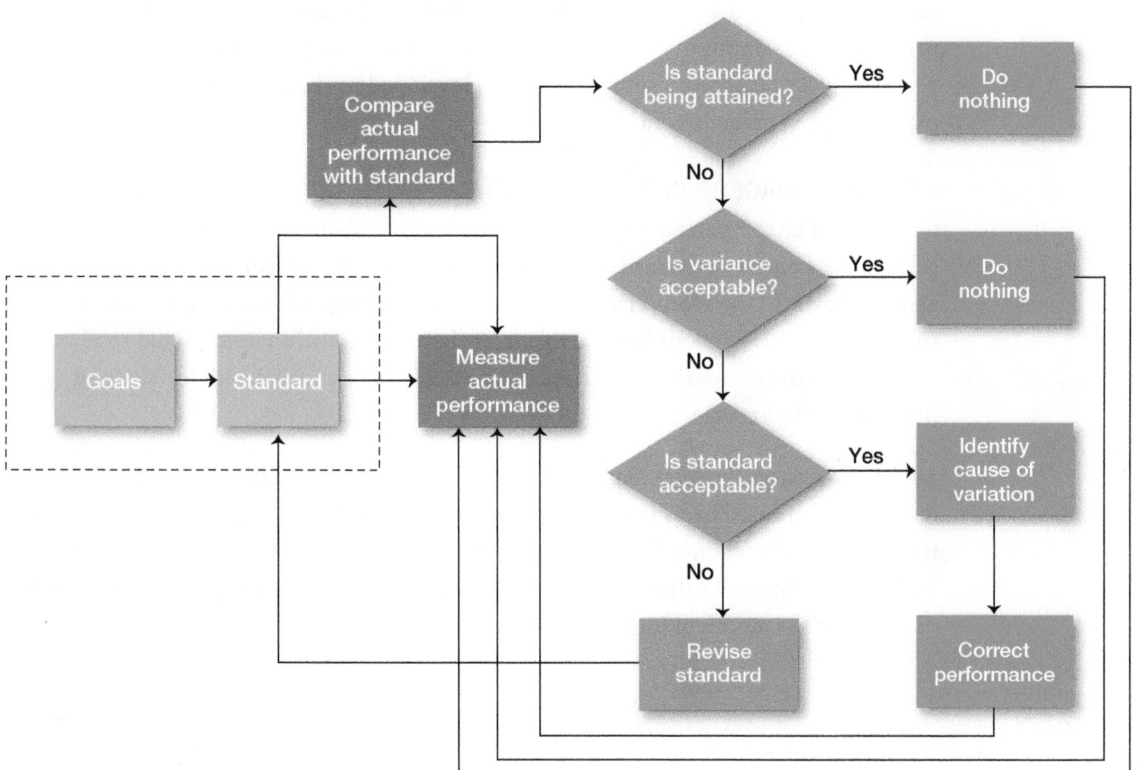

FIGURE 9.7

Defining an Acceptable Range of Variation

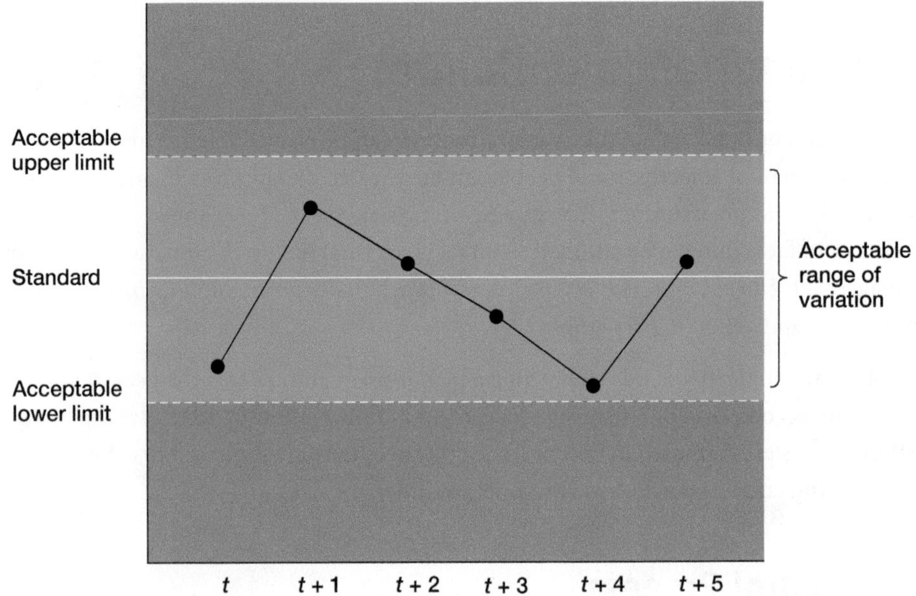

Before we consider each step in detail, you should be aware that the control process assumes that standards of performance already exist, having been created in the planning function. If managers use a clear approach to goal setting (see Guidelines for Establishing Quality Objectives, page 106), then the objectives set are, by definition, tangible, verifiable, and measurable. In such instances, those objectives are the standards against which progress is measured and compared. If goal setting is not practiced, then standards are the specific performance indicators that management uses. Our point is that these standards are developed in the planning function; planning must precede control.

HOW DO MANAGERS COMPARE ACTUAL PERFORMANCE TO PLANNED GOALS? The comparing step determines the degree of discrepancy between actual performance and the standard. Some variation in performance can be expected in all activities; it is, therefore, critical to determine the acceptable **range of variation** (see Figure 9.7). Deviations beyond this range become significant and should receive attention. In the comparison stage, we are particularly concerned with the size and direction of the variation.

range of variation
The acceptable parameters of variance between actual performance and the standard.

Becky Simmons is the sales manager for South Atlantic Distributors. The company distributes imported beers in several states in the South. Becky prepares a report during the first week of each month that summarizes sales for the previous month, classified by brand name. Figure 9.8 displays both the standard and actual sales figures (in hundreds of cases) for the month of July.

FIGURE 9.8

South Atlantic Distributor's Sales Performance for July (hundreds of cases)

BRAND	STANDARD	ACTUAL	OVER (UNDER)
Heineken	1,075	913	(162)
Molson	630	634	4
Beck's	800	912	112
Moosehead	620	622	2
Labatt's	540	672	132
Corona	160	140	(20)
Amstel Light	225	220	(5)
Dos Equis	80	65	(15)
Tecate	170	286	116
TOTAL CASES	4,300	4,464	164

What Managerial Action Can Be Taken?

The third and final step in the control process is managerial action. Managers can choose among four courses of action: (1) They can do nothing, (2) they can correct the actual performance, (3) they can revise the standard of evaluation, or (4) they can revise the work plan. Because doing nothing is fairly self-explanatory, let's look at the latter three choices.

CORRECT ACTUAL PERFORMANCE If the source of the variation has been deficient performance, then you want to take corrective action. Examples of such corrective action might include changes in training programs; the redesign of jobs; or the replacement of personnel.

REVISE THE STANDARD It is also possible that a variance was the result of an unrealistic standard, which is to say the goal may have been too high or too low. In such cases the standard needs corrective attention, not the performance.

REVISE THE WORK PLAN Perhaps the timing, the allocation of resources where not thought out completely. Perhaps the environment changed from when the plan was devised. If changes in the plan are required, then they should be made.

Types of Control

Management can implement controls before an activity commences, while the activity is going on, or after the activity has been completed. The first type is called feedforward control, the second is concurrent control, and the last is feedback control (see Figure 9.9).

FIGURE 9.9

Types of Control

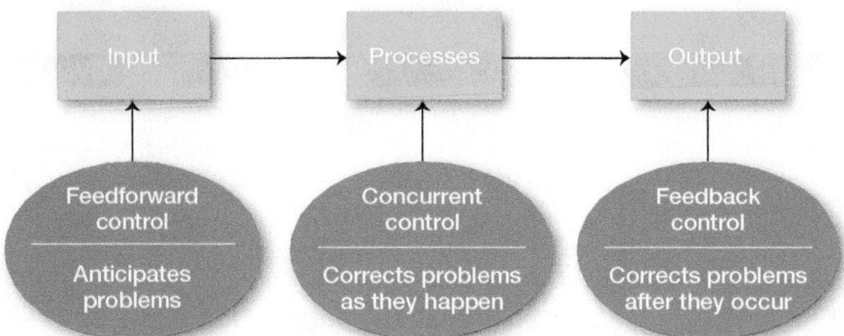

Caterpillar, Inc., which operates in 40 countries on six continents, uses feedforward control in preparing employees for overseas assignments. To erase the negative image of Americans abroad, Caterpillar educates its employees about the different traditions, customs, and diets of each foreign host country where employees will work. The training includes sampling different ethnic food in the cafeteria at Caterpillar's U.S. headquarters in Peoria, Illinois.

PHOTO: AP Photo/Journal Star, David Zalaznik

What Is Feedforward Control?

Feedforward control prevents anticipated problems because it *takes place in advance of the actual activity.* Its future directed. For instance, when McDonald's opened its first restaurant in Moscow, it sent company quality control experts to help Russian farmers learn techniques for growing high-quality potatoes, and sent bakers to teach the processes for baking high-quality breads. Why? Because McDonald's strongly emphasizes product quality no matter what the geographical location.

The key to feedforward control, therefore, is taking managerial action before a problem occurs. Feedforward controls helps to prevent problems rather than having to cure them later.

When Is Concurrent Control Used?

Concurrent control, as its name implies, *takes place while an activity is in progress.* When control is enacted while the work is being performed, management can correct problems before they become too costly.

The best-known form of concurrent control is direct supervision. When a manager directly oversees the actions of an employee, the manager can concurrently monitor the employee's actions and correct problems as they occur. Although some delay between the activity and the manager's corrective response is inevitable, the delay is minimal.

Technical equipment (such as computers and computerized machine controls) can be designed to include concurrent controls. For example, you may have experienced concurrent control when using a computer program such as word processing that alerts you to a misspelled word or incorrect grammatical usage, as you are typing. In addition, many organizational quality programs rely on concurrent controls to inform workers about whether their work output is of sufficient quality to meet standards.

feedforward control
Control established before the work begins that prevents anticipated problems.

concurrent control
Control that takes place while an activity is in progress.

Why Is Feedback Control So Popular?

Feedback Control is the most popular type of control. The control *takes place after the action is completed.* The major drawback of this type of control is that by the time the work is finished any damage or shortfall has occurred. It's analogous to locking the barn door after the horse has been stolen. But for many activities, feedback is the only viable type of control available. For example, year-end financial statements are an example of feedback controls. If, for instance, the income statement shows that sales revenues declined, the decline has already occurred. So at this point, the manager has no opportunity to correct the past performance.

Feedback has two advantages over feedforward and concurrent control. First, feedback provides managers with meaningful information on the ultimate effectiveness of their planning and implementation efforts. Feedback that indicates little variance between standard and actual performance is evidence that planning and implementation were generally on target.

Planning and Scheduling More Complex Projects Using Gantt Charts[8]

Gantt Charts (also known as Gantt Diagrams) are useful tools for analyzing and planning more complex projects. Gantt Charts enable you to do the following and act as a feedforward or a concurrent control:

- Help you to plan out the multiple tasks that need to be completed.
- Give you a basis for identifying and monitoring when these tasks will be started and completed.
- Allow you to plan the allocation of resources needed to complete the project.
- Help you to identify the critical path and key target dates for a project, which must be completed by a particular date.

When a project is under way Gantt Charts help you to monitor whether the project is on schedule. If it is not, it allows you to pinpoint the remedial action necessary to put it back on schedule.

Sequential and Parallel Activities

An essential concept behind project planning (and Critical Path Analysis) is that some activities are dependent on other activities being completed first. For example: It is not a good idea to take a test before you read the materials, attend and participate in the class, and complete the assignments!

These dependent activities need to be completed in a sequence, with each stage being more-or-less completed before the next activity can begin. We can call dependent

FIGURE 9.10A

Gantt Chart Example: Planning a Custom-Written Computer Project

Task	Earliest Start	Length	Type	Dependent on...
A. High level analysis	Week 0	1 week	Sequential	
B. Selection of hardware platform	Week 1	1 day	Sequential	A
C. Installation and commissioning of hardware	Week 1.2	2 weeks	Parallel	B
D. Detailed analysis of core modules	Week 1	2 weeks	Sequential	A
E. Detailed analysis of supporting modules	Week 3	2 weeks	Sequential	D

activities "sequential" or "linear." Other activities are "parallel" tasks. These don't have to be done in sequence, but may sometimes need other tasks to be finished first.

Drawing a Gantt Chart

STEP 1—LIST ALL ACTIVITIES IN THE PLAN For each task, show the earliest start date, estimated length of time it will take, and whether it is parallel(occurs while other tasks are being addressed) or sequential(occurs only after other tasks are completed). Also show which other stages they depend on.

You will end up with a task list like the one in Figure 9.10A. This example shows the task list for a custom-written computer project.

STEP 2—SET UP YOUR GANTT CHART Establish column headers in an Excel sheet with the week starting or ending dates through to task completion.

STEP 3—PLOT THE TASKS ONTO THE CHART Next draw up a rough draft of the Gantt Chart. Plot each task on the rows showing it starting on a given date and ending at a specific date. Draw it as a bar, with the length of the bar being the length of time you expect it will take to complete the task. Above the task bars, make a notation of the time taken to complete each task.

Schedule tasks in such a way that sequential actions are carried out in the required sequence. Ensure that dependent activities do not start until the activities they depend on have been completed.

This will produce an untidy diagram like the one on next page in (see Figure 9.10B).

STEP 4—PRESENTING THE ANALYSIS The last stage in this process is to prepare a final version of the Gantt Chart. This shows how the sets of sequential activities link

FIGURE 9.10B

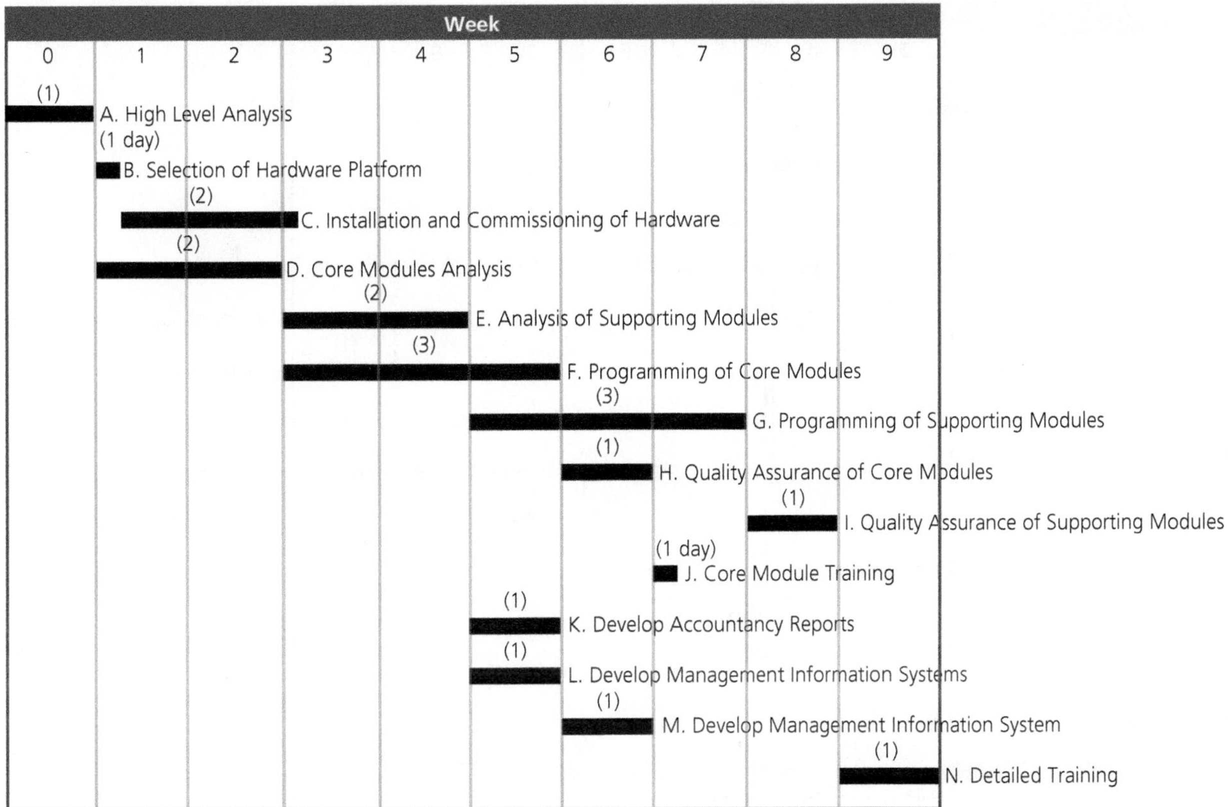

together, and identifies the critical path activities. At this stage you also need to check the sourcing of the various activities. While scheduling, ensure that you make best use of the resources you have available, and do not over-commit your resource.

You can also use color to represent the different resource types that you need to use such as programmers, or analysts.

A redrawn version of the example project is shown in Figure 9.10C.

By drawing this example Gantt Chart, you can see the following:

- If all goes well, the project can be completed in 10 weeks.
- If you want to complete the task as rapidly as possible, you need:
  - One analyst for the first five weeks. (Note that we had to change the scope of activity F so that we could finish this task in two weeks, rather than three. This was because we wanted to complete the project in 10 weeks, and we couldn't commit resources to activities F and G at the same time.
  - One programmer for five weeks starting week 4.
  - One programmer/QA expert for three weeks starting week six. (Note that activities L and M have been moved back a week. This does not affect the critical path, but it does mean that a single programming/QA resource can carry out all three of activities K, L and M.)

FIGURE 9.10C *CONTINUED*

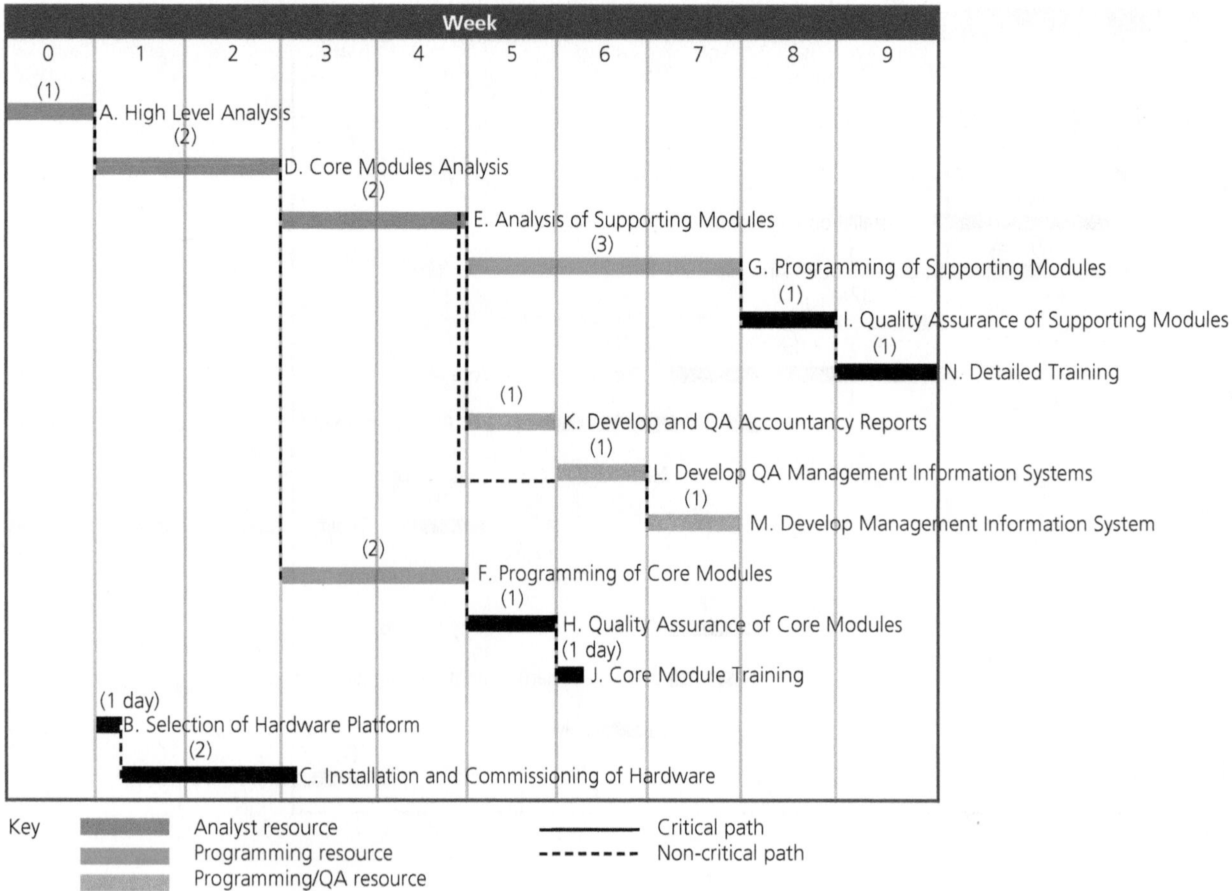

- Analysis, development, and testing of supporting modules are essential activities that must be completed on time.
- Hardware installation and commissioning is not time-critical as long as it is completed before the Core Module Training starts.

Project managers use software tools like Microsoft Excel or Project to create Gantt Charts. Not only do these ease the creation of Gantt Charts, they also make modification of plans easier and provide facilities for identifying who is responsible for each task, monitoring progress against plans, as well as generating resource histograms.

Key Points

Gantt charts are useful tools for planning and scheduling projects. They allow you to visualize how long a project should take, determine the resources needed, and lay out the order in which tasks need to be carried out. They are useful in managing the dependencies between tasks.

When a project is under way, Gantt charts are useful for monitoring its progress. You can immediately see what should have been achieved at a point in time, and can therefore take remedial action to bring the project back on course. This is essential for the successful and profitable implementation of the project.

Conclusion

Control is the final step in the management process. Managers must monitor whether goals that were established as part of the planning process are being accomplished efficiently (proper use of resources) and effectively (achieving the stated objective). That's what they do when they control. Appropriate controls can help managers look for specific performance gaps and areas for improvement.

CHAPTER

10 Strategic Planning[1]

The Importance of Organizational Strategy

Before the early 1970s, managers who made long-range plans generally assumed that better times lay ahead. Plans for the future were merely extensions of where the organization had been in the past. However, the energy crisis, deregulation, accelerating technological change, and increasing global competition as well as other environmental shocks of the 1970s and 1980s undermined this approach to long-range planning.

These changes in the rules of the game forced managers to develop a systematic means of analyzing the environment, assessing their organizations' strengths and weaknesses, and identifying opportunities where the organization could have a competitive advantage.

The value of strategic planning is evident. Those companies that plan strategically appear to have better financial measurements than those organizations that don't. Today, strategic planning has moved beyond the private sector to include government agencies, hospitals, and educational institutions.

A Strategic Framework: Choosing a Niche

When an organization attempts to develop its strategy, senior management goes through the **strategic management process** (see Figure 10.1), a nine-step process that involves strategic planning, implementation, and evaluation. Strategic planning encompasses the first seven steps, but even the best strategies can go awry if management fails to either implement them properly or evaluate their results. Let's look at the various steps in the strategic management process.

strategic management process
A nine-step process that involves strategic planning, implementation, and evaluation.

FIGURE 10.1

The Strategic Management Process

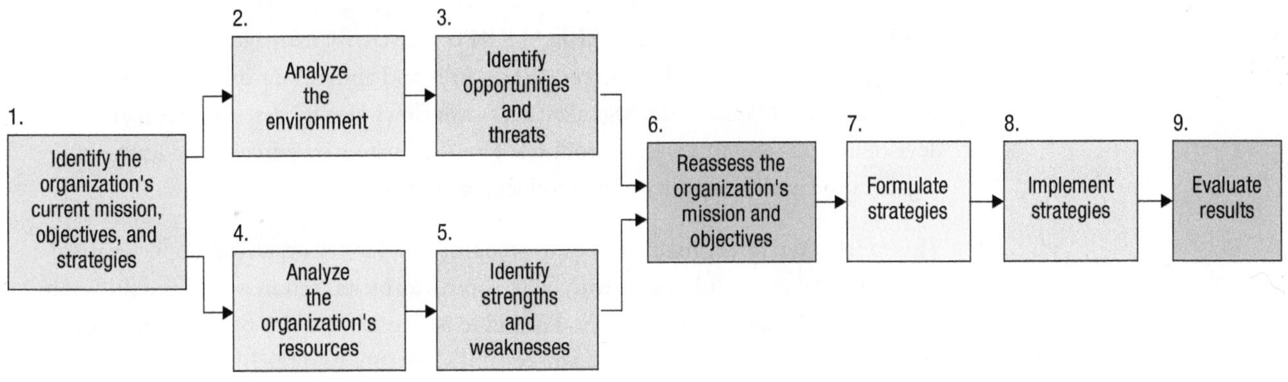

How Does the Strategic Management Process Operate?

STEP 1—EVERY ORGANIZATION HAS A MISSION STATEMENT A **mission statement** defines the purpose and answers the question, "What business or businesses are we in?" Defining the organization's mission forces management to identify the scope of its products or services carefully. For example, the business magazine *Fast Company* established its mission and set its sights "to chronicle the epic changes sweeping across business and to equip readers with the ideas, tools, and tactics that they need to thrive."

mission statement
The purpose of an organization.

STEP 2—ANALYZE THE EXTERNAL ENVIRONMENT Once its mission has been identified, the organization can begin to look outside the company to ensure that its strategy aligns well with the environment. Organizations need to find out what their competition is up to, what pending legislation might affect them, what their customers' desire, and what the supply of labor is like in locations where they operate. By analyzing the external environment, managers are in a better position to define the available strategies that best align with their environment.

Step 2 of the strategy process is complete when management has an accurate grasp of what is taking place in its environment and is aware of important trends that might affect its operations. This awareness is aided by environmental scanning activities and competitive intelligence.

STEP 3—DETERMINE OPPORTUNITIES AND THREATS After analyzing and learning about the environment, management needs to evaluate what it has learned in terms of **opportunities** (strategic) that the organization might exploit and **threats** that the organization faces. In a simplistic way, opportunities are positive external environmental factors, and threats are negative ones.

opportunities
Positive external environmental factors.

threats
Negative external environmental factors.

Keep in mind, however, that the same environment can present opportunities to one organization and pose threats to another in the same or a similar industry because of their different resources or different focus.

STEP 4—ANALYZE THE ORGANIZATION'S RESOURCES Next, we evaluate the organization's internal resources. What skills and abilities do the organization's employees have? What is the organization's cash flow? Has it been successful at developing new and innovative products? How do customers perceive the image of the organization and the quality of its products or services?

This fourth step forces management to recognize that every organization, no matter how large and powerful, is constrained in some way by its resources and the skills it has available. The analysis in Step 4 should lead to a clear assessment of the organization's internal resources, such as capital, worker skills, patents, and the like. It should also indicate organizational departmental abilities such as training and development, marketing, accounting, human resources, research and development, and management information systems.

strengths
Internal resources that are available or things that an organization does well.

core competency
Any of the strengths that represent unique skills or resources that can determine the organization's competitive edge.

weakness
Resources that an organization lacks or important activities that it does not do well.

STEP 5—IDENTIFY STRENGTHS AND WEAKNESSES Internal resources and things the organization does well are **strengths.** Any unique skills or resources that determine the organization's competitive edge are its **core competency,** like Vanguard's "no shareholder structure", which enables it to offer mutual funds at a lower cost, thus providing higher returns to its investor clients.

At UAL, company leaders eliminated their Avolar corporate jet business so that they could return to their core business—commercial aviation. That's because, in part, they lacked certain resources. When an organization lacks certain resources or identifies activities that the firm does not do well, we label it a **weakness.**

Understanding of the organization's resources, or lack of resources, and its culture is a crucial part of Steps 4 and 5. Specifically, managers should be aware that strong and weak cultures have different effects on strategy and that the content of a culture has a major effect on the content of the strategy.

In a strong culture, for instance, almost all employees will have a clear understanding of what the organization is about, and it should be easy for management to convey to new employees the organization's core competency. A department store chain such as Nordstrom, which has a strong culture that embraces service and customer satisfaction, should be able to instill its cultural values in new employees in a much shorter time than can a competitor with a weak culture.

The negative side of a strong culture, of course, is that it is difficult to change. A strong culture may act as a significant barrier to acceptance of a change in the organization's strategies.

SWOT analysis
Assessment of an organization's strengths, weaknesses, opportunities, and threats in order to identify a viable strategy that the organization can pursue.

What Is SWOT Analysis?[2]

The next step of analysis helps you think about the options that the organization could pursue. To do this you compare external opportunities and threats with the internal strengths and weaknesses, as illustrated in the matrix on the following page.[3] To simply identify the internal strengths and weaknesses of an organization with the external opportunities and threats of their business or operating market is not enough. One must identify how the strengths and weaknesses affect the ability to capitalize on opportunities, or mitigate/enhance the existing threats.

This chart helps you identify strategic alternatives that address the following additional questions:

- **Strengths and Opportunities (SO)**—How can you use your strengths to take advantage of the opportunities?
- **Strengths and Threats (ST)**—How can you take advantage of your strengths to mitigate or avoid real and potential threats?
- **Weaknesses and Opportunities (WO)**—How can you use your opportunities to overcome the weaknesses you are experiencing?
- **Weaknesses and Threats (WT)**—How can you minimize your weaknesses and avoid threats?

SWOT Analysis Matrix

	External Opportunities (O) 1. 2. 3. 4.	**External Threats (T)** 1. 2. 3. 4.
Internal Strengths (S) 1. 2. 3. 4.	**SO** *"Maxi-Maxi" Strategy* Strategies that **use strengths** to **maximize opportunities.**	**ST** *"Maxi-Mini" Strategy* Strategies that **use strengths** to **minimize threats.**
Internal Weaknesses (W) 1. 2. 3. 4.	**WO** *"Mini-Maxi" Strategy* Strategies that **minimize weaknesses** by **taking advantage of opportunities.**	**WT** *"Mini-Mini" Strategy* Strategies that **minimize weaknesses** and **avoid threats.**

STEP 6—REASSESS MISSION AND OBJECTIVES[4] Having completed the SWOT analysis, the organization reassesses its mission and objectives (Step 6). Based on the SWOT analysis and identification of the organization's opportunities, management reevaluates whether its mission and objectives are realistic, whether they need modification, and where any needed changes are likely to originate. On the other hand, if no changes are necessary, management is ready to begin the actual formulation of strategies.

STEP 7—STRATEGIES NEED TO BE SET FOR ALL ORGANIZATIONAL LEVELS Management needs to develop and evaluate alternative strategies and then select a set that is compatible at each level and will allow the organization to best capitalize on its resources and the opportunities available in the environment. For most organizations, four primary strategies are available. Frequently called the **grand strategies,** they are growth, stability, retrenchment, and combination strategies.

grand strategies
The four primary types of strategies: growth, stability, retrenchment, and combination.

THE GROWTH STRATEGY If management believes that bigger is better, then it may choose a **growth strategy.** A growth strategy is one in which an organization attempts to increase the level of the organization's operations. Growth can take the form of more sales revenues, more employees, or more market share. Many "growth" organizations achieve this objective through direct expansion, new-product development, or by diversifying—merging with or acquiring other firms. Some, such as Ace Hardware, use franchising opportunities to promote their growth strategies.

growth strategy
A strategy in which an organization attempts to increase the level of its operations; can take the form of increasing sales revenue, number of employees, or market share.

Growth through direct expansion involves increasing company size, revenues, operations, or workforce. This effort is internally focused and does not involve other firms. For example, AmeriSuites is pursuing a growth strategy when it expands. As opposed to purchasing other hotels, AmeriSuites expands by opening hotels in new locations or by franchising to entrepreneurs who are willing to accept and do business the "AmeriSuites" way.

Growth, too, can also come from creating businesses within the organization. When Wal-Mart entered the grocery store business with its supercenters, the company was Figureing a growth strategy by expanding its operations to include food distribution, and it caused competitors such as Safeway and Kroger to make cuts to remain competitive.

merger
Occurs when two companies, usually of similar size, combine their resources to form a new company.

Companies may also grow by merging with other companies or acquiring similar firms. A **merger** occurs when two companies—usually of similar size—combine their resources to form a new company. For example, when the Lockheed and Martin Marietta Corporations merged to form Lockheed Martin, they did so to compete more effectively in the aerospace industry.

acquisition
Occurs when a larger company buys a smaller one and incorporates the acquired company's operations into its own.

Organizations can also acquire another firm, such as PepsiCo purchasing Quaker Oats, J.P. Morgan buying Bank One, or Pfizer buying Pharmacia. An **acquisition,** which is similar to a merger, usually happens when a larger company buys a smaller one—for a set amount of money or stocks, or both, and incorporates the acquired company's operations into its own. These acquisitions demonstrate a growth strategy whereby companies expand through diversification.

The growth strategy of Whole Foods Markets, a natural foods and organic foods supermarket, is expanding geographically through acquisitions. Whole Foods made 18 retail acquisitions to accelerate its growth. With its recent acquisition of Wild Oats Market, Inc., Whole Foods has the opportunity to penetrate key markets in the Pacific Northwest, Rocky Mountains, and Florida and reach its growth goal of $12 billion in sales by 2010.

PHOTO: Getty Images

stability strategy
A strategy that is characterized by an absence of significant change.

THE STABILITY STRATEGY A stability strategy is best known for what it is not; that is, the **stability strategy** is characterized by an absence of significant changes. With this strategy, an organization continues to serve its same market and customers while maintaining its market share. When is a stability strategy most appropriate? It is most appropriate when several conditions exist: a stable and unchanging environment, satisfactory organizational performance, a presence of valuable strengths and absence of critical weaknesses, and NO significant opportunities and threats.

Some organizations successfully employ a stability strategy, but most do not get the "press" that companies using other strategies get. One reason might be that no change means no news. Another might be that the company itself wants to keep a low profile; stakeholders may consider the status quo to be inappropriate, or the strategy may be an indication of rigidity of the planning process. Nonetheless, a company such as Kellogg does use the stability strategy well. Kellogg, intent on exploiting its unique niche, has not moved far from its breakfast food market emphasis. The company also has not demonstrated a desire to diversify into other food markets as have some of its competitors.

THE RETRENCHMENT STRATEGY Before the 1980s, few North American companies ever had to consider anything but how to grow or maintain what they currently had. However, the effects of technological advancements, global competition, and other environmental changes may mean that mergers and acquisitions growth and stability strategies are no longer viable for some companies. Instead, organizations such as Sears, AT&T, General Motors, the U.S. Army, and Apple Computer have had to pursue a **retrenchment strategy.** This strategy is characteristic of an organization that reduces its size or sells off less profitable product lines.

retrenchment strategy
A strategy characteristic of a company that is reducing its size, usually in an environment of decline.

THE COMBINATION STRATEGY

A **combination strategy** is the simultaneous pursuit of two or more of the strategies described earlier; that is, one part of the organization may be pursuing a growth strategy while another is retrenching. For example, Procter & Gamble sold off its Jif and Crisco brands to J. M. Smucker (of jam and jelly fame), allowing the company to better concentrate on its growth strategy of consumer brands market by purchasing the Gillette Company.

combination strategy
The simultaneous pursuit by an organization of two or more of growth, stability, and retrenchment strategies.

DETERMINING A COMPETITIVE STRATEGY The selection of a grand strategy sets the stage for the entire organization. Subsequently, each unit within the organization has to translate this strategy into a set of strategies that will give the organization a competitive advantage. That is, to fulfill the grand strategy, managers will seek to position their units so that they can gain a relative advantage over the company's rivals. This positioning requires a careful evaluation of the competitive forces that dictate the rules of competition within the industry in which the organization operates.

Which strategy management chooses depends on the organization's strengths and weaknesses, compared to those of its competitors. Management should avoid a position in which it has to slug it out with everybody in the industry. Rather, the organization should put its strength where the competition isn't. Success, then, depends on selecting the right strategy, the one that fits the complete picture of the organization and the industry of which it is a part. In so doing, organizations can gain the most favorable competitive advantage.

SUSTAINING A COMPETITIVE ADVANTAGE Long-term success with any one of Porter's competitive strategies requires that the advantage be sustainable. It must withstand both the actions of competitors and the evolutionary changes in the industry, which isn't easy, especially in environments as dynamic as the ones organizations face today.

Technology changes. So, too, do customers' product preferences. And competitors frequently try to imitate an organization's success. Managers need to create barriers that make imitation by competitors difficult or reduce the competitive opportunities. The use of patents, copyrights, or trademarks may assist in this effort. In addition, when strong efficiencies come from economies of scale, reducing price to gain volume is a useful tactic, which may be difficult for competitors to copy.

Organizations can also "tie up" suppliers with exclusive contracts that limit their ability to supply materials to rivals. Or organizations can encourage and lobby for government policies that impose import tariffs that are designed to limit foreign competition. The one thing management cannot do is become complacent. Resting on past successes may be the beginning of serious trouble for the organization. Sustaining a competitive advantage requires constant action by management in order to stay one step ahead of the competition.

STEP 8—IMPLEMENTATION The next-to-last step in the strategic management process is implementation (Step 8). No matter how good a strategic plan, it cannot succeed if it is not implemented properly. Top management leadership is a necessary ingredient in a successful strategy. So, too, is a motivated group of middle- and lower-level managers to carry out senior management's specific plans.

STEP 9—RESULTS MUST BE EVALUATED Finally, results must be evaluated: How effective have the strategies been? How efficiently are resources utilized? What adjustments, if any, are necessary?

effectiveness
The degree to which managers attain organizational objectives.

efficiency
The degree to which organizational resources are utilized and contribute to productivity.

Effectiveness is the degree to which managers attain organizational objectives. **Efficiency** is the degree to which organizational resources are utilized and contribute to productivity. A review of organizational performance based on these standards is essential to enhancing the success of any entity.

Conclusion

No matter what organizational structure you choose for your organization, the design should help employees do their work in the best, most efficient and effective way they can. The structure needs to help, not hinder, organizational members as they carry out the organization's work. After all, the structure is simply a means to an end.

CHAPTER 11

Consumer Behavior[1]

Nothing is more important than understanding consumers and how they make decisions when you need to plan marketing strategy. In this chapter we'll look at the consumer decision-making process and the multitude of factors that influence those choices. And we'll show how understanding consumers boosts ROI as these insights help marketers to figure out the best way to win customers by meeting their needs.

We include consumer insights in many parts of the marketing plan—from what type of product to offer to where to advertise. This knowledge is key when we select a target market. For example, Julie's understanding of (RED)'s consumer base showed her that teens were the most receptive to social marketing and thus an ideal target for the organization's message.

The Consumer Decision-Making Process

Compelling new products, clever packaging, and creative advertising surround us, clamoring for our attention—and our money. But consumers don't all respond in the same way. Each of us is unique, with our own reasons to choose one product over another. Remember: The focus of the marketing concept is to satisfy consumers' wants and needs. To accomplish that crucial goal, first we need to appreciate what those wants and needs are. What causes one consumer to step into Denny's for a huge cholesterol-laden breakfast, while another opts for a quick Starbucks latte and Danish, and a third will only eat a healthy serving of "natural"

Kashi cereal and fruit? And what, other than income, will cause one consumer to buy that box of Kashi cereal only when it's "on deal" while her neighbor never even looks at the price?

consumer behavior
The process involved when individuals or groups select, purchase, use, and dispose of goods, services, ideas, or experiences to satisfy their needs and desire.

Consumer behavior is the process individuals or groups go through to select, purchase, use, and dispose of goods, services, ideas, or experiences to satisfy their needs and desires. Marketers recognize that consumer decision-making is an ongoing process—it's much more than what happens at the moment a consumer forks over the cash and in turn receives a good or service.

Let's go back to the shoppers who want to buy a box of dry cereal. Although this may seem like a simple purchase, in reality there are quite a few steps in the process that cereal marketers need to understand. The first decision in the process is where to buy your cereal. If you eat a lot of it, you may choose to make a special trip to a warehouse-type retailer that sells superduper-sized boxes rather than just picking up a box while you're at the local supermarket. Of course, if you get a craving for cereal in the middle of the night, you may dash to the local convenience store. Then there is the decision of the type of cereal. Do you eat only low-fat, high-fiber bran cereals, or do you go for the sugar-coated varieties with marshmallows? Of course, you may also like to have a variety of cereals available so you can "mix and match."

Marketers also need to know how and when you consume their products. Do you eat cereal only for breakfast, or do you snack on it while you sit in front of the TV at night? Do you eat certain kinds of cereal only at certain times (like sugary "kids' cereals" that serve as comfort food when you're pulling an all-nighter)? What about storing the product (if it lasts that long)? Do you have a kitchen pantry where you can store the supersized box, or is space an issue?

And there's more. Marketers also need to understand the many factors that influence each of these steps in the consumer behavior process—internal factors unique to each of us, situational factors at the time of purchase, and the social influences of people around us. In this chapter, we'll talk about how all these factors influence how and why consumers do what they do. But first we'll look at the types of decisions consumers make and the steps in the decision-making process.

Not All Decisions Are the Same

Traditionally, researchers assumed that we carefully collect information about competing products, determine which products possess the characteristics or product attributes important to our needs, weigh the pluses and minuses of each alternative, and arrive at a satisfactory decision. But how accurate is this picture of the decision-making process? Is this the way you buy cereal?

Although it does seem that people take these steps when they make an important purchase such as a new car, is it realistic to assume that they do this for everything they buy, like that box of cereal? Today we realize that decision makers actually employ a set of approaches that range from painstaking analysis to pure whim, depending on the importance of what they are buying and how much effort they choose to put into the decision.[2] Researchers find it convenient to think in terms of an "effort" continuum that is anchored on one end by habitual decision-making, such as deciding to purchase a box of cereal, and at the other end by extended problem solving, such as deciding to purchase a new car.

When consumers engage in extended problem solving, indeed we do carefully go through the steps Figure 11.1 outlines: problem recognition, information search, evaluation of alternatives, product choice, and post-purchase evaluation.

When we make habitual decisions (also called routine decisions), however, we make little or no conscious effort. We may not search much if at all for more information, and we may not bother to compare alternatives. Rather, we make purchases automatically. You may, for example, simply throw the same brand of cereal in your shopping cart week after week without thinking about it. Figure 11.2 provides a summary of the differences between extended problem solving and habitual decision-making.

Many decisions fall somewhere in the middle and are characterized by limited problem solving, which means that we do some work to make a decision but not a great deal. This is probably how you decide on a new pair of running shoes or a new calculator for math class. We often rely on simple "rules of thumb" instead of painstakingly learning all the ins-and-outs of every product alternative. So, rather than devoting a week of your life to learning all there is to know about calculators, you may use a simple rule like: "Buy a well-known electronics brand."

FIGURE 11.1

The Consumer Decision-Making Process

The consumer decision-making process involves as series of steps.

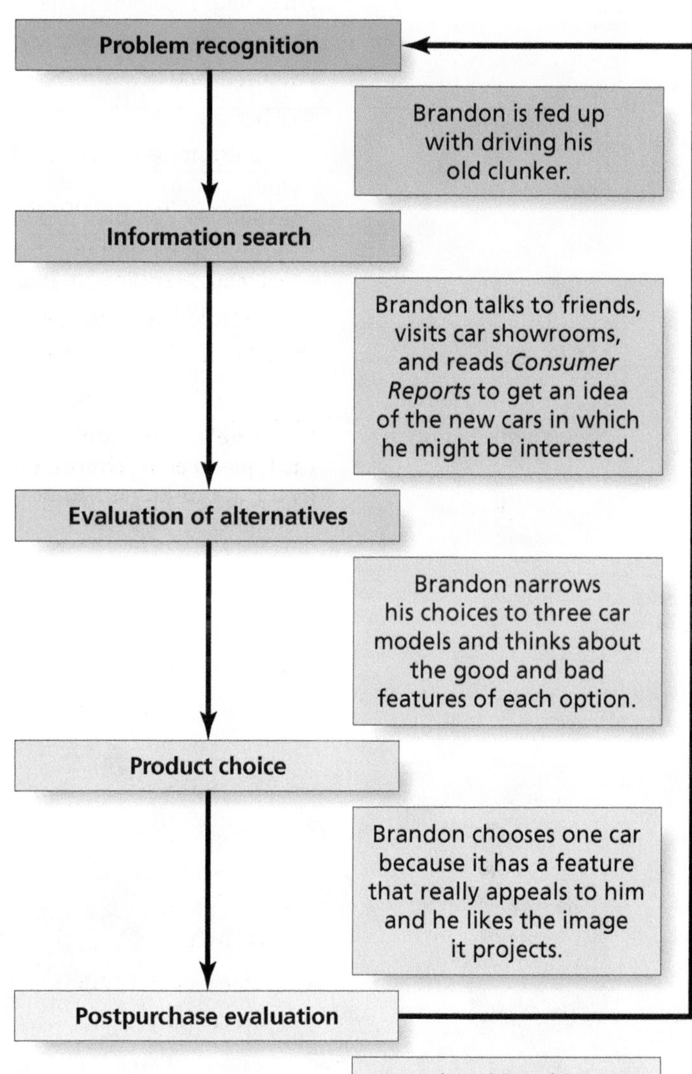

Just how much effort do we put into our buying decisions? The answer depends on our level of **involvement**—how important we perceive the consequences of the purchase to be. As a rule, we are more involved in the decision-making process for products that we think are risky in some way. **Perceived risk** may be present if the product is expensive or complex and hard to understand, such as a new computer or a sports car. Perceived risk also can play a role when we think that making a bad choice will result in embarrassment or social rejection. For example, a person who wears a pair of Skechers on a job interview may jeopardize the job if the interviewer doesn't approve of his footwear.

involvement
The relative importance of perceived consequences of the purchase to a consumer.

perceived risk
The belief that choice of a product has potentially negative consequences, whether financial, physical, and/or social.

When perceived risk is low—such as when we buy a box of cereal—we experience a small amount of involvement in the decision-making process. In these cases we're not overly concerned about which option we choose because it is not especially important

FIGURE 11.2

Extended Problem Solving versus Habitual Decision-Making[3]

Decisions characterized as extended problem solving versus habitual decision-making differ in a number of ways.

	Extended Problem Solving	*Habitual (Routine) Decision Making*
Product	New car	Box of cereal
Level of involvement	High (important decision)	Low (unimportant decision)
Perceived risk	High (expensive, complex product)	Low (simple, low-cost product)
Information processing	Careful processing of information (search advertising, magazines, car dealers, Web sites)	Respond to environmental cues (store signage or displays)
Learning model	Cognitive learning (use insight and creativity to use information found in environment)	Behavioral learning (ad shows product in beautiful setting, creating positive attitude)
Needed marketing actions	Provide information via advertising, salespeople, brochures, Web sites. Educate consumers to product benefits, risks of wrong decisions, etc.	Provide environmental cues at point-of-purchase, such as product display

or risky. The worst-case scenario is that you don't like the taste and pawn off the box on your unsuspecting roommate! In *low-involvement* situations, the consumer's decision is often a response to environmental cues, such as when you decide to try a new type of cereal because the grocery store prominently displays it at the end of the aisle. Under these circumstances, managers must concentrate on how a store displays products at the time of purchase to influence the decision maker. For example, a cereal marketer may decide to spend extra money to be sure its brand stands out in a store display or feature a cool athlete like Olympic speed skater Apolo Ohno on the box so consumers notice it.

Marketers at the beginning of the walking shoe craze assumed that all recreational walkers were just burned-out joggers. Subsequent psychographic research that examined the AIOs of these walkers showed that there were actually several psychographic segments within the larger group who engaged in the activity for very different reasons. These different motivations included walking for fun, walking to save money, and walking for exercise. This research resulted in walking shoes for different segments, from Footjoy Walkers to Nike Healthwalkers.

PHOTO: Zuma Press/Newscom

For *high-involvement* purchases, such as when we buy a house or a car, we are more likely to carefully process all the available information and to have thought about the decision well before we buy the item. The consequences of the purchase are important and risky, especially because a bad decision may result in significant financial losses, aggravation, or embarrassment. Most of us would not just saunter into a real estate agent's office at lunchtime and casually plunk down a deposit on a new house. For high-involvement products, managers must start to reduce perceived risk by educating the consumer about why their product is the best choice well in advance of the time that the person is ready to make a decision.

To understand each of the steps in the decision-making process, we'll follow the fortunes of a consumer named Brandon, who, as Figure 11.1 shows, is in the market for a new ride—a highly involving purchase decision, to say the least.

Step 1: Problem Recognition

Problem recognition occurs whenever a consumer sees a significant difference between his or her current state of affairs and some desired or ideal state. A woman whose 10-year-old Hyundai lives at the mechanic's shop has a problem, as does the man who thinks he'd have better luck getting dates if he traded his Hyundai for a new sports car. Brandon falls into the latter category—his old clunker runs okay, but he wants to sport some wheels that will get him admiring stares instead of laughs.

problem recognition
The process that occurs whenever the consumer sees a significant difference between his current state of affairs and some desired or ideal state; this recognition initiates the decision-making process.

information search
The process whereby a consumer searches for appropriate information to make a reasonable decision.

Do marketing decisions have a role in consumers' problem recognition? Although most problem recognition occurs spontaneously or when a true need arises, marketers often develop creative advertising messages that stimulate consumers to recognize that their current state (that old car) just doesn't equal their desired state (a shiny, new convertible). Figure 11.3 provides examples of marketers' responses to consumers' problem recognition and the other steps in the consumer decision-making process.

Campbell's asks, "What shape are your kids in?" This question kick-starts problem recognition for parents who may need to reconsider what they feed their children.

PHOTO: Campbell Soup Company

Step 2: Information Search

Once Brandon recognizes his problem—he wants a newer car!—he needs adequate information to resolve it. **Information search** is the step of the decision-making process in which the consumer checks his memory and surveys the environment to identify what options are out there that might solve his problem. Advertisements in newspapers, on TV or the radio, information we "Google" on the Internet, or a video on YouTube often provide valuable guidance during this step. Brandon might rely on recommendations from his friends, Facebook drivers' clubs, information he finds at www.caranddriver.com, in brochures from car dealerships, or on the manufacturers' Web sites.

THE INTERNET AS A SEARCH TOOL Increasingly, consumers use the Internet to search for information about products. Search engines, sites such as Google (**www.google.com**) and Bing (**www.Bing.com**), help us locate useful information as they search millions of Web pages for key words and return a list of sites that contain those key words.

Of course, the problem for marketers is that consumers seldom follow up on more than a page or two of results they

FIGURE 11.3

Responses to Decision Process Stages

Understanding the consumer decision process means marketers can develop strategies to help move the consumer from recognizing a need to being a satisfied customer.

Stage in the Decision Process	Marketing Strategy	Example
Problem recognition	Encourage consumers to see that existing state does not equal desired state	• Create TV commercials showing the excitement of owning a new car
Information search	Provide information when and where consumers are likely to search	• Target advertising on TV programs with high target-market viewership • Provide sales training that ensures knowledgeable salespeople • Make new-car brochures available in dealer showrooms • Design exciting, easy-to-navigate, and informative Web sites • Provide information on blogs and social networks to encourage word-of-mouth strategies • Use search marketing to ensure that your Web site has preferential search engine positioning • Participate in consumer review/advisory Web sites such as tripadvisor.com
Evaluation of alternatives	Understand the criteria consumers use in comparing brands and communicate own brand superiority	• Conduct research to identify most important evaluative criteria • Create advertising that includes reliable data on superiority of a brand (e.g., miles per gallon, safety, comfort)
Product choice	Understand choice heuristics used by consumers and provide communication that encourages brand decision	• Advertise "Made in America" (country of origin) • Stress long history of the brand (brand loyalty)
Postpurchase evaluation	Encourage accurate consumer expectations	• Provide honest advertising and sales presentations

get from these searches—we're all bombarded by way too much information these days to ever look at all of it. This has led marketers to develop sophisticated **search marketing** techniques. With **search engine optimization (SEO)** marketers first find what key words consumers use most in their searches. Then they edit their site's content or HTML to increase its relevance to those keywords so they can try to place their site high up in the millions of sites the search might generate. With **search engine marketing (SEM)** the search engine company charges marketers to display **sponsored search ads** that appear at the top or beside the search results.

search marketing
Marketing strategies that involve the use of Internet search engines.

search engine optimization (SEO)
A systematic process of ensuring that your firm comes up at or near the top of lists of typical search phrases related to your business.

search engine marketing (SEM)
Search marketing strategy in which marketers pay for ads or better positioning.

sponsored search ads
Paid ads that appear at the top or beside the Internet search engine results.

Comparison shopping agents (or **shopbots**) such as **Shopzilla.com** and **NexTag.com** are Web applications that can help online shoppers to find what they are looking for at the lowest price. In addition to listing where a product is available and the price, these sites often provide customer reviews and ratings of the product and the sellers. They enable consumers to view both positive and negative feedback about the product and the online retailer from other consumers. Increasingly consumers also search out other consumers' opinions and experience through networking Web sites such as YouTube and Facebook. We'll talk more about these sites and others similar to them later in the chapter.

comparison shopping agents or shopbots
Web applications that help online shoppers find what they are looking for at the lowest price and provide customer reviews and ratings of products and sellers.

BEHAVIORAL TARGETING During information search, the marketer's goal is to make the information consumers want and need about their product easily accessible. The challenge today is how to get the right message to the right consumer. One answer to this challenge is **behavioral targeting,** a strategy that presents individuals with advertisements based on their Internet use. In other words, with today's technology it has become fairly easy for marketers to tailor the ads you see to Web sites you've visited.

behavioral targeting
The marketing practice by which marketers deliver advertisements for products a consumer is looking for by watching what the consumer does online.

Cable TV stations offer the newest behavioral targeting strategy. Using existing systems in digital set-top boxes, cable companies can deliver ads to specific households based on such demographic data as income, ethnicity, gender, and household size. For example, an ad for diapers would only go to households with infants, while one for the Lexus SC convertible (beginning price of over $68,000) would target high-income households. In addition, a viewer will be able to press a button on her remote to get more information about a product, see a movie trailer, view a demonstration video of a new product, or order a sample or a coupon.

Some critics feel this is a mixed blessing because of privacy issues. While most agree using demographic information is acceptable, many fear that viewing habits will be tracked and also used in behavioral targeting. What do you think?

When a consumer recognizes a problem such as the need to shed a few pounds, he or she will be more receptive to products that offer to help.

PHOTO: Campbell Soup Company

Step 3: Evaluation of Alternatives

Once Brandon has identified his options, it's time to decide on a few true contenders. There are two components to this stage of the decision-making process. First, a consumer armed with information identifies a small number of products in which he is interested. Then he narrows down his choices as he decides which of the possibilities are feasible and by comparing the pros and cons of each remaining option.

Brandon has always wanted a red Ferrari. But, after he allows himself to daydream for a few minutes, he returns to reality and reluctantly admits that an Italian sports car is probably not in the cards for him right now. He decides that the cars he likes—and can actually afford—are the Scion, the Ford Focus, and the Honda Element. He has narrowed down his options by considering only affordable cars that come to mind or that his buddies suggest.

evaluative criteria
The dimensions consumers use to compare competing product alternatives.

Now it's decision time! Brandon has to look more systematically at each of the three possibilities and identify the important characteristics, or **evaluative criteria,** that he will use to decide among them. The criteria may be power, comfort, price, the style of the car, and even safety. Keep in mind that marketers often play a role in educating consumers about which product characteristics they should use as evaluative criteria—usually they will "conveniently" emphasize the dimensions in which their product excels. To make sure customers like Brandon come to the "right" conclusions in their evaluation of the alternatives, marketers must understand which criteria consumers use, and which are more or less important. With this information, sales and advertising professionals can point out a brand's superiority on the most important criteria as *they* have defined them.

Step 4: Product Choice

When Brandon examines his alternatives and takes a few test drives, it's time to "put the pedal to the metal." Deciding on one product and acting on this choice is the next step in the decision-making process. After agonizing over his choice for a few weeks, Brandon decides that even though the Element and the Scion have attractive qualities, the Focus has the affordability he needs and its carefree image is the way he wants others to think about him. All this thinking about cars is "driving" him crazy, and he's relieved to make a decision to buy the Focus and get on with his life.

So, just how do consumers like Brandon choose among the alternatives they consider? These decisions often are complicated because it's hard to juggle all the product characteristics in your head. One car may offer better gas mileage, another is $2,000 cheaper, while another boasts a better safety record. How do we make sense of all these qualities and arrive at a decision?

heuristics
A mental rule of thumb that leads to a speedy decision by simplifying the process.

We saw earlier that consumers often rely on decision guidelines when they weigh the merits of competing brands claims that companies make. These **heuristics,** or mental rules-of-thumb, provide consumers with shortcuts that simplify the decision-making process. One such brand because they assume that if it costs more, it must be better (even though this isn't always true).

brand loyalty
A pattern of repeat product purchases, accompanied by an underlying positive attitude toward the brand, based on the belief that the brand makes products superior to those of its competition.

Perhaps the most common heuristic is **brand loyalty;** this occurs when we buy the same brand over and over, and as you can guess it's the Holy Grail for marketers. Consumers who have strong brand loyalty feel that it's not worth the effort to consider competing options. People form preferences for a favorite brand and then may never change their minds in the course of a lifetime. Needless to say, this makes it extremely difficult for rivals to persuade them to switch.

Still another heuristic is based on country-of-origin. We assume that a product has certain characteristics if it comes from a certain country. In the car category, many people associate German cars with fine engineering and Swedish cars with safety. Brandon assumed that the Japanese-made Honda would be a bit more reliable than the Ford or Saturn, so he factored that into his decision.

Sometimes a marketer wants to encourage a country association even when none exists. For example, U.S. firm General Mills offers consumers Swiss-sounding Yoplait yogurt while Stonyfield Farms has introduced its Greek-sounding Oikos Organic Greek Yogurt. Häagen-Dazs ice cream comes from that exotic Scandinavian area we call . . . New Jersey.

When you're dieting and you'll only consider low-calorie options, taste becomes an evaluative criterion.

Step 5: Postpurchase Evaluation

In the last step of the decision-making process, the consumer evaluates just how good a choice he made. Everyone has experienced regret after making a purchase ("What was I *thinking*?"), and (hopefully) we have all been pleased with something we've bought. The evaluation of the product results in a level of **consumer satisfaction/dissatisfaction.** This refers to the overall feelings, or attitude, a person has about a product after she purchases it.

consumer satisfaction/ dissatisfaction
The overall feelings or attitude a person has about a product after purchasing it.

Just how do we decide if we're satisfied with what we bought? The obvious answer would be, "That's easy. The product is either wonderful or it isn't." However, it's a little more complicated than that. When we buy a product, we have some *expectations* of product quality. How well a product or service meets or exceeds these expectations determines customer satisfaction. In other words, we tend to assess product quality by comparing what we have bought to a preexisting performance standard. We form this standard via a mixture of information from marketing communications, informal information sources such as friends and family, and our own prior experience with the product category. That's why it's very important that marketers create accurate expectations of their product in advertising and other communications.

Even when a product performs to expectations, consumers may suffer anxiety or regret, or **cognitive dissonance,** after making a purchase. When we reject product alternatives with attractive features, we may second-guess our decision. Brandon, for example, might begin to think, "Maybe I should have chosen the Honda Element—everyone says Hondas are great cars." To generate satisfied customers and remove dissonance, marketers often seek to reinforce purchases through direct mail or other personalized contacts after the sale.

cognitive dissonance
The anxiety or regret a consumer may feel after choosing from among several similar attractive choices.

So, even though Brandon's new Focus is not exactly as powerful as a Ferrari, he's still happy with the car, because he never really expected a fun little car to eat up the highway like a high-performance sports car that costs ten times as much. Brandon has "survived" the consumer decision-making process: He recognized a problem, conducted an informational search to resolve it, identified the (feasible) alternatives available, made a product choice, and then evaluated the quality of his decision.

Apart from understanding the mechanics of the consumer decision-making process, marketers also try to ascertain what influences in consumers' lives affect this process. There are three main categories: internal, situational, and social influences. In Brandon's case, for example, the evaluative criteria he used to compare cars and his feelings about each were influenced by:

1. Internal factors such as the connection he learned to make between a name like Ford Focus and an image of "slightly hip, yet safe and solid"
2. Situational factors such as the way the Ford salesperson treated him.
3. Social influences such as his prediction that his friends would be impressed when they saw him cruising down the road in his new wheels.

FIGURE 11.4

Influences on Consumer Decision-Making

A number of different factors in consumers' lives influence the consumer decision-making process. Marketers need to understand these influences and which ones are important in the purchase process.

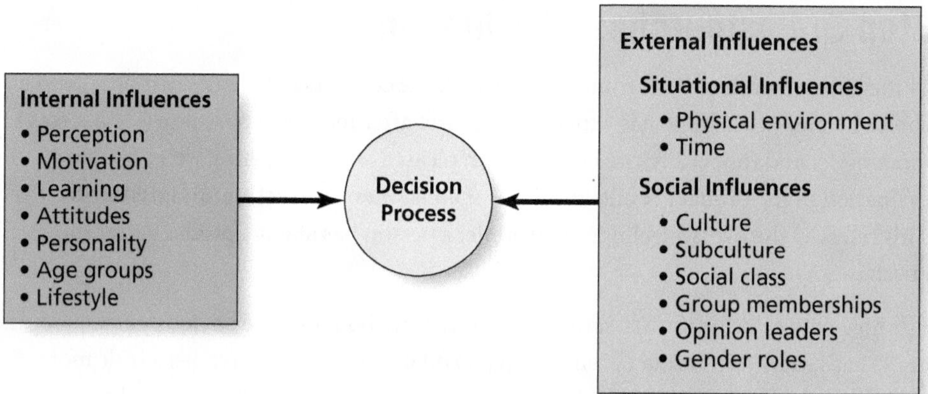

Figure 11.4 shows the influences in the decision-making process and emphasizes that all these factors work together to affect the ultimate choice each person makes. Now, let's consider how each of these three types of influences work, starting with internal factors.

Internal Influences on Consumers' Decisions

Like Brandon, your dream ride may be a sporty Ferrari. However, your roommate dreams of a pimped-out Escalade and your dad is set on owning a big Mercedes. As the saying goes, "That's why they make chocolate and vanilla." We can attribute much of these differences to internal influences on consumer behavior—those things that cause each of us to interpret information about the outside world, including which car is the best, differently from one another. Let's see how internal factors relating to the way people absorb and interpret information influence the decision-making process.

Perception

perception
The process by which people select, organize, and interpret information from the outside world.

Perception is the process by which people select, organize, and interpret information from the outside world. We receive information in the form of sensations, the immediate response of our sensory receptors—eyes, ears, nose, mouth, and skin—to basic stimuli such as light, color, odors, touch, and sound. We try to make sense of the sensations we receive as we interpret them in light of our past experiences. For example, when we encounter a new product, we look at and perhaps touch the product or its package. Then we interpret that product based on our past experiences—or lack of experiences—with similar products.

Take the computer keyboard, for example. When typewriters were introduced in the 1870s the keys got stuck if you typed too fast. Then in 1874 an inventor named

Christopher Latham Sholes developed the QWERTY keyboard (named for the first six letters on the top row); this layout arranged the letters of the alphabet so that it decreased how fast a person could type. We don't have physical keys in computers and cell phones, so why do we still use QWERTY keyboards? Because we're used to them and it would be a hassle to learn a different configuration.

We are bombarded with information about products—thousands of ads, in-store displays, special offers, our friends' opinions, and on and on. The perception process has important implications for marketers: As we absorb and make sense of the vast quantities of information that compete for our attention, the odds are that any single message will get lost in the clutter. And, if we do notice the message, there's no guarantee that the meaning we give it will be the same one the marketer intended. The issues that marketers need to understand during this process include exposure, attention, and interpretation.

EXPOSURE The stimulus must be within range of people's sensory receptors to be noticed; in other words, people must be physically able to see, hear, taste, smell, or feel the stimulus. For example, the lettering on a highway billboard must be big enough for a passing motorist to read easily, or the message will be lost. **Exposure** is the extent to which a person's sensory receptors are capable of registering a stimulus.

exposure
The extent to which a stimulus is capable of being registered by a person's sensory receptors.

Marketers work hard to achieve exposure for their products, but sometimes it's just a matter of making sure that cool people use your product—and that others observe them doing this. After finding out that a close friend was flying to Los Angeles to audition for the film *Any Given Sunday*, the president of the high-performance sportswear company Under Armour sent along with him a bunch of free samples of its athletic wear to give to the film's casting director as a gift. The director liked the quality of the clothes so much he gave them to the wardrobe company the filmmakers hired and they also really liked the clothes. The next thing you know, the movie (starring Al Pacino and Jamie Foxx) featured both the actors wearing Under Armour clothes on screen—and there was even a scene in the film when Jamie Foxx undressed in the locker room with a clear shot of the Under Armour logo on his jock strap. After the movie's release, hits on Under Armour's Web site spiked, and, as they say, the rest is history.[4]

Many people believe that even messages they can't see will persuade them to buy advertised products. Claims about **subliminal advertising** of messages hidden in ice cubes (among other places) have been surfacing since the 1950s.A survey of American consumers found that almost two-thirds believe in the existence of subliminal advertising, and over one-half are convinced that this technique can get them to buy things they don't really want.[5]

subliminal advertising
Supposedly hidden messages in marketers' communications.

There is very little evidence to support the argument that this technique actually has any effect at all on our perceptions of products. But still, concerns persist. In 2006 ABC rejected a commercial for KFC that invites viewers to slowly replay the ad to find a secret message, citing the network's long-standing policy against subliminal advertising. The ad (which other networks aired) is a seemingly ordinary pitch for KFC's $.99 Buffalo Snacker chicken sandwich. But if you replay it slowly on a digital video recorder or VCR, it tells you that viewers can visit KFC's Web site to receive a coupon for a free sandwich. Ironically, this technique is really the opposite of subliminal advertising because instead of secretly placing words or images in the ad, KFC blatantly publicized its campaign by informing viewers that it contains a message and how to find it.[6] The short story: Hidden messages are intriguing and fun to think about (if a little scary), but they don't work. Sorry for the letdown.

attention
The extent to which a person devotes mental processing to a particular stimulus.

ATTENTION As you drive down the highway, you pass hundreds of other cars. But to how many do you pay attention? Probably only one or two—the bright pink and purple VW Bug and the Honda with the broken taillight that cut you off at the exit ramp. **Attention** is the extent to which we devote mental-processing activity to a particular stimulus. Consumers are more likely to pay attention to messages that speak to their current needs. For example, you're far more likely to notice an ad for a fast-food restaurant when you're hungry, while smokers are more likely than nonsmokers to block out messages about the health hazards of smoking.

Grabbing consumers' attention is becoming harder than ever, because people's attention spans are shorter than ever. Now that we are accustomed to multitasking, flitting back and forth between our e-mails, TV, IMs, and so on, advertisers have to be more creative by mixing up the types of messages they send. That's why we see both long (60-second) commercials that almost feel like miniature movies and short (some as brief as five seconds) messages that are meant to have surprise value: They are usually over before commercial-haters can zap or zip past them. Indeed, brief blurbs that are long enough to tantalize viewers but short enough not to bore them are becoming commonplace. In contrast to the old days when most commercials on television networks were 30-second spots, today more than one-third run for only 15 seconds.[7]

interpretation
The process of assigning meaning to a stimulus based on prior associations a person has with it and assumptions he or she makes about it.

INTERPRETATION **Interpretation** is the process of assigning meaning to a stimulus based on prior associations we have with it and assumptions we make about it. Extra Strength Maalox Whip Antacid flopped, even though a spray can is a pretty effective way to deliver this kind of tummy ache relief. But to consumers, aerosol whips mean dessert toppings, not medication.[8] If we don't interpret the product the way it was intended because of our prior experiences, the best marketing ideas will be "wasted."

Motivation

motivation
An internal state that drives us to satisfy needs by activating goal-oriented behavior.

Motivation is an internal state that drives us to satisfy needs. Once we activate a need, a state of tension exists that drives the consumer toward some goal that will reduce this tension by eliminating the need.

Think again about Brandon and his old car. He began to experience a gap between his present state (he owns an old car) and a desired state (he craves a car that gets him noticed and is fun to drive). This activated the need for a new car, which in turn motivated Brandon to test different models, to talk with friends about different makes, and finally to buy a new car.

hierarchy of needs
An approach that categorizes motives according to five levels of importance, the more basic needs being on the bottom of the hierarchy and the higher needs at the top.

Psychologist Abraham Maslow developed an influential approach to motivation.[9] He formulated a **hierarchy of needs** that categorizes motives according to five levels of importance, the more basic needs being on the bottom of the hierarchy and the higher needs at the top. The hierarchy suggests that before a person can meet needs at a given level, he must first meet the lower level's needs—somehow those hot new Seven jeans don't seem as enticing when you don't have enough money to buy food.

FIGURE 11.5

Maslow's Hierarchy of Needs and Related Products

Abraham Maslow proposed a hierarchy of needs that categorizes motives. Savvy marketers know they need to understand the level of needs that motivates a consumer to buy a particular product or brand.

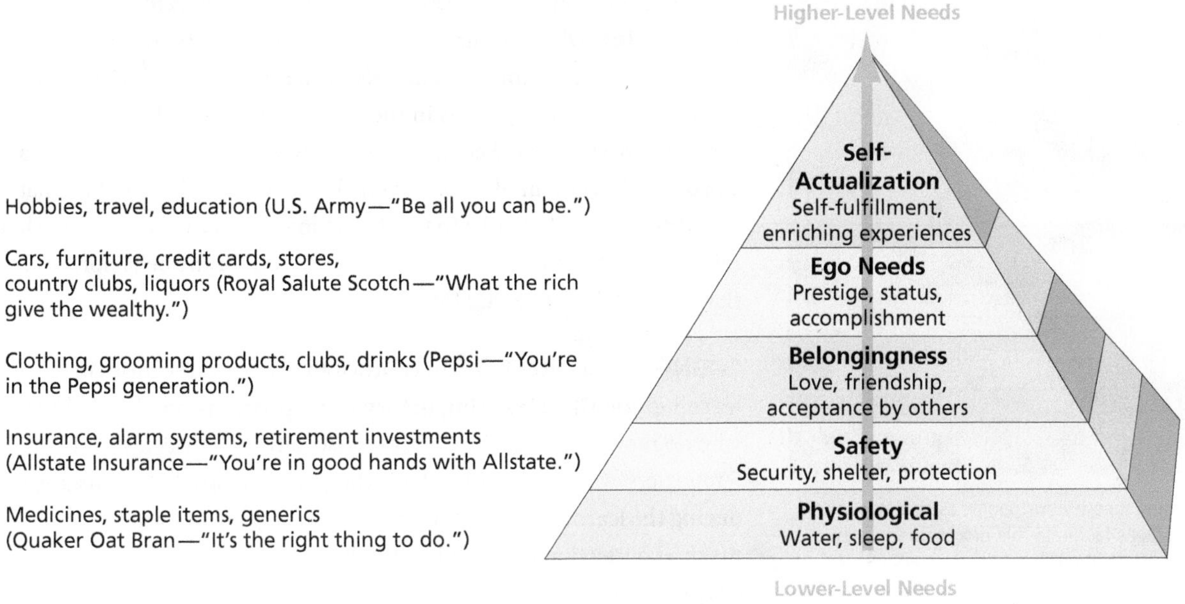

As you can see from Figure 11.5, people start at the lowest level with basic physiological needs for food and sleep. Then they progress to higher levels to satisfy more complex needs, such as the need to be accepted by others or to feel a sense of accomplishment. Ultimately, they can reach the highest-level needs, where they will be motivated to attain such goals as self-fulfillment. As the figure shows, if marketers understand the level of needs relevant to consumers in their target market, they can tailor their products and messages to them.

Learning

Learning is a change in behavior caused by information or experience. Learning about products can occur deliberately, as when we set out to gather information about different MP3 players before we buy one brand. We also learn even when we don't try. Consumers recognize many brand names and can hum many product jingles, for example, even for products they themselves do not use. Psychologists who study learning have advanced several theories to explain the learning process, and these perspectives are important because a major goal for marketers is to "teach" consumers to prefer their products. Let's briefly review the most important perspectives on how people learn.

learning
A relatively permanent change in behavior caused by acquired information or experience.

behavioral learning theories
Theories of learning that focus on how consumer behavior is changed by external events or stimuli.

classical conditioning
The learning that occurs when a stimulus eliciting a response is paired with another stimulus that initially does not elicit a response on its own but will causes a similar response over time because of its association with the first stimulus.

BEHAVIORAL LEARNING **Behavioral learning theories** assume that learning takes place as the result of connections we form between events. In one type of behavioral learning, **classical conditioning,** a person perceives two stimuli at about the same time. After a while, the person transfers his response from one stimulus to the other. For example, an ad shows a product and a breathtakingly beautiful scene so that (the marketer hopes) you will transfer the positive feelings you get when you look at the

Cognitive learning theory views people as problem-solvers. Marketing messages facilitate this process when they provide factual information to help consumers make decisions.

PHOTO: Photography by Staudinger & Franke/Marge Casey & Associates

scene to the advertised product. Hint: Did you ever notice that car ads often show a new auto on a beautiful beach at sunset or speeding down a mountain road with brightly colored leaves blowing across the pavement?

Another common form of behavioral learning is **operant conditioning,** which occurs when people learn that their actions result in rewards or punishments. This feedback influences how they will respond in similar situations in the future. Just as a rat in a maze learns the route to a piece of cheese, consumers who receive a reward such as a prize in the bottom of a box of cereal will be more likely to buy that brand again. We don't like to think that marketers can train us like lab mice, but that kind of feedback does reward us for the behavior. Will that be American or Swiss for you?

COGNITIVE LEARNING In contrast to behavioral theories of learning, **cognitive learning theory** views people as problem-solvers who do more than passively react to associations between stimuli. Supporters of this viewpoint stress the role of creativity and insight during the learning process. *Cognitive learning* occurs when consumers make a connection between ideas or by observing things in their environment.

Observational learning occurs when people watch the actions of others and note what happens to them as a result. They store these observations in memory and at some later point use the information to guide their own behavior. Marketers often use this process to create advertising and other messages that allow consumers to observe the benefits of using their products. Health clubs and manufacturers of exercise equipment feature well-muscled men and women pounding away on treadmills, while mouthwash makers show that fresh breath is the key to romance.

operant conditioning
Learning that occurs as a result of rewards or punishments.

cognitive learning theory
Theory of learning that stresses the importance of internal mental processes and that views people as problem solvers who actively use information from the world around them to master their environment.

observational learning
Learning that occurs when people watch the actions of others and note what happens to them as a result.

Now we've discussed how the three internal processes of perception, motivation, and learning influence how consumers absorb and interpret information. But the results of these processes—the interpretation the consumer gives to a marketing message—differ depending on unique consumer characteristics. Let's talk next about some of these characteristics: existing consumer attitudes, the personality of the consumer, and consumer age groups.

Attitudes

An **attitude** is a lasting evaluation of a person, object, or issue.[10] Consumers have attitudes toward brands, such as whether McDonald's or Wendy's has the best hamburgers. They also evaluate more general consumption-related behaviors such as whether high-fat foods, including hamburgers, are a no no in a healthy diet. A person's attitude has three components: affect, cognition, and behavior.

attitude
A learned predisposition to respond favorably or unfavorably to stimuli on the basis of relatively enduring evaluations of people, objects, and issues.

Affect is the feeling component of attitudes. This term refers to the overall emotional response a person has to a product. Affect is usually dominant for expressive products, such as perfume, where we choose a fragrance if it makes us feel happy.

affect
The feeling component of attitudes; refers to the overall emotional response a person has to a product.

Some marketing researchers are trying to understand how consumers' emotional reactions influence how they feel about products. A company called Sensory Logic, for example, studies videotapes of people's facial reactions—to products and commercials—in increments as fleeting as 1/30 of a second. Staffers look for the difference between, say, a true smile (which includes a relaxation of the upper eyelid) and a social smile (which occurs only around the mouth). Whirlpool hired the company to test consumers' emotional reactions to its Duet washers and dryers. Its (perhaps ambitious) goal was to design appliances that would actually make people happy. The research led Whirlpool to change some design options on the Duet products, including geometric patterns and certain color combinations. Smile, it's Laundry Day! More recently, Disney has built a lab where it will measure heart rate and skin conductivity and track the eye gaze of consumers while they view ads over the Internet, mobile devices, and their TVs.[11]

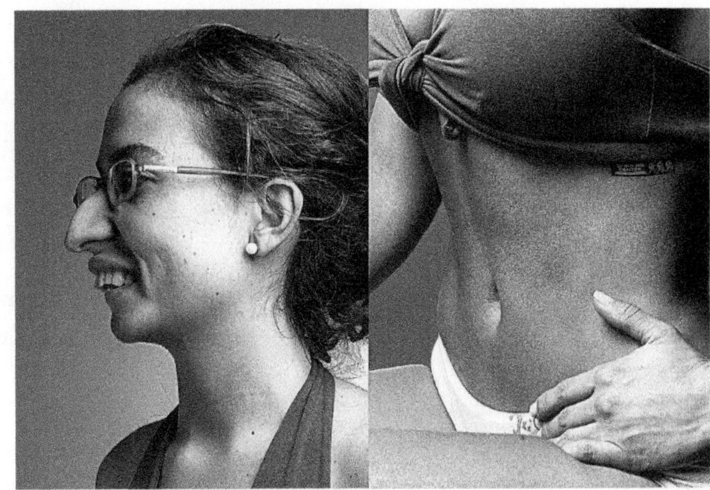

Marketers often try to influence our attitudes via the affect component when they use images that arouse either negative or positive feelings. This ad for a gym in Bogota, Colombia, focuses on consumers' emotional reactions to unattractive faces and attractive bodies.

PHOTO: Copywriter: Hugo Corredor, Art Director: Giovanni Martinez, Photography: Alfonso Torres

Cognition, the knowing component, refers to the beliefs or knowledge a person has about a product and its important characteristics. You may believe that a Mercedes is built better than most cars, or (like Brandon) that a Ford Focus is slightly hip, yet solid. Cognition is important for complex products, such as computers, for which we may develop beliefs on the basis of technical information.

cognition
The knowing component of attitudes; refers to the beliefs or knowledge a person has about a product and its important characteristics.

Behavior, the doing component, involves a consumer's intention to do something, such as the intention to purchase or use a certain product. For products such as cereal, consumers act (purchase and try the product) on the basis of limited information and then form an evaluation of the product simply on the basis of how the product tastes or performs.

behavior
The doing component of attitudes; involves a consumer's intention to do something, such as the intention to purchase or use a certain product.

Personality and the Self: Are You What You Buy?

Personality is the set of unique psychological characteristics that consistently influences the way a person responds to situations in the environment. One adventure-seeking consumer may always be on the lookout for new experiences and cutting-edge products, while another is happiest in familiar surroundings using the same brands over and over. Today, popular online matchmaking services like **match.com, Matchmaker.com,** and **Tickle.com** offer to create your "personality profile" and then hook you up with other members whose profiles are similar.

personality
The set of unique psychological characteristics that consistently influences the way a person responds to situations in the environment.

It makes sense to assume that consumers buy products that are extensions of their personalities. That's why marketers try to create brand personalities that will appeal to different types of people. For example, consider the different "personalities" fragrance marketers invent: A brand with a "wholesome, girl-next-door" image such as Clinique's Happy would be hard to confuse with the sophisticated image of Christian Dior's Dolce Vita.

This German ad appeals directly to the self-concepts of potential customers who want to shed a few pounds.
PHOTO: Courtesy of Jung von Matt, Berlin

A person's **self-concept** is his attitude toward himself. The self-concept is composed of a mixture of beliefs about one's abilities and observations of one's own behavior and feelings (both positive and negative) about one's personal attributes, such as body type or facial features. The extent to which a person's self-concept is positive or negative can influence the products he buys and even the extent to which he fantasizes about changing his life.

Self-esteem refers to how positive a person's self-concept is. Alberto Culver uses a self-esteem pitch to promote its Soft & Beautiful, Just for Me hair relaxer for children. The company's Web site "Mom's Blog" encourages mothers to provide affirmation of their daughters' beauty to encourage their self-esteem. The site also provides "conversation starters" to help parents talk to their daughters about self-image.[12]

self-concept
An individual's self-image that is composed of a mixture of beliefs, observations, and feelings about personal attributes.

Age

A person's age is another internal influence on purchasing behavior. Many of us feel we have more in common with those of our own age because we share a common set of experiences and memories about cultural events, whether these involve Woodstock, Woodstock II, or even Woodstock III.

Goods and services often appeal to a specific age group. Although there are exceptions, it is safe to assume that most buyers of Lil' Kim's CDs are younger than those who buy Barbra Streisand disks. Thus, many marketing strategies appeal to the needs of different age groups such as children, teenagers, the middle-aged, and the elderly. These various needs result in different types of consumer behavior both offline and now online as many people incorporate the Web into their shopping patterns.

Age is important, but actually regardless of how old we are, what we buy often depends more on our current position in the family life cycle—the stages through which family members pass as they grow older. Singles (of any age) are more likely to spend money on expensive cars, entertainment, and recreation. Couples with small children purchase baby furniture, insurance, and a larger house, while older couples whose children have "left the nest" are more likely to buy a retirement home in Florida.

Lifestyle

lifestyle
The pattern of living that determines how people choose to spend their time, money, and energy and that reflects their values, tastes, and preferences.

A **lifestyle** is a pattern of living that determines how people choose to spend their time, money, and energy and that reflects their values, tastes, and preferences. We express our lifestyles in our preferences for activities such as sports, interests such as music, and opinions on politics and religion. Consumers often choose goods, services, and activities that they associate with a certain lifestyle. Brandon may drive a Ford Focus, hang out in Internet cafes, and go extreme skiing during Spring Break because he views these choices as part of a cool college student lifestyle.

If lifestyles are so important, how do marketers identify them so that they can reach consumers who share preferences for products that they associate with a lifestyle that appeals to them? *Demographic* characteristics, such as age and income, tell marketers *what* products people buy, but they don't reveal *why.* Two consumers can share the same demographic characteristics, yet be totally different people—all 20-year-old male college students are hardly identical to one another. That's why it is often important to further profile consumers in terms of their passions and how they spend their leisure time.

Marketers recognize that it's often helpful to group people into market segments based on similarities in lifestyle preferences. For example, skateboarding has morphed from an activity we associate with the lawbreaking daredevils from the movie *Dogtown* and *Z-Boys* depicted to become a full-fledged lifestyle, complete with a full complement of merchandise that boarders need to live the life. Shows on MTV feature professional skateboarders, and sales of a skateboarding video game, Tony Hawk by Activision, are over $1 billion. Many kids happily fork over $20 for T-shirts and more than $60 for skate shoes in addition to the hundreds they may spend on the latest boards.[13]

PHOTO: Jordan Strauss/WireImage/Getty Images

To breathe life into demographic analyses, marketers turn to **psychographics,** which groups consumers according to psychological and behavioral similarities. One way to do this is to describe people in terms of their activities, interests, and opinions (**AIOs**). These dimensions are based on preferences for vacation destinations, club memberships, hobbies, political and social attitudes, tastes in food and fashion, and so on. Using data from large samples, marketers create profiles of customers who resemble one another in terms of their activities and patterns of product use.[14]

psychographics
The use of psychological, sociological, and anthropological factors to construct market segments.

AIOs
Measures of consumer activities, interests and opinions used to place consumers into dimensions.

Situational and Social Influences on Consumers' Decisions

We've seen that internal factors such as how people perceive marketing messages, their motivation to acquire products, and their unique personalities, age groups, family life cycle, and lifestyle influence the decisions they make. In addition, situational and social influences—factors external to the consumer—have a big impact on the choices consumers make and how they make them.

Situational Influences

When, where, and how consumers shop—what we call *situational influences*—shape their purchase choices. Some important situational cues are our physical surroundings and time pressures.

Marketers know that dimensions of the physical environment, including factors such as decor, smells, lighting, music, and even temperature, can significantly influence consumption. If you don't believe this, consider that one study found that pumping certain odors into a Las Vegas casino actually increased the amount of money patrons fed into slot machines.[15] **Sensory marketing** is becoming big business. Westin Hotels spray a blend of green tea, geranium, and black cedar into hotel lobbies while Sheraton uses a combination of jasmine, clove, and fig. Sony scents its stores with orange, vanilla, and cedar, and Cadillac puts that "new car" smell into its autos artificially, all to influence the consumer's decision process.[16]

sensory marketing
Marketing techniques that link distinct sensory experiences such as a unique fragrance with a product or service.

Let's see how some other situational factors influence the consumer decision-making process.

THE PHYSICAL ENVIRONMENT It's no secret that physical surroundings strongly influence people's moods and behaviors. Despite all their efforts to pre-sell consumers through advertising, marketers know that the store environment influences many purchases. For example, one classic study showed that consumers decide on about two out of every three of their supermarket product purchases in the aisles (so always eat before you go to the supermarket).[17] A more recent study in Germany showed that almost 70 percent of shoppers decide what to buy at the point of sale. The messages consumers receive at the time and their feelings about being in the store strongly influence these decisions.

Two dimensions, *arousal* and *pleasure,* determine whether a shopper will react positively or negatively to a store environment. In other words, the person's surroundings can be either dull or exciting (arousing) and either pleasant or unpleasant. Just because the environment is arousing doesn't necessarily mean it will be pleasant—we've all been in crowded, loud, hot stores that are anything but. Maintaining an upbeat feeling in a pleasant context is one factor behind the success of theme parks such as Disney World, which tries to provide consistent doses of carefully calculated stimulation to visitors.[18]

The importance of these surroundings explains why many retailers focus on packing as much entertainment as possible into their stores. For example, Bass Pro Shops, a chain of outdoor sports equipment stores, features giant aquariums, waterfalls, trout ponds, archery and rifle ranges, putting greens, and free classes in everything from ice fishing to conservation. A company called Privy Promotions and others like it even sell ad space on restroom walls in stadiums. According to the company's president, "It's a decided opportunity for an advertiser to reach a captive audience."[19] Guess so.

TIME Time is one of consumers' most limited resources. We talk about "making time" or "spending time," and we remind one another that "time is money." Marketers know that the time of day, the season of the year, and how much time a person has to make a purchase affects decision-making.

Indeed, many consumers believe that they are more pressed for time than ever before. This sense of **time poverty** makes consumers responsive to marketing innovations that allow them to save time, including services such as one-hour photo processing, drive-through lanes at fast-food restaurants, and ordering products on the Web. A number of Web sites, including Apple's iTunes and even Walmart, now offer consumers the speed and convenience of downloading music or movies. These sites allow consumers

time poverty
Consumers' belief that they are more pressed for time than ever before.

to browse through thousands of titles, preview selections, and order and pay for them—all without setting foot inside a store. This saves the customer time, plus the "store" is always open.

Social Influences on Consumers' Decisions

Although we are all individuals, we are also members of many groups that influence our buying decisions. Families, friends, and classmates often sway us, as do larger groups with which we identify, such as ethnic groups and political parties. Now let's consider how social influences such as culture, social class, influential friends and acquaintances, and trends within the larger society affect the consumer decision-making process.

culture
The values, beliefs, customers, and tastes a group of people values.

CULTURE We think of **culture** as a society's personality. It is the values, beliefs, customs, and tastes a group of people produce or practice. Although we often assume that what people in one culture (especially our own) think is desirable or appropriate will be appreciated in other cultures as well, that's far from the truth. Middle Eastern youth may not agree with U.S. politics, but they love Western music and find Arab TV music channels boring. Enter MTV Arabia, a 24-hour free satellite channel. Sure, many U.S. and European videos have to be cleaned up for the Arab audience and many are simply too edgy to air. To meet the values of the Middle Eastern audience, bad language and shots of kissing, revealing outfits, or people in bed are blurred or removed and sometimes replaced by a more acceptable copy.[20] Culture matters.

RITUALS Every culture associates specific activities and products with its rituals, such as weddings and funerals. Some companies are more than happy to help us link products to cultural events. Consider the popularity of the elaborate weddings Disney stages for couples who want to reenact their own version of a popular fairy tale. At Disney World, the princess bride wears a tiara and rides to the park's lakeside wedding pavilion in a horse-drawn coach, complete with two footmen in gray wigs and gold lamé pants. At the exchange of vows, trumpets blare as Major Domo (he helped the Duke in his quest for Cinderella) walks up the aisle with two wedding bands in a glass slipper on a velvet pillow. Disney stages about 2,000 of these extravaganzas each year.[21]

In most countries, rituals are involved in the celebration of holidays. American purchase and/or cook turkeys, cranberry sauce, and pumpkin pies to have the perfect Thanksgiving dinner. In Christian cultures, the Christmas ritual is so strongly tied to gifts, Christmas trees, lights, and decorations that it becomes the make-or-break sales season of the year for retailers. In many Muslim countries, the Ramadan season means fasting during the day but consuming gigantic amounts of food after sunset each day. And New Year's Eve parties all around the globe must include fancy party dresses and champagne. Is it any wonder that marketers of so many companies study consumer rituals?

Our culture rewards skinny people.
PHOTO: Dreyer's Grand Ice Cream

VALUES (AGAIN) Cultural values are deeply held beliefs about right and wrong ways to live.[22] Marketers who understand a culture's values can tailor their product offerings accordingly. Consider, for example, that the values for collectivist countries differ greatly from those of individualistic cultures where immediate gratification of one's own needs come before all other loyalties. In collectivist cultures, loyalty to a family or a tribe overrides personal goals. Collectivist cultures put value on self-discipline, accepting one's position in life, and honoring parents and elders. Individualist cultures, on the other hand, stress equality, freedom, and personal pleasure. Today, we see the economic growth of some collectivist countries such as India, Japan, and China, making many consumers more affluent—and individualistic. For marketers, this means growth opportunities for products such as travel, luxury goods, sports activities like tennis and golf, and entertainment.

subculture
A group within a society whose members share a distinctive set of beliefs, characteristics, or common experiences.

microcultures
Groups of consumers who identify with a specific activity or art form.

SUBCULTURES A **subculture** is a group that coexists with other groups in a larger culture but whose members share a distinctive set of beliefs or characteristics, such as members of a religious organization or an ethnic group. **Microcultures** are groups of consumers who identify with a specific activity or art form. These form around music groups such as the Dave Matthews Band, media creations such as *World of Warcraft*, or leisure activities such as extreme sports. Social media has been a real boon to subcultures and microcultures; it provides an opportunity for like-minded consumers to share their thoughts, photographs, videos, and so on. More on these important new sharing platforms later in the book.

For marketers, some of the most important subcultures are racial and ethnic groups because many consumers identify strongly with their heritage, and products that appeal to this aspect of their identities appeal to them. To grow its business, cereal maker General Mills targets Hispanic consumers. The company hopes to reach mothers who want better ways to nurture their children through its Que Vida Rica marketing program that tells mothers about the benefits of its products and offers nutrition tips and recipe suggestions. Advertising for General Mills' Nature Valley brand shows Hispanic couples "savoring nature instead of conquering it."[23]

EMERGING LIFESTYLE TRENDS: CONSUMERISM AND ENVIRONMENTALISM
Powerful new social movements within a society also contribute to how we decide what we want and what we don't. One such influence is **consumerism,** the social movement directed toward protecting consumers from harmful business practices. Many consumers are becoming very aware of the social and environmental consequences of their purchases—and making their decisions accordingly.

consumerism
A social movement that attempts to protect consumers from harmful business practices.

Organized activities that bring about social and political change are not new to the American scene. Women's right to vote, child labor laws, the minimum wage, equal employment opportunity, and the ban on nuclear weapons testing all have resulted from social movements in which citizens, public and private organizations, and businesses worked to change society. In today's connected world, criticisms from consumerists can be especially damaging. A company's best way to combat such attacks and maintain a good image is to be proactive by practicing good business.

environmentalism
A broad philosophy and social movement that seeks conservation and improvement of the natural environment.

Related to the consumerism movement is **environmentalism;** this is a social movement that grows out of the worldwide growing concern for the many ways in which our consumption behaviors impact the physical world in which we live. Environmentalists seek solutions that enable companies to manage resources responsibly.

The **Kyoto Protocol** is an agreement the United Nations Framework Convention on Climate Change (UNFCCC) crafted in 1997. The Kyoto Protocol covers 170 countries worldwide. It aims to reduce greenhouse gases that create climate change. The protocol has been ratified by 175 countries. The United States has not ratified the agreement because of objections that China, as a developing country, is exempt from the emissions requirements of the agreement even though it is the world's second largest emitter of carbon dioxide. It's unlikely that the United States will ratify the Kyoto Protocol before it expires in 2012. In November 2009, the United Nations Climate Change Conference (referred to as the Copenhagen Summit) was unable to reach consensus on a post-2012 agreement.

Kyoto Protocol
A global agreement among countries that aims at reducing greenhouse gases that create climate change.

Still, global concerns are mounting and a lot of businesses are acting even in the absence of government regulations because they understand that consumers will reward companies who do. Many firms now assume a position of **environmental stewardship** when they make socially responsible business decisions that also protect the environment. A **green marketing** strategy describes efforts to choose packages, product designs, and other aspects of the marketing mix that are earth-friendly but still profitable.

environmental stewardship
A position taken by an organization to protect or enhance the natural environment as it conducts its business activities.

green marketing
A marketing strategy that supports environmental stewardship, thus creating a differential benefit in the minds of consumers.

Green marketing practices can indeed result in black ink for a firm's bottom line. As mainstream marketers recognize this change, they are starting to alter their practices to satisfy Americans' desires for healthy and earth-friendly products. Coca-Cola, for example, demonstrated its commitment to the environment during the 2010 Vancouver Olympics. The company sponsored a 100 percent environmentally sustainable, carbon-neutral café. It featured bottles, furniture, and other products made from recycled material. Going even further, Coke made every aspect of its involvement with the Olympics green—from staff uniforms to delivery trucks to compostable coffee cups.[24]

SOCIAL CLASS **Social class** is the overall rank of people in a society. People who are within the same class tend to exhibit similarities in occupation, education, and income level, and they often have similar tastes in clothing, decorating styles, and leisure activities. Class members also share many political and religious beliefs as well as preferences for AIOs.

social class
The overall rank or social standing of groups of people within a society according to the value assigned to factors such as family background, education, occupation, and income.

Many marketers design their products and stores to appeal to people in a specific social class. Working-class consumers tend to evaluate products in more utilitarian terms like sturdiness or comfort instead of trendiness or aesthetics. They are less likely to experiment with new products or styles, such as modern furniture or colored appliances, because they tend to prefer predictability to novelty. Marketers need to understand these differences and develop product and communication strategies that appeal to different social classes.

Luxury goods often serve as **status symbols;** visible markers that provide a way for people to flaunt their membership in higher social classes (or at least to make others believe they are members). The bumper sticker, "He who dies with the most toys wins," illustrates the desire to accumulate these badges of achievement. However, it's important to note that over time, the importance of different status symbols rises and falls. For

status symbols
Visible markers that provide a way for people to flaunt their membership in higher social classes (or at least to make others believe they are members).

example, when James Dean starred in the movie *Giant,* the Cadillac convertible was the ultimate status symbol car in America. Today, wealthy consumers who want to let the world know of their success are far more likely to choose a Mercedes, a BMW, or an Escalade. The "in" car five years from now is anyone's guess—perhaps with today's emphasis on the environment the Prius and other hybrids will emerge as the new status symbols?

In addition, traditional status symbols today are available to a much wider range of consumers around the world with rising incomes. This change fuels demand for mass consumed products that still offer some degree of panache or style. Think about the success of companies like Nokia, H&M, Zara, ING, Dell Computers, Gap, Nike, EasyJet, or L'Oréal. They cater to a consumer segment that analysts have labeled **mass-class.** This term refers to the hundreds of millions of global consumers who now enjoy a level of purchasing power that's sufficient to let them afford high-quality products offered by well-known multinational companies.

mass-class
The hundreds of millions of global consumers who now enjoy a level of purchasing power that's sufficient to let them afford high-quality products—except for big-ticket items like college educations, housing, or luxury cars.

reference group
An actual or imaginary individual or group that has significant effect on an individual's evaluations, aspirations, or behavior.

opinion leader
A person who is frequently able to influence others' attitudes or behaviors by virtue of his or her active interest and expertise in one of more product categories.

GROUP MEMBERSHIP Anyone who's ever "gone along with the crowd" knows that people act differently in groups than they do on their own. When there are more people in a group, it becomes less likely that any one member will be singled out for attention, and normal restraints on behavior may evaporate (think about the last wild party you attended). In many cases, group members show a greater willingness to consider riskier alternatives than they would if each member made the decision alone.[25]

A **reference group** is a set of people a consumer wants to please or imitate. Consumers "refer to" these groups when they decide what to wear, where they hang out, and what brands they buy. This influence can take the form of family and friends, respected statesmen like Martin Luther King Jr., celebrities like Angelina Jolie, or even (dare we say it!) your professors.

Since we consume many of the things we buy in the presence of others, group behaviors are very important to marketers. Sometimes group activities create new business opportunities. Consider, for example, the increasing popularity of tailgating during football games, long a tradition at some college campuses. Now many companies have figured out that there's as much, if not more, money to be made in the stadium parking lot as on the field. Coleman sells grills designed just for tailgating as part of its RoadTrip line. The *American Tailgater* catalog features tailgate flags, tailgate tents, and even a gas-powered margarita blender. Ragu offers tailgating training camps that John Madden hosts, and Jack Daniels sponsors parking-lot contests. The National Football League sells over $100 million per year of tailgating merchandise, including keg-shaped grills.[27]

PHOTO: Scott Boehm/Getty Images

OPINION LEADERS If, like Brandon, you are in the market for a new car, is there a certain person to whom you'd turn for advice? An **opinion leader** is a person who influences others' attitudes or behaviors because they believe that he possesses expertise about the product.[26] Opinion leaders usually exhibit high levels of interest in the product category. They continuously update their knowledge as they read blogs, talk to salespeople, or subscribe to podcasts about the topic. Because of this involvement, opinion leaders are valuable information sources.

Unlike commercial endorsers, who are paid to represent the interests of just one company, opinion leaders have no ax to grind and can impart both positive and negative information about the product (unless they're being compensated to blog on behalf of a brand, which is not unheard of these days!). In addition, these knowledgeable consumers often are among the first to buy new products, so they absorb much of the risk and reduce uncertainty for others who are not as courageous.

GENDER ROLES Some of the strongest pressures to conform come from our **gender roles,** society's expectations regarding the appropriate attitudes, behaviors, and appearance for men and women.[28] Of course, marketers play a part in teaching us how society expects us to act as men and women. Marketing communications and products often portray women and men differently. These influences teach us what the "proper" gender roles of women or men should be and which products are appropriate for each gender. Some of these "sex-typed" products have come under fire from social groups. For example, feminists claim the Barbie doll reinforces unrealistic ideas about what women's bodies should look like—even though a newer version of the doll isn't quite as skinny and buxom.

gender roles
Society's expectations regarding the appropriate attitudes, behaviors, and appearance for men and women.

Sex roles constantly evolve—in a complex society like ours we often encounter contradictory messages about "appropriate" behavior. We can clearly see this in the messages girls have been getting from the media for the last several years: It's cool to be overly provocative. Role models like Paris Hilton, Lindsay Lohan, Britney Spears, and even Bratz dolls convey standards about how far preteens and teens should go to broadcast their sexuality. Now we see signs of a backlash. At the Pure Fashion Web site, girls get style tips including skirts and dresses that fall no more than four fingers above the knee and no tank tops without a sweater or jacket over them. Several other sites such as **ModestApparelU.S.A.com** advocate a return to styles that leave almost everything to the imagination.[29] Is our culture moving from a celebration of "girls gone wild" to "girls gone mild"?

Men's sex roles are changing too. For one, men are concerned as never before with their appearance. Guys spend $7.7 billion on grooming products globally each year. In Europe, 24 percent of men younger than age 30 use skincare products—and 80 percent of young Korean men do. In fact, no doubt one of the biggest marketing buzzwords over the past few years is the **metrosexual**—a straight, urban male who is keenly interested in fashion, home design, gourmet cooking, and personal care. But just how widespread is the metrosexual phenomenon?

metrosexual
A straight, urban male who is keenly interested in fashion, home design, gourmet cooking, and personal care.

Clearly, our cultural definition of masculinity is evolving as men try to redefine sex roles while they stay in a "safety zone" of acceptable behaviors bounded by danger zones of sloppiness at one extreme and effeminate behavior at the other. For example, a man may decide that it's okay to use a moisturizer but draw the line at an eye cream that he considers too feminine.[30] And, much like the "girls gone milder" trend we just discussed, some cultural observers report the emergence of "retrosexuals"—men who want to

This ad from New Zealand reinforces a widely held assumption about the male gender role.
PHOTO: Courtesy of Barnes, Catmur & Friends

emphasize their old-school masculinity as they get plastic surgery to create a more rugged look that includes hairier chests and beards, squarer chins, and more angular jaw lines.[31]

Miller Genuine Draft conducted a survey of American men aged 21 to 34 to try to get a handle on these new definitions so that it could position its brand to appeal to them. The company found that, indeed, many "average Joes" are moving on from the days of drinking whatever beer is available and wearing baseball hats backward, but they also don't want to sacrifice their identities as regular guys. They care more about preparing a good meal, meeting friends for a beer, and owning a home than they do about amassing shoes, savoring fine wine, or dining at expensive restaurants. This new man is discerning when it comes to some important everyday and lifestyle decisions but isn't overly concerned about fitting into cultural molds or trends.[32]

Conclusion

Consumer behavior is the process individuals or groups go through to select, purchase, use, and dispose of goods, services, ideas, or experiences to satisfy their needs and desires. Consumer decisions differ greatly, ranging from habitual, repeat (low-involvement) purchases to complex, extended problem-solving activities for important, risky (high-involvement) purchases.

Several internal factors influence consumer decisions. Perception is how consumers select, organize, and interpret stimuli. Motivation is an internal state that drives consumers to satisfy needs. Learning is a change in behavior that results from information or experience. Behavioral learning results from external events, while cognitive learning refers to internal mental activity. An attitude is a lasting evaluation of a person, object, or issue and includes three components: affect, cognition, and behavior. Personality traits such as innovativeness, materialism, self-confidence, sociability, and the need for cognition may be used to develop market segments. Situational influences include our physical surroundings and time pressures. Dimensions of the physical environment including decor, smells, lighting, music, and even temperature can influence consumption. The time of day, the season of the year, and how much time one has to make a purchase also affect decision-making.

Consumers' overall preferences for products are determined by the culture in which they live and their membership in different subcultures. Consumerism is a social movement directed toward protecting consumers from harmful business practices. Environmentalism, another social movement, seeks ways to protect the natural environment. Firms practice environmental stewardship when they make decisions that protect the environment. Green marketing strategies include earth-friendly packaging and product designs. Social class, group memberships, and opinion leaders are other types of social influences that affect consumer choices. A reference group is a set of people a consumer wants to please or imitate, and this affects the consumer's purchasing decisions. Purchases also often result from conformity to real or imagined group pressures. Another way social influence is felt is in the expectations of society regarding the proper roles for men and women. Such expectations have led to many gender-typed products.

CHAPTER 12

Individual Behavior[1]

This chapter addresses the subject of **individual behavior** and **organizational behavior,** which is the study of the actions of people at work.

organizational behavior
The study of the actions of people at work.

individual behavior
The actions of people.

One of the challenges in understanding organizational behavior (OB) is that it addresses issues that aren't obvious. Like an iceberg, OB has a small visible dimension and a much larger hidden portion. (See Figure 12.1.) What we see when we look at an organization is its visible aspects: strategies, objectives, policies and procedures, structure, technology, formal authority relationships, and chain of command. But under the surface are other elements that managers need to understand—elements that also influence how employees behave at work. As we'll show, OB provides managers with considerable insights into these important, but hidden, aspects of the organization.

What Is the Role of Organizational Behavior?

Organizational behavior focuses on three major areas:

- First, OB looks at *individual behavior.* Based predominantly on contributions from psychologists, this area includes such topics as attitudes, personality, perception, learning, and motivation.

FIGURE 12.1

Organization as Iceberg

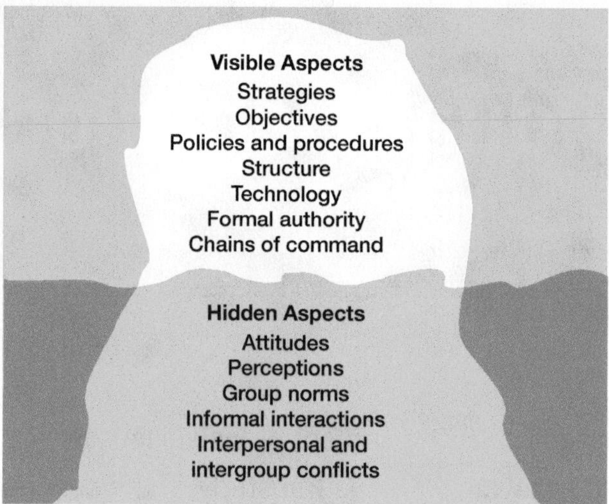

- Second, OB is concerned with *group behavior,* which includes norms, roles, team building, leadership, and conflict. Our knowledge about groups comes basically from the work of sociologists and social psychologists.
- Finally, OB also looks at *organizational* aspects including structure, culture, and human resource policies and practices.

What Are the Goals of Organizational Behavior?

The goals of OB are to *explain, predict,* and *influence* behavior. Managers need to be able to *explain* why employees engage in some behaviors rather than others, *predict* how employees will respond to various actions and decisions, and *influence* how employees behave.

Five important organizational behaviors are productivity, absenteeism, turnover, organizational citizenship, and workplace misbehavior.

- **Productivity** is a performance measure of both work efficiency and effectiveness. Managers want to know what factors will influence the efficiency (use of resources) and effectiveness (achievement of objectives) of organizations.
- **Absenteeism** is the failure to show up, mentally or physically, for work. It's difficult for work to get done if members don't show up physically or mentally.
- **Turnover** is the voluntary and involuntary permanent withdrawal from an organization. It is a problem because of increased recruiting, selection and training costs, and work disruptions.
- **Organizational citizenship** is discretionary behavior that's not part of a person's formal job requirements, but which promotes the effective functioning of the organization. Examples of good Organizational Citizenship include helping others on one's work team, volunteering for extended job activities, avoiding unnecessary conflicts, and making constructive statements about one's work group and the organization

- **Workplace misbehavior** is any intentional member behavior that is potentially harmful to the organization or individuals within the organization. Misbehavior ranges from playing loud music, texting during a meeting, and other behaviors that irritate coworkers and sabotage the team's ability to work effectively and efficiently.

The following addresses how an understanding of four psychological factors—(1) attitudes, (2) personality, (3) perception, and (4) learning—can help predict and explain team member behaviors.

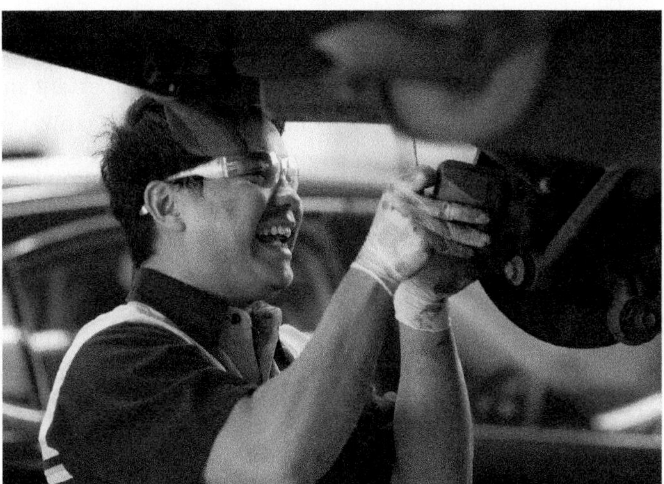

Organizational behavior focuses on job satisfaction and how it influences employee productivity, absenteeism, and turnover. Job satisfaction is high at the Lexus of Westminster auto dealership where Trung Pham, shown here, works as a mechanic. Pham and the dealership's 125 other employees have a positive feeling about their jobs and the company they work for. They say their employer, a family-owned and operated business, values the contributions they make, treats them with respect and integrity, and entrusts them with great responsibility in providing customers with a world-class Lexus ownership experience. Satisfied employees help the dealership maintain low absenteeism and turnover rates and high worker productivity.

What Role Do Attitudes Play in Job Performance?

Attitudes are evaluative statements, either favorable or unfavorable, concerning objects, people, or events. They reflect how an individual feels about something. When a person says, "I like my job," he or she is expressing an attitude about work.

Three Components of an Attitude

The three components of attitude are: cognition, affect, and behavior. The **cognitive component** of an attitude is made up of the beliefs, opinions, knowledge, and information held by a person. For example, shortly after the September 11, 2001, attacks on the World Trade Center and the Pentagon, Congress debated for weeks as to whether airport baggage screeners should be federal employees. Evidence presented during the debate showed that knives, pepper spray, and loaded guns were missed by private airport screeners. The belief held by some congressional leaders that private screeners were ineffective is an example of the cognitive component.

cognitive component
The part of an attitude made up of the beliefs, opinions, knowledge, and information held by a person.

The **affective component** is the emotional or feeling part of an attitude. This component would be reflected in the statement, "I don't like Erica because she is in a competing sorority." There is little if any knowledge of Erica, the attitude is based on emotion, perhaps due to a rivalry between sororities.

affective component
The part of an attitude that's the emotional or feeling part.

The **behavioral component** of an attitude refers to an intention to behave in a certain way toward someone or something. So, to continue our example, I might choose to avoid Erica because of my feelings about her.

behavioral component
The part of an attitude that refers to an intention to behave in a certain way toward someone or something.

Looking at attitudes as being made up of three components—cognition, affect (emotion), and behavior—helps to illustrate the complexity of attitudes. For the sake of clarity, keep in mind that the term usually refers only to the affective component.

Job-Related Attitudes

The three most important and most studied job-related attitudes are job satisfaction, job involvement, and organizational commitment.

- **Job satisfaction** is a person's general attitude toward his or her work. When people speak of employee attitudes, more often than not they mean job satisfaction.
- **Job involvement** is the degree to which a person identifies with his or her job, actively participates in it, and considers the quality of his or her work performance an important reflection of their self-worth.
- **Organizational commitment** represents an person's orientation toward the organization in terms of his or her loyalty to, identification with, and involvement in the organization.

Highly engaged people are passionate about and deeply connected to their work. Disengaged people have essentially "checked out" and don't care. They show up for work, but have no energy or passion for it.

Having highly engaged team members produces significant benefits. Highly engaged people are two-and-a-half times more likely to be top performers than their less-engaged coworkers.

Do Individuals' Attitudes and Behaviors Need to Be Consistent?

Research generally concludes that people seek consistency between their attitudes and their behavior. Individuals try to reconcile differing attitudes and align their attitudes and behavior so that they appear rational and consistent. *They do so by altering either the attitudes or the behavior or by developing a rationalization for the discrepancy.*

cognitive dissonance
Any incompatibility or inconsistency between attitudes or between behavior and attitudes.

COGNITIVE DISSONANCE THEORY Cognitive dissonance theory, proposed by Leon Festinger in the 1950s, sought to explain the relationship between attitudes and behavior.[2] **Cognitive dissonance** is any incompatibility or inconsistency between attitudes or between behavior and attitudes. The theory argued that inconsistency is uncomfortable and that individuals will try to reduce the discomfort and thus, the dissonance.

Did you ever notice how people change what they say so that it doesn't contradict what they do? Perhaps a friend of yours had consistently argued that American-manufactured cars were poorly built and that he'd never own anything but a foreign import. Then his parents gave him a late model American-made car, and suddenly they weren't so bad.

Or when going through sorority rush, a new freshman believes that sororities are good and that pledging a sorority is important. If she's not accepted by a sorority, however, she may say, "Sorority life isn't all it's cracked up to be anyway."

Of course, no one can completely avoid dissonance. You know you should floss your teeth every day, but don't do it. There's an inconsistency between attitude and behavior.

HOW DO PEOPLE COPE WITH COGNITIVE DISSONANCE? The theory proposed that no matter how hard we might try to reduce dissonance it is determined by three things:

1. The *importance* of the factors creating the dissonance.
2. The degree of *influence* the individual believes he or she has over those factors.
3. The *rewards* that may be involved in dissonance.

Cognitive Dissonance refers to any incompatibility or inconsistency between attitudes and behaviors. For example, most people may believe that they are safe drivers, yet many may create potentially unsafe road conditions by driving and texting at the same time. To reduce the dissonance, these drivers may either stop their habit of driving and texting, or they may rationalize that driving and texting doesn't really pose any threat to others' safety, that they are in control of the situation, or that everyone else is doing the same thing.

PHOTO: Robert Crum/Shutterstock

If the factors creating the dissonance are relatively unimportant, the pressure to correct the inconsistency will be low. However, if those factors are important, individuals may change their behavior, conclude that the dissonant behavior isn't so important, change their attitude, or identify compatible factors that outweigh the dissonant ones.

How much influence individuals believe they have over the factors also affects their reaction to the dissonance. If they perceive the dissonance is something about which they have no choice, they won't be receptive to attitude change or feel a need to do so. If, for example, the dissonance-producing behavior was required as a result of a manager's order, the pressure to reduce dissonance would be less than if the behavior had been performed voluntarily. Although dissonance exists, it can be rationalized and justified by the need to follow the manager's orders—that is, the person had no choice or control.

Finally, rewards also influence the degree to which individuals are motivated to reduce dissonance. Coupling high dissonance with high rewards tends to reduce the discomfort by motivating the individual to believe that there is consistency.

Let's look at an example. Tracey Ford, a corporate manager, believes strongly that no company should lay off employees. Unfortunately, Tracey has to make decisions that trade off her company's strategic direction against her convictions on layoffs. She knows that organizational restructuring means some jobs may no longer be needed. She also knows layoffs are in the best economic interest of her firm. What will she do? Undoubtedly, Tracey is experiencing a high degree of cognitive dissonance. Because of the *importance* of the issues in this example, she can't ignore the inconsistency.

To deal with her dilemma, she can follow several steps. She can change her behavior (lay off employees). Or she can reduce dissonance by concluding that the dissonant behavior is not so important after all ("I've got to make a living, and in my role as a decision maker, I often have to place the good of my company above that of individual organizational members"). She might also change her attitude ("There is nothing wrong in laying off employees"). Finally, another choice would be to seek out more consonant elements to outweigh the dissonant ones ("The long-term benefits to the surviving employees from our restructuring more than offset the associated costs"). Let's explain her behavior.

The *degree of influence* that Tracey believes she has also impacts how she reacts to the dissonance. If she perceives the dissonance to be uncontrollable—something about which she has no choice—she's less likely to feel she needs to change her attitude. If, for example, her boss told her that she had to lay off employees, the pressure to reduce dissonance would be less than if Tracey was performing the behavior voluntarily. Dissonance would exist but it could be rationalized and justified. This tendency illustrates why it's critical in today's organizations for leaders to establish an ethical culture. Without the leaders' influence and support, employees won't feel as much dissonance when faced with decisions of whether to act ethically or unethically.

Finally, *rewards* also influence how likely Tracy is to reduce dissonance. High dissonance, when accompanied by high rewards, tends to reduce the tension inherent in the dissonance. The reward reduces dissonance by adding to the consistency side of the individual's balance sheet. Tracey might feel because she is well compensated in her job that she sometimes has to make hard decisions, such as laying off employees. So what can we say about dissonance and employee behavior? These moderating factors suggest that although individuals experience dissonance, they won't necessarily move toward consistency, that is, toward reducing the dissonance. If the issues underlying the dissonance are of minimal importance, if an individual perceives that the dissonance is externally imposed and is substantially uncontrollable, or if rewards are significant enough to offset the dissonance, the individual will not be under great tension to reduce the dissonance.

How Can an Understanding of Attitudes Help Managers Be More Effective?

Managers should be interested in understanding and influencing attitudes because they influence behavior. We can say with some certainty that the correlation between satisfaction and productivity is fairly strong. Satisfied workers do perform better on the job. So managers should focus on those factors that have been shown to be conducive to high levels of job satisfaction: (1) making work challenging and interesting, (2) providing equitable rewards, (3) and creating supportive working conditions and supportive colleagues.

Managers should also survey their team members about their attitudes. As one study put it, "A sound measurement of overall job attitude is one of the most useful pieces of information an organization can have about its employees." Note that research has also shown that attitude surveys can be more effective at pinpointing employee dissatisfaction if done multiple times rather than just at one point in time.

Personality: What Do Managers Need to Know about Personality?

"Incoming Bowling Green State University freshmen Erica Steele and Katelyn Devore had never met. But after they scored a 95 percent match on an online compatibility test, they signed up to room together." If you've ever shared a living space with someone else (family or nonfamily), you know how important it can be for roommates to be compatible and to get along with each other. This compatibility is affected and influenced by our own and by other people's personalities.

We all have a personality. Some of us are quiet and passive; others are loud and aggressive. When we describe people using terms such as *quiet, passive, loud, aggressive, ambitious, extroverted, loyal, tense,* or *sociable,* we're describing their personalities. An individual's **personality** is a unique combination of emotional, thought, and behavioral patterns that affect how a person reacts to situations and interacts with others. Personality is most often described in terms of measurable traits that a person exhibits. We're interested in looking at personality because just like attitudes, it affects how and why people behave the way they do.

personality
A unique combination of emotional, thought, and behavioral patterns that affect how a person reacts to situations and interacts with others.

The Big Five Personality Traits Model

The Big Five Model is a personality trait model that examines five traits: extraversion, agreeableness, conscientiousness, emotional stability, and openness to experience.

1. **Extraversion** A personality dimension that describes the degree to which someone is sociable, talkative, and assertive.
2. **Agreeableness** A personality dimension that describes the degree to which someone is good-natured, cooperative, and trusting.
3. **Conscientiousness** A personality dimension that describes the degree to which someone is responsible, dependable, persistent, and achievement oriented.
4. **Emotional stability** A personality dimension that describes the degree to which someone is calm, enthusiastic, and secure (positive) or tense, nervous, depressed, and insecure (negative).
5. **Openness to experience** A personality dimension that describes the degree to which someone is imaginative, artistically sensitive, and intellectual.

The Big Five model provides more than just a personality framework. Research has shown that important relationships exist between these personality dimensions and job performance. For example, one study reviewed five categories of occupations: professionals (e.g., engineers, architects, attorneys), police, managers, sales, and semiskilled and skilled employees. Job performance was defined in terms of employee performance ratings, training competency, and personnel data such as salary level. *The results of the study showed that **conscientiousness** predicted job performance for all five occupational groups.*

Predictions for the other personality dimensions depended on the situation and the occupational group. For example, extraversion predicted performance in managerial and sales positions, in which high social interaction is necessary. Openness to experience was found to be important in predicting training competency. Ironically, emotional security was not positively related to job performance. Although it would seem logical that calm and secure workers would be better performers, that wasn't the case. Perhaps it's a function of the likelihood that emotionally stable workers often keep their jobs and emotionally unstable people may not. Given that all those participating in the study were employed, the variance on that dimension was probably small.

Locus of Control—A Driver of Behavior

locus of control
The degree to which people believe they control their own fate.

Who has control over an individual's behavior? Some people believe that they control their own fate. Others see themselves as pawns of fate, believing that what happens to them in their lives is due to luck or chance. The **locus of control** in the first case (control their own fate) is internal. In the second case (pawns of fate), it is external; these people believe that their lives are controlled by outside forces. One might also expect to find that externals blame a poor performance evaluation on their boss's prejudice, their coworkers, or other events outside their control, whereas "internals" explain the same evaluation in terms of their own actions.

What Is Perception and What Influences It?

"L ke y ur b ain, the n w L nd Rov r autom tic lly adj sts to anyth ng." This advertisement for a Land Rover SUV illustrates the perceptual process at work. You were likely able to read the sentence even with the missing letters because you recognized the word patterns and organized and interpreted them in a way that made sense.

perception
A process by which we give meaning to our environment by organizing and interpreting sensory impressions.

Perception is a process by which we give meaning to our environment by organizing and interpreting sensory impressions. Research on perception consistently demonstrates that individuals may look at the same thing yet perceive it differently. One manager, for instance, can interpret the fact that her assistant regularly takes several days to make important decisions as evidence that the assistant is slow, disorganized, and afraid to make decisions. Another manager with the same assistant might interpret the same tendency as evidence that the assistant is thoughtful, thorough, and deliberate. The first manager would probably evaluate her assistant negatively; the second manager would probably evaluate the person positively. The point is that none of us see reality. We interpret what we see and call it reality. And, of course, as the example shows, we behave according to our perceptions.

What Influences Perception?

How do we explain the fact that Cathy, a marketing supervisor for a large commercial petroleum products organization, age 52, noticed Bill's nose ring during his employment interview, and Sean, a human resources recruiter, age 23, didn't? A number of factors operate to shape and sometimes distort perception. These factors can reside in the perceiver, in the object or target being perceived, or in the context of the situation in which the perception is made.

When an individual looks at a target and attempts to interpret what he or she sees, that individual's personal characteristics will heavily influence the interpretation. These personal characteristics include attitudes, personality, motives, interests, past experiences, and expectations.

The characteristics of the target being observed can also affect what is perceived. Loud people are more likely than quiet people to be noticed in a group. So, too, are extremely attractive or unattractive individuals. Because targets are not looked at in isolation, the relationship of a target to its background also influences perception (see Figure 12.2 for an example), as does our tendency to group close things and similar things together.

FIGURE 12.2

Perceptual Challenges—What Do You See?

Old woman or young woman? Two faces or an urn? A knight on a horse?

The context in which we see objects or events is also important. The time at which an object or event is seen can influence attention, as can location, lighting, temperature, and any number of other situational factors.

Our perceptions of people differ from our perceptions of such inanimate objects as computers, robots, or buildings because we make inferences about the actions of people that we don't, of course, make about inanimate objects. When we observe people, we attempt to develop explanations of why they behave in certain ways. Our perception and judgment of a person's actions, therefore, will be significantly influenced by the assumptions we make about the person's internal state. Many of these assumptions have led researchers to develop attribution theory.

WHAT IS ATTRIBUTION THEORY? **Attribution theory** has been proposed to explain how we judge people differently depending on what meaning we attribute to a given behavior. Basically, the theory suggests that when we observe an individual's behavior, we attempt to determine whether it was internally or externally caused. Internally caused behavior is believed to be under the control of the individual. Externally caused behavior results from outside causes; that is, the person is seen as having been forced into the behavior by the situation. *That determination, however, depends on three factors: distinctiveness, consensus, and consistency.*

attribution theory
A theory used to explain how we judge people differently, based on what meaning we attribute to a given behavior.

Distinctiveness refers to whether an individual displays a behavior in many situations or whether it is particular to one situation. Is the employee who arrived late to work today also the person coworkers see as a goof-off? What we want to know is whether this behavior is unusual. If it is, the observer is likely to give the behavior an external attribution. If this action is not unique, it will probably be judged as internal.

Consensus exists if everyone who is faced with a similar situation responds in the same way. Then we can say the behavior shows *consensus.* Our tardy employee's behavior would meet this criterion if all employees who took the same route to work today were also late. If consensus is high, you would be expected to give an external attribution to the employee's tardiness, whereas if other employees who took the same route made it to work on time, you would conclude the reason to be internal.

Consistency in an employee's actions exists when the individual engages in the behaviors regularly. Does the employee respond the same way over time? Coming in 10 minutes

FIGURE 12.3

Attribution Theory

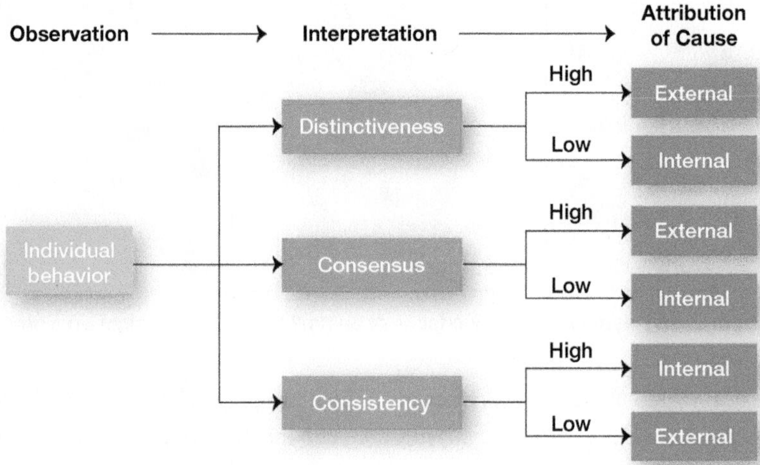

late for work is not perceived in the same way if, for one employee, it represents an unusual case (she hasn't been late for several months), but for another it is part of a routine pattern (he is late two or three times a week). The more consistent the behavior, the more the observer is inclined to attribute it to internal causes.

Figure 12.3 summarizes the key elements in attribution theory. It would tell us, for instance, that if an employee, Mr. Flynn, generally performs at about the same level on other related tasks as he does on his current task (low distinctiveness), if other employees frequently perform differently—better or worse—than Mr. Flynn does on that current task (low consensus), and if Mr. Flynn's performance on this current task is consistent over time (high consistency), his manager or anyone else who is judging Mr. Flynn's work is likely to hold him primarily responsible for his task performance (internal attribution).

FUNDAMENTAL ATTRIBUTION ERROR One of the more interesting findings drawn from attribution theory is that errors or biases distort attributions. For instance, substantial evidence supports the hypothesis that when we make judgments about the behavior of other people, we have a tendency to underestimate the influence of external factors and overestimate the influence of internal or personal factors.

fundamental attribution error The tendency to underestimate the influence of external factors and overestimate the influence of internal factors when making judgments about the behavior of others.

This **fundamental attribution error** can explain why a sales manager may be prone to attribute the poor performance of her sales agents to laziness rather than to the innovative product line introduced by a competitor.

self-serving bias The tendency for individuals to attribute their successes to internal factors while putting the blame for failure on external factors.

SELF-SERVING BIAS Individuals also tend to attribute their own successes to internal factors such as ability or effort while putting the blame for failure on external factors such as luck. This **self-serving bias** suggests that feedback provided to others in performance reviews will be predictably distorted by them, whether it is positive or negative.

PERCEPTUAL SHORTCUTS, ERRORS All of us use a number of shortcuts to judge others. Perceiving and interpreting people's behavior is a lot of work, so we use shortcuts

FIGURE 12.4

Perceptual Shortcuts

SHORTCUT	WHAT IT IS	DISTORTION
Selectivity	People assimilate certain bits and pieces of what they observe depending on their interests, background, experience, and attitudes	"Speed reading" others may result in an inaccurate picture of them
Assumed similarity	People assume that others are like them	May fail to take into account individual differences, resulting in incorrect similarities
Stereotyping	People judge others on the basis of their perception of a group to which the others belong	May result in distorted judgments because many stereotypes have no factual foundation
Halo effect	People form an impression of others on the basis of a single trait	Fails to take into account the total picture of what an individual has done

to make the task more manageable. Such shortcuts can be valuable when they let us make accurate perceptions quickly and provide valid data for making predictions. However, they aren't perfect. They can and do get us into trouble. What are these perceptual shortcuts? (See Figure 12.4 for a summary.)

SELECTIVE PERCEPTION Individuals can't assimilate all they observe, so they're selective in their perception. They absorb bits and pieces. These bits and pieces are not chosen randomly; rather, they're selectively chosen depending on the interests, background, experience, and attitudes of the observer. **Selective perception** allows us to "speed read" others but not without the risk of drawing an inaccurate picture.

selective perception
The tendency for people to only absorb parts of what they observe, which allows us to "speed read" others.

ASSUMED SIMILARITY It's easy to judge others if we assume that they're similar to us. In **assumed similarity,** or the "like me" effect, the observer's perception of others is influenced more by the observer's own characteristics than by those of the person observed. For example, if you want challenges and responsibility in your job, you'll assume that others want the same. People who assume that others are like them can, of course, be right, but not always.

assumed similarity
An observer's perception of others influenced more by the observer's own characteristics than by those of the person observed.

STEREOTYPING When we judge someone on the basis of our perception of a group he or she is part of, we're using the shortcut called **stereotyping.** For instance, "Married people are more stable employees than single persons" or "Older employees are absent more often from work" are examples of stereotyping. To the degree that a stereotype is based on fact, it may produce accurate judgments. However, many stereotypes aren't factual and distort our judgment.

stereotyping
When we judge someone on the basis of our perception of a group to which that person belongs.

HALO EFFECT When we form a general impression about a person on the basis of a single characteristic, such as intelligence, sociability, or appearance, we're being influenced by the **halo effect.** This effect frequently occurs when students evaluate their classroom instructor. Students may isolate a single trait such as enthusiasm and allow their entire evaluation to be slanted by the perception of this one trait. If an instructor who is quiet, assured, knowledgeable, and highly qualified has a classroom teaching style that lacks enthusiasm, that instructor might be rated lower on a number of other characteristics.

halo effect
When we form a general impression of a person on the basis of a single characteristic.

Conclusion

One of the challenges in understanding organizational behavior is that it addresses issues that aren't obvious. Like an iceberg, OB has a small visible dimension and a much larger hidden portion—that is, what we see when we look at an organization is its visible aspects: strategies, objectives, policies and procedures, structure, technology, formal authority relationships, and chain of command. But under the surface are other elements that we need to understand—elements that also influence how we behave at work.

CHAPTER 13

Marketing Research

Marketing Information and Customer Insights

To create value for customers and build meaningful relationships with them, marketers must first gain fresh, deep insights into what customers need and want. Such customer insights come from good marketing information. Companies use these customer insights to develop a competitive advantage.

For example, Apple wasn't the first company to develop a digital music player. However, Apple's research uncovered two key insights: people wanted personal music players that let them take all of their music with them, and they wanted to be able to listen to it unobtrusively. Based on these insights, Apple applied its design and usability magic to create the phenomenally successful iPod. The expanded iPod and iPod Touch lines now capture a 76 percent share of the U.S. MP3 player market. The iPod insights also spawned other Apple blockbusters such as the iPhone and iPad.[1]

Key customer insights, plus a dash of Apple's design and usability magic, have made the iPod a blockbuster. It now captures 76 percent of the market and has spawned other Apple blockbusters such as the iPhone and iPad.

PHOTO: Newscom

Although customer and market insights are important for building customer value and relationships, these insights can be very difficult to obtain. Customer needs and buying motives are often anything but obvious—consumers themselves usually can't tell you exactly what they need and why they buy. To gain good customer insights, marketers must effectively manage marketing information from a wide range of sources.

Today's marketers have ready access to plenty of marketing information. With the recent explosion of information technologies, companies can now generate information in great quantities. Moreover, consumers themselves are now generating tons of marketing information. Through e-mail, text messaging, blogging, Facebook, Twitter, and other grassroots digital channels, consumers are now volunteering a tidal wave of bottom-up information to companies and to each other. Companies that tap into such information can gain rich, timely customer insights at lower cost.

Far from lacking information, most marketing managers are overloaded with data and often overwhelmed by it. For example, when a company such as Pepsi monitors online discussions about its brands by searching key words in tweets, blogs, posts, and other sources, its servers take in a stunning six million public conversations a day, more than two billion a year.[2] That's far more information than any manager can digest. Thus, marketers don't need *more* information; they need *better* information. And they need to make better *use* of the information they already have.

The real value of marketing research and marketing information lies in how it is used—in the **customer insights** that it provides. Based on such thinking, many companies are now restructuring their marketing research and information functions. They are creating *customer insights teams*, headed by a vice president of customer insights and composed of representatives from all of the firm's functional areas. For example, Coca-Cola's marketing research group is headed by a vice president of marketing strategy and insights. And at Unilever, marketing research is done by the Consumer and Market Insight division, which helps brand teams harness information and turn it into customer insights.

Customer insights groups collect customer and market information from a wide variety of sources, ranging from traditional marketing research studies to mingling with and observing consumers to monitoring consumer online conversations about the company and its products. Then they *use* this information to develop important customer insights from which the company can create more value for its customers.

Thus, companies must design effective marketing information systems that give managers the right information, in the right form, at the right time and help them to use this information to create customer value and stronger customer relationships. A **marketing information system (MIS)** consists of people and procedures dedicated to assessing information needs, developing the needed information, and helping decision makers use the information to generate and validate actionable customer and market insights.

Figure 13.1 shows that the MIS begins and ends with information users—marketing managers, internal and external partners, and others who need marketing information. First, it interacts with these information users to *assess information needs*. Next, it interacts with the marketing environment to *develop needed information* through internal company databases, marketing intelligence activities, and marketing research. Finally, the MIS helps users to *analyze and use* the information to develop customer insights, make marketing decisions, and manage customer relationships.

Assessing Marketing Information Needs

The marketing information system primarily serves the company's marketing and other managers. However, it may also provide information to external partners, such as suppliers, resellers, or marketing services agencies. For example, Walmart's Retail Link system gives key suppliers access to information on everything from customers' buying patterns and store inventory levels to how many items they've sold in which stores in the past 24 hours.[3]

A good MIS balances the information users would *like* to have against what they really *need* and what is *feasible* to offer. Some managers will ask for whatever information they

FIGURE 13.1

The Marketing Information System

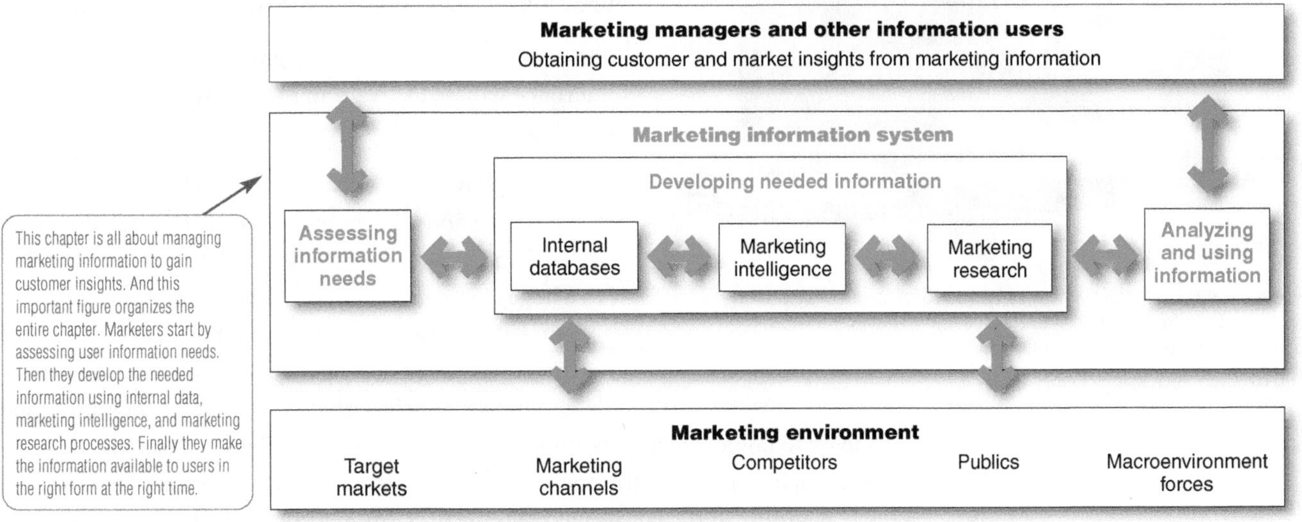

can get without thinking carefully about what they really need. Too much information can be as harmful as too little. Other managers may omit things they ought to know, or they may not know to ask for some types of information they should have. For example, managers might need to know about surges in favorable or unfavorable consumer discussions about their brands on blogs or online social networks. Because they do not know about these discussions, they do not think to ask about them. The MIS must monitor the marketing environment to provide decision makers with information they should have to better understand customers and make key marketing decisions.

Finally, the costs of obtaining, analyzing, storing, and delivering information can quickly mount. The company must decide whether the value of insights gained from additional information is worth the costs of providing it, and both value and cost are often hard to assess.

Developing Marketing Information

Marketers can obtain the needed information from *internal data, marketing intelligence,* and *marketing research.*

Internal Data

Many companies build extensive **internal databases**, electronic collections of consumer and market information obtained from data sources within the company's network. Information in the database can come from many sources. The marketing department furnishes information on customer characteristics, sales transactions, and Web site visits. The customer service department keeps records of customer satisfaction or service problems. The accounting department provides detailed records of sales, costs, and cash flows. Operations reports on production, shipments, and inventories. The sales force

Internal data: Financial services provider USAA uses its extensive database to tailor its services to the specific needs of individual customers, creating incredible loyalty.
PHOTO: Courtney Young

reports on reseller reactions and competitor activities, and marketing channel partners provide data on point-of-sale transactions. Harnessing such information can provide powerful customer insights and competitive advantage.

For example,financial services provider USAA uses its internal database to create an incredibly loyal customer base:[4]

> USAA provides financial services to U.S. military personnel and their families, largely through direct marketing via the telephone and Internet. It maintains a huge customer database built from customer purchasing histories and information collected directly through customer surveys, transaction data, and browsing behavior at its Web site. USAA uses the database to tailor direct marketing offers to the needs of individual customers. For example, for customers looking toward retirement, it sends information on estate planning. If the family has college-age children, USAA sends those children information on how to manage their credit cards.
>
> One delighted reporter, a USAA customer, recounts how USAA even helped him teach his 16-year-old daughter to drive. Just before her birthday, but before she received her driver's license, USAA mailed a "package of materials, backed by research, to help me teach my daughter how to drive, help her practice, and help us find ways to agree on what constitutes safe driving later on, when she gets her license." What's more, marvels the reporter, "USAA didn't try to sell me a thing. My take-away: that USAA is investing in me for the long term." Through such skillful use of its database, USAA serves each customer uniquely, resulting in high customer satisfaction and loyalty. The $18 billion company retains 98 percent of its customers. For the past four years, *Bloomberg BusinessWeek* magazine has ranked USAA among its top two "Customer Service Champs," highlighting its legendary customer service. And MSN Money recently ranked USAA number one on its Customer Service Hall of Fame list.

Internal databases usually can be accessed more quickly and cheaply than other information sources, but they also present some problems. Because internal information is often collected for other purposes, it may be incomplete or in the wrong form for making marketing decisions. Data also ages quickly; keeping the database current requires a major effort. Finally, managing the mountains of information that a large company produces requires highly sophisticated equipment and techniques.

Competitive Marketing Intelligence

Competitive marketing intelligence is the systematic collection and analysis of publicly available information about consumers, competitors, and developments in the marketplace. The goal of competitive marketing intelligence is to improve strategic decision making by understanding the consumer environment, assessing and tracking competitors' actions, and providing early warnings of opportunities and threats. Marketing intelligence techniques range from observing consumers firsthand to quizzing the company's own employees, benchmarking competitors' products, researching the Internet, and monitoring Internet buzz.

Mission control: PepsiCo's Gatorade brand has created an extensive control center to monitor real-time brand-related social media activity.

PHOTO: Pepsi-Cola North America, Inc.

Good marketing intelligence can help marketers gain insights into how consumers talk about and connect with their brands. Many companies send out teams of trained observers to mix and mingle personally with customers as they use and talk about the company's products. Other companies routinely monitor consumers' online chatter. For example, PepsiCo's Gatorade brand has created an extensive control center to monitor brand-related social media activity.[5]

> The Gatorade Mission Control Center, deep within the company's Chicago headquarters, serves as a nerve center in which Gatorade's four-member Mission Control team monitors the brand in real-time across social media. Whenever someone mentions anything related to Gatorade (including competitors, Gatorade athletes, and sports nutrition-related topics) on Twitter, Facebook, a blog, or in other social media, it pops up in various visualizations and dashboards on one of six big screens in Mission Control. Staffers also monitor online-ad and Web site traffic, producing a consolidated picture of the brand's Internet image.
>
> Gatorade uses what it sees and learns at Mission Control to improve its products, marketing, and interactions with customers. For example, while monitoring its "Gatorade Has Evolved" campaign, the team quickly saw that a commercial featuring a song by rap artist David Banner was being heavily discussed in social media. Within 24 hours, they had worked with Banner to put out a full-length version of the song and distribute it to Gatorade followers and fans on Twitter and Facebook. In another case, the brand knew to bulk up on production of its recovery drinks because of complaints they were selling out. Beyond just monitoring social media conversations, the Mission Control team sometimes joins them, as when staffers recently jumped into a Facebook conversation to answer a poster's questions about where to buy products.

Many companies have even appointed *chief listening officers*, who are charged with sifting through online customer conversations and passing along key insights to marketing decision makers. Dell created a position called *Listening Czar* two years ago. "Our chief listener is critical to making sure that the right people in the organization are aware of what the conversations on the Web are saying about us, so the relevant people in the business can connect with customers," says a Dell marketing executive.[6]

Companies also need to actively monitor competitors' activities. Firms use competitive marketing intelligence to gain early warnings of competitor moves and strategies, new-product launches, new or changing markets, and potential competitive strengths and weaknesses. Much competitor intelligence can be collected from people inside the company—executives, engineers and scientists, purchasing agents, and the sales force. The company can also obtain important intelligence information from suppliers, resellers, and key customers. It can monitor competitors' Web sites and use the Internet to search specific competitor names, events, or trends and see what turns up. And tracking consumer conversations about competing brands is often as revealing as tracking conversations about the company's own brands.

Intelligence seekers can also pour through any of thousands of online databases. Some are free. For example, the U.S. Security and Exchange Commission's database provides a huge stockpile of financial information on public competitors, and the U.S. Patent Office and Trademark database reveals patents that competitors have filed. For a fee, companies can also subscribe to any of the more than 3,000 online databases and information search services, such as Hoover's, LexisNexis, and Dun & Bradstreet. Today's marketers have an almost overwhelming amount of competitor information only a few keystrokes away.

The intelligence game goes both ways. Facing determined competitive marketing intelligence efforts by competitors, most companies are now taking steps to protect their own information. The growing use of marketing intelligence also raises ethical issues. Although the preceding techniques are legal, others may involve questionable ethics. Clearly, companies should take advantage of publicly available information. However, they should not stoop to snoop. With all the legitimate intelligence sources now available, a company does not need to break the law or accepted codes of ethics to get good intelligence.

Marketing Research

In addition to marketing intelligence information about general consumer, competitor, and marketplace happenings, marketers often need formal studies that provide customer and market insights for specific marketing situations and decisions. For example, Budweiser wants to know what appeals will be most effective in its Super Bowl advertising. Yahoo! wants to know how Web searchers will react to a proposed redesign of its site. Or Samsung wants to know how many and what kinds of people will buy its next-generation, ultrathin televisions. In such situations, managers will need marketing research.

Marketing research is the systematic design, collection, analysis, and reporting of data relevant to a specific marketing situation facing an organization. Companies use marketing research in a wide variety of situations. For example, marketing research gives marketers insights into customer motivations, purchase behavior, and satisfaction. It can help them to assess market potential and market share or measure the effectiveness of pricing, product, distribution, and promotion activities.

Some large companies have their own research departments that work with marketing managers on marketing research projects. In addition, these companies—like their smaller counterparts—frequently hire outside research specialists to consult with management on specific marketing problems and to conduct marketing research studies. Sometimes firms simply purchase data collected by outside firms to aid in their decision making.

FIGURE 13.2

The Marketing Research Process

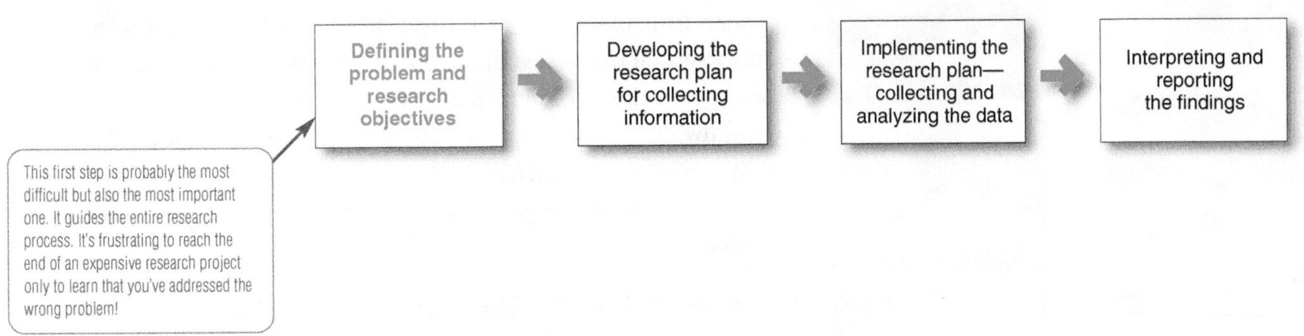

The marketing research process has four steps (see Figure 13.2): defining the problem and research objectives, developing the research plan, implementing the research plan, and interpreting and reporting the findings.

Defining the Problem and Research Objectives

Marketing managers and researchers must work closely together to define the problem and agree on research objectives. The manager best understands the decision for which information is needed, whereas the researcher best understands marketing research and how to obtain the information. Defining the problem and research objectives is often the hardest step in the research process. The manager may know that something is wrong, without knowing the specific causes.

After the problem has been defined carefully, the manager and the researcher must set the research objectives. A marketing research project might have one of three types of objectives. The objective of **exploratory research** is to gather preliminary information that will help define the problem and suggest hypotheses. The objective of **descriptive research** is to describe things, such as the market potential for a product or the demographics and attitudes of consumers who buy the product. The objective of **causal research** is to test hypotheses about cause-and-effect relationships. For example, would a 10 percent decrease in tuition at a private college result in an enrollment increase sufficient to offset the reduced tuition? Managers often start with exploratory research and later follow with descriptive or causal research.

The statement of the problem and research objectives guides the entire research process. The manager and the researcher should put the statement in writing to be certain that they agree on the purpose and expected results of the research.

Developing the Research Plan

Once researchers have defined the research problem and objectives, they must determine the exact information needed, develop a plan for gathering it efficiently, and present the plan to management. The research plan outlines sources of existing data and spells out the specific research approaches, contact methods, sampling plans, and instruments that researchers will use to gather new data.

A decision by Red Bull to add a line of enhanced waters to its already successful mix of energy drinks would call for marketing research that provides lots of specific information.

PHOTO: Red Bull North America

Research objectives must be translated into specific information needs. For example, suppose that Red Bull wants to conduct research on how consumers would react to a proposed new vitamin-enhanced water drink that would be available in several flavors and sold under the Red Bull name. Red Bull currently dominates the worldwide energy drink market with a more than 40 percent market share worldwide.[7] A new line of enhanced waters—akin to Coca Cola's Vitaminwater—might help Red Bull leverage its strong brand position even further. The proposed research might call for the following specific information:

- The demographic, economic, and lifestyle characteristics of current Red Bull customers. (Do current customers also consume enhanced-water products? Are such products consistent with their lifestyles? Or would Red Bull need to target a new segment of consumers?)
- The characteristics and usage patterns of the broader population of enhanced-water users: What do they need and expect from such products, where do they buy them, when and how do they use them, and what existing brands and price points are most popular? (The new Red Bull product would need strong, relevant positioning in the crowded enhanced-water market.)
- Retailer reactions to the proposed new product line: Would they stock and support it? Where would they display it? (Failure to get retailer support would hurt sales of the new drink.)
- Forecasts of sales of both the new and current Red Bull products. (Will the new enhanced waters create new sales or simply take sales away from current Red Bull products? Will the new product increase Red Bull's overall profits?)

Red Bull's marketers will need these and many other types of information to decide whether or not to introduce the new product and, if so, the best way to do it.

The research plan should be presented in a *written proposal*. A written proposal is especially important when the research project is large and complex or when an outside firm carries it out. The proposal should cover the management problems addressed, the research objectives, the information to be obtained, and how the results will help management's decision making. The proposal also should include estimated research costs.

To meet the manager's information needs, the research plan can call for gathering secondary data, primary data, or both. **Secondary data** consist of information that already exists somewhere, having been collected for another purpose. **Primary data** consist of information collected for the specific purpose at hand.

Gathering Secondary Data

Researchers usually start by gathering secondary data. The company's internal database provides a good starting point. However, the company can also tap into a wide assortment of external information sources.

Companies can buy secondary data from outside suppliers. For example, Nielsen sells shopper insight data from a consumer panel of more than 250,000 households in 25 countries worldwide, with measures of trial and repeat purchasing, brand loyalty, and buyer demographics. Experian Simmons carries out a full spectrum of consumer studies that provide a comprehensive view of the American consumer. The MONITOR service by Yankelovich sells information on important social and lifestyle trends. These and other firms supply high-quality data to suit a wide variety of marketing information needs.[8]

Consumer database services such as Experian Simmons sell an incredible wealth of information on everything from the products consumers buy and the brands they prefer to their lifestyles, attitudes, and media preferences. Experian Simmons "provides the most comprehensive view of the American consumer."

PHOTO: Experian Consumer Research

Using *commercial online databases*, marketing researchers can conduct their own searches of secondary data sources. General database services such as Dialog, ProQuest, and LexisNexis put an incredible wealth of information at the keyboards of marketing decision makers. Beyond commercial Web sites offering information for a fee, almost every industry association, government agency, business publication, and news medium offers free information to those tenacious enough to find their Web sites.

Internet search engines can also be a big help in locating relevant secondary information sources. However, they can also be very frustrating and inefficient. For example, a Red Bull marketer Googling "enhanced water products" would come up with more than 50,000 hits. Still, well-structured, well-designed Web searches can be a good starting point to any marketing research project.

Secondary data can usually be obtained more quickly and at a lower cost than primary data. Also, secondary sources can sometimes provide data an individual company cannot collect on its own—information that either is not directly available or would be too expensive to collect. For example, it would be too expensive for Red Bull's marketers to conduct a continuing retail store audit to find out about the market shares, prices, and displays of competitors' brands. But those marketers can buy the InfoScan service from SymphonyIRI Group, which provides this information based on scanner and other data from 34,000 retail stores in markets around the nation.[9]

Secondary data can also present problems. Researchers can rarely obtain all the data they need from secondary sources. For example, Red Bull will not find existing information regarding consumer reactions about a new enhanced-water line that it has not yet placed on the market. Even when data can be found, the information might not be very usable. The researcher must evaluate secondary information carefully to make certain it is *relevant* (fits the research project's needs), *accurate* (reliably collected and reported), *current* (up-to-date enough for current decisions), and *impartial* (objectively collected and reported).

Primary Data Collection

Secondary data provide a good starting point for research and often help to define research problems and objectives. In most cases, however, the company must also collect primary data. Table 13.1 shows that designing a plan for primary data collection calls for a number of decisions on *research approaches, contact methods*, the *sampling plan*, and *research instruments*.

RESEARCH APPROACHES Research approaches for gathering primary data include observations, surveys, and experiments. We discuss each one in turn.

Observational Research. **Observational research** involves gathering primary data by observing relevant people, actions, and situations. For example, Trader Joe's might evaluate possible new store locations by checking traffic patterns, neighborhood conditions, and the locations of competing Whole Foods, Fresh Market, and other retail chains.

Researchers often observe consumer behavior to glean customer insights they can't obtain by simply asking customers questions. For instance, Fisher-Price has established an observation lab in which it can observe the reactions little tots have to new toys. The Fisher-Price Play Lab is a sunny, toy-strewn space where lucky kids get to test Fisher-Price prototypes, under the watchful eyes of designers who hope to learn what will get them worked up into a new-toy frenzy.

Marketers not only observe what consumers do but also observe what consumers are saying. As discussed earlier, marketers now routinely listen in on consumer conversations on blogs, social networks, and Web sites. Observing such naturally occurring feedback can provide inputs that simply can't be gained through more structured and formal research approaches.

A wide range of companies now use **ethnographic research**. Ethnographic research involves sending observers to watch and interact with consumers in their "natural environments." The observers might be trained anthropologists and psychologists or company researchers and managers (see Marketing at Work 13.1).

TABLE 13.1

Planning Primary Data Collection

RESEARCH APPROACHES	CONTACT METHODS	SAMPLING PLAN	RESEARCH INSTRUMENTS
Observation	Mail	Sampling unit	Questionnaire
Survey	Telephone	Sampling size	Mechanical instruments
Experiment	Personal	Sampling procedure	
	Online		

Marketing at Work 13.1

Ethnographic Research: Watching What Consumers *Really* Do

A girl walks into a bar and says to the bartender, "Give me a Diet Coke and a clear sight line to those guys drinking Miller Lite in the corner." If you're waiting for a punch line, this is no joke. The "girl" in this situation is Emma Gilding, corporate ethnographer at ad agency Ogilvy & Mather. In this case, her job is to hang out in bars around the country and watch groups of guys knocking back beers with their friends. No kidding. This is honest-to-goodness, cutting-edge marketing research—ethnography style.

> As a videographer filmed the action, Gilding kept tabs on how close the guys stood to one another. She eavesdropped on stories and observed how the mantle was passed from one speaker to another, as in a tribe around a campfire. Back at the office, a team of trained anthropologists and psychologists pored over more than 70 hours of footage from five similar nights in bars from San Diego to Philadelphia. One key insight: Miller is favored by groups of drinkers, while its main competitor, Bud Lite, is a beer that sells to individuals. The result was a hilarious series of ads that cut from a Miller Lite drinker's weird experiences in the world—getting caught in the subway taking money from a blind musician's guitar case or hitching a ride in the desert with a deranged trucker—to shots of him regaling friends with tales over a brew. The Miller Lite ads got high marks from audiences for their entertainment value and emotional resonance.

Today's marketers face many difficult questions: What do customers *really* think about a product and what do they say about it to their friends? How do they *really* use it? Will they tell you? *Can* they tell you? All too often, traditional research simply can't provide accurate answers. To get deeper insights, many companies use ethnographic research by watching and interacting with consumers in their "natural environments."

Ethnographers are looking for "consumer truth." In surveys and interviews, customers may state (and fully believe) certain preferences and behaviors, when the reality is actually quite different. Ethnography provides an insider's tour of the customer's world, helping marketers get at what consumers *really* do rather than what they say they do. "That might mean catching a heart-disease patient scarfing down a meatball sub and a cream soup while extolling the virtues of healthy eating," observes one ethnographer, "or a diabetic vigorously salting his sausage and eggs after explaining how he refuses jelly for his toast."

By entering the customer's world, ethnographers can scrutinize how customers think and feel as it relates to their products. Here's another example:

> Kelly Peña, also known as "the kid whisperer," was digging through a 12-year-old boy's dresser drawer one recent afternoon. Her undercover mission: to unearth what makes him tick and help the Walt Disney Company reassert itself as a cultural force among boys. Peña, a Disney researcher, heads a team zeroed in on a ratty rock 'n' roll T-shirt. Black Sabbath? "Wearing it makes me feel like I'm going to

Ethnographic research: To better understand the challenges faced by elderly shoppers, this Kimberly-Clark executive tries to shop while wearing vision-impairment glasses and bulky gloves that simulate arthritis.

PHOTO: Lauren Pond/The Photo Pond

an R-rated movie," said Dean, the shy redheaded boy under scrutiny. Jackpot! Peña and her team of anthropologists have spent 18 months peering inside the heads of incommunicative boys in search of just that kind of psychological nugget.

Disney is relying on Peña's insights to create new entertainment for boys ages 6 to 14, who account for $50 billion a year in spending worldwide. With the exception of *Cars*, Disney—home to more girl-focused fare such as the "Princesses" merchandising line, "Hannah Montana," and "Pixie Hollow"—has been notably weak on hit entertainment for boys. Peña's research is sometimes conducted in groups; sometimes it involves going shopping with a teenage boy and his mother. Walking through Dean's house, Peña looked for unspoken clues about his likes and dislikes. "What's on the back shelves that he hasn't quite gotten rid of will be telling," she said beforehand. "What's on his walls? How does he interact with his siblings?" One big takeaway from the two-hour visit: Although Dean was trying to sound grown-up and nonchalant in his answers, he still had a lot of little kid in him. He had dinosaur sheets and stuffed animals at the bottom of his bed. "I think he's trying to push a lot of boundaries for the first time," Peña said later.

Children can already see the results of Peña's scrutiny on Disney XD, a new cable channel and Web site. It's no accident, for instance, that the central character on "Aaron Stone" is a mediocre basketball player. Peña told producers that boys identify with protagonists who try hard to grow. "Winning isn't nearly as important to boys as Hollywood thinks," she said.

Ethnographic research often yields the kinds of intimate details that just don't emerge from traditional focus groups and surveys. For example, focus groups told the Best Western hotel chain that it's men who decide when to stop for the night and where to stay. But videotapes of couples on cross-country journeys showed it was usually the women. And observation can often uncover problems that customers don't even know they have. By videotaping consumers in the shower, plumbing fixture maker Moen uncovered safety risks that consumers didn't recognize—such as the habit some women have of shaving their legs while holding on to one unit's temperature control. Moen would find it almost impossible to discover such design flaws simply by asking questions.

Experiencing firsthand what customers experience can also provide powerful insights. To that end, consumer products giant Kimberly-Clark even runs a program that puts executives from retail chains such as Walgreens, Rite Aid, and Family Dollar directly into their customers' shoes—literally. The executives shop in their own stores with glasses that blur their vision, unpopped popcorn in their shoes, and bulky rubber gloves on their hands. It's all part of an exercise designed to help marketers understand the physical challenges faced by elderly shoppers, who will represent 20 percent of the total U.S. population by 2030.

The vision-blurring glasses simulate common vision ailments such as cataracts, macular degeneration, and glaucoma. Unpopped popcorn in shoes gives a feel for what it's like to walk with aching joints. And the bulky gloves simulate the limitations to manual dexterity brought on by arthritis. Participants come back from these experiences bursting with ideas for elderly-friendly store changes, such as bigger typefaces and more eye-friendly colors on packaging and fliers, new store lighting and clearer signage, and instant call buttons near heavy merchandise such as bottled water and laundry detergent.

Thus, more and more, marketing researchers are getting up close and personal with consumers—watching them closely as they act and interact in natural settings or stepping in to feel firsthand what they feel. "Knowing the individual consumer on an intimate basis has become a necessity," says one research consultant, "and ethnography is the intimate connection to the consumer."

Sources: Adapted excerpts and other information from Brooks Barnes, "Disney Expert Uses Science to Draw Boy Viewers," *New York Times*, April 14, 2009, p. A1; Linda Tischler, "Every Move You Make," *Fast Company*, April 2004, pp. 73–75; Ellen Byron, "Seeing Store Shelves Through Senior Eyes," *Wall Street Journal*, September 14, 2009, p. B1; and Natasha Singer, "The Fountain of Old Age," *New York Times*, February 6, 2011, p. BU 1.

Also consider this example:[10]

> Kraft Canada recently sent its president and other high-level Kraft executives to observe actual family life in a dozen diverse Canadian homes. "We went out with the purpose of understanding the Canadian family, what's going on in their homes,

particularly the kitchen," says Kraft Canada's vice president of consumer insights and strategy. After viewing hours of video of all 12 families visited, the consumer insights group found some unifying themes across Kraft's diverse markets. It learned that almost all families faced the same "mad rush to have something ready to feed the family, a hectic-ness, last-minute decisions, the need to balance the child's needs and different food needs." Kraft shared a compilation of the videos with marketing and sales teams, who used it as a basis for brainstorming sessions, and even put the video on an internal Web site for Kraft's 4,500 employees across Canada to view. The experience of "living with customers" helped Kraft's marketers and others understand how the company's brands help customers by providing more convenient products that reduce the stress of getting meals on the table.

Ethnographic research: Kraft Canada sent out its president (above center) and other high-level executives to observe actual family life in diverse Canadian homes. Videos of their experiences helped marketers and others across the company to understand the role Kraft's brands play in people's lives.

PHOTO: Michael Stuparyk/GetStock.com

Beyond conducting ethnographic research in physical consumer environments, many companies now routinely conduct *Netnography* research—observing consumers in a natural context on the Internet. Observing people as they interact on and move about the Internet can provide useful insights into both online and offline buying motives and behavior.[11]

Observational and ethnographic research often yield the kinds of details that just don't emerge from traditional research questionnaires or focus groups. Whereas traditional quantitative research approaches seek to test known hypotheses and obtain answers to well-defined product or strategy questions, observational research can generate fresh customer and market insights that people are unwilling or unable to provide. It provides a window into customers' unconscious actions and unexpressed needs and feelings.

In contrast, however, some things simply cannot be observed, such as feelings, attitudes, motives, or private behavior. Long-term or infrequent behavior is also difficult to observe. Finally, observations can be very difficult to interpret. Because of these limitations, researchers often use observation along with other data collection methods.

Survey Research. Survey research, the most widely used method for primary data collection, is the approach best suited for gathering descriptive information. A company that wants to know about people's knowledge, attitudes, preferences, or buying behavior can often find out by asking them directly.

The major advantage of survey research is its flexibility; it can be used to obtain many different kinds of information in many different situations. Surveys addressing almost any marketing question or decision can be conducted by phone or mail, in person, or on the Web.

However, survey research also presents some problems. Sometimes people are unable to answer survey questions because they cannot remember or have never thought about what they do and why they do it. People may be unwilling to respond to unknown interviewers or about things they consider private. Respondents may answer survey questions even when they do not know the answer just to appear smarter or more informed. Or they may try to help the interviewer by giving pleasing answers. Finally, busy people may not take the time, or they might resent the intrusion into their privacy.

Experimental Research. Whereas observation is best suited for exploratory research and surveys for descriptive research, **experimental research** is best suited for gathering causal information. Experiments involve selecting matched groups of subjects, giving them different treatments, controlling unrelated factors, and checking for differences in group responses. Thus, experimental research tries to explain cause-and-effect relationships.

For example, before adding a new sandwich to its menu, McDonald's might use experiments to test the effects on sales of two different prices it might charge. It could introduce the new sandwich at one price in one city and at another price in another city. If the cities are similar, and if all other marketing efforts for the sandwich are the same, then differences in sales in the two cities could be related to the price charged.

CONTACT METHODS Information can be collected by mail, telephone, personal interview, or online. Table 13.2 shows the strengths and weaknesses of each contact method.

Mail, Telephone, and Personal Interviewing. *Mail questionnaires* can be used to collect large amounts of information at a low cost per respondent. Respondents may give more honest answers to more personal questions on a mail questionnaire than to an unknown interviewer in person or over the phone. Also, no interviewer is involved to bias respondents' answers.

However, mail questionnaires are not very flexible; all respondents answer the same questions in a fixed order. Mail surveys usually take longer to complete, and the response rate—the number of people returning completed questionnaires—is often very low. Finally, the researcher often has little control over the mail questionnaire sample.

TABLE 13.2

Strengths and Weaknesses of Contact Methods

	MAIL	TELEPHONE	PERSONAL	ONLINE
Flexibility	Poor	Good	Excellent	Good
Quantity of data that can be collected	Good	Fair	Excellent	Good
Control of interviewer effects	Excellent	Fair	Poor	Fair
Control of sample	Fair	Excellent	Good	Excellent
Speed of data collection	Poor	Excellent	Good	Excellent
Response rate	Poor	Poor	Good	Good
Cost	Good	Fair	Poor	Excellent

Source: Based on Donald S. Tull and Del I. Hawkins, *Marketing Research: Measurement and Method*, 7th ed. (New York: Macmillan Publishing Company, 1993). Adapted with permission of the authors.

Even with a good mailing list, it is hard to control *whom* at a particular address fills out the questionnaire. As a result of the shortcomings, more and more marketers are now shifting to faster, more flexible, and lower cost e-mail and online surveys.

Telephone interviewing is one of the best methods for gathering information quickly, and it provides greater flexibility than mail questionnaires. Interviewers can explain difficult questions and, depending on the answers they receive, skip some questions or probe on others. Response rates tend to be higher than with mail questionnaires, and interviewers can ask to speak to respondents with the desired characteristics or even by name.

However, with telephone interviewing, the cost per respondent is higher than with mail or online questionnaires. Also, people may not want to discuss personal questions with an interviewer. The method introduces interviewer bias—the way interviewers talk, how they ask questions, and other differences that may affect respondents' answers. Finally, in this age of do-not-call lists and promotion-harassed consumers, potential survey respondents are increasingly hanging up on telephone interviewers rather than talking with them.

Personal interviewing takes two forms: individual interviewing and group interviewing. *Individual interviewing* involves talking with people in their homes or offices, on the street, or in shopping malls. Such interviewing is flexible. Trained interviewers can guide interviews, explain difficult questions, and explore issues as the situation requires. They can show subjects actual products, advertisements, or packages and observe reactions and behavior. However, individual personal interviews may cost three to four times as much as telephone interviews.

Group interviewing consists of inviting six to ten people to meet with a trained moderator to talk about a product, service, or organization. Participants normally are paid a small sum for attending. A moderator encourages free and easy discussion, hoping that group interactions will bring out actual feelings and thoughts. At the same time, the moderator "focuses" the discussion—hence the name **focus group interviewing**.

In traditional focus groups, researchers and marketers watch the focus group discussions from behind a one-way mirror and record comments in writing or on video for later study. Focus group researchers often use videoconferencing and Internet technology to connect marketers in distant locations with live focus group action. Using cameras and two-way sound systems, marketing executives in a far-off boardroom can look in and listen, using remote controls to zoom in on faces and pan the focus group at will.

Along with observational research, focus group interviewing has become one of the major qualitative marketing research tools for gaining fresh insights into consumer thoughts and feelings. In focus group settings, researchers not only hear consumer ideas and opinions, they can also observe facial expressions, body movements, group interplay, and conversational flows. However, focus group studies present some challenges. They usually employ small samples to keep time and costs down, and it may be hard to generalize from the results. Moreover, consumers in focus groups are not always open and honest about their real feelings, behavior, and intentions in front of other people.

To overcome these problems, many researchers are tinkering with the focus group design. Some companies use *immersion groups*—small groups of consumers who interact directly and informally with product designers without a focus group moderator present. Other researchers are changing the environments in which they conduct focus groups

New focus group environments: Lexus general manager Mark Templin hosts "An Evening with Lexus" dinners with luxury car buyers to figure out why they did or didn't become Lexus owners.

PHOTO: Courtesy of Lexus

to help consumers relax and elicit more authentic responses. For example, Lexus recently hosted a series of "An Evening with Lexus" dinners with groups of customers in customers' homes:[12]

> Nothing like citrus-cured sardines with Escabeche vegetables or baked halibut with a quail egg to get the conversation flowing. Indeed, Mark Templin, Lexus group vice president and general manager, figures the best way to get up close and personal with customers is to dine with them—in their homes and in style. At the first dinner, held in Beverly Hills, 16 owners of Lexus, Mercedes, BMW, Audi, Land Rover, and other high-end cars traded their perceptions of the Lexus brand. Through lively talk over a sumptuous meal catered by a famous chef, Templin hoped to learn why people did or didn't become Lexus owners.
>
> While feasting on the cuisine, the high-end car consumers gave Templin many actionable insights. For example, he heard that Lexus vehicles often are tagged with being unexciting. "Everyone had driven a Lexus at some point and had a great experience," Templin says. "But the Lexus they [had] wasn't as fun to drive as the car they have now. It's our challenge to show that Lexus is more fun to drive today than it was 15 years ago." Templin was also startled by the extent to which luxury car buyers allow their grown children to decide what car they should purchase. Templin says Lexus marketing in the future also will have to aim at young adults who may not be buying luxury cars but who may strongly influence their parents' decisions.

Individual and focus group interviews can add a personal touch as opposed to more numbers-oriented research. "We get lots of research, and it tells us what we need to run our business, but I get more out of talking one-on-one," says Lexus's Templin. "It really comes to life when I hear people say it."

Online Marketing Research. The growth of the Internet has had a dramatic impact on how marketing research is conducted. Increasingly, researchers are collecting primary data through **online marketing research**: Internet surveys, online panels, experiments, and online focus groups and brand communities.

Online research can take many forms. A company can use the Web as a survey medium: It can include a questionnaire on its Web site or use e-mail to invite people to answer questions, create online panels that provide regular feedback, or conduct live discussions or online focus groups. Researchers can also conduct experiments on the Web. They can experiment with different prices, headlines, or product features on different Web sites or at different times to learn the relative effectiveness of their offers. They can set up virtual shopping environments and use them to test new products and marketing programs. Or a company can learn about the behavior of online customers by following their click streams as they visit the Web site and move to other sites.

The Internet is especially well suited to *quantitative* research—for example, conducting marketing surveys and collecting data. More than three-quarters of all Americans now have access to the Web, making it a fertile channel for reaching a broad cross-section of consumers.[13] As response rates for traditional survey approaches decline and costs increase, the Web is quickly replacing mail and the telephone as the dominant data collection methodology.

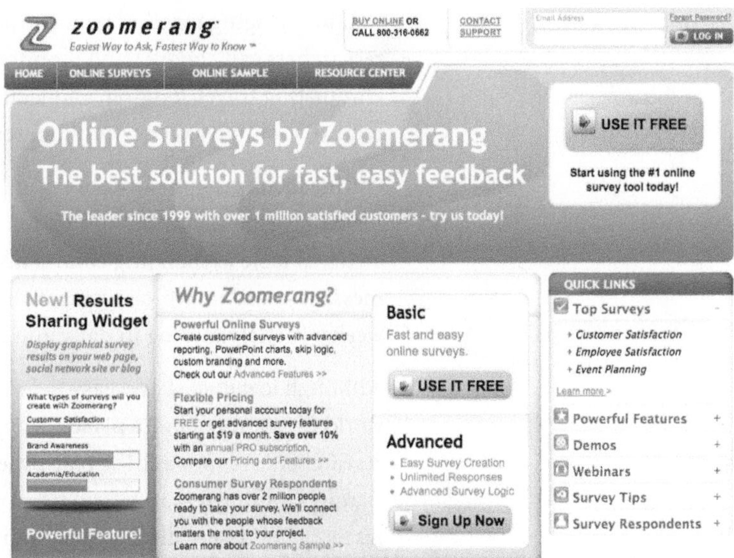

Online research: Thanks to survey services such as Zoomerang, almost any business, large or small, can create, publish, and distribute its own custom surveys in minutes.
PHOTO: Zoomerang, a MarketTools Company

Web-based survey research offers many advantages over traditional phone, mail, and personal interviewing approaches. The most obvious advantages are speed and low costs. By going online, researchers can quickly and easily distribute Internet surveys to thousands of respondents simultaneously via e-mail or by posting them on selected Web sites. Responses can be almost instantaneous, and because respondents themselves enter the information, researchers can tabulate, review, and share research data as the information arrives.

Online research also usually costs much less than research conducted through mail, phone, or personal interviews. Using the Internet eliminates most of the postage, phone, interviewer, and data-handling costs associated with the other approaches. Moreover, sample size has little impact on costs. Once the questionnaire is set up, there's little difference in cost between 10 respondents and 10,000 respondents on the Web.

Its low cost puts online research well within the reach of almost any business, large or small. In fact, with the Internet, what was once the domain of research experts is now available to almost any would-be researcher. Even smaller, less sophisticated researchers can use online survey services such as Zoomerang (*www.zoomerang.com*) and SurveyMonkey (*www.surveymonkey.com*) to create, publish, and distribute their own custom surveys in minutes.

Web-based surveys also tend to be more interactive and engaging, easier to complete, and less intrusive than traditional phone or mail surveys. As a result, they usually garner higher response rates. The Internet is an excellent medium for reaching the hard-to-reach consumer—for example, the often-elusive teen, single, affluent, and well-educated audiences. It's also good for reaching working mothers and other people who lead busy lives. Such people are well represented online, and they can respond in their own space and at their own convenience.

Just as marketing researchers have rushed to use the Internet for quantitative surveys and data collection, they are now also adopting *qualitative* Internet-based research approaches, such as online focus groups, blogs, and social networks. The Internet can provide a fast, low-cost way to gain qualitative customer insights.

A primary qualitative Web-based research approach is **online focus groups**. Such focus groups offer many advantages over traditional focus groups. Participants can log in from anywhere—all they need is a laptop and a Web connection. Thus, the Internet works well for bringing together people from different parts of the country or world. Also, researchers can conduct and monitor online focus groups from just about anywhere, eliminating travel, lodging, and facility costs. Finally, although online focus groups require some advance scheduling, results are almost immediate.

Online focus groups can take any of several formats. Most occur in real time, in the form of online chat room discussions in which participants and a moderator sit around a virtual table exchanging comments. Alternatively, researchers might set up an online message board on which respondents interact over the course of several days or a few weeks. Participants log in daily and comment on focus group topics.

Although low in cost and easy to administer, online focus groups can lack the real-world dynamics of more personal approaches. To overcome these shortcomings, some researchers are now adding real-time audio and video to their online focus groups. For example, online research firm Channel M2 "puts the human touch back into online research" by assembling focus group participants in people-friendly "virtual interview rooms." At the appointed time, participants sign on via their webcam-equipped computer, view live video of other participants, and interact in real-time. Researchers can "sit in" on the focus group from anywhere, seeing and hearing every respondent.[14]

Although growing rapidly, both quantitative and qualitative Internet-based research have some drawbacks. One major problem is controlling who's in the online sample. Without seeing respondents, it's difficult to know who they really are. To overcome such sample and context problems, many online research firms use opt-in communities and respondent panels. For example, Zoomerang offers an online consumer and business panel profiled on more than 500 attributes.[15]

Alternatively, many companies are now developing their own custom social networks and using them to gain customer inputs and insights. For example, in addition to picking customers' brains in face-to-face events such as "An Evening with Lexus" dinners in customers' homes, Lexus has built an extensive online research community called the Lexus Advisory Board.[16]

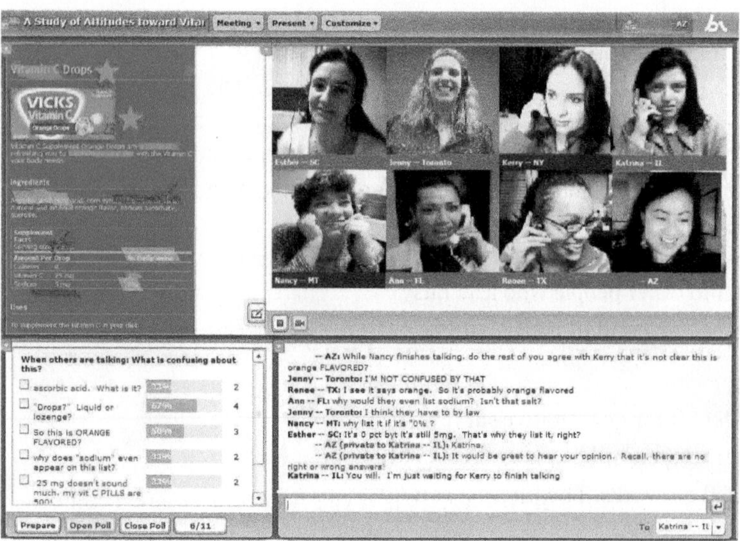

Some researchers have now added real-time audio and video to their online focus groups. For example, Channel M2 "puts the human touch back into online research" by assembling focus group participants in people-friendly "virtual interview rooms."

The Lexus Advisory Board consists of 20,000 invitation-only Lexus owners representing a wide range of demographics, psychographics, and model ownership. Lexus surveys the group regularly to obtain owner input on everything from perceptions of the brand and input on new models and features to the Lexus ownership experience and customer relationships with dealers. "As a Lexus owner, your opinion is invaluable to us," says the invitation, "which is why Lexus is inviting you to join our exclusive online research panel. By becoming a member of the Lexus Advisory Board, your feedback will help shape future product development, customer service, and marketing communications." Says a Lexus marketing executive, "This is a great way of listening to customers."

Thus, in recent years, the Internet has become an important tool for conducting research and developing customer insights. But today's marketing researchers are going even further—well beyond structured online surveys, focus groups, and Web communities. Increasingly, they are listening to and watching consumers by actively mining the rich veins of unsolicited, unstructured, "bottom up" customer information already coursing around the Web.

This might be as simple as scanning customer reviews and comments on the company's brand site or on shopping sites such as Amazon.com or BestBuy.com. Or it might mean using sophisticated Web-analysis tools to deeply analyze mountains of consumer comments and messages found in blogs or on social networking sites, such as Facebook or Twitter. Listening to and watching consumers online can provide valuable insights into what consumers are saying or feeling about brands. As one information expert puts it, "The Web knows what you want."[18] (See Marketing at Work 13.2.)

SAMPLING PLAN Marketing researchers usually draw conclusions about large groups of consumers by studying a small sample of the total consumer population. A **sample** is a segment of the population selected for marketing research to represent the population as a whole. Ideally, the sample should be representative so that the researcher can make accurate estimates of the thoughts and behaviors of the larger population.

Designing the sample requires three decisions. First, *who* is to be studied (what *sampling unit*)? The answer to this question is not always obvious. For example, to learn about the decision-making process for a family automobile purchase, should the subject be the husband, the wife, other family members, dealership salespeople, or all of these? Second, *how many* people should be included (what *sample size*)? Large samples give more reliable results than small samples. However, larger samples usually cost more, and it is not necessary to sample the entire target market or even a large portion to get reliable results.

Marketing at Work 13.2

Listening Online: The Web Knows What You Want

Thanks to the burgeoning world of blogs, social networks, and other Internet forums, marketers now have near-real-time access to a flood of online consumer information. It's all there for the digging—praise, criticism, recommendations, actions—revealed in what consumers are saying and doing as they ply the Internet. Forward-looking marketers are now mining valuable customer insights from this rich new vein of unprompted, "bottom-up" information.

Whereas traditional marketing research provides insights into the "logical, representative, structured aspect of our consumers," says Kristin Bush, senior manager of consumer and market knowledge at P&G, online listening "provides much more of the intensity, much more of the . . . context and the passion, and more of the spontaneity that consumers are truly giving you [when they offer up their opinions] unsolicited."

Listening online might involve something as simple as scanning customer reviews on the company's brand site or on popular shopping sites such as Amazon.com or BestBuy.com. Such reviews are plentiful, address specific products, and provide unvarnished customer reactions. Amazon.com alone features detailed customer reviews on everything it sells, and its customers rely heavily on these reviews when making purchases. If customers in the market for a company's brands are reading and reacting to such reviews, so should the company's marketers. Many companies are now adding customer review sections to their own brand sites. Both positive and negative feedback can help the company learn what it is doing well and where improvement is needed.

At a deeper level, marketers now employ sophisticated Web-analysis tools to listen in on and mine nuggets from the churning mass of consumer comments and conversations in blogs, in news articles, in online forums, and on social networking sites such as Facebook or Twitter. But beyond monitoring what customers are *saying* about them online, companies are also watching what customers are *doing* online. Marketers scrutinize consumer Web-browsing behavior in precise detail and use the resulting insights to personalize shopping experiences. Consider this example:

> A shopper at the retail site FigLeaves.com takes a close look at a silky pair of women's slippers. Next, a recommendation appears for a man's bathrobe. This could seem terribly wrong—unless, of course, it turns out to be precisely what she wanted. Why the bathrobe? Analysis of FigLeaves.com site behavior data—from mouse clicks to search queries—shows that certain types of female shoppers at certain times of the week are likely to be shopping for men.
>
> What a given customer sees at the site might also depend on other behaviors. For example, shoppers who seem pressed for time (say, shopping from work and clicking rapidly from screen to screen) might see more simplified pages with a direct path to the shopping cart and checkout. Alternatively, more leisurely shoppers (say, those shopping from home or on weekends and browsing product reviews) might receive pages with more features, video clips, and comparison information. The goal of such analysis is to teach Web sites "something close to the savvy of a flesh-and-blood sales clerk," says a Web-analytics expert. "In the first five minutes in a store, the sales guy is observing a customer's body language and tone of voice. We have to teach machines to pick up on those same insights from movements online."

More broadly, information about what consumers do while trolling the vast expanse of the Internet—what searches they make, the sites they visit, what they buy, with whom they connect—is pure gold to marketers. And today's marketers are busy mining that gold.

> On the Internet today, everybody knows who you are. In fact, legions of Internet companies know your gender, your age, the neighborhood you live in, who your Facebook and Twitter friends are, that you like pickup trucks, and that you spent, say, three hours and 43 seconds on a Web site for pet lovers on a rainy day in January. All that data streams through myriad computer networks, where it's sorted, cataloged, analyzed, and then used to deliver ads aimed squarely at you, potentially anywhere you travel on the Internet. It's called *behavioral targeting*—tracking consumers' online behavior and using it to target ads to them. So, for example, if you place a cell phone in your Amazon.com shopping cart but don't buy it, you might expect to see some ads for that very type of phone the next time you visit your favorite ESPN site to catch up on the latest sports scores.

Marketers watch what consumers say and do online, then use the resulting insights to personalize online shopping experiences. Is it sophisticated Web research or "just a little creepy"?
PHOTO: Andresr/Shutterstock

That's amazing enough, but the newest wave of Web analytics and targeting takes online eavesdropping even further—from *behavioral* targeting to *social* targeting. Whereas behavioral targeting tracks consumer movements across Web sites, social targeting also mines individual online social connections. Research shows that consumers shop a lot like their friends and are five times more likely to respond to ads from brands friends use. Social targeting links customer data to social interaction data from social networking sites. So, instead of just having a Zappos.com ad for running shoes pop up because you've recently searched for running shoes (behavioral targeting), an ad for a specific pair of running shoes pops up because a friend that you're connected to via Twitter just bought those shoes from Zappos.com last week (social targeting).

Online listening. Behavioral targeting. Social targeting. All of these are great for marketers as they work to mine customer insights from the massive amounts of consumer information swirling around the Web. The biggest question? You've probably already guessed it. As marketers get more adept at trolling blogs, social networks, and other Web domains, what happens to consumer privacy? Yup, that's the downside. At what point does sophisticated Web research cross the line into consumer stalking?

Proponents claim that behavioral and social targeting benefit more than abuse consumers by feeding back ads and products that are more relevant to their interests. But to many consumers and public advocates, following consumers online and stalking them with ads feels more than just a little creepy. Behavioral targeting, for example, has already been the subject of congressional and regulatory hearings. The FTC has recommended the creation of a "Do Not Track" system (the Internet equivalent to the "Do Not Call" registry), which would let people opt out of having their actions monitored online.

Despite such concerns, however, online listening will continue to grow. And, with appropriate safeguards, it promises benefits for both companies and customers. Tapping into online conversations and behavior lets companies "get the unprompted voice of the consumer, the real sentiments, the real values, and the real points of view that they have of our products and services," says P&G's Bush. "Companies that figure out how to listen and respond . . . in a meaningful, valuable way are going to win in the marketplace." After all, knowing what customers really want is an essential first step in creating customer value. And, as one online information expert puts it, "The Web knows what you want."

Sources: Adapted excerpts, quotes, and other information from Stephen Baker, "The Web Knows What You Want," *BusinessWeek*, July 27, 2009, p. 48; Piet Levy, "The Data Dilemma," *Marketing News*, January 30, 2011, pp. 20–21; Brian Morrissey, "Connect the Thoughts," *Adweek*, June 29, 2009, pp. 10–11; Paul Sloan, "The Quest for the Perfect Online Ad," *Business 2.0*, March 2007, p. 88; David Wiesenfeld, Kristin Bush, and Ronjan Sikdar, "Listen Up: Online Yields New Research Pathway," *Nielsen Consumer Insights*, August 2009, http://en-us.nielsen.com/; Elizabeth A. Sullivan, "10 Minutes with Kristin Bush," *Marketing News*, September 30, 2009, pp. 26–28; Eric Picard, "Why Consumers Think Online Marketing Is Creepy," *iMedia Connection*, December 9, 2010, www.imediaconnection.com/content/28158.asp; and Douglas Karr, "Do Not Track: What Marketers Need to Know," *Marketing Tech Blog*, January 26, 2011, www.marketingtechblog.com/technology/do-not-track/.

TABLE 13.3

Types of Samples

PROBABILITY SAMPLE	
Simple random sample	Every member of the population has a known and equal chance of selection.
Stratified random sample	The population is divided into mutually exclusive groups (such as age groups), and random samples are drawn from each group.
Cluster (area) sample	The population is divided into mutually exclusive groups (such as blocks), and the researcher draws a sample of the groups to interview.
NONPROBABILITY SAMPLE	
Convenience sample	The researcher selects the easiest population members from which to obtain information.
Judgment sample	The researcher uses his or her judgment to select population members who are good prospects for accurate information.
Quota sample	The researcher finds and interviews a prescribed number of people in each of several categories.

Finally, *how* should the people in the sample be *chosen* (what *sampling procedure*)? Table 13.3 describes different kinds of samples. Using *probability samples*, each population member has a known chance of being included in the sample, and researchers can calculate confidence limits for sampling error. But when probability sampling costs too much or takes too much time, marketing researchers often take *nonprobability samples*, even though their sampling error cannot be measured. These varied ways of drawing samples have different costs and time limitations as well as different accuracy and statistical properties. Which method is best depends on the needs of the research project.

RESEARCH INSTRUMENTS In collecting primary data, marketing researchers have a choice of two main research instruments: *questionnaires* and *mechanical devices.*

Questionnaires. The questionnaire is by far the most common instrument, whether administered in person, by phone, by e-mail, or online. Questionnaires are very flexible—there are many ways to ask questions. Closed-end questions include all the possible answers, and subjects make choices among them. Examples include multiple-choice questions and scale questions. Open-end questions allow respondents to answer in their own words. In a survey of airline users, Southwest Airlines might simply ask, "What is your opinion of Southwest Airlines?" Or it might ask people to complete a sentence: "When I choose an airline, the most important consideration is. . . ." These and other kinds of open-end questions often reveal more than closed-end questions because they do not limit respondents' answers.

Open-end questions are especially useful in exploratory research, when the researcher is trying to find out *what* people think but is not measuring *how many* people think in a certain way. Closed-end questions, on the other hand, provide answers that are easier to interpret and tabulate.

Researchers should also use care in the *wording* and *ordering* of questions. They should use simple, direct, and unbiased wording. Questions should be arranged in a logical order. The first question should create interest if possible, and difficult or personal questions should be asked last so that respondents do not become defensive.

Mechanical Instruments. Although questionnaires are the most common research instrument, researchers also use mechanical instruments to monitor consumer behavior. Nielsen Media Research attaches people meters to television sets, cable boxes, and satellite systems in selected homes to record who watches which programs. Retailers likewise use checkout scanners to record shoppers' purchases.

Other mechanical devices measure subjects' physical responses. For example, consider Disney Media Networks' new consumer research lab in Austin, Texas:[18]

> A technician in a black lab coat gazed at the short, middle-aged man seated inside Disney's secretive new research facility, his face shrouded with eye-tracking goggles. "Read ESPN.com on that BlackBerry," she told him soothingly, like a nurse about to draw blood. "And have fun," she added, leaving the room. In reality, the man's appetite for sports news was not of interest. (The site was a fake version anyway.) Rather, the technician and her fellow researchers from Disney Media Networks—which includes ABC, ESPN, and other networks—were eager to know how the man responded to ads of varying size. How small could the banners become and still draw his attention? A squadron of Disney executives scrutinized the data as it flowed in real time onto television monitors in an adjacent room. "He's not even looking at the banner now," said one researcher. The man clicked to another page. "There we go, that one's drawing his attention." The tools are advanced: In addition to tracking eye movement, the research team uses heart-rate monitors, skin temperature readings, and facial expressions (probes are attached to facial muscles) to gauge reactions. The goal: to learn what works and what does not in the high-stakes game of new media advertising.

Still other researchers are applying *neuromarketing*, measuring brain activity to learn how consumers feel and respond. Marketing scientists using MRI scans and EEG devices have learned that tracking brain electrical activity and blood flow can provide companies with insights into what turns consumers on and off regarding their brands and marketing. "Companies have always aimed for the customer's heart, but the head may make a better target," suggests one neuromarketer. "Neuromarketing is reaching consumers where the action is: the brain."[19]

Companies ranging from PepsiCo and Disney to Google and Microsoft now hire neuromarketing research companies such as NeuroFocus and EmSense to help figure out what people are really thinking. For example, PepsiCo's Frito-Lay unit uses neuromarketing to test commercials, product designs, and packaging. Recent EEG tests showed that, compared with shiny packages showing pictures of potato chips, matte beige bags showing potatoes and other healthy ingredients trigger less activity in an area of the brain associated with feelings of guilt. Needless to say, Frito-Lay quickly switched away from the shiny packaging. And eBay's PayPal began pitching its online payment service as "fast" after brain-wave research showed that speed turns consumers on more than security and safety, earlier themes used in eBay ad campaigns.[20]

Although neuromarketing techniques can measure consumer involvement and emotional responses second by second, such brain responses can be difficult to interpret. Thus, neuromarketing is usually used in combination with other research approaches to gain a more complete picture of what goes on inside consumers' heads.

Mechanical instruments: To find out what ads work and why, Disney researchers have developed an array of devices to track eye movement, monitor heart rates, and measure other physical responses.

PHOTO: Erich Schlegel/Redux Pictures

Implementing the Research Plan

The researcher next puts the marketing research plan into action. This involves collecting, processing, and analyzing the information. Data collection can be carried out by the company's marketing research staff or outside firms. Researchers should watch closely to make sure that the plan is implemented correctly. They must guard against problems created through interacting with respondents, with the quality of participants' responses, and with interviewers who make mistakes or take shortcuts.

Researchers must also process and analyze the collected data to isolate important information and insight. They need to check data for accuracy and completeness and code it for analysis. The researchers then tabulate the results and compute statistical measures.

Interpreting and Reporting the Findings

The market researcher must now interpret the findings, draw conclusions, and report them to management. The researcher should not try to overwhelm managers with numbers and fancy statistical techniques. Rather, the researcher should present important findings and insights that are useful in the major decisions faced by management.

However, interpretation should not be left only to researchers. Although they are often experts in research design and statistics, the marketing manager knows more about the problem and the decisions that must be made. The best research means little if the manager blindly accepts faulty interpretations from the researcher. Similarly, managers may be biased. They might tend to accept research results that show what they expected and reject those that they did not expect or hope for. In many cases, findings can be interpreted in different ways, and discussions between researchers and managers will help point to the best interpretations. Thus, managers and researchers must work together closely when interpreting research results, and both must share responsibility for the research process and resulting decisions.

SPEED BUMP **LINKING THE CONCEPTS**

Whew! We've covered a lot of territory. Hold up a minute, take a breather, and see if you can apply the marketing research process you've just studied.

- What specific kinds of research can Red Bull's brand managers use to learn more about its customers' preferences and buying behaviors? Sketch out a brief research plan for assessing potential reactions to a new Red Bull enhanced-water line.
- Could you use the marketing research process to analyze your own career opportunities and job possibilities? (Think of yourself as a "product" and employers as potential "customers.") What would your research plan look like?

>> END SPEED BUMP

Analyzing and Using Marketing Information

Information gathered in internal databases and through competitive marketing intelligence and marketing research usually requires additional analysis. Managers may need help applying the information to gain customer and market insights that will improve their marketing decisions. This help may include advanced statistical analysis to learn more about the relationships within a set of data. Information analysis might also involve the application of analytical models that will help marketers make better decisions.

Once the information has been processed and analyzed, it must be made available to the right decision makers at the right time. In the following sections, we look deeper into analyzing and using marketing information.

Customer Relationship Management

The question of how best to analyze and use individual customer data presents special problems. Most companies are awash in information about their customers. In fact, smart companies capture information at every possible customer *touch point*. These touch points include customer purchases, sales force contacts, service and support calls, Web site visits, satisfaction surveys, credit and payment interactions, market research studies—every contact between a customer and a company.

Unfortunately, this information is usually scattered widely across the organization. It is buried deep in the separate databases and records of different company departments. To overcome such problems, many companies are now turning to **customer relationship management (CRM)** to manage detailed information about individual customers and carefully manage customer touch points to maximize customer loyalty.

CRM consists of sophisticated software and analytical tools from companies such as Oracle, Microsoft, Salesforce.com, and SAS that integrate customer information from all sources, analyze it in depth, and apply the results to build stronger customer relationships. CRM integrates everything that a company's sales, service, and marketing teams know about individual customers, providing a 360-degree view of the customer relationship.

CRM analysts develop *data warehouses* and use sophisticated *data mining* techniques to unearth the riches hidden in customer data. A data warehouse is a company-wide electronic database of finely detailed customer information that needs to be sifted through for gems. The purpose of a data warehouse is not only to gather information but also to pull it together into a central, accessible location. Then, once the data warehouse brings the data together, the company uses high-powered data mining techniques to sift through the mounds of data and dig out interesting findings about customers.

These findings often lead to marketing opportunities. For example, grocery chain Kroger works with the data mining firm Dunnhumby, which it co-owns with successful London-based retailer Tesco, to dig deeply into data obtained from customer loyalty cards. It uses the customer insights gained for everything from targeting coupons to locating stores and adjusting inventories to specific locations:[21]

> Although the recent Great Recession revived penny-pinching, Americans are still redeeming only 1 percent to 3 percent of paper coupons. In contrast, Kroger says as many as *half* the coupons it sends to regular customers do get used. Kroger digs deep into the reams of information from its more than 55 million shopper cards and uses the resulting insights, augmented with customer interviews, to guide strategies for tailored promotions, pricing, placement, and even stocking variations from store to store. For example, 95 percent of mailings are tailored to specific households, containing coupons for items they usually load into their carts. Such personalization creates more value for customers and makes them feel more appreciated. In turn, Kroger's ability to turn data into insights builds customer loyalty and drives profitable sales. Says Kroger's CEO, "This level of personalization is a direct link to our customers that no other U.S. grocery retailer can [match]."

Grocery chain Kroger works with data mining firm Dunnhumby to dig deeply into data obtained from customer loyalty cards. It uses the customer insights gained for everything from targeting coupons to locating and stocking its stores.

PHOTO: With permission of The Kroger Co.

By using CRM to understand customers better, companies can provide higher levels of customer service and develop deeper customer relationships. They can use CRM to pinpoint high-value customers, target them more effectively, cross-sell the company's products, and create offers tailored to specific customer requirements.

CRM benefits don't come without costs or risk, either in collecting the original customer data or in maintaining and mining it. The most common CRM mistake is to view CRM as a technology and software solution only. Yet technology alone cannot build profitable customer relationships. Companies can't improve customer relationships by simply installing some new software. Instead, CRM is just one part of an effective overall *customer relationship management strategy*. "There's lots of talk about CRM and these days it usually has to do with a software solution," says one analyst. But marketers should start by adhering to "some basic tenets of actual customer relationship management and *then* empower them with high-tech solutions."[22] They should focus first on the R—it's the *relationship* that CRM is all about.

Distributing and Using Marketing Information

Marketing information has no value until it is used to gain customer insights and make better marketing decisions. Thus, the marketing information system must make the information readily available to managers and others who need it. In some cases, this means providing managers with regular performance reports, intelligence updates, and reports on the results of research studies.

But marketing managers may also need nonroutine information for special situations and on-the-spot decisions. For example, a sales manager having trouble with a large customer may want a summary of the account's sales and profitability over the past year. Or a brand manager may want to get a sense of the amount of online buzz surrounding the launch of a recent advertising campaign. These days, therefore, information distribution involves entering information into databases and making it available in a timely, user-friendly way.

Many firms use company *intranet* and internal CRM systems to facilitate this process. These systems provide ready access to research and intelligence information, customer contact information, reports, shared work documents, and more. For example, the CRM system at phone and online gift retailer 1-800-Flowers gives customer-facing employees real-time access to customer information. When a repeat customer calls, the system immediately calls up data on previous transactions and other contacts, helping reps make the customer's experience easier and more relevant. For instance, "If a customer usually buys tulips for his wife, we [talk about] our newest and best tulip selections," says the company's vice president of customer knowledge management. "No one else in the business is able to connect customer information with real-time transaction data the way we can."[23]

In addition, companies are increasingly allowing key customers and value-network members to access account, product, and other data on demand through *extranets*. Suppliers, customers, resellers, and select other network members may access a company's extranet to update their accounts, arrange purchases, and check orders against inventories to improve customer service. For example, Penske Truck Leasing's extranet site, MyFleetAtPenske.com, lets Penske business customers access all the data about their fleets in one spot and provides an array of tools and applications designed to help fleet managers manage their Penske accounts and maximize efficiency.[24]

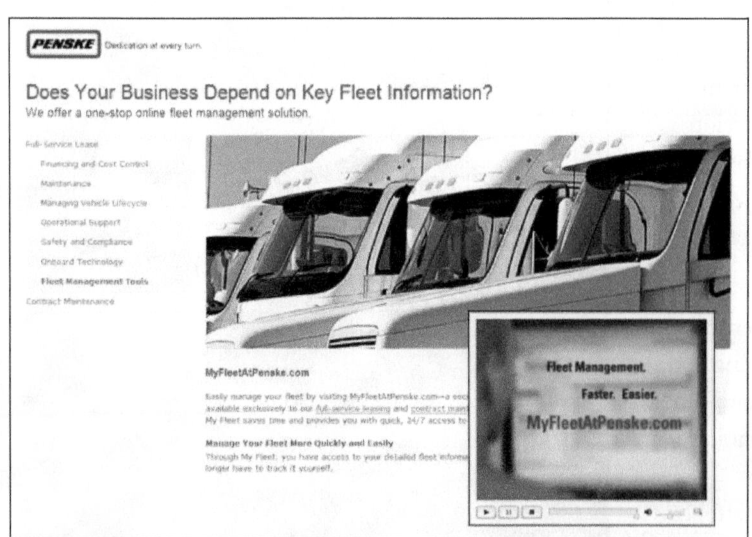

Extranets: Penske Truck Leasing's extranet site, MyFleetAtPenske.com, lets Penske customers access all of the data about their fleets in one spot and provides tools to help fleet managers manage their Penske accounts and maximize efficiency.

PHOTO: Penske Truck Leasing Co., LP

Thanks to modern technology, today's marketing managers can gain direct access to a company's information system at any time and from virtually anywhere. They can tap into the system from a home office, hotel room, or the local Starbucks—anyplace they can connect on a laptop or smartphone. Such systems allow managers to get the information they need directly and quickly and tailor it to their own needs.

Feedback: Supportive Communication[1]

CHAPTER 14

The Focus on Accuracy

Much of the writing on interpersonal communication focuses on the *accuracy* of the information being communicated. The emphasis is generally on making certain that messages are transmitted and received with little alteration or variation from original intent. The communication skill of most concern is the ability to transmit clear, precise messages. The following incidents illustrate problems that result from inaccurate communication:

> *A motorist was driving on the Merritt Parkway outside New York City when his engine stalled. He quickly determined that his battery was dead and managed to stop another driver who consented to push his car to get it started.*
>
> *"My car has an automatic transmission," he explained, "so you'll have to get up to 30 or 35 miles an hour to get me started."*
>
> *The second motorist nodded and walked back to his own car. The first motorist climbed back into his car and waited for the good Samaritan to pull up behind him.*
>
> *He waited—and waited. Finally, he turned around to see what was wrong. There was the good Samaritan—coming up behind his car at about 35 miles an hour!*
>
> *The damage amounted to $3,800. (Haney, 1992, p. 285)*

Many individuals feel that they are very effective communicators. They perceive that communication problems are a product of others' weaknesses, not their own (Carrell & Willmington, 1996)

When accuracy is the primary consideration, attempts to improve communication generally center on improving the mechanics: senders and receivers, encoding and decoding, choices of mediums, and reducing or eliminating noise.

Ineffective communication may lead individuals to misinterpret meanings, be offended, lose confidence, and disagree with each other, as well as cause a host of other interpersonal problems. These interpersonal problems, in turn, generally lead to restricted communication flow, more inaccurate messages, and misinterpretations of meanings.

To illustrate, consider the following situation. Latisha is introducing a new goal-setting program to the organization as a way to overcome some productivity problems. After Latisha's carefully prepared presentation in the management council meeting, Jose raises his hand. "In my opinion, this is a poor approach to solving our productivity issues. The considerations are much more complex than Latisha seems to realize. I don't think we should waste our time by pursuing this plan any further."

Jose's opinion may be justified, but the manner in which he delivers the message will probably eliminate any hope of its being dealt with objectively. Instead, Latisha will probably hear a message such as, "You're naive," "You're stupid," or "You're incompetent." Therefore, we wouldn't be surprised if Latisha's response was defensive or even hostile. Any good feelings between the two have probably been jeopardized, and their communication will probably be reduced to self-image protection. The merits of the proposal will be smothered by personal defensiveness. Future communication between the two will probably be minimal and superficial.

What Is Supportive Feedback?

Supportive feedback is interpersonal communication that helps you articulate accurately and honestly, especially in difficult circumstances, without jeopardizing interpersonal relationships. It is not so difficult to communicate supportively—to express confidence, trust, and openness—when things are going well. But when you have to correct someone else's behavior, when you have to deliver negative feedback, or when you have to point out shortcomings of another person, communicating in a way that builds and strengthens the relationship is more difficult.

Supportive feedback seeks to preserve or enhance a positive relationship between the communicating parties while still addressing a problem, giving negative feedback, or tackling a difficult issue. It allows you to communicate information to others that addresses an observed behavior that is not acceptable, or to resolve an uncomfortable issue with another person but, in the process, strengthen their performance and your relationship.

We focus on five attributes of supportive feedback which are summarized in Table 14.1. When supportive feedback is used, not only is a message delivered accurately, but the relationship between the two communicating parties is supported, even enhanced, by the interchange. Positive interpersonal relationships result. People feel energized and uplifted, even when the information being communicated is focused on observed behaviors that are negative.

TABLE 14.1
THE FIVE ATTRIBUTES OF SUPPORTIVE COMMUNICATION

■ **Descriptive**—(a) specific behavior-event, (b) effect on you/team, and (c) consequence
■ **Problem Oriented**—Focus on actions that can change NOT personalities or traits
■ **Validating**—Engage the other party-respectful, collaborative, Build mutual solutions.
■ **Owned**—Based on YOUR opinion-beliefs-observations . . . NOT Hearsay
■ **Timely**—Close to the event so the information is relevant to the receiver

Qualities of Supportive Feedback

Researchers have found that organizations fostering supportive interpersonal communications enjoy higher productivity, faster problem solving, higher-quality outputs, and fewer conflicts. Five qualities best exemplify supportive communications.

1. Descriptive Feedback

Descriptive feedback is designed to reduce the tendency to evaluate and to perpetuate a defensive interaction, and involves three steps summarized in Table 14.2.

Step 1, *describe objectively your observation of the event that occurred or the behavior that you think needs to be modified.* As objectively and dispassionately as possible, talk about the event, the behavior that happened instead of about the person involved. Behavior should be compared to accepted standards rather than to personal opinions or preferences.

Second, *describe your (or others') reactions to the behavior or describe the consequences of the behavior.* Rather than projecting onto another person the cause of the problem, focus on the consequences the behavior produced. This requires that communicators are aware of their own reactions and are able to describe them. Using one-word descriptions for feelings is often the best method: "I'm concerned about our productivity." "Your level of accomplishment frustrates me because. . . ."

Similarly, the consequences of the behavior can be pointed out: "Profits are off this month," "Department quality ratings are down," or "Two customers (A & B) have called in to express dissatisfaction." Describing feelings or consequences also lessens the likelihood of defensiveness since the problem is framed in the context of the communicator's feelings and objective consequences, not the attributes of the other

TABLE 14.2
DESCRIPTIVE FEEDBACK

Step 1: Describe objectively the event, behavior, or circumstance.

- Avoid accusations.
- Present specific data or evidence.

Example: Three clients (X, Y, and Z) have complained to me this month that you have not responded to their requests.

Step 2: Focus on the behavior and the effect on you and the team, not on the other person's attributes.

- Describe your reactions and feelings.
- Describe the objective consequences that have resulted or will result from the observed behavior.

Example: I'm worried because each client has threatened to go elsewhere if we aren't more responsive.

Step 3: Focus on solutions.

- Avoid discussing who's right or wrong.
- Solicit suggestions from the other party for an acceptable alternative.
- Be open to multiple alternatives.

Example: We need both to win back their confidence and to show them you are responsive. What do you suggest we do to accomplish that?

person. If those feelings or consequences are described in a non-accusing way, the energies of the communicators can be focused on problem solving rather than on defending against evaluations.

Third, solicit suggestions for *an acceptable alternative.* This focuses the discussion on the suggested alternative, not on the person. It also helps the other person save face and avoid feeling personally criticized because the individual is separated from the behavior. Self-esteem is preserved because it is the behavior—something controllable—not the person, that should be modified.

Of course, care should be taken not to give the message, "I don't like the way things are, so what are *you* going to do about it?" The change need not be the responsibility of only one of the communicating parties. Instead, the emphasis should be on mutually finding a solution that is acceptable to both people, not on deciding who is right and who is wrong or who should change and who shouldn't. For example, "I would like to help you identify the things that are standing in the way of higher performance."

Effective communicators who provide supportive feedback do not abandon the three steps. They simply switch the focus. They might respond, "I'm surprised to hear you say that you don't care how I/we feel about this problem (step 1). Your response concerns me, and I think it might have important implications for the productivity of our team (step 2). I suggest we spend some time trying to identify the obstacles you feel might be inhibiting our ability to work together on this problem (step 3)."

2. Problem-Oriented Feedback

Problem-oriented feedback focuses on problems and solutions rather than on personal traits. Person- oriented feedback focuses on the characteristics of the individual, not the event. "This is the problem" rather than "You are the problem" illustrates the difference between problem and person orientation.

Problem-oriented feedback is useful because it focuses on behaviors and events. Person-oriented feedback, on the other hand, often focuses on personal attributes, things that cannot be changed or controlled, and it can send the message that the individual is inadequate.

Statements such as "You are dictatorial" and "You are insensitive" describe the person, while "I am being left out of decision making" and "We don't seem to see things the same way" describe problems. Imputing motives is person-oriented ("It's because you want to control other people"), whereas describing overt behaviors is problem-oriented ("You made several sarcastic comments in the meeting today").

Problem-oriented feedback should also be linked to accepted standards or expectations rather than to personal opinions. Personal opinions are more likely to be interpreted as person-oriented and arouse defensiveness than statements in which the behavior is compared to an accepted standard or performance.

For example, the statement, "I don't like the way you write" is an expression of a personal opinion and will probably create resistance, especially if the listener does not feel that the communicator's opinions are any more legitimate than his or her own. On the other hand, "Your writing style is not in keeping with the team's standards," is a comparison to external standards that have some legitimacy. Feelings of defensiveness are less likely to arise since the problem, not the person, is being addressed. In addition, other people are more likely to support a statement based on a commonly accepted standard.

3. Supportive Feedback Validates the Individual

Validating feedback helps people feel recognized, understood, accepted, and valued. Feedback that is **invalidating** arouses negative feelings about self-worth, identity, and relatedness to others. It denies the presence, uniqueness, or importance of other individuals.

Non-Validating feedback can take the form of put-downs, in which others are made to look bad so that the communicator looks good. Or it can take the form of "one-upmanship," in which the communicator tries to elevate him- or herself in the esteem of others. One form of one-upmanship is withholding information, either boastfully ("If you knew what I knew, you would feel differently") or coyly to trip people up ("If you had asked me, I could have told you the executive committee would disapprove of your proposal"). Boasting almost always makes others uncomfortable, mainly because it is designed to convey superiority.

Speaking a foreign language in the presence of individuals who don't understand it may also be done to create the impression of exclusiveness or superiority. In most circumstances, using words or language that a listener can't understand is bad manners because it invalidates the other person.

Another major type of invalidation is dealing in absolutes or being rigid. The communication is portrayed as unequivocal, or unquestionable. No other opinion or point of view could possibly be considered. Individuals who communicate in dogmatic, "know-it-all" ways often do so in order to minimize others' contributions or to invalidate others' perspectives. It is possible to communicate rigidity, however, in ways other than just being dogmatic. Rigidity is also communicated in the following ways:

- Reinterpreting all other viewpoints to conform to one's own.
- Never saying, "I don't know," but having an answer for everything.
- Appearing unwilling to tolerate criticisms or alternative points of view.
- Resistance to receiving personal feedback.

Validating, respectful, feedback helps others realize that they have a stake in identifying problems and resolving them. Validating feedback recognizes others as worthwhile, competent, and insightful and emphasizes joint problem solving rather than projecting a superior position. This can be achieved merely by asking for opinions, suggestions, and ideas.

4. Supportive Feedback Is Owned

Taking responsibility for one's statements and acknowledging that the source of the ideas is oneself and not another person or group is **owning feedback.** Using first-person words, such as "I," "me," "mine," indicates ownership. **Disowning feedback** is suggested by use of third-person or first-person-plural words: "We think," "They said," or "One might say." Disowned feedback is attributed to an unknown person, group, or to some external source (e.g., "Lots of people think"). The communicator avoids taking responsibility for the message and therefore avoids investing in the interaction. This may convey the message that the communicator is aloof or uncaring about the receiver or is not confident enough in the ideas expressed to take responsibility for them.

One result of disowned feedback is that the listener is never sure whose point of view the message represents: "How can I respond if I don't know to whom I am responding?" "If I don't understand the message, whom can I ask since the message represents someone else's point of view?" Owned communication, indicates a willingness to invest oneself in a relationship and to act as a colleague or helper.

5. Supportive Feedback Is Timely

The positive or constructive feedback is provided to the recipient close to the timing of the event as possible so that the information is relevant to the receiver and thay can adjust or replicate the behaviors.

Feedback Matrix

The Feedback Matrix, as shown below, is a useful tool that helps with self-exploration. It encourages you to examine both the positive and negative aspects of feedback, and then connect the comments back to what you already know about yourself, and what you did not know and need to explore more fully.

	Positive	Negative
Expected		
Unexpected		

Feedback generally falls into one of the categories in the matrix:

POSITIVE/EXPECTED We often have a good idea of what we do well, because we receive regular positive feedback about these things. But instead of simply hearing this familiar praise and doing nothing with it, ask yourself:

- Can I use these positive traits to understand myself better?
- Can these positive traits help me improve my job performance?
- Can I use my strengths to help others who are struggling?

NEGATIVE/EXPECTED If we're honest with ourselves, we're often aware of some of the areas in our life that need improvement. If our boss asks for a meeting, chances are we know and expect what will be discussed. In fact, we're often more critical of ourselves than others are, but we just don't know how to improve without some help. To apply this expected feedback and make a positive change, ask yourself:

- What actions can I take to address my weaknesses?
- Have my actions been successful?
- What else do I need to do to achieve the results I want?
- What will happen in my life or at my job if I don't make changes?

POSITIVE/UNEXPECTED Receiving positive feedback that we don't expect is like a surprise birthday present. It creates a wonderful feeling when we learn or hear something positive that was totally unexpected. But after the initial joy, it's important to examine this feedback further by asking yourself:

- What surprised me about the positive feedback?
- Why did I never notice this quality in myself before?
- How can I celebrate this new quality?
- How can I apply this quality to the rest of my life?

NEGATIVE/UNEXPECTED This feedback is the most difficult to hear and understand. But it can also be the source of much self-discovery, if we're open to it. This unexpected feedback often comes from areas that we don't want to acknowledge, or aren't prepared to face, and it can cause some strong emotions. However, when we learn to deal with it, we can take big steps forward on our journey of self-improvement. Some further questions to explore include:

- What more do I need to know to make use of this feedback?
- What kind of support do I need to make use of this feedback?
- What sorts of changes can I make immediately?
- How can knowing these things help me in the rest of my life?

Download our **feedback matrix template (www.mindtools.com)** to use this technique. When you give or receive feedback, use this matrix to improve your experience – and your outcomes.

Key Points

Feedback is meant to be the first step toward change. Unfortunately, the result is often too much or too little change, which doesn't help you achieve your goals.

The Feedback Matrix helps you get the most from any feedback session. It leads you to examine the negative and positive aspects of the feedback, and ask yourself what you did and did not expect. It challenges you to take advantage of the expected positives, commit to working harder on the expected negatives, celebrate the unexpected positives, and fully explore the unexpected negatives. With this tool, you can use feedback effectively to achieve significant, positive change.

Conclusion

Arguably, the most important skill in building and strengthening positive relationships is the ability to communicate with people in a way that enhances feelings of trust, openness, and support. This chapter focused on helping your develop and improve this skill—the ability to communicate supportively.

CHAPTER 15

Segmentation, Targeting, and Positioning[1]

Segmentation Explained

There was a time when large companies such as McDonald's, Procter & Gamble, and Coca-Cola could market and sell their products by considering only the broad wants and needs of large groups of the U.S. population, if not the entire market. These companies could advertise their messages through a small number of radio and television stations that reached much of the population. This strategy is known as mass marketing.

Mass marketing is communicating a product or service message to as broad a group of people as possible with the purpose of positively influencing sales. The idea of mass marketing is that the broader the audience, the more potential for sales. In the past, this strategy proved successful for some businesses. Today, there are several problems with mass marketing. For one, there is no longer the ability to easily reach a large audience. Secondly, there are an increasingly vast number of product and brand choices for the consumer.

Communicating with the entire U.S. market or a large segment within the market was much easier decades ago. For example, in the 1960s, businesses could run advertising on three major television networks, ABC, CBS, and NBC, and reach 80% of U.S. women.[2] Reaching a similar level today would require advertising on over 100 television channels.[3] Even if a business purchased enough advertising and was able to reach such a large audience, it is not enough to tell consumers that the business exists and invite them to buy its products or services. Many product categories contain hundreds of different brand choices and consumers are often overwhelmed with options. Consider a typical supermarket shelf. Many brands in product categories offer specific attributes that appeal to certain consumers, but do not appeal to others.

Consumers differ in their wants, needs, perceptions, values, and expectations. It is these differences that form the foundation for segmentation. Segmentation identifies groups of consumers who have similar market responses, such as reacting to advertising or personal selling, within their group, but whose responses differ from other groups.[4] A response could be to product characteristics, or to a projected image, or the way a group learns about, purchases, and consumes a product or service.

To qualify as a true segment, a group should fulfill several criteria:[5]

- Be a homogeneous set
- Be different from other segments
- Be a critical mass
- Have core similarities of attitude, behavior, and economics
- Be robust and replicable over time

Segmentation Applied

Market **segmentation** allows businesses to look at consumers as several different groups, instead of one mass market. Correctly segmenting consumers allows companies to target their marketing dollars effectively. The value of market segmentation can be measured through increased market share for a given segment, for example, an increase in sales for women ages 24–35.

segmentation (also referred to as market segmentation)
The division of consumer markets into meaningful and distinct customer groups.

The most basic form of market segmentation involves demographic or psychographic criteria, such as age or gender. However, consumers seldom make purchase decisions based solely on demographics or psychographics. Instead, they rely on a wide range of other criteria, such as attitudes or values. There are similar levels of complexity in segmenting business markets (for B2B transactions) and segmenting international markets.

Businesses generally conduct market segmentation through marketing research studies among consumers or businesses. Large numbers of consumers or businesses are surveyed on a wide range of issues and the results are used to create segments based on a variety of factors.

EXAMPLE **SEGMENTATION**

PHOTO: Deklofenak/Shutterstock

Smartwater is the number one premium bottled water brand in the United States and is part of Glaceau's leading portfolio, along with Vitaminwater and Vitaminenergy, in the enhanced water category. Founded in 1996, Glaceau targets its products at people on the go who want to feel better, perform better, and live healthier lives through better hydration. Smartwater is targeted to healthy individuals who carefully watch what they put into their bodies. Smartwater is a zero-calorie, vapor-distilled, electrolyte enhanced water product. As the segment of individuals who value health and wellness increases, Smartwater has differentiated its market position from spring water by having the lowest measurement of total dissolved solids, including minerals and metals, of any water on the market. Smartwater partnered with Jennifer Aniston, known for her healthy lifestyle including yoga and organic cooking, in 2007 to reinforce the product's market position.[6]

>> END EXAMPLE

Segmentation Base Explained

segmentation base
A group of characteristics that is used to assign segment members.

The choice of a **segmentation base** can be one of the most critical decisions that influence the success of market segmentation. Consumers are divided into groups for marketing purposes. For example, if you market Smartwater, as we saw in the opening example, then you would market to health-conscious individuals who ascribe a high value to quality ingredients. You would focus your marketing in an effort to sell more units of Smartwater. Consumers are typically divided into groups by demographic, psychographic, values, behavioral, and needs variables.

Demographic segmentation divides the market into groups, based on criteria such as age, gender, family size, family life cycle, income, occupation, education, religion, ethnicity, generation, nationality, and sexual orientation. For example, some companies offer distinct products or marketing approaches for different age cohorts or life-stage groups, such as selling child insurance policies to new parents. Some may market to affluent consumers with premium goods or services. Others may market to men or women with gender-specific products or services.

Demographic criteria provide the most common bases for segmenting customer groups and, while use of such criteria is typically the initial method of segmenting, other criteria can be used within demographic segments. Demographics can be the easiest information to obtain, but may not provide the greatest amount of insight into why consumers behave differently. A hypothetical example of demographic segmentation output that reflects the percentage of age groups that watch 20 hours or more of television each week is shown in Figure 15.1.

EXAMPLE **DEMOGRAPHIC SEGMENTATION**

Curves, the largest fitness franchise in the world, is designed to provide one-stop fitness facilities and exercise and nutritional information for women. With over 10,000 locations in 70 countries serving 4 million women, Curves offers a variety of products, including its 30-minute workout. By segmenting the market by gender, Curves has carefully defined itself to consumers and has made many women, both experienced athletes and novices alike, feel more comfortable about working out.[7]

>> END EXAMPLE

PHOTO: Deklofenak/Shutterstock

Psychographic segmentation assigns buyers into different groups, based on lifestyle, class, or personality characteristics. People belonging to a particular demographic group can have dramatically different psychographic characteristics. For example, 18- to 24-year-old males represent a wide range of lifestyles that can dramatically influence the likelihood of whether they will select one type of product or service over another. Some may be adventurous and go camping when traveling, while others may enjoy staying in luxury hotels. In fact, these distinct groups of people may have more in common with people from a wide range of age groups rather than their fellow 18- to 24-year-olds.

FIGURE 15.1

Percentage of Age Groups That Watch 20 or More Hours of Television Each Week

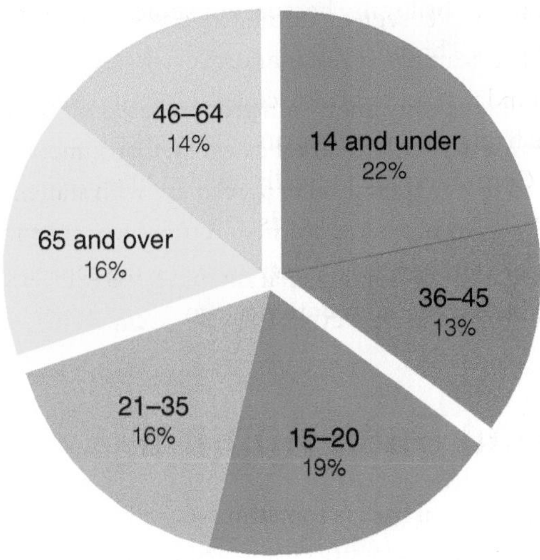

EXAMPLE **PSYCHOGRAPHIC SEGMENTATION**

Moosejaw began as a small outfitter in Keego Harbor, Michigan. Over time, it became an iconic cult brand with sales across the country. Moosejaw flags are a common promotional tool and the company combines a savvy knowledge of consumer behavior with a broad range of products. Moosejaw uses lifestyle, a psychographic segmentation variable, to create an emotional connection with its customers; that connection is called Moosejaw madness. Moosejaw madness involves a variety of activities, such as reviewing proposed advertising copy and having people send in pictures of themselves with a Moosejaw flag in places around the world.[8]

PHOTO: Dana E. Fry/Shutterstock

>> END EXAMPLE

Values segmentation considers what customers prefer and what motivates customer response to marketing activities. Individual values are among the most fundamental determinants of consumer behavior and are considered to be more closely related to motivations than attitudes. Once motivations are understood, behavior becomes easier to predict.[9] Values generally develop over many years and are very difficult to influence through marketing communication. However, values segmentation criteria can be used to segment consumers effectively by reflecting consumer perception. Examples of values variables include an interest in lifelong learning, enjoyment, integrity, respect, self-direction, and honesty.

Behavioral segmentation allocates consumers into groups based on their uses or responses to a product or service. For example, buyers can be grouped according to occasions or life events, such as graduations, when they get the idea to buy a product or service, actually make their purchase, or use the purchased item. Markets can be segmented into nonusers, ex-users, potential users, first-time users, and regular users of a product. Consumers could be grouped into high levels of usage or lower levels of usage. A market can be segmented by loyalty because consumers can be loyal to distribution outlets or product or service brands.

Needs segmentation assigns consumers into groups, based on their current and desired level of interaction with a particular market category. Consumers classified by needs segmentation are asked to rate their level of agreement with statements about how they feel about aspects of the category being studied. Automotive consumers can be classified based on their needs for storage space, horsepower, towing capacity, and many other characteristics of products in the automotive category.

Segmentation Base Applied

The selection of a segmentation base is sometimes done by default if a business is unaware of the different ways to classify customers. Businesses may use readily available information, usually demographics, to conduct segmentation without considering if that available information best represents how consumers think about and interact with their business and the larger category. In many cases, more complex segmentation bases should be considered, such as psychographic, values, behavioral, and needs. Quite often, a combination of different bases provides the most useful segmentation.

Needs segmentation could be utilized to identify specific groups, but those groups could then be classified by demographic, psychographic, and behavioral characteristics. It is important to use a variety of criteria in creating segments because they may overlap in classification criteria. For example, two segments could both be females between the ages of 25 and 35, but the product needs could be completely different. One group may want to drive convertibles and the other group may consist of moms who want minivans. This would certainly require different marketing activities for each group.

Companies, however, can be wrong when trying to determine what different segments want. For example, a company could believe that it has a product that 18- to 25-year-olds will want, but in which 30- to 45-year-olds will not be interested. Believing this, the company targets its ads to the younger age group. However, sales information may indicate that both groups bought the product. For example, Toyota launched the Scion brand assuming young adults would be the primary purchasers. Ultimately, Toyota found that people of all ages were purchasing the product.

Marketers seldom restrict their segmentation analysis to variables from only one type of segmentation base, such as demographic. Instead, they are increasingly using multiple segmentation bases to locate better-defined target groups. For example, a jewelry designer could identify a group of individuals earning over $1 million each year who are interested in his or her products and, within that group, the designer could identify a large subgroup that enjoys tennis. By combining demographic and psychographic bases, the jewelry designer could produce products for high-income individuals that are either created in tennis themes or are marketed and sold at tennis events. Instead of simply targeting high-income individuals, there is another connection—tennis—that creates a stronger level of interest among certain consumers.

Segmenting Business Markets

Business markets can often be segmented using variables similar to consumer markets. The primary business segmentation variables include the following:

- **Demographics**—Business size, industry group
- **Geographics**—Regional, national, international locations
- **Benefits sought**—Desire for extensive service support, cutting-edge technology, financing terms
- **Loyalty**—Share of total purchases
- **Usage rates**—Amount, frequency of purchases

There are some unique business market variables that include the following:

- **Customer operating characteristics**—Customer capabilities and processes, and technology requirements
- **Purchasing approaches**—Where power resides in an organization and general purchasing policies
- **Situational factors**—Size of order, sense of urgency of order
- **Personal characteristics**—Loyalty, risk aversion of customer

Depending on the product, some businesses may place a high value on the service support offered by the supplier. That level of service may make the price less important. Like consumer markets, a combination of variables may provide the most effective segmentation.

EXAMPLE **SEGMENTING BUSINESS MARKETS**

JPMorgan Chase is a leading global financial services firm with assets of $2 trillion. Operating in over 60 countries, Chase offers consumer and business banking offerings. Business services include credit, payroll services, retirement services, and payment processing services. In addition, Chase offers special programs for certain business segments, including not-for-profits (through tax-exempt business retirement program management and access to potential grants through the JPMorgan Chase Foundation) and CPAs (through a dedicated CPA hotline and online access to client banking information). The programs are designed to meet the unique needs of these segments.[10]

PHOTO: David Gilder/Shutterstock

>> END EXAMPLE

Segmenting International Markets

Consumers in one country's market can have more in common with certain segments in another country's market than with consumers in their own country. This could be due to immigration and shared heritage. Some Hispanic consumers in parts of the United States and some consumers in Mexico have the same brand preferences and consume similar media. Global marketing strategies can be successful by identifying consumer needs and wants that span national boundaries by increasing the overall market potential. Segments that span national boundaries can sometimes be more valuable to companies than segments that exist in a single country.

Countries, even those in close proximity, may differ significantly in their cultural, economic, and political composition. The basis for grouping consumers, whether across country borders or across county borders, involves identifying distinct buying needs and behaviors.

EXAMPLE **SEGMENTING INTERNATIONAL MARKETS**

PHOTO: Josh Gow/Shutterstock

Nokia, the world's leading mobile phone manufacturer, has sold over 1 billion phones in over 150 countries. Nokia has a global portfolio that is adapted to meet local customer needs as well as infrastructure and legal requirements. In the Middle East, Nokia launched a selection of mobile applications for the holy month of Ramadan. The Ramadan offering enables users to search, read, bookmark, and listen to Qur'an recitation. Locations of major mosques in Saudi Arabia, Egypt, Morocco, Pakistan, Jordan, and the United Arab Emirates are included through Nokia Maps. Additional mobile content includes wallpaper, ringtones, and Islamic songs. About 14% of Nokia global sales come from the Middle East and Africa.[11]

>> END EXAMPLE

Targeting Explained

Once the segmentation possibilities have been identified, the next step is to determine which customer groups to serve. Businesses often select more than one customer group based on criteria such as the following:

- Ability to meet requirements of the customers
- Overall cost to meet customer requirements
- Potential profitability of serving different customer groups

As many brands face an increasingly competitive and crowded market, the challenges are both strategic and tactical. Strategic questions generally involve "where" and "who" types of questions, such as "Who are those consumers who are most interested in what my brand stands for?" Tactical questions typically involve "what" and "how" types of questions, such as "What type of marketing offer would be most desired by those consumers who are most interested in my brand?"

Although market targeting often begins with an established product or service, target marketing occurs when a business identifies a market segment it wants to serve and then develops a product or service that is appropriate for that segment. For example, Baby Einstein, owned by Disney, has a wide product offering of DVDs and toys and markets its portfolio to moms, with a particular focus on first-time moms. The targeting process involves an understanding of the characteristics of the various segments and draws considerably from the choices made during segmentation. Ultimately, the concept of targeting involves the prioritization of segments and the allocation of resources.[12]

Targeting Applied

Targeting allows businesses to build efficiencies through the use of appropriate advertising media and relevant messages for a given target. Targeting can be accomplished in a variety of methods, but ultimately should be based on the understanding of consumer preferences and needs. The result can be a competitive advantage that is essential to the overall marketing strategy.

With the growing number of ways to segment customers, targeting choices are also increasing. Generational marketing involves grouping consumers by age and socioeconomic factors. Cohort marketing looks at individuals with similar life experiences at different times in their history. Life-stage marketing considers those common events that individuals and families face regardless of age. Behaviors are another aspect, beyond age, that can provide valuable targeting options.

Behavioral targeting is a recent development that optimizes the online advertising potential for products and services. The ultimate idea is to increase interest in a particular product at a point when the consumer is actively shopping within the product category. Behavioral targeting works by placing a cookie, information that a Web site places on your computer to identify you at a later time, on a user's computer. The cookie then makes a note of the user's online behavior. An example would be a consumer searching a variety of automotive sites and then receiving an offer for vehicle insurance.

In some cases, products or services are developed before a market opportunity is sought. There is considerable risk with this scenario, particularly with technology companies.

EXAMPLE **TARGETING**

Iridium LLC, supported by Motorola, spent $5 billion to launch a system of satellites and to establish other infrastructure to support the development of a satellite telephone network in 1998. The global satellite telephone market proved unsustainable for Iridium and others in the late 1990s. Iridium filed for bankruptcy in 1999. While there was some demand for satellite telephones, the pricing structure, performance, and substitute products made companies such as Iridium not viable.[13]

PHOTO: Alistair Cotton/Shutterstock

>> END EXAMPLE

There are several specific targeting choices available, but there are essentially three market coverage choices when targeting: undifferentiated, differentiated, and niche marketing.

Undifferentiated Marketing

Building on the concept of mass marketing introduced at the beginning of this chapter, **undifferentiated marketing** is when a company treats the market as a whole, focusing on what is similar among the needs of customers, rather than on what is different. By using this strategy, companies create products or services to appeal to the greatest number of potential buyers. The benefit of an undifferentiated strategy is that it can be cost-effective because a limited portfolio results in reduced production, advertising, research, inventory, and shipping costs. This strategy is typically most successful when used in a market with limited or no competition or when the product or service has wide appeal and the market is rapidly growing. A wide range of organizations could be classified as having practiced undifferentiated marketing at some point in their history; examples include local libraries, public utilities, Coca-Cola, and Disney.

EXAMPLE **UNDIFFERENTIATED MARKETING**

PHOTO: Rob Wilson/Shutterstock

Henry Ford's early financial backers encouraged him to build cars for the rich to maximize his profits, just as the hundreds of other automotive start-ups were doing. Instead of taking this advice, Ford bought out his backers and embarked on a path that led to the launch of what Ford referred to as "the universal car." The Ford Model T was introduced in 1908 with the intention of being affordable for the general population. Over 15 million Model Ts were produced between 1908 and 1927. Ford practiced undifferentiated marketing that is best represented by his quote: "The customer can have any color he wants, so long as it's black." An excerpt from another quote acknowledges that he understood the market as well: "All Fords are exactly alike, but no two men are just alike. . . ." Ford was able to practice undifferentiated marketing because the automotive market was expanding rapidly and he had a unique selling proposition based on affordability, quality, and safety in the context of the time.[14]

>> END EXAMPLE

Differentiated Marketing

A firm practicing **differentiated marketing** separates and targets different market segments, with a unique product or service tailored to each segment. The result is a distinctive marketing plan for each segment. With a differentiated marketing strategy, companies can generally increase total sales because of broader appeal through greater relevance across market segments and a stronger position within each segment. Sometimes referred to as multi-segment marketing, the strategy not only increases sales potential, but it also increases costs associated with targeting different market segments with relevant messages. Still, if done effectively, there is the potential for greater loyalty, resulting in repeat purchases.

EXAMPLE **DIFFERENTIATED MARKETING**

Just a decade ago, many people could have argued that McDonald's practiced undifferentiated marketing. McDonald's had a standard product portfolio that consisted of foods such as hamburgers, french fries, chicken nuggets, and fish sandwiches and essentially targeted the mass market with a standard marketing mix strategy. In recent years, McDonald's has taken steps to make its brand relevant to increasingly fragmented consumer segments by expanding its offerings. Those now include items such as salads and yogurt parfaits. Simply thinking beyond the core product of a hamburger led McDonald's to realize that convenience and enjoyment were reasons that its customers frequented its stores. These points became the foundation for McDonald's marketing. Today, McDonald's targets a wide range of consumer segments, from diversity groups to young people to healthy people of all ages. A recent entry into the coffee market has targeted yet another segment of the population.[15]

PHOTO: Jim Lopes/Shutterstock

>> END EXAMPLE

Niche Marketing

The third market coverage strategy is known as the niche strategy. Also referred to as concentrated marketing, or focused marketing, **niche marketing** is serving a small but well-defined consumer segment. It is best suited for companies with limited resources, or companies with exclusive products. This approach allows companies to gain a strong position within their segments because they have a better understanding of consumer needs in those specific segments. The marketing plans for niche markets can be quite specialized.

EXAMPLE **NICHE MARKETING**

Movado Group, Inc., was founded in 1967 and designs, markets, and distributes jewelry and watches. The organization's portfolio includes popular watch brands such as Ebel, Concord, Movado, ESQ, Coach, HUGO BOSS, Juicy Couture, Tommy Hilfiger, and Lacoste. In 2007, Movado moved to retarget its premium offering, the almost 100-year-old Concord brand, to an even more upscale target. The Concord offering was reduced to a single line, the recently launched C1. The number of retail outlets was reduced significantly and average retail prices almost tripled to over $9,000. Concord's target was stated to be "hardcore watch aficionados and enthusiasts."[16]

PHOTO: Igor Grochev/Shutterstock

>> END EXAMPLE

Global Targeting

There are many different ways that brands can adopt a global strategy. These methods include the following:

- Standardizing core products or services with limited localization for all markets
- Creating value-added elements for selective markets
- Practicing specific competitive-based strategies for each market
- Implementing a universal targeting strategy and marketing mix.

Many luxury brands are practicing the strategy of targeting a group that exhibits similar characteristics across national boundaries. While this may be efficient, most brands are adopting some level of standardization with localization as necessary to reflect local conditions.

Selecting a Target

When choosing an appropriate market for a given product or service, three general factors should be considered:

- Attractiveness
- Size and growth potential
- Brand objectives and resources to form the basis for competition

The attractiveness of the segment is determined by the level of competition within the segment and the various strategies used by the brands competing in the segment. If many large competitors that practice differentiated marketing exist, it may be difficult for a smaller brand to stake out a particular market space. Alternatively, a small brand may have tremendous successes by entering an undifferentiated market with a specific point of differentiation.

The size and growth potential for the segment includes the variability and viability of the segment. A segment may be subjected to significant technology or legislative changes that might redefine opportunity in the near future. Brand objectives and resources represent the basis on which the company has to compete. There may be limited flexibility in the product portfolio, or there may be limited funding for advertising. Either reality might limit the potential for the brand to succeed, depending on the market being entered.

Positioning Explained

Positioning involves the development of marketing programs to meet the requirements of target customers.[17] Ultimately, positioning is how your target customers define you in relation to your competitors. Therefore, customer perceptions have much to do with a brand's positioning. The process to establish positioning, provided you are not already positioned precisely where you want, involves competing with all your competitors' marketing communications. Communication of a unique selling proposition (USP) can provide a good basis for successful positioning. A USP is an expression of the uniqueness of a brand in a succinct manner. It can be a commitment that others cannot match, or it can be some distinct aspect of your product or service.

There are three types of positioning:

- **Functional positioning** is based on the attributes of products or services and their corresponding benefits and is intended to communicate how customers can solve problems or fulfill needs. An example would be high quality.
- **Symbolic positioning** is based on characteristics of the brands that enhance the self-esteem of customers. An example would be the concept of physical appearance.
- **Experiential positioning** is based on characteristics of the brands that stimulate sensory or emotional connections with customers. An example would be the feeling of joy.

Positioning Applied

The **positioning** of a brand results in a value proposition being presented to the target market. The value proposition is the entire set of benefits upon which the brand is differentiated. Similar to the USP, the value proposition is also unique. However, unlike the USP, it is intended to be specifically relevant to the target. Although a product can be unique, such as being organic or made in the United States, the brand target for that product may not value those characteristics. That same product may be of exceptionally high quality, which may be a desired benefit that could be conveyed in a value proposition. Value can be created from many different positioning strategies. Positioning strategies can be based on specific product attributes, different ways the product or service can be used, different types of users, differences between the product and a competitor's product, and a comparison to other product classes.

positioning
The placement of a product or service offering in the minds of consumer targets.

Sometimes a position needs to evolve, based on customer response. Federal Express invented the concept of delivering packages overnight. A significant point of differentiation was identified to be that the company owned its own fleet of planes. However, customers and potential customers did not care if Federal Express owned its own planes. Once the company determined that the primary benefit was the overnight delivery the positioning was cemented, and the success of Federal Express has been well documented.

EXAMPLE **POSITIONING**

The Apple iPod, with over 200 million units sold, controls the leading position in the global digital music player industry. Launched by Apple Computers in 2001, the iPod has enjoyed success from building on the Apple brand and using the Apple computer as a digital hub for consumers. The idea of a digital hub is that consumers will purchase additional Apple products to connect to their Apple computer. Beyond iPod, iTunes, iPhone, and iPad, there is iLife, iWork, iWeb, and iPhoto, not to mention Apple TV (renamed from iTV). While the iPod basically performs the same functions as the many different brands of MP3 players, it separates itself from other brands by being used by many different influential celebrities, from presidents to rock stars, and by generally being considered "cool." Being positioned as cool and being associated with celebrities have made the product iconic in countries across the world. Just as being popular has helped the iPod increase sales, it is that ubiquity that could, potentially, cause at least some of its consumers to look for less common brands of MP3s to express their individuality. That is where the digital hub strategy is designed to keep adding new and relevant products to the overall Apple offering.[18]

PHOTO: Michael Ledray/ Shutterstock

>> END EXAMPLE

Positioning is also important in an online environment. Since Internet search engines such as Google, Bing, and AltaVista have become ubiquitous, it makes sense to optimize one's position in this important medium. **Search engine optimization,** the process of enhancing Web site traffic through either organic or compensated means, can be an effective marketing tool and can assist in the positioning of your product or service during the consumer shopping process. The critical element of effective search engine optimization is the selection of the keywords, which should be based on the positioning of the product or service.

Using a Perceptual Map

A **perceptual map** defines the market, based on consumer perceptions of attributes, or characteristics, of competing products. Also referred to as a positioning chart, a perceptual map visually represents consumer perceptions of a group of brands by evaluating category attributes such as price, quality, speed, fuel economy, and appearance. Bran ds can be positioned in the context of competing brands on a perceptual map. The perceptual map can identify important competitors and indicate if the current positioning needs to be changed.

EXAMPLE **PERCEPTUAL MAP**

A perceptual map for the relationship between *Consumer Reports'* overall road-test scores and fuel economy ratings for a select list of compact sedans is illustrated in Figure 15.2.

This particular perceptual map combines subjective consumer road-test ratings with established fuel-economy numbers. The map could also have been constructed with two subjective criteria, such as consumer road-test ratings and consumer appearance ratings. In this example, although the Hyundai Elantra has the highest road-test score, the Toyota Prius has a similar road-test score, but with much higher fuel economy. The Toyota Corolla and Honda Civic are clear competitors for those consumers who consider road-test scores and fuel economy as the primary factors in their purchase decisions. This perceptual map assumes that road-test scores and fuel-economy ratings are the only relevant attributes in selecting a vehicle. This is seldom the case. Status, appearance, and ride could all factor into an evaluation. Still, Prius is the leading hybrid vehicle sold in the United States, and Civic and Corolla are two of the leading models in overall sales.[19]

>> END EXAMPLE

FIGURE 15.2

A Perceptual Map

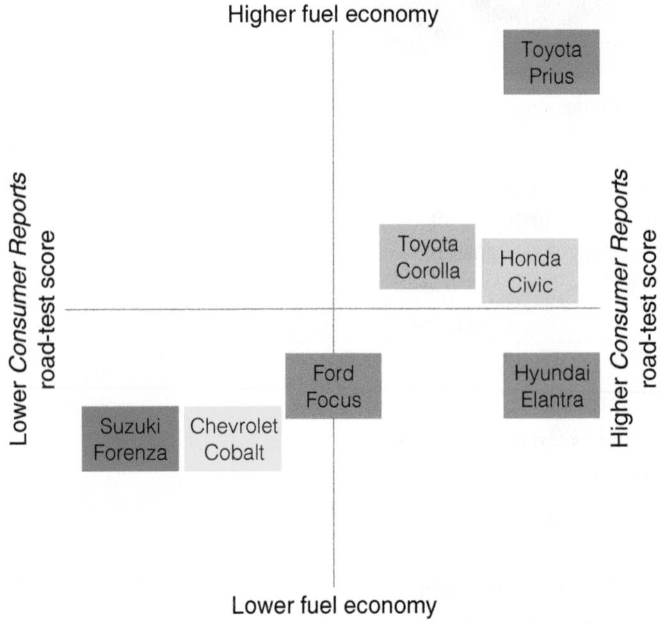

Selecting a Position

The selection of a position should reflect an understanding of the external marketing environment and the competitive advantage that can be created as a result of differentiation. It is necessary to understand how the brands, products, and services satisfy the needs of the target segment, as well as to switch costs for those target consumers who are using competitive products or services. Ultimately, the position selected should do the following:

- Deliver a valued benefit to the target
- Be distinctive with respect to competitors
- Offer a superior benefit that can easily be communicated
- Be difficult for others to copy
- Be affordable to the target
- Provide required revenues and profits to the brand

One way to communicate your position is through a brand position statement.

Developing a Brand Position Statement

The **brand position statement** is a summary of what your brand offers to the market. This statement is not seen by the public and is not the advertising tagline, although the tagline should support the brand position statement. The statement is a guide for marketing communication development and should be developed using the following form: To (consumer segment) our (brand) is (business concept) that (basis for differentiation).[20]

EXAMPLE **BRAND POSITION STATEMENT**

Focus: HOPE has been active as a Detroit-based community organization since 1967. Its brand position statement directed to potential donors is the following: To socially aware people and organizations who desire to financially support an organization dedicated to overcoming racism, poverty, and injustice, Focus: HOPE is the preeminent community-based organization that has a long history of addressing those issues through a holistic process by providing education and training for the disadvantaged, distributing packaged food to low-income seniors and young families, and revitalizing neighborhoods.[21]

PHOTO: Kuzma/Shutterstock

>> END EXAMPLE

Conclusion

The process of segmenting, targeting, and positioning builds on concepts of building a brand and a marketing philosophy. Without a strong brand to which consumers ascribe equity and a company philosophy that places a brand at the forefront of its business, no segmentation effort can be successful. Well-crafted segmentation can provide a company with the means to efficiently identify and target consumers with a value proposition that is differentiated from its competitors. The process of identifying and selecting segments can be expensive and time-consuming, but the rewards can be significant. Ultimately, segmentation advances the marketing goals and creates an organization that grows with its customers.

CHAPTER

16 Branding[1]

Branding Explained

Based on the Nordic word *brandr,* meaning to burn, brands began as a mark of possession that was applied to cattle.[2] Over time, brands have evolved not only to represent ownership, but also to stand for specific attributes that mean something to consumers.

brand
A promise to deliver specific benefits associated with products or services to consumers.

When the attributes that a **brand** possesses form a connection with consumers' desires, a perception of value is created. A brand is more than simply a name; it is a promise. This promise manifests itself in everything that consumers can sense about a brand. If the promise is continually kept, the brand's image is solidified by its reputation. A brand can be represented by a name or symbol and can be perceived positively, negatively, or ambiguously by consumers. This perception is influenced by both marketing communications and experiences with the brand.

Branding Applied

A brand differs considerably from a product or service as it exists in a consumer's mind. Consider the following:

- A product is something produced in a factory, while a brand is created through marketing communications and experience.
- A product can be duplicated by a competitor, while a brand is unique.
- A product can become outdated, while a successful brand is often timeless.
- A product is a generic term, while a brand has personality, characteristics, and associations.

The personality, characteristics, and associations of a brand can be thought of as layers. These layers provide richness to a brand that creates an emotional connection that is not typically generated from a product. The initial layer represents tangible features, while inner layers represent benefits, attitudes, and values. This richness can translate into many opportunities for brands, including the following:[3]

- Ability to command price premium
- Long-term financial strength
- Greater market share
- Higher perceived quality
- Greater supply and distribution chain advantage
- More brand extension opportunities to take an existing brand into a new category
- Greater purchase frequency

As consumers spend an increasing time online, the various mediums used to access online content are being targeted by brands. A **digital brand strategy** is a set of marketing activities that uses digital mediums to connect consumers to brands. A digital brand strategy is more than a Web site. Brand messages can be placed on many different digital devices including personal digital assistants (PDAs), mobile phones, and video games.

Coca-Cola is sold in more than 200 countries. Produced by the Coca-Cola Company, its traditional soft drink product is often referred to simply as Coke. Originally intended as a patent medicine when Dr. John Pemberton created the product in the nineteenth century, Coca-Cola was purchased eventually by businessman Asa Candler, whose marketing efforts led Coke to its leadership in the world soft drink market throughout the twentieth and now twenty-first centuries. Coke is so well known it can be recognized by a letter or two of typeface, or simply the color of the container itself. The Coke name may also convey certain meaning to you that increases value of, and interest in, the Coke product.

PHOTO: RLN/Shutterstock

Brands are also being developed in a multicultural environment. Multicultural brands are brands that are created and managed to be relevant to more than one cultural group. For example, Yankelovich's Multicultural Marketing Study identified that Hispanic and African American consumers were likely to "enjoy looking at or listening to" advertising at a rate almost double of their peers of other races.[4] The study also revealed that marketing was generally perceived as neither culturally nor personally relevant.[5] The challenge for brands is to establish relevancy without over-commercializing culture.

EXAMPLE **BRAND**

Kodak invented the digital camera in 1975. After challenging times in the mid-2000s, Kodak has looked to digital media to help resurrect the company. The famous "Kodak moment" is now shared with others through social media. Kodak sees value both in the product as well as the digital services that can be activated. Kodak created a Web site, kodakmoments.com, where images can be submitted to a contest. Kodak also built functionality into its products to access social media, including share buttons and tagging capability for Flickr, YouTube, Facebook, and e-mail. Kodak has built its brand around its photographic heritage but has made the brand more relevant to consumers through the use of a digital brand strategy.

PHOTO: Photocreo Michal Bednarek/Shutterstock

>> END EXAMPLE

Brand Equity Explained

brand equity
The power of a brand through creation of distinct image, to influence customer behavior.[6]

While brands are different from products and services, they definitely influence the perceived value of a company's products or services. This influence, or equity, can either enhance or diminish a company's position in the marketplace. **Brand equity** reflects the value consumers attach to the promise of the brand and evolves from the layers of the brand. Brand equity extends beyond products and services to include social movements, political parties, not-for-profit organizations, and individuals such as political candidates and other celebrities.

Branding expert Kevin Keller defines brand equity as "the differential effect of brand knowledge on consumer response to the brand's marketing activities. **Brand knowledge** is the set of associations that consumers hold in memory regarding the brand's features, benefits, users, perceived quality, and overall attitude as a result of prior brand marketing activities."[7] Effective marketing programs should apply Keller's brand equity definition to link desired images, perceptions, opinions, and feelings to their respective brands.[8]

Brand Equity Applied

Brand equity can provide a sustainable competitive advantage that can be capitalized on in both good and bad times.[9] Given a competitive industry, a strong brand has the potential to sustain a price war, which is when businesses cut prices to take sales from competitors. Price wars often occur in the airline industry and better-known brands often use aggressive pricing against start-up airlines. Essentially, the brand premium that exists for a strong brand provides a differential position among consumers that lesser-established brands cannot match. The lesser brands generally become identified by the lower price. The stronger brand can trade off its premium tactically by reducing its price, but not to the level of competitors, or it can reinforce the quality of its product and attempt to stabilize the price war. Alternatively, growth opportunities can be capitalized on by a strong brand identity that attracts a large number of brand-loyal consumers. The situation facilitates less elastic demand that resists price changes and can translate into increased profits. Well-established supermarket brands are regularly faced with promotions by lesser-known brands and often use their equity to resist competitive discounting.

Although many companies acknowledge the financial potential of their brands, there is often a lack of understanding of many potential applications of brand equity. These applications include the following:[10]

- Brand alliances with other companies to expand marketing opportunities
- **Channel switching,** creating new product distribution or moving the distribution flow of products from one distribution channel to another, to project equity from one channel to another (A **channel** is a system with few or many steps in which products and services flow from businesses to consumers while payment flows from consumers to businesses.)
- Relationship building to connect faster and closer to customers and distribution partners

- **Brand stretching,** extending a brand to new products, services, or markets, to spread brand building costs across a larger base of activities provided there is a fundamental fit with consumers' perceptions of the brand
- **Outsourcing,** procuring certain services from a third-party supplier, to lower costs and focus resources on core competencies

Brand Valuation

Discussion of the practical importance of branding and brand equity leads us to consider the methods that consumers and businesses use to ascribe value to brands. Brand valuation is the process of quantifying the financial benefit that results from owning a brand. This process is important as companies try to understand what drives value in their business.

The history of modern brand valuation began in the mid-1980s when Interbrand began conducting a brand valuation for a United Kingdom business.[11] Interbrand continues to be involved with the brand valuation industry, including joining with *BusinessWeek* to publish a yearly ranking of the best global brands (see Table 16.1). Eight of the top-ranked global brands are U.S. owned.

Brand valuation has become increasingly important as certain countries require intangible items such as brand value to be included on a business balance sheet. There are two primary methods of brand valuation: additive and inclusive. The former, and more common application, refers to the idea that product and brand are separate, while the latter considers them to be one.[13] The problem with separation can be demonstrated by asking the questions "Can Coke be valued as a soda without the brand?" and "How many Jaguars would be sold without the brand versus with the brand?" An inclusive approach to brand valuation combines the brand with associated product attributes to determine true value. Product attributes can be translated into potential sales revenue in the inclusive approach.

TABLE 16.1
***BUSINESSWEEKS*/INTERBRAND'S ANNUAL RANKING OF THE BEST GLOBAL BRANDS FOR 2009[12]**

RANK	COMPANY	2009 BRAND VALUE $MILLIONS	PERCENT CHANGE (OVER 2008)	COUNTRY OF OWNERSHIP
1	Coca-Cola	68,734	3%	U.S
2	IBM	60,211	2%	U.S.
3	Microsoft	56,647	–4%	U.S.
4	GE	47,777	–10%	U.S.
5	Nokia	34,864	–3%	Finland
6	McDonald's	32,275	4%	U.S.
7	Google	31,980	25%	U.S.
8	Toyota	31,330	–8%	Japan
9	Intel	30,636	–2%	U.S.
10	Disney	28,447	–3%	U.S.

Building Brand Equity

The process of creating or enhancing brand equity involves understanding the value of the brand as well as those factors that can create a positive brand image. These factors include loyalty, commitment, and customer equity.

LOYALTY The equity ascribed to a brand is reflected behaviorally through loyalty. There are two components of brand loyalty: purchase loyalty and attitudinal loyalty. Attitudinal loyalty leads to a higher relative price while purchase loyalty leads to greater market share. These factors combine to influence brand profitability.[14]

COMMITMENT The psychological attachment that a consumer has to a brand will be a function of how relevant it is to that consumer, that is, does it touch on things that are truly important to him or her. Brand relationships can be placed in a continuum of very committed users to uninterested nonusers.

CUSTOMER EQUITY Brand equity is also created from consumer knowledge that is translated into consumer behavior.[15] Customer-based brand equity is defined as the differential effect that brand knowledge has on the customer response to marketing efforts.[16] This concept is based on the idea that brand equity extends from what consumers have learned, heard, felt, and seen about a brand through their cumulative experiences. If this brand equity resides in the consumer's mind, managing and influencing experiences are critical.

EXAMPLE **BRAND EQUITY**

PHOTO: Ken Inness/Shutterstock

Victoria's Secret, a leading specialty retailer of intimate apparel with over 1,000 stores across the United States, launched the Pink brand in 2004 to target a younger audience of high school and college students. The Pink brand targeted a new audience for Victoria's Secret and has grown to become the leading loungewear brand in the world. The Pink brand is actively promoted across college campuses through its Pink Collegiate Collection, and through relationships with MTV; a co-branded merchandise arrangement with Major League Baseball; and on social media sites such as Facebook (with over 1.25 million fans for its VSPink page), MySpace, and other blogs that are frequented by its target consumers. Victoria's Secret is using the Pink brand to build loyalty that extends into the Victoria's Secret brand as girls grow older.[17]

>> END EXAMPLE

Global Brand Equity

The concepts of loyalty, commitment, and customer equity and their contribution to building brand equity gain increased complexity when considered in a global context. Global brand equity is influenced by elements of the traditional marketing mix as well as additional issues such as geography, culture, legal and business environments, and political and economic realities. Four central ideas influence strategies to create global brand equity:[18]

- Identifying emerging global customers
- Building stronger links between country-specific marketing activities that support a global infrastructure
- Realizing opportunities to transfer products, brands, and ideas throughout various countries
- Gaining economies of scale by sharing human and financial resources in creating and managing brands

---

EXAMPLE **BRAND EQUITY**

IKEA, a Swedish furniture company, has cultivated unique global brand equity through its contemporary designs, creative promotions, and affordable pricing strategies. IKEA has grown steadily to over 220 stores in Europe, Asia, Australia, and North America by focusing on its consumers' lifestyles. The formula of quality, affordable contemporary furniture seems to reach across borders. IKEA endeavors to design and sell products that are aesthetically pleasing yet inexpensive and functional. Founded in 1943, the brand has not always fared well entering new markets. An entry into the United States in the early 1990s was met with challenges, including beds that were measured only in centimeters, sofas that were not deep enough, kitchens that did not accommodate U.S.-sized appliances, and curtains that were too short.[19]

PHOTO: Alexey Kashin/Shutterstock

>> END EXAMPLE

Business-to-Business Brand Equity

Brands are as important in the business-to-business (B2B) environment as they are in the business-to-consumer (B2C) environment. As has been discussed in previous chapters, the purchase process is more formal in the B2B markets than in the B2C markets. However, the question remains as to how certain brands are selected for inclusion in the sourcing process. That decision is often based on the unique requirements of the contract, past experiences with brands in the appropriate category, and the established brand equity of potential brands. Successful brands like Cisco, Intel, and Akamai have all established clear B2B positions and have translated those positions into financial success. Businesses selling to other businesses tend to present their products and services while discussing more rational elements, such as product characteristics, than do B2C brands, but they also focus on both economic value and emotional benefits.

Building Strong Brands Explained

Is there an innate purpose for brands? If there were such a reason, then companies could create demand for their brands by appropriately managing their image. It is possible that consumers are in need of brands as much as companies are in need of them. The clutter of products in the marketplace and the extensive choices available could drive consumers to look for reassurance in brands with which they have positive associations.[20]

strong brand
Occupies a distinct position in consumers' minds based on relevant benefits and creates an emotional connection between business and consumers.

Strong brands provide three things to consumers: They save time during the shopping process, they project the right message, and they provide an identity.[21] Consumers have established perspectives on known brands and, unless a unique new product or service has entered the market or there has been a large price adjustment or drastic change in the market, it is easy to repurchase a brand that has previously been selected and performed as expected. A brand can be used to project security, convenience, quality, or something else to consumers that can reinforce the ability of a product or service to meet consumer needs. The brand provides consumers with the ability to project style and preferences to others through the choices made.

The large numbers of brands that have stood the test of time demonstrate the value of brands. Over 60% of the best-known brands in the United States are 50 years old or older.[22]

The power of a long-lasting brand can often resist but not necessarily prevent decline if not properly supported. Research that tracks consumer memorability of brands often identifies a latent memory of a brand's advertising even if it has not advertised for months or even years. Still, it is possible for a brand to be damaged beyond repair, such as the failed former energy giant Enron. Enron grew through the 1990s to a $70 billion company by operating gas lines and power plants as well as engaging in trading businesses for a variety of commodities. In 2001, it was revealed that Enron had misstated its income and that its value was billions less than its balance sheet claimed. Enron claimed bankruptcy and ultimately went out of business.[23]

Apparently, brands are just as important to CEOs as to consumers. A Marsh Inc. and Oxford University study conducted in 2000, based on input from senior business executives, revealed that 85% considered brands to be their company's most important asset. Brand management expert Leslie de Chernatony has identified three essential elements of a powerful brand:

- The values that will characterize the brand
- The purpose for the brand other than making money—the brand's reason for being
- The future environment that the brand aims to facilitate
- A business with a powerful brand understands what its brand should stand for, what it does stand for, and what it can stand for in the future

Building Strong Brands Applied

How can a company capitalize on its brand and achieve a leading market position? This can be achieved, arguably, through a strong business model with desirable products and services of appropriate quality and a strong financial position, as well as strong brands. Strong brands can be built by considering the competitive category, level, and type of competitors; ability to differentiate; relevance to consumers; management acumen; corporate strategy; and corporate assets.[24] The nature of the category dictates the success criteria for competing businesses including consumer desires. The existing competitive environment, whether filled with many or few competitors, also influences the creation of strong brands. The basis for a brand to differentiate from competitors through elements such as patents, expensive or unique production equipment, or weaker elements can assist in creating strong brands. The relevancy of the brand to consumers, often presented using advertising and the characteristics of the product or service, also influences the strength of the brand. Business capabilities such as having capable management, having a clear vision, and possessing financial and human assets are additional factors that influence the creation of a strong brand.

Brand Positioning

The creation of a strong brand involves several different steps that collectively answer the question "What should my brand stand for?" The first step involves placing the brand in a distinct position in consumers' minds. **Brand positioning,** the location that a brand occupies in the marketplace relative to competitors, can be achieved on a hierarchy of three levels (see Figure 16.1).[25]

Attributes (either product or service) are the most basic levels of positioning and include smells, tastes, textures, and ingredients. Competitors can usually copy attribute positioning unless there is some type of intellectual property involved. The motivation for purchasing such products is typically what the attribute offers to the consumer instead of the brand itself.

The second level of positioning is benefit positioning, which involves focusing on the benefits that the attributes provide. Security, quality, performance, convenience, and value are all examples of benefits that products and services can provide. The benefits can also be communicated as a problem/solution position.

The third level is value positioning, which involves creating an emotional connection between the brand and consumer. Unlike beliefs and attitudes, values are the least likely to change. This type of positioning can appeal to aspirations as well. Each level creates value but the value positioning can create a relationship that engenders brand loyalty, commitment, and strong consumer equity.

FIGURE 16.1

Positioning Levels

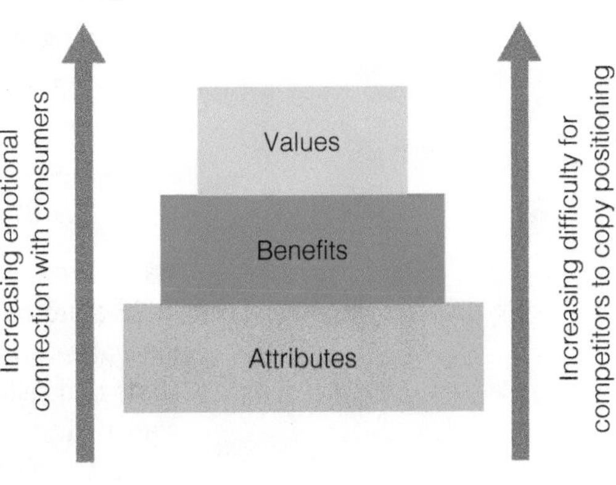

Brand positioning is also strengthened if the positioning reflects the personality of the brand. **Brand personality** consists of characteristics that make a brand unique, much like human personality. Brand personalities vary widely, including rugged, sexy, and sophisticated.

Brand Name Selection

The right brand name can provide a tremendous advantage for the product or service. The brand name should fit with the attributes and benefits of the product or service and be relevant to the target consumers. Some important guidelines for brand name selection include the following:

- Use the name to distinguish as well as describe the product or service.
- Select a name that is memorable and distinctive yet appropriate for the category.
- Avoid limiting business opportunities to a particular market segment with a name that cannot be extended into new segments.
- Choose a name that is exportable to international markets.
- Ensure the name can be protected as intellectual property.

In many cases, a company is faced with a decision to create a new brand name for a new product or service or to add the product to an existing portfolio. This is a question regarding the company's brand architecture. **Brand architecture** involves the naming and organizing of brands within a broader portfolio. Sometimes these decisions are so critical that companies need to be hired to assist with naming research.

Brand Sponsorship

A product or service can be launched in two basic forms: manufacturer (national) brand and private label (retailer, reseller) brand. While the manufacturer, retailer, or reseller typically develops its own brand, some brands are licensed from other companies and others are co-branded with other brands. There are strategic advantages and disadvantages to each form and the most appropriate form must be carefully selected.

COMPARING MANUFACTURER BRANDS TO PRIVATE LABEL BRANDS

Manufacturer brands, which are owned by a manufacturer as opposed to a retailer or reseller, have traditionally dominated the brand choices available to consumers at retail stores. However, **private label** brands created by either a retailer or reseller have increasingly appeared in the retail environment. Private label brands have almost completely absorbed the "generic" or non-branded products of the 1980s and 1990s by realizing that branding can provide incremental profitability that non-branded products cannot. It is difficult to attach a brand promise to an unbranded product. This growth of private brands has expanded to small and midsize retailers primarily due to the profitability of these private label brands. Since retailers control more customer contact than manufacturers, they have the opportunity to realize the increased profit potential of private label products. Considerable effort goes into creating private brand products, from identifying and selecting a product to negotiating with the supplier and assessing and approving the product's level of safety and performance characteristics.

EXAMPLE **BRAND SPONSORSHIP**

Trader Joe's, established in 1958, has grown to 280 stores in 23 states. The company's strategy has included offering innovative, hard-to-find food with employees wearing Hawaiian shirts and selling in an environment that feels like a local market. The company also brands over 80% of its offerings as private label products, which allows development of the Trader Joe's brand as opposed to supplier brands and allows better control of advertising and promotion costs associated

PHOTO: Shutterstock

with the Trader Joe's brand. Trader Joe's private label strategy is part of the company's brand character. The net result is a loyal brand following translating into significant financial success. Interestingly enough, Trader Joe's has achieved its success without having to invest in traditional advertising. The company's only promotional effort is its newsprint circular.[26]

>> END EXAMPLE

LICENSING An alternative to the significant expense of creating and developing a brand is licensing. Licensing involves assigning rights, generally for a fee, for one company to use another company's brand for specific products and for a specific period. An existing brand can be used to provide brand equity and enhance the chances for the new product to be more rapidly accepted by consumers. The primary motivator for choosing which particular brand to license, beyond affordability, is the stature of the brand (including awareness, familiarity, and opinion) and the consistency and relevancy of the image to the company's target consumers and category. Typical types of properties that are licensed include characters, corporate trademarks and brands, fashion, sports, and art.

EXAMPLE **LICENSING**

Southern Comfort, a whiskey manufacturer, licensed its brand to Kemps Ice Cream, which created two products: Southern Comfort eggnog flavored ice cream and Southern Comfort vanilla spice flavored ice cream. Southern Comfort eggnog and Southern Comfort gourmet coffees are also in the marketplace. The benefit to the licensees is the unique brand flavor and brand equity. The Southern Comfort brand, founded in 1874, has also expanded to nonfood product categories including apparel.[27]

PHOTO: Ljupco Smokovski/ Shutterstock

>> END EXAMPLE

CO-BRANDING Co-branding involves the collaboration of multiple brands in the marketing of one specific product. The idea is that the attributes of each brand can be blended and loyalty from the separate brands may extend to the co-branded product. Any shortcomings of one brand may also be mitigated by positive equity from the other brand. These types of arrangements are seen in market sectors including automotive, fashion, hotels, financial service, and food products. A co-branding strategy can work for different reasons including generating marketplace exposure, positioning against private label brands, and sharing promotion costs with a partner. Many co-branding efforts are based on brand alliances. A brand alliance is a relationship, short of a merger, that is formed by two or more businesses to create market opportunities that would not have existed without the alliance. A brand alliance is one form of a brand extension.

EXAMPLE **CO-BRANDING**

Ford Motor Company and Eddie Bauer, a popular American sportswear company founded in 1920, have been involved in a co-branding relationship since 1983 with the Eddie Bauer edition vehicles offered by Ford. The 1984 Ford Bronco II was the first model to feature the Eddie Bauer premium trim package that was designed to reflect Eddie Bauer's brand character of unpretentious style and rugged capability. Other

PHOTO: Krivosheev Vitaly/ Shutterstock

Ford models have subsequently offered the Eddie Bauer trim level, including the Aerostar minivan, F-Series truck, and Explorer, Expedition, and Excursion sport utility vehicles. Eddie Bauer edition vehicles offer unique paint schemes, special wheels, custom seats, and a variety of special interior and exterior features. Ford sells the vehicles through its dealer network while Eddie Bauer features the vehicles in its catalogs, promotional brochures, store displays, and on its Web site.[28]

>> END EXAMPLE

Brand Development

Brand equity can be developed and maximized not only for a single brand but also for a portfolio of brands. When a company has multiple brands, the decisions on the correct combination of brand names and attributes across the entire portfolio is part of a comprehensive brand strategy. **Brand strategy** is the process where "the offer is positioned in the consumer's mind to produce a perception of advantage."[29] The brand strategy defines the brand architecture that is used for brand development. The development of brands involves several different strategic options: line extensions, brand extensions, multi-brand offerings, and entirely new brands.

LINE EXTENSIONS A **line extension** is an addition to an existing product line that retains the currently utilized brand name. Companies often use line extensions because they believe such use will keep customers from switching brands and allow firms to retain or increase their margins.

There are two primary methods to extend product lines: horizontal and vertical. The product attributes selected to distinguish the products will determine which method is being used. A vertical line extension involves varying the product line by price and quality. A horizontal line extension maintains products within a similar price and quality level but varies other attributes such as flavor or smell. Line extensions can provide new opportunities to reach different consumers but can also expose a brand to new levels of competition. Growth needs must be matched with any increased risks.

PHOTO: Judy Kennamer/Shutterstock

EXAMPLE **LINE EXTENSIONS**

Crayola, known for its crayons that made their initial debut in 1903, has a variety of products including clay, paints, markers, and coloring books for children. Silly Putty is also a Crayola brand offering. Crayola practices vertical line extension with its portfolio products marketed to adults and artists with an upscale version of its drawing pencils, oil pastels, colored pencils, acrylic paints, and watercolors. The use of a vertical line extension allows Crayola to present products to different market segments and to market different product characteristics and benefits while still building the overall Crayola brand.[30]

>> END EXAMPLE

Bundling is a way to present the portfolio to customers without necessarily adding to the product lines. Bundling refers to the "practice of marketing two or more products and/or services in a single 'package.'"[31] The principle behind bundling is that a bundled offering is perceived by customers to offer more value than the individual components of the bundle sold separately.

BRAND EXTENSIONS A **brand extension** involves taking an existing brand into a new category. This practice can save marketing investment in a new brand and could build additional brand stature. The risks include losing focus of the core attributes and positioning of the brand and failing in the new category, which could damage perceptions of the brand. The greatest chance for success is if the brand is well positioned with consumers based on an emotional connection. Without an emotional connection, the brand can risk being overextended. Known for disposable razors, pens, and lighters, BIC attempted to extend its brand into women's underwear rather unsuccessfully.[32]

EXAMPLE **BRAND EXTENSIONS**

Entertainment and media giant Disney has extended its venerable brand with significant financial success. Disney has traditionally been involved in theme parks, television, and merchandising and recently has expanded into many different market segments. Disney uses its brand to enhance its relationships with its loyal customers by offering brand extensions such as Disney Vacation Club, Disney Cruise Line, and Radio Disney Network.[33]

PHOTO: Travelshots.com/Alamy Images

>> END EXAMPLE

MULTIBRANDS Some companies elect to launch several brands in the same category to appeal to the varying wants of the consumers and to take advantage of business conditions. In a fragmented market, a company may elect to compete with itself with the reasoning that owning 5 out of 14 brands will result in greater aggregate market share than owning 1 out of 10. Having individual brand names, while potentially expensive to develop, offers considerable flexibility in positioning different product attributes. **Cannibalization** is one particular problem associated with a multi-brand approach. Cannibalization is the loss of sales of an existing product within a portfolio to a new product in the same portfolio. However, the risks of competing with oneself can be acceptable if there is a net overall gain. Many consumer product companies launch new products knowing that some sales will be cannibalized.

NEW BRANDS A company can elect to create an entirely new brand because of an existing brand suffering from poor equity or because an existing brand does not extend well into a new category. New brands can offer a clean slate for positioning but require considerable financial investment to develop. Sometimes a new brand can be created based on the experience and positioning of another brand in the company's portfolio and positioned into a unique market niche.

EXAMPLE **NEW BRANDS**

PHOTO: Supri Suharjoto/Shutterstock

In some market conditions, such as intense competition with clearly defined market segments, a new brand, often called a **flanker brand**, is created to expand an organization's portfolio into a new segment of an existing market category while retaining relevance with current customers. The idea is that the new brand will increase overall sales in a particular category by targeting consumers who are not currently purchasing products or services from a particular organization. In some cases, a brand currently owned by a parent organization is relaunched to compete as a flanker brand. Sprint Nextel Corporation, one of the largest telecommunications companies in the United States, relaunched Boost Mobile, a wholly owned subsidiary brand that was mainly a regional business in the United States until 2006 when it became known nationally for its unlimited talk plan, as an unlimited talk time prepaid product. A flanker brand for Sprint Nextel in the expanding prepaid phone market, Boost Mobile offered unlimited calling, texting, and Web access for $50 at its 2009 relaunch. The new position for Boost directly competed with prepaid brands MetroPCS Communications Inc. and Leap Wireless International Inc. and put pressure on other large mobile phone companies such as AT&T and Verizon that did not have similar offers to the Boost Mobile product.[34]

>> END EXAMPLE

Conclusion

The process of creating, cultivating, and strategically managing brands builds on concepts of value creation, consumer decision-making, and consumer insights. Strong brands provide a consumer with relevant and desired benefits and possess a distinct position in the consumer mind. Ultimately, brands form a connection between companies and consumers that, if properly nurtured, can provide the means to realize the financial potential of the company.

CHAPTER 17

Communication[1]

The importance of effective communication cannot be overemphasized for one specific reason: Everything we do involves communicating. Not some things but everything! Organizations can't formulate strategy or make decisions without communicating information. Once a decision is made, communication must again take place to ensure all parties involved are aware of the decision and actions to take. The best idea, the most creative suggestion, or the finest plan cannot be effectively developed or implemented without communication. Note that good communication skills alone do not make a manager or any person successful. However, ineffective communication skills will lead to a continuous stream of problems for any person or manager.

How Does the Communication Process Work?

Communication can be thought of as a process or flow. Communication problems occur when deviations or blockages disrupt that flow. Before communication can take place, a purpose, expressed as a message to be conveyed, is needed. It passes between a source (the sender) and a receiver. The message is encoded (converted to symbolic form) and is passed by way of some medium (channel) to the receiver, who retranslates (decodes) the message initiated by the sender. The result is **communication,** which is a transfer of understanding and meaning from one person to another.[2]

communication
A transfer of understanding and meaning from one person to another.

Asako Hoskino, corporate vice president of Japan's Nissan Motor Company, chooses to use oral communication by holding a meeting in her Tokyo office with company managers and executives. For Hoshino, communicating verbally gives her and her coworkers the opportunity to share information, discuss what they hear, and ask questions and receive answers to ensure that what is said has been received and understood. In addition to a built-in feedback mechanism, oral communication has the advantage of conveying more information in less time than written communication.

FIGURE 17.1

The Communication Process

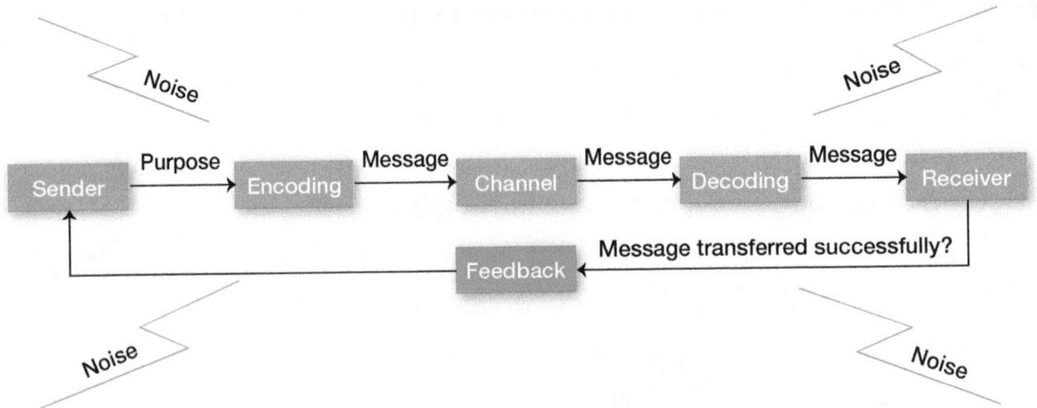

communication process
The seven-part process of transferring and understanding of meaning.

encoding
Converting a message into symbolic form of words, pictures, sounds, designs, etc.

Figure 17.1 depicts the **communication process.** This model has seven parts: (1) the communication source or sender, (2) encoding, (3) the message, (4) the channel, (5) decoding, (6) the receiver, and (7) feedback.

The sender initiates a message by **encoding** a thought. Four conditions affect the encoded message: skill, attitudes, knowledge, and the social cultural system. Our message in our communication to you in this book depends on our writing *skills,* if we don't have the requisite writing skills, our message will not reach you in the form designed. Keep in mind that a person's total communication success includes speaking, reading, listening, and reasoning skills as well.

Our attitudes influence our behavior. We hold predisposed ideas on numerous topics, and our communications are affected by those *attitudes.* Furthermore, we're restricted in our communicative activity by the extent of our *knowledge* of the particular topic. We can't communicate what we don't know, and should our knowledge be too extensive, it's possible that our receiver will not understand our message. Clearly, the amount of knowledge the source holds about his or her subject will affect the message he or she seeks to transfer and the receiver's ability to properly decode the message. Finally, just as attitudes influence our behavior, so does our position in the *social cultural system* in which we exist. Your beliefs and values, all part of your culture, act to influence you as a communicative sender and receiver.

The **message** is the actual product emanating from the sender that conveys some information. When we speak, the words we use influence the message. When we write, the style of writing affects the message. The environment, the context, in which we deliver a message affects its decoding (understanding) by the receiver. When we gesture, the movements of our arms, the expressions on our faces become a part of the message.[3] Our message is affected by the group of symbols we employ to transfer meaning, the content of the message itself, and the decisions that we make in selecting and arranging both content and context.[4]

message
A communication in writing, in speech, or by signals

The **channel** is the medium through which the message travels. It's selected by the sender, who must determine whether to use a formal or an informal channel. Formal channels are established by the organization and transmit messages that pertain to the job-related activities of members. They traditionally follow the authority network within the organization. Other forms of messages, such as personal or social, follow the informal channels in the organization.

channel
The medium by which a message travels.

The receiver is the person to whom the message is directed. However, before the message can be effectively received, the symbols in it must be translated and understood by the receiver, which is the **decoding** of the message. Just as the encoder was limited by his or her skills, attitudes, knowledge, and social cultural system, the receiver is equally restricted. A person's knowledge, attitudes, and cultural background influence his or her ability to receive, just as they do the ability to send.

decoding
Translating a received message.

The final link in the communication process is a feedback loop. **Feedback** is the check on how successful we have been in transferring the meaning of our messages as originally intended. Feedback identifies whether understanding has been achieved. Given the cultural diversity that exists in our workforce today, the importance of effective feedback to ensure proper communications cannot be overstated.[5]

feedback
Checking to see how successfully a message has been understood.

Written versus Verbal Communications

Written communications include memos, letters, email, and other forms of digital communication. A value of written communication is that it is tangible, verifiable, and more permanent than the oral variety. Typically, both sender and receiver have a record of the communication. Most written messages can be stored for an indefinite period of time or converted to digital versions. If questions arise about the content of the message, it's physically available for later reference. This feature is particularly important for complex or lengthy communications. For example, the marketing plan for a new product is likely to contain a number of tasks spread out over several months. By putting it in writing, those who have to carry out the plan can readily refer to the document over the life of the plan.

Another benefit or written communication comes from the process itself. Generally, more care is taken with the written word than with the spoken word. Having to put something in writing forces a person to think more carefully about what he or she wants to convey. Therefore, written communications are more likely to be well thought out, logical, and clear.

Of course, written messages have their drawbacks. Writing may be more precise, but it generally consumes more time than oral communication. A student could convey far more information to their college instructor in a one-hour oral exam than in a one-hour written exam. In fact, they could probably say in 10 to 15 minutes what it takes an hour to write.

The other major disadvantage of written communication is timely feedback or, rather, lack of it. Oral communications allow receivers to respond rapidly to what they think they hear. However, written communications, even text and e-mail, don't have a built-in feedback mechanism. Sending a memo or e-mail is no assurance that it will be received and, if it is received, no guarantee that the recipient will interpret it as the sender meant. The latter point is also relevant in oral communications, but it's easier in oral communication cases merely to ask the receiver to summarize what you have said. An accurate summary presents feedback evidence that the message has been received and understood.

Is the Grapevine an Effective Way to Communicate?

The **grapevine** is the unofficial way that communications take place in an organization. It's neither authorized nor supported by the organization. Rather, information is spread by word of mouth—and even through electronic means. Ironically, good information passes among us rapidly, but bad information travels even faster.[6] The grapevine gets information out to organizational members as quickly as possible.

How Do Nonverbal Cues Affect Communication?

Some of the most meaningful communications are neither spoken nor written. They are nonverbal communications. A loud siren or a red light at an intersection tells you something without words. A college instructor doesn't need words to know that students are not paying attention; their eyes get glassy or they begin to text or open their computers during class (but not our class!). Similarly, when papers start to rustle and notebooks begin to close, the message is clear: Class time is about over. The size of a person's office and desk or the clothes he or she wears also convey messages to others. However, the best-known areas of nonverbal communication are body language and verbal intonations.

body language
Nonverbal communication cues such as facial expressions, gestures, and other body movements.

Body language refers to gestures, facial configurations, and other movements of the body.[7] A frown, for example, says something different from a smile. Hand motions, facial expressions, and other gestures communicate emotions or temperaments such as happiness, aggression, fear, shyness, arrogance, and confusion.[8]

verbal intonation
An emphasis given to words or phrases that conveys meaning.

Verbal Intonation refers to the emphasis someone gives to words or phrases. To illustrate how intonations can change the meaning of a message, consider the student who asks the instructor a question during class. The instructor replies, "What do you mean by that?" The student's reaction will vary, depending on the tone of the instructor's response. A soft, smooth tone creates a different meaning from one that is abrasive or sarcastic with a strong emphasis on the last word. Most of us would view the first intonation as coming from someone who sincerely sought clarification, whereas the second suggests that the person is aggressive or defensive. The adage, "it's not what you say but how you say it," is something to remember when we communicate.

The fact that every oral communication also has a nonverbal message cannot be overemphasized.[9] It is often the nonverbal component that is likely to carry the greater influence on the decoding of the message. Research indicates that between 65 and 90 percent of the decoding of every face-to-face conversation is interpreted through body language. Without complete agreement between the spoken words and the body language that accompanies it, receivers are more likely to react to body language as the "true meaning."[10]

Barriers That Keep Communication from Being Effective

A number of interpersonal and intrapersonal barriers affect why the message decoded by a receiver is often different from what the sender intended. We summarize the more prominent barriers to effective communication in Figure 17.2 and briefly describe them here.

FILTERING refers to the way that a sender manipulates information so that it will be seen more favorably by the receiver. For example, when a person tells their boss or instructor what he feels that person wants to hear, they are filtering information. Does filtering happen much in organizations? Sure it does. As information is passed up or through the channels it becomes condensed and synthesized. Those doing the condensing filter communications through their own personal interests and perceptions of what's important.

filtering
Deliberately manipulating information to make it appear more favorable or acceptable to the receiver.

The extent of filtering tends to be the function of the organization's culture and perhaps the number of vertical levels in the organization. More vertical levels in an organization provide more opportunities for filtering (think of the children's' game of "Whisper

FIGURE 17.2

Barriers to Effective Communication

BARRIER	DESCRIPTION
Filtering	The deliberate manipulation of information to make it appear more favorable to the receiver.
Selective Perception	Receiving communications on the basis of what one selectively sees and hears depending on his or her needs, motivation, experience, background, and other personal characteristics.
Information Overload	When the amount of information one has to work with exceeds one's processing capacity.
Emotions	How the receiver feels when a message is received.
Language	Words have different meanings to different people. Receivers will use their definition of words being communicated.
Gender	How males and females react to communication may be different, and they each have a different communication style.
National Culture	Communication differences arising from the different languages that individuals use to communicate and the national culture of which they are a part.

down the lane"). An organizational culture encourages or discourages filtering by the type of behavior it rewards. The more that organizational rewards emphasize style and appearance over the content and logic/rationale, the more people will be motivated to filter communications in their favor.

selective perception
Selectively perceiving or hearing a communication based on your own needs, motivations, experiences, or other personal characteristics.

SELECTIVE PERCEPTION AFFECTS COMMUNICATION We've mentioned selective perception before in this book (see "Individual Behavior). We discuss it again here because the receivers in the communication process selectively see and hear based on their needs, motivations, experience, background, and other personal characteristics. Think of selective perception as the receiver's side of the "Filtering" coin. Receivers also project their interests and expectations into communications as they decode them. For example: The employment interviewer who believes a female job applicant will put their family ahead of their career is likely to see that tendency in all female applicants, regardless of whether the applicants would do so or not.

INFORMATION OVERLOAD AFFECTS COMMUNICATION Individuals have a finite capacity for processing data. For instance, consider the manager of Nordstroms who at the end of a busy day finds that she still has more than 100 emails providing her with information and/or waiting for her responses. It's not possible to fully read and respond to each one of those messages without facing **information overload.**

information overload
What results when information exceeds processing capacity.

In today's environment there are frequent complaints of information overload.[11] The demands on business persons of keeping up with email, phone calls, faxes, texts, tweets, meetings, and professional reading create an onslaught of data that is nearly impossible to process and assimilate. What happens when you have more information than you can sort out and use? You're likely to select out, ignore, pass over, or forget information. Or you may put off further processing until the overload situation is over. In any case, the result is lost information and less effective communication.

EMOTIONS AFFECT COMMUNICATION How a receiver feels when a message is received influences how he or she interprets it. You'll often interpret the same message differently, depending on whether you're happy or distressed. Extreme emotions are most likely to hinder effective communications. In such instances, we often disregard our rational and objective thinking processes and substitute emotional judgments. It's best to avoid reacting to a message when you're upset because you're not likely to be thinking clearly.

LANGUAGE AFFECTS COMMUNICATON Words mean different things to different people. Age, education, and cultural background are three of the more obvious variables that influence the language a person uses, their familiarity with and definitions he or she applies to words.

In an organization, especially large global entities and universities, people often come from diverse backgrounds and, therefore, have different patterns of speech. Many cultural subsets develop their own **jargon.** In large organizations, members are also frequently widely dispersed geographically—even operating in different countries—and individuals in each locale will use terms and phrases that are unique to their area.[12] The language of business executives can be mystifying to individuals not familiar with their industry's jargon.

jargon
Technical language, specific to a culture, discipline, or industry.

Keep in mind that while we may speak the same language, our use of that language is far from uniform. Senders tend to assume that the words and phrases they use mean the same to the receiver as they do to them. This assumption, of course, is incorrect and creates communication barriers. Knowing how each of us modifies the language would help minimize those barriers.

Convergys Corporation provides customer service and sales support for clients in more than 70 countries speaking nearly 35 languages. Even though the call-center employees shown here at the company's facility in Gurgaon, India, and their clients speak the common language of English, communication barriers exist because of differences among country cultures, language accents, and different patterns of speech. To overcome these barriers, Convergys employees receive multi-cultural skills-based training and accent-neutralization training so they can be more easily understood by their calling clients.

CULTURE AFFECTS COMMUNICATION

Communication differences also arise from the different languages that individuals use to communicate and the national culture of which they're a part.[13] For example, let's compare countries that place a high value on individualism (such as the United States) with countries where the emphasis is on collectivism (such as Japan).[14]

In the United States, communication patterns tend to be oriented to the individual and clearly spelled out. Business people in the United States rely heavily on memoranda, announcements, position papers, and other formal forms of communication to state their positions on issues. Supervisors here may hoard information in an attempt to make themselves look good (filtering) and as a way of persuading their employees to accept decisions and plans. And for their own protection, lower-level employees also engage in this practice.

In collectivist countries, such as Japan, there's more interaction for its own sake and a more informal manner of interpersonal contact. The Japanese manager, in contrast to the U.S. manager, engages in extensive verbal consultation with employees over an issue first and draws up a formal document later to outline the agreement that was made. The Japanese value decisions by consensus, and open communication is an inherent part of the work setting. Also, face-to-face communication is encouraged.[15]

How to Overcome Communication Barriers

The following suggestions should help make communication more effective (see also Figure 17.3).

Seek Feedback

Many communication problems are directly attributed to misunderstanding and inaccuracies. These problems are less likely to occur if we seek confirming feedback, both verbal and nonverbal.

FIGURE 17.3

Overcoming Barriers to Effective Communication

Use Feedback	Check the accuracy of what has been communicated—or what you think you heard.
Simplify Language	Use words that the intended audience understands.
Listen Actively	Listen for the full meaning of the message without making premature judgment or interpretation—or thinking about what you are going to say in response.
Constrain Emotions	Recognize when your emotions are running high. When they are, don't communicate until you have calmed down.
Watch Nonverbal Cues	Be aware that your actions speak louder than your words. Keep the two consistent.

Ask open-ended questions about a message to determine whether it was received and understood as intended. Ask the receiver to restate the message in his or her own words. If you hear the person restate what was intended for them to receive, understanding and accuracy are present. Feedback can also be more subtle as general comments can give you a sense of the receiver's reaction to a message.

Feedback doesn't have to be verbal. If a sales manager emails information about a new monthly sales report that all sales representatives will need to complete and return and some of them don't turn it in, the sales manager has received feedback. This feedback perhaps suggests that either the sales manager needs to clarify the initial communication, or perhaps that some of the sales force should start looking for another job.

SIMPLIFIED LANGUAGE SHOULD BE USED Complex language can be a barrier. Consider the audience to whom the message is directed and tailor the language to them. Remember, effective communication is achieved when a message is both received and *understood*. For example, a business student should always try to communicate in clear, easily understood terms and to use language tailored to the receiving groups. Messages to the faculty should be purposefully different from those directed to the sorority sisters or other peers. Jargon can facilitate understanding if it's used within a group that knows what it means, but can cause problems and create "noise" when used outside that group.

LISTEN ACTIVELY When someone talks, we hear. But too often we don't listen. Listening is an active search for meaning, whereas hearing is passive. In listening, the receiver is also putting effort into the communication.

Many of us are poor listeners and most of us would rather do the talking. Listening, in fact, is often more mentally challenging than talking. Unlike "simply hearing", active listening, which is listening for full meaning without making premature judgments or interpretations, demands total concentration. The average person normally speaks at a rate of about 125 to 200 words per minute. However, the average listener can comprehend up to 400 words per minute.[16] The difference leaves lots of idle brain time and opportunities for the mind to wander ("noise").

Active listening is enhanced by developing empathy with the sender—that is, by putting yourself in the sender's position. Because senders differ in attitudes, interests, needs, and expectations, empathy makes it easier to understand the actual content of a message.

An empathetic listener reserves judgment on the message's content and carefully listens to what is being said. The goal is to improve one's ability to get the full meaning of a communication without distorting it by premature judgments or interpretations.

Other specific behaviors that active listeners use include making eye contact, exhibiting affirmative nods and appropriate facial expressions, avoiding distracting actions or gestures that suggest boredom, asking questions, paraphrasing using your own words, avoiding interrupting the speaker, not talking too much, and making smooth transitions between being a speaker and a listener.

CONSTRAIN EMOTIONS It would be naïve to assume that we always communicate in a rational manner. We know that emotions can cloud and distort communication. A person who is upset over an issue is more likely to misconstrue incoming messages and fail to communicate his or her outgoing messages clearly and accurately. What to do? The simplest answer is to calm down and get emotions under control before communicating.

Business Writing Skills: Getting Your Message Across Clearly[17]

A colleague has just sent you an email relating to a meeting you're having in one hour's time. The email is supposed to contain key information that you need to present at the meeting, as part of the business case for an important project. But there's a problem: The email is so poorly written that you can't find the data you need. There are misspellings and incomplete sentences, and the paragraphs are so long and confusing that it takes you three times more than it should to find the information you want.

As a result, you're under-prepared for the meeting, and it doesn't go as well as it should.

Have you ever faced a situation similar to this? In today's information overload world, it's vital to communicate clearly, concisely and effectively. People don't have time to read book-length emails,half-page long paragraphs and they don't have the patience to scour badly constructed emails, memos, or reports for "buried" points.

The better your writing skills are, the better the impression you'll make on the people around you–including your professors, your colleagues, and your employers. You never know how far these good impressions will take you! The following provides tips on how you can improve your writing skills and avoid common mistakes.

Audience and Format

The first step to writing clearly is choosing the appropriate format. Do you need to send an informal email? Write a detailed report? Create advertising copy? Or write a formal letter?

The format, as well as your audience, will define your "writing voice"–that is, how formal or relaxed the tone should be. For instance, if you write an email to a professor or client, should it have the same tone as an email to a friend? Definitely not. With everything you write, your readers, or recipients, should define your tone as well as aspects of the content.

Composition and Style

Once you know why you're writing, and for whom you're writing, you actually have to start writing.

A blank, white computer screen is often intimidating. And it's easy to get stuck because you don't know how to start. Try these tips for composing and styling your document:

- **Start with your audience**—Remember, your readers may know nothing about what you're telling them. What do they know and what do they need to know?
- **Create an outline**—This is especially helpful if you're writing a longer document such as a report, presentation, or speech. Outlines help you identify which steps to take in which order, and they help you break the task up into manageable pieces of information.
- **Use AIDA**—If you're writing something that must inspire action in the reader, follow the Attention-Interest-Desire-Action (AIDA) formula. These four steps can help guide you through the writing process. (See www.mindtools.com for detailed information.)
- **Try some empathy**—For instance, if you're writing a proposal for prospective clients, why should they care about your product or proposal? What's the benefit for them? Remember your audience's needs at all times. If you're trying to persuade someone to do something, make sure that you communicate why people should listen to you, pitch your message in a way that engages your audience, and present information rationally and coherently.
- **Identify your main theme**—If you're having trouble defining the primary theme of your message, pretend that you have 15 seconds to explain your position. What do you say? This is likely to be your main theme.
- **Use simple language**—It is best to use simple, direct language. Don't use long words just to impress people.

Structure

Your document should be as "reader friendly" as possible. **Use headings, subheadings, bullet points, and numbering whenever possible to break up the text.**

After all, what's easier to read–a page full of long paragraphs, or a page that's broken up into short paragraphs, with section headings and bullet points? A document that's easy to scan will get read more often than a document with long, dense paragraphs of text.

Headers (such as **"Structure" above**) grab the reader's attention and inform them of the focus of the content that follows. In emails and proposals, use short, factual headings and subheadings, like the ones in this text.

Adding simple, clear graphs and charts is also an effective way to break up your text, keep the reader engaged and convey information. These visual aids not only keep the reader's eye engaged, but they can communicate important information much more quickly than text.

Grammatical Errors

You probably don't need us to tell you that errors in your document will make you look unprofessional. It's essential to use proper grammar and to avoid common mistakes that your spell checker won't find. Here are some examples of commonly misused words:

- Affect/effect
  - "Affect" is a verb meaning to influence. (Example: The economic forecast will affect our projected income.)
  - "Effect" is a noun meaning the result or outcome. (Example: What is the effect of the proposal?)
- Then/than
  - "Then" is typically an adverb indicating a sequence in time. (Example: We went to dinner, then we saw a movie.)
  - "Than" is a conjunction used for comparison. (Example: The dinner was more expensive than the movie.)
- Your/you're
  - "Your" is a possessive. (Example: Is that your file?)
  - "You're" is a contraction of "you are." (Example: You're the new manager.)
  - Note: Also watch out for other common homophones (words that sound alike but have different spellings and meanings) - such as their/they're/there, to/too/two, and so on.
- Its/it's
  - "Its" is a possessive. (Example: Is that its motor?)
  - "It's" is a contraction of "It is." (Example: It's often that heavy.) (Yes, it is this way around!)

Proofing

The enemies of good proofreading are speed and over confidence. Many people rush through their documents, and miss mistakes. Follow these guidelines to check what you've written:

- **Proof your headers and sub-headers**—People often skip these and focus on the text alone. Just because headers are big and bold doesn't mean they're error free!
- **Read the document out loud**—This forces you to go more slowly, so that you're more likely to catch mistakes.
- **Use your finger, or a pointer, to follow text as you read**—This is another trick that helps you slow down.
- **Start at the end of your document**—Proofread one sentence at a time, working your way from the end to the beginning. This helps you focus on errors, not on content.

Conclusion

More than ever, it's important to know how to communicate your point quickly and professionally. You spend a lot of time talking, writing, listening and reading, so the better you are at these forms of communication, the more successful you're likely to be.

Identify your audience before you start creating your message. If you feel that there's too much information to include, create an outline to help organize your thoughts. Learning grammatical and stylistic techniques will also help you write and speak more clearly. Be sure to proof the final document or script. Like most things, the more you consciously work on improving your communication sending and receiving skills, the better you're going to be!

CHAPTER 18

Approaches to Leadership[1]

Ideally, all managers should possess and demonstrate leadership skills. However, not all leaders necessarily have capabilities in other managerial functions and, thus, not all should hold managerial positions. The fact that an individual can influence others does not mean that he or she can also plan, organize, and control.

We will pursue the subject of leadership from a managerial perspective. Therefore, by **leaders** we mean those who are able to influence others and who possess managerial authority and responsibility.

leaders
People who are able to influence others and who possess managerial authority.

Trait Theories of Leadership

Ask the average person on the street what comes to mind when he or she thinks of leadership. You're likely to get a list of qualities such as intelligence, charisma, decisiveness, enthusiasm, strength, bravery, integrity, and self-confidence. These responses represent, in essence, **trait theories of leadership.** The search for traits or characteristics that differentiate leaders from non-leaders, dominated the early research efforts in the study of leadership and the selection of leader-managers.

trait theories of leadership
Theories that isolate characteristics that differentiate leaders from non-leaders.

Is it possible to isolate one or more traits in individuals who are generally acknowledged to be leaders? We may agree that certain individuals meet our definition of a leader, but they exhibit significantly different characteristics. If the concept of traits were to prove a valid indicator then all leaders would have to possess specific characteristics.

FIGURE 18.1

Six Traits That Differentiate Leaders from Non-leaders

1. **Drive.** Leaders exhibit a high effort level. They have a relatively high desire for achievement, they're ambitious, they have a lot of energy, they're tirelessly persistent in their activities, and they show initiative.
2. **Desire to lead.** Leaders have a strong desire to influence and lead others. They demonstrate the willingness to take responsibility.
3. **Honesty and integrity.** Leaders build trusting relationships between themselves and followers by being truthful or nondeceitful and by showing high consistency between word and deed.
4. **Self-confidence.** Followers look to leaders for an absence of self-doubt. Leaders, therefore, need to show self-confidence in order to convince followers of the rightness of goals and decisions.
5. **Intelligence.** Leaders need to be intelligent enough to gather, synthesize, and interpret large amounts of information and to be able to create visions, solve problems, and make correct decisions.
6. **Job-relevant knowledge.** Effective leaders have a high degree of knowledge about the company, industry, and technical matters. In-depth knowledge allows leaders to make well-informed decisions and to understand the implications of those decisions.

Source: Reprinted from "Leadership: Do Traits Really Matter?" by S. A. Kirkpatrick and E. A. Locke by permission of *Academy of Management Executive*, May 1991, pp. 48–60.

Attempts to identify a set of traits that would always differentiate leaders from followers and effective leaders from ineffective leaders failed. Perhaps it was a bit optimistic to believe that a set of consistent and unique personality traits could apply across the board to all effective leaders, whether they were in charge of a basketball team, a university, a hospital, a stock exchange, a country, or a business team.

However, attempts to identify traits consistently associated with leadership have been more successful. Six traits on which leaders are seen to differ from non-leaders include drive, the desire to lead, honesty and integrity, self-confidence, intelligence, and job-relevant knowledge. These traits are briefly described in Figure 18.1.

Yet traits alone do not sufficiently explain leadership. Explanations based solely on traits ignore situational factors. Possessing the appropriate traits only makes it more likely that an individual will be an effective leader-manager. He or she still has to make thoughtful decisions, communicate effectively, solve problems, work with and through others, and take the right actions. Just to confound the issue, managerial leaders function in an environment where what is the right action to take in one situation is not necessarily right for another situation.

Behavioral Theories of Leadership

The inability to explain leadership solely by traits led researchers to look at the behavior of specific leaders. Researchers wondered whether effective leaders exhibited something unique in their behavior. For example, do leaders tend to be more democratic than autocratic?

A number of studies looked at behavioral styles. We shall briefly review three of the most popular studies: Kurt Lewin's studies at the University of Iowa, the Ohio State group, and the University of Michigan studies. Then we will see how the concepts those studies developed could be used to create a grid for appraising leadership styles.

Identifiable Leadership Behaviors

One of the first studies of leadership behavior was done by Kurt Lewin and his associates at the University of Iowa. In their studies, the researchers explored three leadership behaviors or styles: autocratic, democratic, and laissez-faire.

- An **autocratic style** is that of a leader who typically tends to centralize authority, dictate work methods, make unilateral decisions, and limit employee participation.
- A **democratic style** is one that tends to involve employees in decision making, delegates authority, encourages participation in deciding work methods and goals, and uses feedback as an opportunity to coach employees. The democratic style can be further classified in two ways: consultative and participative.
    - A *democratic-consultative leader* seeks input and hears the concerns and issues of employees but makes the final decision him- or herself. In this capacity, the democratic-consultative leader is using the input as an information-seeking exercise.
    - A *democratic-participative leader* often allows employees to have a say in what's decided. Here, decisions are made by the group, with the leader providing one input to that group.
- Finally, the **laissez-faire** leader generally gives his or her employees complete freedom to make decisions and to complete their work in whatever way they see fit. A laissez-faire leader might simply provide necessary materials and answer questions.

autocratic style of leadership
The term used to describe a leader who centralizes authority, dictates work methods, makes unilateral decisions, and limits employee participation.

democratic style of leadership
The term used to describe a leader who involves employees in decision making, delegates authority, encourages participation, to differing degrees, in deciding work methods and goals, and uses feedback to coach employees.

laissez-faire style of leadership
The term used to describe a leader who generally gives his or her employees complete freedom to make decisions and to complete their work in whatever way they see fit.

Lewin and his associates wondered which one of the three leadership styles was most effective. On the basis of their studies of leaders from boys' clubs, they concluded that the laissez-faire style was ineffective on every performance criterion when compared with both democratic and autocratic styles. Quantity of work done was equal in groups with democratic and autocratic leaders, but work quality and group satisfaction were higher in democratic groups. The results suggest that a democratic leadership style could contribute to both good quantity and high quality of work.

In subsequent studies, group members' satisfaction levels were generally higher under a democratic leader than under an autocratic one. Did this finding mean that managers should always exhibit a democratic style of leadership? Two researchers, Robert Tannenbaum and Warren Schmidt, attempted to provide that answer.

The autocratic style describes the leader behavior at this restaurant in Beijing, China, where employees gather each morning for a briefing of their work tasks and a motivational talk. Leaders using the autocratic style tend to centralize authority, dictate work methods, make decisions, and limit employee participation.
PHOTO: © Michael Wolf/Redux

FIGURE 18.2

Continuum of Leader Behavior

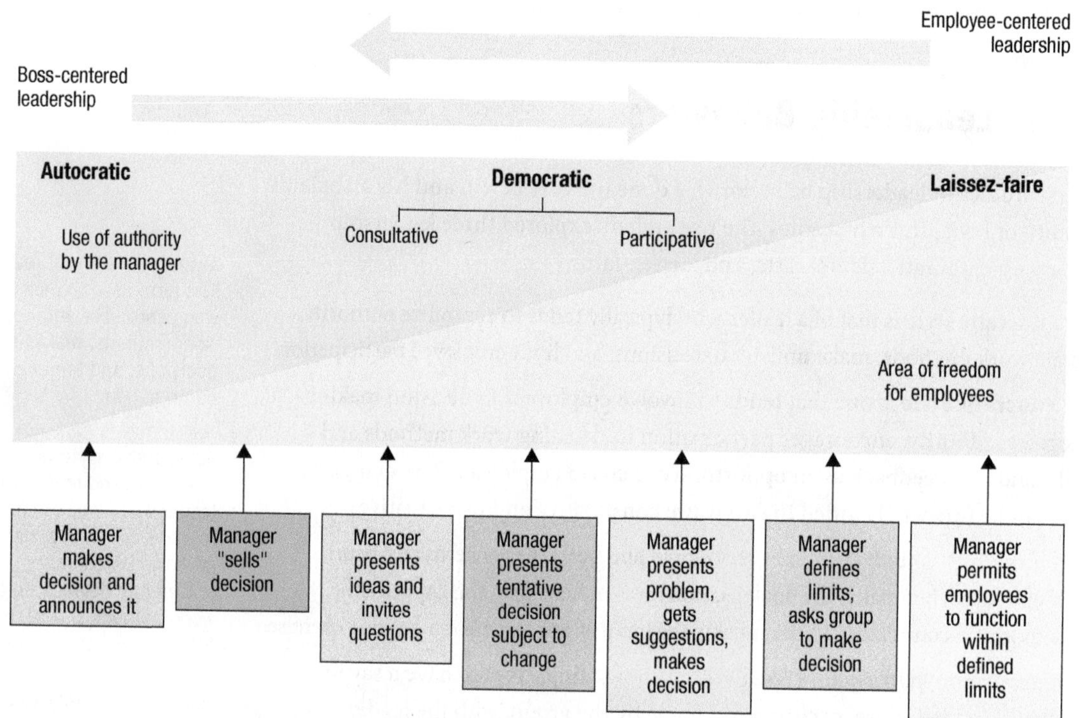

Source: Adapted and reprinted by permission of the *Harvard Business Review*. An Exhibit from "How to Choose a Leadership Pattern" by R. Tannenbaum and W. Schmidt, May–June 1973. Copyright © 1973 by the President and Fellows of Harvard College.

Tannenbaum and Schmidt developed a continuum of leader behaviors (see Figure 18.2). The continuum illustrates that a range of leadership behaviors, all the way from boss centered (autocratic) on the left side of the model to employee centered (laissez-faire) on the right side of the model, is possible. In deciding which leader behavior from the continuum to use, Tannenbaum and Schmidt proposed that managers look at (1) forces within themselves (such as comfort level with the chosen leadership style), (2) forces within the employees (such as readiness to assume responsibility), and (3) forces within the situation (such as time pressures). They suggested that managers should move toward more employee-centered styles in the long run because such behavior would increase employees' motivation, decision quality, teamwork, morale, and development.

This dual nature of leader-manager behaviors—that is, focusing on the work to be done and focusing on the employees—is also a key characteristic of the Ohio State and University of Michigan studies.

The Ohio State Studies

The most comprehensive and replicated of the behavioral theories resulted from research that began at Ohio State University in the late 1940s. These studies sought to identify independent dimensions of leader behavior. Beginning with more than 1,000 dimensions, the researchers eventually narrowed the list down to two categories that accounted for most of the leadership behavior described by employees. They called these two dimensions initiating structure and consideration.

Initiating structure (Task Focus) refers to the extent to which a leader is likely to define and structure his or her role and those of employees in the search for goal attainment. It includes behavior that attempts to organize work, work relationships, and goals. For example, the leader who is characterized as high in initiating structure assigns group members to particular tasks, expects workers to maintain definite standards of performance, and emphasizes the meeting of deadlines.

initiating structure
The extent to which a leader defines and structures his or her role and the roles of employees to attain goals.

Consideration (Relationship Focus) is defined as the extent to which a leader has job relationships characterized by mutual trust and respect for employees' ideas and feelings. A leader who is high in consideration helps employees with personal problems, is friendly and approachable, and treats all employees as equals. He or she shows concern for his or her followers' comfort, well being, status, and satisfaction.

consideration
The extent to which a leader has job relationships characterized by mutual trust, respect for employees' ideas, and regard for their feelings.

Extensive research based on these definitions found that a leader who is high in both initiating structure and consideration (a high-high leader) achieved high employee performance and satisfaction more frequently than one who rated low on either consideration, initiating structure, or both. However, the high-high style did not always yield positive results. For example, leader behavior characterized as high on initiating structure led to greater rates of grievances, absenteeism, and turnover, and lower levels of job satisfaction for workers performing routine tasks.

Catherine Mrowiec, general manager of The Bedford Renaissance Hotel in Boston, scores high on consideration. The day after the September 11 terrorist attacks, Mrowiec noticed that the hotel's Middle Eastern employees were avoiding eye contact with her. After talking with them about the hotel's values and what they should expect from management, the employees began to seek her out. Mrowiec's friendly and approachable leadership showed regard for employees' feelings, offered help with their personal problems, and treated all employees as equals.
PHOTO: © Joanne Rathe/The Boston Globe

Other studies found that high consideration was negatively related to performance ratings of the leader by his or her manager. In conclusion, the Ohio State studies suggested that the high-high style generally produced positive outcomes, but enough exceptions were found to indicate that situational factors needed to be integrated into the theory.

The Leadership Dimensions of the University of Michigan Studies

Leadership studies undertaken at the University of Michigan's Survey Research Center, at about the same time as those being done at Ohio State, had similar research objectives: to locate the behavioral characteristics of leaders that were related to performance effectiveness.

The Michigan group also came up with two dimensions of leadership behavior, which they labeled employee oriented and production oriented. Leader-Managers who were **employee oriented (Relationship Focus)** emphasized interpersonal relations; they took a personal interest in the needs of their employees and accepted individual differences among members. The **production-oriented (Task Focus)** leader-Managers, in contrast, tended to emphasize the technical or task aspects of the job, were concerned mainly with accomplishing their group's tasks, and regarded group members as a means to that end.

employee oriented
A leader-manager who emphasizes interpersonal relations, takes a personal interest in the needs of employees, and accepts individual differences.

production oriented
A leader-manager who emphasizes the technical or task aspects of a job, is concerned mainly with accomplishing tasks, and regards group members as a means to accomplishing goals.

The conclusions of the Michigan researchers strongly favored leaders who were employee oriented. Employee-oriented leader-managers were associated with higher group productivity and higher job satisfaction. Production-oriented leaders were associated with lower group productivity and lower worker satisfaction.

The Managerial Grid

managerial grid
A two-dimensional view of leadership style that is based on concern for people versus concern for production.

The **managerial grid** is a two-dimensional view of leadership style developed by Robert Blake and Jane Mouton. They proposed a managerial grid based on the styles of "concern for people" and "concern for production," which essentially represent the Ohio State dimensions of consideration and initiating structure and the Michigan dimensions of employee orientation and production orientation.

The grid, depicted in Figure 18.3 has nine possible positions along each axis, creating 81 different positions into which a leader's style may fall. The grid does not show the results but rather the dominating factors in a leader's thinking in regard to getting the results. That is, although the grid has 81 positions, the five key positions identified by Blake and Mouton focus on the four corners of the grid and a middle-ground area.

Blake and Mouton concluded that managers perform best using a 9,9 style. Unfortunately, the grid offers no answers to the question of what makes an effective

FIGURE 18.3

The Managerial Grid

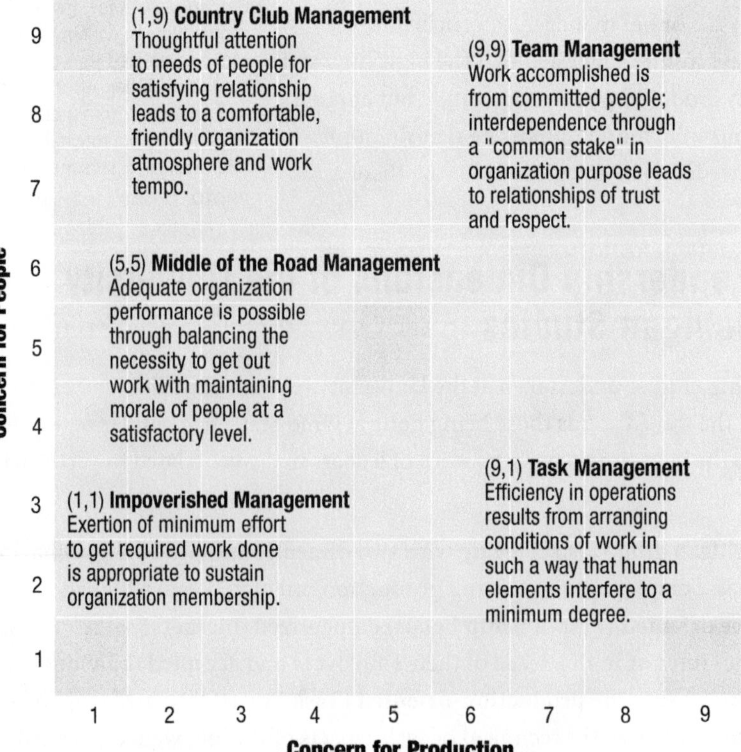

Source: Adapted and reprinted by permission of the Harvard Business Review. An exhibition from "Breakthrough in Organization Development" by R.R. Blake, J.A. Mouton, L.B. Barnes, and L.E. Greine, November–December 1964, p. 136. Copyright © 1964 by the President and Fellows of Harvard College; all rights reserved.

leader but only a framework for conceptualizing leadership style. In fact, little substantive evidence supports the conclusion that a 9,9 (High Concern for People + High Concern for Production) style is most effective in all situations.

The Behavioral Theories' Insights to Leadership

We have described the most popular and important attempts to explain leadership in terms of behavior. Problems associated with the behavioral theories were that they had little success in identifying consistent relationships between patterns of leadership behavior and successful performance. General statements could not be made because results would vary over different ranges of circumstances.

What was missing was a consideration of the situational factors that influence success or failure. For example, would Mother Teresa have been a great leader of the poor at the turn of the century? Would Ralph Nader have risen to lead a consumer activist group had he been born in 1834 rather than in 1934 or in Costa Rica rather than in Connecticut? It seems quite unlikely, yet the behavioral approaches we have described could not clarify such situational factors. These uncertainties, the application of certain leadership styles in all situations, led researchers to try to better understand the influence of the situation on effective leadership styles.

Contingency Theories of Leadership

The failure to obtain consistent results utilizing behavioral theories alone led to a new focus on influences on leadership styles. The relationship between leadership style and effectiveness suggested that under condition "A", style "X" would be appropriate, whereas style "Y" would be more suitable for condition "B", and style "Z" for condition "C". But what were the conditions a, b, c, and so forth? It was one thing to say that leadership effectiveness depended on the conditions and another to be able to isolate those conditions.

Several approaches to isolating key variables have proved more successful than others and, as a result, have gained wider recognition. We shall consider three: the Fiedler contingency model, path-goal theory, and Hersey and Blanchard's situational leadership theory.

The Fiedler Contingency Model

The first comprehensive contingency model for leadership was developed by Fred Fiedler. His model proposes that effective group performance depends on the proper match between the leader's style of interacting with his or her subordinates and the degree to which the situation gives control and influence to the leader.

Fiedler developed an instrument, which he called the **least-preferred coworker (LPC) questionnaire,** which purports to measure the leader's behavioral orientation—either task oriented or relationship oriented. Then he isolated three work-place criteria—*leader-member relations, task structure,* and *position power*—that which could be manipulated so as to create the proper match with the behavioral orientation of the leader.

least-preferred coworker (LPC) questionnaire
A questionnaire that measures whether a person is task or relationship oriented.

Fiedler contingency model
The theory that effective group performance depends on the proper match between the leader's style of interacting with employees and the degree to which the situation gives control and influence to the leader.

In a sense, the **Fiedler contingency model** is an outgrowth of trait theory, because the LPC questionnaire is a simple psychological test. Fiedler, however, went significantly beyond trait and behavioral approaches in attempting to isolate situations, relating his personality measure to his situational classification and then predicting leadership effectiveness as a function of the two. This description of the Fiedler model is somewhat abstract (see Details on a Management Classic on the following page).

The Fiedler contingency model of leadership proposed matching an individual's least preferred coworker score and an assessment of three contingency variables to achieve maximum leadership. In his studies of more than 1,200 groups, in which he compared relationship versus task oriented leadership styles in each of eight work place environments Fiedler concluded that task-oriented leaders tend to perform best in situations that are either very favorable or very unfavorable to them (see Figure 18.4). Fiedler predicted that, when faced with a category I, II, III, VII, or VIII situation, task-oriented leaders would perform well. Relationships-oriented leaders, however, perform best in moderately favorable situations—categories IV through VI.

Remember that according to Fiedler, an individual's leadership style is fixed. Therefore, there are really only two ways in which to improve leader effectiveness.

- First, you can change the leader to fit the situation. For example, if a group situation rates as highly unfavorable to the leader but is currently led by a relationship-oriented manager, the group's performance could be improved by replacing that manager with one who is task oriented; or...
- The second alternative would be to change the situation to fit the leader by restructuring the tasks or by increasing or decreasing the power that the leader has to control such factors as salary increases, promotions, and disciplinary actions.

FIGURE 18.4

The Findings of the Fiedler Model

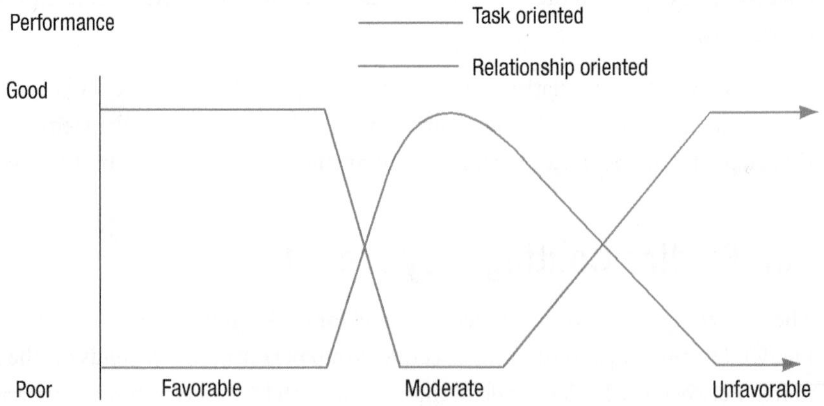

Category	I	II	III	IV	V	VI	VII	VIII
Leader–member relations	Good	Good	Good	Good	Poor	Poor	Poor	Poor
Task structure	High	High	Low	Low	High	High	Low	Low
Position power	Strong	Weak	Strong	Weak	Strong	Weak	Strong	Weak

Considerable evidence supports at least substantial parts of the model. Even though Fielder may not have identified all the contextual variables that affect leadership, the ones he did identify do appear to contribute substantially to our understanding of influential situational factors.

The Fiedler Contingency Model of Leadership

Fiedler assumed that an individual's leadership style is fixed—that is, either relationship oriented or task oriented. This assumption is important because it means that if a situation requires a task-oriented leader and the person in that leadership position is relationship oriented, either the situation has to be modified or the leader replaced for optimum effectiveness. Fiedler argued that leadership style is innate to a person, i.e. you can't change your style to fit changing situations.

It is necessary to match the leader with the situation. The three situational factors or contingency dimensions identified by Fiedler are defined as follows:

Leader-member relations. The degree of confidence, trust, and respect employees have in their leader.

Task structure. The degree to which the job assignments of employees are structured or unstructured.

Position power. The degree of influence a leader has over power variables such as hiring, firing, discipline, promotions, and salary increases.

An essential step in utilizing the Fiedler model is to evaluate the situation in terms of these three contingency variables. **Leader-member relations** are either good or poor, **task structure** either high or low, and **position power** either strong or weak.

Fiedler stated that the better the leader–member relations, the more highly structured the job; and the stronger the position power, the more control or influence the leader has. For example, a very favorable situation (in which the leader has a great deal of control) might involve a payroll manager who is well respected and whose subordinates have confidence in him or her (good leader–member relations); where the activities to be done—such as wage computation, check writing, report filing—are specific and clear (high-task structure); and where the job provides considerable freedom to reward and punish subordinates (strong-position power).

On the other hand, an unfavorable situation might be that of the disliked leader of a voluntary fundraising team. In this job, the leader has little control. All together, by mixing the three contingency variables, there are potentially eight different situations or categories in which a leader could find him- or herself. Fiedler concluded that task-oriented leaders perform best in situations that are very favorable or very unfavorable to them. A moderately favorable situation, however, is best handled through relationship-oriented leadership.

The Path-Goal Theory

One of the most respected approaches to leadership is **Path-Goal Theory,** developed by Robert House.

Path-Goal Theory
The theory that it is a leader's job to assist followers in attaining their goals and to provide the necessary direction and support.

The essence of the theory is that it is the leader's job to assist his or her followers in attaining their goals and to provide the necessary direction and support to ensure that their goals are compatible with the overall objectives of the group or organization. The term *path-goal* is derived from the belief that effective leaders clarify the path to help their followers get from where they are to the achievement of their work goals and make the journey along the path easier by reducing roadblocks and pitfalls.

According to Path-Goal Theory:

- A leader's behavior is acceptable to the degree that employees view it as an immediate source of satisfaction or as a means of future satisfaction.

Boeing CEO James McNerney adopts the path-goal approach to leadership by helping employees attain their goals and providing the necessary direction and support. He views himself as a value-added facilitator in charting the course for his employees, helping them get better, and inspiring them to reach performance goals. McNerney believes that a company's performance begins with the growth and development of its people rather than its strategy or products.

PHOTO: Olivier Leban-Mattei/AFP/Getty Images

- A leader's behavior is motivational to the degree that it (1) makes employee need satisfaction contingent on effective performance and (2) provides the coaching, guidance, support, and rewards that are necessary for effective performance.

House identified four leadership behaviors.

- The *directive leader* lets employees know what is expected of them, schedules work to be done, and gives specific guidance as to how to accomplish tasks. This type of leadership closely parallels the Ohio State dimension of initiating structure.
- The *supportive leader* is friendly and shows concern for the needs of employees. This type of leadership is essentially synonymous with the Ohio State dimension of consideration.
- The *participative leader* (á la Lewin's democratic consultative style) consults with employees and uses their suggestions before making a decision.
- The *achievement-oriented* leader sets challenging goals and expects employees to perform at their highest levels.

In contrast to Fiedler's view of a leader's behavior, House assumes that leaders are flexible. Path-goal theory implies that the same leader can display any or all of these leadership styles, depending on the situation.

As Figure 18.5 illustrates, Path-Goal Theory proposes two classes of situational or contingency variables that influence the leadership behavior:

- **Environmental variables** that are outside the control of the employee (task structure, the formal authority system, and the work group).
- **Employee variables** that are part of the personal characteristics of the employee (locus of control, experience, and perceived ability).

Environmental factors determine the type of leader behavior required if employee outcomes are to be maximized, and employee variables (personal characteristics of the employee) determine how the environment and leader behavior are interpreted. The theory proposes that leader behavior will be ineffective when it is redundant to sources of environmental structure or incongruent with subordinate characteristics.

The majority of the evidence supports the logic underlying the Path-Goal theory. That is, employee performance and satisfaction are likely to be positively influenced when

FIGURE 18.5

Path-Goal Theory

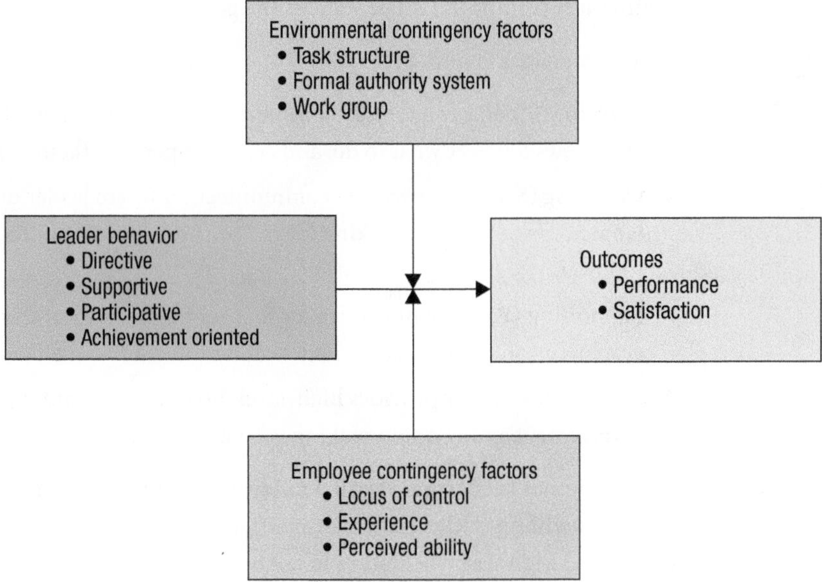

the leader compensates for shortcomings with the employee or the work setting. But if the leader spends time explaining tasks when those tasks are already understood or the employee has the ability and experience to handle them without interference, the employee is likely to see such directive behavior as redundant or even insulting, at least as non-productive.

Situational Leadership

Paul Hersey and Kenneth Blanchard's leadership model has gained a strong following among management development specialists. Called **Situational Leadership®,** it shows how a leader should adjust his or her leadership style to reflect what followers need. This model has been incorporated into leadership training programs at many *Fortune* 500 companies, and more than 10 million managers a year from a wide variety of organizations learn its basic elements.

situational leadership®
A model of leadership behavior that reflects how a leader should adjust his or her leadership style in accordance with the readiness (ability and willingness) of followers.

Situational Leadership theory focuses on the situation of the followers. Successful leadership is achieved by the leader-manager selecting the appropriate style, which is contingent on the follower's level of readiness.

Before we proceed, let's clarify two points: Why focus on the followers? And what is meant by the term *readiness*?

- The emphasis on the followers in leadership effectiveness reflects the reality that it is the followers who accept or reject the leader. Regardless of what the leader does, effectiveness depends on the actions of his or her followers. This important dimension has been overlooked or underemphasized in most leadership theories.
- **Readiness**, as defined by Hersey and Blanchard, refers to the extent that people have the ability and the willingness (or commitment) to accomplish a specific task.

readiness
The extent to which people have the ability and the willingness (or commitment) to accomplish a task.

FIGURE 18.6

Hershey and Blanchard's Situational Leadership Model®

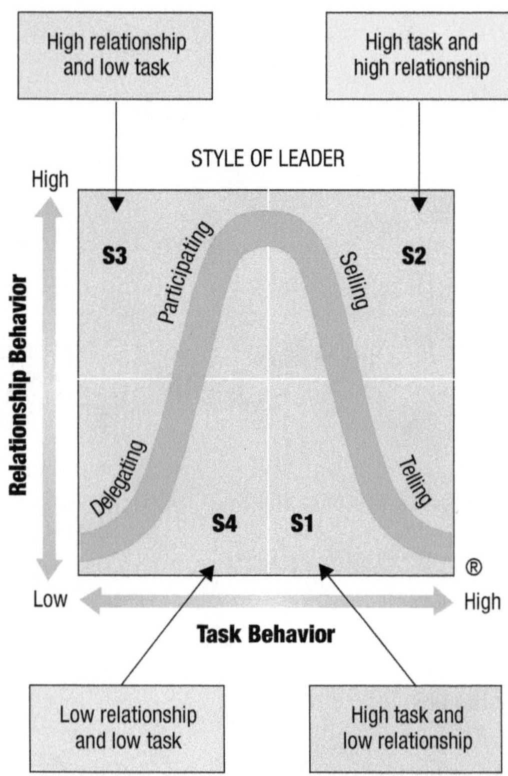

Source: Reprinted with permission from the Center for Leadership Studies. Situational Leadership® is a registered trademark of the Center for Leadership Studies, Escondido, California.

Hersey and Blanchard identify four specific leader-manager behaviors (see Figure 18.6). Effective leadership behavior depends on it being appropriately matched with a follower's ability and willingness (commitment) to achieve the goal.

Leader-Manager Styles:

- Directing (Telling)—one-way communication where leader tells and shows follower what to do, and closely supervises them doing it.
- Coaching (Selling)—two-way communication where leader directs what needs to be done, seeking ideas and suggestions from the follower.
- Supporting (Participating)—leader focuses on motivation and employee confidence issues and leaves task decisions to follower.
- Delegating—leader provides high-level direction only and further involvement and decision making is controlled by follower.

So, Situational Leadership says if a follower is significantly unable and/or unwilling (lacking commitment), the leader needs to display a (Directive) high task orientation to compensate for the follower's lack of ability and/or willingness. The leader-manager's high task and low relationship orientation is needed to get the follower to understand what needs to be done and to accomplish it.

At the other end of the readiness spectrum, if followers are very able and very willing, the leader doesn't need to do much to enhance their performance so the preferred leader-manager style would be (Delegating) reflecting a low task and low relationship orientation.

Situational Leadership has an intuitive appeal. It acknowledges the importance of followers' attitudes and abilities and builds on the idea that leaders need to adjust their behaviors to the ability and motivation levels of their followers.

A difference between Path-Goal and Situational approaches is that a Path-Goal leader-manager considers employee factors **AND** environmental factors that take into consideration the influence of specific factors of the working environment. In comparison the Situational leader-manager focuses only on the employee factors (readiness). However, the four leader-manager behaviors (Directive, Supportive, Participative, Delegating/Achievement) they can adopt, based on the different inputs are very similar.

Building Trust: The Essence of Leadership[2]

Trust, or lack of trust, is an increasingly important issue in today's organizations. The actions by leaders at WorldCom, Adelphia, and Enron in the early part of the decade led to a precipitous drop in the public's trust in corporate leaders. Many individuals simply see such leaders as greedy and opportunistic. Those characteristics do not lead to developing trusting relationships!

This chapter explores how trust is a vital component of effective leadership.

The Basis of Trust

Trust is a positive expectation that another will not—through words, actions, or decisions—act opportunistically. The phrase *positive expectation* in our definition assumes knowledge of and familiarity with the other party.

trust
The belief in the integrity, character, and ability of a leader.

Trust is a history-dependent process based on relevant but limited samples of experience. It takes time to form, building incrementally and accumulating (see Developing Your

Developing Your Trust-Building Skill

About the Skill
Given the importance trust plays in the leadership equation, today's leaders should actively seek to build trust with their followers. Here are some suggested actions for building and maintaining trust.

Trust Building Actions

1. **Practice openness.** Mistrust comes as much from what people don't know as from what they do know. Openness leads to confidence and trust. So keep people informed; make clear the criteria on how decisions are made; explain the rationale for your decisions; be candid about problems; and fully disclose relevant information.
2. **Be fair.** Before making decisions or taking actions, consider how others will perceive them in terms of objectivity and fairness. Give credit where credit is due; be objective and impartial in performance appraisals; and pay attention to equity perceptions in reward distributions.
3. **Speak your feelings.** Leaders who convey only hard facts come across as cold and distant. When you share your feelings, others will see you as real and human. They will know who you are and their respect for you will increase.
4. **Tell the truth.** If honesty is critical to credibility, you must be perceived as someone who tells the truth. Followers are more tolerant of being told something they "don't want to hear" than of finding out that their leader lied to them.
5. **Be consistent.** People want predictability. Mistrust comes from not knowing what to expect. Take the time to think about your values and beliefs. Then let them consistently guide your decisions. When you know your central purpose, your actions will follow accordingly, and you will project a consistency that earns trust.
6. **Fulfill your promises.** Trust requires that people believe that you are dependable. So you need to keep your word. Promises made must be promises kept.
7. **Maintain confidences.** You trust those whom you believe to be discrete and whom you can rely on. If people make themselves vulnerable by telling you something in confidence, they need to feel assured that you won't discuss it with others or betray that confidence. If people perceive you as someone who leaks personal confidences or someone who can't be depended on, you won't be perceived as trustworthy.
8. **Demonstrate confidence.** Develop the admiration and respect of others by demonstrating technical and professional ability. Pay particular attention to developing and displaying your communication, negotiating, and other interpersonal skills.

Practicing the Skill-Situation
You are a new manager. Your predecessor, who was popular and who is still with your firm, concealed from your team how far behind they are on their goals this quarter. As a result, your team members are looking forward to a promised day off that they are not entitled to and will not be getting.

It's your job to tell them the bad news. How will you do it, while utilizing the previously noted trust building action steps?

Trust-Building Skill below). Most of us find it hard, if not impossible, to trust someone immediately if we don't know anything about him or her. At the extreme, in the case of total ignorance, we can gamble but we can't trust. But as we get to know someone and the relationship matures, we gain confidence in our ability to make a positive expectation.

There is inherent risk and vulnerability in any trusting relationship. Trusts involves making oneself vulnerable as when, for example, we disclose intimate information or rely on another's promises. By its very nature, trust provides the opportunity to be disappointed or to be taken advantage of. Trust is a willingness to take risk. So when we trust someone, we expect that he or she will not take advantage of us. This willingness to take risks is common to all trust situations.

Patricia Woertz knows that the effectiveness of her leadership depends on her ability to gain the trust of followers. Woertz is the new CEO of Archer Daniels Midland, a $37 billion food-processing company and the largest U.S. ethanol producer. Woertz spent her first few months as CEO meeting with more than 4,000 employees at 32 ADM locations. "My objective in my first 100 days has been to listen and learn and build trust," she says.

PHOTO: Schmid Schurter/The New York Times

Trust Is Critical to Leadership

Trust appears to be a primary attribute associated with leadership. In fact, if you look back at our discussion of leadership traits, honesty and integrity were found to be among the six traits consistently associated with leadership.

Part of the leader's task is to work with other people to find and solve problems. Whether leaders gain access to the knowledge and creative thinking they need to solve problems depends on how much people trust them. Trust and trustworthiness modulate the leader's access to knowledge and cooperation.

When followers trust a leader-manager, they are willing to be vulnerable to the leader's actions, confident that their rights and interests will not be abused. People are unlikely to look up to or follow someone who they perceive as dishonest, inconsistent or who is likely to take advantage of them. Honesty, for instance, consistently ranks at the top of most lists of characteristics admired in leaders.

Now, more than ever, managerial and leadership effectiveness depends on the ability to gain the trust of followers. Moreover, contemporary management practices such as empowerment and the use of work teams require trust to be effective. A survey of employees by a firm in Chicago found 40 percent agreed with the statement: "I often don't believe what management says." In times of change and instability, people turn to personal relationships for guidance, and the quality of these relationships is largely determined by level of trust.

There Are Three Types of Trust

The three types of trust in organizational relationships are deterrence based, knowledge based, and identification based. Let's briefly look at each of these.

deterrence-based trust
Trust based on fear of reprisal if the trust if violated.

DETERRENCE-BASED TRUST The most fragile relationships are founded on **deterrence-based trust.** One violation or inconsistency can destroy the relationship. This form of trust is based on fear of reprisal if the trust is violated. Individuals who are in this type of relationship act because they fear the consequences of not following through on their obligations.

Deterrence-based trust will work only to the degree that (1) some form of punishment is possible, (2) consequences are clear, and (3) the punishment is actually imposed if the trust is violated. To be sustained, the potential loss of future interaction with the other party must outweigh the profit potential that comes from violating expectations. Moreover, the potentially harmed party must be willing to introduce harm (for example, I have no qualms about speaking badly of you if you betray my trust).

Most new relationships begin on a base of deterrence.

An example of deterrence-based trust is a new manager–employee relationship. As an employee, you typically trust a new boss even though you have little experience upon which to base that trust with this person. The bond that creates this trust is based in the authority held by the boss and the punishment, or lack of rewards he or she can impose if you fail to fulfill your job-related obligations.

KNOWLEDGE-BASED TRUST Most organizational relationships are rooted in **knowledge-based trust.** That is, trust is based on the behavioral predictability that comes from a history of limited interaction. It exists when you understand someone well enough to be able to accurately predict his or her behavior in multiple situations.

knowledge-based trust
Trust based on the behavioral predictability that comes from a history of interaction.

Knowledge-based trust relies on information and experience, rather than deterrence. Knowledge of the other party and predictability of his or her behavior replaces the actual or implied contracts, penalties, and legal arrangements more typical of deterrence-based trust. This knowledge develops over a period of time, largely as a function of shared experience that builds confidence of trustworthiness and predictability.

The better you know someone, the more accurately you can predict what he or she will do. Predictability enhances trust even if the other person is predictably untrustworthy because the ways that the other will violate the trust can be predicted. The more communication and regular interaction you have with someone, the more this form of trust can be developed and depended upon.

Interestingly, at the knowledge-based level, trust is not necessarily broken by inconsistent behavior. If you believe you can adequately explain or understand another's apparent violation, you can accept it, forgive the person, and move on in the relationship. However, the same inconsistency at the deterrence level is likely to irrevocably break the trust.

In an organizational context, most manager–employee, or co-worker relationships are knowledge based. Both parties have enough experience working with each other to know what to expect. A long history of consistently open and honest interactions, for instance, is not likely to be permanently destroyed by a single violation.

IDENTIFICATION-BASED TRUST The highest level of trust is achieved when a deep emotional connection is made between the parties. It allows one party to act as an agent for the other and substitute for that person in interpersonal transactions and is called **identification-based trust.** In this case, trust exists because the parties understand each other's intentions and values, and empathize with the other's wants and desires. This mutual understanding is developed to the point that each can effectively act for the other. Controls are minimal at this level. You don't need to monitor the other party because unquestioned loyalty exists.

identification-based trust
Trust based on a deep emotional, values based connection between the parties.

An example of identification-based trust is a long-term, happy marriage or relationship. A person comes to learn what is important to his or her partner and anticipates those actions. The partner, in turn, realizes this understanding and incorporates it into their behaviors. Increased identification enables each to think like the other, feel like the other, and respond like the other.

Conclusion

You see identification-based trust occasionally in organizations among people who have worked together for very long periods of time and have a depth of experience that allows them to know each other inside and out. This type of trust is also what managers ideally seek in teams when the members have worked together for years, share the same values and are so comfortable and trusting of each other that they can anticipate each other and freely act in each other's' place.

Realistically, in the current work world, most large corporations have broken the bonds of identification trust that they may have built with long-term employees. Broken promises have led to a breakdown in what was, at one time, a bond of unquestioned loyalty. It's likely to have been replaced with knowledge-based trust.

CHAPTER

19

Motivation

This discussion on **motivation** takes a look at the key theories of what drives people to act, or not to act. It shows you how the current understanding of motivation has come about, so that you can better identify the approaches needed for success in today's complex workplace.

motivation
The internal or external force that propels you to act.

Historical Motivational Theories

If we're to understand the current view of motivation, we need to understand its history. This is important because ideas have changed radically over the past 70 years. Approaches that might have been valid in the mid-20th century have been replaced with more applicable approaches, which are reflective of society today.

Maslow's Hierarchy of Needs[1]

Maslow's Hierarchy of Needs was significant in that it established that humans have a range of different needs that they seek to satisfy.

Importantly, Maslow grouped these needs together into levels. The most basic level starts with the physiological need for food, water, and shelter. This is followed by security and social needs. Maslow believed that the higher level needs, such as self-esteem and self-fulfillment, could only be met after the lower level needs had been satisfied. The diagram on the next page, Figure 19.1, shows Maslow's Hierarchy:

FIGURE 19.1

MASLOW'S HIERARCHY OF NEEDS

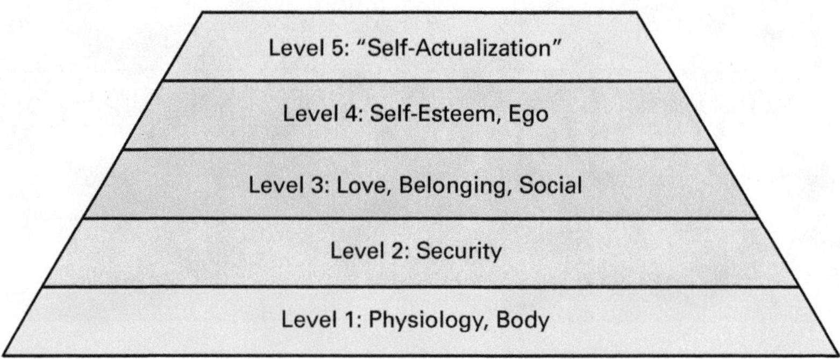

Maslow's hierarchical levels are explained below:

LEVEL 1—BODY, PHYSIOLOGY This level represents the basic things you need to stay alive. It includes needs like having enough food, water and shelter to survive.

LEVEL 2—SECURITY Level 2 represents safety and security—the need to be safe from physical and psychological harm in the present and future. This includes the need to feel secure in one's job.

LEVEL 3—BELONGING, SOCIAL This level stands for the need to feel a valued member of one's team, and the need to enjoy good relationships with the people around you.

LEVEL 4—SELF-ESTEEM Level 4 corresponds to a feeling of self-respect and self-acceptance, and encompasses the need for recognition and the desire to feel important.

LEVEL 5—"SELF-ACTUALIZATION" This represents the need for self-fulfillment, and the desire to realize your full potential and become the best you can be.

The basis of Maslow's Hierarchy is that people progress from level to level: Once needs for security are met, people are then motivated by the search for belonging. And once they feel they belong, they are motivated by self-esteem.

Now this has strong intuitive appeal, and some element of truth within it. And as a general approach, it reminds us that if we want to have people be motivated all these different levels of need should be considered.

Maslow's Theory in Practice

However, do not stick too rigidly to Maslow's hierarchy:

- In reality, people don't work through these levels one-at-a-time; they are much less structured in the way they satisfy their needs
- Different people with different cultural backgrounds and in different situations may have different hierarchies of need

FIGURE 19.2

THEORY X AND THEORY Y PREMISES

THEORY X: A MANAGER WHO VIEWS EMPLOYEES FROM A THEORY X (NEGATIVE) PERSPECTIVE BELIEVES:

1 Employees inherently dislike work and, whenever possible, will attempt to avoid it.
2 Because employees dislike work, they must be coerced, controlled, or threatened with punishment to achieve desired goals.
3 Employees will shirk responsibilities and seek formal direction whenever possible.
4 Most workers place security above all other factors associated with work and will display little ambition.

THEORY Y: A MANAGER WHO VIEWS EMPLOYEES FROM A THEORY Y (POSITIVE) PERSPECTIVE BELIEVES:

1 Employees can view work as being as natural as rest or play.
2 Men and women will exercise self-direction and self-control if they are committed to the objectives.
3 The average person can learn to accept, even seek, responsibility.
4 The ability to make good decisions is widely dispersed throughout the population and is not necessarily the sole province of managers.

McGregor's Factor X/Y Theory

Shortly after Maslow published his hierarchy of needs, Douglas McGregor published his Factor X/Y Theory. McGregor noted that managers generally had two beliefs about employees and their attitudes toward their jobs:

- **Theory X,** by which managers assume that the majority of employees dislike work, and would be idle if they could be: Because of this, employees need to be closely managed; and
- **Theory Y,** which assumes that employees will work hard, seek responsibility, and show initiative without the need for much supervision.

Theory X (McGregor)
The assumptions that employees dislike work, are lazy, seek to avoid responsibility, and must be coerced to perform.

Theory Y (McGregor)
The assumptions that employees are creative, seek responsibility, and can exercise self-direction.

McGregor's Factor X/Y Theory taps into the age-old wisdom that a happy employee is a better performer and will be more motivated, concluding that a constructive working environment is key to motivational success.

In many cases Theory X management destroys motivation, while Theory Y management unlocks strong performance.

McGregor's Theory in Practice

Now, stop and ask yourself how you perceive your co-workers and your team. When you think about them as individuals, which of the two approaches would you use to manage each person (see Figure 19.2)?

Most likely you'll end up with a mixture of approaches, and probably a few people who sit in between the two extremes. However, if you find you tend more towards Theory X than Theory Y, then you probably need to take ideas of motivation much more seriously: Think of it as a great opportunity to improve the productivity of your team.

McGregor's broad approach was taken much further by Frederick Herzberg, a well-respected researcher who closely studied the sources of employee motivation in the 1950s and 1960s.

hygiene factor
Herzberg's terms for factors, such as working conditions and salary, that, when adequate, may eliminate job dissatisfaction but do not necessarily increase job satisfaction.

motivators
Herzberg's term for factors, such as recognition and growth, which increase job satisfaction.

Herzberg's Motivation-Hygiene (Two-Factor) Theory

Frederick Herzberg produced great work on job satisfaction and employee satisfaction. This is an important part of the foundation on which most successful motivation efforts are now built.

Herzberg's findings revealed that certain characteristics of a job are consistently related to job satisfaction, while different factors are associated with job dissatisfaction. See Figure 19.3 below.

Remedying the causes of dissatisfaction will not create satisfaction. Nor will adding the factors of job satisfaction eliminate job dissatisfaction. If you have a hostile work environment, giving someone a promotion will not make him or her satisfied. If you create a healthy work environment but do not provide members of your team with any of the satisfaction factors, the work they're doing will still not be satisfying.

According to Herzberg, the factors leading to job satisfaction are "separate and distinct from those that lead to job dissatisfaction." Therefore, if you set about eliminating dissatisfying job factors you may create peace, but not necessarily enhance performance. This placates your workforce instead of actually motivating them to improve performance.

Herzberg's Theory in Practice

Herzberg's "Hygiene Factors" (the things that make us unhappy and demotivated) are obstructive company policy, unhelpful administration, intrusive supervision,

FIGURE 19.3

HERZBERG'S TWO-FACTOR, MOTIVATION-HYGIENE THEORY

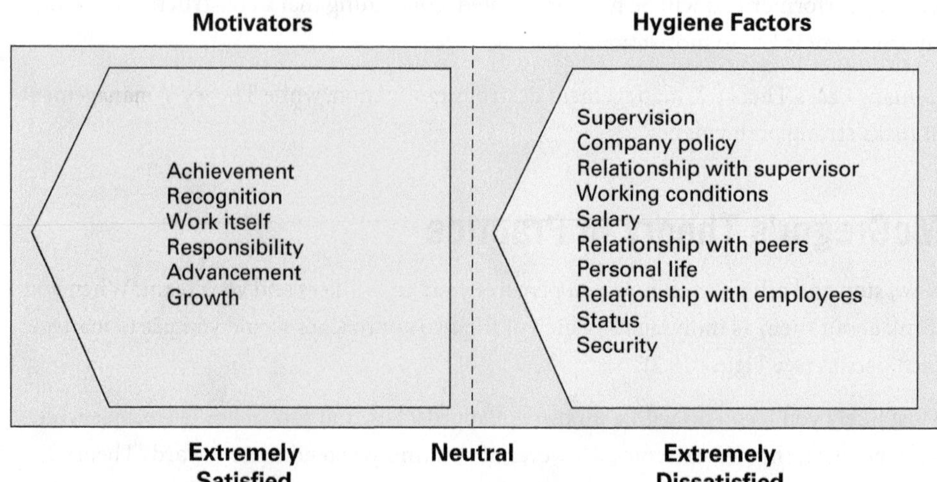

bad working relationships, poor conditions, uncompetitive salaries, low status and job insecurity. By fixing these problems you can get rid of much demotivation and unhappiness, but you will not build high motivation.

To start motivating people, these demotivating factors need to be controlled. But then to build real motivation, you need to give opportunities for and recognize achievement; provide intrinsically rewarding work; and give opportunities for responsibility, growth and advancement.

Despite its wide acceptance, Herzberg's theory has its detractors. Some say its methodology does not address the notion that when things are going well people tend to look at the things they enjoy about their job. When things are going badly, however, they tend to blame external factors.

Another common criticism is the fact that the theory assumes a strong correlation between job satisfaction and productivity. Herzberg's methodology did not address this relationship, therefore the assumption needs to be proven as correct for his findings to have practical relevance.

Job Characteristics Model (JCM)

What differentiates one job from another? We know that an airline pilot's job is different from that of an emergency room nurse. And we know that both of those jobs have little in common with the job of an editor in a newsroom or that of a component assembler on a production line. The job characteristics model (JMC), designed by J. Richard Hackman and Greg R. Oldham. JMC is based on the idea that the design of the task itself is essential to employee motivation.

It states that there are five core job characteristics (skill variety, task identity, task significance, autonomy, and feedback), which affect three critical psychological states (experienced meaningfulness, experienced responsibility for outcomes, and knowledge of the actual results), in turn influencing work outcomes (job satisfaction, absenteeism, work motivation, etc.). According to Hackman and Oldham, any job can be described in terms of the following five core job dimensions:

- **Skilled variety.** Requires different skills/talents (meaningfulness of the work).
- **Task identity.** Responsible for the task start to finish (meaningfulness of the work).

FIGURE 19.4

JOB CHARACTERISTICS MODEL

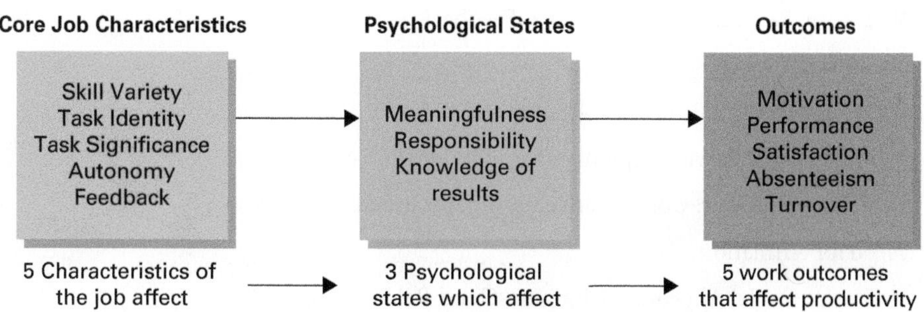

- **Task significance.** Tasks are important — they matter (meaningfulness of the work).
- **Autonomy.** Self-determine how and when to do it (responsibility for outcomes).
- **Feedback.** Receives direct and clear performance feedback (knowledge of results).

Job Characteristics Theory in Practice

Specifically, a boring and monotonous job stifles motivation to perform well, whereas a challenging job enhances motivation.

Variety, autonomy and decision authority are three ways of adding challenge to a job. Job enrichment and job rotation are ways of adding variety.

Contemporary Theories of Motivation

Some contemporary theories have reasonable degrees of valid supporting documentation. The following theories represent the contemporary views of employee motivation.

McClelland's Acquired Needs Theory

Three-Needs theory
McClelland's theory that the needs for achievement, power, and affiliation are major motives in work.

Need for achievement
The drive to excel, to achieve in relation to a set of standards, and to strive to succeed.

Need for power
The need to make others behave in a way that they would not have behaved otherwise.

Need for affiliation
The desire for friendly and close interpersonal relationships.

The Acquired Needs (or Three-Needs Theory) was developed by psychologist, David McClelland. He made the very important observation that we each have varying needs for achievement, affiliation, and power.

People who are high achievers need or want to solve problems and challenge themselves. They are goal oriented, task focused, and they desire recognition.

People with a high-power need or want to have control and influence over their environment. They desire to be influential in a group or to be responsible for others.

People with a high-affiliation need or want acceptance and productive working relationships with others. They desire social interaction and cooperation in the workplace.

Since motivational factors differ from one person to another, a manager must first identify the three acquired-need profiles of those employees working with him/her before they can leverage these insights in the workplace (see Figure 19.5).

FIGURE 19.5

ACQUIRED NEEDS

- Need for Achievement
  - Desire: Responsibility-Challenge-Feedback
- Need for Power
  - Desire: Control, Influence, Responsibility for…
    - **Personal Power**: Exploitive-for individual objectives
    - **Social Power**: Collaborative for organizational objectives
- Need for Affiliation
  - Desire: Social Approval-Belonging-Good Relationships

McClelland's Acquired Needs Theory in Practice

The value of McClelland's Three-Need Theory is its simplicity. It is easy to understand and apply in the real world of work. For example, some individuals do not have further educational goals (Achievement) so a tuition reimbursement benefit does little to excite them. Other individuals are embarrassed by public attention and do not want to be singled out from their work team so they do not value the Employee of the Month award (Affiliation) as much as others. Finally, other employees do not want more authority so giving them increased responsibilities (Power) in the organization does little to motivate them.

Finding a strategy to meet the motivational needs of all employees can be difficult.

Equity Theory

This theory is built on the belief that employees become de-motivated, both in relation to their job and their employer, if they feel as though their inputs (what they put into the task) are greater than the outputs (what they receive) in comparison to others is the same or similar situations. Employees can be expected to respond to this in different ways, (generally to the extent the employee perceives the disparity between the inputs and the outputs exist), including de-motivation, which can be exhibited through reduced effort, becoming disgruntled, or, in more extreme cases, perhaps disruptive behavior or quitting.

FIGURE 19.6

ADAM'S EQUITY THEORY DIAGRAM—JOB MOTIVATION

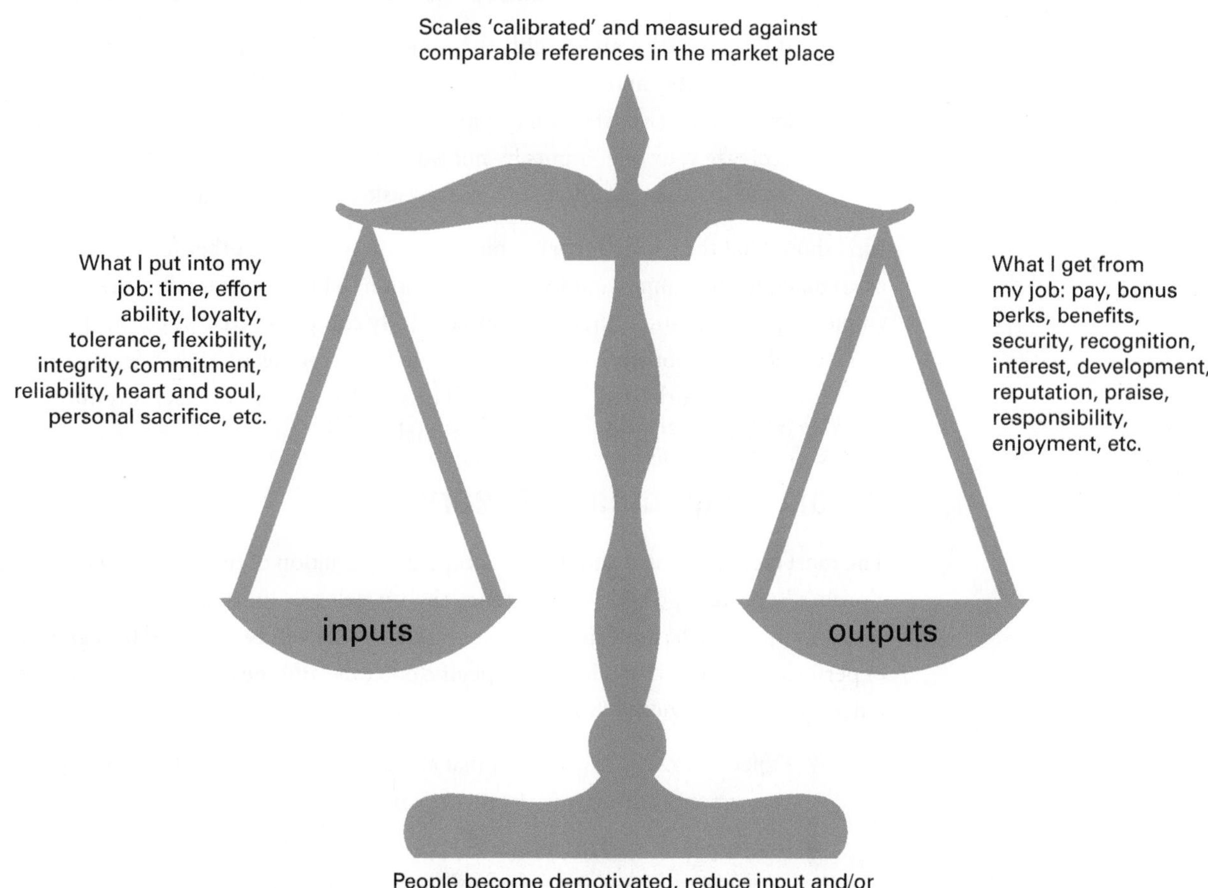

FIGURE19.7

EQUITY THEORY: INDIVIDUAL JUDGMENTS

When people perceive an inequity they may react in the following ways:

- Change their inputs (efforts). Induce others to change their inputs (efforts).
- Distort the perceived value of inputs or outcomes.
- Distort their perception of others.
- Choose a different comparison referent.
- Quit their job...change their environment.

Adam's Theory in Practice

Equity refers to the distribution of rewards in direct equality to the contribution of each person to the organization. Everyone needs not receive the same rewards, but the rewards should be in accordance with individual contributions. According to the theory, the idea of equity is as follows:

1. First, a development of an input-to-outcome ratio. Inputs are the things that are contributed to the organization. Outcomes are the things we get from the organization, e.g. a hard working person who is well paid by the organization.
2. Next, a comparison of this ratio is made with what we perceive as the input-to-outcome ratio for some other person, called the comparison other.
3. If the two ratios are roughly the same, you feel that the organization is treating you equitably and are motivated to leave things as they are. If our ratio is the lower of the two, you will feel under rewarded. To change things you may decrease your own inputs by not working so hard, leave the work situation or try to increase our total outcomes by asking for a raise in pay.

This shows that the equity theory is most relevant to pay and other forms of recognition as an outcome. It is important for an organization to know how much work each employee produces and if they are **comparatively** compensated. It is certainly not fair if a person who does not work hard gets rewarded at the same, or higher, level as another person who does work hard. Not only will this under-rewarded person get unmotivated but it might lead to their physical or emotional resignation from the company.

Vroom's Expectancy Theory

The most comprehensive and widely accepted explanation of motivation to date is Victor Vroom's Expectancy Theory. Expectancy theory states an individual tends to act in a certain way on the basis of the expectation that the act will be followed by a given level of performance, which will lead to a specific outcome and the attractiveness of that outcome to the individual. It includes three variables or relationships:

- **Expectancy.** The expectation that effort is sufficient and will lead to successful performance (Effort—Performance Link).
- **Instrumentality.** That successful performance will lead to certain outcomes (rewards and avoidance of punishment (Performance—Reward Link).
- **Valance.** The person's perceived value of the outcomes (Reward—Value Link).

The belief here is that where employees are confident that hard work will generate good outcomes, employees will want to work hard.

Building this link between effort and outcome is a two-stage process:

- First, a link needs to be made between high effort and high performance. In some cases this will be easy and self-evident, but in others it will involve training and coaching while someone is brought "up to speed;"
- Secondly, managers need to build a link between high performance and good outcomes.

Where both of these hold true, then the *hard work: good outcome* link is created.

Unfortunately, the reality is that the world is not always like this—factors outside hard work (such as inferior resources, lack of talent, or external factors) can break this link. Effort alone does not lead to successful performance, the person needs to possess the necessary talent and the effort needs to be proportionate to the task.

Expectancy theory implies that in this case a manager must be careful to nurture the linkage. Where an employee has failed despite intense hard work, the manager must take care to explain the internal or external factors that caused failure. Conversely, where an employee has been successful while still being idle, the manager reinforces the link either by showing that other factors, external to the employee's effort contributed to the positive outcome, or by pointing out how much more successful things would have been if the employee had been better prepared or worked harder.

Expectancy Theory has several useful guidelines for managers. It suggests that managers must recognize the following assumptions:

- Employees work for a variety of reasons.
- These reasons, or expected outcomes, may change over time.
- It is necessary to clearly show employees how they can attain the outcomes they desire.

Expectancy Theory in Practice

A short scenario is given below to illustrate this model of motivation. This scenario involves two airline sales reservations agents, Bill and Susan, who are candidates for promotion to the position of manager of Sales Reservations.

Bill is very talented, has had a very good sales record and always gets good performance evaluations **(effort-performance link)**. He knows that his performance is equal with Susan's and qualifies him to be promoted **(performance-reward link)**. **However,** he is not too excited about the prospects of being promoted because it would require being away from home, a great deal of travel, longer working hours, and much stress and pressure **(reward–value link).**

Susan's sales performance is tops in the company and equal to Bill's **(effort-performance link)** and her evaluations are among the best in the company. Because of her excellent performance she is also a candidate for the promotion **(performance-reward link)**. Susan really wants the position of manager. It means more money and the opportunity to travel; both are very attractive to her **(reward–value link)**.

According to expectancy theory, Bill is not very motivated to seek the promotion, but Susan is very motivated to seek the promotion, because of the reward—value linkage. In Bill's case that linkage is not positive, he does not value the travel that accompanies the promotion, yet Susan does.

Expectancy theory is complex because each action that is taken is likely to lead to several different outcomes, some that we may want and others that we may not want. For example, if people work hard and put in a lot of extra hours, several things may happen. They may get a pay raise, they may be promoted, they may gain valuable new job skills or it might have undesirable outcomes such as having less time to spend with their families and then need to cut back on their social life.

The implication for management is that it is very important to ensure the employees can in fact do the work at the desired level of performance, or be trained to do so within an acceptable period of time (**effort-performance link**). Work should be structured so that rewards are achievable and can be attained through quality performance that meets expectations (**performance-reward link**). Lastly, ensure that the rewards are valued by the employees and realize that not all persons find the same rewards attractive (**reward-value link**). When all three of the conditions for expectancy theory are fulfilled, motivation will exist. However if any one of the conditions is not fulfilled, then motivation is not present.

The Simple Answer for Motivational Success

So how can you better motivate your team members to achieve the success you desire? As simple as it may seem, the answer may lie in talking with them.

The importance of this cannot be overstated. If you don't make a point of listening to your team members, you can miss huge opportunities both for removing obstacles and for motivation. Team members may be upset by tiny points of bureaucracy of which you're not even aware. Or there may be simple actions that you could take that would have a positive affect on people's morale.

But what questions should you ask?

Ask questions that will help you learn more about their individual goals and their views as they pertain to their responsibilities. (For large groups, gather everyone and distribute a questionnaire that asks these questions in the simplest, most direct way possible).

Keep in mind that achievement, recognition, growth, meaningful work, equity and camaraderie are likely to be high on most people's list of motivators. This, of course, is aside from the obvious, which is that employees must have a safe working environment, a practical workload, comfortable working conditions, a reasonable degree of job security, satisfactory compensation and benefits, respectful treatment, credible and consistent management, and the opportunity to voice their concerns, to achieve even minimal motivation. After all, these are the basics and should be considered not so much as motivational factors, but as basic necessities, which create dissatisfaction if not present.

You should also ask team members if they feel challenged at work and if they feel they are able to use their skills and apply their knowledge. Determine if there is adequate room for growth for your employees. Do they have the opportunity to expand their knowledge and learn new skills? Do they perceive their job to be important? Do they receive recognition for their performance? And, are they proud to work for the team and proud of their contribution?

Also, strive to learn more about their relationships within the workplace. Do your best to ensure your employees have consistently positive interactions with other members of the team. By having regular one-to-one chats with team members, managers can quickly pick up and resolve issues before they become significant, as well as taking the opportunity to praise achievement.

Conclusion

Remember, your goal with the team is to learn what will build a higher morale, generate enthusiasm, and increase productivity. Just look at companies when they're performing at their best. What you'll most often find as a common denominator is the high morale of the workers.

Simply put, to motivate team members, help them be productive and be the best they can be, let them know how they are doing, make an investment in them and help them grow.

Considering that employee enthusiasm is directly related to employee performance, this becomes a never-ending cycle, one that when spun the right way, will yield unmatched results for all members of the organization.

Motivational success can seldom be achieved by applying just one theory, or just one approach. Different people in different situations in different cultures think and behave in different ways. For when it comes to motivating, what leads to success can be as wide-ranging as the theories that make up this important managerial tool.

We have used examples to provide a better understanding of some of the most important ideas in motivation, thereby helping you see both the value of these ideas and their limitations.

CHAPTER

20 Integrated Marketing Communications[1]

One-to-Many: The Traditional Communication Model

Test your advertising memory:*

1. What energy drink "gives you wiiings?"
2. What product advertises that "Even a caveman can do it?"
3. What character do Energizer battery ads feature?
4. At Burger King, you can have it "________________," whereas at Hardees the burgers are "_____________" broiled.
5. Which paper towel brand is "The Quicker Picker-Upper?"[2]

Did you get them all right? You owe your knowledge about these and a thousand other trivia questions to the efforts of people who specialize in marketing communication. Of course today, these slogans are "old school" as marketers have followed consumers onto Facebook and Twitter and into virtual worlds to talk with their customers.

promotion
The coordination of a marketer's communication efforts to influence attitudes or behavior.

Promotion is the coordination of marketing communication efforts to influence attitudes or behavior. This function is one of the famous Four Ps of the marketing mix and it plays a vital role—whether the goal is to sell hamburgers, insurance, ringtones, or healthy diets. Of course, virtually everything an organization says and does is a form of marketing communication. The ads it creates, the packages it designs, the uniforms its employees wear, and what other consumers say about their experiences with the firm contribute to the thoughts and feelings people have of the company and its products. In fact, savvy marketers should consider that every element of the marketing mix is actually a form of communication. After all, the price of a product, where it is sold, and of course the quality of the product itself contributes to our impression of it.

Previously we talked about creating, managing, and pricing tangible and intangible products. But it's not enough just to produce great products—successful marketing plans must also provide effective marketing communication strategies. Just what do we mean by communication? Today messages assume many forms: quirky television commercials, innovative Web sites, viral videos, sophisticated magazine ads, funky T-shirts, blimps blinking messages over football stadiums—even do-it-yourself, customer-made advertising. Some marketing communications push specific products (like the Apple iPad) or actions (like donating blood), whereas others try to create or reinforce an image that represents the entire organization (like General Electric or the Catholic Church).

Promotion takes many forms, including humorous print ads like this one for a German company that makes pens.

PHOTO: JungVonMatt-Hamburg

Marketing communication in general performs one or more of four roles:

1. It *informs* consumers about new goods and services.
2. It *reminds* consumers to continue using certain brands.
3. It *persuades* consumers to choose one brand over others.
4. It *builds* relationships with customers.

Many marketing experts now believe a successful promotional strategy should blend several diverse forms of marketing communication. **Integrated marketing communication (IMC)** is the process that marketers use "to plan, develop, execute, and evaluate coordinated, measurable, persuasive brand communication programs over time"[3] to plan, develop, execute, and evaluate coordinated, measurable, persuasive brand communication programs over time to targeted audiences. The IMC approach argues that consumers come in contact with a company or a brand in many different ways before, after, and during a purchase. Consumers see these points of contact or *touchpoints* as we described in Chapter 7—a TV commercial, a company Web site, a coupon, an opportunity to win a sweepstakes, or a display in a store—as a whole, as a single company that speaks to them in different places and different ways. IMC marketers understand that to achieve their marketing communication goals, they must selectively use some or all of these touchpoints to deliver a consistent message to their customers in a **multichannel promotional strategy** where they combine traditional advertising, sales promotion, and public relations activities with online buzz-building activities. That's a lot different from most traditional marketing communication programs of the past that made little effort to coordinate the varying messages consumers received. When an advertising campaign runs independently of a sweepstakes, which in turn has no relation to a NASCAR racing sponsorship, consumers often get conflicting messages that leave them confused and unsure of the brand's identity. With IMC, marketers seek to understand what information consumers want as well as how, when, and where they want it—and then to deliver information about the product using the best combination of communication methods available to them.

integrated marketing communication (IMC)
A strategic business process that marketers use to plan, develop, execute, and evaluate coordinated, measurable, persuasive brand communication programs over time to targeted audiences.

multichannel promotional strategy
A marketing communication strategy where they combine traditional advertising, sales promotion, and public relations activities with online buzz-building activities.

It's great to talk about a multichannel strategy, but that still leaves a lot of questions about how we get our customers to understand what we're trying to say. And, in today's high-tech world these questions get even more complicated because the communication options available to marketers change literally almost every day—there will probably be new formats that appear on the scene between the time you start and finish this course!

FIGURE 20.1

Three Models of Marketing Communication

Marketers today make use of the traditional one-to-many communication model and the updated many-to-many communication model as well as talking one-to-one with consumers and business customers.

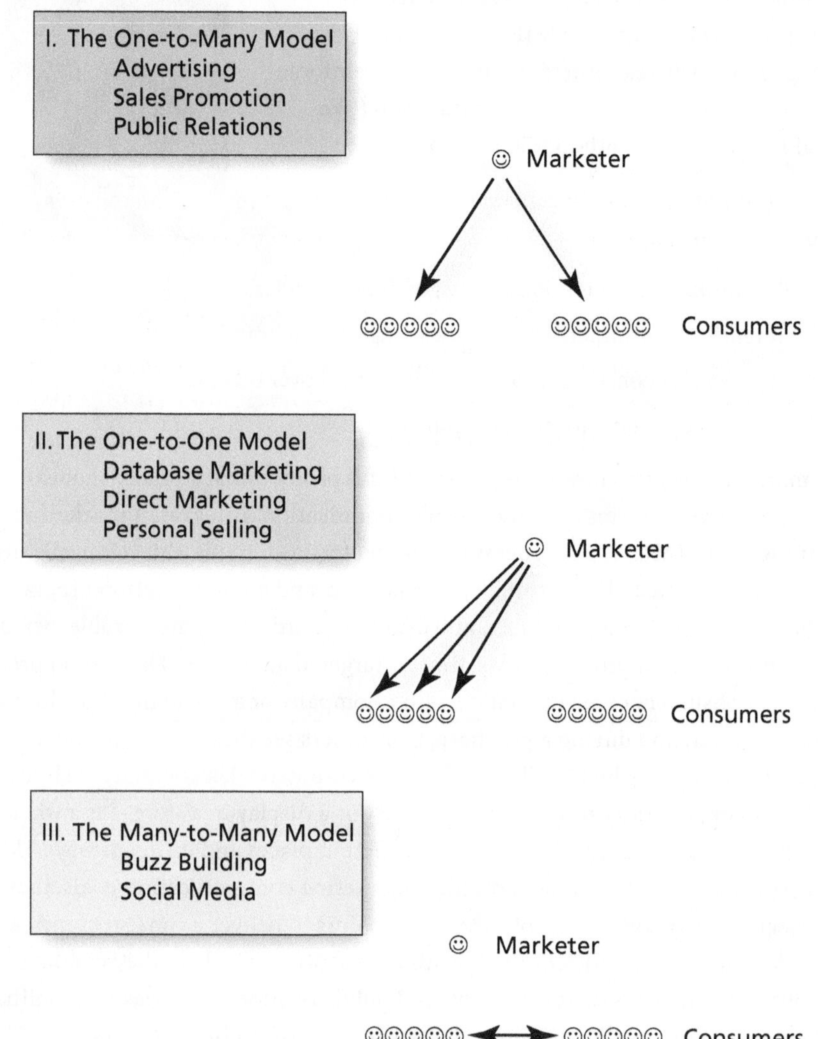

It helps to understand these options when we look at how we as consumers get our information. Figure 20.1 shows three communication models. The first, traditional communication model is a "One-to-Many" view in which a single marketer develops and sends messages to many, perhaps even millions of consumers at once. The one-to-many approach involves traditional forms of marketing communication such as *advertising* including traditional mass media (TV, radio, magazines, and newspapers), *out-of-home* (like billboards), and Internet advertising. This model also benefits from *consumer sales promotions* such as coupons, samples, rebates, or contests; and press releases and special events that *public relations* professionals organize.

Today, these traditional methods still work in some circumstances—but there are a lot of other options available that often mesh better with our "wired" 24/7 culture. When you take a break from posting to your friends on Facebook, you'll recognize that you also learn about products and services from your own social network in addition to ads, billboards, or coupons. For this reason we need to consider an updated communication model where marketing messages are what we think of as many-to-many. This newer perspective recognizes the huge impact of **word-of-mouth communication** where consumers look to each other for information and recommendations. Many of us are more likely to choose a new restaurant based on users' reviews we read on Yelp than because we saw a cool commercial for the place on TV. Ditto for nail salons, bike stores, and maybe even cars.

word-of-mouth communication When consumers provide information about products to other consumers.

In the updated model, marketers add new tools to their communications toolbox including *buzz-building* activities that use *viral* and *evangelical marketing techniques* as well as new social media platforms such as *brand communities, product review sites,* and *social networking sites.* The odds are you're using many of these platforms already, though you may not call them by these names. By the end of this section, you will.

We also need to expand our traditional communication model to include *one-to-one marketing,* where marketers speak to consumers and business customers individually. The one-to-one forms of marketing communication include personal selling, trade sales promotion activities used to support personal selling, and a variety of database marketing activities that include direct marketing.

The Communication Model

Wired or not, the **communication model** in Figure 20.2 is a good way to understand the basics of how any kind of message works. In this perspective, a *source* transmits a *message* through some *medium* to a receiver who (we hope) listens and understands the message. The basic idea is that any way a marketer reaches out to consumers—a hat with a Caterpillar tractor logo on it, a personal sales pitch from a Mary Kay representative, or a televised fashion show with supermodels strutting their stuff for Victoria's Secret—this is part of the basic communication process.

communication model The process whereby meaning is transferred from a source to a receiver.

The communication model specifies the elements necessary for effective communication to occur: a source, a message, a medium, and a receiver. Regardless of how a marketer sends messages, her objective is to capture receivers' attention and relate to their needs.

THE SOURCE ENCODES Let's start to explore this basic model from a good place: the beginning. **Encoding** is the process by which a source translates an idea into a form of communication that conveys the desired meaning. The **source** is the organization or individual that sends the message. It's one thing for marketers to form an idea about a product in their own minds, but it's not quite as simple to express the idea to their customers. To make their messages more believable or more attractive to consumers, marketers sometimes choose a real person (like the computer users that appeared in Microsoft's "Windows 7 Was My Idea" advertising), hire an actor or a model (William Shatner of *Star Trek* fame for **Priceline.com** or Queen Latifah for Cover Girl Cosmetics) or create a character (the GEICO gecko with the Cockney accent) to represent the source.[4]

In other cases the message features actual customers. In advertising to counter negative consumers' responses to Toyota's massive recall, the company used ads in which Toyota customers told why they were going to continue to buy the cars.

FIGURE 20.2

The Communication Model

The communication model explains how organizations create and transmit messages from the marketer (the source) to the consumer (the receiver) who (we hope) understands what the marketer intends to say.

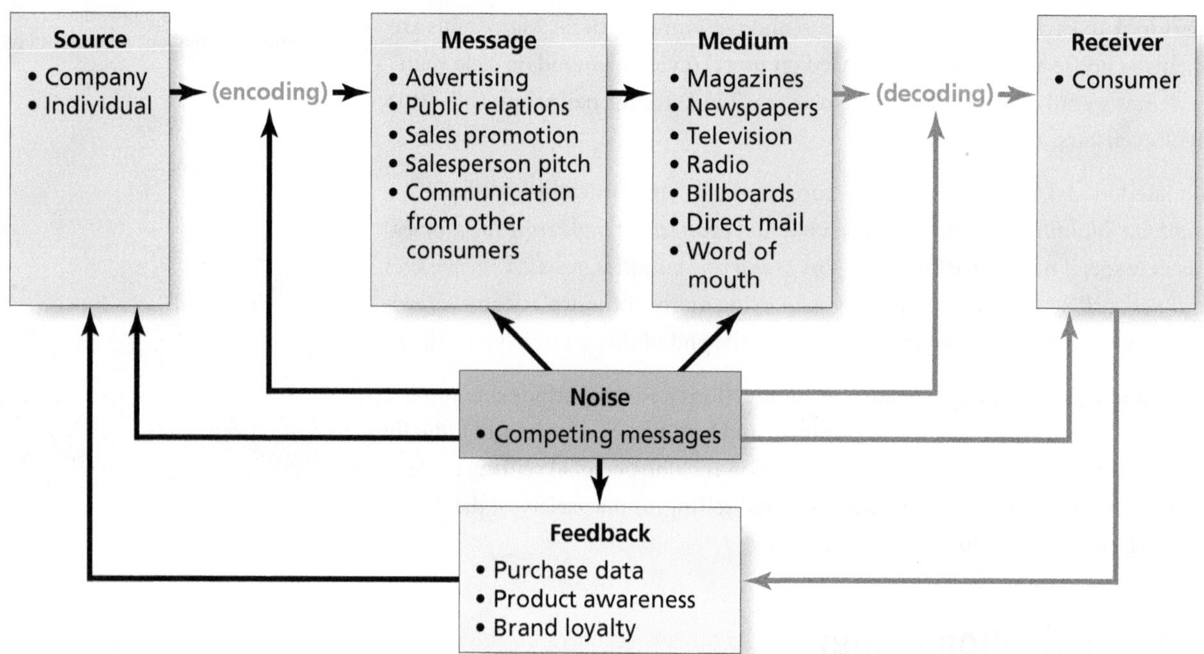

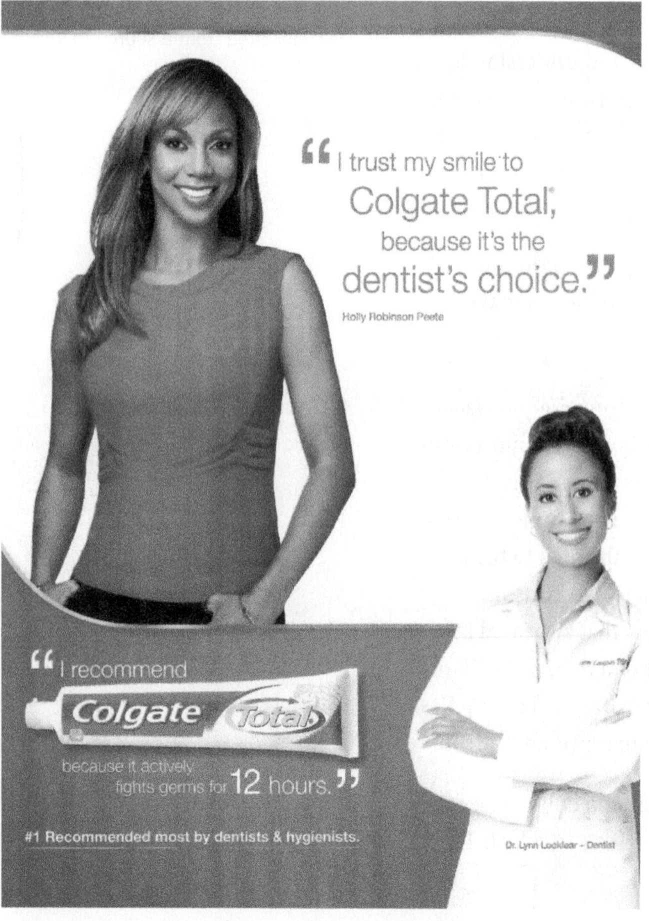

Many marketing messages rely on an expert of highly credible source to encourage recipients to take them seriously.

THE MESSAGE The **message** is the actual content that goes from the source to a receiver. It includes information necessary to persuade, inform, remind, or build a relationship. Advertising messages may include both verbal and nonverbal elements, such as beautiful background scenery or funky music. The marketer must select the ad elements carefully so that the message connects with end consumers or business customers in its target market. Otherwise effective communication simply does not occur and the organization just wastes its money.

THE MEDIUM No matter how the source encodes the message, it must then transmit it via a **medium,** a communication vehicle that reaches members of a target audience. This vehicle can be television, radio, social media sites such as Facebook or Twitter, a magazine, a company Web site, an Internet blog, a personal contact, a billboard, or even a coffee mug that displays a product logo. Marketers face two major challenges when they select a medium. First, they must make sure the target market will be exposed to the medium—that the intended receivers actually read the magazine or watch the TV show where the message appears. Second, the attributes of the advertised product should match those of the medium. For example, magazines with high prestige are more effective to communicate messages about overall product image and quality, whereas specialized magazines do a better job when they convey factual information.[5]

An Italian candy ad communicates the product's caffeine content quite vividly.
PHOTO: Courtesy of Procter & Gamble, Co

THE RECEIVER DECODES If a tree falls in the forest and no one hears it, did it make a sound? Zen mysteries aside, communication cannot occur unless a **receiver** is there to get the message. The receiver is any individual or organization that intercepts and interprets the message. Assuming that the customer is even paying attention (a big assumption in our overloaded, media-saturated society), she interprets the message in light of her unique experiences. **Decoding** is the process whereby a receiver assigns meaning to a message; that is, she translates the message she sees or hears back into an idea that makes sense to her.

Marketers hope that the target consumer will decode the message the way they intended, but effective communication occurs only when the source and the receiver share a mutual frame of reference. Too often sources and receivers aren't on the same page, and the results can range from mildly embarrassing to downright disastrous. This mismatch is especially likely to happen when the source and the receiver don't share the same cultural background or language.

NOISE The communication model also acknowledges that noise—anything that interferes with effective communication—can block messages. As the many arrows between noise and the other elements of the communication model in Figure 20.2 indicate, noise can occur at any stage of communication. It can pop up at the encoding stage if the source uses words or symbols that the receiver will not understand. Or a nearby conversation may distract the receiver. There may be a problem with transmission of the message through the medium—especially if it's drowned out by the chorus of other marketers clamoring for us to look at their messages instead. Marketers try to minimize noise when they place their messages where there is less likely to be distractions or competition for consumers' attention. Calvin Klein, for example, will often buy a block of advertising pages in a magazine so that the reader sees only pictures of its clothing as she leafs through that section.

Gillette employs a creative medium to get its message to customers.
PHOTO: Courtesy of Procter & Gamble, Co

FEEDBACK To complete the communication loop, the source gets **feedback** from receivers. Feedback is a reaction to the message that helps marketers gauge the effectiveness of the message so they can fine-tune it. Sometimes consumers eagerly provide this feedback—especially if they are unhappy. They may call a toll-free number or post an e-mail to the manufacturer to resolve a problem. More often, though, marketers must actively seek their customers' feedback. The need for this "reality check" reminds us of the importance of conducting marketing research to verify that a firm's strategies are working. And, keep in mind that even though nobody likes to be yelled at, we actually want customers to complain so that we have an opportunity to address their concerns before they say negative things to others.

The Traditional Promotion Mix

As we said earlier, promotion, or marketing communication, is one of the Famous Four Ps. Marketers use the term **promotion mix** to refer to the communication elements that the marketer controls. These elements of the traditional promotion mix include:

- Advertising
- Sales promotion
- Public relations
- Personal selling
- Direct marketing

Just as a DJ combines different songs or phrases to create an entertainment experience, the term mix implies that a company's promotion strategy focuses on more than one element. And as we said, promotion works best when the marketer/DJ skillfully combines all of the elements of the promotion mix to deliver a single consistent message about a brand.

For effective decoding to occur, the course and the receiver must share a mutual frame of reference. In this ad the receiver needs to understand the meaning of a "white flag" in order for the message to make sense.

PHOTO: CLOROX® is a registered trademark of The Clorox Company. Used with permission

Another challenge is to be sure that the promotion mix works in harmony with the overall marketing mix to combine elements of promotion with place, price, and product to position the firm's offering in people's minds. For example, marketers must design ads for luxury products such as Rolex watches or Jaguar automobiles to communicate that same luxury character of the product, and the ads should appear in places that reinforce that upscale image. A chic commercial that appears before a showing of the latest *Jackass* movie just won't cut it.

Marketers have a lot more control over some kinds of marketing communication messages than they do others. As Figure 20.3 shows, *mass media advertising* and *sales promotion* are at one end of the continuum, where the marketer has total control over the message she delivers. At the other end is *word-of-mouth (WOM) communication,* where everyday people rather than the company run the show. WOM is a vitally important component of the brand attitudes consumers form—and of their decisions about what and what not to buy. Sandwiched between the ends we find *personal selling* and *direct marketing,* where marketers have some but not total control over the message they deliver, and *public relations,* where marketers have even less control. Table 20.1 presents some of the pros and cons of each element of the promotion mix.

FIGURE 20.3

Control Continuum

The messages that consumers receive about companies and products differ in terms of how much the marketers can control the content.

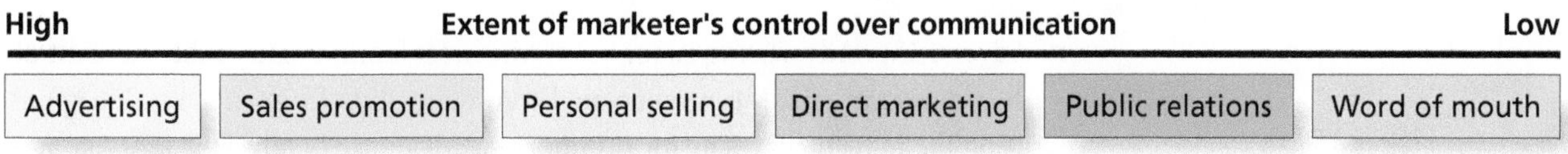

High	Extent of marketer's control over communication				Low
Advertising	Sales promotion	Personal selling	Direct marketing	Public relations	Word of mouth

TABLE 20.1
A COMPARISON OF ELEMENTS OF THE TRADITIONAL PROMOTION MIX

PROMOTIONAL ELEMENT	PROS	CONS
Advertising	■ The marketer has control over what the message will say, when it will appear, and who is likely to see it.	■ Because of the high cost to produce and distribute, it may not be an efficient means of communicating with some target audiences. ■ Some ads may have low credibility and/or be ignored by audience.
Sales promotion	■ Provides incentives to retailers to support one's products. ■ Builds excitement for retailers and consumers. ■ Encourages immediate purchase and trial of new products. ■ Price-oriented promotions cater to price-sensitive consumers.	■ Short-term emphasis on immediate sales rather than a focus on building brand loyalty. ■ The number of competing promotions may make it hard to break through the promotional clutter. ■ If marketers use too many price-related sales promotion activities, consumers' perception of a fair price for the brand may be lowered.
Public relations	■ Relatively low cost ■ High credibility	■ Lack of control over the message that is eventually transmitted and no guarantee that the message will ever reach the target. ■ It is difficult to measure the effectiveness of PR efforts.
Personal selling	■ Direct contact with the customer gives the salesperson the opportunity to be flexible and modify the sales message to coincide with the customer's needs. ■ The salesperson can get immediate feedback from the customer.	■ High cost per contact with customer. ■ Difficult to ensure consistency of message when it is delivered by many different company representatives. ■ The credibility of salespeople often depends on the quality of their company's image, which has been created by other promotional strategies.
Direct marketing	■ Targets specific groups of potential customers with different offers. ■ Marketers can easily measure the results. ■ Provides extensive product information and multiple offers within a single appeal. ■ Provides a way for a company to collect feedback about the effectiveness of its messages in an internal database.	■ Consumers may have a negative opinion of some types of direct marketing. ■ Costs more per contact than mass appeals.

MASS COMMUNICATION Some elements of the promotion mix include messages intended to reach many prospective customers at the same time. Whether a company offers customers a coupon for 50 cents off or airs a television commercial to millions, it promotes itself to a mass audience. These are the elements of the promotion mix that use **mass communication,** i.e., TV radio, magazines, and newspapers:

- **Advertising:** Advertising is, for many, the most familiar and visible element of the promotion mix. It is nonpersonal communication from an identified sponsor using the mass media. The most important advantage of advertising is that it reaches large numbers of consumers at one time. In addition, advertising can convey rich and dynamic images that establish and reinforce a distinctive brand identity. This helps marketers bond with customers and boost sales. Advertising also is useful to communicate factual information about the product or to remind consumers to buy their favorite brand. However, it sometimes suffers from a credibility problem: Cynical consumers tune out messages they think are biased or are intended to sell them something they don't need. Advertising can also be very expensive, so firms must ensure that their messages deliver the best bang for the buck.
- **Sales promotion:** Consumer sales promotion includes programs such as contests, coupons, or other incentives that marketers design to build interest in or encourage purchase of a product during a specified period. Unlike other forms of promotion, sales promotion intends to stimulate immediate action (often in the form of a purchase) rather than build long-term loyalty.
- **Public relations:** Public relations describe a variety of communication activities that seek to create and maintain a positive image of an organization and its products among various publics, including customers, government officials, and shareholders. Public relations programs also include efforts to present negative company news in the most positive way so that this information will have less damaging consequences. In contrast to sales promotion, public relations components of the promotion mix usually do not seek a short-term increase in sales. Instead, they try to influence feelings, opinions, or beliefs for the long term.

Advertising can convey rich and dynamic images that establish and reinforce a distinctive brand identity.

PHOTO: Courtesy of Heinz World Headquarters

PERSONAL COMMUNICATION Sometimes marketers want to communicate with consumers on a personal, one-on-one level. The most immediate way for a marketer to make contact with customers is simply to tell them how wonderful the product is. This is part of the *personal selling* element of the promotion mix we mentioned previously. It is the direct interaction between a company representative and a customer that can occur in person, by phone, or even over an interactive computer link.

Salespeople are a valuable source of communication because customers can ask questions and the salesperson can immediately address objections and describe product benefits. Personal selling can be tremendously effective, especially for big-ticket consumer items and for industrial products for which the "human touch" is essential.

Marketers also use direct mail, telemarketing, and other direct marketing activities to create personal appeals. Like personal selling, direct marketing provides direct communication with a consumer or business customer. Because direct marketing activities seek to gain a direct response from individual consumers, the source can target a communication to market segments of a few or—with today's technology—even segments of one.

Communications Mix Explained[6]

The various elements companies can use to communicate with the target market are referred to as the communications mix. These elements include advertising, public relations, sales promotion, and personal selling. Marketers must decide how to integrate these elements in an effective way to deliver the right marketing message at the right time. While one company will focus all its communication efforts on a single element, such as advertising, others will use two, three, or even all four elements in concert with each other

EXAMPLE **COMMUNICATIONS MIX**

Hoping to reinvigorate a long neglected brand, Old Spice launched its "The Man Your Man Could Smell Like" ad campaign during the 2010 Super Bowl. Although the ad, featuring Isaiah Mustafa, scored with viewers during the game, no one could imagine that the ad would become an online sensation almost overnight. Within months, the commercial was viewed over 10 million times on YouTube, with subsequent commercials also being released online. Looking to maintain the buzz, Old Spice turned to Facebook and Twitter by inviting people to post questions to Mustafa. Over a two-day period the former NFL wide receiver responded, in near real-time, with over 180 video responses to select messages he received. Those responses have been viewed over 40 million times and the Old Spice brand has received over 110 million brand Web views.[7]

PHOTO: Christina Leohr/ Shutterstock

>> END EXAMPLE

Communications Mix Applied

Deciding which communication element to use depends on several factors, including the marketing objectives, target market, type and age of product, and promotional resources. For example, limited financial resources will generally exclude a national television campaign as a consideration. High-priced products, such as automobiles, typically employ personal selling because buyers prefer more interaction to gain information and access to product demonstration (test drive). Brands in the early stages of the product lifecycle benefit from increased awareness, which can be accomplished through advertising.

Companies typically establish the communications mix based on a set of objectives. These objectives guide the marketer in determining what message should be sent and how to send it. Determining objectives requires that marketers understand that before consumers buy they first must be aware of the product. The AIDA model, which is an acronym for Awareness, Interest, Desire, and Action, assists the marketer in

FIGURE 20.4

AIDA Model and the Effectiveness of Communication Tools

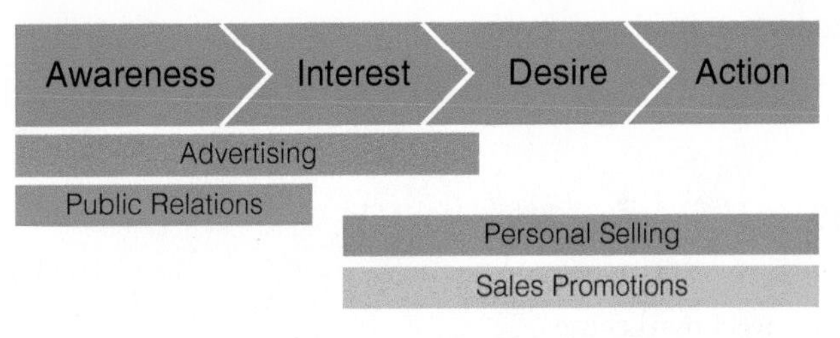

	Awareness	Interest	Desire	Action
Advertising	High	High	Limited	None
Public Relations	High	Limited	None	None
Personal Selling	None	Limited	High	High
Sales Promotions	None	Limited	High	High

FIGURE 20.5

Push-Pull Strategies

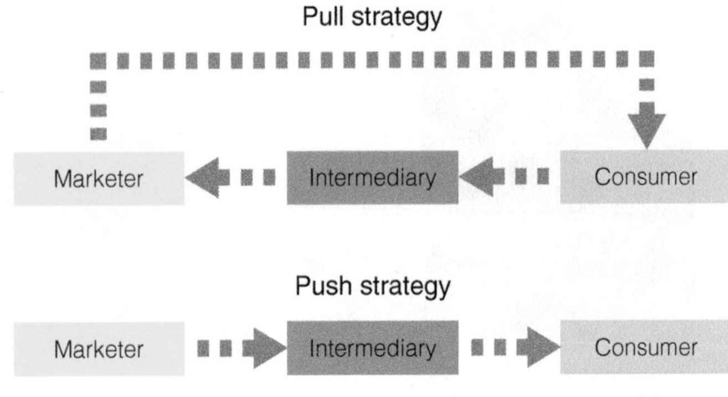

developing the communications mix. Each element of the communications mix is beneficial at one stage of the AIDA model, but is ineffective at another. Figure 20.4 shows that advertising and public relations are effective at generating awareness, but they lack the capability to move consumers to take action or buy. Personal selling and sales promotions are effective at stimulating desire and encouraging action, but do little in the way of building awareness. As such, multiple elements of the communications mix are often needed to reach the desired objectives.

In many cases, companies must decide whether to use a pull or push strategy. Companies use a **pull strategy** by promoting directly to consumers, who then request the product from retailers. Retailers in turn request the product from the wholesaler, who orders it from the manufacturer. A **push strategy**, on the other hand, targets wholesalers and retailers and encourages them to order the product, thus pushing it through the channel to consumers (see Figure 20.5). A pull strategy often employs advertising and consumer sales promotion while personal selling and trade promotions are used with a push strategy.

Companies should also consider the time that some objectives require. For example, communication tools such as advertising and public relations require longer periods of time for maximum benefits to be realized. The same is true for building brand loyalty and strong customer relationships. Sales promotions, on the other hand, are designed for short-term sales increases. However, sales promotions should be used wisely and on a limited basis. Because promotions typically result in lower prices, their continued use will run the risk of shifting the expected price of a product downward.

The media environment is constantly evolving, and marketers must understand how members of the target market use media. For example, 30 years ago, media options were relatively limited. Network television dominated the American media landscape, along with print (including newspapers and magazines), radio, and outdoor advertising such as billboards. In the twenty-first century, television still plays a role in consumers' media choices, but new forms of communication are rapidly emerging, creating a variety of choices for consumers. As evidence, consider the complexity of an average American's media habits:[8]

- Americans spend more than 3,200 hours a year consuming some form of media.
- Over 1,900 hours are spent watching television (including broadcast, cable, and satellite).
- Over 550 hours are spent listening to the radio.
- Almost 350 hours are spent on the Internet.

- About 158 hours are spent reading newspapers.
- Over 90 hours are spent reading magazines or books.
- Over 220 hours are spent playing video games.

To make things even more complicated, some consumers use multiple types of media at the same time. It is not uncommon for consumers to simultaneously watch TV, talk or text on their cell phones, and surf the Internet on a laptop. As consumers gain more control over media and have a broader range of media choices, companies will need to alter where media dollars are spent. Many companies have already begun to shift from traditional media, such as TV and radio, toward digital media such as the Internet and mobile (see Figure 20.6).[9]

Although our media choices are increasing, our ability to pay attention remains limited because no one has found a way to add hours to a day. To communicate effectively, marketers need to create innovative media strategies that deliver relevant messages to consumers wherever and whenever they are prepared to receive them.

FIGURE 20.6

PAST AND FUTURE MEDIA MIX

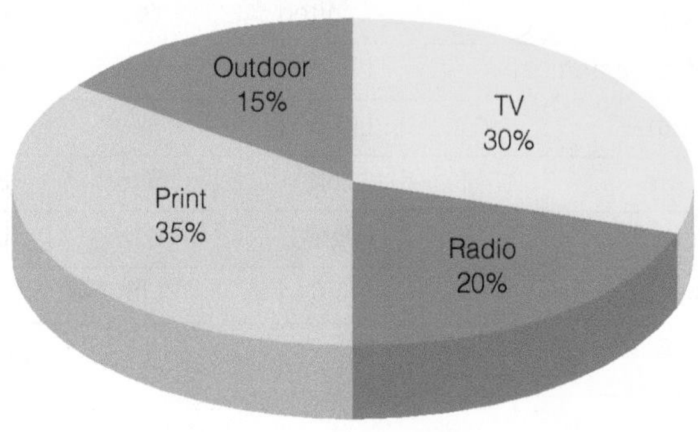

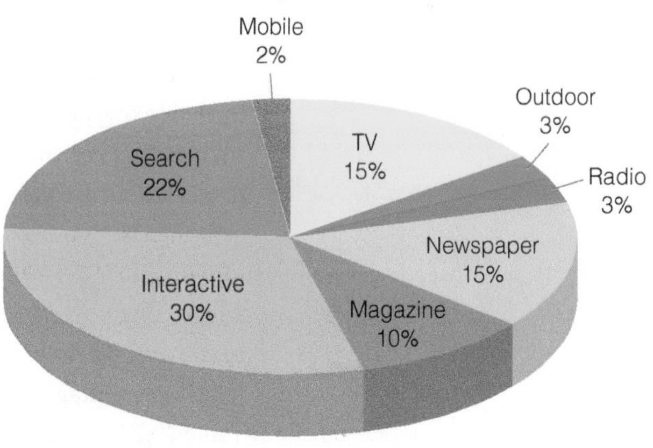

Media Types Explained

The various forms of media enable people to have options for how they receive news, sports, or entertainment. While many people spend a lot of time watching shows or movies on TV, many others use their TVs for video games. While some people read newspapers, others turn to the Web. Technological advances such as satellites and the Internet have created a wide range of media options from which to choose.

Media can be classified in numerous ways. For mass communications, the major categories of media are:

- **Broadcast**—Includes network TV, cable TV, and radio.
- **Print**—Includes newspapers, magazines, and direct mail.
- **Out-of-home (OOH)**—Includes display advertising such as billboards, signs, and posters.
- **Digital media**—Includes media such as e-mail, Web advertising, and Web sites.
- **Branded entertainment** —Incorporates brand messages into entertainment venues such as movies or TV shows.

Media Types Applied

With so many types of media from which to choose, how do marketers decide which ones to use? Media efficiency measures how effective a media vehicle is at reaching a particular customer segment, compared to the cost. Because media budgets are not infinite, marketers weigh efficiency carefully. More efficient forms of media are less expensive, but less able to finely target niche demographics or behavioral segments.

TABLE 20.2
CAPABILITIES AND LIMITATIONS OF MAJOR MEDIA TYPES

	TELEVISION	RADIO	NEWSPAPERS	MAGAZINES	INTERNET	OUT-OF-HOME
Reach mass audience	Yes	No	No	No	Yes	No
Target market	Limited	Yes	Limited	Yes	Yes	No
Target geographically	Limited	Yes	Yes	Limited	Limited	No
Lead time	Long	Short	Short	Long	Short	Limited
Shelf life	Short	Short	Short	Long	Short	Long
Expense	High	Low	Low	High	Low	High
Measureable results	Limited	Limited	Limited	Limited	High	None

Media impact is a qualitative assessment of the value of a message exposed in a particular medium. For example, consumers might view an ad in the *New York Times* as having more credibility than if it appeared in the *National Enquirer.* Marketing research companies collect measures of **media engagement,** which evaluates how attentively audiences read, watch, or listen to media. Two television shows might deliver audiences of equal size, but viewers of one show might be significantly more engaged and involved in their experience than viewers of another show. For example, viewers of drama shows, such as *NCIS or Grey's Anatomy,* are more actively involved in the show from week to week than are viewers of other genres such as news or comedy. Product or service characteristics are also taken into account. Does the product need to be demonstrated for consumers to understand what it does? If so, visual media such as television or online advertising are required. Are customers located in a fairly tight geographic area? If so, local newspapers or local radio would be a great solution. Each type of medium has relative advantages and disadvantages that are weighed when developing a media mix.[10] Table 20.2 highlights the capabilities and limitations of the major media types.

Broadcast

For decades, broadcast was the media type of choice among U.S. advertisers. Broadcast sends messages to large numbers of people extremely quickly, at a fraction of the cost of other media. The two traditional forms of broadcast are television and radio.

Network television (for example, CBS, NBC, ABC, and FOX) refers to the over-the-air broadcast of programming and paid advertising through a nationwide series of affiliate television stations. Although network television commands the majority of broadcast spending, **cable television** (for example, CNN, MTV, and USA Network) is gaining advertising dollars. Unlike network television, which started by broadcasting over free public airwaves, cable TV networks require cable or satellite dishes to deliver their signals. Some cable networks are funded by paid ads, whereas others charge viewers a fee to watch.

Among all types of media, television has the greatest capability to deliver audiences en masse. **Reach** measures the number of people who could potentially receive an ad through a particular media vehicle. It can be expressed as a raw number of individuals or as a percentage of a target audience. An **impression** is a single delivery of an advertising message. Another way to think about television is that it offers high reach, because it can generate a huge number of impressions. Nielsen Media reports television and radio ratings that are the percentage of the total available audience watching a television show or tuned in to a radio program.[11]

Television is also attractive to marketers because it serves up big audiences at a low cost per viewer. **CPM (or cost per thousand)** is a metric that calculates the cost for any media vehicle to deliver one thousand impressions among a group of target customers. The "M" in CPM comes from the Latin word mille, which stands for thousand. To calculate CPM, all a marketer needs to know is total media cost and the number of impressions. Cost is then divided by impressions converted into thousands.

EXAMPLE **CPM**

An advertising campaign costs $4,000 and generates 120,000 impressions. The CPM can be calculated using the following formula:[12]

$$\text{Cost per Thousand (CPM)} \frac{\text{Advertising}}{(\text{Impressions Generated}/1{,}000)}$$

$$= \frac{\$4{,}000}{(120{,}000/1{,}000)}$$

$$= \frac{\$4{,}000}{120} = \$33.33$$

>> END EXAMPLE

Despite its strengths, television has a few disadvantages. In addition to concerns over declining viewership, marketers balk at the high up-front costs of television advertising. Production expenses on a polished TV commercial will often run into millions of dollars. In addition, television is a better choice for marketers targeting broad population groups, such as adults aged 18–54. As targets become smaller and more narrowly defined, the efficiency of television is lost.

Growth in the use of DVRs (digital video recorders) also poses a threat to television advertising. Time-shifting is the practice of recording a television program at one time to replay it at another. Research shows that during playback, 53% of viewers with DVRs skip over the commercials, which is troubling to networks with business models based on television advertising.[13] If fewer people are watching commercials, advertisers will demand lower rates or will shift advertising dollars to other forms of media.

In contrast with television, radio is a low-cost medium. Media rates to advertise on radio stations are much lower than for network or cable television. Network and cable signals may cover an entire country, but radio broadcasts are mostly confined to the geographic reach of a station's signal transmitter. Radio ads are also purchased to target specific local or regional areas. It should therefore come as no surprise that local businesses like automotive dealers or restaurants use significant amounts of radio advertising.

Radio also does an excellent job of targeting audiences with specific interests. Programming ranges across diverse genres such as music, talk, sports, and news. Even within the music format, listeners can find almost any kind of channel they want, from hip-hop to classical music. This ability to target audiences is why marketers who segment customers based on their lifestyles or interests find radio appealing.

A major disadvantage of radio is that advertising messages cannot include visuals. The entire ad must succeed, or fail, based on a virtual "theater of the mind" where consumers imagine products or services based solely on what they hear. This poses a creative challenge for many ad agencies, but radio ads have a significant impact on listeners when done well. Because they involve only the sense of hearing, radio ads may also leave a more fleeting impression on listeners. This problem is compounded because our attention is usually divided while listening to radio. Most of us are doing something else, such as driving a car or cooking, while tuned in.

Because of the increasing popularity of digital media, spending on broadcast-station-based terrestrial radio will continue to decline. However, this does not mean that radio will disappear. Both television and radio are looking for new ways to distribute their programming content. Some television networks and radio stations are broadcasting or streaming shows online to laptops or mobile devices. Satellite radio is a fairly recent addition to the media landscape and uses space-based satellites to broadcast instead of local antennas. As the listener base increases, satellite radio companies might begin to offer limited on-air advertising opportunities to marketers.

Print

Magazines and newspapers are the two most frequently used forms of print advertising. Posters, flyers, signs, and other printed communications are included under the heading of "print" but are used by marketers much less frequently.

There are thousands of magazines published in the United States every year. You can find a magazine devoted to almost any interest or hobby imaginable. If you're a news junkie, you can read *Time Magazine* or *The Week*. If you love pets, then perhaps you should check out Pet Fancy. Are you a high school science teacher? *Science Teacher* magazine might be right for you. Companies selling products or services related to occupations, lifestyles, or interests use magazines because they can pinpoint their target audiences. For instance, it would be efficient and effective for a business manufacturing yoga mats to run ads in *Yoga* magazine.

Magazines also have a degree of credibility and prestige, due in part to their capability to reproduce high-quality images. As any reader of *GQ* or *Vogue* will testify, there is no medium with ads as beautiful as those found in glossy magazines. The credibility of such magazines is further enhanced by the professionally written stories and editorials they contain. Magazines also have fairly long lives; monthlies may be kept around and read for 30 days or longer.

The number of published and distributed copies of a magazine is called its **circulation.** A magazine's circulation can be thought of as a measure of its readership, or reach. The long life span of magazines creates a pass-along effect, where a single issue might have multiple readers. Copies of magazines that you might read in a doctor's office are an example of a single issue "passing along" from one patient to another.

One disadvantage of magazines is their high CPM relative to other types of media. Marketers justify the added expense of magazines based on their capability to deliver specific target audiences, their credibility, and their longer life spans. Lead time is the amount of preparation time a media type requires before an advertisement can be run. Four-color magazines require longer lead times than television or newspapers, and the position—for example, front cover or back cover—of an ad in a particular issue is usually not guaranteed.

EXAMPLE **MEDIA TYPES**

Instead of emotional appeals, new ads emphasize the fact that Welch's has twice the antioxidant power of orange juice. With a total budget of $10 million and the need to provide consumers with an information-intensive message, a breakthrough approach to media was also needed. Special print ads with "Peel 'n Taste" strips attached appeared in magazines such as *People* and *Cookie*, inviting readers to experience Welch's bold flavor. After peeling back the strip and then licking it, consumers were able to read about the juice's health benefits. News coverage for the innovative ad included stories in the *Wall Street Journal* and on *Good Morning America*, and dramatically expanded the campaign's reach. Best of all, during the campaign period, sales of Welch's grape juice increased 10%.[14]

>> END EXAMPLE

Grape juice sales have been falling due to rising competition and parents' concerns over beverages with high sugar content. Marketers for Welch's brand noticed that traditional media plans emphasizing television ads with pictures of smiling, happy kids weren't as effective as in the past. Welch's revamped its entire message and media strategy.
PHOTO: David P. Smith/Shutterstock

Local newspapers focus the bulk of their coverage on a city or regional area, like the *Chicago Tribune or Miami Herald.* Messages that are relevant to specific geographic areas, like ads for 24-hour sales at a neighborhood furniture store, are well suited to local papers. Similar to magazines, ads in newspapers are surrounded by independently written stories that may lend credibility to their marketing messages. Newspapers also have more advertising flexibility than magazines because they usually publish on a daily basis. Compared with television, local papers are a somewhat less expensive media option, but this advantage can be offset by their limited geographic coverage. National newspapers like *USA Today* or the *Wall Street Journal* can achieve nationwide coverage; however, readers tend to be more upscale, such as businesspeople and travelers. They offer the same advantages of timeliness and credibility as local newspapers, but their overall audience numbers are small when compared with television or other types of media.

A major drawback of using newspapers as part of a media mix is their declining readership. Fewer people are reading newspapers, as evidenced in a study by the Pew Research Center for the People & the Press. In 2008, only 34% of people reported reading a newspaper the previous day, down 6% from just two years prior.[15]

Web readership is increasing, but there are not yet sufficient numbers of online readers to offset declines in printed newspapers. To offset weaker ad sales, publishers are creating online versions of their papers as new outlets for content. Over the next decade, advertising spending on online newspaper sites is expected to grow to $10 billion.[16]

Compared with a magazine, the average newspaper has a very short life. Readers may be exposed to an ad for only a single day before a paper is consigned to the recycle bin. As a result, opportunities for pass-along readership are limited. Image reproduction quality is also relatively poor. To keep newspaper prices low, publishers use less expensive paper and most ads are printed in black and white.

Out-of-Home

Media channels aren't limited to delivering messages into our homes or into our hands. Because people are often in transit at some point during the day, marketers place brief advertising messages along people's travel routes. Out-of-home (OOH) media is a term that covers the following three main types of media:[17]

- **Outdoor boards** are large ad display panels, usually near highways or other heavily trafficked locations.
- **Posters** are smaller than outdoor boards and are frequently used at bus or train stops.
- **Transit advertising** appears on and inside buses, in air terminals, in taxis, and wherever people are being transported from one place to another.

OOH is a popular type of media among advertisers, with spending exceeding $8 billion annually. This is due in part to the implementation of new OOH technology like digital billboards, which can rotate ad messages, generating 10 times the advertising revenue of a static board.[18] As an example of applying new technology to outdoor advertising, Nike installed an electronic billboard in New York's Times Square that displayed a tennis shoe that passersby could modify by using their cell phones. One advantage of out-of-home media is that it can result in high message frequency among people who often travel the same route past an outdoor board or transit ad. **Frequency** is message by a media vehicle.

Marketers use OOH media when they have a short message that needs to be exposed to a broad audience. OOH media does an excellent job of delivering sheer numbers of impressions at a low CPM. It is also a good choice for messages that have a geographic component, such as an ad sited along a highway that says "For a great meal, exit here!" The OOH media environment is fairly uncluttered compared with magazines or television. Marketers also have total control over the location of their messages; they choose the size, site, and duration of their advertising. Some boards are even movable, allowing expanded market coverage.

Although its CPM is low, OOH advertising can have significant out-of-pocket costs. In a top national market, the monthly cost for outdoor boards can add up to millions of dollars. The time for passersby to process messages is also fleeting, so advertising copy must be kept to a minimum. If you need a lot of words to explain your product or service, then outdoor advertising is not the most appropriate medium.

Digital Media

Digital media are certainly the new media "kid on the block," with broadband penetration in the United States estimated at 48.3% (or 139.4 million people).[19] Definitions and categories of digital media change almost daily, but some of the most frequently recognized types are as follows:

- **Banner advertising**—The placement of advertisements (called banners) onto various Web sites that link to the sponsor's Web page.
- **Classified advertising**—The online version of traditional classified ads.
- **Search marketing**—The optimization of Web site keywords and marketing agreements with search engines to drive traffic to Web sites.
- **Mobile advertising**—Refers to advertisements delivered over portable communication devices such as mobile phones and PDAs.

- **User-generated content**—Social networks (such as Facebook or MySpace), user blogs, and filesharing (such as Flickr or Snapfish) are sources of both word-of-mouth communications and advertising.

Digital media spending topped $22.7 billion in 2009,[20] propelled mainly by display ads, search, and online classifieds.[21]

One of the most attractive aspects of digital media for marketers is the capability to target Web users based on their previous behavior, interests, or other factors. To give a simple example, a search of Google for "refrigerators" might serve up a banner ad for a GE refrigerator along with the results. CPM per contact can also be fairly low, and the message result can be immediate. Unlike ads in any other form of media, customers can interact directly with ads, clicking or texting in response to a sponsor's messages. This characteristic adds another level of accountability for digital media, which is vital for marketers who must prove a return on investment from their advertising campaigns.

Social networks, such as Facebook and MySpace, connect people with common interests and those who are looking to make friends online. These sites are growing in popularity, and marketers are experimenting with their advertising potential. Electronic publishing, such as blogs, e-magazines, and e-books, are also emerging marketing opportunities. Marketers are even exploring virtual worlds, such as SecondLife or CyWorld, where users have avatars that act as cyberspace "selves" who work, play, and interact online. Advertisements may be placed or virtual market tests conducted in these new media environments.

Digital media also has some limitations. Penetration of digital media is growing, but large portions of the U.S. population are not yet online. Research has shown that on the question of television or Internet advertising, the answer is not "either/or," but "both." There are parts of the population who can be reached only through the Web. And there are others who can be reached only by using traditional media communications. Campaigns have been proven to be more effective when using combinations of media instead of using one type exclusively.

Marketers need to adopt a completely different perspective when thinking about digital media. For the most part, consumers are in control of the communication process. At any given time, consumers' personal interests dictate when and where they will end up on the Web. Most advertisements are not so much "transmitted" in an Internet world as they are "found." In addition, surfers are only a click away from any ad they find offensive or boring.

EXAMPLE **DIGITAL MEDIA**

The United States Air Force stages recruiting events at state fairs and other locations around the country. At many of these events, real fighter jets are often available for attendees to touch, and thus increase excitement about the Air Force. But once a potential recruit leaves an event, how does the USAF maintain that excitement and interest? One way is through the use of mobile media. Event attendees can download 17 different types of USAF-related content to their cell phones, including videos, wallpaper, and ringtones. Signs at events display SMS short codes, which can be

PHOTO: Tebnad/Shutterstock

sent as phone text messages to unlock videos detailing specific careers in the Air Force. Quick response (QR/2D) code messaging is also possible, whereby attendees with phones containing special software may scan a bar code granting them access to USAF promotional material. Event staffers are also on hand to provide visitors with training in the use of these advanced features, if needed. For prospects who will not or cannot attend formal events, the USAF also places a variety of ads on mobile sites from channels such as MTV and Comedy Central, which direct viewers to resources offering additional content.[22]

>> END EXAMPLE

Branded Entertainment

The integration of brands or brand messages into entertainment vehicles, such as movies, television shows, video games, or sporting events, is referred to as branded entertainment. Companies spent over $24 billion in 2009 on product placement, product integration, and event sponsorships, which are some of the elements of branded entertainment. This use of branded entertainment can be used to develop a connection with an audience in a much deeper way than traditional advertising. Well-known examples include a can of Coke being prominently displayed on American Idol (product placement), James Bond driving an Aston Martin in *Casino Royale* (product integration), and Dodge Ram sponsoring the 2010 Kentucky Derby (event sponsorships).[23]

Branded entertainment can deliver a large number of impressions and is well suited for brands that already have mass awareness, so marketers don't need to worry if audiences understand a product's basic purpose. But exposure in entertainment lends an aura of prestige or credibility, especially if a well-known movie, music, or TV star is using the product. In addition, many audience members might prefer to avoid advertising, but will sit for two hours watching a movie embedded with brands. Product placements are immune to DVR or TiVO as well, because viewers may zip past ads, but they would never skip their recorded programs.

Like television advertising, branded entertainment ventures have low CPM but often carry high initial costs. Studios and publishers are quite aware of the value of branded entertainment, and the price for its use is rising. These prices are inflated as marketers bid against each other for the right to appear in the hottest properties. In the majority of instances, onscreen brand impressions are fleeting, so the impact of audience exposures may be questionable. Even the most savvy media maven can't accurately predict the success or failure of a film, song, book, or TV show. Branded entertainment is partially a "roll of the dice" because marketers have to guess a year or more in advance which are the special properties that audiences, listeners, and readers will embrace.

PHOTO: Konstantin Sutyagin/ Shutterstock

EXAMPLE **BRANDED ENTERTAINMENT**

Even branded entertainment can become a cluttered media environment. In the 2001 film *Driven*, Brandchannel identified 102 different brand or product placements. These included both paid and unpaid brand exposures, which can be frustrating for those companies who invested significant dollars to be part of the movie. Brands represented in this movie included Kool-Aid, Marlboro, Snapple, and Nextel.

In part, this was due to the film's storyline about racing, which naturally contains a large number of brand identifications. Unfortunately for everyone involved, the film only grossed $54.7 million on a production budget of $94 million.[24]

>> END EXAMPLE

The effectiveness of any mass media advertising campaign can be greatly increased through the use of personal selling, sales promotions, and direct marketing. Personal selling involves marketing messages delivered face-to-face, from salespeople to customers. The impact of a mass-media campaign is multiplied when salespeople are able to clarify and build on its basic message at the point of sale. With personal selling, communication with prospects is customizable on the spot. Questions can be answered, products demonstrated, or additional information provided.

On a CPM basis, however, personal selling is expensive because its reach is extremely limited. Training is required to ensure that salespeople have the knowledge needed to deliver the right messages, which increases the total cost for the campaign. The quality of personal selling also varies; it depends on an individual salesperson's personality, knowledge, and selling ability.

Direct marketing is another useful complement to broader-reach media. Similar to personal selling, direct marketing is highly targeted, because each recipient is pre-selected based on his or her product usage, demographics, interests, or geography. Marketers leverage the wider audience of mass media like broadcast or even print, and then reinforce the impact of this advertising with specific target audiences via direct marketing.

Media Selection Explained

Marketing communication campaigns involve the definition of a target customer, specification of communication objectives, development of a creative strategy, and media selection. Because the first part of this list has previously been discussed, the remainder of this chapter focuses on media selection, implementation, and measurement. Marketers follow a step-by-step process to select, implement, and measure advertising media (see Figure 20.7).

The process starts by establishing a media budget and media objectives. A media budget is a subset of the marketing communications budget, which also includes funds for nonmedia activities such as sales force support and public relations. In turn, the marketing communications budget is a portion of the company's overall **marketing budget.** The media budget specifies the total amount a firm will spend on all types of advertising media.

As a first step, along with the media budget, an understanding of **media objectives** is required. A media objective is a clear, unambiguous statement as to what media selection

FIGURE 20.7

Media Selection

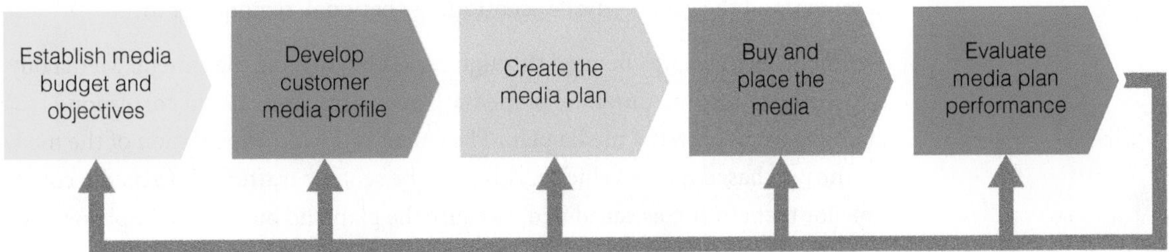

and implementation will achieve. This statement should convey, in as much detail as possible, what the media will accomplish and when. Some examples of media objectives are as follows:[25]

- Within the $10 million budget, create national awareness for our product before the end of the year.
- During the launch period, reach 80% of target customers an average of five times, and reach 50% of target customers an average of three or more times.
- Sustain product awareness by reaching 30% of target customers at least once a month.

Media budgets and media objectives are interrelated, because it would be impossible to fully achieve an objective without sufficient funding. The optimal way to set budgets is by using a task-and-objective approach and by allocating dollars sufficient to attain media objectives. In reality, many firms have limited budgets, and simply decide to use an easily calculated method, for example, a percentage of sales revenue, or to spend whatever they can afford.

Media Selection Applied

Marketing decisions should be based on an in-depth understanding of the customer, and media are no exception. The next step in the media-selection process is to build a detailed profile of the target customers and their media habits. This profile will include data on the following characteristics of target customers:

- **Demographics**—Who are they?
- **Geographic location**—Where do they live?
- **Media consumption habits**—What types of media do they consume? At what times of day?
- **Lifestyles and interests**—How do they live? What are their likes and dislikes?

Marketers use these profiles to guide their media-selection decisions. A hypothetical profile may suggest that a target customer is a heavy user of print media, an occasional user of the Internet, and never listens to radio. The target may also live on the West Coast of the United States and make product purchases twice a month. All these findings will have implications for media strategy.

Once the media objectives have been established, the media budget has been set, and the target customer media profile has been developed, then media planning can begin (see Figure 20.8). **Media planning** involves the creation of a **media plan,** which is a document that describes how an advertiser plans to spend its media budget to reach its objectives. A media plan specifies the types and amounts of media to be used, the timing of media, and the geographic concentration—national, regional, or local.

The media plan is implemented through media buying and placement. Media buying is the negotiation and purchase of media. These purchases should correspond to the direction as given in the media plan. Placement is the implementation of the media plan via the purchased media vehicles. Ads must be sent (or trafficked) to media companies in time for them to run as scheduled. Because the plan and buying are implemented in real time, their performance is monitored and evaluated. Real-time conclusions and insights from the plan are fed back into the process for continuous improvement.

Media Planning

Media planning is a complicated activity; it requires advertisers to balance many different inputs. For a large advertiser, the planning department of the company's advertising agency writes the media plans. A **media planner** has extensive knowledge about media vehicles and expertise in formulating media plans.

Planners consider several issues when building a media plan. When formulating a plan, media planners take into account not only the suitability of each medium, but how different types could work together to deliver the advertising message. The impact of a message viewed on television is multiplied when heard on the radio or seen on a billboard. Working with creative teams, planners also look for ways to combine or link media vehicles. For instance, TV ads sometimes contain Web addresses directing customers to the Internet or to 800 numbers to call to obtain additional product information or make purchases.

Some advertisers include special codes in magazine ads that readers can scan with Webcams or enter into cell phones to unlock additional online content.

Gross Rating Points (GRPs) are a way for planners to approximate the impact of media decisions. A GRP is the product of reach multiplied by frequency. For example, if an ad is scheduled to air two times in a single TV show (frequency), where the show has a 5.0 rating (reach), the plan will result in 10 GRPs. Demographics are always specified for GRPs (like ratings among adults aged 25–54).

A **media flowchart** (or **media footprint**) is a visual representation of the media plan. Expressed in worksheet or project software, the flowchart is essentially a calendar with time periods as columns and media types as rows. Whenever the plan dictates a media vehicle should be used, the column and row intersection contains estimated GRPs and a budget allocated to that media type. Multiple levels of geography may be shown on a single footprint or separately. The footprint allows planners to view at a glance the complete media plan. An example of a media flowchart for a women's athletic shoe brand can be seen in Figure 20.8.[26]

Media Buying

Based on the media plan, a group of agency experts called media buyers negotiate and purchase media properties. All media are sold on an open market, with media companies trying to sell their properties for top dollars and advertisers looking to scoop

FIGURE 20.8

Media Flowchart

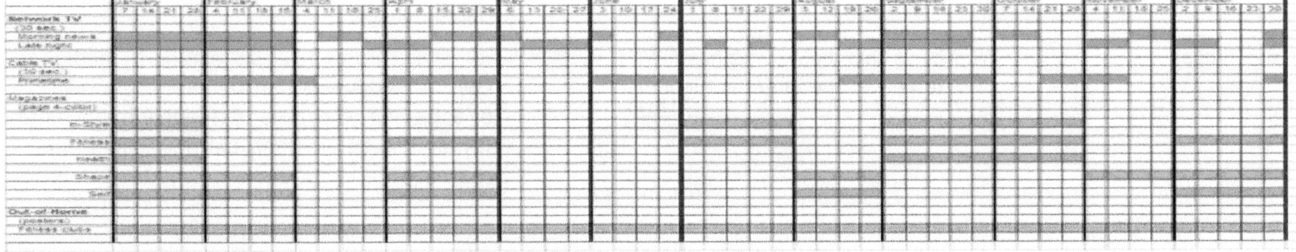

up the best deals. Media prices vary according to marketplace demand and the skill of negotiators on both sides of the table.

The bulk of network television is sold in an **upfront market**, which is a long-lead marketplace where TV networks and advertisers negotiate media prices for the fourth quarter of the current year, plus the first three quarters of the following year. In an upfront market, advertisers commit to purchase media and, in return, the networks set aside ad time for their upcoming programs. Advertisers can usually lock in the best pricing and programming by participating in an upfront market, but their ability to cancel or sell off any commitments is limited. Ads that are not purchased in advance via an upfront market, but are secured on a quarterly basis, are called scatter buys. Although scatter buys can be less efficient, media buyers can use them to react to changes in the marketplace and they allow greater spending flexibility.

Magazines, newspapers, radio, and OOH are purchased on the basis of **rate cards,** which are officially published prices for different types of media. Rate cards are often negotiable, and with the merger of large media companies, packages featuring a single price for combined offline and online media buys are increasingly common.

Internet advertising is usually priced on a CPM basis, and prices vary according to the size and type of ad. Advertisements could take many forms, such as banners or interstitial ads (also called "pop-ups"). Search advertising operates differently, with advertisers paying search engines or directories only after Web surfers have clicked their ad or link.

TABLE 20.3
STRATEGIC QUESTIONS IN MEDIA SELECTION

ISSUE	STRATEGIC QUESTIONS (EXAMPLES)	IMPACT
Reach versus frequency	Should the plan maximize the number of customer impressions (reach), the number of times each customer is communicated with (frequency), or both?	Maximizing reach will require heavy investments in mass media, such as broadcast; maximizing frequency may more heavily employ vehicles with less reach.
Scheduling	Should the plan be continuous, where advertising is running constantly? Should the plan involve a flight, where advertising is running for only brief periods? Should the plan be some combination of the two?	Continuous plans can be expensive, but are well suited to products or services in demand year-round, for example, food, beverages, and telecommunications. Flights are less expensive and are good for products that are more seasonal, for example, Halloween costumes and snow blowers, or for brand-reminder advertising.
Geography	Should the plan cover the entire world? A single country? Regions within a country? Cities or localities?	A plan could have national, regional, or local coverage, or combinations of any of the three. The media plan's geographic coverage is determined by the location of target customers.
Product type	How frequently is the product purchased? How much information do customers need?	Products that are used frequently require more continuous media. Ones that are information intensive suggest plans that employ print, digital, or direct media.
Media cost	What does this media type cost? What is its CPM to deliver the target audience?	All issues are weighed in relation to media cost. A media type may be effective in terms of achieving objectives, but highly inefficient. It may also be efficient, but do a poor job of reaching the target audience.

After media have been purchased, the advertising agency or marketing firm must deliver ads to the various media companies for broadcast, publication, or posting. The procedure for getting finished ads to the correct media firms is called **ad trafficking** because ads are "routed" on their way to implementation.

For a list of strategic questions in media selection, see Table 20.3.

Measuring Marketing Explained[27]

A popular quotation, attributed to department store merchant John Wanamaker, is "Half the money I spend on advertising is wasted; the trouble is I don't know which half." Although the quote refers to advertising, the idea behind it is often extended to all marketing activities. The challenges to measuring marketing effectiveness are significant:[28]

- Difficulty in isolating marketing activities in complex distribution channels, such as when a manufacturer and retailer concurrently engage in advertising that could either complement or contradict the efforts of the other
- Significant investment required to implement information technology to support gathering marketing information
- A variety of marketing activities acting simultaneously with possibly different brand messages

Early marketing measurement efforts considered consumer attitudes such as brand awareness and intention to purchase, which could be calculated through surveys.[29] Current efforts to measure the effectiveness of marketing expenditures involve linking sales performance with marketing actions such as advertising.

By choosing to measure marketing activities, organizations are committing to relating their marketing activities to specific marketing objectives. An appreciation of how brand relationships are influenced by marketing communications and how the elements of marketing communication work together is also necessary. Understanding marketing measurement also requires a commitment to explore the financial implications of marketing decisions on individual advertising executions, complete advertising campaigns, and brands.

Effective measurement of marketing activities requires a more contemporary perspective on the role of marketing within an organization. A measurement-focused marketing activity is concerned with actions such as developing marketing campaigns that generate revenues and profits with a level of risk that is consistent with other business investments. This is in contrast to simply generating brand awareness or creating innovative artistic renderings of the brand.

Marketing measurement has both process and structural implications for a business. Process issues include how marketing information is generated and analyzed and how employees are rewarded for using measurement data. Structurally, staff needs to be assigned to perform the necessary measurement tasks and dedicated and qualified individuals are needed who ensure insights generated from marketing measurement are comprehended.

Organizations generally decide on activities to measure and the types of measurements to collect for each activity based on marketing objectives. Key performance indicators (KPIs) are measurements that assist an organization in quantifying progress toward achievement of marketing objectives. Examples of KPIs include average revenue per customer, cost to acquire a new customer, and cost to retain a customer. KPIs can be connected to the strategic planning process through models such as the balanced scorecard.

Measuring Marketing Applied

The Adworks 2 study identified that, among the top 10% of consumer packaged-goods companies, TV advertising returned only 32 cents on the dollar for their brands. The fundamental choice resulting from that study was either TV is not returning an adequate amount on its investment or the value of marketing is not being properly measured by current industry standards.

Managers need to know that their investment will increase sales or profitability before they engage in an expensive marketing campaign. Businesses create and administer customer relationship management (CRM) programs to build and maintain profitable relationships with customers, invest in consumer influence campaigns that can involve one or more media types, and implement marketing-mix strategies. Many customer KPIs are identified and managed through CRM programs. Firms attempt to measure the impact of marketing activities on loyalty, customer value, and, importantly, sales. Companies such as Coca-Cola, Kraft, and Procter & Gamble all have ways to measure marketing investment. Marketing measurement tools include advertising copy tests, brand health tracking studies, and return on marketing investment models. These terms are defined and discussed on the following pages.

EXAMPLE **MEASURING MARKETING**

Cadillac, which was founded in 1902 and is one of General Motors' most prestigious brands, regularly evaluates how consumers view its advertising prior to launching a new advertising campaign. The company does this by presenting a sample of target consumers with a collection of finished advertisements or artistic renderings of key elements of advertisements to determine consumer reactions such as interest in the advertisement, impact on interest in the brand, and impact on interest in competitors' brands. Low-rated advertisements are then changed or cancelled prior to launch. Cadillac also monitors consumers' attitudes toward its brand and products through regular consumer surveys.

PHOTO: Dongliu/Shutterstock

>> END EXAMPLE

Measuring Advertising Explained

For most organizations, advertising is one of the largest marketing expenditures. The most important measure of advertising if its level of effectiveness in meeting marketing objectives such as increasing market share, building brand awareness, and changing brand perceptions. Advertising effectiveness can be considered on two levels, strategically and behaviorally. From a strategic perspective, attaining the communications objectives is paramount. Communications objectives range from introducing a new idea to asking consumers to act. The construction of an advertising campaign depends entirely on the communication objectives. The length of time to determine success of an advertising campaign varies with the communication objectives. Informing consumers and building the brand relationship is typically a longer-term effort, whereas call to action advertising is asking for an immediate response that often involves a sale of a product or service.

From a behavioral perspective, the effectiveness of advertising can be measured more specifically through outcomes up to and including sales. Advertising influences measurable items such as brand awareness and advertising awareness. Brand attributes, such as quality and convenience, can also assist in predicting consumer behavior since attributes define the positioning of one brand versus another. It is important to consider both the strategic and behavioral elements of advertising effectiveness.

Advertising effectiveness is ultimately measured as the ability to persuade. The influencing factors in moving from establishing an advertising objective to persuading consumer action include:

- Brand perception
- Category interest
- Consumer engagement
- Integrated marketing

The cumulative effect of advertising evolves from both short-term advertising actions, such as a direct mail offers, and longer-term advertising actions, such as magazine advertising.

Measuring Advertising Applied

Advertising managers and advertising agency representatives alike would seldom question the necessity and benefits of advertising. Although advertising often has a significant impact on marketing results, it is important to evaluate critically the contribution that advertising makes to a product or service such as building brand equity. Advertising effectiveness can be measured qualitatively, such as by conducting focus groups, and quantitatively, such as through surveys.

A product category provides either an initial opportunity or a significant challenge when choosing advertising to assist in shaping consumer behavior. Customer loyalty ranges from pet food at 54% loyalty to soft drinks at 41% to canned goods at 14%.[30] The greater the loyalty, the stronger are the existing brand relationships, whereas the lower the levels of loyalty, the greater the opportunities to gain sales.

TABLE 20.4
ADVERTISING REPORT CARD

ADVERTISING REPORT CARD					
ADVERTISING EXECUTION	RECOGNITION %	BRAND LINKAGE %	ENTERTAINMENT (1–10)	CREATIVITY (1–10)	GRADE
Execution 1	30	65	4	2	C+
Execution 2	38	63	6	2	B–
Execution 3	30	50	6	8	B–

Many advertising campaigns take advantage of a variety of media channels. A successful integrated marketing campaign that uses different media channels must include consistent messaging. Certain media is more effective than others for a given brand's marketing strategies. It may be the case that a brand is most efficient on radio but feels that it must be on TV simply because it is a big brand. The risk is sub-optimizing marketing expenditures by overlooking efficient, less costly media and spending marketing dollars on more expensive but relatively inefficient media choices.

Individual advertising also can be examined for effectiveness. Within a TV or radio spot, it is possible that a small percentage of the advertisement will account for a large percentage of recall. It is essential that the elements of the advertisement that are recalled contain both the brand and the critical messages. Music can serve as the component that induces recall. "Like a Rock" is attached to Chevrolet and the song, even without additional advertising content, can induce recall. Businesses often use a process known as copy testing to explore advertising effectiveness.

Copy testing is a survey-based process that can assist in measuring advertising and campaign effectiveness. The assessment of effectiveness can be performed prior to the airing of advertising, during the advertising campaign, and after the campaign. Testing before media is launched to the public is particularly important so as not to expend advertising dollars for an advertisement that does not work toward the campaign objectives.

Often called a report card, such as the example in Table 20.4, by advertising agency creative directors, copy testing can be simply a report card or it can be a diagnostic tool to help evolve creative development into successful advertising campaigns. The more direct explanation of copy testing is the process of evaluating how well an advertising execution communicates the brand's strategic positioning and accomplishes the brand's objectives. In the report card example, Execution 2 is better recognized and better linked to the appropriate brand than Execution 3, but Execution 3 is considered to be considerably more creative. A decision still needs to be made based on desired quality level of the execution and the better fit to brand position and objectives.

Copy testing can explore alternative advertising campaign ideas, as well as the communication effectiveness of different campaigns. Copy testing can reveal connections between executional elements and performance dimensions while identifying what works and what does not. Ultimately, copy testing can suggest what elements might warrant changing to achieve optimal performance against stated objectives.

Ultimately, the copy test process must be versatile enough to address the needs of different advertising objectives. New product introduction advertising should be evaluated on criteria like basic enjoyment and brand awareness. Public service announcements can be evaluated differently based on whether they are related to established brands with a consistent message or if brand and message are relatively new or require an immediate response.

The measurement of new media, such as interactive advertising, is becoming increasingly important as a greater percentage of marketing budgets are being allocated to new media platforms. Everything from viral video to blogs to video game sponsorship are targets for research. Currently there is no standard tool to copy test the wide range of diverse media platforms.

EXAMPLE **MEASURING ADVERTISING**

Millward Brown, a leading global research agency specializing in advertising, marketing communications, media, and brand equity research and part of communications services giant WPP, has conducted over 65,000 advertising copy tests over 20 years using its proprietary model known as Link. Link exposes respondents to advertising in various forms of development and then asks a series of questions including what message was recalled, what brand was doing the advertising, and ability to recount the elements of the advertisement. Link also includes an interest trace, a process where respondents use a computer mouse to indicate what they like and what they dislike as the commercial plays, to address nonverbal measures that lead to persuasion, including involvement, integration, and interest.[31]

PHOTO: Helder Almeida/Shutterstock

>> END EXAMPLE

Measuring Brand Health Explained

Advertising and other marketing activities as well as customer experience have a cumulative effect, over time, on consumer attitudes toward an organization and its products and services. This effect is often measured as the health of an organization's brand. Remember, a brand is essentially a promise to consumers. That promise provides context to everything that consumers can sense about a brand. If the promise is regularly fulfilled, then the brand's image is solidified and its reputation established and reinforced. This reputation can be enhanced or diminished depending on the ability of an organization to deliver on its brand promise.

Quantitative brand tracking among consumers is one means to monitor brand health. A brand tracking process typically begins with assessing the recognition and influence of advertising and other forms of marketing communications such as sponsorship and public relations on consumer attitudes toward the advertising brand and its competitors. By translating marketing communications into a linear communications model, a content outline can be developed for a brand tracking study. In Figure 20.9, media recognition—referring to which media channels on which consumers claim

FIGURE 20.9

Brand Tracking Model

FIGURE 20.10

THE PURCHASE FUNNEL

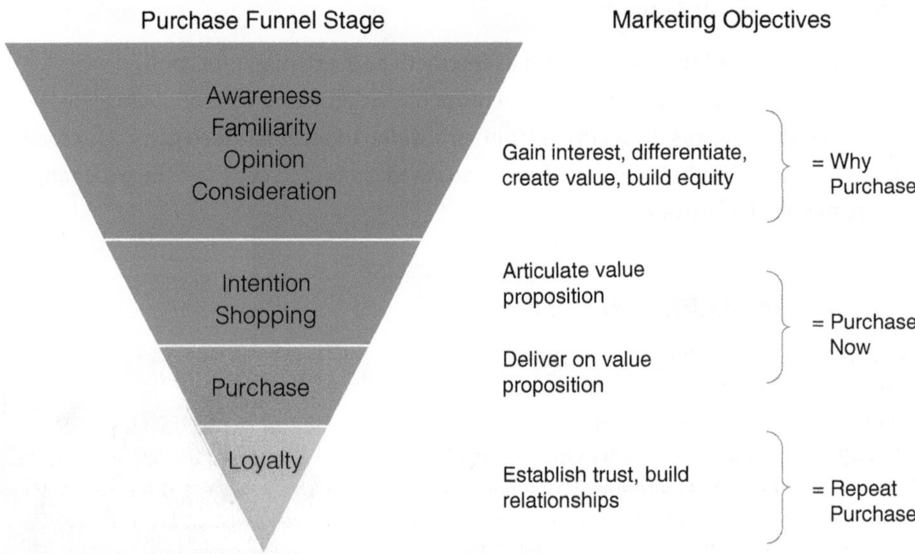

to see a brand advertised, brand recognition, and brand attributes associated with the brand—form the basic architecture for a brand tracking process.

Measuring Brand Health Applied

Brand tracking studies are common among large companies. These studies typically measure aspects of brand health and marketing communications and the interplay between the two. Some brands are tracked on a continuous basis with monthly or quarterly reports while others are measured once or twice each year. Reports are provided to a marketing or brand manager and the marketing team on issues such as the **purchase funnel,** a sequential consumer decision-making model encompassing awareness to loyalty (see Figure 20.10). Consider the stages in the purchase funnel and the associated marketing objectives. Different marketing activities would be appropriate for different stages and objectives. Sponsorship may help build awareness for a brand while a direct mail offer may assist in the shopping stage and a reward program may assist in the loyalty stage.

Consider a situation where there is 15% unaided awareness for a brand of speedboat, meaning that only 15% could name the specific brand in question when asked "Thinking about brands of speed boats, which brands come to mind?" What if 90% of those aware of the boat subsequently purchased the boat? The purchase funnel would be very narrow and vertical. One possible interpretation is that the product is so desirable that the more people that become aware, the more sales that will be generated. If this interpretation is correct one might wish to increase advertising focused on increasing awareness.

Alternatively, if the unaided awareness is 80% yet purchases are only 5%, the purchase funnel is wider than the one portrayed in Figure 20.10. In this case, one may interpret a problem lower in the purchase funnel because people are aware yet not satisfied about some aspect of the speedboat. Possibly the price is too high based on the value of the product or perhaps there is an inadequate distribution network. The purchase funnel can be a very useful tool in assessing brand health.

Other measures often tracked include brand image statements exploring topics such as value, convenience, and quality. Data from various measures are often trended—collected at specific time intervals such as every business quarter or every year—to determine if any change in market perception relative to a brand's competitors has occurred. The trending aspect is critical to the viability of the brand health data. If the topics studied change each month, then no trending is possible and there is limited strategic marketing value.

EXAMPLE **MEASURING BRAND HEALTH**

Tropicana, owned by PepsiCo, changed its packaging in January 2009 to reflect fresh taste with a simpler, cleaner design. There was extensive public outcry through letters and social media claiming that the brand looked generic and even "ugly." After sales plummeted and brand perceptions diminished, Tropicana quickly dropped the redesign and returned to the original packaging. By continually assessing brand health, Tropicana was able to identify a problem in its purchase funnel where a change in packaging altered opinions, which subsequently reduced purchase levels.[32]

>> END EXAMPLE

PHOTO: Martin Poole/ Thinkstock Royalty Free

Return on Marketing Investment Explained

ROMI is used to inform decisions on future marketing investments by measuring the overall effectiveness of marketing activities. Models are typically created to measure performance against near and long-term objectives. A near-term objective could be to have a sale to lower inventory levels and a long-term objective could include a market share growth target of 10% higher than the current level. The primary difference between a traditional marketing evaluation perspective and ROMI perspective is that financial performance metrics are established with ROMI as opposed to typically intangible objective criteria such as brand awareness.

ROMI provides insights into which types of marketing activities most effectively deliver on marketing objectives. ROMI should lead to improved marketing effectiveness, increased financial performance, and increased market share for the equivalent marketing expenditure without ROMI. ROMI models are developed over extended periods (often 18 months or greater) due to the considerable time it takes to measure the short- and long-term effects of different media channels on sales and can provide insights for brand marketing and media planning. Examples of specific benefits of ROMI include:

- Advertising investment can be allocated to the most efficient media executions.
- Advertising investment can be optimized to avoid overspending.
- Concurrent advertising activities can be measured to ensure they work together to achieve campaign objectives.

- Media placement and media weight can be scheduled to optimally influence sales.
- Campaign wear-out can be identified relative to other marketing activities.

Return on Marketing Investment Applied

In practice, a ROMI model is generally used to explain the relative contribution of various marketing efforts to sales. Proper funding can then be allocated to the most effective marketing activity depending on the marketing objective such as sales revenue or market share. Based on the output from a ROMI model and efficiency projections of various media campaign elements, allocation of marketing funds can be made based on budgetary limitations and not guesswork. Although there are no specific industry standards, it is logical that ROMI should return something better than a 1-to-1 relationship between minimum expected incremental revenue from a specific marketing program in relation to the amount to be invested in that marketing program.

Consider a company that spends $300,000 for a direct marketing campaign that delivers $1,200,000 in incremental revenue. The ROMI factor is 4. If the incremental contribution margin based on the incremental revenue for the direct marketing campaign is 50%, then the program returns $2 (50% X 4) for each additional marketing dollar invested. Typically, there are ROMI factors for a set of alternative campaigns representing different media. Depending on the marketing objective and program **hurdle rate,** the minimum amount of financial return that an organization requires before making a financial investment, the direct marketing campaign will be evaluated relative to the financial return of any alternatives. Generally, the campaign with the highest financial return that meets marketing objectives is implemented.

Conclusion

Firms use promotion and other forms of marketing communication to inform consumers about new products, remind them of familiar products, persuade them to choose one alternative over another, and build strong customer relationships. Recognizing that consumers come in contact with a brand at many different touch points, firms today often practice integrated marketing communication to reach consumers through a multichannel promotional strategy. Because marketers understand the impact of word-of-mouth communication, they are likely to supplement the traditional one-to-many communication model with a newer many-to-many model and also talk one-to-one with consumers.

The traditional communication model includes a message source that creates an idea, encodes the idea into a message, and transmits the message through some medium. The message is delivered to the receiver, who decodes the message and ma y provide feedback to the source. Anything that interferes with the communication is called "noise."

The promotion mix refers to the marketing communication elements that the marketer controls. Advertising, sales promotion, and public relations use the mass media to reach many consumers at a single time while personal selling and direct marketing allow marketers to communicate with consumers one-on-one.

Advertising, Sales Promotion, and Public Relations[1]

CHAPTER 21

Advertising: The Image of Marketing

Advertising is so much a part of marketing that many people think of the two as the same thing. Remember, product, price, and distribution strategies are just as important as marketing communications. And, there are many ways to get a message out to a target audience in addition to advertising. Make no mistake—traditional advertising is still important, even during hard economic times. In 2009, U.S. marketers spent just over $125 billion on advertising, down 12.3 percent from $142.9 billion in 2008.[2] As a result, U.S. advertising and marketing firms cut 7.9% of their staff or over 58,000 jobs.[3]

In today's competitive environment even the big guys like Procter & Gamble and General Motors are rethinking how much they want to invest in pricey ad campaigns as they search for alternative ways to get their messages out there. Indeed, while total ad spending declined, spending on Internet advertising increased 7.3 percent among all advertisers and a whopping 34 percent among the top 100 U.S. advertisers.[4]

One thing is sure—as the media landscape continues to change, so will advertising. Sales of Internet-ready and 3-D TVs are booming, as is the number of households with digital video recorders (DVRs) that let viewers skip through the commercials. Nielsen reported that in the first quarter of 2010, 138 million consumers watched video on the Internet and 20.3 million viewed mobile video.[5]

With all of this bleak news, is traditional advertising dead? Don't write any obituaries yet. Mass media communications are still the best way to reach a large audience. For that reason, producers of FMCGs (fast-moving consumer goods) such as P&G and Unilever will continue to rely on these traditional channels of communication to reach their customers. They will just be more creative as they mix-and-match different platforms to reach various target markets.

Indeed, wherever we turn advertising bombards us. Television commercials, radio spots, banner ads, and huge billboards scream, "Buy me!" Advertising is nonpersonal communication. An identified sponsor pays for that uses mass media to persuade or inform an audience.[6] Advertising can be fun, glamorous, annoying, informative—and hopefully an effective way to let consumers know what a company is selling and why people should run out and buy it today. Advertising is also a potent force that creates desire for products; it transports us to imaginary worlds where the people are happy, beautiful, or rich. In this way, advertising allows the organization to communicate its message in a favorable way and to repeat the message as often as it deems necessary to have an impact on receivers.

A long-running Virginia Slims cigarettes advertising campaign proclaimed, "You've come a long way, baby!" We can say the same about advertising itself. Advertising has been with us a long time. In ancient Greece and Rome, ad messages appeared on walls, were etched on stone tablets, or were shouted by criers, interspersed among announcements of successful military battles or government proclamations. Would the ancients have believed that today we get messages about products almost wherever we are, whether we cruise down the road or around the Web? Some of us even get advertising messages on our mobile phones or in public restrooms. It's hard to find a place where ads don't try to reach us.

Types of Advertising

Although almost every business advertises, some industries are bigger spenders than others. Retail advertising tops the list with spending on measured advertising (magazines, newspapers, radio, television, and Internet) of over $15 billion in 2009, down 11.5 percent from 2008. The automotive industry with its recent problems cut measured ad spending 23 percent to a little over $12 billion in 2009. In contrast, the telecommunications industry's 2009 spending was up 1.5 percent from the previous year to $10.2 billion while medicine and remedies and financial services finished up the top five ad spenders with a little over $8 billion each, down 4.9 and 16.4 percent respectively. Because they spend so much on advertising, marketers must decide which type of ad will work best to get their money's worth given their organizational and marketing goals. As Figure 21.1 shows, the advertisements an organization runs can take many forms, so let's review the most common kinds.

FIGURE 21.1

Types of Advertising

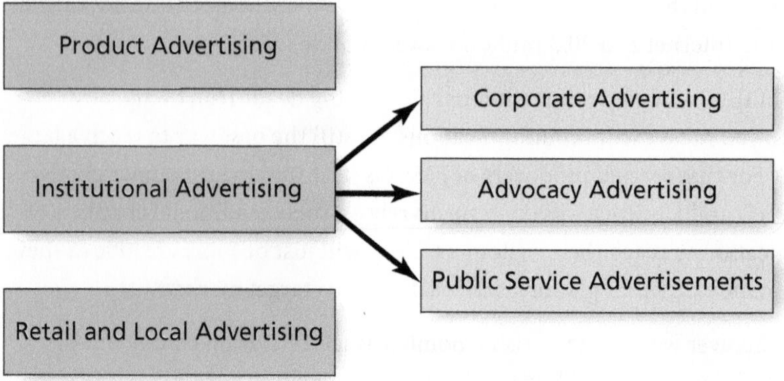

PRODUCT ADVERTISING When people give examples of advertising, they are likely to recall the provocative poses in Victoria's Secret ads or the cheeky reminders from the GEICO gecko. These are examples of **product advertising,** where the message focuses on a specific good or service. While not all advertising features a product or a brand, most of the advertising we see and hear is indeed product advertising.

Product advertising focuses on a specific good or service.

INSTITUTIONAL ADVERTISING Rather than a focus on a specific brand, **institutional advertising** promotes the activities, personality, or point of view of an organization or company. **Corporate advertising** promotes the company as a whole instead of the firm's individual products. Some firms, in fact, do not advertise specific products at all but have built their businesses with only corporate advertising. Cisco, for example, uses corporate advertising to brand itself as "the human network." Other firms like Dow Chemical Co. use corporate advertising in addition to product advertising. Dow boosted its brand equity 25 percent through its "Human Element" corporate advertising campaign that said it is the "human element" that can solve some of the world's problems such as climate change and lack of clean water.[7]

Some institutional messages state an organization's position on an issue to sway public opinion, a strategy we call **advocacy advertising.** For example, U.S. governors joined together in a campaign to get Congress to pass climate change legislation. The campaign included a 30-second TV commercial starring three governors, including California governor and *Terminator* movie star Arnold Schwarzenegger.[8]

Other messages take the form of **public service advertisements (PSAs)** that the media run free of charge. These messages promote not-for-profit organizations that serve society in some way, or they champion an issue such as increasing literacy or discouraging drunk driving. Advertising agencies often take on one or more public service campaigns on a *pro bono* (for free, not the U2 singer) basis. Little League baseball aired a 15-second PSA on ESPN that featured a 10-year old at the plate. In the stands the father yells, "Come on, son. Hit the ball." The boy rolls his eyes, turns around to face his dad, and yells back, "DAD, IS THAT THE BEST YOU CAN DO?! THAT'S PATHETIC. I DON'T EVEN KNOW WHY YOU BOTHER SHOWING UP! WHY CAN'T YOU BE MORE LIKE JIMMY'S DAD?! ALL THE OTHER PARENTS ARE GOING TO LAUGH AT YOU! YOU MAKE ME SICK!" The ad ends with a supertitle, "Now you know how it feels. Just let them play."[9]

RETAIL AND LOCAL ADVERTISING Both major retailers and small, local businesses advertise to encourage customers to shop at a specific store or use a local service. Local advertising informs us about store hours, location, and products that are available or on sale. These ads may take the form of popup ads online or perhaps newspaper circulars that fill out your Sunday newspaper.

product advertising
Advertising messages that focus on a specific good or service.

institutional advertising
Advertising messages that promote the activities, personality, or point of view of an organization or company.

corporate advertising
Advertising that promotes the company as a whole instead of a firm's individual products.

advocacy advertising
A type of public service advertising where an organization seeks to influence public opinion on an issue because it has some stake in the outcome.

public service advertisements (PSAs)
Advertising run by the media for not-for-profit organizations or to champion a particular cause without charge.

Who Creates Advertising?

advertising campaign
A coordinated, comprehensive plan that carries out promotion objectives and results in a series of advertisements placed in media over a period of time.

An **advertising campaign** is a coordinated, comprehensive plan that carries out promotion objectives and results in a series of advertisements placed in various media over a period of time. Although a campaign may be based around a single ad idea, most use multiple messages with all ads in the campaign having the same look-and-feel. Some campaigns run for only a short period of time while others remain with us for many years. Take, for example, GEICO's advertising campaigns. In recent years the insurance company has mounted a total of four different advertising campaigns; the messages often run simultaneously. These four are (1) the GEICO gecko campaign, (2) the caveman campaign that even spawned a short-lived TV sitcom ("so easy a caveman can do it"), (3) the "money you could be saving" campaigns with the googly-eyed dollar bills, and (4) the "Rhetorical Questions" campaign that includes ads featuring Charlie Daniels, Elmer Fudd, and the Waltons. While all of these campaigns promote the same company and its products and all use the same tag line, "Fifteen minutes could save you 15 percent or more on car insurance," they are each creatively distinct. Each includes multiple ads (there have been at least 22 caveman TV commercials), but each ad is obviously part of a coordinated campaign.

limited-service agency
An agency that provides one or more specialized services, such as media buying or creative development.

full-service agency
An agency that provides most or all of the services needed to mount a campaign, including research, creation of ad copy and art, media selection, and production of the final messages.

Although some firms create their own advertising in-house, in many cases several specialized companies work together to develop an advertising campaign. Typically the firm retains one or more outside advertising agencies to oversee this process. A **limited-service agency** provides one or more specialized services, such as media buying or creative development. In contrast, a **full-service agency** supplies most or all of the services a campaign requires, including research, creation of ad copy and art, media selection, and production of the final messages. The largest global agencies are Dentsu (based in Japan), McCann Worldwide Group, BBDO Worldwide, and DDB Worldwide, each with over 2 billion in billings.[10]

account executive (account manager)
A member of the account management department who supervises the day-to-day activities of the account and is the primary liaison between the agency and the client.

account planner
A member of the account management department who combines research and account strategy to act as the voice of the consumer in creating effective advertising.

creative services
The agency people (creative director, copywriters, and art director) who dream up and produce the ads.

A campaign has many elements; it requires the services of many different people to pull it all together. Big or small, an advertising agency hires a range of specialists to craft a message and make the communication concept a reality:

- **Account management:** The **account executive,** or account manager, is the "soul" of the operation. This person supervises the day-to-day activities on the account and is the primary liaison between the agency and the client. The account executive has to ensure that the client is happy while verifying that people within the agency execute the desired strategy. The **account planner** combines research and account strategy to act as the voice of the consumer in creating effective advertising. It is the job of the account planner to use market data, qualitative research, and product knowledge to become intimately familiar with the consumer and to translate what customers are looking for to the creative teams who create the ads.
- **Creative services:** *Creatives* are the "heart" of the communication effort. These are the people who actually dream up and produce the ads. They include the agency's creative director, copywriters, and art director. Creatives are the artists who breathe life into marketing objectives and craft messages that (hopefully) will interest consumers.

- **Research and marketing services:** *Researchers* are the "brains" of the campaign. They collect and analyze information that will help account executives develop a sensible strategy. They assist creatives in getting consumer reactions to different versions of ads or by providing copywriters with details on the target group.
- **Media planning:** The media planner is the "legs" of the campaign. He helps to determine which communication vehicles are the most effective and recommends the most efficient means to deliver the ad by deciding where, when, and how often it will appear.

research and marketing services
Advertising agency department that collects and analyzes information that will help account executives develop a sensible strategy and assist creatives in getting consumer reactions to different versions of ads.

media planners
Agency personnel who determine which communication vehicles are the most effective and efficient to deliver the ad.

More and more agencies practice integrated marketing communication (IMC), in which advertising is only one element of a total communication plan. Because IMC includes more than just advertising, client teams composed of people from account services, creative services, media planning, research, public relations, sales promotion, and direct marketing may work together to develop a plan that best meets the communication needs of each client.

User-Generated Advertising Content

The latest promotional craze is to let your customers actually create your advertising for you. **User-generated content** (UGC), also known as **consumer-generated media** (CGM), includes the millions of online consumer comments, opinions, advice, consumer-to-consumer discussions, reviews, photos, images, videos, podcasts and webcasts, and product-related stories available to other consumers through digital technology. Marketers that embrace this strategy understand that it's okay to let people have fun with their products. For example, join the millions of others who checked out the infamous YouTube videos where "mad scientists" mix Mentos candies with Diet Coke for explosive results (such as http://www.youtube.com/watch?v5hKoB0MHVBvM).

user-generated content (UGC) or consumer-generated media (CGM)
Online consumer comments, opinions, advice and discussions, reviews, photos, images, videos, podcasts, webcasts, and product, related stories available to other consumers.

Marketers need to monitor (and sometimes encourage) UGC for two reasons. First, consumers are more likely to trust messages from fellow consumers than what companies tell them. In fact, they're more likely to say they "trust completely" product information they receive from other consumers than from any other source. Second, we've already seen in the last chapter how social media is proliferating everywhere; a person who searches online for a company or product name is certain to access any number of blogs, forums, homegrown commercials, or online complaint sites that the product manufacturer had nothing to do with. Some companies resist this trend when they restrict access to their material or even sue consumers who talk about them because they fear they will lose control over their brand messages. They really need to get over it and recognize that in our digital world their messages (like your Facebook page) are almost impossible to control. In Web 2.0, you're either on the train or under it!

To take advantage of this phenomenon, some marketers encourage consumers to contribute their own **do-it-yourself (DIY) ads.** When Frito-Lay sponsored a contest for 2010 Super Bowl ads, two of the winners, "House Rules" and "Underdog," turned out to be the most watched ads of the game.[11] In its "Priceless" campaign, MasterCard invited consumers to write their own ad copy for two filmed commercials—all entries had to end with the word "Priceless." Converse allowed customers to send homemade

do-it-yourself (DIY) ads
Product ads that are created by consumers.

commercials to its Web site, then ran several of them on television.[12] Other companies that have experimented with do-it-yourself (DIY) advertising are L'Oréal ("You Make the Commercial"), JetBlue ("Travel Stories"), and McDonald's ("Global Casting").[13]

For advertisers do-it-yourself advertising offers several benefits. First, consumer-generated spots cost only one-quarter to one-third as much as professional TV and Internet ads—about $60,000 compared to the $350,000 or more to produce a traditional 30-second spot. This can be especially important for smaller businesses and emerging brands. Equally important, even to large companies with deep pockets, is the feedback on how consumers see the brand and the chance to gather more creative ideas to tell the brand's story.[14]

crowdsourcing
A practice in which firms outsource marketing activities (such as selecting an ad) to a community of users.

Crowdsourcing is a practice in which firms outsource marketing activities (such as selecting an ad) to a community of users, that is, a crowd. When the D.C. Lottery created a new game with new ways to win, it decided to update its 28-year-old logo at the same time. To get the public involved and to select a logo that would be inviting to lottery "customers," the organization invited visitors to its Web site to vote on which of six logos they preferred.[15]

To get the ball rolling, an agency typically solicits ideas from online communities that people access because they are fans of a product or a specific brand. The idea behind crowdsourcing is that if you want to know what consumers think and what they like, the most logical thing to do is to ask them. First the agency shares a challenge with a large number of people who have varying degrees of expertise. Whether motivated by money, competition, or obsession, individuals then submit their solution to the problem.

Kraft, a global marketer of fast-moving-consumer goods including Lacta, a chocolate brand in Greece, recently enlisted a crowdsourcing technique to develop a branded film. Kraft first asked consumers to submit real love tales that might be the subject of a short film that would feature Lacta. A story about two strangers, a young soldier and a musician, meeting on a train was the winner out of the 1,307 real love tales submitted. Next Kraft used online polls for voters to select screen tests, names of characters, and costumes. The film created so much buzz that when Greece's #1 TV station ran the film for free, over 335,000 people watched it.[16]

Ethical Issues in Advertising

Advertising, more than any other part of marketing, has been sharply criticized for decades. Such criticism certainly may be based less on reality than on the high visibility of advertising and the negative attitudes of consumers who find ads an intrusion in their lives. The objections to advertising are similar to those some people have to marketing in general. Here are the main ones:

- *Advertising is manipulative:* Advertising causes people to behave like robots and do things against their will—to make purchases they would not otherwise make were it not for the ads. However, consumers are not robots. Since they are consciously aware of appeals made in advertising, they are free to choose whether to respond to an ad or not. Of course, consumers can and often do make bad decisions that advertising may influence, but that is not the same as manipulation.

- *Advertising is deceptive and untruthful:* Deceptive advertising means that an ad falsely represents the product and that consumers believe the false information and act on it. Indeed, there is some false or deceptive advertising, but as a whole advertisers try to present their brands in the best possible light while being truthful. In the United States, both government regulation and the industry itself strongly encourage honesty.

To protect consumers from being misled, the Federal Trade Commission (FTC) has specific rules regarding unfair or deceptive advertising. Some deceptive ads make statements that can be proven false. For example, the FTC fined Volvo and its ad agency $150,000 each for an ad containing a "rigged" demonstration. The Volvo "Bear Food" ad campaign showed a monster truck running over a row of cars and crushing all but the Volvo station wagon. The Volvos, however, had been structurally reinforced, while the structural supports in some of the other cars had been cut.[17]

In addition to fining firms for deceptive advertising, the FTC also has the power to require firms to run **corrective advertising**, messages that clarify or qualify previous claims.[18] Yaz, a best-selling birth control pill by Bayer, was accused of overstating its ability to improve women's moods and clear up acne and not adequately communicating the drug's health risks. As a result the Food and Drug Administration and the attorneys general of 27 states required Bayer to spend $20 million over six years in corrective advertising, telling consumers that they should not take the pill to cure pimples or premenstrual syndrome.

corrective advertising
Advertising that clarifies or qualifies previous deceptive advertising claims.

Other ads, although not illegal, may create a biased impression of products when they use **puffery**—claims of superiority that neither sponsors nor critics of the ads can prove are true or untrue. For example, Nivea bills itself as "the world's number 1 name in skin care," Neutrogena claims that its cream cleanser produces "the deepest feeling clean," and DuPont says that its Stainmaster Carpet is "a creation so remarkable, it's practically a miracle."

puffery
Claims made in advertising of product superiority that cannot be proven true or untrue.

Does this mean that puffery is an unethical marketing practice? Not really. In fact, both advertisers and consumers generally accept puffery as a normal part of the advertising game. Although a little exaggeration may be reasonable, in most cases the goal is to create marketing communications that are both honest and that present the products in the most positive way possible. This approach works to the firm's advantage in the long run since it prevents consumers from becoming overly cynical about the claims it makes.

- *Advertising is offensive and in bad taste:* To respond to this criticism, we need to recognize that what is offensive or in bad taste to one person may not be to another. Yes, some TV commercials are offensive to some people, but then news and program content in the media can be and often is even more explicit or in poor taste. While advertisers seek to go the distance using humor, sex appeals, or fear appeals to get audiences' attention, most shy away from presenting messages that offend the very audience they want to buy their products.
- *Advertising creates and perpetuates stereotypes:* Some advertising critics assert that advertising portrays certain groups of consumers in negative ways. For example, advertising has portrayed women more often as homemakers than as industry leaders. While there is evidence that advertising (and media program content) is guilty of perpetuating stereotypes, it is important to recognize that these stereotypes already exist in the culture. Advertising doesn't create them so much as it reflects them.

Ripped from the Headlines

Ethics/Sustainable Decisions in the Real World

Many consumers today are concerned about **greenwashing**: a practice in which companies promote their products as environmentally friendly when in truth the brand provides little ecological benefit. This practice may refer to a company that boasts in its corporate image advertising of the cutting-edge research it does to save the planet when in fact this work accounts for only a small fraction of its activities. Hotels claim they are "green" because they allow guests to choose not to have clean sheets and clean towels in their rooms every day. And grocery stores claim to be green because you can return your plastic bags there.

Critics of greenwashing single out Huggies Pure and Natural disposable diapers because the brand claims to be more environmentally friendly and safer for a baby. Its advertising claims that it offers parents the "pure bliss of a diaper that includes gentle, natural materials." However, the only real difference in the Pure and Natural Huggies from the original is a piece of organically grown cotton fabric that is on the outside of the diaper, not where it touches the baby's skin.

But are such claims ethical? Are consumers being deceived into buying products that they think make a real difference to the environment when in reality the products are not substantially different? Those who are accused of greenwashing would argue that even small efforts toward "going green" are important and that such claims are justified. If you were a marketer, would you try to promote your product as more environmentally friendly even though differences between your product and those of the competition are very minor?

greenwashing
A practice in which companies promote their products as environmentally friendly when in truth the brand provides little ecological benefit.

- Advertising causes people to buy things they don't really need: The truth of this criticism depends on how you define a "need." If we believe that all consumers need is the basic functional benefits of products—the transportation a car provides, the nutrition we get from food, and the clean hair we get from shampoo—then advertising may be guilty as charged. If, on the other hand, you think you need a car that projects a cool image, food that tastes fantastic, and a shampoo that makes your hair shine and smell ever so nice, then advertising is just a vehicle that communicates those more intangible benefits.

FIGURE 21.2

Steps to Develop an Advertising Campaign

Developing an advertising campaign includes a series of steps that will ensure that the advertising meets communication objectives.

Develop the Advertising Campaign

The advertising campaign is about much more than creating a cool ad and hoping people notice it. The campaign should be intimately related to the organization's overall communication goals. That means the firm (and its outside agency if it uses one) must have a good idea of whom it wants to reach, what it will take to appeal to this market, and where and when it should place its messages. Let's examine the steps required to do this, as Figure 21.2 shows.

Step 1: Understand the Target Audience

The best way to communicate with an audience is to understand as much as possible about them and what turns them on and off. An ad that uses the latest "hip-hop" slang may relate to teenagers but not to their parents—and this strategy may backfire if the ad copy reads like an "ancient" 40-year-old trying to sound like a 20-year-old.

As we discussed, marketers often identify the target audience for an advertising campaign from research. Researchers (like Jim Multari, the director of research for PBS Kids Sprout) try to get inside the customer's head to understand just how to create a message that he will understand and to which he will respond. For example, an account executive working on a campaign for Pioneer Stereo was assigned to hang out with guys who were likely prospects to buy car stereos. His observations resulted in an advertising campaign that incorporated the phrases they actually used to describe their cars: "My car is my holy temple, my love shack, my drag racer of doom."[19]

Step 2: Establish Message and Budget Objectives

Advertising objectives should be consistent with the overall communication plan. That means that both the underlying message and its costs need to relate to what the marketer is trying to say about the product and what the marketer is willing or able to spend. Thus, advertising objectives generally will include objectives for both the message and the budget.

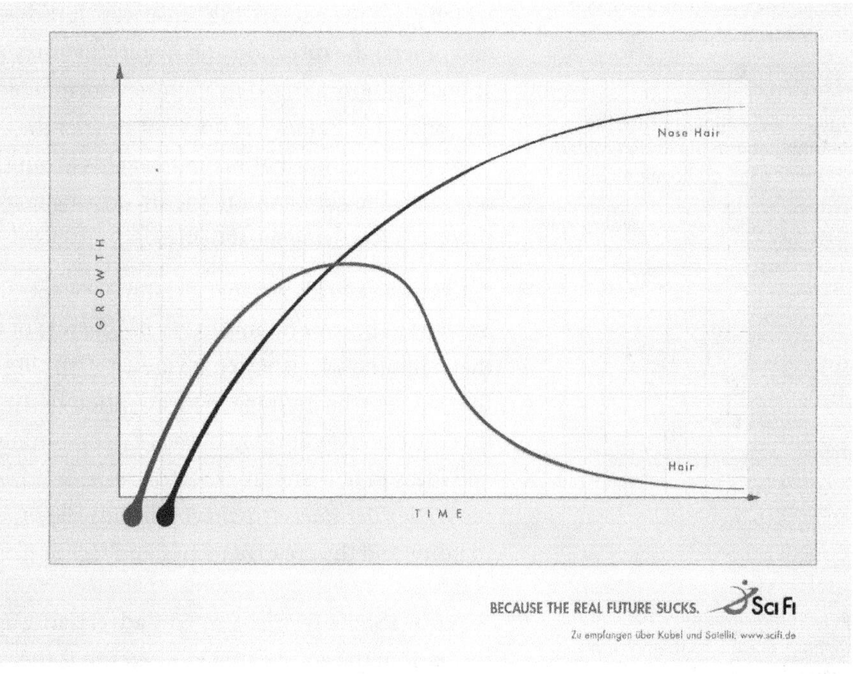

This German ad speaks to many of the viewers the SciFi channel hopes to reach.

SET MESSAGE OBJECTIVES As we noted earlier, because advertising is the most visible part of marketing, many people assume that marketing is advertising. In truth, advertising alone is quite limited in what it can achieve. What advertising can do is inform, persuade, and remind. Accordingly, some advertisements are informational—they aim to make the customer knowledgeable about features of the product or how to use it. At other times, advertising seeks to persuade consumers to like a brand or to prefer one brand over the competition. But many, many ads simply aim to keep the name of the brand in front of the consumer—reminding consumers that this brand is the one to choose when they look for a soft drink or a laundry detergent.

SET BUDGET OBJECTIVES Advertising is expensive. Procter & Gamble, which leads all U.S. companies in advertising expenditures, spends almost $5 billion per year while second- and third-place ad spenders AT&T and General Motors each spend well over $3 billion each.[20]

An objective of many firms is to allocate a percentage of the overall communication budget to advertising, depending on how much and what type of advertising the company can afford. The major approaches and techniques to setting overall promotional budgets, such as the percentage-of-sales and objective-task methods as well as set advertising budgets.

Major corporations like General Motors advertise heavily on expensive media such as television to promote multiple products throughout the year. Other companies may be more selective, and smaller firms may want to put their advertising dollars into cheaper media outlets such as direct mail or trade publications. Or a firm may decide to blow its entire advertising budget in one grand gesture—as the Web site host company **GoDaddy.com** does when it buys airtime during the Super Bowl.

Step 3: Create the Ads

creative strategy
The process that turns a concept into an advertisement.

creative brief
A guideline or blueprint for the marketing communication program that guides the creative process.

The creation of the advertising begins when an agency formulates a **creative strategy**, which gives the advertising "creatives" (art directors, copywriters, photographers, and others) the direction and inspiration they need to begin the creative process. The strategy is summarized in a written document known as a **creative brief**, a rough blueprint that guides but does not restrict the creative process. It provides only the most relevant information and insights about the marketing situation, the advertising objective, the competition, the advertising target and, most importantly, the message that the advertising must deliver.

It's one thing to know what a company wants to say about itself or its products and another to figure out how to say it. The role of the creative brief is to provide the spark that helps the ad agency come up with "the big idea," the visual and/or verbal concept that delivers the message in an attention-getting, memorable, and relevant manner. From this the creatives develop the ads by combining already-known facts, words, pictures, and ideas in new and unexpected ways. Specifically, to come up with finished ads, they must consider four elements of the ads shown in Figure 21.3: the appeal, the format, the tonality, and the creative tactics and techniques.[21]

advertising appeal
The central idea or theme of an advertising message.

ADVERTISING APPEALS An **advertising appeal** is the central idea of the ad and the basis of the advertising messages. It is the approach used to influence the consumer. Generally, we think of appeals as informational or emotional.

unique selling proposition (USP)
An advertising appeal that focuses on one clear reason why a particular product is superior.

Informational or rational appeals relate to consumers' practical need for the product. They emphasize the features of the product and/or the benefits we receive from using it. Often informational appeals are based on a **unique selling proposition (USP)** that gives consumers a clear, single-minded reason why the advertiser's product is better than other products at solving a problem. For example, "M&Ms melt in your mouth, not in your hands" is a USP. In general, a USP strategy is effective if there is some clear product advantage that consumers can readily identify and that is important to them.

Because consumers often buy products based on social or psychological needs, advertisers frequently use emotional appeals instead where they try to pull our heartstrings rather than make us think differently about a brand. Emotional appeals focus on an emotional or social benefit the consumer may receive from the product such as safety, love, excitement, pleasure, respect, or approval.

FIGURE 21.3

Creative Elements of Advertising

Creating good ads includes making decisions about the four different ad elements.

Creative Element	Element Options
Appeals	Rational (Unique Selling Proposition) Emotional Reminder Advertising Teaser Ads
Execution Formats	Comparison Demonstration Testimonial Slice of Life Lifestyle
Tonality	Straightforward Humor Dramatic Romantic Apprehension/Fear
Creative Tactics and Techniques	Animation and Art Celebrities Music, Jingles, and Slogans

Of course, not all ads fit into these two appeal categories. Well-established brands often use **reminder advertising** just to keep their name in people's minds or to be sure that consumers repurchase the product as necessary. For example, Arm & Hammer baking soda reminds us to replace the open box many of us keep in our refrigerators to absorb odors on a regular basis.

reminder advertising
Advertising aimed at keeping the name of a brand in people's minds to be sure consumers purchase the product as necessary.

Sometimes advertisers use **teaser** or **mystery ads** to generate curiosity and interest in a to-be-introduced product. Teaser ads draw attention to an upcoming ad campaign without mentioning the product. Before the creative team can craft and polish the words and visuals to bring the big idea to life, they still must choose the most appropriate format and tonality of the advertising. We'll turn to those ideas next.

teaser or mystery advertising
Ads that generate curiosity and interest in a to-be-introduced product by drawing attention to an upcoming ad campaign without mentioning the product.

EXECUTION FORMATS **Execution format** describes the basic structure of the message. Some of the more common formats, sometimes used in combination, include the following:

execution format
The basic structure of the message such as comparison, demonstration, testimonial, slice-of-life, and lifestyle.

- *Comparison:* A comparative advertisement explicitly names one or more competitors. Pizza Hut's recent "America's Favorite Pizza" spots claimed that consumers preferred its hand-tossed pizzas 2 to 1 over both number two Domino's and number three Papa John's. Ads showed rival pizza delivery drivers eating Pizza Hut pizza at the Pizza Hut driver's home. Papa John's countered with claims that its crust was made fresh while Pizza Hut's was frozen.[22]

Comparative ads can be very effective, but there is a risk of turning off consumers who don't like the negative tone. While in many countries comparative advertising is illegal, it's a widely used tactic in the United States. This format is best for brands that have a smaller share of the market and for firms that can focus on a specific feature that makes them superior to a major brand. When market leaders use comparative advertising, there is the risk consumers will feel they are "picking on the little guy." One exception is the "cola wars" advertising by Coca-Cola and Pepsi. In the recent Pepsi Max ad which features the song "Why Can't We Be Friends?" by War, delivery drivers for Coke and Pepsi meet in a diner; the Coke driver samples Pepsi Max and prefers it.

- *Demonstration:* The ad shows a product "in action" to prove that it performs as claimed: "It slices, it dices!" Demonstration advertising is most useful when consumers are unable to identify important benefits except when they see the product in use.
- *Testimonial:* A celebrity, an expert, or a "man in the street" states the product's effectiveness. The use of a celebrity endorser is a common but expensive strategy.
- *Slice of life:* A slice-of-life format presents a (dramatized) scene from everyday life. Slice-of-life advertising can be effective for everyday products such as peanut butter and headache remedies that consumers may feel good about if they see "real" people buy and use them.
- *Lifestyle:* A lifestyle format shows a person or persons attractive to the target market in an appealing setting. The advertised product is "part of the scene," implying that the person who buys it will attain the lifestyle. For example, a commercial on MTV might depict a group of "cool" California skateboarders who take a break for a gulp of milk and say, "It does a body good."

tonality
The mood or attitude the message conveys (straightforward, humor, dramatic, romantic, sexy, and apprehension/fear).

Humorous, witty, or outrageous ads can be an effective way to break through advertising clutter.

TONALITY **Tonality** refers to the mood or attitude the message conveys. Some common tonalities include:

- *Straightforward:* Straightforward ads simply present the information to the audience in a clear manner. Informative ads are frequently used in radio but less often in TV.
- *Humor:* Humorous, witty or outrageous ads can be an effective way to break through advertising clutter. But humor can be tricky, because what is funny to one person may be offensive or stupid to another. Different cultures also have different senses of humor. A recent Reebok commercial showed women at a basketball game checking out the all-male cheerleading squad. The spot was witty, but people from countries that don't feature cheerleaders at sports events (you don't find too many pom-poms at soccer matches) might not "get it."

Perhaps the major benefit of humorous advertising is that it attracts consumers' attention and leaves them with a pleasant feeling. Of course, humor in advertising can backfire. In the United Kingdom, a Renault Megane 225 ad that featured people in everyday situations shaking uncontrollably as the car passed was banned by the government's Office of Communications: Viewers complained that the ad mocked people with illnesses such as Parkinson's disease.[23]

- *Dramatic:* A dramatization, like a play, presents a problem and a solution in a manner that is often exciting and suspenseful—a fairly difficult challenge in 30 or 60 seconds.
- *Romantic:* Ads that present a romantic situation can be especially effective at getting consumers' attention and at selling products people associate with dating and mating. That's why fragrance ads often use a romantic format.

Gillette uses a romantic theme in China.

- *Sexy:* Some ads appear to sell sex rather than products. In a Guess jeans ad, a shirtless man lies near an almost shirtless woman. Ads such as these rely on sexuality to get consumers' attention. Sex appeal ads are more likely to be effective when there is a connection between the product and sex (or at least romance). For example, sex appeals will work well with a perfume but are less likely to be effective when you're trying to sell a lawn mower.
- *Apprehension/Fear:* Some ads highlight the negative consequences of not using a product. Some fear appeal ads focus on physical harm, while others try to create concern for social harm or disapproval. Mouthwash, deodorant, and dandruff shampoo makers and life insurance companies successfully use fear appeals. So do ads aimed at changing behaviors, such as messages discouraging drug use or encouraging safe sex. In general, fear appeals can be successful if the audience perceives there to be an appropriate level of intensity in the fear appeal. For example, horrible photos of teens lying on the highway following an auto accident can be quite effective in PSAs designed to persuade teens not to drink and drive, but they are likely to backfire if an insurance company tries to "scare" people into buying life insurance.

CREATIVE TACTICS AND TECHNIQUES In addition to ad formats and tonality, the creative process may also include a number of different creative tactics and techniques. The following are some of these:

- *Animation and art:* Not all ads are executed with film or photography. Sometimes a creative decision is made to use art, illustration, or animation to achieve the desired look of a print ad or TV commercial or to attract attention. For example, Coke used the popular *Simpsons* cartoon characters in its Super Bowl ads in 2010.[24]
- *Celebrities.* Sometimes they just appear in testimonials, or for endorsements such as Marie Osmond's pitches for NutriSystem. Other times using a celebrity is simply a casting decision—a technique to make an ad more interesting or appealing, such as when the actor Luke Wilson shows up in commercials for AT&T mobile phones.
- *Music, jingles and slogans.* **Jingles** are original words and music written specifically for advertising executions. Many of us remember classic ad jingles such as "I wish I were an Oscar Mayer Wiener" (Oscar Mayer) and ad slogans such as "Finger lickin' good" (KFC), "Got milk?" (initially created for the

jingles
Original words and music written specifically for advertising executions.

California Milk Processor Board), and "Just do it" (Nike). Jingles aren't used as often as they were in the past, but many advertisers still like to set their slogan to original music at the end of a commercial. These are called "musical buttons" or "tags." A currently popular technique is to add a few appropriate measures of a popular song near the end of a commercial to emphasize the message.

slogans
Simple, memorable linguistic devices linked to a brand.

Slogans link the brand to a simple linguistic device that is memorable (jingles do the same but set the slogan to music). We usually have no trouble reciting successful slogans (sometimes years after the campaign has ended); think of such die-hards as "Please don't squeeze the Charmin," "Double your pleasure, double your fun," and "Even a caveman can do it." Firms such as Clorox, Allstate, and Procter & Gamble find that the songs they use in their commercials can become popular on their own; now they offer consumers the opportunity to purchase full-length versions of the music.[25]

Step 4: Pretest What the Ads Will Say

pretesting
A research method that seeks to minimize mistakes by getting consumer reactions to ad messages before they appear in media.

Now that the creatives have performed their magic, how does the agency know if the campaign ideas will work? Advertisers try to minimize mistakes by getting reactions to ad messages before they actually place them. Much of this **pretesting,** the research that goes on in the early stages of a campaign, centers on gathering basic information that will help planners be sure they've accurately defined the product's market, consumers, and competitors. This information comes from quantitative sources, such as surveys, and qualitative sources, such as focus groups.

In these two executions from the U.K. the creatives borrow a nostalgic look from an earlier era.

In addition, some researchers use physiological measures to pretest ads. For example, the ad agency Bark Group employs eye movement tracking, skin responses, and brain responses to gauge consumers' emotional responses to ads in order to produce ad campaigns that result in a stronger emotional reaction.[26] The idea is to be able to identify the colors, sounds, images and words that elicit the strongest responses—even in some cases when viewers aren't consciously aware of how they're feeling.

Step 5: Choose the Media Type(s) and Media Schedule

media planning
The process of developing media objectives, strategies, and tactics for use in an advertising campaign.

Media planning is a problem-solving process that gets a message to a target audience in the most effective way. Planning decisions include audience selection and where, when, and how frequent the exposure should be. Thus, the first task for a media planner is to find out when and where people in the target market are most likely to be exposed to the communication. Many college students read the campus newspaper in the morning (believe it or not, sometimes even during class!), so advertisers may choose to place ad messages aimed at college students there.

There is no such thing as one perfect medium for advertising. The choice depends on the specific target audience, the objective of the message, and, of course, the budget. For the advertising campaign to be effective, the media planner must match the profile of the target market with specific media vehicles. For example, many Hispanic American consumers, even those who speak English, are avid users of Spanish-language media. Marketers that wish to reach this segment might allocate a relatively large share of their advertising budget to buying Spanish-language newspapers, magazines, TV, and Spanish webcasts available to broadband Internet users.

The choice of the right media mix is no simple matter, especially as new options including videos and DVDs, video games, personal computers, the Internet, MP3 players, hundreds of new TV channels, and even satellite radio now vie for our attention. Consider that in 1965, advertisers could reach 80 percent of 18- to 49-year-olds in the United States with three 60-second TV spots! That kind of efficiency is just a pipe dream in today's highly fragmented media marketplace.

WHERE TO SAY IT: TRADITIONAL MASS MEDIA What does a 50-inch plasma TV with Dolby Surround Sound have in common with a matchbook? Each is a media vehicle that permits an advertiser to communicate with a potential customer. Depending on the intended message, each medium has its advantages and disadvantages. In this section we'll take a look at the major categories of traditional mass media; then we'll look at Internet advertising and some less traditional indirect forms of advertising. Table 21.1 summarizes some of the pros and cons of each type.

- *Television:* Because of television's ability to reach so many people at once, it's often the medium of choice for regional and national companies. However, advertising on a television network can be very expensive. The cost to air a 30-second ad on a popular primetime network TV show one time normally ranges between \$200,000 and \$750,000 or more depending on the size of the show's audience. In 2008, ads for a near-finale episode of *American Idol,* the number one TV show for four years, went for \$1 million or more.[27] Advertisers

TABLE 21.1
PROS AND CONS OF MEDIA VEHICLES

VEHICLE	PROS	CONS
Television	■ TV is extremely creative and flexible. ■ Network TV is the most cost-effective way to reach a mass audience. ■ Cable and satellite TV allow the advertiser to reach a selected group at relatively low cost. ■ A prestigious way to advertise. ■ Can demonstrate the product in use. ■ Can provide entertainment and generate excitement. ■ Messages have high impact because of the use of sight and sound.	■ The message is quickly forgotten unless it is repeated often. ■ The audience is increasingly fragmented. ■ Although the relative cost of reaching the audience is low, prices are still high on an absolute basis—often too high for smaller companies. A 30-second spot on a prime-time TV sitcom costs well over $250,000. ■ Fewer people view network television. ■ People switch from station to station and zap commercials. ■ Rising costs have led to more and shorter ads, causing more clutter.
Radio	■ Good for selectively targeting an audience. ■ Is heard outside the home. ■ Can reach customers on a personal and intimate level. ■ Can use local personalities. ■ Relatively low cost, both for producing a spot and for running it repeatedly. ■ Because of short lead time, radio ads can be modified quickly to reflect changes in the marketplace. ■ Use of sound effects and music allows listeners to use their imagination to create a vivid scene.	■ Listeners often don't pay full attention to what they hear. ■ Difficulty in buying radio time, especially for national advertisers. ■ Not appropriate for products that must be seen or demonstrated to be appreciated. ■ The small audiences of individual stations means ads must be placed with many different stations and must be repeated frequently.
Newspapers	■ Wide exposure provides extensive market coverage. ■ Flexible format permits the use of color, different sizes, and targeted editions. ■ Provides the ability to use detailed copy. ■ Allows local retailers to tie in with national advertisers. ■ Readers are in the right mental frame to process advertisements about new products, sales, etc. ■ Timeliness, i.e., short lead time between placing ad and running it.	■ Most people don't spend much time reading the newspaper. ■ Readership is especially low among teens and young adults. ■ Short life span—people rarely look at a newspaper more than once. ■ Offers a very cluttered ad environment. ■ The reproduction quality of images is relatively poor. ■ Not effective to reach specific audiences.
Magazines	■ Audiences can be narrowly targeted by specialized magazines. ■ High credibility and interest level provide a good environment for ads. ■ Advertising has a long life and is often passed along to other readers. ■ Visual quality is excellent. ■ Can provide detailed product information with a sense of authority.	■ With the exception of direct mail, it is the most expensive form of advertising. The cost of a full-page, four-color ad in a general-audience magazine typically exceeds $100,000. ■ Long deadlines reduce flexibility. ■ The advertiser must generally use several magazines to reach the majority of a target market. ■ Clutter.
Directories	■ Customers actively seek exposure to advertisements. ■ Advertisers determine the quality of the ad placement because larger ads get preferential placement.	■ Limited creative options. ■ May be a lack of color. ■ Ads are generally purchased for a full year and cannot be changed.

TABLE 21.1
CONTINUED

VEHICLE	PROS	CONS
Out-of-home media	■ Most of the population can be reached at low cost. ■ Good for supplementing other media. ■ High frequency when signs are located in heavy traffic areas. ■ Effective for reaching virtually all segments of the population. ■ Geographic flexibility.	■ Hard to communicate complex messages because of short exposure time. ■ Difficult to measure advertisement's audience. ■ Controversial and disliked in many communities. ■ Cannot pinpoint specific market segments.
Internet Web sites	■ Can target specific audiences and individualize messages. ■ Web user registration and cookies allow marketers to track user preferences and Web site activity. ■ Is interactive—consumers can participate in the ad campaign; can create do-it-yourself ads. ■ An entertainment medium allowing consumers to play games, download music, etc. ■ Consumers are active participants in the communication process, controlling what information and the amount and rate of information they receive. ■ Web sites can facilitate both marketing communication and transactions. ■ Consumers visit Web sites with the mindset to obtain information. ■ Banners can achieve top of mind awareness (TOMA), even without click-throughs.	■ Limited to Internet users only. ■ Banners, pop-ups, unsolicited e-mail, etc., can be unwanted and annoying. ■ Declining click-through rates for banners—currently less than 0.03 percent. ■ If Web pages take too long to load, consumers will abandon the site. ■ Phishing is e-mail sent by criminals to get consumers to go to phony Web sites that will seek to gain personal information such as credit card numbers. ■ Because advertisers' costs are normally based on the number of click-throughs, competitors may engage in click fraud by clicking on a sponsored link. ■ Difficult to measure effectiveness.
Place-based media	■ Effective for certain markets such a pharmaceutical companies to reach their target audience. ■ In retail locations it can reach customers immediately before purchase; this provides a last opportunity to influence the purchase decision. ■ In locations such as airports, it receives a high level of attention because of lack of viewer options.	■ Limited audience. ■ Difficult to measure effectiveness.
Branded entertainment	■ Brand presented in a positive context. ■ Brand message presented in a covert fashion. ■ Less intrusive and thus less likely to be avoided. ■ Connection with a popular movie plot or TV program and with entertaining characters can help a brand's image. ■ Can build emotional connection with the audience. ■ Can create a memorable association that serves to enhance brand recall.	■ Little control of how the brand is positioned—is in the hands of the director. ■ Difficult to measure effectiveness. ■ Costs of placement can be very high.
Advergaming	■ Companies can customize their own games or incorporate brands into existing popular games. ■ Some game producers now actively pursue tie-ins with brands. ■ Millions of gamers play an average of 40 hours per game before they tire of it. ■ Millions of consumers have mobile phones "in their hands."	■ Audience limited to gamers.
Mobile phones	■ A large variety of different formats using different mobile phone apps.	■ Consumers may be unwilling to receive messages through their phones.

Sources: Adapted from J. Thomas Russell and Ron Lane, Kleppner's Advertising Procedure, 15th ed. (Upper Saddle River, NJ: Prentice Hall, 2002); Terence A. Shimp, Advertising, Promotion and Supplemental Aspects of Integrated Marketing Communications, 8th ed. (Australia: Thomson Southwestern, 2010); and William Wells, John Burnett, and Sandra Moriarty, Advertising: Principles and Practice, 6th ed. (Upper Saddle River, NJ: Prentice Hall, 2003).

may prefer to buy cable, satellite, or local television time rather than network time because it's cheaper or because they want to reach a more targeted market, such as "foodies," who are into cooking. Nevertheless, 78 percent of advertisers say TV advertising has become less effective as DVRs and video-on-demand grow in popularity.[28]

While viewing of traditional broadcast TV is down dramatically in recent years, people spend a lot more time watching cable and satellite channels. This explains why the companies that own broadcast networks also are buying up major cable channels—General Electric's NBC owns MSNBC, CNBC, Bravo, SciFi, and USA TV channels; Walt Disney Co., which owns ABC, also owns ESPN and ABC Family and also is a partial owner for Lifetime, A&E, and E! cable channels; and Viacom Inc. owns MTV, VH1, Comedy Central, Showtime, The Movie Channel, and Nickelodeon along with CBS.[29]

- *Radio:* Radio as an advertising medium dates back to 1922, when a New York City apartment manager went on the air to advertise properties for rent. One advantage of radio advertising is flexibility. Marketers can change commercials quickly, often on the spot by an announcer and a recording engineer.[30]
- *Newspapers:* The newspaper is one of the oldest communication platforms. Retailers in particular have relied on newspaper ads since before the turn of the 20th century to inform readers about sales and deliveries of new merchandise. While most newspapers are local, *USA Today,* the *Wall Street Journal,* and the *New York Times* have national circulations and provide readerships in the millions. Newspapers are an excellent medium for local advertising and for events (such as store sales) that require a quick response. Today, most newspapers also offer online versions of their papers to expand their exposure. Some, such as the *New York Times,* offer online subscribers downloads of the actual newspaper including all the ads at a much lower cost than the paper version. Rates for newspapers vary depending on the circulation of the paper. Most newspapers help advertisers in putting their ads together, a real advantage to the small business. However, the newspaper industry is in serious trouble as more people choose to get their news online and many major papers are closing their doors or struggling.
- *Magazines:* Today, in addition to general audience magazines such as *Readers Digest,* there are literally thousands of special-interest magazines. Approximately 92 percent of adults look through at least one magazine per month. New technology such as selective binding allows publishers to personalize their editions so that they can include advertisements for local businesses in issues they mail to specific locations. For advertisers, magazines also offer the opportunity for multi-page spreads as well as the ability to include special inserts so they can deliver samples of products such as perfumes and other "scratch-and-sniff" treats. Kimberly Clark's Viva brand paper towels, for example, included samples of the product stitched into copies of *Readers Digest* as part of a six-page spread.[31]

digital media
Media that are digital rather than analog including Web sites, mobile or cellular phones, and digital video such as YouTube.

WHERE TO SAY IT: DIGITAL MEDIA The term **digital media** refers to any media that are digital rather than analog. The more popular types of digital media advertisers use today include Web sites, mobile or cellular phones, and digital video such as YouTube.

Owned, Paid, and Earned Media Internet media can be classified as owned, paid, and earned.[32] Companies can control their **owned media** that includes Web sites, blogs, Facebook, and Twitter accounts. The advantage of these owned media is that they are effective means for companies to build relationships with their customers. **Paid media**, the most similar model to traditional media, includes display ads, sponsorships, and paid key word searches. Consumers generally dislike the paid ads making their effectiveness less of a sure thing. Earned media refers to word of mouth (WOM) or buzz using social media. The positive of **earned media** is that it is the most credible to consumers. The challenge is that marketers have no control over earned media; they can only listen and respond.

owned media
Internet sites such as Web sites, blogs, Facebook, and Twitter accounts that are owned by an advertiser.

paid media
Internet media such as display ads, sponsorships, and paid key word searches that are paid for by an advertiser.

earned media
Word-of-mouth or buzz using social media where the advertiser has no control.

Website Advertising Online advertising no longer is a novelty; companies now spend over $21 billion a year to communicate via digital media. Major firms like General Mills and Kraft Foods are boosting their spending and the number of brands they promote online.[33] The reason? Fifteen percent of the time U.S. consumers spend with all media is now online—and of course for some segments such as college students, that figure is much higher.[34]

Online advertising offers several advantages over other media platforms. First, the Internet provides new ways to finely target customers. Web user registrations and cookies allow sites to track user preferences and deliver ads based on previous Internet behavior. In addition, because the Web site can track how many times an ad is "clicked," advertisers can measure in real time how people respond to specific online messages.

Finally, online advertising can be interactive—it lets consumers participate in the advertising campaign, and in some cases they can even become part of the action. Viewers who logged on to a special Web site were able to "direct" TV commercials for the Ford Probe by picking the cast and plotlines that Ford's ad agency then used to create actual spots. Similarly, during its "whatever.com" campaign, Nike sent consumers to the Web to pick the endings of three cliffhanger TV spots.[35]

Alaska Airlines developed a system to create unique ads for individual Web surfers based on their geographic location, the number of times that person has seen an Alaska Airlines ad, the consumer's purchase history with the airline, and his experience with lost bags, delays, and flight cancellations. The program can offer different prices to different customers, even prices below the lowest published fares.[36]

Specific forms of Internet advertising include banners, buttons, pop-up ads, search engines and directories, and e-mail:

- **Banners**, rectangular graphics at the top or bottom of Web pages, were the first form of Web advertising.
- **Buttons** are small banner-type advertisements that a company can place anywhere on a page.
- A **pop-up ad** is an advertisement that appears on the screen while a Web page loads or after it has loaded. Because these messages take up part of the screen's "real estate" while surfers wait for the desired page to load, they are difficult to ignore. Many surfers find pop-ups a nuisance, so most Internet access software provides an option that blocks all pop-ups. Web advertisers are typically charged only if people actually click through to the ad.

banners
Internet advertising in the form of rectangular graphics at the top or bottom of Web pages.

buttons
Small banner-type advertisements that can be placed anywhere on a Web page.

pop-up ad
An advertisement that appears on the screen while a Web page loads or after it has loaded.

search engines
Internet programs that search for documents with specified keywords.

- **Search engines and directory listings** are ways for people to find Web pages of interest to them. A Web **search engine** is a program that searches for documents with specified keywords. Because there are millions of Web pages that include a particular word or phrase, most search engines use some method to rank their search results and provide users with the most relevant results first. Firms are increasingly paying search engines for more visible or higher placement on results lists. Google, which has 65% of all U.S. web searches, has total global revenues of nearly $30 billion. In June, 2010, BP spent nearly $3.6 million for Google advertising following the Gulf oil spill while Google's top client, AT&T spent $8.08 million on Google's AdWords to support its launch of the iPhone 4.38. Unlike search engines, a **Web directory** does not display lists of Web pages based on keywords but instead lists sites by categories and subcategories. Google, for example, offers its users the Google Directory in addition to its search engine. Who have you Googled today?

web directory
Internet program that lists sites by categories and subcategories.

e-mail advertising
Advertising messages sent via e-mail to large numbers of people simultaneously.

spam
The use of electronic media to send unsolicited messages in bulk.

permission marketing
E-mail advertising in which on-line consumers have the opportunity to accept or refuse the unsolicited e-mail.

- **E-mail advertising** that transmits messages to very large numbers of inboxes simultaneously is one of the easiest ways to communicate with consumers—it's basically the same price whether you send ten messages or ten thousand. Recipients might be drawn from an organization's list or they may have "opted-in" to receive notifications of a company's discounts and promotions. One downside to this platform is the explosion of **spam**. The industry defines this practice as sending unsolicited e-mail to five or more people not personally known to the sender. Many Web sites that offer e-mail give surfers the opportunity to refuse unsolicited e-mail via junk e-mail blockers. This **permission marketing** strategy gives the consumer the power to opt in or out. Marketers in the United States send about 200 billion e-mails to consumers every year, so they hope that a good portion of these will be opened and read rather than being sent straight to the recycle bin.[37]

mobile advertising
A form of advertising that is communicated to the consumer via a handset.

Mobile Advertising The Mobile Marketing Association defines **mobile advertising** as "a form of advertising that is communicated to the consumer via a handset."[38] Mobile marketing offers advertisers a variety of ways to speak to customers including Mobile Web sites, mobile applications, mobile messaging, and mobile video and TV.

Mobile advertising has just begun to boom, much energized by Apple's iPhone and all the apps that go with it. Begun with Apple's iAd, today's mobile advertising has moved from tiny static banner ads to rich media that brings motion, interactivity, sound, video, or Flash, to mobile advertising.[39] In the U.K., Kellogg's used mobile advertising for its "The Big Bake" campaign.[40] Messages on Kellogg's cereal boxes encouraged consumers to use their mobile phones to send in photos of themselves cooking recipes that include Kellogg's cereals. Winners of the contest were given the opportunity to star in a Kellogg's TV or print ad. And, before Oprah left TV, she made herself available to fans through a smartphone app that included a weekly calendar of what was on the show, information about availability of reservations for the show, and access to articles and photos from Oprah.com and *O Magazine* and to her tweets.[41]

Newer phones with global positioning system (GPS) features that pinpoint your location allow additional mobile advertising opportunities. Outdoor apparel retailer North Face, for example, used location-based mobile ads to lure consumers to its stores.[42] When customers who opt in are close to one of the chain's stores, they receive a text message about new arrivals or an in-store promotion such as a free water bottle with a purchase.

Video Sharing: Check It Out on YouTube **Video sharing** describes the strategy of uploading video recordings or **vlogs** (pronounced vee-logs) to Internet sites such as YouTube so that thousands or even millions of other Internet users can check them out. These videos are a powerful way to break through the clutter. To understand how, let's take a look at how Blendtec, a small electric blender manufacturer, used this strategy to grab a lot of attention quickly and cheaply. The company uploaded a vlog that showed its president dropping a brand-new iPhone into one of its appliances—presto! Within 24 hours, over a million people had watched as presto! purée of phone resulted.[43]

video sharing
Uploading video recordings on to Internet sites such as YouTube so that thousands or even millions of other Internet users can see them.

vlogs
Video recordings shared on the Internet.

For marketers, YouTube provides vast opportunities to build relationships with consumers. For example, Home Depot provides do-it yourselfers with free educational videos that promote Home Depot products while these vlogs position the company as a trusted expert. The University of Phoenix uses YouTube to post hundreds of video testimonials. The Boone Oakley advertising agency has established its Web site on YouTube. The interactive video allows potential clients to view its work in an easily accessible way and is especially appealing to companies that want a nontraditional marketing communications program.

Where to Say It: Branded Entertainment As we noted earlier, more and more marketers rely on paid product placements in TV shows and movies to grab the attention of consumers who tune out traditional ad messages as fast as they see them. These placements are an important form of branded entertainment, a strategy where marketers integrate products into all sorts of venues including movies, television shows, videogames, novels, and even retail settings. For one promotion a group of 7-Eleven convenience stores literally became Kwik-E-Marts just like the store Homer loves to frequent in the TV show *The Simpsons*. Real-world customers could buy such exotic delicacies as "Squishees," "Buzz Cola," and "Krusty-Os cereal." The KFC fast-food chain paid two cities in Indiana to put founder Colonel Sanders's face on their hydrants and fire extinguishers to promote its new "fiery" chicken wings.[44] And the Twentieth Century Fox movie studio even managed to place a plug for the romantic comedy *I Love You, Beth Cooper* in a high school valedictorian's speech (she got paid $1,800 to mention one of the main characters).[45] Product placement has also moved to social media as many firms are paying YouTube celebrities to push their products. Because consumers trust what these YouTubers say, companies including giants AT&T, GE, Ford, Colgate, Lancôme Paris, McDonalds, and Coca-Cola are paying $75,000 or more to some YouTube stars.[46]

augmented reality
A form of technology where a view of a real-world environment joins a layer of virtual computer-generated imagery to create a mixed reality.

The Cutting Edge

Augmented Reality

Ever wonder how they make those yellow first-down lines in televised football games that spectators in the stadium can't see? Or how about the trail of the puck in broadcasts of hockey games? The answer is **augmented reality** (AR), a form of technology where a view of a real-world environment joins a layer of virtual computer-generated imagery to create a mixed reality.

Adidas is one of several companies experimenting with AR in its marketing program.[47] **Adidas.com** uses augmented reality to create three online games for Adidas sneaker customers. One is a skateboard game where the gamer's sneaker navigates through the city. Other Adidas games include a *Star Wars*–like game and a music game. To play all three games, the consumer holds the tongue of the sneaker up to a computer webcam and an implanted code activates a virtual 3-D world that the person sneaks into. The iPhone now offers users at least ten AR apps. Hold your phone up to the stars and the app will map the constellations with their names for you while the Firefighter 360 game app sets your location on fire and then allows you to put the fire out and save passers-by to make you a hero.[48]

Is branded entertainment a solid strategy? The idea is that when consumers see a popular celebrity who uses a specific brand in their favorite movie or TV program, they might develop a more positive attitude toward that brand. Successful brand placements include the BMW Z3 James Bond drove, the Nike shoes Forrest Gump wore, and the Ray-Ban sunglasses Tom Cruise sported in *Risky Business.* Audi recently promoted its R8 sports car in the movie *Iron Man: Superhero* Tony Stark drives the car, while Gwyneth Paltrow as Virginia "Pepper" Potts drives the Audi S5 sports sedan.[49]

But placing a Pepsi can in a TV show is only one form of branded entertainment. Today advertisers also take a more active role in developing new television programs to showcase their products. For example, TNT and Dodge paired up to produce *Lucky Chance,* a branded mini-series about an undercover Drug Enforcement Agency agent who drives a 2009 Dodge Challenger to transport money to a mob boss.[50]

advergaming
Brand placements in video games.

Beyond movies and television shows, what better way to promote to the video generation than through brand placements in video games? The industry calls this technique **advergaming.** If you are a video game hound, watch for placements of real-life brands such as Ford, Radio Shack, General Motors, Toyota, and Sony embedded in the action of your game. Quiksilver, a clothing manufacturer for extreme-sport participants, now puts its shirts and shorts into video games such as Tony Hawk's *Pro Skater 3.*

support media
Media such as directories or out-of-home media that may be used to reach people who are not reached by mass media advertising.

Where to Say It: Support Media While marketers (and consumers) normally think of advertising as mass media messages, in reality many of the ads we see today show up in our homes, our workplaces, and in public venues like restroom walls, on signs that trail behind airplanes, or in movies and television programs. **Support media** reach people who may not have been reached by mass media advertising, and these platforms also support the messages traditional media delivers. Here we'll look at some of the more important support media advertisers use.

- **Directories**: Directory advertising is the most "down-to-earth," information-focused advertising medium. In 1883, a printer in Wyoming ran out of white paper while printing part of a telephone book, so he substituted yellow paper instead. Today, the Yellow Pages, including the online Yellow Pages, posts revenues of more than $16 billion in the United States and over $45 billion globally.[51] Often consumers look through directories just before they are ready to buy.

out-of-home media
Communication media that reach people in public places.

digital signage
Out-of-home media that use digital technology to change the message at will.

- **Out-of-home media** includes outdoor advertising (billboards and signs), transit advertising (signs placed inside and/or outside buses, taxis, trains, train stations, and airports) and other types of messages that reach people in public places. In recent years, outdoor advertising has pushed the technology envelope with **digital signage** that enables the source to change the message at will. In a first for out-of-home media, CBS Outdoor installed a high-definition 3-D projection display in New York's Grand Central Terminal where 70,000 commuters a day were able to view 3-D commercials (yes, with 3-D glasses) for Visa.[52] Of course, many consumers dislike out-of-home media, especially outdoor advertising, because they feel it is unattractive.

place-based media
Advertising media that transmit messages in public places, such as doctors' offices and airports, where certain types of people congregate.

- **Place-based media** like "The Airport Channel" transmit messages to "captive audiences" in public places, such as doctors' offices and airport waiting areas. Place-based video screens are now in thousands of shops, offices, and health clubs across the country including stores like CompUSA, Best Buy, Borders, Foot Locker, and Target. The Walmart TV Network has more than 125,000 screens in

2,850 Walmart stores, and patients who wait in over 10,800 doctors' offices watch medical programming and ads. NBC Universal has its shows on screens installed in office building elevators and on United Airlines flights.[53]

- And now, some retailers can even follow you around the store to deliver more up-close and personal messages: *RFID* technology (radio frequency identification) uses tiny sensors embedded in packages or store aisles to track customers as they pass. An unsuspecting shopper might hear a beep to remind him that he just passed his family's favorite peanut butter.[54] You're not paranoid; they really are watching you!

When to Say It: Media Scheduling After she chooses the advertising media, the planner then creates a **media schedule** that specifies the exact media the campaign will use as well as when and how often the message should appear. Figure 21.4 shows a hypothetical media schedule for the promotion of a new video game. Note that much of the advertising reaches its target audience in the months just before Christmas, and that much of the expensive television budget focuses on advertising during specials just prior to the holiday season.

The media schedule outlines the planner's best estimate of which media will be most effective to attain the advertising objective(s) and which specific media vehicles will do the most effective job. The media planner considers qualitative factors such as the match between the demographic and psychographic profile of a target audience and the people a media vehicle reaches, the advertising patterns of competitors, and the capability of a medium to adequately convey the desired information. The planner must also consider factors such as the compatibility of the product with editorial content. For example, viewers might not respond well to a lighthearted ad for a new snack food during a somber documentary on world hunger.

media schedule
The plan that specifies the exact media to use and when to use it.

There are also a number of quantitative factors, which the media planner uses to develop the media schedule. **Reach** is the percentage of the target market that will be exposed to the media vehicle at least once during a given period of time, usually four weeks.

reach
The percentage of the target market that will be exposed to the media vehicle.

FIGURE 21.4

Media Schedule for a Video Game

Media planning includes decisions on where, when, and how much advertising to do. A media schedule such as the one for a video game shows the plan visually.

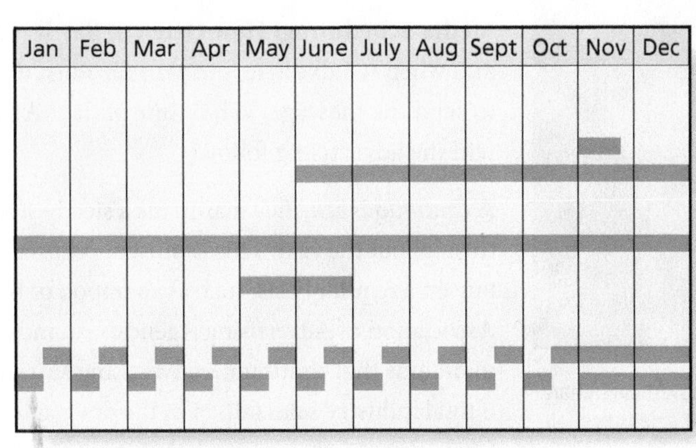

For example, if the target market includes 100 million adults age 18 and over and a specific TV program has an audience that includes 5 million adults in this age group, the program has a reach of 5. Developing a media plan with high reach is particularly important for widely used products when the message needs to get to as many consumers as possible.

frequency
The average number of times a person in the target group will be exposed to the message.

Frequency is the average number of times that an individual or a household will be exposed to the message. Note that this is the average. For example, while some members of a target market may be exposed to an ad 2 or 4 or 20 times and others see an ad only once, the average and thus the frequency might be 4. High levels of frequency are important for products that are complex or those that are targeted to relatively small markets for which multiple exposures to the message are necessary to make an impact.

gross rating points (GRPs)
A measure used for comparing the effectiveness of different media vehicles: average reach x frequency.

cost per thousand (CPM)
A measure used to compare the relative cost-effectiveness of different media vehicles that have different exposure rates; the cost to deliver a message to 1,000 people or homes.

Gross rating points (GRPs) are a measure of the quantity of media included in the media plan. Just as we talk about buying 15 gallons of gas or a pound of coffee, media planners talk about a media schedule that includes the purchase of 250 gross rating points of radio and 700 GRPs of TV. We calculate gross rating points by multiplying a media vehicle's rating by the number of planned ad insertions. As we see in Table 21.2, if 30 percent of a target audience watches *American Idol* and you place eight ads on the show, you buy 240 GRPs of that show.

Although some media vehicles deliver more of your target audience, they may not be cost-efficient. More people will see a commercial aired during the Super Bowl than during a 3:00 A.M. rerun of a *Tarzan* movie. But the advertiser could run late-night commercials every night for a year for the cost of one 30-second Super Bowl spot. To compare the relative cost-effectiveness of different media and of spots run on different vehicles in the same medium, media planners use a measure they call **cost per thousand (CPM).** This figure reflects the cost to deliver a message to 1,000 people.

Assume that the cost of each 30-second commercial on American Idol is $400,000 but the number of target audience members the show reaches is 20 million or 20,000 X 1,000. The CPM of *American Idol* is $400,000/20,000 — $20 CPM. Compare this to the cost of advertising in *Fortune* magazine: A full-page 4-color ad costs approximately $115,000 and the readership includes approximately 2 million members of our target audience. The cost per thousand for *Fortune* is $115,000/2000—$57.50. Thus, *American Idol,* while having a much higher total cost, actually is a more efficient buy.

The long-running Got Milk? Campaign avoids advertising wear-out because it uses a steady stream of different celebrities (all with milk mustaches, of course) over time.

Media Scheduling: How Often to Say It After she decides where and when to advertise, the planner must decide how often she wants to send the message. What time of day? And what overall pattern will the advertising follow?

A *continuous schedule* maintains a steady stream of advertising throughout the year. This is most appropriate for products that we buy on a regular basis, such as shampoo or bread. The American Association of Advertising Agencies, an industry trade group, maintains that continuous advertising sustains market leadership even if total industry sales fall.[55] On the downside, some messages can suffer from advertising wear-out because people tune out the same old ad

TABLE 21.2
A (HYPOTHETICAL) MEDIA SCHEDULE

MEDIA VEHICLE	RATING (PERCENTAGE OF TARGET AUDIENCE REACHED)	NUMBER OF AD INSERTIONS DURING THE PERIOD	GRPS (RATING × NUMBER OF INSERTIONS)
American Idol TV show	30	8 (2 ads on each week's show for 4 weeks)	240 GRPs
NBC Nightly News	10	40 (2 ads each weeknight for 4 weeks)	400
The Today Show	20	40 (2 ads each weekday morning for 4 weeks)	800
Newsweek magazine	20	4 (1 ad in each of 4 editions during the 4-week period)	80
Fortune magazine	12	2 (1 ad in each of the 2 editions each month)	24
USA Today newspaper	7	8 (1 ad each Monday and Thursday during the 4-week period)	56
Total GRPs			1600

messages. A pulsing schedule varies the amount of advertising throughout the year based on when the product is likely to be in demand. A suntan lotion might advertise year-round but more heavily during the summer months. *Flighting* is an extreme form of pulsing, in which advertising appears in short, intense bursts alternating with periods of little to no activity. It can produce as much brand awareness as a steady dose of advertising at a much lower cost if consumers noticed the messages from the previous flight and these made an impact.

Step 6: Evaluate the Advertising

John Wanamaker, a famous Philadelphia retailer, once complained, "I am certain that half the money I spend on advertising is completely wasted. The trouble is, I don't know which half."[56] Now that we've seen how advertising is created and executed, let's step back and see how we decide if it's working.

There's no doubt that a lot of advertising is ineffective. Ironically, as marketers try harder and harder to reach their customers, these efforts can backfire. Many consumers have a love–hate relationship with advertising. Over half the respondents in a survey said they "avoid buying products that overwhelm them with advertising and marketing," and 60 percent said their opinion of advertising "is much more negative than just a few years ago."[57] With so many messages competing for the attention of frazzled customers, it's especially important for firms to evaluate their efforts to increase the impact of their messages. How can they do that?

posttesting
Research conducted on consumers' responses to actual advertising messages they have seen or heard.

Posttesting means conducting research on consumers' responses to advertising messages they have seen or heard (as opposed to pretesting, which as we've seen collects reactions to messages before they're actually placed in "the real world"). Ironically, many creative ads that are quirky or even bizarre make an advertising agency look good within the industry (and on the résumé of the art director), but are ultimately unsuccessful because they don't communicate what the company needs to say about the product itself. We may remember that weird ad, but have no idea what product it advertised. Three ways to measure the impact of an advertisement are unaided recall, aided recall, and attitudinal measures:

unaided recall
A research technique conducted by telephone survey or personal interview that asks whether a person remembers seeing an ad during a specified period without giving the person the name of the brand.

aided recall
A research technique that uses clues to prompt answers from people about advertisements they might have seen.

attitudinal measures
A research technique that probes a consumer's beliefs or feelings about a product before and after being exposed to messages about it.

1. **Unaided recall** tests by telephone survey or personal interview whether a person remembers seeing an ad during a specified period without giving the person the name of the brand.
2. An **aided recall** test uses the name of the brand and sometimes other clues to prompt answers. For example, a researcher might show a group of consumers a list of brands and ask them to choose which items they have seen advertised within the past week.
3. **Attitudinal measures** probe a bit more deeply by testing consumers' beliefs or feelings about a product before and after they are exposed to messages about it. If, for example, Pepsi's messages about "freshness-dating" make enough consumers believe that the freshness of soft drinks is important, marketers can consider the advertising campaign successful.

Public Relations

Public relations (PR) is the communication function that seeks to build good relationships with an organization's publics; these include consumers, stockholders, legislators, and other stakeholders in the organization. Today marketers use PR activities to influence the attitudes and perceptions of various groups not only toward companies and brands but also toward politicians, celebrities, and not-for-profit organizations.

The basic rule of good PR is, Do something good, and then talk about it. A company's efforts to get in the limelight—and stay there—can range from humanitarian acts to sponsoring band tours. The big advantage of this kind of communication is that when PR messages are placed successfully, they are more credible than if the same information appeared in a paid advertisement. As one marketing executive observed, "There's a big difference between hearing about a product from a pitchman and from your trusted local anchorman."[58]

publicity
Unpaid communication about an organization that appears in mass media.

Public relations strategies are crucial to an organization's ability to establish and maintain a favorable image. Proactive PR activities stem from the company's marketing objectives. For example, marketers create and manage **publicity**, unpaid communication about an organization that gets media exposure. It's interesting to note that this aspect of PR is blending into other promotional strategies as social media continue to mushroom. Essentially, buzz marketing is also one form of public relations because it tries to motivate consumers to talk up a brand or service to one another (ideally for free).

crisis management
The process of managing a company's reputation when some negative event threatens the organization's image.

As many of the other function of public relations blend into buzz marketing activities, perhaps the most important function it still "owns" is **crisis management**. This refers to the process of managing a company's reputation when some negative and often unplanned event threatens the organization's image. Think about the unfortunate BP executives, for example, who had to communicate to the public as the explosion of an oil rig in the Gulf of Mexico took the shape of an epic environmental disaster, or those who had to reassure a formerly loyal Toyota customer base that faulty accelerator pedals would not in fact cause their cars to speed out of control.

The goal in such situations is to manage the flow of information to address concerns so that consumers don't panic and distributors don't abandon the product. Although some organizations don't seem to learn this lesson, typically the best strategy is to be honest about the problem and to quickly take responsibility for correcting it. For example, a few years ago PepsiCo was rocked by claims that consumers had found hypodermic needles in Diet Pepsi cans. The company assembled a crisis team to map out a response and supplied video footage of its bottling process to show that it was impossible for foreign objects to find their way into cans before they were sealed at the factory. The claims proved false, and PepsiCo ran follow-up ads reinforcing the findings. Pepsi's calm, coordinated response averted a PR disaster.

Even a single negative event can cause permanent damage to a company, the success of its products, and its stockholder equity. While it didn't have the magnitude of a massive oil spill such as the one BP confronted, Wendy's was faced with a similar public image disaster when a customer said she found a finger in a bowl of its chili.[59] The woman and her husband were both sent to prison after investigators discovered that he had actually obtained the finger from a co-worker who had lost it in a workplace accident. While the claim proved false, it still cost the company $2.5 million in lost sales.[60] In another incident, a man stuffed a dead mouse in a Taco Bell burrito in an attempt to extort money from the fast-food chain.[61] Supersize that!

Public relations professionals know that when a firm handles a crisis well, it can minimize damage and help the company make things right. Thus, a vitally important role of PR is to prepare a crisis-management plan. This is a document that details what an organization will do if a crisis occurs—who will be the spokesperson for the organization, how the organization will deal with the press, and what sort of messages it will deliver to the press and the public.

Plan a Public Relations Campaign

A **public relations campaign** is a coordinated effort to communicate with one or more of the firm's publics. This is a three-step process that develops, executes, and evaluates PR objectives. Let's review each step and then we'll examine some of the more frequently used objective and tactics shown in Figure 21.5.

public relations campaign
A coordinated effort to communicate with one or more of the firm's publics.

Like an advertising campaign, the organization must first develop clear objectives for the PR program that define the message it wants people to hear. For example the International Apple Institute, a trade group devoted to increasing the consumption of apples, had to decide if a campaign should focus on getting consumers to cook more with apples, drink more apple juice, or simply to buy more fresh fruit. Because fresh apples brought a substantially higher price per pound to growers than apples used for applesauce or apple juice, the group decided to push the fresh fruit angle. It used the theme "An apple a day..." (sound familiar?) as it mounted a focused campaign to encourage people to eat more apples by placing articles in consumer media extolling the fruit's health benefits.

FIGURE 21.5

Objectives and Tactics of Public Relations

Successful PR campaigns include clearly defined objectives and the use of the right PR activities.

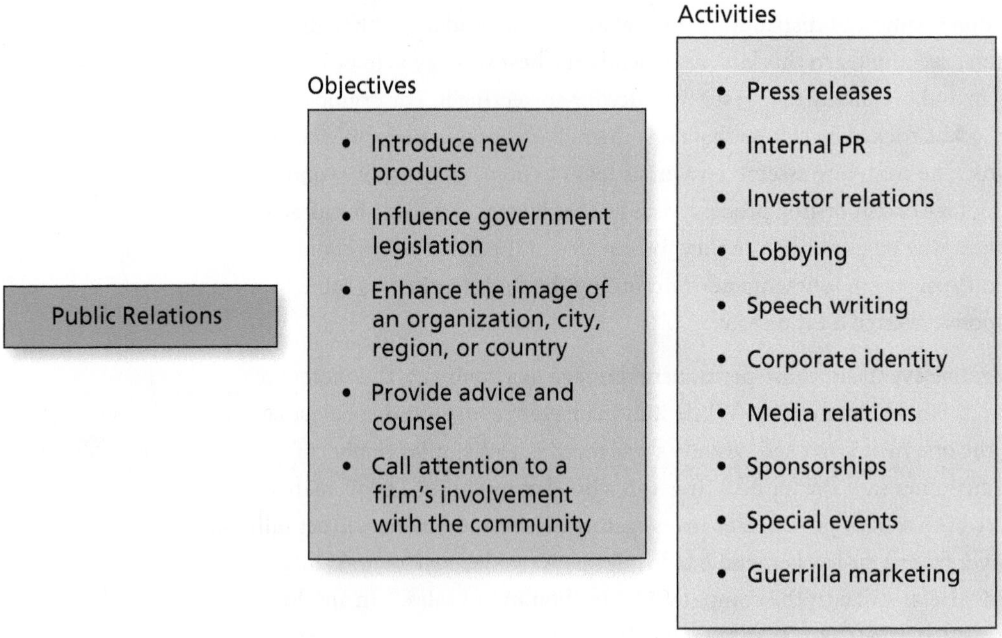

Public Relations

Objectives

- Introduce new products
- Influence government legislation
- Enhance the image of an organization, city, region, or country
- Provide advice and counsel
- Call attention to a firm's involvement with the community

Activities

- Press releases
- Internal PR
- Investor relations
- Lobbying
- Speech writing
- Corporate identity
- Media relations
- Sponsorships
- Special events
- Guerrilla marketing

Execution of the campaign means deciding precisely how to communicate the message to the targeted public(s). An organization can get out its positive messages in many ways: news conferences, sponsorship of charity events, and other attention-getting promotions.

One of the barriers to greater reliance on PR campaigns is evaluation; compared to many other forms of marketing communications, it's difficult to devise metrics to gauge their effectiveness. Who can say precisely what impact an appearance by Steve Carell on *The Tonight Show* to plug his new movie exerts on ticket sales, or whether Virgin's sponsorship of the London Marathon boosted purchases of airline tickets? It is possible to tell if a PR campaign gets media exposure, though compared to advertising it's much more difficult to assess bottom-line impact. Table 21.3 describes some of the most common PR measurement techniques.

Public Relations Objectives

Marketing communication experts know that PR strategies are best used in concert with advertising, sales promotion, and personal selling to send a consistent message to customers and other stakeholders. As part of the total marketing communication plan, they often rely on PR to accomplish the following objectives:

- *Introduce new products to retailers and consumers.* To make the most of the introduction of the iPad in January 2010, Apple staged a live press conference hosted by CEO Steve Jobs in his trademark blue jeans and black turtleneck.[62]
- *Influence government legislation.* Airplane maker Boeing spent over a decade in public relations activities to persuade regulators that jetliners with two engines

TABLE 21.3
MEASURING THE EFFECTIVENESS OF PUBLIC RELATIONS (PR) TACTICS

METHOD	DESCRIPTION	EXAMPLE	PROS	CONS
Personal (subjective) evaluation of PR activities	Evaluation of PR activities by superiors may occur at all levels of the organization.	Items in employee annual reviews relate to the successful fulfillment of PR role.	Simple and inexpensive to complete; assures an annual assessment will be completed.	Subjective nature of the evaluation may result in biased appraisal. Employees may focus on the annual review to the exclusion of some important PR goals.
Matching of PR activity accomplishments with activity objectives	Simple counts of actual PR activities accomplished compares with activity goals set for the period.	Goal: to obtain publication of three feature articles in major newspapers in the first quarter of the year. Result: four articles published.	Focuses attention on the need for quantitative goals for PR activities and achievements. Easy and inexpensive to measure.	Focuses on activity goals rather than image or communication goals. Ignores image perception or attitudes of the firm's publics.
Evaluation of communication objectives through opinion surveys among the firm's publics	Surveys are used to determine if image/ communication goals are met within key groups.	Goal: to achieve an improved image of the organization among at least 30 percent of financial community stakeholders.	Causes PR professionals to focus on actual communication results of activities.	May be difficult to measure changes in perceptions among the firm's publics. Factors not under the control of PR practitioners may influence public perceptions. It is relatively expensive. Results may take many months, thus preventing corrective actions in PR activities.
Measurement of coverage in print and broadcast media, especially those generated by PR activities	Systematic measurement of coverage achieved in print media (column inches/pages) and broadcast media (minutes of air time).	Total number of column inches of newspaper articles resulting from PR releases. Total number of articles including those not from PR releases. Total amount of positive print and broadcast coverage. Total amount of negative print and broadcast coverage. Ratio of negative to positive print and broadcast coverage.	Very objective measurements with little opportunity for bias. Relatively inexpensive.	Does not address perceptions, attitudes, or image issues of the organization.
Impression measurement	Measure the size of the audience for all print and broadcast coverage. Often assessment includes comparisons in terms of advertising costs for same number of impressions.	Network news coverage during the time period equaled over 15 million gross impressions. This number of impressions through advertising would have cost $4,500,000.	Objective, without any potential bias in measurement; provides a monetary measure to justify the expenditures of the PR office or consultant. Relatively inexpensive.	Does not differentiate between negative and positive news coverage. Does not consider responses of publics to the coverage. Assumes advertising and PR communication activities are equal.

are as safe as those with three or four engines even for nonstop international flights, some as long as 16 hours.[63]

- *Enhance the image of an organization.* The Ladies Professional Golf Association (LPGA) used a variety of public relations and other promotion activities—from product endorsements to player blogs to sexy calendars—in its "These Girls Rock" campaign. The program to change the image of ladies' golf to a hip sport seems to be working, as both tournament attendance and television audiences have increased.[64]
- *Provide advice and counsel.* Because of their expertise and understanding of the effects of communication on public opinion, PR professionals also provide advice and counsel for top management. When a firm needs to shut down a plant or to build a new one, to discontinue a product or add to the product line, to fire a vice president, or to give an award to an employee who spends hundreds of hours a year doing volunteer work in his community, it needs the advice of its PR staff. What is the best way to handle the situation? How should the announcement be made? Who should be told first? What is to be said and how?
- *Enhance the image of a city, region, or country.* To promote Vancouver, British Columbia, and Canada around the world, the not-for-profit business organization Tourism Vancouver used a large variety of PR activities to make the most of the Winter Olympics in Vancouver in 2010.[65]
- *Manage a crisis.* PR specialists handle the crucial but often difficult task of communicating with stakeholders when something goes wrong, such as when BP is involved in a massive oil spill or Toyota issues a massive recall of cars with faulty accelerator pedals. Organizations respond in many ways, ranging from (unfortunately) complete denial or silence to full disclosure. For example, when Toyota started to receive reports of unsafe cars in the U.K., the director of the carmaker's operations there posted a five-minute video apologizing to consumers.[66]
- *Call attention to a firm's involvement with the community.* U.S. marketers spend about $15 billion a year to sponsor sporting events, rock concerts, museum exhibits, and the ballet. PR specialists work behind the scenes to ensure that sponsored events receive ample press coverage and exposure. We'll talk more about sponsorships later in this section.

Public Relations Tactics

In order to accomplish their objectives, PR professionals choose from a variety of tactics as shown in Figure 21.5. These activities include press releases, activities aimed at specific internal and external stakeholder groups, speech writing and corporate communications, sponsorships and special events, and guerilla marketing activities.

press release
Information that an organization distributes to the media intended to win publicity.

PRESS RELEASE The most common way for PR specialists to communicate is by a **press release. This is a report of some event or activity that an organization** writes and sends to the media in the hope that it will be published for free. A newer version of this idea is a video news release (VNR) that tells the story in a film format instead. Some of the most common types of press releases include the following:

- *Timely topics* deal with topics in the news, such as Levi Strauss's efforts to promote "Casual Fridays" to boost sales of its Dockers and Slates casual dress pants by highlighting how different corporations around the country are adopting a relaxed dress code.
- *Research project stories* are published by universities to highlight breakthroughs by faculty researchers.
- *Consumer information* releases provide information to help consumers make product decisions, such as helpful tips from Butterball about how to prepare dishes for Thanksgiving dinner.

INTERNAL PR AND EXTERNAL STAKEHOLDERS **Internal PR** activities target employees; they often include company newsletters and closed circuit television to keep people informed about company objectives, successes, or even plans to "downsize" the workforce. Often company newsletters also are distributed outside the firm to suppliers or other important publics.

internal PR
PR activities aimed at employees of an organization.

Investor relations activities focus on communications to those whose financial support is critical; this is especially vital for publicly held companies. It is the responsibility of the PR department to develop and distribute annual and quarterly reports and to provide other essential communications with individual and corporate stockholders, with investment firms, and with capital market organizations.

Investor relations
PR activities such as annual and quarterly reports aimed at a firm's investors.

Lobbying means talking with and providing information to government officials to persuade them to vote a certain way on pending legislation or even to initiate legislation or regulations that would benefit the organization.

lobbying
Talking with and providing information to government officials in order to influence their activities relating to an organization.

SPEECH WRITING AND CORPORATE COMMUNICATIONS An important job of a firm's PR department is **speech writing**; specialists provide speeches for company executives to deliver. While some executives do actually write their own speeches, it is more common for a speechwriter on the PR staff to develop an initial draft of a speech to which the executive might add her own input. PR specialists also provide input on **corporate identity** materials, such as logos, brochures, building design, and even stationery that communicates a positive image for the firm.

speech writing
Writing a speech on a topic for a company executive to deliver.

corporate identity
Materials such as logos, brochures, building design, and stationery that communicate an image of the organization.

One of the tasks of the PR professional is to develop close **media relations** to ensure the organization will receive the best media exposure possible for positive news, such as publicizing the achievements of an employee who has done some notable charity work or for a product the company developed that saved someone's life. And, as we've seen, good media relations can be even more important when things go wrong. News editors are less inclined to present a story of a crisis in its most negative way if they have a good relationship with PR people in the organization.

media relations
A PR activity aimed at developing close relationships with the media.

SPONSORSHIPS AND SPECIAL EVENTS **Sponsorships** are PR activities through which companies provide financial support to help fund an event in return for publicized recognition of the company's contribution. Many companies today find

sponsorship
PR activities through which companies provide financial support to help fund an event in return for publicized recognition of the company's contribution.

that their promotion dollars are well spent to sponsor a golf tournament, a NASCAR driver, a symphony concert, or global events such as the Olympics or World Cup soccer competition. These sponsorships are particularly effective because they allow marketers to reach customers during their leisure time; people often appreciate these efforts because the financial support makes the events possible in the first place.

special events
Activities—from a visit by foreign investors to a company picnic—that are planned and implemented by a PR department.

A related task is to plan and implement special events. Companies find **special events** useful for a variety of purposes. For example, a firm might hold a press conference to increase interest and excitement in a new product or other company activity. A city or state may hold an annual event such as the strawberry festivals in Florida and California or the National Cherry Blossom Festival in Washington, D.C. to promote tourism. A company outing like the huge road rallies Harley-Davidson's Harley Owner's Group (H.O.G.) sponsors reinforces loyalty toward an existing product. Other special events aim simply to create buzz and generate publicity. For New York City shoppers, Unilever created its "All Small & Mighty Clothes Bus," a 40-foot bus it covered in all the shirts, shorts, and socks that one bottle of super-concentrated All laundry detergent can wash. Consumers who spotted the bus during its 12-day campaign could "clean up" if they entered a sweepstakes to win a $5,000 shopping spree or $200 gift cards.[67]

guerilla marketing
Marketing activity in which a firm "ambushes" consumers with promotional content in places they are not expecting to encounter this kind of activity.

GUERRILLA MARKETING Organizations with tiny advertising budgets need to develop innovative—and cheap—ways to capture consumers' attention. **Guerrilla marketing** activities are an increasingly popular way to accomplish this objective. No, this term doesn't refer to marketers making monkeys out of themselves (that's "gorilla marketing"). A guerrilla marketing strategy involves "ambushing" consumers with promotional content in places where they don't expect to encounter these messages. These activities include putting advertising stickers on apples, placing product-related messages on the backs of theater tickets and flags on golf courses, or even staging elaborate dance routines in train stations. T-Mobile pulled this off at the Liverpool station in the U.K. as 350 pedestrians suddenly congregated in the center and launched into an elaborate group routine as the song *Shout!* played on huge speakers (check out the video at **http://www.youtube.com/watch?v5VQ3d3KigPQM&feature5player_embedded#at530).**

Today, big companies buy into guerrilla marketing strategies big time. Burger King recently decided to increase sales in its Asia-Pacific stores by 25 percent. The company sent CDs with quirky marketing suggestions to local restaurant managers. These included putting on T-shirts and placing the shirts on Ronald McDonald, placing large footprints from McDonald's stores to Burger King outlets, placing signs on empty benches saying "gone to BK—Ronald," and placing large signs at BK locations that are near KFC locations that read, "It's why the chicken crossed the road."[68]

Companies use guerrilla marketing to promote new drinks, cars, clothing styles, or even computer systems. Much to the annoyance of city officials in San Francisco and Chicago, IBM painted hundreds of "Peace Love Linux" logos on sidewalks to publicize the company's adoption of the Linux operating system. Even though the company got hit with a hefty bill to pay for cleaning up the "corporate graffiti," one marketing journalist noted that they "got the publicity they were looking for."[69] Given the success of many of these campaigns that operate on a shoestring budget, expect to see even more of these tactics as other companies climb on the guerrilla bandwagon.

Sales Promotion

Sometimes when you walk through your student union on campus you might get assaulted by a parade of people eager for you to enter a contest, taste a new candy bar, or take home a free T-shirt with a local bank's name on it. These are examples of **sales promotion**, programs that marketers design to build interest in or encourage purchase of a good or service during a specified period.[70]

sales promotion
Program designed to build interest in or encourage purchase of a product during a specified period.

How does sales promotion differ from advertising? Both are paid messages from identifiable sponsors to change consumer behavior or attitudes. In some cases, a traditional advertising medium actually publicizes the sales promotion, as when Denny's restaurant used Super Bowl advertising to tell consumers about its free breakfast offer. But while marketers carefully craft advertising campaigns to create long-term positive feelings about a brand, company, or store, sales promotions are more useful if the firm has an *immediate* objective, such as bolstering sales for a brand quickly or encouraging consumers to try a new product.

Marketers today place an increasing amount of their total marketing communication budget into sales promotion. Several reasons account for this increase. First, due to the growth of very large grocery store chains and mass merchandisers such as Walmart, there has been a shift in power in the channels. These large chains can pressure manufacturers to provide deals and discounts. A second reason for the growth in sales promotion is declining consumer brand loyalty. This means that consumers are more likely to purchase products based on cost, value, or convenience. Thus a special sales promotion offer is more likely to cause price-conscious customers to switch brands.

Marketers target sales promotion activities either to ultimate consumers or to members of the channel such as retailers that sell their products. Thus we divide sales promotion into two major categories: consumer-oriented sales promotion and trade-oriented sales promotion. You'll see some examples of common consumer-oriented sales promotions in Table 21.4.

Sales Promotion Directed toward Consumers

As we said, one of the reasons for an increase in sales promotion is because it works. For consumer sales promotion, the major reason for this is that most promotions temporarily change the price/value relationships. A coupon for 50 cents off the price of a bottle of ketchup reduces the price while a special "25 percent more" jar of peanuts increases the value. And if you get a free hairbrush when you buy a bottle of shampoo, this also increases the value. Even the prize in the bottom of the box of cereal increases its value exponentially as every mother (unfortunately) knows. As shown in Figure 21.6, we generally classify consumer sales promotions as either price-based or attention-getting promotions.

Price-Based Consumer Sales Promotion

Many sales promotions target consumers where they live—their wallets. They emphasize short-term price reductions or rebates that encourage people to choose a brand—at

TABLE 21.4
CONSUMER SALES PROMOTION TECHNIQUES: A SAMPLER

TECHNIQUE	DESCRIPTION	EXAMPLE
Coupons (newspaper, magazine, in-the-mail, on product packages, in-store, and on the Internet)	Certificates for money off on selected products, often with an expiration date, are used to encourage product trial.	Crest offers $5 off its WhiteStrips.
Price-off packs	Specially marked packages offer a product at a discounted price.	Tide laundry detergent is offered in a specially marked box for 50 cents off.
Rebates/refunds	Purchasers receive a cash reimbursement when they submit proofs of purchase.	Uniroyal offers a $40 mail-in rebate for purchasers of four new Tiger Paw tires.
Continuity/loyalty programs	Consumers are rewarded for repeat purchases through points that lead to reduced price or free merchandise.	Airlines offer frequent fliers free flights for accumulated points; a carwash offers consumers a half-price wash after purchasing 10 washes.
Special/bonus packs	Additional amount of the product is given away with purchase; it rewards users.	Maxell provides 10 free blank CDs with purchase of a pack of 50.
Contests/sweepstakes	Offers consumers the chance to win cash or merchandise. Sweepstakes winners are determined strictly by chance. Contests require some competitive activity such as a game of skill.	Publisher's Clearing House announces its zillionth sweepstakes.
Premiums: Free premiums include in-pack, on-pack, near pack, or in-the-mail premiums; consumers pay for self-liquidating premiums	A consumer gets a free gift or low-cost item when a product is bought; reinforces product image and rewards users.	A free makeup kit comes with the purchase of $20 worth of Clinique products.
Samples (delivered by direct mail, in newspapers and magazines door-to-door, on or in product packages, and in-store)	Delivering an actual or trial-sized product to consumers in order to generate trial usage of a new product.	A free small bottle of Clairol Herbal Essences shampoo arrives in the mail.

FIGURE 21.6

Types of Consumer Sales Promotion

Consumer sales promotions are generally classified as price-based or attention-getting promotions.

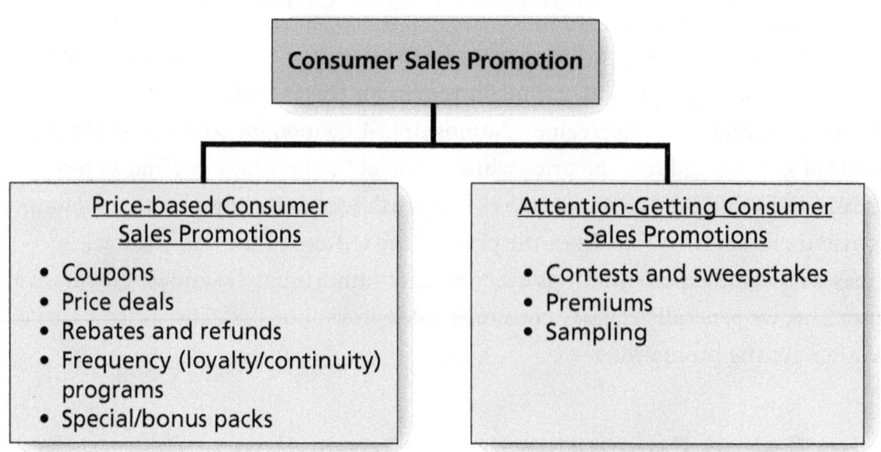

least during the deal period. Price-based consumer promotions, however, have a downside similar to trade promotions that involve a price break. If a company uses them too frequently, this "trains" its customers to purchase the product at only the lower promotional price. Price-based consumer sales promotion includes the following:

- *Coupons:* Try to pick up any Sunday newspaper without spilling some coupons. These certificates, redeemable for money off a purchase, are the most common price promotion. Indeed, they are the most popular form of sales promotion overall. Companies distribute billions of them annually in newspapers, magazines, in the mail, in stores, by e-mail, and through the Internet. One company, Val-Pak, has created an entire business around coupons. You've probably received a Val-Pak envelope in the mail—it's the one with dozens of coupons and other offers inside. Even industries such as pharmaceuticals that never tried this approach before now use it in a big way. This industry mails coupons that customers can redeem for free initial supplies of drugs. Coupons are also available through sites such as **Viagra.com** and **Purplepill.com**. Companies use the coupons to prompt patients to ask their physician for the specific brand instead of a competing brand or a more economical generic version.[71]
- *Price deals, refunds, and rebates:* In addition to coupons, manufacturers often offer a temporary price reduction to stimulate sales. This price deal may be printed on the package itself, or it may be a price-off flag or banner on the store shelf. Alternatively, companies may offer refunds or **rebates** that allow the consumer to recover part of the purchase price via mail-ins to the manufacturer. Today, many retailers such as Best Buy print the rebate form for you along with your sales receipt. After you mail it in, you can track whether the check has been sent to you by visiting the retailer's Web site.

rebate
Sales promotions that allow the customer to recover part of the product's cost from the manufacturer.

- *Frequency (loyalty/continuity) programs:* **Frequency programs**, also called loyalty or continuity programs, offer a consumer a discount or a free product for multiple purchases over time. Mike Gunn, former vice president of marketing at American Airlines, is widely credited with developing this concept in the early 1980s when he coined the phrase "frequent flyer" miles. Of course, all the other airlines were quick to follow suit, as were a host of other firms, including retailers, auto rental companies, hotels, restaurants—you name it, and they have a customer loyalty program. Virgin Atlantic has gone one step further with its frequent flyer program, which allows Virgin Atlantic Flying Club members the chance to redeem miles for a trip to outer space—only 2 million miles required![72] La Croissanterie, a French-style fast-food chain in Paris, offers an enhanced customer loyalty program that allows customers to identify themselves with a paper pass, a smart-phone application or their public transportation pass—no problem if you happen to leave the loyalty card at home.[73]
- *Special/bonus packs:* Another form of price promotion involves giving the shopper more product instead of lowering the price.[74] How nice to go to Walgreen's and find an 8-ounce bottle of Nivea lotion packaged with another 4 ounces free! A special pack also can be in the form of a unique package such as a reusable decorator dispenser for hand soap.

Ben & Jerry's uses a game as part of its campaign to control global warming.

Attention-Getting Consumer Sales Promotions

Attention-getting consumer promotions stimulate interest in a company's products. Some typical types of attention-getting promotions include the following:

- *Contests and sweepstakes:* According to their legal definitions, a contest is a test of skill, while a sweepstakes is based on chance.
- Ben & Jerry's, famous for ice cream flavors such as Chunky Monkey and Phish Food, launched a contest for consumers to create an original flavor ice cream. Consumers enter the "Do Us a Flavor" contest by submitting their flavor name and description through Ben & Jerry's Web site.[75]
- As part of the kickoff of Disney's global marketing campaign themed "Where Dreams Come True," Disney offered consumers an online *Keys to the Magic Kingdom* sweepstakes. The winning family received a trip to Walt Disney World Resort and a day at the Magic Kingdom.[76]
- Oreo included consumers as not only the contestants, but also the judges in its Oreo & Milk Jingle Contest. The top five contestants' renditions of the Oreo song were posted on the **Oreo.com** Web site. Consumers entered part of an Oreo package UPC to vote for their favorite; the winner received $10,000 and a recording session for an Oreo radio spot and a trip to Los Angeles to visit with *American Idol* judge Randy Jackson.[77]

Cooking contests (such as the "bourboncuing" contest sponsored by Jim Beam) are a popular way to let consumers "strut theier stuff" and create buzz about the company's products.

- *Premiums:* **Premiums** are items you get free when you buy a product. The prize in the bottom of the box of cereal—the reason many college students open the box from the bottom—is a premium. Prepaid phone cards have become highly popular premiums. Companies that jump on the phone card bandwagon offer cards emblazoned with pictures of sports heroes, products, and rock bands. Phone cards make ideal premiums because they are compact, they can display brand logos or attractive graphics, and they provide opportunities for repeat exposure. And an important benefit for the marketer is the ability to build databases by tracking card usage. Your "good neighbor" State Farm agent used to send you a calendar on your birthday—now you're likely to get a phone card with 30 long-distance minutes on it, adorned with a reminder of your agent's phone number to be sure you won't forget who sent it to you.

premiums
Items offered free to people who have purchased a product.

- *Sampling:* How many starving college students at one time or another have managed to scrape together an entire meal by scooping up free food samples at their local grocery store? Some stores, like Publix and Sam's Club, actually promote Saturdays as sampling day in their advertising. **Product sampling** encourages people to try a product by distributing trial-size and sometimes regular-size versions in stores, in public places such as student unions, or through the mail. Many marketers now distribute free samples through sites on the Internet. Companies like Procter & Gamble, Unilever, S.C. Johnson, and GlaxoSmithKline are readily taking advantage of Web sites such as **www.freesamples.com** and **www.startsampling.com** that distribute the firms' samples and then follow up with consumer-satisfaction surveys.

Oscar Mayer created an eye-catching promotion with its Weinermobile—guaranteed to draw attention from hot dog lovers.

product sampling
Distributing free trial-size versions of a product to consumers.

Conclusion

In this chapter you learned about a variety of sales promotion techniques aimed directly at consumers. Now you can describe the process of developing an advertising campaign and how marketers evaluate advertising. You can explain the role of public relations and the steps in developing a public relations campaign, as well as describe what a sales promotion is and explain the different types of consumer sales promotional activities.

CHAPTER

22

Personal Selling[1]

Personal Selling Explained

Whether it was homemade lemonade, Girl Scout cookies, or wrapping paper for a school fundraiser, almost everyone has sold something. And no matter which career path you choose, you will be engaged in personal selling at different times throughout your life. For example, when searching for your first job, you will assume the role of a salesperson in selling yourself to an employer.

Personal selling is one of the oldest and most effective forms of marketing communication. What makes it effective is that it allows a representative of the company, a salesperson, to have a one-on-one interaction with a customer or prospect (a potential customer). This interaction allows the salesperson to present the features and benefits of the product based on the specific needs of the customer. A salesperson can also alter the message, or provide additional information, based on the immediate feedback gained during a sales call.

More and more companies are relying on personal selling to generate product sales. These salespeople are employed in a number of industries and meet with customers in a variety of locations such as:

- A retail environment, for example, store, bank, or a dealership
- A business environment, for example, client office, sales office, real estate site, or job site
- A nonbusiness environment, for example, trade show, event, fair, golf course, restaurant, or new home site
- A customer's or prospect's home, for example, door-to-door selling or personal consultation
- On the phone
- Over the Internet

Personal Selling Applied

Although personal selling can be the most expensive promotional activity, it offers numerous advantages over other forms, such as advertising. Personal selling allows the company to:

- Develop long-term, personal relationships with customers
- Precisely target the most desirable customers
- Directly address customers' questions or concerns
- Demonstrate the product firsthand
- Deliver complex information to the customer

Salespeople not only deliver information, they also gain information. By being out in the field, members of the sales team are often the first to learn of new opportunities and potential threats that often arise in the market. For example, a salesperson can learn about the customer's plans for expansion or is informed about a competitor's new product. Just by being out of the office, a salesperson can discover potential new customers.

The biggest disadvantage of personal selling is the high average cost of a sales call. Some estimates place this figure as high as $300 in the B2B market. Given that a salesperson may need to make multiple trips before a prospect becomes a customer, the costs of gaining a new customer can approach $1,500 or more. The cost of a sales call involves more than the salesperson's compensation. Other costs, including travel expenses, sales support, sales training, employee retention, and the recruitment of salespeople, must also be taken into account.

Richard Santulli, CEO of NetJets, a company that specializes in fractional jet ownership, once telephoned a prospective customer who was worried that he would never be important to NetJets. The prospect told him, "You guys are big and successful, and I'm just a little guy." Richard said that it was 12:10 P.M., and that he was getting married at 1:00 P.M. that day. As he spoke, his wife-to-be was yelling at him to get off the phone. Richard said, "I insisted that I give you a call to show you we do care." The prospect has been a customer since 1998—and a happy one.[2]

PHOTO: USTIN/Shutterstock

For many companies, and in many industries, recruiting salespeople is an expensive and ongoing process. A high turnover rate, which is the percentage of the sales force that leaves a company per year, can significantly increase the costs of personal selling. Attracting and training new salespeople takes time, which often leaves a sales territory without a salesperson. This usually results in little to no sales being generated. It can also have a long-term impact if a customer decides to switch to a competitor.

Further, the customer may have established a personal, working relationship with the salesperson, and in some cases salespeople may "take the customer with them" if they are hired by a competitor.

Personal selling can be used for a wide variety of products and services in both the consumer and business market. However, personal selling is best used when the product or service:

- Is complex
- Is purchased infrequently
- Is expensive

- Is customized
- Requires a "push" strategy
- Has a long consideration period
- Has a small target market
- Has a purchase price that is negotiable

EXAMPLE **PERSONAL SELLING**

According to *Selling Power* magazine, the top 500 companies in America, based on the size of their salesforce, employ a total of 21 million salespeople. These firms are found across a variety of industries, including services, manufacturing, and direct selling. The greatest number of salespeople are employed by direct-sales firms such as Amway, Mary Kay, and Tupperware. The top 30 firms in this sector employ just over 19 million salespeople. The service sector, composed of companies such as AFLAC, AT&T, and Citigroup, have a total of 662,250 salespeople. Firms such as Microsoft, Coca-Cola, and Pfizer make up the manufacturing sector, which employs just over 500,000 salespeople. As far as productivity goes, each salesperson in the manufacturing sector generates an average of $7.6 million in sales, while the average sales per salesperson in the service sector is $3.9 million.

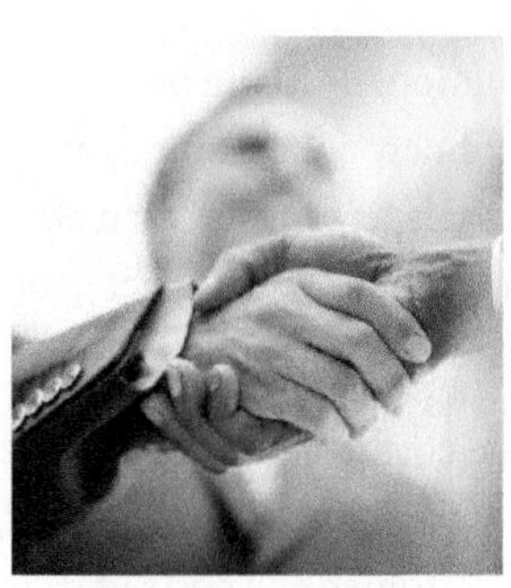

PHOTO: Yuri Arcurs/ Shutterstock

>> END EXAMPLE

Personal Selling Process Explained

A company's growth, and often its survival, depends on the ability of the sales team to obtain new customers. And although they may be offering different products, to distinct groups of customers, virtually every salesperson follows the personal selling process to recruit new business for their company.

Personal Selling Process Applied

In the seven-step process, shown in Figure 22.1, the salesperson identifies (prospecting), researches (preapproach), and contacts (approach) potential customers. During her meeting with the prospective customer (the sales presentation) the salesperson outlines the benefits of the product and responds to any issues raised by the prospect (overcomes objectives). After the salesperson has addressed the concerns of the prospect, she asks for the order (closes the sale). Even at this point, the personal selling process is not over. The salesperson needs to contact the customer (follow-up) to ensure that the order was delivered as promised. Whereas each particular company may use unique terms, descriptions, or requirements, the general process is widely accepted.

FIGURE 22.1

Steps in the Personal Selling Process

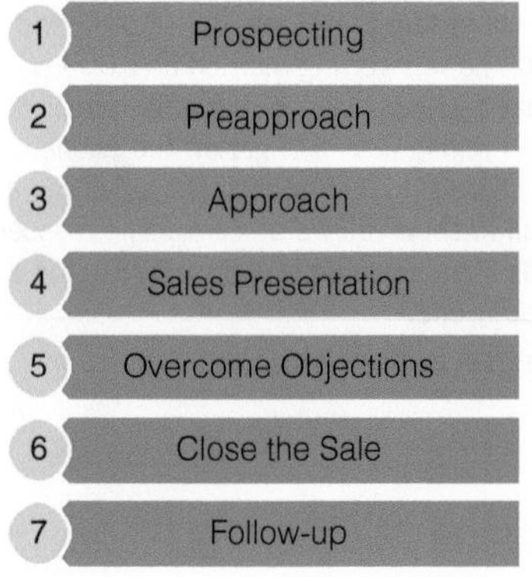

Step 1: Prospecting

Because they have limits on their time, salespeople must be able to identify those individuals or companies that are most likely to be interested in the products or services being offered. This process, called **prospecting,** results in a list of potential customers, or prospects, for the salesperson to pursue.

prospecting
Identifying those who are most likely to be interested in the products or services being offered.

A prospect list can be developed through external or internal sources. External sources include lists from trade associations (e.g., American Hospital Association), business research firms (e.g., Hoovers, Inc.), or commercial databases (e.g., InfoUSA.com). Many companies generate their own prospect list by using other elements of the promotion mix such as advertising or trade shows. A prospect list that was generated internally is often considered more valuable because the prospect must take action to be included.

Professional online social networks, such as **LinkedIn.com, Ryze.com, Biznik.com,** or **WomanOwned.com,** are becoming valuable tools for sales professionals. These sites allow salespeople to network online with people they already know, and to also request "introductions" to people they want to know. Professional social networking is a fast, efficient way to establish a connection with people to whom salespeople might not otherwise have access. Today, many salespeople are using social networking as a replacement for cold calling.

Step 2: Preapproach

The objective of the preapproach step is for the salesperson to learn as much as possible about the prospect. For business prospects, this includes identifying the prospect's business needs and challenges and determining how to help solve the problem and add value to the prospect's business. This step also includes identifying the correct person in the organization with whom to make initial contact, as well as identifying other key decision makers and key influencers who will have an impact on the final purchasing decision.

Sources such as financial analysis firms (e.g., Standard & Poor's), local and national business publications (e.g., *Wall Street Journal*), and the company's own Web site are ideal places to build knowledge of the prospect. A salesperson may also find information on a prospect from an internal company database. Here, the salesperson can learn if there was any previous contact with the prospect and, if so, the timing of the contact, the response, and the reasons the prospect chose not to purchase at that time. This is why it is critical that salespeople maintain excellent records of their activities.

Step 3: Approach

After a prospect has been qualified and researched, the salesperson is ready to approach the prospect. The approach is the first formal contact with the prospect and allows salespeople to make a professional introduction of themselves and their company. The approach provides a great opportunity for salespeople to enhance their understanding of the prospect's needs. The approach phase is a critical step in the personal selling process because the prospect will decide whether to go to the next step, which is agreeing to a formal meeting with the salesperson. The old saying, "you never get a second chance to make a first impression," is never more true than during the approach phase.

Step 4: Sales Presentation

The **sales presentation,** or sales call, is the formal meeting between the salesperson and the prospect. A sales call is not just about presenting information; it also serves as a means of gaining information. A question that broadly addresses the prospect's need and offers an all-encompassing solution can be effective at the beginning of a sales presentation. This ensures that the salesperson accurately understands the needs of the prospect. This type of questioning can also signal to the prospect that the salesperson engages in **consultative selling,** in which the salesperson is focused more on solving the problems of the prospect rather than just trying to sell a product. A problem-solving approach will generally result in long-term relationships that are mutually beneficial.

Because it can take multiple sales calls before a prospect places an order, the initial sales call is the first step in building a professional relationship. As such, the salesperson should seek to build rapport with the prospect in order to build understanding and to develop trust. This can be accomplished by observing the décor of the prospect's office. Most people will have some items of personal interest in their office that can offer cues as to what topics will be of interest to the prospect that can be used to break the ice.

Step 5: Overcome Objections

Prospects will almost always raise objections when the salesperson asks for the order. The most frequent objections given relate to price, quality, timing, or existing contracts. A good salesperson has already anticipated these objections prior to the sales presentation and developed a means to overcome them. In handling objections, the salesperson should ask questions of the prospect to clarify the concerns. In many cases, the objections can be overcome if the salesperson fully understands the prospect's concerns by providing new information. Supporting information such as testimonials, references, and case studies can help salespeople successfully overcome objections.

Step 6: Close the Sale

If all objections have been satisfied, the salesperson should close the sale by asking for the order. Although this task may seem daunting to inexperienced salespeople, the close is a natural outcome of the well-prepared sales effort. Deciding when to close is perhaps the most difficult part of this step, but often prospects provide signals to indicate they are ready to buy. These buying cues can be verbal, such as questions about price or credit terms, or nonverbal, such as relaxed facial muscles or a natural smile.

A variety of techniques can be used to close the sale. Many times a salesperson will use a trial close to gauge the prospect's interest. Under a trial close the salesperson might ask, "Now that your concerns have been addressed, is there anything else that can impact your decision to buy?" The alternative close seeks to have the prospect make a choice not between buy or not buy, but rather between product features or options. For example, the salesperson could ask the prospect "Would you prefer it in red or blue?" or "Should I have it delivered tomorrow or next Tuesday?" The assumptive close takes a more direct approach by asking the prospect specific questions such as "Will 200 cases be enough for the first order?"

Step 7: Follow-up

After the sale has been made, the salesperson needs to finalize the process by following up with the customer to ensure that the order was received on time and the product was delivered to the customer as promised. This simple effort can serve multiple purposes, including solving any problems that may have occurred with the order and also to show the customer that the salesperson cares as much after the sale as before receiving the order. This is especially true if the salesperson wishes to have future business with the new customer.

EXAMPLE **PERSONAL SELLING PROCESS**

At Pitney Bowes, a global provider of physical and digital mailing products and services, sales representatives rely on vital customer and inventory information available on their mobile devices. They can, for example, get information about their next sales call, ensure they have the proper parts and inventory within their vans, and access client sales and service histories. Sales reps are able to make more calls in a day because they spend less time on each call.[3]

PHOTO: Galina Barskkaya/Shutterstock

>> END EXAMPLE

Sales Management Explained

Because sales are the lifeblood of every company, proper sales management is a requirement for success. Sales management clearly communicates company objectives, strategies, and product information so the salespeople can communicate with customers. For most companies, a senior sales executive, with titles such as vice president of sales or general sales manager, is responsible for overseeing the selling function. These executives organize, motivate, and lead the sales team, with the purpose of ensuring that sales targets or objectives are met. Many companies split their sales team into regions, which are led by regional sales managers. These midlevel executives will manage a small group of district managers, who in turn supervise groups of 8 to 10 salespeople.

Sales Management Applied

Effective sales managers provide leadership, which, in turn, outlines priorities and direction to salespeople. Sales managers are constantly looking for ways to reduce nonselling functions, such as paperwork and internal meetings, so salespeople have more time to focus on selling activities, such as meeting with customers and prospects.

Sales managers use an organizational structure to help provide accountability and increase salesperson productivity. Although all sales forces are not structured exactly the same, some general functions are used by most selling organizations. Sales managers may oversee different types of salespeople. Salespeople who are physically located inside the office and rarely, if ever, have face-to-face contact with customers or prospects are called **inside sales.** Salespeople who spend the majority of their time outside the office meeting with customers and prospects are called **outside sales.** Sales managers may exclusively use one type of sales force or combine the two types, based on the company's sales strategy and financial structure. An inside sales force is usually less expensive because it does not generate travel expenses. However, outside salespeople enable the development of personal relationships with customers, which generates long-term benefits for the company.

Some key sales roles include order taker, customer service representative, technical or product specialist, sales representative, sales support, and new business development. All these roles can be performed either as inside or outside sales functions.

EXAMPLE **SALES MANAGEMENT**

Rebecca Herwick, CEO of Harley-Davidson licensee Global Products, knew her sales strategy wasn't working when seven of her nine independent sales representatives quit carrying her products during August 2006. Herwick had been using independent sales reps to sell her products—everything from Harley-Davidson–branded bandanas to coffee mugs—to over 800 Harley dealerships nationwide. Although the use of independent sales reps was a cost-effective strategy, there were problems, including a lack of clear expectations, a limited performance tracking system, and few penalties for violating established rules. The independent sales reps were selling other product lines that didn't compete with her products, but she still felt that her company wasn't getting the attention it deserved. Rather than hiring a dedicated but expensive internal sales staff, she learned to better manage her independent sales reps. She laid down ground rules, including new commission rates, new requirements for customer visits, and customer feedback surveys to help assess sales representative performance. The changes are paying off. Sales are up, and more important, customers have noticed a difference in attention and service.[4]

PHOTO: Kaspars Grinvalds/Shutterstock

>> END EXAMPLE

Sales Management Process

Establishing a sales force requires long-term vision on the part of senior sales executives. The decisions they make at the start will determine the structure and size of the sales force. However, the sales management process should be examined from the operational perspective, which determines how salespeople are recruited, compensated, trained, managed, motivated, and evaluated. The goal of the sales management process is to ensure that the sales force is organized to effectively and efficiently meet the sales objectives of the company.

Sales Management Process Applied

The sales management process entails four key areas, and the decisions made provide the blueprint to manage salespeople and deliver results.

SETTING SALES FORCE OBJECTIVES The overall sales objectives for a company are established on an annual basis by the firm's top management team. However, the objectives that are set for the sales force will vary depending on the goals of the company. While one company will set its objectives based on sales volume, another company may focus the sales force on generating new customers. Once established, the objectives will filter down to individual salespeople who will be responsible for meeting their specific objectives.

Take, for example, a company with a national sales team that is structured around five regional offices. If the overall objective of the company is to increase sales by $10 million, then, on average, each regional office is responsible for $2 million in additional sales. If each regional office has five districts, then each district must increase sales by $400,000. Taking this further, if each district has eight salespeople, then each salesperson is responsible for $50,000 in additional sales. Of course, this is a very simple example. A more likely scenario would be to allocate a percentage of the $10 million objective based on each region's previous year's sales, with larger regions and districts being expected to account for a larger share. These objectives express exactly what the sales force needs to accomplish and by when.

Objectives also help sales managers develop even more specific goals for each salesperson in terms of how many sales should be generated from each existing customer, how many sales should come from new customers, and how many new business calls must be made to meet the overall sales objective. The specific sales objectives then become the basis of sales staff compensation.

Developing the Sales Force Strategy

The sales force strategy is the approach that sales management uses to meet a company's sales objectives. To develop this strategy, sales managers determine the number and type of sales positions needed to meet sales objectives. These people and positions must then be organized in the most efficient manner possible. Sales managers can organize their sales forces by:

- **Geography.** This approach ensures there is coverage in all key geographic areas. This so-called geographic or territory strategy is common because it is among the most cost-efficient approaches in that it minimizes the amount of time salespeople spend traveling between calls.
- **Product line.** This means that each salesperson specializes in selling a particular product or product line. This strategy is effective in putting the focus on individual products or product lines, but it can be difficult and expensive to implement because it means that each salesperson might have to travel to various geographic areas to meet with customers or prospects. This approach may also require that some customers or prospects have multiple salespeople calling on them from the same company.

- **Industry.** In organizing by industry, each salesperson calls on companies in a single industry, such as retail, financial services, or pharmaceuticals. This strategy is successful when products or services are complex and have different applications in different industries. Here, salespeople have the opportunity to learn from each customer and apply this knowledge to help others in the industry.
- **Key accounts.** This strategy recognizes that the major customers of a product or service are the most important, so those customers should receive dedicated personal-selling resources. The key account strategy can be used alone, or it can be supplemented with any of the strategies mentioned earlier. For instance, a company may have some salespeople dedicated to calling on key accounts, while the balance of its sales force may be organized by territory, product line, or industry.

Recruiting, Compensating, Training, and Motivating the Sales Force

Building a successful sales force is key to meeting the company's objectives.

RECRUITING Recruiting and hiring the right salespeople is one of the most important activities a sales manager can perform. The salesperson is an ambassador for the company and, in many cases, the customer's exclusive point of contact with the company. A salesperson can make the difference between success and failure in meeting both the customer's and his or her company's objectives. Most companies therefore make a significant investment in training, managing, motivating, and recognizing salespeople.

Salespeople must possess specific characteristics, such as good personal and listening skills, the ability to work both independently and as part of a team, the ability to manage a budget, and the ability to resolve problems in a timely manner. They must also be able to identify and research a qualified prospect, close a sale, and follow up. They must have the drive and passion to move forward, even when everything is not going smoothly.

There is no ironclad method for hiring the right salespeople. Some companies administer tests to see whether sales candidates have the characteristics and skills needed to succeed. Other companies use an extensive interviewing process in which the candidates meet with several people inside the company and accompany existing staff on sales calls.

COMPENSATING In most companies, the sales function is based on a pay-for **performance compensation strategy.** This strategy means that a large part or all of a salesperson's income is based on the amount of sales or profit he or she delivers to his or her company in a given timeframe. When this is the case, salespeople are paid on commission. Commission is a percentage of the sales or profit the salesperson generates. In some companies, a salesperson may earn commission, plus an incentive or bonus for sales or profit delivered over a stated goal. A bonus may be an additional commission rate, a set dollar amount, a trip, or some other incentive. In many companies, there is no limit to how much money a salesperson can make, because the company wants to sell as much of its products and services as possible.

TRAINING To ensure that their salespeople are successful, most companies invest in training for all members of the sales force. There are several types of training. Usually, sales management provides a combination of types of training for salespeople on an ongoing basis. The types of training include the following:

- Product training is information about the features and benefits of specific products or product lines.
- Sales training can focus on information about the company, its product offerings, or specific skills that help salespeople improve their relationship building or closing skills.
- Personal-development training includes exposure to areas that help prepare salespeople to advance to the next level. This can include topics such as management training and leadership skills.

Sales meetings are the traditional method used to train salespeople. A sales meeting allows salespeople to meet their peers; all salespeople hear the company message at the same time and feel the energy of the meeting. In addition, technology plays a significant role in all types of sales training, with the use of webinars, podcasts, video conferences, audio conferences, on-demand training videos, Web-based knowledge centers, and video games. Sales managers know that in-person meetings with technology-based training can be a powerful combination.

MOTIVATING Maintaining a highly motivated sales force is key for any company. Although money and incentives can be effective, the effect is generally short-lived. Great sales managers realize that it takes more than money or prizes to motivate and engage salespeople. Rather, motivating a sales force requires constant communication and recognition. Communication keeps an organization on track by maintaining the focus on goals and providing updates about successes. One of the best ways to motivate and retain salespeople is to recognize them for their efforts. Many companies have recognition programs that highlight high achievers in a variety of areas. For instance, in addition to recognizing sales achievements, many companies also recognize salespeople who have provided extraordinary customer service, supported other employees, or otherwise gone above and beyond the call of duty. Recognition programs may include rewards such as being invited to a recognition dinner, receiving a plaque, or being inducted as a member of a performance "club."

Evaluating the Sales Force

The last area that sales managers focus on—evaluating the sales force—links back to the first step in the process. Each salesperson will have one or a series of objectives for the sales territory set by the sales manager. Typical objectives used include sales volume, average number of sales calls per day, sales per customer, or new customer orders. Once the objectives are established, regular reports must be made available to all salespeople so that they can track their performance.

Evaluation is an ongoing process. Formal evaluations usually take place on a regular basis, such as monthly, quarterly, or annually. New objectives for the upcoming time period are established, based on each salesperson's performance. Some companies are beginning to include customer feedback as a means to evaluate salespeople. In these cases, the company issues a survey (by mail, phone, or online) and gathers feedback about the performance of the company and the salesperson.

Conclusion

The power of targeted marketing is demonstrated in personal selling. These methods allow marketers to target and communicate directly with potential customers who are most likely to respond. Either on their own, or as part of the overall communication plan, personal selling can be effective at generating sales.

Direct, Interactive, and Social Media Marketing[1]

CHAPTER 23

Direct Marketing Explained

Direct marketing is an interactive process that uses communication that is addressed to an individual consumer to generate an action or response from that consumer. The desired response could be an order, a request for further information, or a visit to a store or other place of business to purchase a product.[2] Direct marketing is considered interactive because the consumer actually interacts with the marketer as a direct result of the marketing communication.

Direct marketing is sometimes referred to as "one-to-one" marketing because marketers can target the communication and even personalize the message to each individual. Direct marketing can employ this high degree of targeting because it involves the use of consumer databases. A database may include demographic information, such as name, address, income, age, gender, number of children in the household, home ownership status, and prior purchases of specific products or services. Some consumer databases also include psychographic information, such as hobbies, travel preferences, personal aspirations, or perceptions of certain products, services, brands, or stores. Direct marketers use the information in such databases to target specific messages to specific consumers at specific times to increase the likelihood of getting the desired response. Marketers can create their own proprietary databases of customer information based on previous inquiries, transactions (such as frequent purchasers), and surveys; this type of database is called a **house file**. Alternatively, marketers can rent consumer information from companies that collect and maintain databases. These rented lists are called **outside lists**, and they can be used alone or in conjunction with a house file.

Direct Marketing Applied

The types of direct marketing can be seen in Table 23.1. The key benefits of direct marketing are as follows:

- **Targeting**—As previously discussed, direct marketing allows marketers to deliver their message only to those consumers who meet their target audience characteristics.

TABLE 23.1
TYPES OF DIRECT MARKETING

TYPE	RESPONSE RATE	COST PER ORDER	ADVANTAGES	DISADVANTAGES	EXAMPLES
Mail Order					
Catalogs	2.5%	Mid	Can present a wide selection of products, can target specific groups of buyers	High cost to produce and mail, saturation of mail pieces	Pottery Barn, L.L. Bean, TigerDirect
Direct Mail	1%–3%	Mid	Personalized message, high control, wide coverage, flexible	Delivery delays, saturation	Financial/insurance offers
Phone-based					
Telemarketing	6%–10%	Highest	Interactive, personal, high impact, wide reach	Negative image, high costs for equipment/ training, use of caller ID, Do Not Call list	For-profit and nonprofit organizations
Direct Response Advertising					
DRTV Infomercials	4%	High	Ability to demonstrate product, holds attention	High production costs, long lead time	ShamWow, OxiClean, George Foreman Grill
Internet					
E-mail	1.7%	Mid	Lower costs, quick to implement, can be targeted, broad reach, easy response	Negative image, low response rate, spam filters can block messages	Variety
Paid Search	3.8% (clickthru)	Low	Can target specific search terms, measurable results	High competition, click fraud	Variety
Internet Display	4.4% (clickthru)	Low	Ability to reach target market, flexible, quick to implement, measurable results	Difficult to gain and maintain attention of viewer	Variety

- **Measurability**—Direct marketing is trackable and measurable. Marketers can calculate a true ROI (return on investment) based on the consumer responses.
- **Testing**—With direct marketing, marketers can test offers, creative approaches, and responsiveness of specific customer segments. Testing makes it possible to fine-tune a company's marketing efforts before launching a full campaign.
- **High ROI**—The Direct Marketing Association reports that, on average, direct marketing generates a return on investment of $11.69, compared to $5.24 for nondirect marketing expenditures.[3]

On the other hand, the key weaknesses of direct marketing include the following:

- **Expensive**—The cost per contact (that is, the cost to reach each consumer) is usually higher for direct marketing than for other media. Paper, printing, and postage have a significant impact on the costs of direct marketing. Although the upfront cost of direct marketing is high, the return on the investment is high and helps offset the expense.
- **Low response rates**—Direct marketing usually yields a response rate of 1%–5%. That means that 95%–99% of the consumers who receive a particular direct marketing communication do not respond to it.

- **Lack of general brand awareness**—When companies use direct marketing alone, consumers who do not receive the direct marketing may not be aware of the brand or product.

Direct marketing should be considered as part of the communication mix when one or more of the following conditions holds true:

- The product or service is used only by a clearly defined segment or portion of consumers.
- The product or service purchase is time sensitive.
- The product or service is available in a particular geographic location.
- The marketer wants to reach previous purchasers of the product or service to encourage a repeat purchase or trial of a related product.
- The marketer wants to make an offer to a select group of consumers.

Direct marketing includes catalogs, direct mail, direct response TV and radio, infomercials, and the Internet. Direct marketing has evolved significantly over the years. What started with a flyer sent to customers about products in the nineteenth century has developed into sophisticated and customized communications to consumers on the Internet, via mobile phones, and even on video game consoles. Technology has become a major force behind the evolution of direct marketing, with over 1.8 billion people around the world using the Internet. The diversity of direct marketing is discussed in the following sections.[4]

Mail Order

In 1872, Aaron Montgomery Ward and two partners created a one-page flyer that listed their merchandise with prices, hoping to generate some interest in their retail store.[5] But it was Richard Sears, who in 1888 published a flyer to advertise his watches and jewelry, truly revolutionized the direct marketing business. Sears promised his customers that "we warrant every American watch sold by us, with fair usage, an accurate time keeper for six years—during which time, under our written guarantee we are compelled to keep it in perfect order free of charge."[6] It was the promise of satisfaction guaranteed that changed the face of mail-order marketing.

Today, mail order includes two types of marketing—catalogs and direct mail. The term **mail order** describes "the business of selling merchandise through the mail."[7] Catalogs are a common marketing strategy for many marketers, such as Pottery Barn, J. Crew, and PC Mall. Over 19 billion catalogs are distributed annually.[8] They provide marketers an opportunity to showcase a large selection of product and service offerings to their target audience.

Catalogs are an effective element in the communication mix because they are targeted, can generate high returns per catalog mailed, and can be accurately measured for the sales and profit they generate. However, catalogs are extremely expensive to print and mail; costs range from $0.50 to over $3.00 or more per catalog mailed, depending on the number of pages, quantity printed, and paper quality.

Direct mail differs from catalogs because it does not showcase an entire assortment of products. Instead, direct mail usually involves only a pamphlet or flyer that focuses on a specific product or service. Direct mail may also include a postcard, letter, brochure, or product sample. Charities, political groups, retail stores, and packaged goods companies are major users of direct mail. Some Internet companies such as Netflix also use direct mail to drive traffic to their Web sites.

Although there are many variations of direct mail, all successful direct mail campaigns include three major elements:

- **Offer**—A compelling offer should be apparent to the recipient. An offer is usually promotional in nature to provide incentive for the recipient to respond. Examples of common offers are "Save 20%," "Free shipping," or "Buy One, Get One Free."
- **Mailing list**—When conducting a direct-mail campaign, identifying the proper target is as important as crafting the message. The mailing list should include only those consumers who have the highest likelihood of responding. For example, if a local grocer wants to mail coupons for baby products, the mailing list should include only those households with children under the age of one that are located within a five-mile radius of each store.
- **Call to action**—A call to action describes the response the company wants to elicit from the consumer. Examples of a call to action are the following: "Call 800-555-5555 to make an appointment," "Visit www.si.com and order today," or "Visit your nearest Lexus dealership." The call to action should be clear and easy to act on.

Direct mail can be an effective medium because it is targeted. However, like catalogs, direct mail can be an expensive option due to the cost of paper, printing, and postage.

Telemarketing

Telemarketing, direct marketing conducted over the phone, can be an effective part of a marketer's media mix because it provides a real-time, personal conversation with a potential customer. The types of marketers that often rely on telemarketing include charities, political parties, financial services, and retailers. Because of the negative perceptions of telemarketing that stem from calls being received at inconvenient times and the use of unscrupulous selling techniques, some marketers avoid telemarketing. Telemarketing is an expensive means of communicating with potential customers. Many firms, in order to reduce the cost, have turned to specialized firms that benefit from economies of scale. One key reason that many firms have abandoned telemarketing was the passage of the national Do Not Call Registry in 2003. This legislation, which was updated in 2008, prohibits telemarketers from calling any phone number registered with the Federal Trade Commission.

Direct-Response Advertising

Direct-response advertising is designed to have customers respond to specific offers or calls to action by marketers. The deliver of the enticement is through broadcast media, including newspapers and magazines, TV, radio, and the new medium of choice, the Internet. The benefit of direct-response advertising is that the effectiveness of different campaigns and media is quantifiable.

DRTV (direct-response TV) includes any form of television commercial or home shopping television show that advertises a product or service and allows the viewer to purchase the product or service directly. Although the investment in production and media can be significant, when produced and targeted properly DRTV can be an effective marketing tool. Companies such as QVC and Home Shopping Network made DRTV mainstream. Newer forms of DRTV are emerging that can deliver targeted television commercials based on selected criteria and provide a personalized call to action.

Infomercials, television shows that are a combination of an information session and a commercial, are considered direct-response marketing when they include a method for viewers to purchase the product or service directly. Infomercials vary in their length and can range from a few minutes to an hour or more. The growth of cable television has provided a significant amount of programming time, which has appealed to producers of infomercials. Once the flagship of entrepreneurs and some unscrupulous marketers, infomercials have come of age; they now generate over $1 billion in sales annually. Major marketers such as Volkswagen, American Airlines, and Procter & Gamble successfully use this format to drive consumer response, such as a dealer visit or request for additional information.

Infomercials are effective because they are targeted based on the television or radio stations on which they air. In addition, they give marketers an opportunity to describe and demonstrate the features and benefits of a product or service. Infomercials are well suited for new product introductions as well as complex products because the format provides more selling time than a traditional 30-second commercial. However, producing, testing, and airing infomercials can be expensive.

EXAMPLE **DIRECT-RESPONSE ADVERTISING**

Billy Mays was one of the most successful direct-response marketing salespersons, often called pitchmen, in history. Prior to his death in 2009, Mays was a regular presence on television advertisements with his emotional sales pitch, distinctive voice, and trademark beard selling products including Orange Glo, OxiClean, and a wide range of home-based cleaning and maintenance products. Mays and Anthony Sullivan, another well-known direct response personality, starred in a 2009 Discovery Channel series *Pitchmen*. In each episode, the pitchmen became potential backers for inventors' products such as a broken-screw extractor and shark repellent device.

>> END EXAMPLE

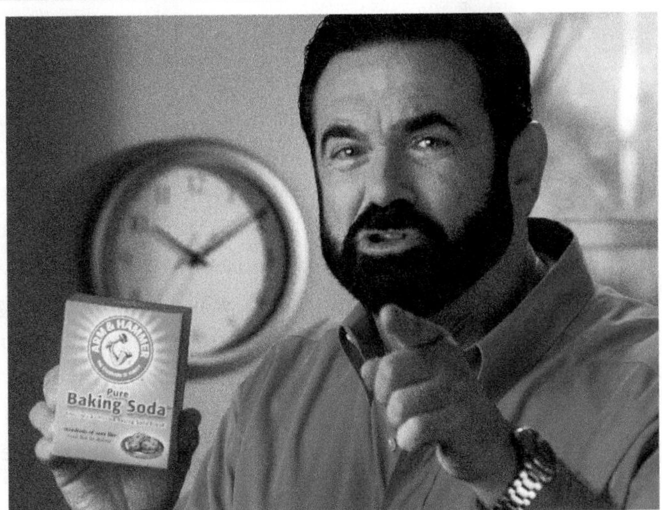

PHOTO: s70/ZUMA Press/Newscom

A Wired World[9]

The World Internet Usage Statistics site estimates that there are just over 1.7 billion Internet users worldwide. Asia hosts the most Internet users with 42.6 percent of the world's online population, followed by Europe with 23.1 percent and North America with 13.6 percent. According to the Pew Internet & American Life Project in 2009, 74 percent of Americans were online (it's safe to assume that percentage is even higher today). Although North America lags behind Asia and Europe in percentage of total users, it has the highest Internet penetration rate, the measure of the percentage of a population with Internet access. Asia's penetration rate is just 19.4 percent and Europe's is 52.0 percent. Australia makes up a measly 1.2 percent of all Internet users, but boasts a 60 percent penetration rate.

Table 23.2 summarizes who is online in the United States and who isn't (yet). As you might expect, younger people are more likely to be active online. Fully 93 percent of teens and young adults aged 12–29 are online, compared to 81 percent of adults aged 30–49 and 70 percent of adults aged 50–64. It's only when we consider elderly groups that we see a lack of Internet penetration—just 38 percent of adults 65 and over are online. Even so, this means more than one out of every three "senior citizens" surfs the Web!

Thousands of people join the online world every day. What's more, their quality of access has improved dramatically. Just a few years ago, you had to dial in to a slow connection to get online, while today most of us have high-speed access via cable modems and DSL-enabled phone lines. We've gotten used to the luxury of seeing pages load in seconds and many of us just assume that we can jump online almost anywhere we travel (even on airplanes). In addition, Internet access has gone mobile for many as we continue to snap up wireless devices such as netbooks and smartphones. These changes in access to the Internet equate to increased access to target audiences for social media marketers. In other words, our reach is now extensive online. Reach refers to the percentage of the target audience that can be accessed using a form of media. In the early days of the Internet, reach was small and the medium was not considered as attractive.

What We Do Online

For decades, Westerners spent most of their media time watching television. Now, those who are connected spend about the same amount of time online instead of being glued to the Boob tube. Consumers perceive the Internet as the most essential of all media. Table 23.3 provides a list of the most common activities people engage in online. When we look at this list, it is easy to see how user behavior drives marketing efforts online. For example, Internet users spend much of their time emailing, so many advertisers send permission emails. Permission emails are the direct mail of the digital age—they are personalized email offers sent to individuals who "opt in" to receiving marketing communications. Opting in is an agreement activity in which an individual gives his or her permission for the source to send relevant messages.

These advertisers might also embed display ads in some email sites. Display ads are advertisements shown on websites. They may be simple banner ads that appear above, below, or on the side of a site; rich media ads that include streaming video; or text ads that present short, clickable headlines. If you use Google's email client, Gmail, you've likely noticed the text ads that appear along the side of your email inbox.

TABLE 23.2

PEW CHART OF GENERATIONS ONLINE

The Pew Internet & American Life Project is a think tank devoted to monitoring the increasingly digital lives of Americans. Its research provides an unbiased and holistic view of digital life in the United States, as it seeks to provide a sort of census on Internet adoption and activities for Americans of all backgrounds.

Generations Online 2010: Summary

The following chart shows the popularity of Internet activities among Internet users in each generation.

90–100%	40–49%
80–89%	30–39%
70–79%	20–29%
60–69%	10–19%
50–59%	0–9%

Key: % of Internet users in each generation who engage in this online activity.

MILLENNIALS AGES 18–33	GEN X AGES 34–45	YOUNGER BOOMERS AGES 46–55	OLDER BOOMERS AGES 56–64	SILENT GENERATION AGES 65–73	G.I. GENERATION AGE 74+
Email	Email	Email	Email	Email	Email
Search	Search	Search	Search	Search	Search
Social network sites	Health info	Health info	Health info	Health info	Health info
Use SNS	Get news	Get news	Get news	Get news	Buy a product
Watch video	Govt website	Govt website	Govt website	Travel reservations	Get news
Get news	Travel reservations	Travel reservations	Buy a product	Buy a product	Travel reservations
Buy a product	Watch video	Buy a product	Travel reservations	Gov't website	Gov't website
Instant Message (IM)	Buy a product	Watch video	Bank online	Watch video	Bank online
Listen to music	Social network sites	Bank online	Watch video	Financial info	Financial info
Travel reservations	Bank online	Social network sites	Social network sites	Bank online	Religious info
Online classifieds	Online classifieds	Online classifieds	Online classifieds	Rate things	Watch video
Bank online	Listen to music	Listen to music	Financial info	Social network sites	Play games
Gov't website	IM	Financial info	Rate things	Online classifieds	Online classifieds
Play games	Play games	IM	Listen to music	IM	Social network sites
Read blogs	Financial info	Religious info	Religious info	Religious info	Rate things
Financial info	Religious info	Rate things	IM	Play games	Read blogs
Rate things	Read blogs	Read blogs	Play games	Listen to music	Donate to charity
Religious info	Rate things	Play games	Read blogs	Read blogs	Listen to music
Online auction	Online auction	Online auction	Online auction	Donate to charity	Podcasts
Podcasts	Donate to charity	Donate to charity	Donate to charity	Online auction	Online auction
Donate to charity	Podcasts	Podcasts	Podcasts	Podcasts	Blog
Blog	Blog	Blog	Blog	Blog	IM
Virtual worlds	Virtual worlds	Virtual worlds	Virtual worlds	Virtual worlds	Virtual worlds

Source: Kathryn Zickuhr, *Generation 2010,* Pew Internet & American Life Project, December 16, 2010, http://pewinternet.org/Reports/2010/Generations2010/Activities/Summary.aspx, accessed December 31, 2010. Used by permission of Pew Internet & American Life Project.

TABLE 23.3
PARTICIPATION RATES IN POPULAR ONLINE ACTIVITIES

ACTIVITY	PERCENT OF INTERNET USERS
Send or read email	94%
Use a search engine to find information	87
Look for information online about a service or product you are thinking of buying	78
Get news	75
Go online just for fun or to pass the time	72
Buy a product	72
Watch a video on a video sharing site such as YouTube or Google Video	66
Use an online social networking site such as MySpace, Facebook, or LinkedIn	61
Look for information on Wikipedia	53
Use online classified ads or sites such as Craigslist	53
Send instant messages	47
Upload photos to a website so you can share them with others online	46
Play online games	35
Read someone else's online journal or blog	32
Rate a product, service, or person using an online rating system	32
Post a comment or review online about a product you bought or a service you received	32
Share something online that you created yourself	30
Pay to access or download digital content online	28
Categorize or tag online content such as a photo, news story, or blog post	28
Post comments to an online news group, website, blog, or photo site	26
Download a podcast so you can listen to it or view it later	21
View live images online of a remote location or person, using a webcam	17
Use Twitter or other status-update service	17
Create or work on web pages or blogs for others, including friends, groups you belong to, or for work	15
Take material you find online—such as songs, text, or images—and remix it into your own artistic creation	15
Download or share files using peer-to-peer file-sharing networks, such as BitTorrent or LimeWire	15
Sell something online	15
Create or work on your own web page	14
Create or work on your own online journal or blog	14
Participate in an online discussion, a listserv, or other online group forum that helps people with personal issues or health problems	7
Visit virtual worlds such as Second Life	4

Source: Adapted from *Pew Internet & American Life Project, Online Activities/Total,* www.pewinternet.org/Static-Pages/Trend-Data/Online-Activites-Total.aspx, accessed December 31, 2010. Used by permission of Pew Internet & American Life Project.

Another popular activity is online search, which simply means using a search engine to find information using key words. Millions of us instinctively check search engines such as Google and Yahoo! to answer almost any kind of question—so much so that the word "Google" has become a verb as well as a noun. Search engine advertising leverages that behavior by presenting display ads associated with the search terms entered by the user.

Setting Up an Online Presence[10]

One way or another, most companies have now moved online. Companies conduct online marketing in any or all of the five ways shown in Figure 23.1: creating Web sites, placing ads and promotions online, setting up or participating in online social networks, sending e-mail, or using mobile marketing.

Creating Web Sites

For most companies, the first step in conducting online marketing is to create a Web site. However, beyond simply creating a Web site, marketers must design an attractive site and find ways to get consumers to visit the site, stay around, and come back often.

Web sites vary greatly in purpose and content. The most basic type is a **corporate** (or **brand**) **Web site**. This type of site is designed to build customer goodwill, collect customer feedback, and supplement other sales channels rather than to sell the company's products directly. It typically offers a rich variety of information and other features in an effort to answer customer questions, build closer customer relationships, and generate excitement about the company or brand.

corporate (or brand) web site
A Web site designed to build customer goodwill, collect customer feedback, and supplement other sales channels rather than sell the company's products directly.

For example, you can't buy anything at Nestlé's colorful Wonka.com site, but you can learn about different Nestlé candy products, enter the latest contest, or hang around a while and doodle with Nerds, "paint your dreams" with the Wonka imaginator, or post Wonka-inspired digital art. Similarly, you can't buy anything at GE's corporate Web site. Instead, the site serves as a global public face for the huge company. It presents a

FIGURE 23.1

Setting Up for Online Marketing

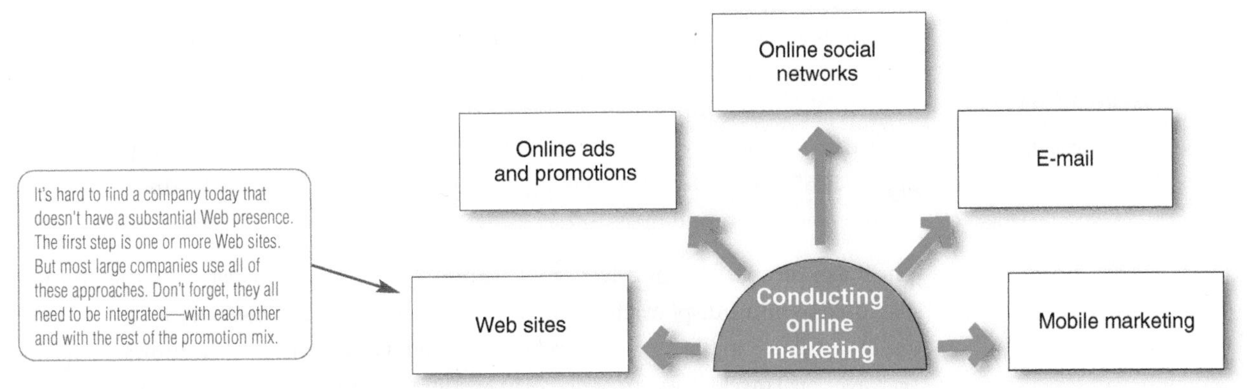

Corporate Web sites: You can't buy anything at Nestlé's colorful Wonka.com site, but you can learn about different Nestlé candy products or just hang around for a while and "feed your imagination."

PHOTO: Screen capture courtesy of Nestlé

massive amount of product, service, and company information to a diverse audience of customers, investors, journalists, and employees. It's both a B-to-B site and a portal for consumers, whether it's a U.S. consumer researching a microwave, an Indonesian business buyer checking into eco-friendly locomotives, or a German investor looking for shareholder information.

marketing web site
A Web site that interacts with consumers to move them closer to a direct purchase or other marketing outcome.

Other companies create a **marketing Web site.** These sites interact with consumers to move them closer to a direct purchase or other marketing outcome. For example, MINI USA operates a marketing Web site at www.miniusa.com. Once a potential customer clicks in, the carmaker wastes no time trying to turn the inquiry into a sale and then into a long-term relationship. The site offers a garage full of useful information and interactive selling features, including detailed and fun descriptions of current MINI models, tools for designing your very own MINI, information on dealer locations and services, and even tools for tracking your new MINI from factory to delivery.

Creating a Web site is one thing; getting people to visit the site is another. To attract visitors, companies aggressively promote their Web sites in offline print and broadcast advertising and through ads and links on other sites. But today's Web users are quick to abandon any Web site that doesn't measure up. The key is to create enough value and excitement to get consumers who come to the site to stick around and come back again. At the very least, a Web site should be easy to use, professional looking, and physically attractive. Ultimately, however, Web sites must also be *useful.* When it comes to Web browsing and shopping, most people prefer substance over style and function over flash. Thus, effective Web sites contain deep and useful information, interactive tools that help buyers find and evaluate products of interest, links to other related sites, changing promotional offers, and entertaining features that lend relevant excitement.

Placing Ads and Promotions Online

online advertising
Advertising that appears while consumers are browsing the Web, including display ads, search-related ads, online classifieds, and other forms.

As consumers spend more and more time on the Internet, companies are shifting more of their marketing dollars to **online advertising** to build their brands or attract visitors to their Web sites. Online advertising has become a major medium. Total U.S. Internet advertising spending will reach an estimated $31 billion this year and is expected to approach $50 billion by 2015, making it the second largest medium behind TV—ahead of even newspapers and magazines.[11]

The major forms of online advertising are search-related ads, display ads, and online classifieds. Online display ads might appear anywhere on an Internet user's screen and are often related to the information being viewed. For instance, while browsing vacation packages on Travelocity.com, you might encounter a display ad offering a free upgrade on a rental car from Enterprise Rent-A-Car. Or while visiting the Yahoo! Finance site, a flashing E*TRADE ad might promise a free BlackBerry smartphone when you open a new account. Internet display ads have come a long way in recent years in terms of attracting and holding consumer attention. New *rich media* ads now incorporate animation, video, sound, and interactivity.

The largest form of online advertising is *search-related ads* (or *contextual advertising*), which accounted for 46 percent of all online advertising spending last year. In search advertising, text-based ads and links appear alongside search engine results on sites such as Yahoo! and Google. For example, search Google for "LCD TVs." At the top and side of the resulting search list, you'll see inconspicuous ads for ten or more advertisers, ranging from Samsung and Dell to Best Buy, Sears, Amazon.com, Walmart.com, and Nextag.com. Nearly all of Google's $29 billion in revenues last year came from ad sales. Search is an always-on kind of medium. And in today's tight economy, the results are easily measured.[12]

A search advertiser buys search terms from the search site and pays only if consumers click through to its site. For instance, type "Coke" or "Coca-Cola" or even just "soft drinks" or "rewards" into your Google or Yahoo! search engine and almost without fail "My Coke Rewards" comes up as one of the top options. This is no coincidence. Coca-Cola supports its popular online loyalty program largely through search buys. The soft drink giant started first with traditional TV and print advertising but quickly learned that search was the most effective way to bring consumers to its www.mycokerewards.com Web site to register. Now, any of dozens of purchased search terms will return MyCokeRewards.com at or near the top of the search list.

Other forms of online promotions include content sponsorships and viral advertising. Using content sponsorships, companies gain name exposure on the Internet by sponsoring special content on various Web sites, such as news or financial information or special interest topics. For example, Alamo sponsors the "Vacation and Travel Planner and Guides" on Weather.com. And Marriott sponsors a "Summer to the Rescue!" microsite at Travelocity.com. Sponsorships are best placed in carefully targeted sites where they can offer relevant information or service to the audience.

viral marketing
The Internet version of word-of-mouth marketing: a Web site, video, e-mail message, or other marketing event that is so infectious that customers will seek it out or pass it along to friends.

Finally, online marketers use **viral marketing**, the Internet version of word-of-mouth marketing. Viral marketing involves creating a Web site, video, e-mail, mobile message, advertisement, or other marketing event that is so infectious that customers will seek it out or pass it along to their friends. Because customers find and pass along the message or promotion, viral marketing can be very inexpensive. And when the information comes from a friend, the recipient is much more likely to view or read it.

Viral marketing: Sometimes a well-made regular ad can go viral. For example, Volkswagen's clever "The Force" Super Bowl ad, featuring a pint-sized Darth Vader, received more than 18 million online hits the week before it aired on TV during the Super Bowl.

PHOTO: LUCASFILM/MCT/Newscom

For example, P&G's Old Spice brand created a viral sensation with its "Smell like a man, man" campaign featuring Isaiah Mustafa. The campaign consisted of TV ads and made for-the-Web videos designed to go viral on YouTube, Facebook, and other social media. The initial campaign garnered tens of millions of viral views. A second campaign, which consisted of nearly 200 videos in which Mustafa responded personally to digital inquiries from users including Ellen DeGeneres and Alyssa Milano, scored 21 million views in only its first week. It increased the brand's Facebook interaction by 800 percent and OldSpice.com traffic by 300 percent. After the introduction of these videos, Old Spice's YouTube page became the all-time-most-viewed channel on the site.[13]

Sometimes a well-made regular ad can go viral with the help of targeted "seeding." For example, Volkswagen's clever "The Force" Super Bowl ad, featuring a pint-sized Darth Vader using The Force to start a VW Passat, turned viral after a team at VW's ad agency seeded it to selected auto, pop culture, and *Star Wars* sites the week before the sporting event. By the time the ad aired during the Super Bowl, it had received more than 18 million hits online.

However, marketers usually have little control over where their viral messages end up. They can seed messages online, but that does little good unless the message itself strikes a chord with consumers. For example, why did the seeded VW Darth Vader ad explode virally? Because the sentimental ad appeals to parents—the car's target demographic—who want a responsible suburban family ride. And it appeals to the child inside the parent, who may have once been wowed by *Star Wars* and now wants a car with a little bit of magic. Says one creative director, "you hope that the creative is at a high enough mark where the seeds grow into mighty oaks. If they don't like it, it ain't gonna move. If they like it, it'll move a little bit; and if they love it, it's gonna move like a fast-burning fire through the Hollywood hills."[14]

Creating or Participating in Online Social Networks

online social networks
Online communities where people congregate, socialize, and exchange views and information.

The popularity of the Internet has resulted in a rash of **online social networks** or *Web communities.* Countless independent and commercial Web sites have arisen that give consumers online places to congregate, socialize, and exchange views and information. These days, it seems, almost everyone is buddying up on Facebook, checking in with Twitter, tuning into the day's hottest videos at YouTube, or checking out photos on Flickr. And, of course, wherever consumers congregate, marketers will surely follow. Most marketers are now riding the huge social networking wave.

Marketers can engage in online communities in two ways: They can participate in existing Web communities or they can set up their own. Joining existing networks seems the easiest. Thus, most major brands—from Dunkin' Donuts and Harley-Davidson to Nissan and Victoria's Secret—have created YouTube channels. GM and other companies have posted visual content on Flickr. Coca-Cola's Facebook page has 26 million fans.

Some of the major social networks are huge. The largest social network—Facebook—by itself commands 70 percent of all social network traffic. Forty-seven percent of the online population visits Facebook every day. That rivals the 55 percent who watch any TV channel and trounces the percentage listening to radio (37 percent) and reading newspapers (22 percent) daily. Now at more than 720 million members, Facebook aims to reach one billion members by 2012.[15]

Although large online social networks such as Facebook, YouTube, and Twitter have grabbed most of the headlines, a new breed of more focused niche networks has emerged. These networks cater to the needs of smaller communities of like-minded people, making them ideal vehicles for marketers who want to target special interest groups. There's at least one social network for just about every interest or hobby.[16]

Yub.com and kaboodle.com are for shopaholics; moms advise and commiserate at CafeMom.com; and PassportStamp.com is one of several sites for avid travelers. GoFISHn, a community of 4,000 anglers, features maps that pinpoint where fish are biting and a photo gallery where members can show off their catches.

At Dogster, 700,000 members set up profiles of their four-legged friends, read doggy diaries, or just give a dog a bone. On Ravelry.com, 1.4 million registered knitters, crocheters, designers, spinners, and dyers share information about yarn, patterns, methods, and tools.

Some niche sites cater to the obscure. Passions Network is an "online dating niche social network" with 600,000 members and 145 groups for specific interests, including *Star Trek* fans, truckers, atheists, and people who are shy. Others reach more technical communities: More than a million scientists use ResearchGATE to coordinate research in areas such as artificial intelligence and cancer biology. And at myTransponder.com, pilots find work, students locate flight instructors, and trade-specific advertisers—such as aviation software maker ForeFlight—hone in on a hard-to-reach audience of more than 2,000 people who love aviation. The myTransponder community aims to "make aviation more social."

Thousands of social networking sites have popped up to cater to specific interests, backgrounds, professions, and age groups. At Dogster, 700,000 members set up profiles of their four-legged friends, read doggy diaries, or just give a dog a bone.

PHOTO: Dogster.com

But participating successfully in existing online social networks presents challenges. First, most companies are still experimenting with how to use them effectively, and results are hard to measure. Second, such online networks are largely user controlled. The company's goal is to make the brand a part of consumers' conversations and their lives. However, marketers can't simply muscle their way into consumers' online interactions—they need to earn the right to be there. A brand has no right to be there unless the conversation is already about that brand. Rather than intruding, marketers must learn to become a valued part of the online experience.

To avoid the mysteries and challenges of building a presence on existing online social networks, many companies have created their own targeted Web communities. For example, on Nike's Nike+ Web site, more than 4 million runners with more than 375 million miles logged in 243 countries join together online to upload, track, and compare their performances. Nike plans eventually to have 15 percent or more of the world's 100 million runners actively participating in the Nike+ online community.[17]

Similarly, *Men's Health* magazine created a Web community in conjunction with its Belly Off! program (http://my.menshealth.com/bellyoff/). The magazine's long-running program helps readers develop a solid plan for exercise and diet over a set schedule. The community Web site incorporates user-generated content and offers workout and eating plans, reports on progress, how-to videos, and success stories. In all, the Belly Off!

Site serves a community of nearly 125,000 members who share similar weight-loss and fitness goals. Since 2001, the program has helped 400,000 people lose nearly 2 million pounds.[18]

Sending E-Mail

e-mail marketing
Sending highly targeted, tightly personalized, relationship-building marketing messages via e-mail.

E-mail marketing is an important and growing online marketing tool. E-mail is a much-used communication tool; by one estimate, the number of worldwide e-mail accounts will grow from the current 2.9 billion to more than 3.8 billion over the next five years. Not surprisingly, then, a recent study by the DMA found that 79 percent of all direct marketing campaigns employ e-mail. U.S. companies now spend more than $660 million a year on e-mail marketing, and this spending will grow by an estimated 13.6 percent annually through 2014.[19]

When used properly, e-mail can be the ultimate direct marketing medium. Most bluechip marketers use it regularly and with great success. E-mail lets these marketers send highly targeted, tightly personalized, relationship-building messages. For example, the National Hockey League (NHL) sends hyper-targeted e-newsletters to fans based on their team affiliations and locations. It sends 62 versions of the e-newsletter weekly—two for each of the 30 teams, tailored to fans in the United States and Canada, respectively, and two generic league e-newsletters for the two countries. Another NHL e-mail campaign promoting the start of single-game ticket sales had 930 versions.[20]

spam
Unsolicited, unwanted commercial e-mail messages.

But there's a dark side to the growing use of e-mail marketing. The explosion of **spam**—unsolicited, unwanted commercial e-mail messages that clog up our e-mailboxes—has produced consumer irritation and frustration. According to one research company, spam now accounts for almost 75 percent of all e-mail sent.[21] E-mail marketers walk a fine line between adding value for consumers and being intrusive.

To address these concerns, most legitimate marketers now practice *permission-based e-mail marketing,* sending e-mail pitches only to customers who "opt in." Many companies use configurable e-mail systems that let customers choose what they want to get. Amazon.com targets opt-in customers with a limited number of helpful "we thought you'd like to know" messages based on their expressed preferences and previous purchases. Few customers object, and many actually welcome such promotional messages. Similarly, StubHub redesigned its e-mail system to make certain that its e-mails go only to consumers who actually want to receive them:

As a start-up almost a decade ago, online ticket merchant StubHub ran "batch-and-blast" e-mail campaigns focused on building awareness. For years, sheer volume far outweighed e-mail relevancy. But StubHub has now learned the value of carefully targeted, relevant

E-mail can be an effective marketing tool. But there's dark side—spam unwanted commercial e-mail that clogs up our inboxes and causes frustration.

PHOTO: (left) iStock International; (right) ICP/incamerastock/Alamy

> e-mail messages. It now lets customers opt in for e-mail at registration, during purchases, and at sign-up modules throughout the StubHub site. Using opt-in customer data, StubHub targets designated consumer segments with ticket and event information closely aligned with their interests. Incorporating customer data produced immediate and stunning results. E-mail click-through rates quickly jumped 30 percent, and the company saw a 79 percent year-over-year increase in ticket sales despite having sent fewer e-mails. "The results speak for themselves," says a StubHub marketer. "These [new targeted campaigns] are driving 2,500 percent more revenue per e-mail than [our] average marketing campaigns."[22]

Given its targeting effectiveness and low costs, e-mail can be an outstanding marketing investment. According to the DMA, e-mail marketing produces the greatest return on investment of all direct marketing media.[23]

Using Mobile Marketing

Mobile marketing features marketing messages and promotions delivered to on-the-go consumers through their mobile devices. Marketers use mobile marketing to reach and interact with customers anywhere, anytime during the buying and relationship-building processes. The widespread adoption of mobile devices and the surge in mobile Web traffic have made mobile marketing a must for most brands.

mobile marketing
Marketing to on-the-go consumers through mobile phones, smartphones, tablets, and other mobile communications devices.

With the recent proliferation of mobile phones, smartphone devices, and tablet PCs, more than 96 percent of U.S. households own some sort of mobile device. Nearly 27 percent of U.S. households are currently mobile-only households; this means they have no landline and instead depend on mobile devices to make and receive all calls. Furthermore, about 63 million people in the United States own a smartphone device, and about 35 percent of smartphone users use it to access the mobile Internet. They not only browse the mobile Web but are also avid mobile application users. The mobile apps market is exploding: The Apple App Store offers 425,000 iPhone apps plus another 90,000 iPad apps. Android Market offers upwards of 150,00 apps.[24]

A recent study estimates that mobile advertising spending in the United States will grow from $743 million in 2010 to $2.5 billion by 2014. Marketers of all kinds—from Pepsi and Nordstrom to nonprofits such as the ASPCA to the local bank or supermarket—are now integrating mobile platforms into their direct marketing. Sixty percent of mobile users currently click on a mobile ad at least once a week.[25]

A mobile marketing campaign might involve placing display ads, search ads, or videos on relevant mobile Web sites and online communities such as Facebook or YouTube. Today's rich media mobile ads can create substantial impact and involvement. For example, HBO ran engaging mobile ads for the season premiere of its *True Blood* series:[26]

> Imagine browsing through the Flixter app looking for a movie or browsing the Variety app, and the first touch of the screen turns into a bloody fingerprint. Touch again and get another fingerprint, then the blood pours down and takes over the screen and the activation pops up, a tap-to-watch-trailer call-to-action screen with a banner ad at the bottom. HBO's *True Blood* mobile ad campaign sent chills down consumers' spines and increased viewership 38 percent; 5.1 million viewers tuned in to view the season premiere.

A mobile marketing effort might be as simple as inviting people to text a number, such as when the Red Cross asked for Japan earthquake and tsunami relief donations (text "JAPAN" to 90999 to donate $10). It might involve texting promotions to consumers—anything from retailer announcements of discounts, brand coupons, and gift suggestions to mobile games and contests. Many marketers have also created their own mobile Web sites, optimized for specific phones and mobile service providers. Others have created useful or entertaining mobile apps to engage customers with their brands and help them shop (see Marketing at Work 15.2). For example, Nike gained unprecedented direct access to runners with a Nike+ GPS iPhone app for real-time tracking of runs and bike rides.

As with other forms of direct marketing, however, companies must use mobile marketing responsibly or risk angering already ad-weary consumers. "If you were interrupted every two minutes by advertising, not many people want that," says a mobile marketing expert. "The industry needs to work out smart and clever ways to engage people on mobiles." The key is to provide genuinely useful information and offers that will make consumers want to opt in or call in. One study found that 42 percent of cell phone users are open to mobile advertising if it's relevant.[27]

In all, online marketing continues to offer both great promise and many challenges for the future. Its most ardent apostles still envision a time when the Internet and online marketing will replace magazines, newspapers, and even stores as sources for information and buying. Most marketers, however, hold a more realistic view. To be sure, online marketing has become a successful business model for some companies—Internet firms such as Amazon.com, Facebook, and Google, as well as direct marketing companies such as GEICO and Netflix. However, for most companies, online marketing will remain just one important approach to the marketplace that works alongside other approaches in a fully integrated marketing mix.

Marketing at Work 23.1

Mobile Marketing: Customers Come Calling

You're at the local Best Buy checking out portable GPS navigation systems. You've narrowed it down to the latest Garmin nüvi versus a less-expensive competing model, but you're not certain that Best Buy has the best prices. Also, you'd love to know how other consumers rate the two brands. No problem. Just pull out your smartphone and launch your Amazon Mobile app, which lets you browse the brands you're considering, read customer reviews, and compare prices of portable GPS systems sold by Amazon.com and its retail partners. The application even lets you snap a photo or scan a barcode from an item; Amazon.com employees will then search for a similar item available from Amazon. If Amazon.com offers a better deal, you can make the purchase directly from the application.

Welcome to the new world of mobile marketing. Today's new smartphones are changing the way we live—including the way we shop. And as they change how we shop, they also change how marketers sell to us.

A growing number of consumers—especially younger ones—are using their mobile phones as a "third screen" for texting, browsing the mobile Web, watching videos and shows, and checking e-mail. According to one expert, "the mobile phone ... is morphing into a content device, a kind of digital Swiss army knife with the capability of filling its owner's every spare minute with games, music, live and on-demand TV, Web browsing, and, oh yes, advertising." Says the president of the Mobile Marketing Association, "It's only a matter of time before mobile is the 'first screen.'" According to another industry insider:

Mobile phones, iPads, and other mobile devices have quietly become the hottest new frontier for marketers, especially those targeting the coveted 18- to 34-year-old set. TV networks are prodding viewers to send text messages to vote for their favorite reality TV character. Wireless Web sites are lacing sports scores and news digests with banner ads for Lexus, Burger King, and Sheraton. A few companies are even customizing 10-second video ads for short, TV-style episodes that are edging their way onto mobile phones. For advertisers, the young audience is just one selling point. Mobile gadgets are always on, ever-present accessories. The fact that a phone or other device is tethered to an individual means that ads can be targeted. And users can respond instantly to time-sensitive offers. The mobile phone is very personal, and it's always with you.

Mobile marketing: Zipcar's iPhone app lets members find and book a Zipcar, honk the horn (so they can find it in a crowd), and even lock and unlock the doors—all from their iPhones.

Marketers large and small are weaving mobile marketing into their direct marketing mixes. For example, Walmart uses text message alerts to spread the news about sales; once you receive a text, you can click on links within the messages to go to the retailer's mobile Web site and check on details. Unilever phones out mobile coupons for Ragu pasta sauce, Dove body wash, Breyers ice cream, and its other brands: Just hold up your mobile phone at the checkout, and the cashier will scan the barcode off the screen. Tide's Stain Brain app helps customers find ways to remove stains. A Sit or Squat app that directs people to nearby public restrooms opens with a splash page for Charmin bathroom tissue.

Beyond helping you buy, other mobile marketing applications provide helpful services, useful information, and entertainment. USAA's mobile banking app lets you check your balance, transfer funds, and even deposit a check via phone by taking a photo of the front and back of the check and hitting "send." Zipcar's app lets members find and reserve a Zipcar, honk the horn (so they can find it in a crowd), and even lock and unlock the doors—all from their phones. REI's The Snow and Ski Report app gives ski slope information for locations throughout the United States and Canada, such as snow depth, snow conditions, and the number of open lifts. The app also links you to "Shop REI," for times "when you decide you can't live without a new set of K2 skis or a two-man Hoo-Doo tent."

For entertainment, carmaker Audi offers the Audi A4 Driving Challenge game for the iPhone, iPod, and iPod Touch, which features a tiny A4 that maneuvers its way through different driving courses—to steer, you tilt your phone right or left. Similarly, Audi's "Truth in 24" app lets you in on the action behind the notorious 24 Hours of Le Mans Audi auto race, including an iPhone game that "puts the excitement of LeMans racing right in the palm of your hand." For customers interested in reviewing Audi's cars, Audi A4 and A8 "Experience" apps let you explore these models interactively inside and out. Audi claims that such apps have been downloaded millions of times, drawing hundreds of thousands of visitors to its mobile Web sites.

One of the most effective mobile marketing applications is Kraft's iFood Assistant, which provides easy-to-prepare recipes for food shoppers on the go, how-to videos, a recipe box, and a built-in shopping list. iFood Assistant supplies advice on how to prepare some 7,000 simple but satisfying meals—at three meals a day, that's almost 20 years worth of recipes. The iFood Assistant will even give you directions to local stores. Of course, most of the meals call for ingredients that just happen to be Kraft brands. The iFood Assistant app cost Kraft less than $100,000 to create but has engaged millions of shoppers, providing great marketing opportunities for Kraft and its brands.

Increasingly, consumers are using their phones as in-store shopping aids, and retailers are responding accordingly. For example, while strolling among the bookshelves at the local Barnes & Noble store, you can now snap a photo of any book cover that strikes your interest and use a Barnes & Noble app to learn more about it. The app uses image recognition software to recognize the book and then almost instantly pulls up user reviews from barnesandnoble.com to help shoppers decide whether to buy. "We've seen a huge uplift in reservations of books for purchase in physical stores, as well as buying, from the . . . app since we launched it," says the chain's vice president for digital devices.

Many consumers are initially skeptical about mobile marketing. But they often change their minds if mobile marketers deliver value in the form of useful brand and shopping information, entertaining content, or discounted prices and coupons for their favorite products and services. Most mobile marketing efforts target only consumers who voluntarily opt in or who download apps. In the increasingly cluttered mobile marketing space, customers just won't do that unless they see real value in it. The challenge for marketers: Develop useful and engaging mobile marketing apps that make customers come calling.

Sources: Adapted extract, quotes, and other information from Christine Birkner, "Mobile Marketing: This Time It's Different," *Marketing News,* January 30, 2011, pp. 17–18; Richard Westlund, "Mobile on Fast Forward," *Brandweek,* March 15, 2010, pp. M1–M5; Todd Wasserman, "I'm on the Phone!" *Adweek,* February 23, 2009, pp. 6–7; Alice Z. Cuneo, "Scramble for Content Drives Mobile," *Advertising Age,* October 24, 2005, p. S6; Jen Arnoff, "Wising Up to Smart Phones," *News & Observer (Raleigh),* April 22, 2009, p. 5B; Carol Angrisani, "Priced to Cell," *Supermarket News,* June 1, 2009, p. 28; Reena Jana, "Retailers Are Learning to Love Smartphones," *Businessweek,* October 26, 2009, p. 49; and www.usaa.com/inet/pages/usaa_mobile_main, accessed August 2011.

The 5th P of Marketing[28]

Social media offers marketers opportunities to reach consumers where they work and live. Just as in the other aspects of our lives we've already discussed, the element of participation is key in this context also: Social media enables consumers to have more of a say in the products and services that marketers create to meet their needs.

Let's take a step back: **Marketing** is the activity, set of institutions, and processes for creating, communicating, delivering, and exchanging offerings that have value for customers, clients, partners, and society at large.[29] The classic view is that organizations accomplish these goals through a **marketing mix** that includes the so-called **4 Ps**: Product, Price, Promotion, and Place (or distribution).

As social media marketing techniques continue to sprout around us, today we need to add a fifth P: **Participation**. It's fair to say that just as social media is changing the way consumers live on a daily basis, so too these new platforms transform how marketers go about their business. Whether our focus is to improve customer service, maintain customer relationships, inform consumers of our benefits, promote a brand or related special offer, develop a new product, or influence brand attitudes, new social media options play a role. **Social media marketing** is the utilization of social media technologies, channels, and software to create, communicate, deliver, and exchange offerings that have value for an organization's stakeholders.

Marketing Communication: From Top-Down to Bottom-Up

Just as the horizontal revolution changed the way society communicates, the advent and adoption of social media changes the way brands and consumers interact. Traditional marketing focuses on **push messaging** (one-way communication delivered to the target audience) using a large dose of broadcast and print media to reach a mass audience. There are minimal opportunities for interaction and feedback between customers and the organization, and what is possible is facilitated by **boundary spanners** (employees who interact directly with customers) who operate in service roles. The brand message is controlled in a top-down manner by brand leadership within the organization.

Believe it or not, when the Internet first began to catch on there were many skeptics who declared it was just a fad! Even as digital technology developed in the 1990s and beyond, marketers still essentially applied the traditional 4Ps model to reach customers. Over time they embraced the Internet as an environment for promotion and distribution. **E-commerce** began to blossom as an alternative to other forms of promotion such as television or radio. Consumers increasingly began to learn about products online—and to purchase them online as well. E-commerce sites are websites that allow customers to examine (onscreen) different brands and to conduct transactions via credit card.

This explosion in e-commerce activity was a boon to manufacturers, retailers, and nonprofit organizations because it offered greater speed, cost efficiencies, and access to **micromarkets**. A micromarket is a group of consumers once considered too small and inaccessible for marketers to pursue. Suddenly it became feasible for even a small company that offered a limited inventory to reach potential customers around the globe. The Internet enables efficient access to these markets, and in turn allows customers to search for very specialized products (e.g., music tracks by bands that recorded bassline music in Sheffield, England, between 2002–2005, or steampunk science fiction novels written by K. W. Jeter). This allows marketers to offer **niche products** that appeal to small, specialized groups of people.

As it became clear that the Internet was not going to go away, marketers flocked to cyberspace. However, most of them still applied the familiar model of the 4 Ps to the digital domain. This form of marketing, **tradigital marketing**, is characterized by improvements in interactivity and measurement, but it retains the primarily vertical flow of power in the channels of communication and distribution. Digital online messages made it possible for consumers to respond directly to an online display ad by clicking through to the e-commerce website. **Search advertising** grew during this time too, making it possible for online advertising to target both mass and niche audiences. Direct marketers widely adopted email marketing as a complement to direct mail and telemarketing. Despite these developments, modes of communication were still primarily vertical, one-way "mass communication," largely impersonal, and delivered from one to many. Whether you read the front page of the *New York Times* online at www.nytimes.com or peruse the physical newspaper at your kitchen table, the content from the publisher is delivered vertically through the channel of communication.

Both traditional and tradigital marketing work on the basis of the interruption-disruption model we discussed earlier. This means that the source of a communication delivers messages to audiences whether they want to receive them or not, and regardless of whether these messages are directly relevant to their unique needs. By design, an advertising message interrupts some prior activity: A commercial for Axe body deodorant suddenly appears during the latest episode of MTV's *Jersey Shore,* or perhaps a pop-up bubble asks you to click on a link to learn more about low rates on car insurance while you browse a website. Why would Internet users tolerate these disruptions as they surf the Web? For the same reason television viewers and radio listeners have for decades. The ad as interruption provides a stream of revenue for the media provider, which enables this sponsor to provide the content of interest at little or no cost to the audience. Television programming exists to draw audiences, which enables the network to sell space to advertisers who wish to reach that audience. The audience in turn accepts the presence of the advertising in order to consume the desired programming. This "you scratch my back and I'll scratch yours" relationship also describes traditional Internet advertising: Before you can watch a full episode of Gossip Girl on your laptop, you might sit through a 15-second ad for Verizon Wireless. Just like television and radio broadcasting, the Web 1.0 Internet relies upon the interruption-disruption model to earn revenue.

In contrast, social media empowers consumers. It isn't enough to interrupt the consumer experience and steal a few moments of attention. With social media marketing, the ability for consumers to interact and engage with brands is greatly enhanced. Social media channels give consumers unparalleled access. Consumers discuss, contribute, collaborate, and share—with brands and with each other. The culture of marketing has shifted to an informal one focused on the belief that customers are in control. Marketing guru Peter Drucker once famously said, "The purpose of a business is to create a customer." With the reach and community influence of social media, we can expand this definition: The purpose of a business is to create customers who create other customers.[30] *That Participation in the process is the new fifth P of marketing.*

In the few years of social media's existence, social media marketing has expanded rapidly as much for its efficiency given its low absolute costs as for its potential business applications as a tool for garnering customer attention, managing customer relationships, developing new product ideas, promoting brands, driving store (online and off) traffic, and converting consumers to customers. Social media are not a substitute for traditional marketing communications, but they are also more than a complement to traditional methods as you'll see throughout this book. This shift from traditional to tradigital to social media is illustrated in Figure 23.2.

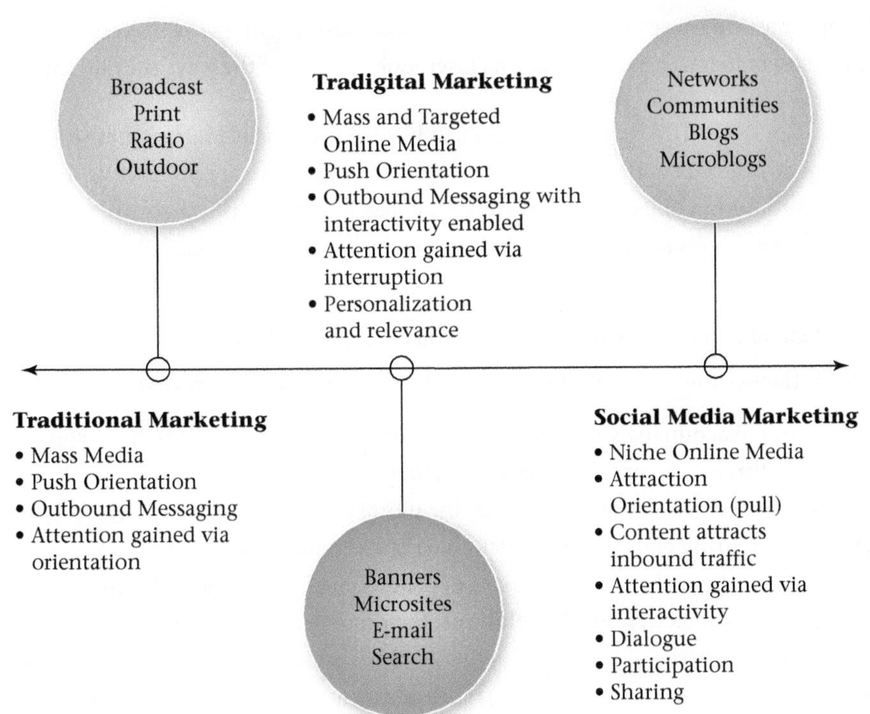

FIGURE 23.2

The Evolution of Marketing Communication

Source: Based on David Armano (May 21, 2009), Social Engagement Spectrum, http://darmano.typepad.com/logic_emotion/2009/05/socialengagement-spectrum.html, accessed November 8, 2011.

FIGURE 23.3

Brand Applications Across Social Media Zones

Social Media Achieves Marketing Objectives

As social media marketing has accelerated over the last few years, the objectives organizations can accomplish also have expanded. Figure 23.3 shows these objectives cross a range of marketing activities that include promotion and branding, customer service, relationship management, retailing and commerce, and marketing research. Just as the digital lives of consumers intersect across the four zones of social media, brands reach consumers in those same spaces to build awareness, promote themselves, and encourage users to try them. Let's take a closer look at some of the ways they do this.

PROMOTION AND BRANDING Marketers have many possible techniques to promote goods, services, ideas, places, or people. Though there are potentially dozens of specific promotion objectives marketers may seek to accomplish, there are two overarching objectives relevant to the use of social media marketing as part of a brand's promotional mix:

1. Extend and leverage the brand's media coverage, and
2. Influence the consumer throughout the decision-making process.

When it comes to acquiring space in media to distribute brand messages, marketers have access to three core types of media: (1) paid, (2) owned, and (3) earned. Marketers are assessed monetary fees for **paid media**, including purchasing space to deliver brand messages and securing endorsements. Paid media are traditionally the purview of **advertising**, defined as the paid placement of promotional messages in channels capable of reaching a mass audience. **Public relations**, the promotional mix component tasked with generating positive publicity and goodwill, may also utilize paid media in the form of sponsorships. Television commercials, radio ads, magazine print ads, newspaper ads, billboards, Internet display ads, and **search engine marketing (SEM)** all represent examples of paid media that may be incorporated in a brand's promotional plan. As we'll see in later chapters, other emerging formats include paying for messages in online games like Happy Pets or offering branded virtual goods to inhabitants of virtual worlds. And traditional sales promotions such as coupons and contests get a new life on social media platforms.

Owned media are channels the brand controls. Corporate websites and e-commerce sites, corporate blogs, advergames, and ARGs all represent forms of owned media. Just as Best Buy's brick-and-mortar retail stores are owned and controlled by the organization, so is its website.

Earned media are those messages that are distributed at no direct cost to the company and by methods beyond the control of the company. **Word-of-mouth (WOM)** communication (called **influence impressions** in social media) and publicity are important forms of earned media. Companies release content through press releases and paid channels, participate in community events and causes, create stunts designed to generate media attention and buzz, and offer exceptional service quality, all with the hope that a brand message will spread. Table 23.4 explains the forms of paid, earned, and owned media possible in each of the zones of social media marketing.

A major objective related to using social media marketing for promotional purposes is to assist in moving the consumer through the purchase process. Marketers target various stages of this cycle to increase brand awareness, enhance brand liking and image, build brand equity, incite desire, and move consumers to action. They can influence consumer attitudes and movement through the process with promotional messages targeted

TABLE 23.4
TYPES OF MEDIA

ZONE	PAID MEDIA	EARNED MEDIA	OWNED MEDIA
1: Social Communities	■ Ads	■ Conversations in communities ■ Shared content ■ Influence impressions ■ Likes, followers, fans	■ Controlled profiles
2: Social Publishing	■ Endorsements ■ Branded channels in media sharing sites	■ Embeds ■ Comments ■ Shares ■ Links ■ Search rankings	■ Corporate blogs ■ Brand-controlled media sharing sites
3: Social Entertainment	■ Ads in games	■ In-game interactions	■ Advergames and branded ARGs
4: Social Commerce	■ Sales promotions	■ Reviews and ratings ■ Recommendations and referrals ■ Group buys ■ Social shopping interactions	■ Advergames and branded ARGs ■ Social storefronts

throughout the social media channels. Let's take a brief look at how this works at each stage of the purchase process.

1. **Increase Awareness**: Brands can increase awareness with social media marketing by maintaining an active presence in the social spaces where target consumers "live." That means engaging in social communities and publishing content as well as encouraging word of mouth communication and consumer reviews. It may even include social entertainment.
2. **Influence Desire**: Social media promotions can be used much like advertising, catalog marketing, and feature events to persuade consumers to recognize a sense of desire. The fashion brand Black Horn posts each new collection on Facebook, Flickr, and YouTube. Visitors can tour pictures of its designs, fresh from each photo shoot. It's like being in the pages of *Vogue*.
3. **Encourage Trial**: Social media can even be used to support sampling and loyalty programs. Sampling means to offer a free trial of a product; these are usually mailed to consumers' homes or distributed in stores or on the street. Social media can be used to recruit interested prospects to qualify for samples. Emergen-C, a health supplement, used this tactic to promote free samples. Whenever a user on Twitter tweeted something like "need energy" or "need

to focus" Emergen-C sent a tweet requesting the person's mailing address. A couple of days later, the tired tweeter received a gift of three samples.

4. **Facilitate Purchase**: Social media serves as a distribution channel and venue for many sales promotion incentives including deals and group offers. Many customers "like" or follow brands in social networks in order to qualify for special deals. Here's a recent tweet from Best Buy: "Save $330 on an LG 32" Class HDTV + Wireless Adapter package: http://bbyurl.us/t3svia @BestBuy_deals." Kohl's distributes thousands of coupons by posting announcements on its Facebook Fan Page. Fans visit the page, download the coupon, and store traffic increases.
5. **Cement brand loyalty**: Social media venues offer engaging activities for consumers that can ensure they spend more time with the brand, hopefully resulting in higher levels of brand loyalty. Look no farther than social games that offer rewards for the most loyal visitors. That's just what FourSquare does. Starbucks "mayors" earn one dollar off a cup of coffee when they visit. Tasti D-Lite, a regional ice cream chain, went even further when it developed its social media loyalty program.[31] Customers use TreatCards—which also double as gift cards—to earn points for purchases, and those that opt in to the social media bonuses automatically earn additional points. Twitter and Foursquare accounts are updated each time the card is swiped and points are earned or redeemed. As a customer earns points, he or she can redeem them for free cones.

Setting a Social Media Campaign Strategy

To develop a social experience worthy of participation and worthy of sharing, social media planners ask and answer several questions:

- What are the campaign goals and/or communication tasks? Objectives have been set for the campaign and the use of social media identified as a possibility. Here the planner reviews these decisions and provides a succinct overview of the goals.
- How is the brand positioned? What is unique and special about its position in the marketplace? As in a traditional creative brief, any campaign work should leverage the brand's positioning strategy and build on the brand's strengths.
- Who is the target audience? You've profiled the target already. Now consider what you want the audience to do. Do you want them to talk to the brand? Create and share content? Spread the message to their network? On what devices (e.g., iPad, smartphone, desktop) will they interact with your brand? What could you offer of value in exchange for their cooperation?
- Is there another group of people who can persuade the target audience to follow them? This group is your influencers—the people who will propagate your message. Why would these people want to share your message with others? What's in it for them?

- What are the existing creative assets? How can the brand's creative foster a social experience? Most brands already have some creative assets that drive their paid and owned media. For example, a well-known and popular brand spokescharacter such as the GEICO gecko is a creative asset that the insurance company has developed in its traditional advertising, so he might be employed in a social media campaign to give the company a head start in terms of consumer recognition as it tries to break through the clutter of competing messages. The planner should list the creative assets that already exist and identify the assets he or she still needs to extend the brand's story. How can the creative assets already available be used and/or leveraged in a social media context?
- How can we integrate with other branded media being used by the organization, and how long do we have to execute? This is a question that references how the campaign can integrate best with the brand's paid and owned media.
- What experiences are possible given target market needs and motives, the available channels, and the creative assets? How can we design these experiences to maximize device portability and access? Creative used in social media campaigns should inspire activity and interactivity. These questions ask what types of activities could be engaging for the target audience using multiple devices and worth sharing with their network.
- What content will be needed? Social media are content-driven. What content will be relevant to the campaign and what will be the source? Comments? Questions and polls? Video? Images? Stories? Apps?
- How will experience engagement be extended and shared throughout the social channels? For instance, will engagement activity auto-post to status updates (e.g., "Tracy likes Cole Haan")?

What Matters Is Measured[32]

We've shown you throughout this book that brands can benefit when they participate in the social media space. With social media, brands can engage consumers, enhance brand reputation and image, build positive brand attitudes, improve organic search rankings, service customers, and drive traffic to brand locations, both online and off. But no social media marketing campaign can identify the right measures to use. It's harder than it sounds—in fact, marketers continue to wrestle with these decisions as they seek concrete ways to illustrate the value of these techniques to others in their organizations who hold the purse strings.

Not that long ago, social media marketers felt that there were no standard metrics we could apply to social media marketing campaigns. Some believed that applying metrics to something as organic as social media was "mission impossible"—the metrics were bound to be meaningless at best because social media was not about quantitative monetary accomplishments. Social media is meant to be about participation and relationships between brands and consumers. In a short period of time, we've developed a host of valuable metrics, but these also come with an important caveat. The metrics we use must be appropriate for the objectives we set for the campaign. Counting followers and fans, retweets, and blog comments is only relevant if those behaviors relate to the goals of the brand's social media activity.

In many ways, social media marketing mimics online advertising in terms of the viable metrics available to measure how effective these messages are. Advertisers can measure the reach (the number people exposed to the message) and frequency (the average number of times someone is exposed), and analyze site stickiness (the ability of a site to draw repeat visits and to keep people on a site) and the relative pull (a comparison of how well different creative executions generate a response) of creative advertising. Brands can monitor clickthroughs (the number of people exposed to an online ad or link who actually click on it), sales conversions (the number of people who click through who go on to purchase the product), and viewthroughs (the number of people who are exposed and do not click through, but who later visit the brand's website).

A First Date or a Marriage?

Some metrics such as number of unique visitors, page views, frequency of visits, average visit length, and clickthrough rates may be irrelevant or simply fail to capture information appropriate to the reasons we use them. When we want to demonstrate the value of what we're doing, we love to count—we count impressions, visitors, friends, posts, players, even how often we count! There's no doubt that numbers are important. For instance, when we know the number of community members involved in brand-related conversations this measure can serve as an indicator of exposure, and the number of message threads and lines of text within a thread can serve as proxies of conversation depth.

However, simply counting the quantity of interactions consumers have with a brand doesn't tell us much about the *quality* of these touchpoints. We also need to know the degree of **engagement** people feel during and after the interaction, and how these exposures influenced their feelings about the brand. For this reason we also try to collect other numbers that are a bit more diagnostic, such as measures of brand likeability, brand image, brand awareness, brand loyalty, brand affiliation, congruency, and purchase intent. Hershey's Bliss, a brand we will look at closer later in this chapter, may have more than 32,000 Facebook friends, but what does the number of friends tell us about how the target audience *feels* about Hershey's Bliss chocolate? As one analyst observed, "Four thousand two hundred and thirty-one is a measurement. Without context, it is merely a number. When compared with your personal best, company expectations, or your competitors' efforts, that number becomes a metric. It is now indicative of value, importance or a change in results."[33]

Engagement is a complex construct made up of several individual accomplishments. The Engagement Food Chain illustrates the hierarchy of effects we seek from our target audience as they reach increasing levels of engagement with our brand. Figure 23.4 demonstrates how we look for different outcomes depending upon the consumer's level of engagement with the brand.

Because engagement is such a complex phenomenon, we need to be choosy about just what measures we collect and which ones are important. **Key performance indicators (KPIs)** are those metrics that are tied to organizational objectives.[34] But, there's a catch:

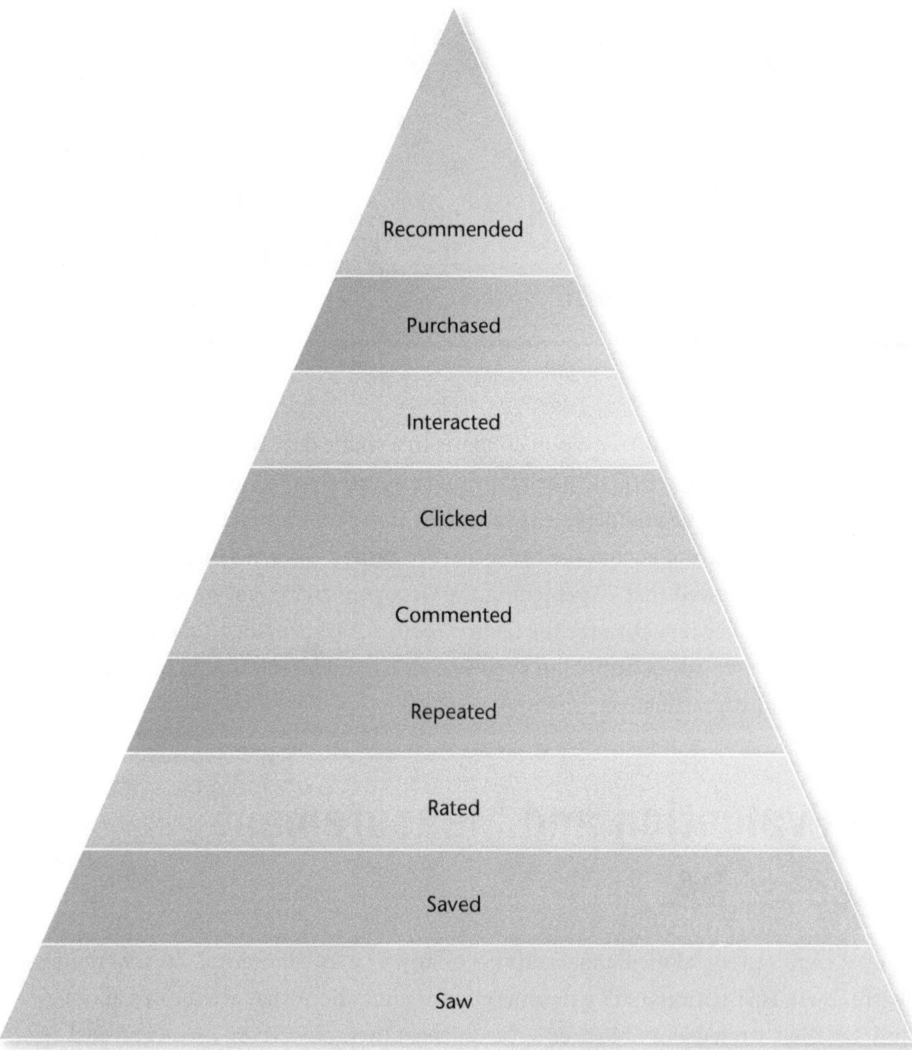

FIGURE 23.4

The Engagement Food Chain

Source: Based on "The Engagement Food Chain," Jim Sterne, 2010, *Social Media Metrics,* p. 109.

In order for KPIs to be valuable, we first must be sure the objectives they're supposed to measure are well-defined. As the old geek saying goes, "Garbage in, garbage out." To review where we are so far:

- Measurements within a defined context are metrics.
- Measurements require context to provide useful feedback.
- Metrics that are tied to objectives are key performance indicators.
- Objectives must be well-defined before we can identify key performance indicators.

Campaign Timelines and Metrics

To make matters a bit more complicated (uh oh!), it's important to remember that the metrics we use may shift as a campaign progresses. For example, in the early days just following launch we primarily may be interested in awareness—are people in cyberspace tuning in to what we're doing? As the campaign progresses, we may not be so impressed with that as the pressure builds to show tangible results such as a boost in sales. For example, when Gap ran a group deal with Groupon offering $50 of Gap apparel for $25,

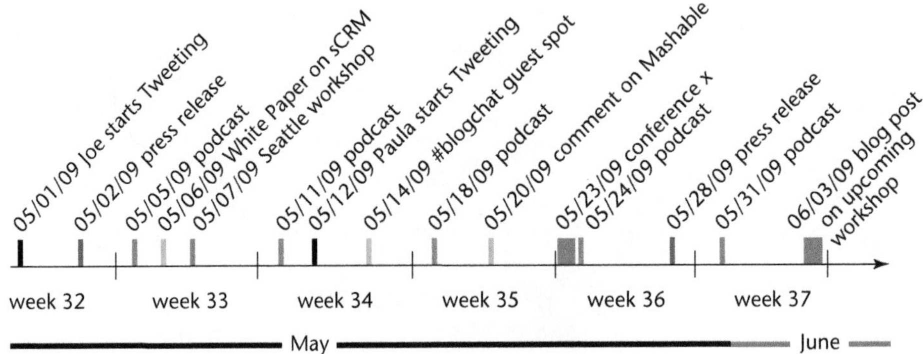

FIGURE 23.5

A Sample Social Media Campaign Timeline

Source: Based on Oliver Blanchard, "Social Media ROI–Part 8: An Introduction to Timelines," *BrandBuilder*, http://thebrandbuilder.wordpress.com/2009/07/21/social-media-r-o-i-part-8-an-introduction-to-timelines/, accessed December 27, 2010.

it was excited to sell 441,000 Groupon coupons in a single day—$11 million in revenue. But Gap's social commerce tactic wasn't meant to act solely as a single sales promotion to improve sales revenue and deplete inventories. Gap also wanted to remind consumers about the Gap brand and encourage consumers to utilize Gap's website. Later measures of the campaign showed that 70 percent of the Groupon users went on to browse Gap online, meeting a key objective for the tactic.[35] Figure 23.5 provides a sample campaign timeline to illustrate how a campaign evolves over time. Metrics should be tied to each stage in the campaign timeline.

The Evaluation and Measurement Process: DATA

When it comes to social media marketing—or any form of marketing, for that matter—measurement isn't optional. It's a necessity for organizations that are serious about adjusting their strategies and tactics to better meet their objectives. Some may feel intimidated about specifying what it is they want to see happen when it comes to their social media activities; perhaps they believe this sets them up to fail because they're not sure they can actually define or attain specific goalposts. Others may still be in the early stage of the social media maturity life cycle; because they're still "playing" with social media, they don't yet feel the need to define what results they would like to see. But ultimately social media will have to answer to the same masters as other kinds of traditional media—the bean counters that need to see value for their money. The investment in social media marketing will require justification. Strategists will want to understand what's working and what isn't in order to decide if a campaign needs fixing or if it's worth continuing at all. Welcome to the cold cruel world of budgets!

In reality, devising a measurement plan is a relatively straightforward process (at least on paper!). We organize our plan according to a four-step process known as the **DATA approach**:[36]

1. **Define:** Define the results that the program is designed to promote.
2. **Assess:** Assess the costs of the program and the potential value of the results.
3. **Track:** Track the actual results and link those results to the program.
4. **Adjust:** Adjust the program based on results to optimize future outcomes.

Let's dive deeper into each of these four steps.

BYTES TO BUCKS **HERSHEY'S BLISS**

Hershey's Bliss worked with the agency House Party to create a campaign with both offline and social online components. The campaign sought to make female consumers aged 25 to 49 who love chocolate aware of the three varieties of Hershey's Bliss chocolate and to position the brand as an everyday indulgence. Further, they wanted to ensure product trial during the campaign and encourage word-of-mouth communication in social communities and on blogs. To pursue this goal, House Party planned 10,000 real parties in the homes of consumers they identified as influentials. Party hosts received a House Party Pack filled with products, gift bags, themed cocktail napkins, and a party photo album. Party hosts and attendees were asked to share the Hershey's Bliss experience online at the House Party microsite and to further share that content with their networks.

>> END EXAMPLE

Define

Our first—and arguably most critical—task is to define just what we want to occur and what we need to measure. Quite simply we have to define the objectives of the social media marketing campaign. After all, if we don't have clear objectives, how do we know when we've reached them? The specific objectives we might identify can vary dramatically from brand to brand but it's likely they will include three overarching issues:

1. *Motivating* some behavior from the target audience (such as visits to a website or purchases of the product),
2. *Influencing* brand knowledge and attitudes (particularly among those who are likely to spread the message to their own networks), and
3. *Accomplishing* the first two objectives with fewer resources than might be required with other methods.

For instance, if we use Twitter to identify customer complaints early on and resolve those complaints online like the Best Buy Twelpforce does, we can potentially influence attitude toward the brand, inspire the customer to share the experience with others, and do so online at a cost far less than it normally takes a call center to resolve. Remember that organizational objectives will tie directly to the applications they've selected. If social media are being used as a customer service venue, we will identify service-oriented results in this step. If social media are a part of the brand's promotional strategy, we will identify communication objectives. If social media are a source of data for customer insight, we specify research objectives.

ARE YOUR OBJECTIVES SMART? How can we be sure our objectives are clear enough that we can adequately measure them? The key is to state them so they have SMART characteristics:

- Specific
- Measurable
- Appropriate
- Realistic
- Time-oriented

To understand how objectives can be SMART or not, consider the following two examples.

> *"We will tell everyone we can about our new Facebook page and see if they like it so much they'll buy more of our product."*
>
> *"We will promote our new Facebook page in print advertisements we will place in the June issues of* Rolling Stone, Sports Illustrated, *and* Maxim. *On July 15 we will count the number of Facebook users who 'like' our brand and compare sales to the same period last year."*

The second objective is SMART; the first, not so much. However, defining objectives in a specific manner is not as easy as it sounds. Even the most desirable of outcomes (brand engagement and cost-efficiency, for instance) must be clearly defined if they are to be useful in assessment. It may seem difficult to shift from thinking about the benefits we can derive from social media marketing to ways we can measure those values. The benefits may seem intangible ("create lots of buzz!"), so an early step is to find a way to quantify results that may not lend themselves to numerical measurement. Here are some examples:

- One benefit of hosting a blog is that the target audience may use it to educate themselves about the company's product line. It is difficult to measure the value of consumer education, but there are tangible benefits we should see from greater knowledge about a brand. Assuming that people like what they see, these efforts should move blog visitors to the e-commerce site and from there to transactions. Thus the benefit of consumer education is valuable if it results in increases in site traffic and sales.
- Another common goal of social media marketing is search engine optimization. We can see whether our site is optimized when we test the search rankings we achieve. In addition, better search results should lead to higher traffic to the site. Aha! Something we can measure.
- Reaching a specific audience with our brand message is a valuable outcome. Here we may need to measure impressions, but we can also compare the cost of reaching the target audience with social media to the cost of doing so using traditional media. Social media are valuable for showing responsiveness to consumer concerns, but what is the value of the increased responsiveness? We can track customer satisfaction and retention to assess this value.

METRICS The next step is to decide on the *metric*, or specific standard of measurement, we will use to measure the objective. When we specify our metrics we need to match these to the results we are concerned about—whether attitude shifts and behavioral responses from our target audience or efficiency and profitability measures resulting from cost savings and/or increased sales. Table 23.5 lists some of the most commonly-used metrics.

A SOCIAL MEDIA MARKETING METRICS MATRIX The list of possible measures applicable to social media can be overwhelming. Applying a framework to manage the types of measures is useful. The matrix shown in Table 23.6 illustrates the types and characteristics of social media metrics. The three types of metrics include activity metrics, interaction metrics, and return (financial) metrics.

TABLE 23.5
COMMONLY-USED SOCIAL MEDIA METRICS

1. WOM Metrics Buzz volume
    a. Number (volume) of posts, comments, retweets/shares, bookmarks by channel
    b. Frequency, momentum, recency, seasonality
2. Asset popularity, virality
    a. Sharing, viewing, bookmarking, downloads, installs, and embedding of branded assets such as videos, pictures, links, articles
    b. Changes over time
3. Media mentions (earned media)
4. Brand liking
    a. Fans, followers, friends
    b. Growth in fans, followers, friends
    c. Likes, favorites, ratings, links back
5. Reach and second degree reach (influence impressions from others)
    a. Readers, viewers
    b. Subscriptions
    c. Mentions, links
6. Engagement
    a. Comment volume
    b. Uploads, contest participation
    c. Subscriptions (RSS, podcasts, video series, document series)
    d. Registrations
    e. Time spent with social pages
7. Quality
    a. Ratings, bookmarks
8. Search engine optimization
9. Web site effectiveness (traffic, clicks, conversions, viewthroughs)
10. Share of voice in social media and overall
11. Influence
12. Sentiment
    a. Nature of comments, tag attributes
    b. Attitudes
13. Customer value
    a. sales changes online, offline;
    b. customer lifetime value shifts, customer retention, lower customer acquisition costs

Based on David Berkowitz, "100 Ways to Measure Social Media," *MediaPost Social Media Insider*, November 17, 2009, www.mediapost.com/publications/?fa=Articles.showArticle&art_aid=117581, accessed October 15, 2010.

- **Activity metrics** measure the actions the organization takes relative to social media. For instance, an organization might set goals in terms of the number and timing of blog posts, white papers, tweets, videos, comment responses, and status updates it may contribute in social venues. Hershey's Bliss House Party campaign set activity metrics for number of parties held, party attendance, blog posts, and content quantity uploaded to the microsite.
- **Interaction metrics** focus on how the target market engages with the social media platform and activities. Interaction measures include the number of followers and fans, comments, likes, recommendations and reviews, and the amount of shared content. Interactions are essentially made up of all the ways in which users can participate in a social media relationship with the brand. Hershey's Bliss House Party included interaction metrics in its' measurement plan too. Brand analysts measured the quantity of shared content and the sentiment of these posts.

TABLE 23.6

A SOCIAL MEDIA METRICS FRAMEWORK

Source: Adapted from Mike Brown, July 14, 2010, 6, "Social Media Metrics You Should Be Tracking," *Social Media Today,* http://www.socialmediatoday.com/mikebrown1/146589/6-social-media-metrics-you-should-be-tracking, accessed September 2011.

Category/Characteristic	Quantitative Measures	Qualitative Measures
Activity (input)	Number, frequency, and recency of Blog posts Updates/posts Comments/reply comments White papers Photo posts Video posts Activity across media channels	Creative messaging and positioning strategy Resonance/fit of campaign appeal Social media involvement
Interaction (responses)	Number, frequency, and recency of: Registrations Bookmarks/favorites/likes/ratings Comments/posts/mentions/tags Links/trackbacks Downloads/installs/embeds Subscriptions Fans/followers/friends Share/forward/invite/refer Reviews/testimonials Traffic/visits/views/impressions Time spent on site Profile development UG content contributed Discount/deal redemption rate Echo effect/virality	Sentiment Engagement Influence effects Recommendations Buzz/virality
Performance (outcome)	Cost/prospects Lead conversion rate Average new revenue per customer Cost efficiencies across marketing functions Customer lifetime value Earned media values Shifts in average sales/site Traffic/search engine ratings Share of voice Return on investment	Attitude toward the brand Brand loyalty Customer satisfaction Service quality perceptions

Source: Adapted from Mike Brown, "Social Media Metrics You Should Be Tracking," *Social Media Today*, July 14, 2010, www.socialmediatoday.com/mikebrown1/146589/6-social-media-metrics-you-should-be-tracking, accessed January 1, 2011.

- **Return metrics** focus on the outcomes (financial or otherwise) that directly or indirectly support the success of the brand. They include return on investment measures, cost reduction measures, and other performance metrics. In addition to these categories, social media data can be characterized as qualitative or quantitative. Using both forms provide the hard numbers that CFOs (chief financial officers) require to fund investments in social media strategy while also valuing the soft benefits of social media such as stories, buzz, and image. Hershey's Bliss House Party didn't disclose its return metrics or the cost of the campaign, but you can bet these figures were calculated. The agency would be sure to calculate the cost to reach 10.1 million consumers in the target audience and the 77 million impressions the campaign earned when it reported return estimates to the client.

A common metric to gauge success is **return on investment (ROI).** ROI is a measure of profitability. It captures how effective a company is at using capital to generate profits. To determine ROI we assign a financial value to the resources we use to execute a strategy, measure financial outcomes, and calculate the ratio between inputs and outcomes. Return on investment answers the question, "How much income was generated from investments in the activities?" When we apply this concept to a brand's investment in social media marketing we call the measure **social media return on investment (SMROI).** SMROI answers the question, "How much income did our investments in social media marketing generate?"

It's natural to want to quantify the value of a corporate activity and to use that value as justification to continue and expand the activity. The challenge when it comes to social media is the qualitative, viral, pervasive nature of the outcomes of social media advertising. Investments in social media generate goodwill, brand engagement, and momentum, and analysts must define how those constructs will be assessed.

Analysts have proposed several ways to calculate SMROI that are appropriate to measure the financial return on social media depending on the objective that is relevant. In addition to SMROI, we can view other returns that may be generated as a result of social media marketing efforts. Let's review some other approaches.[37]

- The **return on impressions model** demonstrates how many media impressions were generated by the social media tactics employed. An impression is simply an "opportunity to see" for the target audience. When a brand buys advertising space, it purchases opportunities for the target market to be exposed to the ad. Social media also provides impressions but the media space is not purchased. The costs are different. The opportunity for exposure to the brand message might be delivered as part of a virtual world event, on a social networking profile site, and with consumer-generated ads, product reviews, and so on. Impressions are valuable, according to this model, because we assume that impressions lead to changes in awareness, followed by changes in comprehension, changes in attitude, and ultimately changes in behavior (sales). Using the percentage of people reached who ultimately purchase as a way to calculate sales value, we can then determine a return on impressions by taking the gross revenue estimated minus the cost of the social media advertising program divided by the cost of the program. For example, if we estimate that Dunkin' Donuts earns $500,000 in gross revenue due to its Twitter presence, at a cost of $100,000 in time investment, the ROI for the microblogging activity is 400 percent.

- The **return on social media impact model** attempts to track coverage across media and in different markets against sales over time. It requires the statistical technique of *advanced multiple regression analysis* to analyze variables that may affect sales, including the mix of advertising and promotional tools used at each time and place. This approach offers the greatest potential for social media marketers, because it can include lagged measurements that control for time order of events taking place online (for instance, the timing of an event in a social world, the point at which a profile was activated, the timing of a contest conclusion, and subsequent posting of consumer-generated ads). Return on social media impact promises to determine how sales can be attributed to each element in a marketing mix and for tactics within the social media advertising strategy. Content generation and consumption is tracked and assigned algorithm scores to dictate weight of relative influence. Sales are also tracked at the same intervals and then statistical analysis is used to determine how sales trends shifted according to the timing of the social media marketing.
- The **return on target influence model** relies upon survey data to assess the effectiveness of social media marketing. Surveys assess whether participants were exposed to the social media tactics and what perceptions they formed as a result of exposure. The model then calls for calculating the change in the probability of purchase based on the exposure.
- The final approach is that of **return on earned media model.** This approach uses a metric called advertising equivalency value to equate publicity in news media outlets to its paid advertising equivalent. In other words, if a brand had paid for a mention in a specific space, what would it have cost? For social media advertising, an AEV would attempt to equate source authority, source prominence, depth of brand mention, and recommendation with a paid advertising value. To calculate advertising equivalency, the cost to purchase a display ad on a site would be used to assign a dollar value to the impressions achieved socially. For example, if a display ad on Facebook costs $50,000, we could assign an earned media value of $50,000 to a thousand page views of our brand profile on Facebook. The value can also be adjusted by the subjective importance of the earned media in question. For example, one might believe that profile visits are more valuable than a display ad rotation because it suggests that visitors sought out the brand interaction. The earned media value can be adjusted to account for variables such as the popularity of the location, the relative influence of the source, and so on. The ROI calculation is then based on the difference between the AEV and the cost of the social media advertising program divided by the cost of the program. If the AEV for the Facebook profile is $50,000 but it cost $5,000 in time for its development and maintenance, the incremental gain is $45,000. The gain divided by the cost of the program expressed as a percentage reveals an ROI of 900 percent. This measure may be among the easiest to execute for those social media spaces that also sell display advertising. However, it is not truly a return on investment measure so much as it is a measure of effective resource utilization.

CHAPTER 24

Ethics in Marketing[1]

Good ethics are a cornerstone of sustainable marketing. In the long run, unethical marketing harms customers and society as a whole. Further, it eventually damages a company's reputation and effectiveness, jeopardizing its very survival. Thus, the sustainable marketing goals of long-term consumer and business welfare can be achieved only through ethical marketing conduct.

Conscientious marketers face many moral dilemmas. The best thing to do is often unclear. Because not all managers have fine moral sensitivity, companies need to develop corporate marketing ethics policies—broad guidelines that everyone in the organization must follow. These policies should cover distributor relations, advertising standards, customer service, pricing, product development, and general ethical standards.

The finest guidelines cannot resolve all the difficult ethical situations the marketer faces. Table 24.1 lists some difficult ethical issues marketers could face during their careers. If marketers choose immediate sales-producing actions in all these cases, their marketing behavior might well be described as immoral or even amoral. If they refuse to go along with any of the actions, they might be ineffective as marketing managers and unhappy because of the constant moral tension. Managers need a set of principles that will help them figure out the moral importance of each situation and decide how far they can go in good conscience.

TABLE 24.1
SOME MORALLY DIFFICULT SITUATIONS IN MARKETING

1. Your R&D department has slightly changed one of your company's products. It is not really "new and improved," but you know that putting this statement on the package and in advertising will increase sales. What would you do?
2. You have been asked to add a stripped-down model to your line that could be advertised to pull customers into the store. The product won't be very good, but salespeople will be able to switch buyers who come into the store up to higher-priced units. You are asked to give the green light for the stripped-down version. What would you do?
3. You are thinking of hiring a product manager who has just left a competitor's company. She would be more than happy to tell you all the competitor's plans for the coming year. What would you do?
4. One of your top dealers in an important territory recently has had family troubles, and his sales have slipped. It looks like it will take him a while to straighten out his family trouble. Meanwhile, you are losing many sales. Legally, on performance grounds, you can terminate the dealer's franchise and replace him. What would you do?
5. You have a chance to win a big account that will mean a lot to you and your company. The purchasing agent hints that a "gift" would influence the decision. Your assistant recommends sending a large-screen television to the buyer's home. What would you do?
6. You have heard that a competitor has a new product feature that will make a big difference in sales. The competitor will demonstrate the feature in a private dealer meeting at the annual trade show. You can easily send a snooper to this meeting to learn about the new feature. What would you do?
7. You have to choose between three advertising campaigns outlined by your agency. The first (a) is a soft-sell, honest, straight-information campaign. The second (b) uses sex-loaded emotional appeals and exaggerates the product's benefits. The third (c) involves a noisy, somewhat irritating commercial that is sure to gain audience attention. Pretests show that the campaigns are effective in the following order: c, b, and a. What would you do?
8. You are interviewing a capable female applicant for a job as salesperson. She is better qualified than the men who have been interviewed. Nevertheless, you know that in your industry some important customers prefer dealing with men, and you will lose some sales if you hire her. What would you do?

But what principle should guide companies and marketing managers on issues of ethics and social responsibility? One philosophy is that the free market and the legal system should decide such issues. Under this principle, companies and their managers are not responsible for making moral judgments. Companies can in good conscience do whatever the market and legal systems allow.

A second philosophy puts responsibility not on the system but in the hands of individual companies and managers. This more enlightened philosophy suggests that a company should have a social conscience. Companies and managers should apply high standards of ethics and morality when making corporate decisions, regardless of "what the system allows." History provides an endless list of examples of company actions that were legal but highly irresponsible.

Each company and marketing manager must work out a philosophy of socially responsible and ethical behavior. Under the societal marketing concept, each manager must look beyond what is legal and allowed and develop standards based on personal integrity, corporate conscience, and long-run consumer welfare.

Dealing with issues of ethics and social responsibility in an open and forthright way helps to build strong customer relationships based on honesty and trust. In fact, many companies now routinely include consumers in the social responsibility process. Consider toy maker Mattel:[2]

> In fall 2007, the discovery of lead paint on several of its best-selling products forced Mattel to make worldwide recalls on millions of toys. Threatening as this was, rather than hesitating or hiding the incident, the company's brand advisors were up to the challenge. Their quick, decisive response helped to maintain consumer confidence in the Mattel brand, even contributing to a 6 percent sales increase over the same period from the year before. Just who were these masterful "brand advisors"? They were the 400 moms with kids ages 3 to 10 who constitute The Playground community, a private online network launched by Mattel's worldwide consumer insights department in June 2007 to "listen to and gain insight from moms' lives and needs." Throughout the crisis, The Playground community members kept in touch with Mattel regarding the product recalls and the company's forthright response plan, even helping to shape the post-recall promotional strategy for one of the affected product lines. Even in times of crisis, "brands that engage in a two-way conversation with their customers create stronger, more trusting relationships," says a Mattel executive.

As with environmentalism, the issue of ethics presents special challenges for international marketers. Business standards and practices vary a great deal from one country to the next. For example, bribes and kickbacks are illegal for U.S. firms, and a variety of treaties against bribery and corruption have been signed and ratified by more than 60 countries. Yet these are still standard business practices in many countries. The World Bank estimates that bribes totaling more than $1 trillion per year are paid out worldwide. One study showed that the most flagrant bribe-paying firms were from India, Mexico, China, and Russia. Other countries where corruption is common include Iraq, Myanmar, and Haiti. The least corrupt were companies from Belgium, Canada, and the Netherlands.[3] The question arises as to whether a company must lower its ethical standards to compete effectively in countries with lower standards. The answer is no. Companies should make a commitment to a common set of shared standards worldwide.

Many industrial and professional associations have suggested codes of ethics, and many companies are now adopting their own codes. For example, the American Marketing Association, an international association of marketing managers and scholars, developed the code of ethics that calls on marketers to adopt the following ethical norms:[4]

- Do no harm. This means consciously avoiding harmful actions or omissions by embodying high ethical standards and adhering to all applicable laws and regulations in the choices we make.
- Foster trust in the marketing system. This means striving for good faith and fair dealing so as to contribute toward the efficacy of the exchange process as well as avoiding deception in product design, pricing, communication, and delivery of distribution.

- Embrace ethical values. This means building relationships and enhancing consumer confidence in the integrity of marketing by affirming these core values: honesty, responsibility, fairness, respect, transparency, and citizenship.

Companies are also developing programs to teach managers about important ethical issues and help them find the proper responses. They hold ethics workshops and seminars and create ethics committees. Furthermore, most major U.S. companies have appointed high-level ethics officers to champion ethical issues and help resolve ethics problems and concerns facing employees.

PricewaterhouseCoopers (PwC) is a good example. In 2002, PwC established a global ethics office and comprehensive ethics program, headed by a high-level global ethics officer. The ethics program begins with a code of conduct called "Doing the Right Thing—the PwC Way." PwC employees learn about the code of conduct and about how to handle thorny ethics issues in comprehensive ethics training programs, which start when the employee joins the company and continue throughout the employee's career. The program also includes ethics champions around the world and channels such programs as ethics helplines to enable people to raise concerns. "It is obviously not enough to distribute a document," says PwC's former CEO, Samuel DiPiazza. "Ethics is in everything we say and do."[5]

Conclusion

Still, written codes and ethics programs do not ensure ethical behavior. Ethics and social responsibility require a total corporate commitment. They must be a component of the overall corporate culture. According to DiPiazza, "I see ethics as a mission-critical issue . . . deeply embedded in who we are and what we do. It's just as important as our product development cycle or our distribution system. . . . It's about creating a culture based on integrity and respect, not a culture based on dealing with the crisis of the day. . . . We ask ourselves every day, 'Are we doing the right things?' "[6]

CHAPTER

25

Distribution, Retailing, and Pricing[1]

Marketing Channels Explained

Think back to the last time you bought groceries. With your shopping list in hand you probably weaved your way through the aisles of a grocery store filling your cart with the items on your list (and probably some that weren't). Could you imagine how different life would be if there were no retailers? The opportunity for you to choose from a wide selection of products, in a single location (such as a grocery store), is made possible through the power of **distribution.** Distribution (or the Place element of the 4 Ps) is the process of making products available to customers. It is essential because without it, products will not be available for customers to purchase.

Several different businesses, or middlemen, participate in the movement of products from production to the point of sale. A marketing channel (or a channel of distribution) includes all the parties that are involved in the distribution process. Channels are composed of one or more intermediaries, such as a wholesaler and a retailer, with each performing a role in producing, collecting, sorting, transporting, promoting, pricing, and selling products to customers. These activities directly relate to the three marketing functions (exchange function, physical function, and facilitating function). Examples of the specific marketing functions performed by channel members include the following:

- **Exchange Function:** Negotiate price; make sales; place orders; develop communications
- **Physical Function:** Transport and store products; break bulk; create assortments
- **Facilitating Function:** Gather information; provide credit and other purchase options

Moving products through a marketing channel is expensive; 30% to 50% of the ultimate selling price of a product is attributed to distribution costs.[2] These costs entail more than freight or storage expenses; they also include the profits earned by intermediaries such as wholesalers and retailers. Manufacturers are willing to share the profits with intermediaries in exchange for the functions that they perform. A manufacturer could decide to keep more of the profits by eliminating wholesalers from the channel, but they cannot eliminate the functions that the intermediary performed.

Marketing Channels Applied

In addition to the functions they perform, channel intermediaries provide significant benefits to manufacturers. One key benefit gained through marketing channels is contact efficiency, which is explained with a hypothetical example. Assume there are six manufacturers of digital cameras and six consumers who want to buy a digital camera. As shown in Figure 25.1, each manufacturer has to directly contact six consumers, resulting in a total of 36 contact points. If a retailer was added to the mix, as shown in Figure 25.2, the number of contact points is reduced to 12. The addition of a retailer decreased the number of contacts by 67%, making the process more efficient for the consumer and the manufacturer. A retailer provides additional benefits to both consumers and other manufacturers by offering accessories for the digital camera, such as tripods, camera bags, batteries, and memory cards.

The use of marketing channels can also help to alleviate the differences between the desires of the manufacturer and those of the customer. For example, in a manufacturer's ideal world, the manufacturer would prefer to sell every product it produces, at the time it is produced, and in the location where it is produced. The customer, on the other hand, wants to buy a single unit of the product, at the time he or she needs it, and as close to home as possible. Marketing channels help overcome these differences.

FIGURE 25.1

Manufacturer-to-Customer Channel

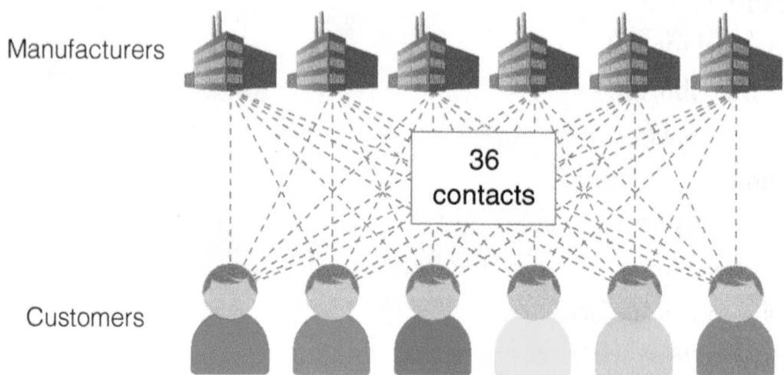

FIGURE 25.2

Manufacturer-to-Retailer-to-Customer Channel

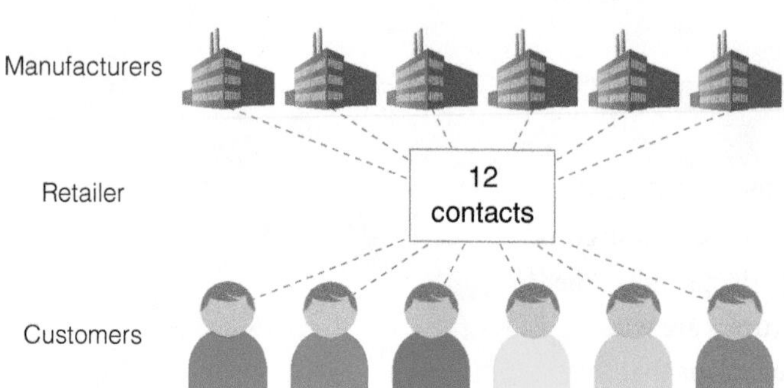

Types of Channel Intermediaries

The role of intermediaries is to improve the overall efficiency and effectiveness of the marketing channel. Channel intermediaries are classified based on whether they take ownership, or title, to the product. Resellers, which include wholesalers and retailers, take ownership of the product, while brokers and facilitators do not.

RESELLERS

- **Wholesalers**—firms that acquire large quantities of products from manufacturers and then sort, store, and resell them to retailers or businesses.
- Retailers—all channel members who are involved in selling products or services to consumers.

BROKERS

- **Agents**—people who facilitate the exchange of products but do not take title (i.e., purchase) anything that they sell.

At midnight on July 21, 2007, the final installment of the Harry Potter series of books, *Harry Potter and the Deathly Hallows*, went on sale in bookstores around the world. Anticipation among fans was palpable; some stood in line for hours so they could be among the first to own a copy. A year earlier, in 2006, the book's publisher, Scholastic, began distribution plans for 12 million copies—a record number of books for a first printing. To keep the book from slipping out in advance of the official release date, every copy had to arrive in customers' hands as close to 12:01 A.M., July 21, 2007, as possible. Given the enormity of the task, and the book's importance to its readers, Scholastic worked with printers, trucking companies, warehouses, and retailers to make Harry's final bow a complete success. If all the trucks delivering the books were lined up end to end, they would have stretched for 15 miles. The publisher used GPS (Global Positioning System) trackers on every truck to prevent shipments from getting lost. Upon receiving the books, Barnes & Noble.com separated copies according to zip code. A complicated formula was used to calculate exactly when to release a copy to the post office or UPS to guarantee simultaneous arrival across the United States.[3]

PHOTO: Scott Rothstein/Shutterstock

FACILITATORS

- Transportation Companies—organizations that assist in the distribution of products but do not take title or negotiate sales.

EXAMPLE **MARKETING CHANNELS**

Have you ever wondered how a bottle of Listerine mouthwash ends up in your local drugstore or grocery store? Every bottle travels through a series of manufacturing and distribution partners that work together to form a marketing channel:

PHOTO: EuToch/Shutterstock

- Warner-Lambert, the maker of Listerine, purchases eucalyptol, synthetic alcohol, sorbitol, menthol, citric acid, and other ingredients. These are transported to Warner-Lambert's manufacturing and distribution facility, where they are mixed together to create Listerine mouthwash.
- The product is bottled, capped, labeled, and then put in large boxes. The boxes are organized into pallets, which are then transported to the distribution center where they will remain for about two to four weeks.
- When Warner-Lambert receives an order from a retailer (such as a drugstore), the order is screened to ensure that it can be filled. Software calculates the price for the order and how much product is already in stock. If there is a shortage, additional production is scheduled.
- When the order can be filled, pallets are transported by forklift to the appropriate shipping door. Trucks are loaded with the product, and those trucks depart for the customer's warehouse.
- The trucks are unloaded at the retailer's warehouse where the Listerine is stored for as long as three weeks until it is needed.
- When one of the retailer's stores begins running low on Listerine, that store requests a shipment of additional product from the warehouse. Another software program optimizes delivery schedules for all the retailer's stores that are requesting product, and boxes of Listerine are shipped.
- Trucks unload their cargo of Listerine at each of the destination stores, where staffers place bottles on shelves.[4]

>> END EXAMPLE

Channel Strategies Explained

The goal of a channel strategy is to determine the best way of making a product available to the target market. However, the strategy must also ensure that the overall marketing objectives of the product are being supported. While a properly crafted channel strategy cannot guarantee the success of a product, an incorrect strategy will generally ensure its failure.

Channel Strategies Applied

Because a principal goal of marketing is to deliver high levels of customer satisfaction, formulating a channel strategy must begin with the target customer. Based on this, marketers must decide on the structure of the channel and how it should be organized.

Channel Structure

One of the initial decisions that marketers face in developing a channel strategy is determining how many levels of intermediaries should be used to connect the manufacturer to the end customer. Figure 25.3 illustrates the various types of business-to-consumer (B2C) and business-to-business (B2B) channels.[5] The shortest possible channel is a direct marketing channel, where the manufacturer sells directly to the end customer. One benefit of a direct channel is that it gives the manufacturer greater control

FIGURE 25.3

Business-to-Consumer and Business-to-Business Channels

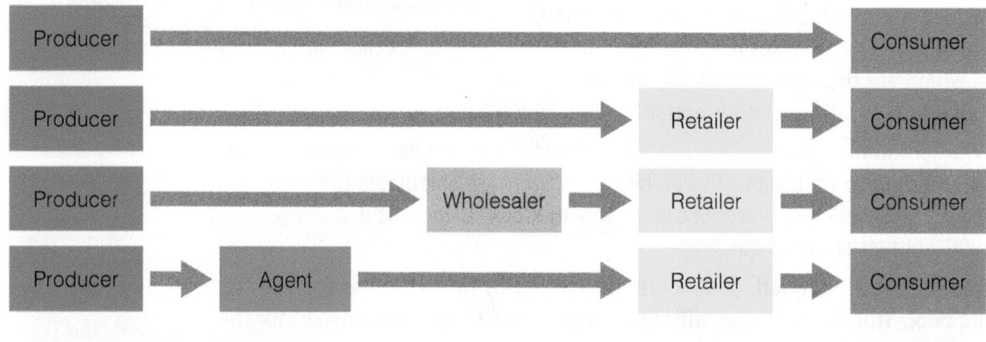

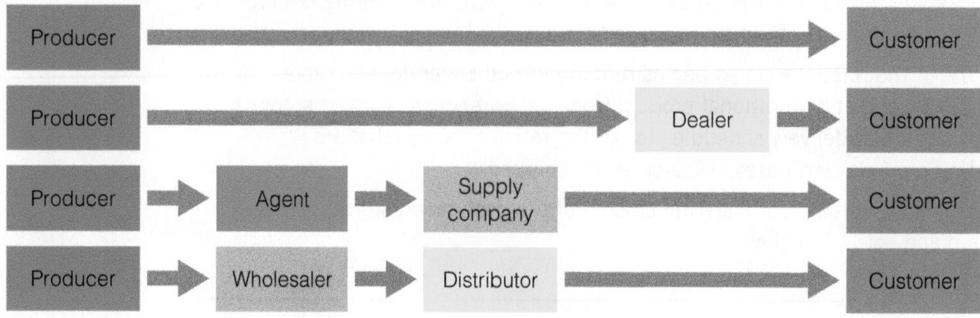

over every step of the distribution process. In this case the manufacturer must perform all the functions normally conducted by intermediaries, including sales, payment processing, delivery, and product returns.

Indirect marketing channels contain at least one intermediary, and allow manufacturers to leverage the growing importance of intermediaries. In a B2C channel, for example, many consumers have a strong affinity for specialized retailers. Stores such as The Home Depot, Best Buy, and Bed Bath & Beyond are increasingly "where customers go first" for hardware, home electronics, or housewares. Indirect channels allow manufacturers to capitalize on the specialized skills of intermediaries in the performance of transportation, storage, return, and transaction functions.

Due to changes in customer preferences and the emergence of new channel options, manufacturers are adopting multichannel distribution systems. The use of multiple distribution channels allows a manufacturer to better satisfy the needs of different customer segments more efficiently than any single channel could offer. For example, a manufacturer can sell directly to consumers through an online store, and sell its products through traditional retailers. The company's own sales force assumes the responsibilities for large retailers, while wholesalers service smaller, local or regional retailers. Under this system the consumer will have multiple locations in which to purchase the product.

In addition to the channel's length, marketers must decide on the distribution intensity, or the width of a channel level. Intensity describes the number of outlets or locations where a product will be sold. Distribution intensity is determined by a combination of a product's classification (recall from Chapter 12 as convenience, shopping, or specialty products) and the branding strategy. Convenience products generally follow an intensive distribution strategy and are sold through a large number of retail outlets so they are readily available. For example, Coca-Cola places its products in a wide variety of locations so consumers can easily locate and purchase its soft drinks. The locations are not limited to retail outlets as Coke has invested heavily in developing and placing vending machines in areas with high foot traffic. In contrast, shopping products employ a more selective distribution strategy. Consumers are willing to exert a bit more time and effort to buy an HD TV or a computer, so these kinds of shopping products are distributed more selectively, through retailers like Best Buy or department stores. Many luxury or high-ticket items use exclusive distribution, where retailers or wholesalers are given exclusive rights to sell a product. This level of intensity is frequently used to maintain a perception of exclusivity and prestige for these products.

Before deciding on the structure of the channel marketers must take several factors into consideration. The nature of the product, the characteristics of the customer, and the capabilities of the organization will all influence the optimal channel structure.

PRODUCT FACTORS The nature of the product influences channel length, type and cost of transportation, and the product's distribution intensity. Short channels (i.e., few channel members) are better suited for products that require extensive technical knowledge before the purchase (such as airplanes) or a high level of service after the purchase (such as automobiles). For products such as perishables (such as flowers or dairy products), only short channels can be used due to the potential for spoilage. Longer channels are often best for products that are standardized, durable, and less expensive.

A long channel structure is beneficial for manufacturers because wholesalers and retailers assume risks by taking ownership of the goods they carry. Products that move through long channels—tubes of toothpaste, for example—are typically purchased in small quantities by consumers, at retailers of all sizes. Establishing a direct channel with consumers, or a sending a sales team to every retailer who sells toothpaste, is impractical for manufacturers.

CUSTOMER FACTORS Marketers must determine how customers prefer to buy the product. For some customers, such as those in the business market, professional buyers prefer to purchase directly from the manufacturer. A face-to-face meeting provides the opportunity to negotiate in areas such as price and payment terms. In the B2C market, consumers are becoming more comfortable purchasing a wide range of products on the Internet. However, these consumers may require that a local retailer carry the product so they can examine the product firsthand. In business markets, if customers are concentrated in a relatively small area a short channel can be used. For example, Silicon Valley, which is located outside of San Francisco, California, is home to a high concentration of companies involved in the high-tech or computer industry. If customers require a high level of service after the sale, a shorter channel is needed. If customers require or prefer a wide assortment of products, longer channels, such as the use of retailers, will be required.

ORGANIZATIONAL FACTORS An organization may select a specific channel structure due to its own limitations. Small firms, or firms with a narrow product line, may have no other option but to utilize middlemen to reach customers. The organization may also decide to focus its efforts on product development and turn over the responsibility for sales and marketing to intermediaries such as agents or wholesalers.

Channel Organization

Channel organization defines how channel members will work together and the role each one should play. Three methods for channel organization are as follows:

- **Conventional**—Under a conventionally organized channel, each member works independently of the others, buying and selling products or services. The channel is self-regulating according to market forces.
- **Vertical Marketing System (VMS)**—A VMS exists when a firm takes on the role of another channel member, either through acquisition or by developing its own distribution capabilities. For instance, a manufacturer could vertically integrate by acquiring its own wholesale or retail business. As a result, the channel becomes more efficient due to reductions in conflict, sharing of information and resources among channel members, and greater collective-bargaining power.
- **Horizontal**—Channels are organized horizontally when two or more channel members at the same level (e.g., two or more wholesalers, two or more retailers) form an alliance. The firms may be related or unrelated in function, but they share resources and services as a means to improve channel performance.

Channel Management

Ensuring that a channel operates smoothly depends on the relationships among the channel members. Unless the manufacturer employs a vertical marketing system, each channel member will have its own objectives and profit targets. At times, the interests of one channel member will conflict with that of another, which can negatively impact the entire channel functions. Even if the conflict is between the wholesaler and a retailer, the manufacturer must be aware of and be willing to work to resolve the issue. Four general types of conflict can occur in a channel:

- **Channel conflict** refers to situations in which there is a disagreement among two or more parties in a distribution channel. For instance, a retailer may think that a wholesaler's terms and conditions are unreasonable.
- **Vertical conflict** occurs between two channel members at different levels. A wholesaler's argument with a manufacturer over access to a popular item is an example.
- **Horizontal conflict** involves channel members at the same level, such as two retailers, arguing over sales territories.
- **Multichannel conflict** refers to conflicts among multiple channel types. A manufacturer selling products through its own Web site might experience conflict with its independent brick-and-mortar retailers over pricing strategy.

A **channel leader** (also called a channel captain) is a firm with sufficient power over other channel members to take a leadership role, enforcing norms and processes. A strong leader who can establish and enforce "rules of engagement" for the channel is also a leader who can reduce conflict. Manufacturers have traditionally been channel leaders due to their ownership of powerful brands, desirable products, and access to customer information. However, retailers are increasingly taking on leadership roles because of the number of customers they influence and the increasing sophistication of their marketing approach.[6]

Marketers who successfully manage their distribution channels carefully select their channel partners on the basis of expertise and ability to cooperate. These successful marketers also work to motivate members to achieve shared objectives for the entire channel, often through training and financial incentives. The performance of channel participants is also carefully measured according to stated objectives, such as volume, profitability, and market share. Underperforming members are removed from the channel and replaced.

EXAMPLE **CHANNEL STRATEGIES**

When Hyundai decided to offer its customers a 10-year warranty on its products, it also had to begin planning for a decade-long period when repair parts might be needed to fulfill this promise.

>> END EXAMPLE

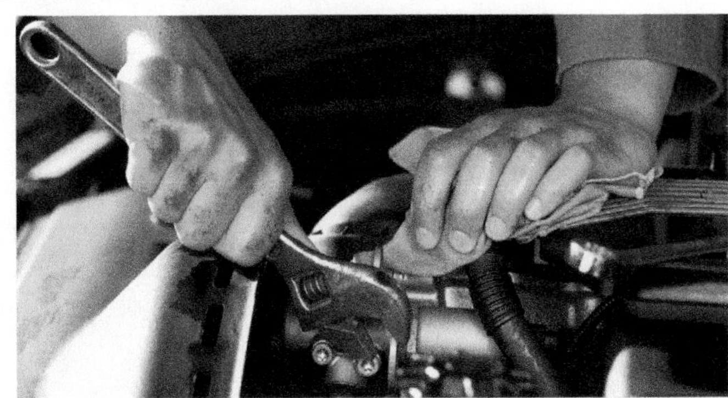

PHOTO: Jamzol/Shutterstock

Retailing Explained

The sale of products to consumers (or retailing) is performed by a broad range of organizations. For example, some manufacturers sell directly to consumers over the Internet or through their own factory outlets, and many wholesalers operate limited retail operations. However, the majority of retail sales are made through retailers, which are businesses whose primary source of revenue is generated through retailing.

Retailing Applied

To understand how important retailing is to the U.S. economy, consider these facts. Retailers generated $4.4 trillion in retail sales in 2008,[7] which represents 6.2% of the U.S. gross national product.[8] They represent almost 10% of the total businesses in the United States and employ 10.5% of the country's workforce. U.S.-based retailers are also major players in the global economy, and five of the world's largest retailers are U.S.-based companies. The top 10 U.S. retailers for 2009 are listed in Table 25.1.

Retailers are typically classified based on the products they offer, the level of service they deliver, or on the prices they charge compared to direct competitors. Products sold at retail are broadly divided into durable and nondurable goods. Durable goods, or hard goods, are products that are expected to last for three or more years. Examples of durable goods include automobiles, appliances, electronics, and furniture. Nondurable, or soft goods, are products that have a short lifespan (less than three years) and include food, apparel, health and beauty aids, and office supplies. The major types of retailers are found in Table 25.2.

TABLE 25.1
TOP 10 U.S. RETAILERS FOR 2009

RANK	NAME	HEADQUARTERS	REVENUE (IN BILLIONS)	STORE COUNT
1	Walmart	Bentonville, AK	$405.0	7,873
2	Kroger	Cincinnati, OH	76.0	3,654
3	Costco	Issaquah, WA	72.5	544
4	Home Depot	Atlanta, GA	71.2	2,274
5	Target	Minneapolis, MN	64.9	1,682
6	Walgreens	Deerfield, IL	59.0	6,934
7	CVS Caremark	Woonsocket, RI	48.9	6,981
8	Lowe's	Mooresville, NC	48.2	1,649
9	Sears	Hoffman Estates, IL	46.7	3,918
10	Best Buy	Richfield, MN	45.0	3,942

Source: www.stores.org/stores-magazine-july-2009/top-100-retailers.

Types of Retailers

Specialty stores concentrate on satisfying the specific needs of a select group of customers. These retailers typically carry a broad range of choices for a narrow product line. Employees will generally have much greater expertise in the product category and offer a higher degree of service. Examples include David's Bridal, Radio Shack, and the 150-year-old toy retailer FAO Schwarz.

Another form of specialty store that has emerged is the **category killer**. These retailers, which include the likes of Staples, Toys "R" Us, Best Buy, and The Home Depot, offer a wide selection of merchandise in a narrow product category. These stores provide a moderate level of service and expertise to customers, and generally offer lower prices than smaller competitors. The size of these stores varies based on the product category. For example, stores for office product retailer Staples average about 20,000 square feet, while home improvement retailer The Home Depot averages 100,000 square feet.

Department stores, such as Nordstrom, Macy's, and Sears, carry a wide selection of products organized by departments, such as housewares, men's and women's apparel, appliances, and luggage. Each department is generally operated as a stand-alone entity inside the store, with each having its own dedicated group of buyers. Department salespeople are usually well trained and typically work under some type of commission structure. Shoppers expect top-of-the-line brands; however, many department stores have begun establishing their own branded product lines in order to capture higher margins. Department stores average about 150,000 square feet of selling space and generate $124 to $160 in sales per square foot. Typically, apparel accounts for 50% or more of total sales.

TABLE 25.2
MAJOR CATEGORIES OF RETAILERS

RETAILER TYPE	EXAMPLES	PRODUCT LINE/ PRODUCT ASSORTMENT	LEVEL OF SERVICE	AVERAGE SIZE (SQ. FT.)	SALES PER SQ. FT.
Specialty Stores	David's Bridal, FAO Schwartz	Narrow/Deep	High	1,000–2,500	$250–$400
Category Killer	Office Max, Home Depot, Toys "R" Us	Narrow/Broad	High	20,000–150,000	$250–$350
Department Stores	Nordstrom, Sears, Kohl's	Broad/Broad	High	150,000	$124–$160
Discount Stores	Walmart, Target, Kmart	Broad/Narrow	Limited	100,000	$300–$450
Off-Price Retailers	T.J. Maxx, Big Lots	Varies	Limited	30,000	$125–$250
Superstores	Walmart Supercenter, SuperTarget	Broad/Broad	Limited	200,000	$300
Warehouse Clubs	Sam's Club, Costco	Broad/Very Narrow	Limited	150,000	$600
Supermarkets	Kroger, Publix, Safeway	Broad/Broad	Limited	47,000	$95–$115
Convenience Stores	Circle K, 7-Eleven	Narrow/Narrow	Limited	2,500	$160

One of the busiest shopping days of the year, the Friday following Thanksgiving, is more commonly referred to as "Black Friday"—a reference to the day retailers begin showing a profit for the year. In 2009, over 80 million shoppers, many of whom camped in line for up to 12 hours, spent more than $10 billion on Black Friday. Retailers spend up to six months planning for this event and, after numerous incidents where employees or shoppers were injured, the focus has been on ensuring that customers have a positive experience. As a result, many retailers have turned to experts experienced at handling events that draw large crowds, such as the Super Bowl or the Olympics, to help them manage the retail spectacle of Black Friday.

PHOTO: Dmitrijs Dmitrijevs/Shutterstock

Discount stores, such as Walmart or Target, share many similarities with department stores in that they offer a wide variety of products and are organized by departments. However, these retailers operate under an entirely different philosophy. Discount stores focus on turning products over more quickly than traditional department stores by offering lower prices.

While lower prices generally mean lower retail margins, discount stores typically have lower expenses as they offer limited service to customers. Discounters also seek cost efficiencies wherever possible. Many of these retailers, most notably Walmart, have focused on supply chain management to keep prices low. The average discount store occupies 100,000 square feet of space and generates $300 to $450 of sales per square foot.

Off-price retailers typically sell name-brand apparel and accessories at prices 20% to 50% less than specialty or department stores. These retailers continuously change the merchandise they carry based on the availability of closeout merchandise, production overruns, or factory seconds, which are products that have slight irregularities. Off-price retailers, including T.J. Maxx, Ross, and Big Lots, can acquire inventory only through manufacturer imperfections, including production mistakes and misjudgments in consumer demand. Apparel designers rely on off-price retailers to sell products that would otherwise be destroyed.

Warehouse clubs carry a limited selection of merchandise, typically about 10% to 20% of the number of items sold in grocery stores. In addition, the products offered by warehouse clubs come in large quantities or multi-packs that deliver higher value for customers and generate greater unit volume for manufacturers. Groceries typically account for the largest portion of sales revenue for warehouse clubs, followed by health and beauty products and apparel. Warehouse clubs have two streams of revenue: margins earned on the sale of products and membership fees received from consumers and businesses. With members paying between $35 to $100 per year just for the opportunity to shop, larger warehouse clubs, such as Sam's Club and Costco, can generate revenue in excess of $3 billion from membership fees alone.

Grocery stores/supermarkets are self-service retailers that carry food and nonfood items. A typical supermarket, or grocery store, can exceed 47,000 square feet and can stock up to 45,000 different SKUs, all of which are arranged in departments. Stores are normally located close to residential centers and are built to serve a relatively small area, typically a radius of between one and five miles. The U.S. retail grocery industry, to which supermarkets belong, generates over $460 billion in revenue per year and is dominated by major chains such as Kroger, Publix, and Safeway. However, the size of the industry has attracted new competitors, including Walmart, which opened a chain of 42,000-square-foot grocery stores known as Neighborhood Markets. Supermarkets face stiff competition from superstores like SuperTarget and Walmart Supercenters, and have begun offering shoppers greater convenience by leasing space to other retailers such as banks, dry cleaners, and hair salons. Grocers are also facing pressure from changes in consumer lifestyles, as Americans are spending more of their food budget eating outside the home.[9] Supermarkets are introducing prepared and ready-to-eat food sections that expand traditional deli offerings and include other ready-to-eat items such as sushi, roasted chicken, and even Thai food.

Superstores are the combination of a discount store and a grocery store. These retailers, including Walmart Supercenters, Meijer, and SuperTarget, require high customer traffic to justify their existence. A typical superstore averages around 200,000 square feet of space and offers a wider variety of products, including food, electronics, housewares, and home and garden supplies, all under a single roof. The inclusion of a broad range of products allows superstores to provide customers greater convenience and lower prices.

Convenience stores are small, self-service retailers that offer few product choices outside their primary offerings of beer, soft drinks, and snacks. These retailers, such as 7-Eleven and Circle K, average 2,500 square feet and have annual sales per square foot of $325 to $650. There are over 140,000 convenience stores in the United States, and the majority are located in high traffic areas and remain open 24 hours a day. However, shoppers pay for this convenience because these stores have higher prices than other retailers offering the same products. Eight out of 10 convenience stores also sell gasoline, and these stores sell an average of 100,000 gallons of gas each month.

Nonstore Retailing

A physical retail location is not always required to sell products to consumers. **Nonstore retailing** involves the sale of products through the use of vending machines, self-serve kiosks, the Internet, and smart phone applications. Nonstore retailing currently accounts for 4% to 6% of all retail sales, and it is expected to grow to 10% of sales within a decade. This growth is due to the key benefit that consumers gain from using nonstore retailers—convenience. Given that consumers face great constraints on their time, the ability to buy products without waiting in line or from the comfort of home is very appealing. Additionally, the shopping behaviors of Gen-Xers and millennials are vastly different from those of babyboomers. Window shopping is out; browsing online is in.

Vending machines generate over $6 billion in revenue each year and sell a wide range of products including soft drinks, snacks, hot and cold meals, gumballs, and toys. An average vending machine costs between $4,000 and $8,000 and generates sales of about $300 per week. Many retailers are installing automated retail stores (upscale vending machines) to vend products that previously could not be stocked due to security concerns. For example, Macy's is now selling personal electronics, such as iPods, GPS units, and digital cameras, through vending machines.[10]

Internet retailers recorded sales in excess of $150 billion in 2009 and this number is expected to reach almost $230 billion by 2014.[11] Retailing via the Internet is becoming more widely accepted by consumers, and 71% of adults in the United States have made a purchase online.[12] While a wide range of products can be purchased online, certain product categories tend to do especially well. For example, in 2008 more than half of all computer hardware and software sales were made online, followed by books (28%), toys and games (16%), and jewelry/luxury goods (14%).[13] Retailing on the Internet has allowed a new breed of retailers to compete without the presence of a physical store. Although Walmart is the world's largest retailer, the $3.5 billion in online sales it recorded pales in comparison to Amazon's $24.5 billion in sales.[14]

The newest form of nonstore retailing, known as **M-Commerce**, is conducted through the use of mobile devices such as smart phones. By the end of 2010, more than 126 million U.S. consumers are expected to own a smart phone. This is nearly double the 51 million smart phones that were being used in 2008. That year, consumers purchased products totaling $346 million using smart phones.[15] To date, the most popular uses of M-Commerce are in financial services such as mobile banking or stock transactions. However, as smart phone ownership grows and cellular network capabilities improve, mobile commerce will allow consumers to purchase movie tickets and snacks from vending machines, and to participate in online auctions. To capitalize on the emergence of M-Commerce, retailers have begun offering customers specially designed "apps" (short for applications) that can be used to conduct transactions with the retailer. For example, eBay offers an app that allows customers to bid on items up for auction.

PHOTO: Khomulo Anna/Shutterstock

EXAMPLE **NONSTORE RETAILING**

Visa Inc., a global payments technology company, released an iPhone application in 2009 that allows consumers to complete mobile financial purchase transactions by waving their handset in front of a contactless payment terminal. According to the Smart Card Alliance, 150,000-plus merchant locations in the United States accept contactless payments, including Office Depot, AMC movie theaters, Walgreens, CVS, 7-Eleven, Arby's, McDonald's, PetCo, and Subway.

>> END EXAMPLE

Retail Strategies Explained

A retail strategy is established in order to satisfy the business objectives of the organization. As the primary business objective is profitability, a retailer must balance its desires with potential margins. A **retail margin** is the difference between a product's retail selling price and its wholesale cost. As such, a retailer's overall profitability is determined by: (1) the amount of merchandise sold, (2) the retail margin on the merchandise, and (3) the store's overall operating expenses. The strategy crafted by the retailer will impact all three of these elements, and each of these elements influences the others. For example, a retailer can't offer top-quality designer clothing, provide a high level of service to customers, and offer discounted prices. While volume may be high, the retail margin will be too small to cover the high operating costs.

Retail Strategies Applied

Developing a retail strategy begins with an understanding of the wants and needs of the target customer. As such, retailers face the same type of decisions that manufacturers address in developing new products. They use segmentation to select a target market and then establish a position in the retail market space that is appealing to target customers. Next, they decide on the elements of the **retail marketing mix**, which are the product, price, place, and promotion. The product in this case involves decisions about **merchandise assortment**, the level of service to offer, and the store's atmospherics, which are the design and décor of the store. The elements of the retail marketing mix are shown in Figure 25.4.

FIGURE 25.4

The Retail Marketing Mix

Merchandise Assortment

Decisions regarding merchandise assortment determine the breadth and depth of product lines to carry, as well as the amount of each product to stock. For example, Toys "R"Us carries a broad selection of products in a single category, while Walmart carries a narrow selection of products across many categories. In making merchandise decisions, retailers must account for target customers, as well as current and future competitors. Merchandise decisions should be made with the goal of attracting a large enough target market while differentiating the retailer from competitors. Retailers must also take into account the demographics of the local population to ensure that the right styles, sizes, and colors are available when customers are ready to purchase. Retailers must determine if the focus will be on well-known name brands or if **private label products** should be offered. Private label goods have grown in importance for retailers over the past few decades as the products offer retailers higher margins. For example, Kirkland Signature, Costco's private label brand, currently accounts for 20% of the retailer's total sales. As margins are significantly higher than national brands, the company is aggressively working to increase private label sales to 37%.

Level of Service

The service level of a retailer typically ranges between full-service and self-service. **Full-service retailers** are typically high-end specialty and department stores where sales personnel provide assistance during, and even after, a customer's visit. Salespeople have a high degree of knowledge of the product category and their expertise is valued by customers. **Self-service retailers**, on the other hand, provide only a minimal level of service; contact between customers and employees is typically limited to when the sale is made. **Limited-service retailers** provide assistance to customers upon request. These retailers, such as Best Buy or Sears, allow customers to serve themselves, but also have knowledgeable sales associates available to offer guidance. The products a retailer stocks typically determine the level of service offered—specialty goods require more services than do convenience goods—however, the retail strategy determines the degree of service provided. For many retailers carrying similar merchandise, especially those competing for the same target customers, offering more services is often the only means of differentiation. Providing more services increases labor costs, resulting in lower margins.

Atmospherics

A store's **atmospherics**, which include layout, furnishings, color scheme, and music, establish the image customers have of a retailer. The physical environment will determine if shoppers enter a retailer and how long they remain. The layout of a store determines how easy it is for shoppers to navigate the aisles. Grocers, such as Kroger, design stores so that shoppers need to navigate through the majority of the store to find the most often purchased products, such as bread, produce, and milk. Fixtures and furnishings also signal the image of the retailer. Warehouse clubs, such as Costco, use steel racks to stack pallets of merchandise. This no-frills, low-expense approach matches the low price expectations of shoppers. High-end specialty stores are appointed with fine wood displays and decorative lighting to convey luxury and elegance.

The music a retailer plays is carefully selected to reinforce the store's image. As such, apparel retailers like American Eagle Outfitters use decidedly different music than upscale women's clothing stores like Ann Taylor. Music is also used to influence shopper behavior. For example, shoppers spend less time, on average, in a store that plays up-tempo music and spend more time in stores that feature slower, softer music. Older shoppers are typically more sensitive to a store's selection of music than are younger shoppers, and 40% of consumers surveyed indicated that they have left a store because of the music being played.[16]

Location

Assuming that the decision has been made to have physical locations, a retailer has a wide range of options regarding where stores are placed. The decision about where to locate a store is determined by multiple factors, including the product and the target customer. For example, many shoppers will drive several hundred miles to visit an Ikea store; however, they will not drive more than a few minutes to visit a grocery store or pharmacy. When making their selection, retailers must balance a location's cost with the area's traffic, which is the number of people or cars that pass by a location. A destination retailer, such as Bass Pro Shops, can choose a low-cost location away from population centers. The retailer's popularity ensures that consumers will shop at their location. However, most retailers require locations with high traffic counts and, thus, locate within malls or shopping centers. Even in the face of competition, many retailers have elected to open locations close to each other to ensure an adequate level of traffic.

Promotion

A retailer's promotional efforts often focus on creating awareness of a store's grand opening or an upcoming sale. Retailers use a wide variety of promotional tools, including advertising, public relations, and sales promotion, to generate customer traffic in the store. No matter the promotional tool, retailers must ensure that the message being sent is consistent with the store image. Because of its local content and customer expectations, newspapers are used by many retailers, especially specialty stores and supermarkets. Retailers are also using the Internet to reach out to customers by providing information on upcoming sales or offering special deals and discounts.

Retail Price Policy

A retail price policy establishes the level at which prices will be set compared to competitors. Retailers must ensure that the policy is consistent with the positioning or image of the store. Retailers can take an upscale approach, trading lower volume for higher margins, or they can offer discount prices that result in higher volume. Retailers can also use parity pricing by setting prices at the same level as competitors.

This strategy is effective if the retailer can differentiate itself in some other way such as service level, merchandise assortment, or location. In many instances, a retailer's pricing strategy is narrowed considerably by the decisions made about the other elements of the retail marketing mix. Retailers with higher expenses, whether due to enhanced services, upscale furnishings, and/or an expensive location, typically require higher retail margins to achieve profitability.

EXAMPLE **RETAIL STRATEGIES**

Known for its innovative approach to cosmetics retailing, Sephora operates more than 750 stores on three continents. Most cosmetics have traditionally been sold in department stores, alongside furniture, electronics, and hardware. Sephora has built a niche for itself as a specialty retailer, similar to chains like Ikea, Best Buy, or The Home Depot. Sephora offers customers a unique shopping experience by focusing its retailing strategy on innovation, exclusivity, and customer service. The following are key points in that strategy:

PHOTO: Brian Chase/Shutterstock

- **Merchandise**—Sephora carries exclusive product brands, such as Benefit Cosmetics, Stila, Philosophy, and Perricone MD, that aren't widely available. As Bare Escentuals CEO Leslie Blodgett said, "Sephora is a trailblazer . . . it takes brands that seemingly no one else will and turns them into stars."
- **Promotion**—Unlike department stores, Sephora doesn't invest heavily in advertising but relies on positive customer experiences to generate favorable word-of-mouth promotion.
- **Location**—Sephora attempts to secure high-traffic locations in cities or malls. Such locations draw people into the stores. There is a Sephora store on the Champs-Elysées in Paris and on Fifth Avenue in New York City.
- **Atmosphere**—The concept for Sephora stores is perhaps its greatest innovation. Products are displayed in an open-sell environment without glass cases, so shoppers can touch, compare, and sample the items. Each store's distinctive black-and-white decorating scheme draws attention to the colorful product packages that are on display.
- **Pricing**—Prices are generally on par with department stores, but Sephora attempts to deliver better value through product selection, store atmosphere, and customer service. Coaches are even trained to create made-to-order products for customers by mixing cosmetics to match individual color and skin tones.
- **Customer service**—Sephora invests heavily in employee training, so that its salespeople become "beauty coaches" who provide detailed information and assistance to customers.

As of 2009, Sephora continues to increase its sales through expansion into worldwide markets.[17]

>> END EXAMPLE

Wholesaling Explained

Wholesaling involves the redistribution of products to retailers, institutions, and government agencies. A **wholesaler** is a firm that purchases products from manufacturers and resells them to retailers and industrial buyers. There are more than 430,000 wholesalers in the United States, and these channel members handle over 50% of all products sold.[18] In addition to the physical movement of products, wholesalers perform other essential functions in distribution channels. They store goods until consumers need them. They simplify product, payment, and information flows between producers and customers. They inject capital into businesses by providing cash in advance of product sales to customers. They may even assume responsibility for technical support and order processing, thereby making life easier for manufacturers.[19]

Wholesaling Applied

Although wholesalers have been in existence for centuries, their widespread use began in the nineteenth century as manufacturers began to mass-produce products. Wholesalers expanded the market coverage area of a manufacturer and enabled regional brands to become national brands. Even today, many retailers would not have access to the products on their shelves without wholesalers. The same is also true for manufacturers because they would not have access to the markets being served by smaller retailers.

Wholesalers sell a variety of products, from components essential for the manufacture of finished goods (e.g., bicycle seats) to supplies used to conduct everyday business activities (e.g., paper clips). Some wholesalers specialize in a particular category of products, while others sell a broad range.

PHOTO: Kenneth V. Pilon/Shutterstock

EXAMPLE **WHOLESALING**

With more than 15 million square feet of storage space spread out across 11 states, C&S Wholesale Grocers is the largest food wholesaler in the United States. The 90-year-old company carries more than 95,000 different products, including produce, meat and dairy products, health and beauty aids, and candy. C&S Wholesale services over 4,000 independent supermarkets and regional chain stores such as Target, Safeway, Pathmark, and Giant Food Stores. In 2008, Forbes magazine ranked C&S Wholesaler the 12th largest private company in the United States. The wholesaler strives to deliver value to its retail customers, and part of the company's vision is to have "Braggingly happy customers."

>> END EXAMPLE

Types of Wholesalers

Wholesalers can be classified in a number of ways. They can be identified based on the products they carry, how products are distributed, or by the services they perform. The most often used method of classifying a wholesaler is based on if they take title, or ownership, of the product. The U.S. Census of Wholesale Trade uses this method and classifies wholesalers as either (1) merchant wholesalers, (2) agents and brokers, or (3) manufacturers' branches. Table 25.3 identifies the types of wholesalers, along with the products they typically carry and their likely customers.

TABLE 25.3
CATEGORIES OF WHOLESALERS

WHOLESALER TYPE	PRODUCTS CARRIED	CUSTOMER	DESCRIPTION
Merchant Wholesalers			
Full-service			
General merchandise	Pharmaceuticals, groceries, machine parts	Supermarkets, hardware stores	Offers high level of service to customers; can offer narrow or broad range of products
Specialty line	Health food, oriental foods	Specialty retailers	Typically offers a single product line, provides high level of service and support
Limited-service			
Cash-and-carry	Groceries, building materials, office supplies	Small businesses	Buyers purchase products at wholesaler's location, pays cash, and self-transports
Mail-order	Computer hardware, jewelry, sporting goods	Small retailers, industrial firms	Catalogs are used in place of a sales force; customers may have no other means of acquiring products
Drop shippers	Bulk products such as coal, timber	Retailers, wholesalers	Take title to products, but generally do not take possession; orders are shipped by manufacturers
Truck jobbers	Produce, bread, milk	Supermarkets, restaurants	Sales of perishable goods to regular group of customers who pay in cash
Rack jobbers	Nonfood items such as toys, magazines and books, health/beauty aids	Supermarkets, small retailers	Merchandise placed in stores on consignment; jobber keeps merchandise in stock and fresh
Agents and Brokers			
Manufacturers' agents	Apparel, furniture, raw materials	Retailers, manufacturers	Are used in place of a manufacturer's sales force; agents work assigned territories; little control over pricing
Selling agents	Coal, textiles, timber	Manufacturers	Assume full marketing duties for the producer; have authority over pricing and promotional decisions
Commission merchants	Agricultural goods such as wheat, livestock	Industrial buyers, manufacturers	Take possession, but not title. Earn a commission on the sale; seek to sell at highest possible price
Merchandise brokers	Food, insurance, real estate	Retailers, manufacturers, developers	Hired by either the buyer or the seller; paid when transaction is completed

Merchant Wholesalers

Merchant wholesalers encompass the broad group of wholesalers that take title to the products that are purchased from manufacturers. While most of these wholesalers take possession of the products, not all do. Wholesalers purchase merchandise in bulk from manufacturers and then sell in smaller quantities to their customers, which are retailers, businesses, or other wholesalers. Wholesalers are typically granted the exclusive rights to sell a manufacturer's products in a protected geographic area. Manufacturers will contract with enough merchant wholesalers to ensure that products are available throughout the entire market. There are two broad types of merchant wholesalers, full-service wholesalers and limited-service wholesalers.

Full-service wholesalers assume many responsibilities that otherwise would be performed by manufacturers. In addition to the sales function, these wholesalers service customers by extending credit and providing delivery of products. Full-service wholesalers usually have a broader understanding of the market and share this expertise with their customers and manufacturers. **General merchandise wholesalers** carry a wide assortment of merchandise in a broad product category, such as pharmaceuticals or groceries. Customers for these wholesalers vary between nationwide retail chains and small regional wholesalers. General merchandise wholesalers work with their customers to help sell more products and may include advertising and promotional allowances or shelf design services. **Specialty line wholesalers** focus on a single product line, such as health food, and may cover a wide geographic area. They are highly knowledgeable about the product category and the consumer. Specialty line wholesalers are willing to share their knowledge with customers to increase product sales.

Limited-service wholesalers perform fewer services for manufacturers but may be the best or only way to reach the markets they serve. **Cash-and-carry wholesalers** provide few services but offer low prices on the limited number of goods they carry. Customers must travel to these wholesalers' locations, pay for their purchases in cash, and transport their purchases back to their retail store or business. For retailers who are unable to establish accounts with larger, full-service wholesalers, cash-and-carry wholesalers offer the only means necessary to acquire products. **Mail-order wholesalers** employ catalogs or the Internet as their salesforce. Many small businesses must use mail-order wholesalers because they lack access to other types of wholesalers due to their location or size. Computer hardware, office supplies, and costume jewelry are all commonly sold through mail-order wholesalers. **Drop shippers** take title to products but never take possession. By taking title, drop shippers assume all risks until the product is delivered to the buyer. These wholesalers carry no inventory, instead placing an order with the manufacturer after a sale is made. Drop shippers are used primarily for products that require a lot of space, such as coal and timber. **Jobbers** are wholesalers that operate on a relatively small scale and sell and provide services primarily to retailers. Jobbers are active in many industries ranging from automotive parts to textiles.

Agents and Brokers

Agents and brokers are independent businesses that may take possession of products but never take title. Compensation is typically commission-based, payable upon the completion of a transaction. Where some agents and brokers perform only sales, others may assume greater responsibilities over all of a manufacturer's marketing activities. **Manufacturers' agents**, for example, are used as a replacement for a manufacturer's sales team. These independent agents are responsible for all sales in an assigned territory, and they represent several manufacturers of noncompeting, related products. Manufacturers' agents have little control over the selling price of the products they carry. **Selling agents**, on the other hand, are often responsible for a wider range of marketing activities in addition to the sales function. These agents have more flexibility with regards to pricing and promotional activities than do manufacturers' agents. **Commission merchants** take physical possession of products but do not take title. Once the products are sold, these merchants collect payment from the buyer, subtract the agreed-upon commission, and then make payment to the seller. They are widely used for commodity products such as copper, livestock, and wheat. In a retail setting, eBay and Sotheby's Art Auction House are examples of commission merchants. **Merchandise brokers** focus on linking buyers and sellers together. They are generally well known in the area they specialize in and can be hired by either the buyer or the seller. Merchandise brokers are often used to assist in the negotiation process and are paid a fee or commission upon the completion of the transaction.

Manufacturers' Branches

In lieu of a wholesaler, many organizations elect to perform all channel duties themselves. A **manufacturer-owned intermediary** offers benefits in a number of ways. For example, manufacturers will earn greater profit margins and have more control over inventory and the sales process by eliminating an intermediary such as a wholesaler. As a form of a vertically integrated channel, manufacturer-owned intermediaries create efficiencies for large firms. A **sales branch** maintains inventory for a company in different geographic areas. On the other hand, **sales offices** carry no inventory but provide selling services for specific geographic areas. A **manufacturer's showroom** is a facility where a firm's products are permanently on display for customers to view. Any purchases are then fulfilled from distribution centers or warehouses.[20]

Establishing Prices Explained

Science fiction author Robert Heinlein is credited with popularizing the acronym TANSTAAFL, which stands for "There Ain't No Such Thing As A Free Lunch."[21] Whether you prefer to eat at Subway or Panera Bread, this saying holds true. Whenever you make a purchase, an exchange is taking place—you are giving up one thing in order to have another. A price is the formal expression of the value of this exchange.

Although consumers weigh a price carefully when making a purchase decision, the literal price is only part of a product's value. It is a product's perceived value that determines whether it will be purchased, not just its price. Value is a consumer's subjective evaluation of the ratio of the benefits of a product or service to its price. This concept is captured in a simple formula:

$$\text{Value} = \frac{\text{Benefits}}{\text{Price}}$$

A "good value" or a "good deal" is an instance where the ratio of product benefits to price is large. These benefits could be functional benefits, emotional benefits, or a combination of both. Your jacket may not only keep you dry in the rain (a functional benefit), but if it carries a prestigious brand name, it may also make you feel special when wearing it (an emotional benefit).

Price is the marketing mix variable that translates a product's or service's value into monetary terms. If a product is seen to have greater value, it should also have a higher price. The converse is also true, because marketers are forced to cut prices when items decline in perceived value.

Value is a relative concept, because customers will compare alternative products to find the one that offers the most benefits at the least cost. Because price is part of the value equation, whenever any competitor in a market raises (or lowers) its price, the value of every other product is affected. Beyond price, marketers add value for customers by improving the following:

- Product reliability
- Product performance
- Longevity
- Cost (both initial cost and lifetime cost)
- User and environmental safety
- Service (delivery reliability, speed, and flexibility)
- Superior aesthetics or design
- Prestige

Fair prices are those consumers perceive as offering good value and meeting personal and social norms. Unfair prices can evoke strong negative emotion. Companies must be careful to establish fair prices, which convey both value and fair dealing, or they risk alienating customers.

The Apple iPod has been an incredible success, with sales ranging from 50 to 60 million units per year. In addition to breakthrough design and innovative advertising, pricing has been a cornerstone of the iPod marketing strategy. Apple follows a price-lining strategy that positions newer versions of its players or those with the most advanced features at higher price points. For example, consider the following:

- The iPod Shuffle is the smallest and most portable version of the iPod, but has the least amount of storage. Its price begins at $49.
- The iPod Nano is larger than the Shuffle, but can hold more songs and play video. Its price starts at $149.
- The iPod Touch responds to touch and movement like the iPhone and has a starting price of $199.
- The iPod Classic boasts 160GB of storage that can hold 40,000 songs, 200 hours of video, or 25,000 photos and begins at $249.

By offering players at a range of prices, Apple has expanded the number of customers who can afford an iPod. An additional benefit is the opportunity to up-sell a consumer to a $149 Nano when that customer was originally interested in a $49 iPod Shuffle. Apple's profit stream does not end with the sale of its MP3 players. By selling individual songs on its iTunes Web site for around a dollar, the company further extends its revenue stream over time and enhances the value of each iPod.[22]

PHOTO: Joseph Moore/Shutterstock

Establishing Prices Applied

Among the elements of the marketing mix, price is most closely linked with revenue. The activities of product development, promotion, and distribution are considered to be costs with, at best, only an indirect ability to encourage sales. For example, although a clever advertising campaign may encourage brand preference over the long term (and possibly an increase in sales), it is easier to understand how a price adjustment leads to a short-term change in revenue.

Prices are dynamic and constantly changing, but they are a clear reflection of marketplace value in a free market system. They are affected by changes in economic conditions, such as recessions, in which the disposable incomes of consumers fall, or to the introduction of a new product by a competitor, which may offer customers a better value. Pricing must also be aligned with the firm's overall marketing strategy and the product's brand positioning. If the products of an upscale brand (like Gucci) are priced too low, are always on sale, or are a "deal," the company risks an erosion of its brand equity. Price can even be an indicator of quality or superiority. The price–quality ratio describes this relationship: Higher-priced products are assumed to have better quality. Lower-priced products are assumed to have lesser quality, regardless of actual product performance. Prices must be carefully calibrated with regard to pricing objectives, market structure, cost, and customer demand.

Market Structure

Market structure refers to the state of a market with respect to competition. Market structure defines the boundaries of a firm's pricing flexibility. In theory, an individual firm is either a price "maker" with the ability to set prices above those of its competitors, or a price "taker" who must accept the marketplace price for its products or services. Economists recognize four types of market structures:

- **Monopoly**—A single firm is able to act as a price "maker," often due to product exclusivity (such as a patent) or high barriers to competitive entry. This gives a monopoly substantial **pricing power**, which is the ability to set a high price without a significant deterioration in market share. For example, patents on new drugs grant pharmaceutical companies monopoly power by restricting competition. Only the owner of a patent can sell the formulation of a drug, and any firms caught copying or simulating the patented product face legal sanctions. Although they are defended as essential for funding advanced drug research and development, monopolies resulting from patent protection can lead to prices almost 10 times above the competitive market price.
- **Oligopoly**—A small group of firms that shares pricing power through its collective ability to control prices, usually by restricting product supply. Cartels such as OPEC are the modern-day equivalent of oligopolies. For oligopolies to function, they depend on cooperation between member companies, who must agree to meet price and production targets. This can lead to a market price for the products of all member firms that is higher than any single company could achieve on its own.
- **Monopolistic competition**—A limited number of firms compete by offering products with varying degrees of differentiation. In this market structure, individual firms have a moderate ability to set higher prices, depending on customer demand for their specific brand. Nike, Reebok, and Adidas all make tennis shoes. But their products differ in terms of design, materials, and brand image. Each company may charge a price premium to the degree that its shoes are more appealing than those of its competitors. At the same time, monopolistic competition cannot function like a monopoly because if prices are raised too high, customers will defect to competitors.
- **Pure competition**—A large number of producers sell mostly undifferentiated products, like wheat or soybeans. No particular brand of wheat or soybeans is preferred by consumers, so no producer has any appreciable pricing power. In purely competitive situations, companies usually deemphasize price as part of the marketing mix.

Due to globalization and the proliferation of product choices, today's marketplace is highly competitive. Evidence of this is the increasing failure of both start-up and long-standing businesses. Once-healthy and vibrant sectors like banks, automobiles, and airlines are under increasing pressure to reduce prices, cut costs, and consolidate operations. In response, some American firms have outsourced portions of their business, such as customer service or finance, to countries with lower labor costs. Economic cycles, globalization, the proliferation of product choices, and business failures lead to increased competition on the basis of price and downward pressure on profits. It is essential for marketing managers to aggressively manage costs in these situations.

Cost-Based Pricing

In addition to market structure, the cost to manufacture a product or deliver a service should be taken into account. Three common ways to group costs are as follows:

- **Fixed costs** (or overhead) are those costs associated with a product incurred regardless of any production or sales taking place.
- **Variable costs** are costs directly attributable to the production of a product or the delivery of a service.
- **Total cost** is the sum of fixed and variable costs.

For example, the Air Transport Association reports the Quarterly Cost Index on U.S. Passenger Airlines, which divides airline operating expenses into various categories. Variable costs such as fuel, food, labor, and marketing add up to about 85% of total operating cost. Insurance, landing fees, aircraft rents, and other miscellaneous items make up the remainder of the costs.[23]

To earn a profit, a firm must generate revenue that exceeds its total costs. The relationship between a company's profit, revenue, and costs is as follows:

$$\text{Profit} = \underset{\substack{\uparrow \\ \boxed{\text{Price}} \times \text{Sales}}}{\text{Revenue}} - \underset{\substack{\uparrow \\ \text{Fixed Cost} \\ + \\ \text{Variable Cost}}}{\text{Total Costs}}$$

A product's **profit margin** is the difference between its price and total cost per unit. Because revenue is a function of sales volume times price per unit, improving the margin will also increase profitability. **Cost-based pricing** (or cost-oriented) approaches to pricing recognize the need to establish a price that offsets costs and results in a reasonable profit margin or rate of return.

A traditional cost-based method for setting margins is the **cost-plus pricing** approach, which adds a fixed amount to the cost of each item sufficient to earn a desired profit. The additional amount, or margin, added to each product is called a **markup** and is calculated as a percentage of unit variable cost. Although some people use the terms interchangeably, a markup is technically not the same thing as a margin. A markup determines a price based on product cost, while a margin is determined by the difference between the final price and unit cost. Table 25.4 compares margin and markup for a hypothetical product.[24] Let's take the first and last examples from the table and demonstrate how margin and markup are calculated:

You buy a $9.00 widget from ACME company and sell it to your customer Sue for $10.00. Your margin is $1.00, or 10% of the sales price of $10.00. Your markup is $1.00, or 11% of your purchase price of $9.00.

Let's say that you buy a $2.50 widget from ACME company and sell it to your customer Sue for $10.00. Your margin is $7.50, or 75% of the sales price of $10.00. Your markup is $7.50, or 300% of your purchase price of $2.50.

TABLE 25.4
RELATIONSHIP BETWEEN MARGIN AND MARKUP

PRICE	COST	MARGIN	MARKUP
$10.00	$9.00	10%	11%
$10.00	$7.50	25%	33%
$10.00	$6.67	33%	50%
$10.00	$5.00	50%	100%
$10.00	$4.00	60%	150%
$10.00	$3.33	67%	200%
$10.00	$2.50	75%	300%

Margin and markup, therefore, are two methods that calculate profit from different perspectives. From this example, you can see that a 10% margin generated more profit than a 10% markup.

Another cost-based technique for setting price is to calculate a product's **break-even point**, which is a projected price and sales volume where a company "breaks even," or earns revenue exactly equal to its total cost.

At the break-even point, profits are zero. If a firm can sell one additional unit beyond the break-even point, it will earn a profit equal to the margin on that product. Because each additional sale contributes to the bottom line, the gap between price and variable cost is also called a **contribution margin.** The formula used to calculate a break-even point (in units) is as follows:

$$\text{Break-Even Volume} = \frac{\text{Fixed Cost}}{\text{Price} - \text{Variable Cost}}$$

For instance, suppose a product sells for $50. If the product costs $10 per unit to manufacture, and the company's fixed costs are $60,000, then break-even volume is 1,500 units, or

$$1{,}500 \text{ units} = \frac{\$60{,}000}{\$50 - 10}$$

Break-even analysis is helpful to marketers because it clarifies, for a given price, the minimum number of products a company must sell to stay in business. When performing a break-even analysis, marketers find it helpful to calculate the break-even formula at various price points. In Figure 25.5, the firm's variable cost per unit is $5, fixed costs are $40,000, and price per unit is $10.

In this example, the break-even point is 8,000 units. It should be immediately apparent that any quantity to the left of the break-even point (below 8,000 units) will result in a net loss for the firm, because total cost will be greater than total revenue (represented by the red shaded area). Any sales volume above 8,000 units will be profitable (the green shaded area). Based on this information, the product price is adjusted upward or downward until a volume is reached that the marketing group believes is both achievable and profitable. A firm might use a rate of return on investment (such as 10% or 15% on total cost) or a target amount of profit as its criteria.

FIGURE 25.5

The Break-Even Formula of Various Price Points

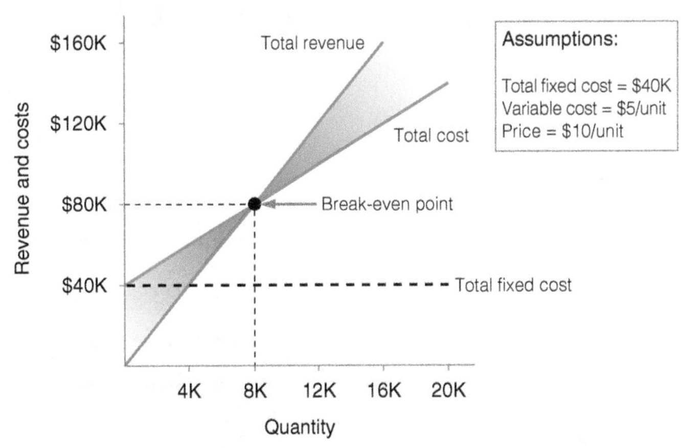

The main advantage to using cost-based pricing methods is that they are relatively easy to calculate. Once costs have been estimated, you simply determine the markup needed to earn a target amount of revenue (or offset fixed costs plus a satisfactory amount of profit). One drawback, however, is that this approach ignores customer demand for the product. It is based solely on cost and desired profit. If fixed or variable costs are too high relative to competition, then using a cost-based approach can lead to an uncompetitive price. If the products offered by competitors are comparable in terms of brand image and performance, a cost-based pricing method will dictate a price that is too high for the marketplace. Customers will not pay a higher price without added benefits. The marketing challenge then becomes how to find a way to make the product more attractive without adding cost, or to reduce fixed, variable, or total costs.

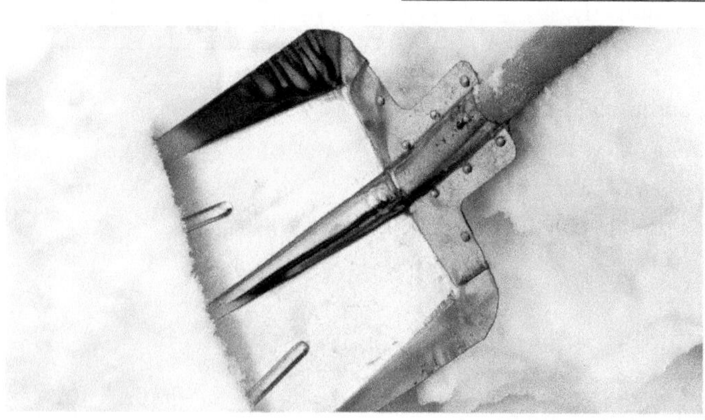

PHOTO: Fedor A. Sidorov/Shutterstock

EXAMPLE **COST-BASED PRICING**

Dr. Sarah Maxwell is an expert in the theory and practice of fair pricing. Two components of fairness are personal fairness and social fairness. Personal fairness is how people perceive that a price affects them personally. Social fairness is how people judge that a price is fair to society in general.

All price increases may be personally unfair to a degree, but the situation can be made worse, depending on how socially unfair they seem. Dr. Maxwell conducted an interesting study that asked two separate groups of people to consider two different imaginary pricing scenarios:

- The first group was told that a hardware store had been selling snow shovels for $15, but raised the price to $20 after a snowstorm. They were then asked to rate this action as completely fair, acceptable, unfair, and very unfair.
- For the second group, the scenario and questions were identical to the first, with the omission of any reference to a snowstorm. When a storm was not mentioned, 69% of people in the second group found the price increase to be unfair, compared with 86% in the first group. Both groups perceived the price increase to be unfair, most likely due to the negative personal impact of paying a higher price (that is, personal fairness). But the second group also saw the price change as socially unfair, as evidenced by the higher percentage who rated the store's action unfavorably. Raising prices to "take advantage" of a snowstorm was perceived as unfair both to individuals and to society.[25]

>> END EXAMPLE

Pricing Strategies Explained

A pricing strategy includes all activities that convey and enhance the value of a purchase. As already discussed, a price must convey a product's value to customers. It also needs to be fair, or consumers will defect to competitors. There are dimensions to pricing strategy that go beyond the traditional notion of a "price," however. Each of the following is also an example of a pricing strategy:

- Offering a discount when a customer pays within 30 days
- Giving a new-car buyer a trade-in value for his or her old vehicle
- Earning points for purchases when using a retailer's credit card

None of these examples change the literal "price" of the product. The quoted or sticker price remains unchanged. But they all have an impact on the perceived value the customer is receiving and, as a result, are part of pricing strategy.

Pricing objectives are goals that keep marketing actions in alignment with overall business objectives. Any marketing strategy or tactic that influences price or perceived customer value should meet the firm's pricing objectives. Different pricing objectives include the following:

- **Profitability**—to maximize profit or to achieve a target profit level
- **Volume**—to maximize volume or market share
- **Meeting competition**—to remove price as a differentiator by matching competitor prices
- **Prestige**—to create an image of exclusiveness and quality by setting a high price

Pricing Strategies Applied

Should the price for a product be set above, equal to, or below its competition? When setting prices, marketers follow a stepwise process:

1. Develop pricing objectives.
2. Estimate demand.
3. Determine costs.
4. Evaluate the pricing environment.
5. Choose a pricing strategy.
6. Develop pricing tactics.

Steps 1 through 4 have already been discussed in this chapter. Step 5 involves choosing the pricing strategy that is most appropriate, given the product or service. Strategies vary depending on the newness of the product, as well as where it will be sold. In Step 6, a company implements its strategy and monitors the results.

EXAMPLE **PRICING STRATEGIES**

Many of us enjoy a really tasty hamburger. But not all hamburgers are created (or priced) qual. Restaurants charge different prices for their burgers, according to the unique characteristics of their products and their pricing objectives. Here are some examples:

PHOTO: Joao Virissimo/Shutterstock

- **Profitability**—Applebee's sells a cheeseburger for about $7. It is not the cheapest burger, nor the most expensive, but it is sold at a price adequate to cover costs and earn a little profit.
- **Volume**—White Castle sells cheeseburgers for about 70 cents. This low price is designed to maximize sales volume—and encourage you to buy a sack full of cheeseburgers!
- **Meeting competition**—Both McDonald's and Burger King sell cheeseburgers for around $1. Because their cheeseburgers are basic, prices are essentially equal,

and marketing emphasis shifts to promotions, for example, movie tie-ins or kids' meal prizes.

- **Prestige**—A Burger Royale at the DB Bistro Moderne in New York City sells for $32. It is a sirloin burger stuffed with short ribs and foie gras (maybe the restaurant will add a slice of cheese gratis). The ingredients are high quality, but customers are also paying for the prestige of a burger prepared by some of New York's top chefs.

>> END EXAMPLE

New Product and Service Pricing Strategies

Suppose that you are planning to introduce a totally new product into the marketplace. Perhaps it is an amazing innovation that offers customers surprising benefits they simply will not be able to find anywhere else. The fixed and variable costs for this product are known to you, but what price should you charge? There is probably a segment of customers who are eager to obtain the product at almost any price, or who will certainly pay a premium for it. At the same time, there is another group who like the product, but are unwilling to pay a higher price. This segment will try the product only if it is sold at a low price, which reduces their risk of purchase.

A **skimming price** is set above the marketplace price for similar products or services, usually with the objective of maximizing revenue or profit. Much like a farmer might skim cream from a pail of milk, this strategy attempts to skim out of the market those customers who are willing to pay a higher price. Early adopters who want the latest and greatest technology will pay more for a new product when it is first introduced, even though prices may fall dramatically 12 to 18 months later. Using a skimming price is only feasible when the new product or service has clear, meaningful advantages over alternatives in the market. The main advantage of a skimming price is that it "does not leave money on the table" and it earns the maximum possible margin for the company on each product sold.

When a **penetration price** is used, the product or service is offered at a low price compared to its competition. Although a product may be sufficiently appealing to command a higher price, and therefore is a candidate for a skimming strategy, a marketer might prefer to set a low price so as to quickly generate sales volume, market segment penetration, and production scale. According to the experience curve theory, costs to manufacture a product will decline as volume increases. This is because when manufacturing is done at higher volumes, companies are able to buy their inputs in larger, cheaper quantities. They also become more skilled and efficient in their manufacturing processes. As a result, even though margins and profits may be slight at first, they should increase over time as costs fall. The firm also gains from brand recognition as a top-selling product in its category. Table 25.5 outlines when a skimming or a penetration price is most appropriate.[26]

Most products and services are not breakthrough, market-changing innovations. Instead, they are incremental improvements to existing products or line extensions under already well-known brand names. Skimming or penetration pricing strategies can be appropriate, but marketers must fully understand consumer perceptions of the product and its pricing power. Marketers should also keep in mind that competitors will react to whatever pricing strategy is employed and attempt to capitalize on vulnerabilities.

TABLE 25.5
PROPER USE OF SKIMMING AND PENETRATION PRICING

USE A SKIMMING PRICE WHEN . . .	USE A PENETRATION PRICE WHEN . . .
■ The product performs better than alternatives.	■ Demand is very elastic.
■ Early adopters will value the product highly.	■ Producing higher quantities can reduce costs.
■ Demand is initially inelastic.	■ The threat of competitor imitation is strong.
■ A company cannot meet expected demand.	■ No segment is willing to pay a higher price.
■ The goal is to position the product as high quality.	■ A low price may prevent competitors from entering the market.
■ A company wants to avoid a price war.	

EXAMPLE **NEW PRODUCT AND SERVICE PRICING STRATEGIES**

PHOTO: Dusan Zidar/Shutterstock

Every day, ballpoint pens are used by millions of people. The basic design of each pen is similar and includes a barrel, ink cartridge, and pocket clip. Simple versions employ a cap to keep ink fresh, while others are spring activated by a push button. For some customers, ballpoint pens are merely a means to an end: a way to write a school paper or a quick note. For other customers, they might be a high-involvement specialty product and convey an image of prestige or exclusiveness based on the brand of pen or its heritage. As a result, marketers of ballpoint pens follow different pricing strategies:

- The BIC brand uses a penetration pricing strategy to generate high sales volume. BIC targets a large segment of consumers who view ballpoint pens as purely functional, disposable devices. A package of 12 BIC pens might sell for $3 to $4 (or as little as 25 cents per pen).
- Mont Blanc targets a smaller group of customers who are highly involved with their pens and view them as fashion items or exclusive collectibles. The brand uses a skimming pricing strategy because its buyers will pay a premium for top quality and craftsmanship. Mont Blanc rollerballs can run $300, or more than 2,000 times the price of a disposable pen.[27]

>> END EXAMPLE

Online and Storefront Pricing Strategies

Before the Internet emerged as another place for customers to buy (or sell) products, people bought the majority of their goods and services through traditional retail channels like grocery stores, mass merchandisers, or other "brick and mortar" businesses. **Storefront pricing** (also called offline pricing) refers to prices established for products or services sold through these kinds of traditional sales channels.

Today, the Internet is an important part of global commerce, with players like Amazon .com becoming a major force in online retailing. **Online pricing** is the process of setting prices for products or services sold over the Internet or through an electronic medium. When developing a pricing strategy, depending on its distribution methods, a firm may use online pricing, offline pricing, or a combination of both.

The Internet's primary effect on pricing strategy has been in the area of **cost transparency**, which is the ability of consumers to understand a firm's true costs. Information about prices is readily abundant, easy to find, and free to anyone with a computer and Internet connectivity. A seller's costs and profit margins become more transparent to its customers. In the past, if you wanted to understand the true cost of a product or whether a price was fair, you had to visit many different storefront locations to collect pricing data. Few customers had the time or willingness to do this. Internet pricing sites like Priceline.com will provide this information quickly and for free. Table 25.6 displays price differences for contact lenses sold both online and offline.[28]

From the marketer's perspective, although cost transparency may be good for consumers' pocketbooks, it also makes online pricing more difficult. Cost transparency has four effects on pricing strategy:[29]

- It erodes high margins because consumers have a better understanding of product costs.
- It can turn products and services into commodities that can be sold only at a common market price.
- It may weaken customer loyalty to brands (if margins are perceived as unfair).
- It can create a perception of price unfairness (if customers feel they are paying too much).

Although marketers can never put the Internet genie back into the bottle, there are strategies marketers can deploy to offset the impact of online cost transparency. A company may use **price lining** (also called **tiered pricing** or **versioning**) to create different prices for different products and services. This technique is commonly used by telecommunications companies that offer various plans at different price points based on customer needs. **Dynamic pricing** (or **"smart" pricing**) is the practice of varying prices based on market conditions, differences in the cost to serve customers, or in the value customers place on a product. When airlines charge a higher fare to business travelers who attempt to book a flight at the last minute, they are leveraging the power of dynamic pricing. Marketers should be cautious in setting dynamic prices, because customers may feel they have been treated unfairly or could even bring accusations of price discrimination.

TABLE 25.6
ONLINE AND STOREFRONT PRICING COMPARISONS FOR CONTACT LENSES

	AVERAGE ALL LENSES	AVERAGE SPHERICAL	AVERAGE SPECIALTY
All online	$ 87.92	$65.51	$119.85
All offline	$107.95	$81.89	$146.36
Offline premium	$ 20.03	$16.38	$ 26.51

Auction Pricing Strategies

"Going once . . . going twice . . . sold!" is the phrase we commonly associate with auctions, in which buyers and sellers engage in an adjudicated process of offer and counteroffer until a price acceptable to both parties is reached. A **forward auction** happens when a buyer puts forth what he or she is seeking to purchase and sellers respond in kind with bids (or prices). Forward auctions end when a bid that is high enough for the seller and low enough for the buyer is reached. In contrast, a **reverse auction** takes place when a buyer communicates not only his or her specifications for the product or service, but also an exact price he or she is willing to pay. If one or more companies are willing to accept the buyer's price, then the reverse auction is complete.

Until recently, the auction process has been used most often in business-to-business contexts. Online auction sites, such as eBay.com, have popularized the notion of negotiating prices in the business-to-consumer and consumer-to-consumer realms. Many customers no longer accept the sticker price and expect that they will be able to negotiate. Respected brands, unique products, and store location (screen placement) can help protect margins. However, new competitors and more powerful price comparison sites are popping up on a daily basis, so marketers must be prepared to negotiate without giving up too much profit.

It is critical for marketers conducting online auctions or price negotiations with customers to understand the **incremental cost** leading to an online sale. These costs include not only the wholesale costs of the product or service, but also the expected click-through fees paid to platforms. **Click-through fees** are the amount one online entity charges another online entity for passing along a Web user who clicks an ad or link. On price-comparison sites, these fees range from 40 cents to as much as $1.50 or more. Knowing the incremental cost helps marketers more accurately gauge their potential profitability during an auction and establish a price "floor," which tells them when to stop or decline a sale.

EXAMPLE **AUCTION PRICING STRATEGIES**

Many consumers view eBay and similar auction services available at Yahoo!, Amazon.com, or Google as the modern-day alternative to classified ads, flea markets, or plain old word of mouth. You do not need to be a corporation with a multi-million-dollar marketing budget to be a retailer. Just make your sales pitch on eBay and see who turns up!

eBay has become the world's most popular online auction site, selling over $60 billion worth of gross merchandise volume annually through its marketplace channels. One of the main selling points for eBay, or for any online auction, is that it keeps prices low by "cutting out the middleman" and encouraging negotiation. Buyers and sellers are able to interact one-on-one without the need for additional markups (except for commissions or listing fees charged by the site). Dedicated shoppers use strategies like sniping, where they hold off making a bid until the last seconds before an auction expires. Professional snipers even install software such as Auction Sentry or HammerSnipe on their PCs to let them monitor multiple auctions simultaneously and bid more quickly.[30]

PHOTO: Dmitriy Shironosov/Shutterstock

>> END EXAMPLE

Portfolio Pricing Strategies

A product portfolio is the collection of all products and services offered by a company. When a company owns a large portfolio of products, pricing decisions focus on whether to charge a similar price across brands or to vary a price according to brand and product type. For example, Samsung sells LCD, plasma, and DLP (digital light projection) televisions under a variety of sub-brand names (such as Series 6). Should all of these products be priced in a similar fashion? Should some have higher percentage margins than others? Should all products within a related product line follow a line pricing strategy?

FIGURE 25.6

Price Ceiling, Price Floor, and Their Effects on Product Pricing

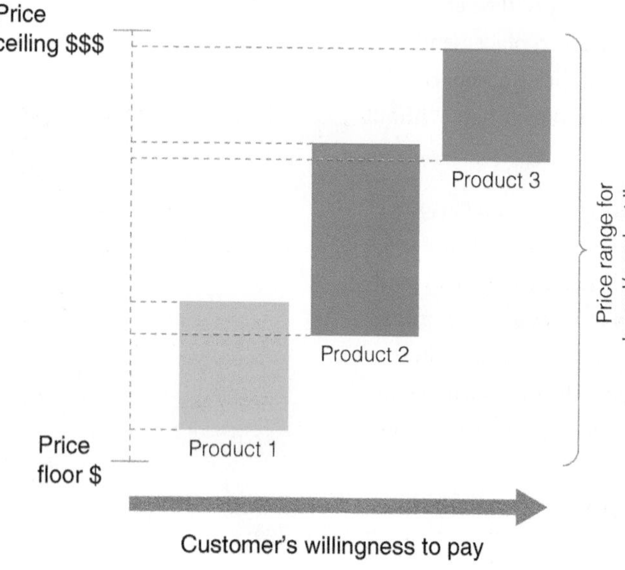

Each product line usually has a price ceiling, which is the price below which all products in that line will be priced. A product line also might have a price floor, which is the price above which all products within a line will be priced. The price ceiling and floor create a price range for the product line, and individual products are priced anywhere between the two bounds. Over time, price ranges come to be associated with brand names. If a marketer sets a price outside the brand's normal price range, either higher or lower, the product's value may be suspect. The brand's image must be broad enough to accommodate this kind of stretch in its price range. Figure 25.6 illustrates how different products may be priced within a brand's price floor and ceiling.

Although there is a degree of overlap in pricing between some products, all prices remain within the price range for the entire product line. They do not exceed the boundaries established by the price ceiling and floor. The same principles apply to portfolios that include multiple product lines and brands. In the illustration, simply replace "Product 1" with "Product Line A" or "Brand X."

As with the majority of pricing questions, a sound portfolio pricing strategy begins with an understanding of customer wants, needs, and willingness to pay. Marketers should then overlay individual product performance compared to competition. If portfolio pricing is not properly managed, then the firm will risk product cannibalization (due to excessive overlaps in price) or erosion in brand equity.

Price Adjustment Strategies

A quoted or sticker price is not necessarily the final price that a customer pays. In some cases, marketers may choose to reduce prices due to competitive pressures, cost advantages, or product improvements. The most straightforward method is to cut the selling price, but once a price is lowered, it may be tough to raise it again. As an alternative, marketers employ several price adjustment strategies to lower the actual price paid by customers, while leaving the MSRP intact:

- **Cash discount**—Customers paying in cash are given a percentage or fixed amount off the quoted price.
- **Quantity discount**—Buying a larger quantity of an item results in a discount per item purchased.
- **Trade-in**—A customer is given cash value for an item in trade toward the new purchase.
- **Rebate**—A manufacturer makes a cash payment back to a customer who has purchased their product at full price.

Reducing prices too often can lead to damaging price wars with other firms. Suppose one firm reduces the price of its products. A competitor may react by lowering its prices in turn. Then, the first company may be tempted to reduce price even further. A price war happens when two firms become locked in a downward spiral of constantly reducing prices in reaction to each other. No one wins a price war because if it continues long enough, it will eventually wipe out everyone's profits.

EXAMPLE **PRICE ADJUSTMENT STRATEGIES**

Pizza restaurants have had difficult times in recent years. Foreign demand for dairy products has sent cheese prices skyrocketing, and droughts in the United States propelled flour prices to all-time highs. All this combined with economic challenges in the U.S. economy have diminished demand.

PHOTO: Hywit Dimyadi/Shutterstock

In the past, product quality and customer service drove market share. With more customers looking for discounts in today's tighter economy, pizza retailers are using low prices as the primary tool to win more business. Combined with higher ingredient costs, price wars among pizza makers are squeezing profit margins.

To avoid the negative consequences of price competition, pizza makers are looking for new ways to maximize revenue and reduce cost. Technology is an answer for some, and more stores are giving customers the option of ordering online or by cell-phone texting. Operators say that check averages for online orders are 10% higher because the Web allows customers to discover items they did not know about. A Papa John's in Louisville, Kentucky, even uses a computer-controlled oven that does not burn at full power until a sufficient number of orders are received.[31]

>> END EXAMPLE

Conclusion

A marketing channel can be short and direct, such as when a manufacturer sells directly to a customer. Or it can include intermediaries, such as wholesales and retailers that facilitate the movement of product from the manufacturer to the end customer. No matter which channel a manufacturer chooses to use, the functions of a channel must be performed by someone.

Retailers and wholesalers provide valuable services to manufacturers, for which they earn a percentage of the retail selling price. From buying merchandise in bulk from manufacturers to providing a location for consumer to buy, the wide assortment of brands that is available to consumers would not be possible without these two channel members. Retailing accounts for a significant portion of America's economy and retailers continuously look for ways to attract customers to their stories.

Pricing is perhaps the most dynamic element of the marketing mix because it is constantly changing in reaction to competitive pressures and marketplace shifts. At the most fundamental level, prices depend on marketplace structure, costs, demand, and price elasticity. Once these factors are understood, marketers overlay pricing practices such as legal or bidding requirements. Final pricing strategies are then developed based on the nature of the product (new or existing), where it will be sold (online offline, or in an auction), its role in a portfolio, and the need to make pricing adjustments.

Marketing and Management by the Numbers[1]

APPENDIX A

Marketing managers are facing increased accountability for the financial implications of their actions. This appendix provides a basic introduction to measuring marketing financial performance. Such financial analysis guides marketers in making sound marketing decisions and in assessing the outcomes of those decisions.

The appendix is built around a hypothetical manufacturer of consumer electronics products—HD. The company is introducing an Internet TV Blu-ray disc player that plays Blu-ray and 3-D video discs as well as videos and television programming streamed over the Internet on high-definition and 3-D televisions. In this appendix, we will analyze the various decisions HD's marketing managers must make before and after the new-product launch.

The appendix is organized into three sections. The *first section* introduces pricing, break-even, and margin analysis assessments that will guide the introduction of HD's new product. The *second section* discusses demand estimates, the marketing budget, and marketing performance measures. It begins with a discussion of estimating market potential and company sales. It then introduces the marketing budget, as illustrated through a *pro forma* profit-and-loss statement followed by the actual profit-and-loss statement. Next, we discuss marketing performance measures, with a focus on helping marketing managers to better defend their decisions from a financial perspective. In the *third section,* we analyze the financial implications of various marketing tactics.

Each of the three sections ends with a set of quantitative exercises that provide you with an opportunity to apply the concepts you learned to situations beyond HD.

Pricing, Break-Even, and Margin Analysis

Pricing Considerations

Determining price is one of the most important marketing-mix decisions. The limiting factors are demand and costs. Demand factors, such as buyer-perceived value, set the price ceiling. The company's costs set the price floor. In between these two factors, marketers must consider competitors' prices and other factors such as reseller requirements, government regulations, and company objectives.

Most current competing Internet TV Blu-ray disc player products sell at retail prices between $100 and $600, but some are over $1,000. We first consider HD's pricing decision from a cost perspective. Then, we consider consumer value, the competitive environment, and reseller requirements.

fixed costs
Costs that do not vary with production or sales level.

variable costs
Costs that vary directly with the level of production.

total costs
The sum of the fixed and variable costs for any given level of production.

DETERMINING COSTS Recall from Chapter 10 that there are different types of costs. **Fixed costs** do not vary with production or sales level and include costs such as rent, interest, depreciation, and clerical and management salaries. Regardless of the level of output, the company must pay these costs. Whereas total fixed costs remain constant as output increases, the fixed cost per unit (or average fixed cost) will decrease as output increases because the total fixed costs are spread across more units of output. **Variable costs** vary directly with the level of production and include costs related to the direct production of the product (such as costs of goods sold—COGS) and many of the marketing costs associated with selling it. Although these costs tend to be uniform for each unit produced, they are called variable because their total varies with the number of units produced. **Total costs** are the sum of the fixed and variable costs for any given level of production.

HD has invested $10 million in refurbishing an existing facility to manufacture the new media phone product. Once production begins, the company estimates that it will incur fixed costs of $20 million per year. The variable cost to produce each device is estimated to be $125 and is expected to remain at that level for the output capacity of the facility.

Setting Price Based on Costs

cost-plus pricing (or markup pricing)
A standard markup to the cost of the product.

HD starts with the cost-based approach to pricing discussed in Chapter 10. Recall that the simplest method, **cost-plus pricing** (or **markup pricing**), simply adds a standard markup to the cost of the product. To use this method, however, HD must specify expected unit sales so that total unit costs can be determined. Unit variable costs will remain constant regardless of the output, but *average unit fixed costs* will decrease as output increases.

To illustrate this method, suppose HD has fixed costs of $20 million, variable costs of $125 per unit, and expects unit sales of 1 million players. Thus, the cost per unit is given by:

$$\text{Unit cost} = \text{variable cost} + \frac{\text{fixed costs}}{\text{unit sales}} = \$125 + \frac{\$20{,}000{,}000}{1{,}000{,}000} = \$145$$

Note that we do *not* include the initial investment of $10 million in the total fixed cost figure. It is not considered a fixed cost because it is not a *relevant* cost. **Relevant costs** are those that will occur in the future and that will vary across the alternatives being considered. HD's investment to refurbish the manufacturing facility was a one-time cost that will not reoccur in the future. Such past costs are *sunk costs* and should not be considered in future analyses.

relevant costs
Costs that will occur in the future and that will vary across the alternatives being considered.

Also notice that if HD sells its product for $145, the price is equal to the total cost per unit. This is the **break-even price**—the price at which unit revenue (price) equals unit cost and profit is zero.

break-even price
The price at which total revenue equals total cost and profit is zero.

Suppose HD does not want to merely break even but rather wants to earn a 25 percent markup on sales. HD's markup price is:[2]

$$\text{Markup price} = \frac{\text{unit cost}}{(1 - \text{desired return on sales})} = \frac{\$145}{1 - 0.25} = \$193.33$$

This is the price at which HD would sell the product to resellers such as wholesalers or retailers to earn a 25 percent profit on sales.

Another approach HD could use is called **return on investment (ROI) pricing** (or **target-return pricing**). In this case, the company *would* consider the initial $10 million investment, but only to determine the dollar profit goal. Suppose the company wants a 30 percent return on its investment. The price necessary to satisfy this requirement can be determined by:

return on investment (ROI) pricing (or target-return pricing)
A cost-based pricing method that determines price based on a specified rate of return on investment.

$$\text{ROI price} = \text{unit cost} + \frac{\text{ROI} \times \text{investment}}{\text{unit sales}} = \$145 + \frac{0.3 \times \$10{,}000{,}000}{1{,}000{,}000} = \$148$$

That is, if HD sells its product for $148, it will realize a 30 percent return on its initial investment of $10 million.

In these pricing calculations, unit cost is a function of the expected sales, which were estimated to be 1 million units. But what if actual sales were lower? Then the unit cost would be higher because the fixed costs would be spread over fewer units, and the realized percentage markup on sales or ROI would be lower. Alternatively, if sales are higher than the estimated 1 million units, unit costs would be lower than $145, so a lower price would produce the desired markup on sales or ROI. It's important to note that these cost-based pricing methods are *internally* focused and do not consider demand, competitors' prices, or reseller requirements. Because HD will be selling this product to consumers through wholesalers and retailers offering competing brands, the company must consider markup pricing from this perspective.

Setting Price Based on External Factors

Whereas costs determine the price floor, HD also must consider external factors when setting price. HD does not have the final say concerning the final price of its product to consumers—retailers do. So it must start with its suggested retail price and work back. In doing so, HD must consider the markups required by resellers that sell the product to consumers.

markup
The difference between a company's selling price for a product and its cost to manufacture or purchase it.

In general, a dollar **markup** is the difference between a company's selling price for a product and its cost to manufacture or purchase it. For a retailer, then, the markup is the difference between the price it charges consumers and the cost the retailer must pay for the product. Thus, for any level of reseller:

$$\text{Dollar markup} = \text{selling price} - \text{cost}$$

Markups are usually expressed as a percentage, and there are two different ways to compute markups—on *cost* or on *selling price*:

$$\text{Markup percentage on cost} = \frac{\text{dollar markup}}{\text{cost}}$$

$$\text{Markup percentage on selling price} = \frac{\text{dollar markup}}{\text{selling price}}$$

To apply reseller margin analysis, HD must first set the suggested retail price and then work back to the price at which it must sell the product to a wholesaler. Suppose retailers expect a 30 percent margin and wholesalers want a 20 percent margin based on their respective selling prices. In addition, suppose that HD sets a manufacturer's suggested retail price (MSRP) of $299.99 for its product.

HD selected the $299.99 MSRP because it is lower than most competitors' prices but is not so low that consumers might perceive it to be of poor quality. In addition, the company's research shows that it is below the threshold at which more consumers are willing to purchase the product. By using buyers' perceptions of value and not the seller's cost to determine the MSRP, HD is using **value-based pricing**. For simplicity, we will use an MSRP of $300 in further analyses.

value-based pricing
Offering just the right combination of quality and good service at a fair price.

To determine the price HD will charge wholesalers, we must first subtract the retailer's margin from the retail price to determine the retailer's cost ($300 – ($300 × 0.30) = $210). The retailer's cost is the wholesaler's price, so HD next subtracts the wholesaler's margin ($210 – ($210 × 0.20) = $168). Thus, the **markup chain** representing the sequence of markups used by firms at each level in a channel for HD's new product is:

markup chain
The sequence of markups used by firms at each level in a channel.

Suggested retail price:	$300
minus retail margin (30%):	–$ 90
Retailer's cost/wholesaler's price:	$210
minus wholesaler's margin (20%):	–$ 42
Wholesaler's cost/HD's price:	$168

By deducting the markups for each level in the markup chain, HD arrives at a price for the product to wholesalers of $168.

Break-Even and Margin Analysis

The previous analyses derived a value-based price of $168 for HD's product. Although this price is higher than the break-even price of $145 and covers costs, that price assumed a demand of 1 million units. But how many units and what level of dollar sales must HD achieve to break even at the $168 price? And what level of sales must be achieved to realize various profit goals? These questions can be answered through break-even and margin analysis.

DETERMINING BREAK-EVEN UNIT VOLUME AND DOLLAR SALES Based on an understanding of costs, consumer value, the competitive environment, and reseller requirements, HD has decided to set its price to wholesalers at \$168. At that price, what sales level will be needed for HD to break even or make a profit on its product? **Break-even analysis** determines the unit volume and dollar sales needed to be profitable given a particular price and cost structure. At the break-even point, total revenue equals total costs and profit is zero. Above this point, the company will make a profit; below it, the company will lose money. HD can calculate break-even volume using the following formula:

break-even analysis
Analysis to determine the unit volume and dollar sales needed to be profitable given a particular price and cost structure.

$$\text{Break-even volume} = \frac{\text{fixed costs}}{\text{price} - \text{unit variable cost}}$$

The denominator (price - unit variable cost) is called **unit contribution** (sometimes called contribution margin). It represents the amount that each unit contributes to covering fixed costs. Break-even volume represents the level of output at which all (variable and fixed) costs are covered. In HD's case, break-even unit volume is:

unit contribution
The amount that each unit contributes to covering fixed costs—the difference between price and variable costs.

$$\text{Break-even volume} = \frac{\text{fixed cost}}{\text{price} - \text{variable cost}} = \frac{\$20{,}000{,}000}{\$168 - \$125} = 465{,}116.2 \text{ units}$$

Thus, at the given cost and pricing structure, HD will break even at 465,117 units.

To determine the break-even dollar sales, simply multiply the unit break-even volume by the selling price:

$$\text{BE sales} = \text{BE}_{vol} \times \text{price} = 465{,}117 \times \$168 = \$78{,}139{,}656$$

Another way to calculate dollar break-even sales is to use the percentage contribution margin (hereafter referred to as **contribution margin**), which is the unit contribution divided by the selling price:

contribution margin
The unit contribution divided by the selling price.

$$\text{Contribution margin} = \frac{\text{price} - \text{variable cost}}{\text{price}} = \frac{\$168 - \$125}{\$168} = 0.256 \text{ or } 25.6\%$$

Then,

$$\text{Break-even sales} = \frac{\text{fixed costs}}{\text{contribution margin}} = \frac{\$20{,}000{,}000}{0.256} = \$78{,}125{,}000$$

Note that the difference between the two break-even sales calculations is due to rounding.

Such break-even analysis helps HD by showing the unit volume needed to cover costs. If production capacity cannot attain this level of output, then the company should not launch this product. However, the unit break-even volume is well within HD's capacity. Of course, the bigger question concerns whether HD can sell this volume at the \$168 price. We'll address that issue a little later.

Understanding contribution margin is useful in other types of analyses as well, particularly if unit prices and unit variable costs are unknown or if a company (say, a retailer) sells many products at different prices and knows the percentage of total sales variable costs represent. Whereas *unit contribution* is the difference between unit price and unit variable costs, *total contribution* is the difference between total sales and total variable costs. The overall contribution margin can be calculated by:

$$\text{Contribution margin} = \frac{\text{total sales} - \text{total variable costs}}{\text{total sales}}$$

Regardless of the actual level of sales, if the company knows what percentage of sales is represented by variable costs, it can calculate the contribution margin. For example, HD's unit variable cost is \$125, or 74 percent of the selling price (\$125 ÷ \$168 = 0.74). That means for every \$1 of sales revenue for HD, \$0.74 represents variable costs, and the difference (\$0.26) represents contribution to fixed costs. But even if the company doesn't know its unit price and unit variable cost, it can calculate the contribution margin from total sales and total variable costs or from knowledge of the total cost structure. It can set total sales equal to 100 percent regardless of the actual absolute amount and determine the contribution margin:

$$\text{Contribution margin} = \frac{100\% - 74\%}{100\%} = \frac{1 - 0.74}{1} = 1 - 0.74 = 0.26 \text{ or } 26\%$$

Note that this matches the percentage calculated from the unit price and unit variable cost information. This alternative calculation will be very useful later when analyzing various marketing decisions.

Determining "Break Even" for Profit Goals

Although it is useful to know the break-even point, most companies are more interested in making a profit. Assume HD would like to realize a \$5 million profit in the first year. How many units must it sell at the \$168 price to cover fixed costs and produce this profit? To determine this amount, HD can simply add the profit figure to fixed costs and again divide by the unit contribution to determine unit sales:

$$\text{Unit volume} = \frac{\text{fixed cost} + \text{profit goal}}{\text{price} - \text{variable cost}} = \frac{\$20{,}000{,}000 + \$5{,}000{,}000}{\$168 - \$125} = 581{,}395.3 \text{ units}$$

Thus, to earn a \$5 million profit, HD must sell 581,396 units. Multiply this amount by price to determine the dollar sales needed to achieve a \$5 million profit:

$$\text{Dollar sales} = 581{,}396 \text{ units} \times \$168 = \$97{,}674{,}528$$

Or use the contribution margin:

$$\text{Sales} = \frac{\text{fixed cost} + \text{profit goal}}{\text{contribution margin}} = \frac{\$20{,}000{,}000 + \$5{,}000{,}000}{0.256} = \$97{,}656{,}250$$

Again, note that the difference between the two break-even sales calculations is due to rounding.

As we saw previously, a profit goal can also be stated as a return on investment goal. For example, recall that HD wants a 30 percent return on its \$10 million investment. Thus, its absolute profit goal is \$3 million (\$10,000,000 × 0.30). This profit goal is treated the same way as in the previous example:[3]

$$\text{Unit volume} = \frac{\text{fixed cost} + \text{profit goal}}{\text{price} - \text{variable cost}} = \frac{\$20{,}000{,}000 + \$3{,}000{,}000}{\$168 - \$125} = 534{,}884 \text{ units}$$

$$\text{Dollars sales} = 534{,}884 \text{ units} \times \$168 = \$89{,}860{,}512$$

Or

$$\text{Dollar sales} = \frac{\text{fixed cost} + \text{profit goal}}{\text{contribution margin}} = \frac{\$20{,}000{,}000 + \$3{,}000{,}000}{0.256} = \$89{,}843{,}750$$

Finally, HD can express its profit goal as a percentage of sales, which we also saw in previous pricing analyses. Assume HD desires a 25 percent return on sales. To determine the unit and sales volume necessary to achieve this goal, the calculation is a little different from the previous two examples. In this case, we incorporate the profit goal into the unit contribution as an additional variable cost. Look at it this way: If 25 percent of each sale must go toward profits, that leaves only 75 percent of the selling price to cover fixed costs. Thus, the equation becomes:

$$\text{Unit volume} = \frac{\text{fixed cost}}{\text{price} - \text{variable cost} - (0.25 \times \text{price})} \text{ or } \frac{\text{fixed cost}}{(0.75 \times \text{price}) - \text{variable cost}}$$

So,

$$\text{Unit volume} = \frac{\$20{,}000{,}000}{(0.75 \times \$168) - \$125} = 20{,}000{,}000 \text{ units}$$

$$\text{Dollar sales necessary} = 20{,}000{,}000 \times \text{units} \times \$168 = \$3{,}360{,}000{,}000$$

Thus, HD would need more than $3 billion in sales to realize a 25 percent return on sales given its current price and cost structure! Could it possibly achieve this level of sales? The major point is this: Although break-even analysis can be useful in determining the level of sales needed to cover costs or to achieve a stated profit goal, it does not tell the company whether it is *possible* to achieve that level of sales at the specified price. To address this issue, HD needs to estimate demand for this product.

Before moving on, however, let's stop here and practice applying the concepts covered so far. Now that you have seen pricing and break-even concepts in action as they relate to HD's new product, here are several exercises for you to apply what you have learned in other contexts.

Marketing by the Numbers Exercise Set One

1. Sanborn, a manufacturer of electric roof vents, realizes a cost of $55 for every unit it produces. Its total fixed costs equal $2 million. If the company manufactures 500,000 units, compute the following:
   a. unit cost
   b. markup price if the company desires a 10 percent return on sales
   c. ROI price if the company desires a 25 percent return on an investment of $1 million
2. An interior decorator purchases items to sell in her store. She purchases a lamp for $125 and sells it for $225. Determine the following:
   a. dollar markup
   b. markup percentage on cost
   c. markup percentage on selling price
3. A consumer purchases a toaster from a retailer for $60. The retailer's markup is 20 percent, and the wholesaler's markup is 15 percent, both based on selling price. For what price does the manufacturer sell the product to the wholesaler?
4. A vacuum manufacturer has a unit cost of $50 and wishes to achieve a margin of 30 percent based on selling price. If the manufacturer sells directly to a retailer who then adds a set margin of 40 percent based on selling price, determine the retail price charged to consumers.

5. Advanced Electronics manufactures DVDs and sells them directly to retailers who typically sell them for $20. Retailers take a 40 percent margin based on the retail selling price. Advanced's cost information is as follows:

DVD package and disc	$2.50/DVD
Royalties	$2.25/DVD
Advertising and promotion	$500,000
Overhead	$200,000

Calculate the following:

a. contribution per unit and contribution margin

b. break-even volume in DVD units and dollars

c. volume in DVD units and dollar sales necessary if Advanced's profit goal is 20 percent profit on sales

d. net profit if 5 million DVDs are sold

Demand Estimates, the Marketing Budget, and Marketing Performance Measures

Market Potential and Sales Estimates

HD has now calculated the sales needed to break even and to attain various profit goals on its new product. However, the company needs more information regarding demand in order to assess the feasibility of attaining the needed sales levels. This information is also needed for production and other decisions. For example, production schedules need to be developed and marketing tactics need to be planned.

total market demand
The total volume that would be bought by a defined consumer group in a defined geographic area in a defined time period in a defined marketing environment under a defined level and mix of industry marketing effort.

The **total market demand** for a product or service is the total volume that would be bought by a defined consumer group in a defined geographic area in a defined time period in a defined marketing environment under a defined level and mix of industry marketing effort. Total market demand is not a fixed number but a function of the stated conditions. For example, next year's total market demand for this type of product will depend on how much other producers spend on marketing their brands. It also depends on many environmental factors, such as government regulations, economic conditions, and the level of consumer confidence in a given market. The upper limit of market demand is called **market potential**.

market potential
The upper limit of market demand.

One general but practical method that HD might use for estimating total market demand uses three variables: (1) the number of prospective buyers, (2) the quantity purchased by an average buyer per year, and (3) the price of an average unit. Using these numbers, HD can estimate total market demand as follows:

$$Q = n \times q \times p$$

Where

Q = total market demand

n = number of buyers in the market

q = quantity purchased by an average buyer per year

p = price of an average unit

A variation of this approach is the **chain ratio method**. This method involves multiplying a base number by a chain of adjusting percentages. For example, HD's product is designed to play high-definition DVD movies on high-definition televisions as well as play videos streamed from the Internet. Thus, consumers who do not own a high-definition television will not likely purchase this player. Additionally, only households with broadband Internet access will be able to use the product. Finally, not all HDTV-owning Internet households will be willing and able to purchase this product. HD can estimate U.S. demand using a chain of calculations like the following:

chain ratio method
Estimating market demand by multiplying a base number by a chain of adjusting percentages.

Total number of U.S. households

× The percentage of HDTV-owning U.S. households with broadband Internet access

× The percentage of these households willing and able to buy this device

The U.S. Census Bureau estimates that there are approximately 113 million households in the United States.[4] HD's research indicates that 60 percent of U.S. households own at least one HDTV and have broadband Internet access. Finally, the company's research also reveals that 30 percent of households possess the discretionary income needed and are willing to buy a product such as this. Then, the total number of households willing and able to purchase this product is:

$$113 \text{ million households} \times 0.60 \times 0.30 = 20.34 \text{ million households}$$

Households will likely only purchase one Internet TV device. Assuming the average retail price across all brands is \$350 for this product, the estimate of total market demand is as follows:

$$20.34 \text{ million households} \times 1 \text{ device per household} \times \$350 = \$7{,}119{,}000{,}000$$

This simple chain of calculations gives HD only a rough estimate of potential demand. However, more detailed chains involving additional segments and other qualifying factors would yield more accurate and refined estimates. Still, these are only *estimates* of market potential. They rely heavily on assumptions regarding adjusting percentages, average quantity, and average price. Thus, HD must make certain that its assumptions are reasonable and defendable. As can be seen, the overall market potential in dollar sales can vary widely given the average price used. For this reason, HD will use unit sales potential to determine its sales estimate for next year. Market potential in terms of units is 20.34 million (20.34 million households × 1 device per household).

Assuming that HD forecasts it will have a 3.66 percent market share in the first year after launching this product, then it can forecast unit sales at 20.34 million units × 0.0366 = 744,444 units. At a selling price of \$168 per unit, this translates into sales of \$125,066,592 (744,444 units × \$168 per unit). For simplicity, further analyses will use forecasted sales of \$125 million.

This unit volume estimate is well within HD's production capacity and exceeds not only the break-even estimate (465,117 units) calculated earlier, but also the volume necessary to realize a \$5 million profit (581,396 units) or a 30 percent return on investment (534,884 units). However, this forecast falls well short of the volume necessary to realize a 25 percent return on sales (20 million units!) and may require that HD revise expectations.

To assess expected profits, we must now look at the budgeted expenses for launching this product. To do this, we will construct a pro forma profit-and-loss statement.

The Profit-and-Loss Statement and Marketing Budget

pro forma (or projected) profit-and-loss statement (or income statement or operating statement) A statement that shows projected revenues less budgeted expenses and estimates the projected net profit for an organization, product, or brand during a specific planning period, typically a year.

All marketing managers must account for the profit impact of their marketing strategies. A major tool for projecting such profit impact is a **pro forma (or projected) profit-and-loss statement** (also called an **income statement** or **operating statement**). A pro forma statement shows projected revenues less budgeted expenses and estimates the projected net profit for an organization, product, or brand during a specific planning period, typically a year. It includes direct product production costs, marketing expenses budgeted to attain a given sales forecast, and overhead expenses assigned to the organization or product. A profit-and-loss statement typically consists of several major components (see **Table A1.1**):

- ***Net sales:*** gross sales revenue minus returns and allowances (for example, trade, cash, quantity, and promotion allowances). HD's net sales for 2012 are estimated to be $125 million, as determined in the previous analysis.
- ***Cost of goods sold*** (sometimes called ***cost of sales***)***:*** the actual cost of the merchandise sold by a manufacturer or reseller. It includes the cost of inventory, purchases, and other costs associated with making the goods. HD's cost of goods sold is estimated to be 50 percent of net sales, or $62.5 million.
- ***Gross margin (or gross profit):*** the difference between net sales and cost of goods sold. HD's gross margin is estimated to be $62.5 million.
- ***Operating expenses:*** the expenses incurred while doing business. These include all other expenses beyond the cost of goods sold that are necessary to conduct business. Operating expenses can be presented in total or broken down in detail. Here, HD's estimated operating expenses include *marketing expenses* and *general and administrative expenses.*
- ***Marketing expenses:*** include sales expenses, promotion expenses, and distribution expenses. The new product will be sold through HD's sales force, so the company budgets $5 million for sales salaries. However, because sales representatives earn a 10 percent commission on sales, HD must also add a variable component to sales expenses of $12.5 million (10 percent of $125 million net sales), for a total budgeted sales expense of $17.5 million. HD sets its advertising and promotion to launch this product at $10 million. However,

TABLE A1.1
PRO FORMA PROFIT-AND-LOSS STATEMENT FOR THE 12-MONTH PERIOD ENDED DECEMBER 31, 2012

			% OF SALES
Net Sales		$125,000,000	100%
Cost of Goods Sold		62,500,000	50%
Gross Margin		$62,500,000	50%
Marketing Expenses			
Sales expenses	$17,500,000		
Promotion expenses	15,000,000		
Freight	12,500,000	45,000,000	36%
General and Administrative Expenses			
Managerial salaries and expenses	$2,000,000		
Indirect overhead	3,000,000	5,000,000	4%
Net Profit before Income Tax		$12,500,000	10%

the company also budgets 4 percent of sales, or $5 million, for cooperative advertising allowances to retailers who promote HD's new product in their advertising. Thus, the total budgeted advertising and promotion expenses are $15 million ($10 million for advertising plus $5 million in co-op allowances). Finally, HD budgets 10 percent of net sales, or $12.5 million, for freight and delivery charges. In all, total marketing expenses are estimated to be $17.5 million + $15 million + $12.5 million = $45 million.

- ***General and administrative expenses:*** are estimated at $5 million, broken down into $2 million for managerial salaries and expenses for the marketing function and $3 million of indirect overhead allocated to this product by the corporate accountants (such as depreciation, interest, maintenance, and insurance). Total expenses for the year, then, are estimated to be $50 million ($45 million marketing expenses + $5 million in general and administrative expenses).
- ***Net profit before taxes:*** profit earned after all costs are deducted. HD's estimated net profit before taxes is $12.5 million.

In all, as Table A1.2 shows, HD expects to earn a profit on its new product of $12.5 million in 2012. Also note that the percentage of sales that each component of the profit-and-loss statement represents is given in the right-hand column. These percentages are determined by dividing the cost figure by net sales (that is, marketing expenses represent 36 percent of net sales determined by $45 million ÷ $125 million). As can be seen, HD projects a net profit return on sales of 10 percent in the first year after launching this product.

Marketing Performance Measures

Now let's fast-forward a year. HD's product has been on the market for one year and management wants to assess its sales and profit performance. One way to assess this performance is to compute performance ratios derived from HD's **profit-and-loss statement** (or **income statement** or **operating statement**).

profit-and-loss statement (or income statement or operating statement)
A statement that shows actual revenues less expenses and net profit for an organization, product, or brand during a specific planning period, typically a year.

Whereas the pro forma profit-and-loss statement shows *projected* financial performance, the statement given in **Table A1.2** shows HD's *actual* financial performance based on actual sales, cost of goods sold, and expenses during the past year. By comparing the profit-and-loss statement from one period to the next, HD can gauge performance against goals, spot favorable or unfavorable trends, and take appropriate corrective action.

The profit-and-loss statement shows that HD lost $1 million rather than making the $12.5 million profit projected in the pro forma statement. Why? One obvious reason is that net sales fell $25 million short of estimated sales. Lower sales translated into lower variable costs associated with marketing the product. However, both fixed costs and the cost of goods sold as a percentage of sales exceeded expectations. Hence, the product's contribution margin was 21 percent rather than the estimated 26 percent. That is, variable costs represented 79 percent of sales (55 percent for cost of goods sold, 10 percent for sales commissions, 10 percent for freight, and 4 percent for co-op allowances). Recall that contribution margin can be calculated by subtracting that fraction from one (1 – 0.79 = 0.21). Total fixed costs were $22 million, $2 million more than estimated. Thus, the sales that HD needed to break even given this cost structure can be calculated as:

$$\text{Break-even sales} = \frac{\text{fixed costs}}{\text{contribution margin}} = \frac{\$22{,}000{,}000}{0.21} = \$104{,}761{,}905$$

TABLE A1.2
PROFIT-AND-LOSS STATEMENT FOR THE 12-MONTH PERIOD ENDED DECEMBER 31, 2012

			% OF SALES
Net Sales		$100,000,000	100%
Cost of Goods Sold		55,500,000	55%
Gross Margin		$45,000,000	45%
Marketing Expenses			
Sales expenses	$15,000,000		
Promotion expenses	14,000,000		
Freight	10,000,000	39,000,000	39%
General and Administrative Expenses			
Managerial salaries and expenses	$2,000,000		
Indirect overhead	5,000,000	7,000,000	7%
Net Profit before Income Tax		($1,000,000)	(–1%)

If HD had achieved another $5 million in sales, it would have earned a profit.

market share
Company sales divided by market sales.

Although HD's sales fell short of the forecasted sales, so did overall industry sales for this product. Overall industry sales were only $2.5 billion. That means that HD's **market share** was 4 percent ($100 million ÷ $2.5 billion = 0.04 = 4 percent), which was higher than forecasted. Thus, HD attained a higher-than-expected market share but the overall market sales were not as high as estimated.

Analytic Ratios

operating ratios
The ratios of selected operating statement items to net sales.

The profit-and-loss statement provides the figures needed to compute some crucial **operating ratios**—the ratios of selected operating statement items to net sales. These ratios let marketers compare the firm's performance in one year to that in previous years (or with industry standards and competitors' performance in that year). The most commonly used operating ratios are the gross margin percentage, the net profit percentage, and the operating expense percentage. The inventory turnover rate and return on investment (ROI) are often used to measure managerial effectiveness and efficiency.

gross margin percentage
The percentage of net sales remaining after cost of goods sold—calculated by dividing gross margin by net sales.

The **gross margin percentage** indicates the percentage of net sales remaining after cost of goods sold that can contribute to operating expenses and net profit before taxes. The higher this ratio, the more a firm has left to cover expenses and generate profit. HD's gross margin ratio was 45 percent:

$$\text{Gross margin percentage} = \frac{\text{gross margin}}{\text{net sales}} = \frac{\$45,000,000}{\$100,000,000} = 0.45 = 45\%$$

Note that this percentage is lower than estimated, and this ratio is seen easily in the percentage of sales column in Table A1.2. Stating items in the profit-and-loss statement as a percent of sales allows managers to quickly spot abnormal changes in costs over time. If there was a previous history for this product and this ratio was declining, management should examine it more closely to determine why it has decreased (that is, because of a decrease in sales volume or price, an increase in costs, or a combination of these). In HD's case, net sales were $25 million lower than estimated, and cost of goods sold was higher than estimated (55 percent rather than the estimated 50 percent).

The **net profit percentage** shows the percentage of each sales dollar going to profit. It is calculated by dividing net profits by net sales:

net profit percentage
The percentage of each sales dollar going to profit—calculated by dividing net profits by net sales.

$$\text{Net profit percentage} = \frac{\text{net profit}}{\text{net sales}} = \frac{-\$1{,}000{,}000}{\$100{,}000{,}000} = -0.01 = -1.0\%$$

This ratio is easily seen in the percent of sales column. HD's new product generated negative profits in the first year, which is not a good situation given that net profits before taxes were estimated at more than $12 million before the product launch. Later in this appendix, we will discuss further analyses the marketing manager should conduct to defend the product.

The **operating expense percentage** indicates the portion of net sales going to operating expenses. Operating expenses include marketing and other expenses not directly related to marketing the product, such as indirect overhead assigned to this product. It is calculated by:

operating expense percentage
The portion of net sales going to operating expenses—calculated by dividing total expenses by net sales.

$$\text{Operating expense percentage} = \frac{\text{total expenses}}{\text{net sales}} = \frac{\$46{,}000{,}000}{\$100{,}000{,}000} = 0.46 = 46\%$$

This ratio can also be quickly determined from the percent of sales column in the profit-and-loss statement by adding the percentages for marketing expenses and general and administrative expenses (39 percent + 7 percent). Thus, 46 cents of every sales dollar went for operations. Although HD wants this ratio to be as low as possible, and 46 percent is not an alarming amount, it is of concern if it is increasing over time or if a loss is realized.

Another useful ratio is the **inventory turnover rate** (also called the **stockturn rate** for resellers). The inventory turnover rate is the number of times an inventory turns over or is sold during a specified time period (often one year). This rate tells how quickly a business is moving inventory through the organization. Higher rates indicate that lower investments in inventory are made, thus freeing up funds for other investments. It may be computed on a cost, selling price, or unit basis. The formula based on cost is:

inventory turnover rate (or stockturn rate)
The number of times an inventory turns over or is sold during a specified time period (often one year)—calculated based on costs, selling price, or units.

$$\text{Inventory turnover rate} = \frac{\text{cost of goods sold}}{\text{average inventory at cost}}$$

Assuming HD's beginning and ending inventories were $30 million and $20 million, respectively, the inventory turnover rate is:

$$\text{Inventory turnover rate} = \frac{\$55{,}000{,}000}{(\$30{,}000{,}000 + \$20{,}000{,}000)/2} = \frac{\$55{,}000{,}000}{\$25{,}000{,}000} = 2.2$$

That is, HD's inventory turned over 2.2 times in 2012. Normally, the higher the turnover rate, the higher the management efficiency and company profitability. However, this rate should be compared to industry averages, competitors' rates, and past performance to determine if HD is doing well. A competitor with similar sales but a higher inventory turnover rate will have fewer resources tied up in inventory, allowing it to invest in other areas of the business.

return on investment (ROI)
A measure of managerial effectiveness and efficiency—net profit before taxes divided by total investment.

Companies frequently use **return on investment (ROI)** to measure managerial effectiveness and efficiency. For HD, ROI is the ratio of net profits to total investment required to manufacture the new product. This investment includes capital investments in land, buildings, and equipment (here, the initial $10 million to refurbish the manufacturing facility) plus inventory costs (HD's average inventory totaled $25 million), for a total of $35 million. Thus, HD's ROI for this product is:

$$\text{Return on investment} = \frac{\text{net profit before taxes}}{\text{investment}} = \frac{-\$1{,}000{,}000}{\$35{,}000{,}000} = -.0286 = -2.86\%$$

ROI is often used to compare alternatives, and a positive ROI is desired. The alternative with the highest ROI is preferred to other alternatives. HD needs to be concerned with the ROI realized. One obvious way HD can increase ROI is to increase net profit by reducing expenses. Another way is to reduce its investment, perhaps by investing less in inventory and turning it over more frequently.

Marketing Profitability Metrics

Given the previous financial results, you may be thinking that HD should drop this new product. But what arguments can marketers make for keeping or dropping this product? The obvious arguments for dropping the product are that first-year sales were well below expected levels and the product lost money, resulting in a negative return on investment.

So what would happen if HD did drop this product? Surprisingly, if the company drops the product, the profits for the total organization will decrease by $4 million! How can that be? Marketing managers need to look closely at the numbers in the profit-and-loss statement to determine the *net marketing contribution* for this product. In HD's case, the net marketing contribution for the product is $4 million; if the company drops this product, that contribution will disappear as well. Let's look more closely at this concept to illustrate how marketing managers can better assess and defend their marketing strategies and programs.

net marketing contribution (NMC)
A measure of marketing profitability that includes only components of profitability controlled by marketing.

NET MARKETING CONTRIBUTION **Net marketing contribution (NMC)**, along with other marketing metrics derived from it, measures *marketing* profitability. It includes only components of profitability that are controlled by marketing. Whereas the previous calculation of net profit before taxes from the profit-and-loss statement includes operating expenses not under marketing's control, NMC does not. Referring back to HD's profit-and-loss statement given in Table A1.2, we can calculate net marketing contribution for the product as:

$$\begin{aligned} \text{NMC} &= \text{net sales} - \text{cost of goods sold} - \text{marketing expenses} \\ &= \$100 \text{ million} - \$55 \text{ million} - \$41 \text{ million} = \$4 \text{ million} \end{aligned}$$

The marketing expenses include sales expenses ($15 million), promotion expenses ($14 million), freight expenses ($10 million), and the managerial salaries and expenses of the marketing function ($2 million), which total $41 million.

Thus, the product actually contributed $4 million to HD's profits. It was the $5 million of indirect overhead allocated to this product that caused the negative profit. Further, the amount allocated was $2 million more than estimated in the pro forma profit-and-loss statement. Indeed, if only the estimated amount had been allocated, the product would have earned a *profit* of $1 million rather than losing $1 million. If HD drops the product, the $5 million in fixed overhead expenses will not disappear—it will simply have to be allocated elsewhere. However, the $4 million in net marketing contribution *will* disappear.

MARKETING RETURN ON SALES AND INVESTMENT To get an even deeper understanding of the profit impact of the marketing strategy, we'll now examine two measures of marketing efficiency—*marketing return on sales* (marketing ROS) and *marketing return on investment* (marketing ROI).[5]

Marketing return on sales (or **marketing ROS**) shows the percent of net sales attributable to the net marketing contribution. For our product, ROS is:

marketing return on sales (or marketing ROS)
The percent of net sales attributable to the net marketing contribution—calculated by dividing net marketing contribution by net sales.

$$\text{Marketing ROS} = \frac{\text{net marketing contribution}}{\text{net sales}} = \frac{\$4{,}000{,}000}{\$100{,}000{,}000} = 0.04 = 4\%$$

Thus, out of every $100 of sales, the product returns $4 to HD's bottom line. A high marketing ROS is desirable. But to assess whether this is a good level of performance, HD must compare this figure to previous marketing ROS levels for the product, the ROSs of other products in the company's portfolio, and the ROSs of competing products.

Marketing return on investment (or **marketing ROI**) measures the marketing productivity of a marketing investment. In HD's case, the marketing investment is represented by $41 million of the total expenses. Thus, marketing ROI is:

marketing return on investment (or marketing ROI)
A measure of the marketing productivity of a marketing investment—calculated by dividing net marketing contribution by marketing expenses.

$$\text{Marketing ROI} = \frac{\text{net marketing contribution}}{\text{marketing expenses}} = \frac{\$4{,}000{,}000}{\$41{,}000{,}000} = 0.0976 = 9.76\%$$

As with marketing ROS, a high value is desirable, but this figure should be compared with previous levels for the given product and with the marketing ROIs of competitors' products. Note from this equation that marketing ROI could be greater than 100 percent. This can be achieved by attaining a higher net marketing contribution and/or a lower total marketing expense.

In this section, we estimated market potential and sales, developed profit-and-loss statements, and examined financial measures of performance. In the next section, we discuss methods for analyzing the impact of various marketing tactics. However, before moving on to those analyses, here's another set of quantitative exercises to help you apply what you've learned to other situations.

Marketing by the Numbers Exercise Set Two

1. Determine the market potential for a product that has 50 million prospective buyers who purchase an average of three per year if the product's price averages $25. How many units must a company sell if it desires a 10 percent share of this market?
2. Develop a profit-and-loss statement for the Westgate division of North Industries. This division manufactures light fixtures sold to consumers through home improvement and hardware stores. Cost of goods sold represents 40 percent of net sales. Marketing expenses include selling expenses, promotion expenses, and freight. Selling expenses include sales salaries totaling $3 million per year and sales commissions (5 percent of sales). The company spent $3 million on advertising last year, and freight costs were 10 percent of sales. Other costs include

$2 million for managerial salaries and expenses for the marketing function and another $3 million for indirect overhead allocated to the division.

a. Develop the profit-and-loss statement if net sales were $20 million last year.

b. Develop the profit-and-loss statement if net sales were $40 million last year.

c. Calculate Westgate's break-even sales.

3. Using the profit-and-loss statement you developed in question 2b, and assuming that Westgate's beginning inventory was $11 million, ending inventory was $7 million, and total investment was $20 million including inventory, determine the following:

a. Gross margin percentage

b. Net profit percentage

c. Operating expense percentage

d. Inventory turnover rate

e. Return on investment (ROI)

f. Net marketing contribution

g. Marketing return on sales (marketing ROS)

h. Marketing return on investment (marketing ROI)

i. Is the Westgate division doing well? Explain your answer.

Financial Analysis of Marketing Tactics

Although the first-year profit performance for HD's new product was less than desired, management feels that this attractive market has excellent growth opportunities. Although the sales of HD's product were lower than initially projected, they were not unreasonable given the size of the current market. Thus, HD wants to explore new marketing tactics to help grow the market for this product and increase sales for the company.

For example, the company could increase advertising to promote more awareness of the new product and its category. It could add salespeople to secure greater product distribution. HD could decrease prices so that more consumers could afford its product. Finally, to expand the market, HD could introduce a lower-priced model in addition to the higher-priced original offering. Before pursuing any of these tactics, however, HD must analyze the financial implications of each.

Increase Advertising Expenditures

HD is considering boosting its advertising to make more people aware of the benefits of this device in general and of its own brand in particular. What if HD's marketers recommend increasing national advertising by 50 percent to $15 million (assume no change in the variable cooperative component of promotional expenditures)? This represents an increase in fixed costs of $5 million. What increase in sales will be needed to break even on this $5 million increase in fixed costs?

A quick way to answer this question is to divide the increase in fixed costs by the contribution margin, which we found in a previous analysis to be 21 percent:

$$\text{Increase in sales} = \frac{\text{increase in fixed cost}}{\text{contribution margin}} = \frac{\$5{,}000{,}000}{0.21} = \$23{,}809{,}524$$

Thus, a 50 percent increase in advertising expenditures must produce a sales increase of almost \$24 million to just break even. That \$24 million sales increase translates into an almost 1 percentage point increase in market share (1 percent of the \$2.5 billion overall market equals \$25 million). That is, to break even on the increased advertising expenditure, HD would have to increase its market share from 4 percent to 4.95 percent (\$123,809,524 ÷ \$2.5 billion = 0.0495 or 4.95 percent market share). All of this assumes that the total market will not grow, which might or might not be a reasonable assumption.

Increase Distribution Coverage

HD also wants to consider hiring more salespeople in order to call on new retailer accounts and increase distribution through more outlets. Even though HD sells directly to wholesalers, its sales representatives call on retail accounts to perform other functions in addition to selling, such as training retail salespeople. Currently, HD employs 60 sales reps who earn an average of \$50,000 in salary plus 10 percent commission on sales. The product is currently sold to consumers through 1,875 retail outlets. Suppose HD wants to increase that number of outlets to 2,500, an increase of 625 retail outlets. How many additional salespeople will HD need, and what sales will be necessary to break even on the increased cost?

One method for determining what size sales force HD will need is the **workload method**. The workload method uses the following formula to determine the sales force size:

workload method
An approach to determining sales force size based on the workload required and the time available for selling.

$$NS = \frac{NC \times FC \times LC}{TA}$$

Where

NS = number of salespeople

NC = number of customers

FC = average frequency of customer calls per customer

LC = average length of customer call

TA = time an average salesperson has available for selling per year

HD's sales reps typically call on accounts an average of 20 times per year for about 2 hours per call. Although each sales rep works 2,000 hours per year (50 weeks per year × 40 hours per week), they spend about 15 hours per week on nonselling activities such as administrative duties and travel. Thus, the average annual available selling time per sales rep per year is 1,250 hours (50 weeks × 25 hours per week). We can now calculate how many sales reps HD will need to cover the anticipated 2,500 retail outlets:

$$NS = \frac{2{,}500 \times 20 \times 2}{1{,}250} = 80 \text{ salespeople}$$

Therefore, HD will need to hire 20 more salespeople. The cost to hire these reps will be \$1 million (20 salespeople × \$50,000 salary per salesperson).

What increase in sales will be required to break even on this increase in fixed costs? The 10 percent commission is already accounted for in the contribution margin, so the contribution margin remains unchanged at 21 percent. Thus, the increase in sales needed to cover this increase in fixed costs can be calculated by:

$$\text{Increase in sales} = \frac{\text{increase in fixed cost}}{\text{contribution margin}} = \frac{\$1{,}000{,}000}{0.21} = \$4{,}761{,}905$$

That is, HD's sales must increase almost $5 million to break even on this tactic. So, how many new retail outlets will the company need to secure to achieve this sales increase? The average revenue generated per current outlet is $53,333 ($100 million in sales divided by 1,875 outlets). To achieve the nearly $5 million sales increase needed to break even, HD would need about 90 new outlets ($4,761,905 ÷ $53,333 = 89.3 outlets), or about 4.5 outlets per new rep. Given that current reps cover about 31 outlets apiece (1,875 outlets ÷ 60 reps), this seems very reasonable.

Decrease Price

HD is also considering lowering its price to increase sales revenue through increased volume. The company's research has shown that demand for most types of consumer electronics products is elastic—that is, the percentage increase in the quantity demanded is greater than the percentage decrease in price.

What increase in sales would be necessary to break even on a 10 percent decrease in price? That is, what increase in sales will be needed to maintain the total contribution that HD realized at the higher price? The current total contribution can be determined by multiplying the contribution margin by total sales:[6]

$$\begin{aligned}\text{Current total contribution} &= \text{contribution margin} \times \text{sales}\\ &= 0.21 \times \$100 \text{ million} = \$21 \text{ million}\end{aligned}$$

Price changes result in changes in unit contribution and contribution margin. Recall that the contribution margin of 21 percent was based on variable costs representing 79 percent of sales. Therefore, unit variable costs can be determined by multiplying the original price by this percentage: $168 × 0.79 = $132.72 per unit. If price is decreased by 10 percent, the new price is $151.20. However, variable costs do not change just because the price decreased, so the contribution and contribution margin decrease as follows:

	Old	**New (reduced 10 percent)**
Price	$168	$151.20
– Unit variable cost	$132.72	$132.72
= Unit contribution	$35.28	$18.48
Contribution margin	$35.28/$168 = 0.21 or 21%	$18.48/$151.20 = 0.12 or 12%

So, a 10 percent reduction in price results in a decrease in the contribution margin from 21 percent to 12 percent.[7] To determine the sales level needed to break even on this price reduction, we calculate the level of sales that must be attained at the new contribution margin to achieve the original total contribution of $21 million:

$$\text{New contribution margin} \times \text{new sales level} = \text{original total contribution}$$

So,

$$\text{New sales level} = \frac{\text{original contribution}}{\text{new contribution margin}} = \frac{\$21,000,000}{0.12} = \$175,000,000$$

Thus, sales must increase by $75 million ($175 million – $100 million) just to break even on a 10 percent price reduction. This means that HD must increase market share to 7 percent ($175 million ÷ $2.5 billion) to achieve the current level of profits (assuming no increase in the total market sales). The marketing manager must assess whether or not this is a reasonable goal.

Extend the Product Line

As a final option, HD is considering extending its product line by offering a lower-priced model. Of course, the new, lower-priced product would steal some sales from the higher-priced model. This is called **cannibalization**—the situation in which one product sold by a company takes a portion of its sales from other company products. If the new product has a lower contribution than the original product, the company's total contribution will decrease on the cannibalized sales. However, if the new product can generate enough new volume, it is worth considering.

cannibalization
The situation in which one product sold by a company takes a portion of its sales from other company products.

To assess cannibalization, HD must look at the incremental contribution gained by having both products available. In the previous analysis, we determined that unit variable costs were $132.72 and unit contribution was just over $35. Assuming costs remain the same next year, HD can expect to realize a contribution per unit of approximately $35 for every unit of the original product sold.

Assume that the first model offered by HD is called HD1 and the new, lower-priced model is called HD2. HD2 will retail for $250, and resellers will take the same markup percentages on price as they do with the higher-priced model. Therefore, HD2's price to wholesalers will be $140 as follows:

Retail price:	$250
minus retail margin (30 percent):	–$ 75
Retailer's cost/wholesaler's price:<	$175
minus wholesaler's margin (20 percent):	–$ 35
Wholesaler's cost/HD's price	$140

If HD2's variable costs are estimated to be $120, then its contribution per unit will equal $20 ($140 – $120 = $20). That means for every unit that HD2 cannibalizes from HD1, HD will *lose* $15 in contribution toward fixed costs and profit (that is, $\text{contribution}_{HD2} - \text{contribution}_{HD1} = \$20 - \$35 = -\$15$). You might conclude that HD should not pursue this tactic because it appears as though the company will be worse off if it introduces the lower-priced model. However, if HD2 captures enough *additional* sales, HD will be better off even though some HD1 sales are cannibalized. The company must examine what will happen to *total* contribution, which requires estimates of unit volume for both products.

Originally, HD estimated that next year's sales of HD1 would be 600,000 units. However, with the introduction of HD2, it now estimates that 200,000 of those sales will be cannibalized by the new model. If HD sells only 200,000 units of the new HD2 model (all cannibalized from HD1), the company would lose $3 million in total contribution (200,000 units × −$15 per cannibalized unit = −$3 million)—not a good outcome. However, HD estimates that HD2 will generate the 200,000 of cannibalized sales plus an *additional* 500,000 unit sales. Thus, the contribution on these additional HD2 units will be $10 million (i.e., 500,000 units × $20 per unit = $10 million). The net effect is that HD will gain $7 million in total contribution by introducing HD2.

The following table compares HD's total contribution with and without the introduction of HD2:

	HD1 Only	**HD1 and HD2**
HD1 contribution	600,000 units × $35 = $21,000,000	400,000 units × $35 = $14,000,000
HD2 contribution	0	700,000 units × $20 = $14,000,000
Total contribution	$21,000,000	$28,000,000

The difference in the total contribution is a net gain of $7 million ($28 million – $21 million). Based on this analysis, HD should introduce the HD2 model because it results in a positive incremental contribution. However, if fixed costs will increase by more than $7 million as a result of adding this model, then the net effect will be negative and HD should not pursue this tactic.

Now that you have seen these marketing tactic analysis concepts in action as they relate to HD's new product, here are several exercises that will allow you to apply what you have learned in this section to other contexts.

Marketing by the Numbers Exercise Set Three

1. Kingsford, Inc. sells small plumbing components to consumers through retail outlets. Total industry sales for Kingsford's relevant market last year were $80 million, with Kingsford's sales representing 10 percent of that total. Contribution margin is 25 percent. Kingsford's sales force calls on retail outlets and each sales rep earns $45,000 per year plus 1 percent commission on all sales. Retailers receive a 40 percent margin on selling price and generate average revenue of $10,000 per outlet for Kingsford.
   a. The marketing manager has suggested increasing consumer advertising by $300,000. By how much would dollar sales need to increase to break even on this expenditure? What increase in overall market share does this represent?
   b. Another suggestion is to hire three more sales representatives to gain new consumer retail accounts. How many new retail outlets would be necessary to break even on the increased cost of adding three sales reps?
   c. A final suggestion is to make a 20 percent across-the-board price reduction. By how much would dollar sales need to increase to maintain Kingsford's current contribution? (See endnote 6 to calculate the new contribution margin.)
   d. Which suggestion do you think Kingsford should implement? Explain your recommendation.

2. PepsiCo sells its soft drinks in approximately 400,000 retail establishments, such as supermarkets, discount stores, and convenience stores. Sales representatives call on each retail account weekly, which means each account is called on by a sales rep 52 times per year. The average length of a sales call is 75 minutes (or 1.25 hours). An average salesperson works 2,000 hours per year (50 weeks per year × 40 hours per week), but each spends 10 hours a week on nonselling activities, such as administrative tasks and travel. How many salespeople does PepsiCo need?
3. Hair Zone manufactures a brand of hair-styling gel. It is considering adding a modified version of the product—a foam that provides stronger hold. Hair Zone's variable costs and prices to wholesalers are:

	Current Hair Gel	**New Foam Product**
Unit selling price	2.00	2.25
Unit variable costs	0.85	1.25

Hair Zone expects to sell 1 million units of the new styling foam in the first year after introduction, but it expects that 60 percent of those sales will come from buyers who normally purchase Hair Zone's styling gel. Hair Zone estimates that it would sell 1.5 million units of the gel if it did not introduce the foam. If the fixed cost of launching the new foam will be $100,000 during the first year, should Hair Zone add the new product to its line? Why or why not?

Endnotes

Chapter 1

1. Adapted from Stephen P. Robbins et al., *Fundamentals of Management: Essential Concepts and Applications,* 8th ed.
2. See, for example, A. Nagurney, J. Dong, and P.L. Mokhtarian, "Multicriteria Network Equilibrium Modeling with Variable Weights for Decision Making in the Information Age with Applications to the Telecommuting and Teleshopping." *Journal of Economic Dynamics and Control* (August 2002), pp. 1629–1650.
3. J. Flinchbaugh, "Surfacing Problems Daily: Advice for Building a Problem-Solving Culture," *Industry Week*, April 2011, p. 12. "Business Analysis Training Helps Leaders Achieve an Enterprise-Wide Perspective," *Leader to Leader*, Fall 2010, pp. 63–65; D. Okes, "Common Problems with Basic Problems," *Business and Economic Review*, April–June 2002, pp. 23–24.
4. See J. Figueira and B. Ray, "Determining the Weights of Criteria in the Electre Type of Methods with a Revised Simons' Procedure," *European Journal of Operational Research*, June 1, 2002, pp. 317–326.
5. E. Teach, "Avoiding Decision Traps," *CFO*, June 2004, pp. 97–99; and D. Kahneman and A. Tversky, "Judgment Under Uncertainty: Heuristics and Biases," *Science* 185 (1974), pp. 1124–1131.
6. Information for this section taken from S.P. Robbins, *Decide & Conquer* (Upper Saddle River, NJH: Financial Times/Prentice Hall, 2004).
7. J. Pfeffer and R.I. Sutton, "Why Managing by Facts Works," *Strategy & Business*, Spring 2006, pp. 9–12.
8. See T. Shavit and A.M. Adam, "A Preliminary Exploration of the Effects of Rational Factors and Behaviorial Biases on the Managerial Choice to Invest in Corporate Responsibility," *Managerial and Decision Economics*, April 2011, pp. 205–213; A. Langley, "In Search of Rationality: The Purposes Behind the Use of Formal Analysis in Organizations," *Administrative Science Quarterly*, December 1989, pp. 298–631; and J.A. Simon, "Rationality in *Psychology and Economics*," *Journal of Business* (October 1986), pp. 209–224.
9. J.G March, "Decision-Making Perspective: Decisions in Organizations and Theories of Choice," in A.H. Van de Ven and W.F. Joyce (eds.), *Perspectives on Organization Design and Behavior* (New York: Wiley-Interscience, 1981), pp. 232–233.
10. "Next: Big Idea," *Fast Company*, December 2010–January 2011, pp. 39–40.
11. R.D. Hof and H. Green, "How Amazon Cleared That Hurdle," *BusinessWeek*, February 4, 2002, p. 59.
12. See, for example, S. Schulz-Hardt, A. Mojzisch, F.C. Brodbeck, R. Kerschreiter, and D. Frey, "Group Decision Making in Hidden Profile Situations: Dissent as a Facilitator for Decision Quality," *Journal of Personality and Social Psychology*, (December 2006), pp. 1080–1083; and C.K.W. DeDreu and M.A. West, "Minority Dissent and Team Innovation: The Importance of Participation in Decision Making," *Journal of Applied Psychology* (December 2001) pp. 1191–1201.
13. S. Mohammed, "Toward an Understanding of Cognitive Consensus in a Group Decision-Making Context," *Journal of Applied Behavioral Science* (December 2001), p. 408.
14. M. J. Fambrough and S.A. Comerford, "The Changing Epistemological Assumptions of Group Theory," *Journal of Applied Behavioral Science* (September 2006), pp. 330–349.

15. R.A. Meyers, D.E. Brashers, and J. Hanner, "Majority-Minority Influence: Identifying Argumentative Pattern and Predicting Argument-Outcome Links," *Journal of Communication* (Autumn 2000), pp. 3–30.
16. I.L. Janis, *Groupthink* (Boston: Houghton Mifflin, 1982). See also J. Chapman, "Anxiety and Defective Decision Making: An Elaboration of the Groupthink Mode," *Management Decision*, October 2006, pp. 1391–1404.
17. See, for example, T.W. Costello and S.S. Zalkind, eds., *Psychology in Administration: A Research Orientation* (Upper Saddle Rive, NJ: Prentice Hall, 1963), pp. 429–430; R. A. Cooke and J.A. Kernagham, "Estimating the Difference Between Group versus Individual Performance on Problem Solving Tasks," *Group and Organization Studies*, September 1987, pp. 319–342; and L.K. Michaelsen, W.E. Watson, and R.H. Black, "A Realistic Test of Individual Versus Group Consensus Decision Making," *Journal of Applied Psychology* (October 1989), pp. 834–839. See also J. Hollenbeck, D.R. Ilgen, J.A. Colquitt, and A. Ellis, "Gender Composition, Situational Strength, and Team Decision-Making Accuracy: A Criterion Decomposition Approach," *Organizational Behavior and Human Decision Processes*, May 2002, pp. 445–475.
18. See, for example, L.K. Michaelsen, W.E. Watson, and R.H. Black, "A Realistic Test of Individual versus Group Consensus Decision Making," *Journal of Applied Psychology* (October 1989) pp. 834–839; and P. W. Pease, M. Beiser, and M.E. Tubbs, "Framing Effects and Choice Shifts in Group Decision Making," *Organizational Behavior and Human Decision Processes*, October 1993, pp. 149–165.
19. J. Wagstaff, "Brainstorming Requires Drinks," *Far Eastern Economic Review*, May 2, 2002, p. 34.
20. T. Kelley, "Six Ways to Kill a Brainstormer," *Across the Board*, March–April 2002, p. 12.
21. K.L. Dowling and R.D. St. Louis, "Asynchronous Implementation of the Nominal Group Technique: Is It Effective," *Decision Support Systems*, October 2000, pp. 229–248.

Chapter 2

1. Taken from *Developing Management Skills,* 8th ed., by David Whetten and Kim S. Cameron.
3. Adapted from www.MindTools.com, "Team Charters: Getting Your Teams Off to a Great Start."
4. Taken from *Developing Management Skills,* Eighth Edition, by David A. Whetten and Kim S. Cameron.

Chapter 3

1. Adapted from *Developing Management Skills,* 8th ed., by David A. Whetten and Kim S. Cameron.
2. Deborah S. Kezsbom, "Managing the Chaos: Conflict Among Project Teams," AACE Transactions (1989): A4.1–A4.8. For an example of how overlapping responsibilities can impact a political organization, see Carolyn Ban and Norma Riccucci, "New York State Civil Service Reform in a Complex Political Environment," *Review of Public Personnel Administration* 15, no. 2 (Spring 1994): 20.
3. Richard Korman, "A Responsibility Gap Crashes at Location C3," *ENR* 250 (2003): 12.
4. Adapted from *Developing Management Skills,* 8th ed., David A. Whetten and Kim S. Cameron.

Chapter 4

1. This information is taken from Certo, Chapter 11, *Modern Management,* 12e, 0-13-217633-5.
2. A. Tacket, "Organizing and Organizations: An Introduction," *The Journal of Operational Research Society* 53 (2002): 1401.
3. Douglas S. Sherwin, "management of Objectives," *Harvard Business Review* (May/June 1976): 149–160 See also Lloyd Sandelands and Robert Drazin, "On the Language of Organization Theory," *Organizational Studies* 10 (1989): 457–77.
4. Tim Peakman, "Organizing the Organization," *Drug Discovery Today* 8 (2003): 673.
5. For a review focusing on division of labor, see "Division of Labor Welcomed," *Business Insurance* 34, No. 10 (March 6, 2000): 8.
6. Jeff Lewis and Walter Knott, "division of Labor: To Gain the Benefits of a Team, Each Member Can't Do Everything," *On Wall Street,* August 1, 2003, 1.
7. Example based on "Painting by Numbers: China's Art Business," *The Economist,* June 10, 2006, 77.
8. C.R. Walker and R.H. Guest," *The Man on the Assembly Line* (Cambridge, MA: Harvard Univesrity Press, 1952). For an excellent example of how technology can affect division of labor, see John P. Walsh, "Technological Change and the Division of Labor: The case of Retail Meatcutters," *Work and Occupations* 16 (May 1989): 165–181.
9. J. Mooney, "The principles of Organization," in *Ideas and Issues in Public Administration,* ed. D. Waldo (New York: McGraw-Hill, 1953), 86. See also Peter Jackson, "Speed versus Heed," *CA Magazine* (November 1994): 56–57. For an application of the coordination principle, see Gail Karet and Tim Stoudt, "Managing Biotech Requires Cross-Functional Coordination," *Research & Development* 43, no. 1 (march 2001): 12–17; see also Jody Gittrel and Leigh Weiaa, "Coordination Networks Within and Across Organizations: A Multi-Level Framework," *The Journal of Management Studies* 41 (2004): 127.
10. Bruce D. Sanders, "Making Work Groups Work," *Computerworld* 24, March 5, 1990 85–89.
11. Lyndall Urwich, *Notes on the Theory of Organization* (New York: American Management Association, 1952). For a recent look at the implication of organizational structure on misbehavior, see Granville King III, "The Implications of an Organization's Structure on Whistleblowing," *Journal of Business Ethics* 20, no 4 (July 1999): 315–326.
12. David Stamps, "Off the Charts," *Training* 34, no. 10 (October 1997): 77–83.
13. For an interesting discussion of a nontraditional organization structure, see David M. Hehmann, "Integrated Enterprise Management: A Look at the Functions, The Enterprise, and the Environment—Can You See the Difference?" *Hospital Material Management Quarterly* 19, no. 4 (May 1998): 22–26.
14. Eric J. Walton, "The Persistence of Bureaucracy: A Meta-Analysis of Weber's Model of Bureaucratic Control," *Organization Studies* 26, no. 4: 569–600.
15. S.R. Maheshwari, "Hierarchy: Key Principle of Organization," *Employment News* 21, no. 49 (March 8-14, 1997): 1–2.
16. For a look at the concept of span of management in public organizations, see Kenneth Meier and John Bohte, "Span of Control and Public Organizations: Implementing Gullick's Research Design," *Public Administration Review* 63 (2003): 61.
17. Harold Koontz, "Making Theory Operational: The Span of Management," *Journal of Management Studies* (October 1966): 229–43; see also John S. McClenahen, "Managing More People in the '90s," Industry Week 238 (March 1989): 30–38.
18. For an account of how Corning Inc. organized its knowledge workers into an effective research and development department that exists to this day, see W. Bernard Carlson and Stuart K. Samms, "Revolution or Evolution?" The Role of Knowledge and Organizations in the Establishment and Growth of R & D at Corning," *Management & Organizational History* 4, no. 3 (2009): 37–65.

19. The U.S. space program offers an interesting study of the forms of work organization—both simple and complex—required to ultimately succeed in putting an astronaut on the moon. See Martin Parker, "Space Age Management," *Management & Organizational History* 4, no. 3 (2009): 317–332.
20. John R. Brandt, "Middle Management: 'Where the Action Will Be'," *Industry Week* (May 2, 1994): 30–36.
21. For a discussion of the benefits of tall structure, see Harold J. Leavitt, "Why Hierarchies Thrive," *Harvard Business Review* 81, no. 3 (2006): 96–102.
22. Andre Nelson, "Have I the Right Stuff to Be a Supervisor?" Supervision 51 (January 1990): 10–12. For a recent responsibility related trend, see "Office Professionals' Responsibilities Set to Soar," *British Journal of Administrative Management* (May/June 2001): 6.
23. Chuck Douros, "Clear Division of Responsibility Defeats Inefficiency," *Nation's Restaurant News* (February 21, 1967): 34–41.

Chapter 5

1. Taken from *Marketing: Defined, Explained, Applied,* 2e, by Michael Levens.
2. www.llbean.com/customerService/aboutLLBean/background.html?nav=In (accessed May 1, 2010).
3. www.reuters.com/article/pressRelease/idUS122196+27-Feb-2008+BW20080227 (accessed April 16, 2010); M. McCarthy, "Vegas Goes Back to Naughty Roots," *USA Today,* April 11, 2005, www.usatoday.com (accessed April 18, 2010).
4. http://adage.com/century/timeline/index.html (accessed April 20, 2010).
5. Ibid.
6. Ibid.
7. R. Jaroslovsky, review of Birth of a Salesman, by Walter A. Friedman, *Wall Street Journal,* "More Than a Shoeshine and a Smile," June 8, 2004.
8. Ibid.
9. "Consumer Interest in Socially Responsible Companies Rising, Survey Finds," July 16, 2007, http://www.GrenBiz.com/news/2007/07/15/consumer-interest-socially-responsible-companies-rising-survey-finds (accessed April 18, 2010).
10. www.firstgencom.com/blog/pepsi/20m-social-compaign/, www.refresheverything.com/ (accessed May 12, 2010).
11. P.F. Drucker, *Innovation and Entrepreneurship: Practice and Principle* (New York, HarperBusiness, 1985).
12. E. Wilson, "Swimsuit for the Olympics Is a New Skin for the Big Dip," *New York Times,* February 13, 2008, www.nytimes.com (accessed August 15, 2008); www.speedousa.com/shop/index.jsp?categoryId=3819798 (accessed May 3, 2010).
13. www.marketingpower.com (accessed May 2, 2010).
14. www.oswegocountybusiness.com/index.php?q=2675 (accessed July 13, 2010).
15. M. Williams, "Timeline: iTunes Store at 10 Billion," *Computerworld* (February 24, 2010) www.computerworld.com/s/article/9162018/Timeline_iTunes_Store_at_10_billion (accessed July 13, 2010); www.apple.com/itunes/what-is/ (accessed July 13, 2010).
16. R.T. Rust and A.J. Zahorik, "Customer Satisfaction, Customer Retention and Market Share," *Journal of Retailing* 69 (Summer 1993) 193–215; Chris Denove and James D. Power IV, *Satisfaction: How Every Great Company Listens to the Voice of the Customer* (New York, NY: Portfolio, 2006).
17. www.southwest.com/about_swa/press/factsheet.html#Recognitions (accessed May 10, 2010).
18. *Sprint Hangs Up on High-Maintenance Customers,* Reuters News Service (July 9, 2007).

19. V. Kumar, J,. Petersen, and R. P. Leone, "How Valuable Is Word of Mouth?" *Harvard Business Review* (October 1, 2007).
20. Purdue University Center for Customer Driven Quality, www.ccdq.com (accessed October 10, 2008).
21. www.wheresyours.com (accessed November 2, 2008).
22. F. Reichheld, *The Loyalty Effect* (Boston: Harvard Business School Press, 1996).
23. www.patronsocialclub.com (accessed November 2, 2008).
24. D. Peppers, M. Rogers, and B. Dorf, "Is Your Company Ready for One-to-One Marketing?" *Harvard Business Review* (January–February 1999).
25. www.marketwire.com/press-release/eMusic-Unveils-New-A-R-Access-Rewards-Benefits-Program-at-SXSW-1134342.htm (accessed June 8, 2010).
26. www.prlog.org/10145504-why-do-most-crm-projects-fail.html (accessed May 10, 2010).

Chapter 6

1. Taken from *Marketing: Defined, Explained, Applied* 2d ed., by Michael Leven.
2. http://www.cia.gov.library/publications/the-world-factbook/geos/us.html (accessed May 24, 2010).
3. P. Kotler and G. Armstrong, *Principles of Marketing* (Upper Saddle Rive, NJ: Prentice Hall, 2008), 239–240.
4. "The Big Ideas Behind Nintendo's Wii," BusinessWeek, November 16, 2006, www.businessweek.com/technology/content/nov2006/1116_750580.htm (accessed August 22, 2008); B. Bremner, "Will Nintendo's Wii Strategy Score?" BusinessWeek, Sept. 20, 2006, www.businessweek.com/globalbiz/content/sep2006/gb20060820_163780.htm (accessed August 22, 2008); "Press Release: Nintendo Wii Is Market Leader in Home Console Business," VGChartz.com, Aug. 22, 2007, http://news.vgchartz.com/news,php?id=508 (accessed October 1, 2008); www.nintendo.com (accessed May 24, 2010).
5. M. Solomon, G. Marshall, and E. Stuart, *Marketing* (Upper Saddle River, NJ: Prentice Hall, 2008), 239–240.
6. P. Kotler and G. Armstrong, *Principles of Marketing* (Upper Saddle River, NJ: Prentice Hall), 220–221.
7. M. Solomon, G. Marshall, and E. Stuart, *Marketing* (Upper Saddle River: NJ, 2008), 244–245.
8. Wrigley Company, 2007 *Annual Report,* http://libaray.corporateir.net/library/92/927/92701/items/278516/Wrigley2007QR.pdf (accessed August 21, 2008).
9. Computer Sciences Corporation (CSC), "Improving Product Success through Effective, Focused Speed to Market," www.csc.com/solutions/managementconsulting/knowledgelibrary/2115.shtml (accessed August 20, 2008).
10. P. Kotler and G. Armstrong, *Principles of Marketing* (Upper Saddle River, NJ: Prentice Hall, 2008), 254–263.
11. J. Quelch, *Cases in Product Management* (Burr Ridge, IL: Richard D. Irwin, Inc., 1995), 3–42.
12. P. Fish, *Marketing Genius* (West Sussex: Capstone, 2006), 214–215.
13. DuPont Company, Winners of the 19th DuPont awards for packaging innovation, www.dupont.com/Packaging/en_US/news_events/19th_dupont_packaging_award_winners.html (accessed August 20, 2008).
14. Target Company, ClearRx, http://sites.target.com/site/en/health/page.jsp?contentId=PRD03-003977 (accessed August 21, 2008).
15. P. Kotler and G. Armstrong, *Principles of Marketing* (Upper Saddle River, NJ: Prentice Hall, 2008), 229–231.
16. The Hershey Company, 2007 *Annual Report to Stockholders/Form 10-K,* February 19, 2008, 1–4.

17. J. Useem, "Internet Defense Strategy: Cannibalize Yourself," *Fortune,* September 6, 1999, http://money.cnn.com/magazines/fortune/fortune_archive/1999/09/06/26528/index.htm (accessed August 20, 2008).
18. M. Solomon, G. Marshall, and E. Stuart, *Marketing* (Upper Saddle River, NJ: Prentice Hall, 2008), 260–261.
19. K. Clancy and P. Krieg, "Product Life Cycle: A Dangerous Idea," *BrandWeek,* March 1, 2004, www.coperniusmarketing.com/about/product_life_cycle.shtml (accessed August 20, 2008).

Chapter 7

1. Taken from *Marketing: Defined, Explained, Applied,* 2d ed., by Michael Levens.
2. www.marketingpower.com (accessed May 1, 2010).
3. "Social Marketing Do's and Don'ts," *Adweek,* October 8, 2007; www.facebook.com (accessed May 2, 2010).
4. http://dpc.senate.gov/healthreformbill/healthbill63.pdf (accessed May 1, 2010); J. Jackson and J. Nolen, "Health Care Reform Bill Summary: A Look at What's in the Bill," *Political Hotsheet,* March 21, 2010, www.cbsnews.com/8301-503544_163-30000846-503544.html (accessed May 2, 2010).
5. www.onstar.com/us_english/jsp/index.jsp (accessed May 12, 2010).
6. J. Verdon, "Government Regulation Creates New Business Niche for Motor Oil Company," The Record, May 2, 2010.
7. www.irs.gov/newsroom/article/0,,id=206869,00.html (accessed May 2, 2010).
8. www.dominos.com/hom/tracker/pizzatracker.jsp (accessed May 1, 2010).
9. www.selig.uga.edu/forecast/GBEC/GBEC0703Q.pdf (accessed August 5, 2008).
10. Ibid.
11. www.marketingpower.com (accessed May 2, 2010).
12. Ibid.
13. Ibid.

Chapter 8

1. Taken from "Running Effective Meetings: Establishing an Objective and Sticking to It," www.mindtools.com.
2. Taken from *Developing Management Skills,* 8th ed., by David A. Whetten and Kim S. Cameron.
3. We are grateful to John Tropman, who prepared this section based on the material the authors had in the previous editions of *Competitive Effectiveness.*

Chapter 9

1. Adapted from *Modern Management: Concepts and Skills,* 12th ed., by Samuel C. Certo and S. Trevis Certo, Ch. 7.
2. For a discussion of U.S. shortsightedness in planning, See Michael T. Jacobs, "A Cure for America's Corporate Short-Termism," *Planning Review* (January/February 1992): 4–9. For a discussion of the close relationship between objectives and planning, see "Mistakes to Avoid: From a Business Owner," *Business Owner* (September/October 1994): 11.
3. For an overview of strategic planning, see Bryan W. Barry, "A Beginner's Guide to Strategic Planning," *The Futurist* 32, no. 3 (April 1998): 33–36.
4. See also Mike Deblieux, "The Challenge and Value of Documenting Performance," *HR Focus* (March 1994): 3. To better understand the role of setting objectives in

compensation plans, see William J. Liccione, "Effective Goal Setting: A Prerequisite for Compensation Plans with Incentive Value," *Compensation & Benefits Management* 13, no. 1 (Winter 1997): 19–25.

5. Robert L. Mathis and John H. Jackson, *Personnel: Human Resource Management* (St. Paul, MN: West Publishing, 1985), 353–355.
6. For an interesting examination of goal specificity, see Gerard J. Seijts, Gary P. Latham, Kevin Tasa, and Brandon W. Latham, "Goal setting and goal orientation: An integration of two different literatures," *Academy of Management Journal* 47, no. 2 (2004): 227–239.
7. The following is taken from *Fundamentals of Management: Essential Concepts and Applications,* Sixth Edition, by Stephen R. Robbins and David A. DeCenzo.
8. This material is adapted from Mindtools (www.mindtools.com), "Gantt Charts, Planning and Scheduling More Complex Projects."

Chapter 10

1. Taken from *Fundamentals of Management: Essential Concepts and Applications,* Sixth Ed., by Stephen P. Robbins and David A. DeCenzo.
2. Adapted from www.mindtools.com, "SWOT Analysis."
3. Ibid.
4. Taken from *Fundamentals of Management: Essential Concepts and Applications,* Sixth Ed., by Stephen P. Robbins and David A. DeCenzo.

Chapter 11

1. Taken from Michael R. Solomon, et al., *Marketing: Real People, Real Choices,* 7th edition.
2. James R. Bettman, "The Decision Maker Who Came in from the Cold," Presidential Address, in *Advances in Consumer Research,* vol. 20, ed. Leigh McAllister and Michael Rothschild (Provo, UT: Association for Consumer Research, 1990); John W. Payne, James R. Bettman, and Eric J. Johnson, "Behavioral Decision Research: A Constructive Processing Perspective," *Annual Review of Psychology* 4 (1992); 87–131; for an overview of recent developments in individual choice models, see Robert J. Meyer and Barbara E. Kahn, "Probabilistic Models of Consumer Choice Behavoir," in *Handbook of Consumer Behavior,* ed. Thomas S. Robertson and Harold J. Kassarjian (Englewood Cliffs, NJ: Prentice Hall, 1991), 85–123.
3. When habitual decision-making is referred to in this text, it also known as "routine" decision-making.
4. Amanda Mark, "Under Armour's Star Presence," *Multichannel Merchant News,* November 1, 2000 http://multichannelmerchant.com/news/marketing_armours_star_presence/ (accessed May 1, 2008).
5. Michael Lev, "No Hidden Meaning Here: Survey See Subliminal Ads," *New York Times,* May 3, 1991, D7.
6. "ABC Rejects KFC Commercial Citing Subliminal Advertising," The Wall Street Journal Interactive Edition, March 2, 2006.
7. Stuart, Elliot, "TV Commercials Adjust to a Shorter Attention Span," *New York Times Online,* April 8, 2005.
8. Robert M. McMath, "image Counts," *American Demographics,* May 1998, 64.
9. Abraham J. Maslow, *Motivation and Personality,* 2nd ed. (New York: Harper & Row, 1970).
10. Robert A. Baron and Donn Byrne, *Social Psychology: Understanding Human Interaction,* 5th ed. (Boston: Allyn & Bacon, 1987).
11. Ryan Nakashima, "Disney to create lab to test ads for ABC, ESPN," USA Today May 12, 2008, http://www.usatoday.com/tech/products/2008-05-121465558386_x.htm (accessed February 24, 2010).

12. http://www.jfmvipclub.com/jfm_styleguide.pdf (accessed February 24, 2010).
13. Bejamin D. Zablocki and Rosabeth Moss Kanter, "Differentiation of Life-Styles," *Annual Review of Sociology* (1976): 267–97; Ben Detrick, "Skateboarding Rolls Out of the Suburbs" *New York Times,* November 11, 2007, http://www.nytimes.com/2007/11/11/fashion/11skaters.html?scp=1&csq=skateboarding&st=nyt (accessed February 10, 2008).
14. Alfred S. Boote, "psychographics: Mind over Matter," American Demographics, April 1980, 26–29; William D. Wells, "Psychographics: A Critical Review," *Journal of Marketing Research,* 12 (May 1975): 196–213.
15. Alan R. Hirsch, "Effects of Ambient Odors on Slot-Machine Usage in a Las Vegas Casino," *Psychology & Marketing* 12, no. 7 (October 1995): 585–94.
16. James Vlahos, "Scent and Sensibility," *New York Times,* September 9, 2007, http://query.nytmes.com/gst/fullpage.html?res=9D07EFDC1E3AA3575AC0A9619C8B63&scp=1&sq=scent%20and%20sensibility&st=cse (accessed February 1, 2008).
17. Marianne Meyer, "Attention Shoppers!" Marketing and Media Decisions 23 (May 1988): 67.
18. Eben Shapiro, "Need a Little Fantasy? A Bevy of New Companies Can Help," *New York Times,* March 10, 1991, F4.
19. Quoted in John P. Cortex, "Ads Head for Bathroom," *Advertising Age,* May 18, 1992, 24.
20. Kerry Capel, "The Arab World Wants Its MTV," *BusinessWeek,* October 11, 2007, http://www.businessweek.com/globalbiz/content/oct2007/gb20071011_342851.htm.
21. Adapted from Michael R. Solomon, *Consumer Behavior: Buying, Having, and Being,* 9th ed. (Upper Saddle River, NJ: Prentice Hall, 2010).
22. Richard W. Pollay, "Measuring the Cultural Values Manifest in Advertising," *Current Issues and Research in Advertising* (1983); 71–92.
23. Emily Bryson York, "General Mills targets Three Groups to Fuel Growth," *Advertising Age,* February 16, 2010, http://adage.com/article?article_id=142138 (accessed February 20, 2010).
24. Ben Berkon, "Coca-Cola Comes Clean about Going Green at Olympic Games," *Brand-Channel,* February 1, 2010, http://www.brandchannel.com/home/post/2010/02/01/Coca-Cola-Comes-Clean-About-Going-Green-At-Olympic-Games.aspx (accessed February 3, 2010).
25. Nathan Kogan and Michael A. Wallach, "Risky Shift Phenomenon in Small Decision-Making Groups: A Test of the Information Exchange Hypothesis," *Journal of Experimental Social Psychology* 3 (January 1967): 75–84; Arch G. Woodside and M. Wayne DeLozier, "Effects of Word-of-Mouth Advertising and Consumer Risk Taking," Journal of Advertising (Fall 1976): 12–19.
26. Everett M. Rogers, *Diffusion of Innovations,* 3rd ed. (New York: Free Press, 1983).
27. Carlo Dellaverson, "Tailgating: It's Bigger Business Than You Think," CNBC.com, December 21, 2006, http://www.cnbc.com/id/16315025/fpr/cnbc (accessed May 6, 2007).
28. Kathleen Debevec and Easwar Iyer, "Sex Roles and Consumer Perceptions of Promotions, Products, and Self: What Do We Know and Where Should We Be Headed," in Advances in Consumer Research, vol. 13, ed. Richard J. Lutz (Provo, UT: Association for Consumer Research, 1986), 210–214; Lynn J. Jaffe and Paul D. Berger, "Impact on Purchase Intent of Sex-Role Identity and Product Positioning," *Psychology & Marketing* (Fall 1988): 259–271.
29. Jennie Yabroff, "Girls Going Mild(er): A New 'Modesty Movement' Aims to Teach Young Women They Don't Have to Be Bad, or Semiclad," *Newsweek* (July 23, 2007), http://bounds.youthnoise.com/eve/forums/a/tpc/f/573295355/m/38310644 (accessed July 18, 2007).
30. Diego Rinallo, "MetroFashion/Tribes of Men: Negotiating the Boundaries of Men's Legitimate Consumption" in B. Cova, R. Kozinets, and A. Shankar, eds., *Consumer Tribes: Theory, Practice and Prospects* (Burlington, MA: Elsevier/Butterworth-Heinemann, 2007); Susan Kaiser, Michael R. Solomon, Janet Hethorn, Basil Englis, Van Dyk Lewis, and Wi-Suk Swon, "Menswear, Fashion, and Subjectivity," paper

presented in Special Session: Susan Kaiser, Michael Solomon, Janet Hethorn, and Basil Englis (Chairs), "What Do Men Want? Media Representations, Subjectibity, and Consumption," at the ACR Gender Conference, Edinburgh, Scotland, June 2006.

31. Catharine Skipp and Arian Campo-Flores, "Looks: A Manly Comeback," Newsweek (August 20, 2007), http://services. Newsweek.com/search.aspx?offset=0&pageSize=10&sortField=pubdatetime&sortDirection=descending&mode=summer&q=Looks%2C+a+manly+comeback (accessed August 17, 2007).
32. "National Poll Reveals the Emergence of a 'New Man'," Miller Brewing Co., PR *Newswire,* http://goliath.ecnext.com/coms2/summary_0199-5364500_ITM (accessed May 14, 2008).

Chapter 12

1. Adapted from *Fundamentals of Management: Essential Concepts and Applications,* 8th ed., by Stephen Robbins, et al.
2. L. Festinger, *A Theory of Cognitive Dissonance* (Stanford, CA: Stanford Univeristy Press, 1957); C. Crossen, "Cognitive Dissonance Became a Milestone in 1950s Psychology," *Wall Street Journal,* December 4, 2006, p. B1; and Y. "Sally" Kim, "Application of the Cognitive Dissonance Theory to the Service Industry," *Services Marketing Quarterly,* April–June 2011, pp. 96–112.

Chapter 13

1. Dan Frommer, "Apple iPod Still Obliterating Microsoft Zune," *Business Insider,* July 12, 2010, http://read.bi/axUYCO.
2. Carey Toane, "Listening: The New Metric," *Strategy,* September 2009, p. 45.
3. Warren Thayer and Michael Sansolo, "Walmart: Our Retailer of the Year," *R&FF Retailer,* June 2009, pp. 14–20; and information from http://walmartstores.com/Suppliers/248.aspx, accessed December 2011.
4. See Scott Horstein, "Use Care with That Database," *Sales & Marketing Management,* May 2006, p. 22; "USAA Announces Mobile RDC App for Android Phones," *TechWeb,* January 27, 2010; "USAA," *Hoover's Company Records,* June 15, 2010; Jean McGregor, "Customer Service Champs: USAA's Battle Plan," *Bloomberg Businessweek,* March 1, 2010, pp. 40–43; "Largest U.S. Corporations," *Fortune,* May 3, 2010, p. F7; and www.usaa.com, accessed September 2011.
5. Based on information from Adam Ostrow, "Inside the Gatorade's Social Media Command Center," June 6, 2010, accessed at http://mashable.com/2010/06/15/gatorade-sical-media-mission-control/; and Valery Bauerlein, "Gatorade's 'Mission': Using Social Media to Boost Sales," *Wall Street Journal Asia,* September 15, 2010, p. 8.
6. Irena Slutsky, "'Chief Listeners Use Technology to Track, Sort Company Mentioned," *Advertising Age,* August 30, 2010, accessed at http://adage.com/digital/article?article_id5145618.
7. See http://biz.yahoo.com/ic/101/101316.html, accessed September 2011.
8. For more on research firms that supply marketing information, see Jack Honomichl, "2010 Honomichl Top 50," special section, *Marketing News,* June 17, 2010. Other information from www.nielsen.com/us/en/measurement/retail-measurement.html and www.yankelovich.com, accessed September 2011.
9. See http://symphonyiri.com/?TabId5159&productid584, accessed September 2011.
10. Example adapted from Dana Flavelle, "Kraft Goes Inside the Kitchen of the Canadian Family," *Toronto Star,* January 16, 2010, www.thestar.com/business/article/751507.

For other examples, see Philip Kotler and Kevin Lane Keller, *Marketing Management*, 14th ed. (Upper Saddle River, NJ: Prentice Hall, 2012), p. 101.

11. For more discussion of online ethnography, see Pradeep K. Tyagi, "Webnography: A New Tool to Conduct Marketing Research," *Journal of American Academy of Business*, March 2010, pp. 262–268; Robert V. Kozinets, "Netnography: The Marketer's Secret Weapon," March 2010, accessed at http://info.netbase.com/rs/netbase/images/Netnography_WP.; and http://en.wikipedia.org/wiki/Online_ethnography, accessed September 2011.
12. Example adapted from information found in "My Dinner with Lexus," *Automotive News*, November 29, 2010, accessed at www.autonews.com/apps/pbcs.dll/article?AID 5/20101129/RETAIL03/311299949/1292.
13. See www.internetworldstats.com/stats14.htm, accessed July 2011.
14. Based on information found at www.channelm2.com/HowOnlineQualitative Research.html, accessed December 2011.
15. See "Online Panel," www.zoomerang.com/online-panel/, accessed December 2011.
16. Derek Kreindler, "Lexus Soliciting Customer Feedback with Lexus Advisory Board," August 24, 2010, accessed at www.autoguide.com/auto-news/2010/08/lexus-soliciting-customer-feedback-with-lexus-advisory-board.html; and "20,000 Customers Sign up for the Lexus Advisory Board," August 30, 2010, accessed at www.4wheelsnews.com/20000-customers-signed-up-for-the-lexus-advisory-board/.
17. Stephen Baker, "The Web Knows What You Want," *BusinessWeek*, July 27, 2009, p. 48.
18. Adapted from Brooks Barnes, "Lab Watches Web Surfers to See Which Ads Work," *New York Times*, July 26, 2009; and "Walt Disney Company's Media Networks to Develop Emerging Media and Advertising Research Lab," accessed at http://corporate.disney.go.com/corporate/moreinfo/media_advertising_research_lab.html, August 2011.
19. Jessica Tsai, "Are You Smarter Than a Neuromarketer?" *Customer Relationship Management*, January 2010, pp. 19–20.
20. For these and other neuromarketing examples and discussion, see Laurie Burkitt, "Neuromarketing: Companies Use Neuroscience for Consumer Insights," *Forbes*, November 16, 2009, www.forbes.com; Ilan Brat, "The Emotional Quotient of Soup Shopping," *Wall Street Journal*, February 17, 2010, p. B6; Natasha Singer, "Making Ads That Will Spur the Brain," *New York Times*, November 14, 2010, p. BU4; and Deena Diggs, "Emotional Marketing," *Editor & Publisher*, January 2010, p. 7.
21. Example adapted from information found in Dan Sewell, "Kroger Uses Shopper Data to Target Coupons," *Huffington Post*, January 6, 2009, www.huffingtonpost.com/2009/01/06/kroger-uses-shopper-data_n_155667.html; and Dan Sewell, "Kroger CEO Often Roams Aisles, Wielding Carte Blanche," *Journal-Gazette* (Ft. Wayne, IN), November 15, 2010, p. C4.
22. Gillian S. Ambroz, "Is This Just: Getting Back to Basics," *Folio*, January 2010, p. 97.
23. "SAS helps 1-800-Flowers.com Grow Deep Roots with Customers," www.sas.com/success/1800flowers.html, accessed September 2011.
24. See www.pensketruckleasing.com/leasing/precision/precision_features.html, accessed September 2011.

Chapter 14

1. This material is adapted from Chapter 15, "Supportive Communications and Feedback," *Competitive Effectiveness*, 0-558-5672-7. This information was originally taken from *Developing Management Skills*, Eight Ed., by David A Whetten and Kim S. Cameron.

Chapter 15

1. Taken from Marketing: Defined, Explained, Applied, 2d ed., by Michael Levens.
2. A. Bianco, "The Vanishing Mass Market," *BusinessWeek,* July 12, 2004, www.businessweek.com/magazine/content/04-28/b3891001_mz001.htm (accessed August 13, 2008).
3. Ibid.
4. W. DeSarbo, "Market Segmentation Practices Are Totally Inadequate," *Ascribe Newsline,* June 15, 2001.
5. A. Dexter, "Egoists, Idealists, and Corporate Animals—Segmenting Business Markets," *International Journal of Market Research* 1, no. 44 (2002): 31.
6. www.glaceau.com (accessed July 11, 2010).
7. www.curves.com (accessed May 23, 2010); "Fitness Club Is Fastest-Growing U.S. Franchise," *Voice of America,* January 27, 2006, www.voanews.com/english/archive/2006-01/2005-01=27-voa18.cfm (accessed August 5, 2008).
8. www.moosejaw.com (accessed May 23, 2010).
9. W. Kamakura and T. Novak, "Value-System Segmentation: Exploring the Meaning of LOV," *Journal of Consumer Research* 19, no. 1 (June 1992): 119–132.
10. www.chase.com (accessed May 23, 2010).
11. K. O'Brien, "Nokia Deal Aimed at Opening Up Mobile Software," *International Herald Tribune,* June 24, 2008, www.iht.com/articles/2008/06/24/business /symbian.php (accessed July 21, 2008; M. Ahmad, "Nokia Middle East and Africa Marks the Holy Month with the Launch of Ramadan Applications for Mobile Users Worldwide," *Business Intelligence Middle East,* July 13, 2008, 222.bi-me.com/main.php?id=23493&t=1&c=129&cg=4&mset=1201 (accessed July 23, 2008); www.nokia.com (accessed May 23, 2010).
12. S. Dibb and L. Simkin, "Market Segmentation: Diagnosing and Treating the Barriers," *International Marketing Management* 30, no. 8 (2001): 21–39.
13. D. Rowell, "All About Satellite Phone Service," *Travel Insider,* April 22, 2008, www.thetravelinsider.info/phones/aboutsatellitephoneservice.htm (accessed August 21, 2008); www.iridium.com (accessed July 24, 2008).
14. www.ford.com (accessed May 23, 2010).
15. www.mcdonalds.com (accessed July 22, 2008).
16. www.movado.com (accessed July 23, 2008).
17. S. Dibb and L. Simkin, "Market Segmentation: Diagnosing and Treating the Barriers," *International Marketing Management* 30, no. 8 (2001): 21–39.
18. www.apple.com (accessed May 23, 2010); D. Coursey, "The Un-Vision: What Steve Jobs Won't Do at Apple," ZDNet, February 7, 2002, http://review.zdnet.com/4520-6033_16_4205922.html (accessed July 24, 2008); R. Hof, "100 Million iPods Sold, But How Many Are Still in Use?" *BusinessWeek,* April 9, 2007, www.businessweek.com/the_thread/techbeat/archives/2007/04/100_million_ipo.html (accessed July 24, 2008).
19. "Gas-Saving Sedans," *Consumer Reports,* July 2008; www.greencarcongress.com/2010/04/hybrids-20100405.html (accessed May 23, 2010).
20. B. Calder and S. Reagan, "Brand Design," in *Kellogg on Marketing,* ed. D. Iacobucci (New York: John Wiley & Sons, 2001), 61.
21. www.focushope.com (accessed May 23, 2010).

Chapter 16

1. Taken from *Marketing: Defined, Explained, Applied,* 2d ed., by Michael Levens.
2. H. Arnold, "Brand Aid," *Financial Management* (November 2001): 33–34.
3. P. Tmeporal, *Advanced Brand Management—From Vision to Valuation* (Singapore: John Wiley & Sons, 2002).

4. "Ethnic Consumers More Receptive Than Peers to Marketing, But Most Believe Messaging Lacks Relevancy, According to New Yankelovich Study," www.hiphoppress.com/2007/09/ethnic-consumer.html (accessed July 30, 2008).
5. Ibid.
6. D. Abrahams and e. Granof, "Respecting Brand Risk," *Risk Management* 4, no. 49 (2002): 40.
7. S. Broniarczyk and A. Gershoff, "The Reciprocal Effects of Brand Equity and Trivial Attributes," *Journal of Marketing Research* (May 2003): 161.
8. S. Hoeffler and K. Keller, "Building Brand Equity Through Corporate Societal Marketing," *Journal of Public Policy and Marketing* 21, no. 1 (2002): 78–89.
9. L. Williams, "What Price a Good Name?" *Business,* May 5, 2002, 23.
10. D. Abrahams and E. Ganof, "Respecting Brand Risk," *Risk Management* 4, no. 49 (2002): 40.
11. Ibid.
12. www.businessweek.com/interactive_reports/best_global_brands_2009.html (accessed May 22, 2010).
13. A. Abela, "additive Versus Inclusive Approaches to Measuring Brand Equity: Practical and Ethical Implications," *Journal of Brand Management* 10, no. 4/5 (2003): 342.
14. A Chaudhuri and M. Holbrook, "The Chain of Effects from Brand Trust and Brand Effect to Brand Performance: the Role of Brand Loyalty," *Journal of Marketing* 65, no. 2 (2001): 81–93.
15. S. Hoeffler and K. Keller, "Building Brand Equity Through Corporate Societal Marketing," *Journal of Public Policy and Marketing* 21, no. 1 (2002): 78–89.
16. Ibid.
17. www.prnewswire.com/news-releases/victorias-secret-pink-and-major-legue-baseball-properties-announce-new-co-branded-collection-87663702.html (accessed May 23, 2010).
18. V. Kamar, "Segmenting Global Markets: Look Before You Leap," *Marketing Research* 13, no. 1 (2001): 8–13.
19. www.ikea.com//us/en (accessed July 30 2008).
20. D. D'Alessandro and M. Owens, *Brand Warfare: 10 Rules for the Killer Brand* (New York: McGraw-Hill, 2002).
21. Ibid.
22. J. Mass, "Pharmaceutical Brands: Do They Really Exist?" *International Journal of Medical Marketing* 2, no. 1 (2001): 8–13.
23. NPR, "The Fall of Enron," www.npr.org/news/specials/enron/ (accessed August 25, 2008).
24. A. Rattray, "Measure for Measure: Brand Value May Be Relative But It Is Measurable, Either from a Company or a Consumer Point of View," *Financial Times,* July 9, 2002, 12.
25. S. Davis, *Brand Asset Management: Driving Profitable Growth Through Your Brands,* 2d ed. (San Francisco: John Wiley & Sons, 2002).
26. www.traderjoes.com (accessed May 23, 2010).
27. www.southerncomfort.com (accessed May 23, 2010); www.kemps.com (accessed May 15, 2010).
28. www.eddiebauer.com/custserv/custserv/jsp?sectinId=601 and www.fordvehivles.com/suvs/expedition/trim/?trim=eddiebaurer&showCategoryTab=viewAll (accessed July 11, 2010).
29. D. Arnold, *The Handbook of Brand Management* (London: Century Business, 1992).
30. www.crayola.com (accessed July 14, 2008).
31. M. Yadav "How Buyers Evaluate Product Bundles: A Model of Anchoring and Adjustment," *Journal of Consumer Research* 21, no. 2 (1994): 342.
32. T. Leopold, "Advertising Builds Character," *CNN.com,* www.cnn.com/2004/SHOWBIZ/08.18/eye.ent.advertising/index.html (accessed August 2, 2008).
33. T. Amobi, "Disney: Mouse on the Move," *BusinessWeek,* May 7, 2007, www.businessweek.com/investor/content/may2007/pi20070507_602321.htm (accessed July 26, 2008).

34. P. Svensson, "Cut Rate Prepaid Plans Shake Up Wireless Industry," *Knoxville News*, April 20, 2009, www.knoxnews.com/news/2009/apr/20/cut-rate-prepaid-plans-shake-wireless-industry/ (accessed May 23, 2010).

Chapter 17

1. Taken from *Fundamentals of Management: Essential Concepts and Applications*, 8th ed., by Stephen P. Robbins, et al.
2. D. K. Berlo, *The Process of Communication* (New York: Holt, Rinehart & Winston, 1960, pp. 30–32.
3. Ibid.
4. See, for instance, "Get the Message: Communication Is Key in Managing Change within Organizations—Yet Ensuring its Effectiveness at Times of High Concerns Can Be Tricky," *Employee Benefits*, February 2002, pp. 58–60.
5. L. R. Birkner and R. K. Birkner, "Communication Feedback: Putting It All Together," *Occupational Hazards*, August 2001, p. 9.
6. L. Hilton, "They Heard It Through The Grapevine," *South Florida Business Journal*, August 18, 2000, p. 53.
7. L. Talley, "Body Language: Read It or Weep," HR Magazine, July 2010, pp. 64–65; and M. Fulfer, "Nonverbal Communication: How to Read What's Plain as the Nose… Or Eyelid…Or Chin…On Their Faces," *Journal of Occupational Excellence* (Spring 2001), pp. 19–38.
8. Ibid; and T. Fernsler, "The Secrets and Science of Body Language," *Nonprofit World*, p. 25.
9. P. Mornell, "*The Sounds of Silence*," *Inc.*, February 2001, p. 117.
10. A. Warfield, "Do You Speak Body Language?" *Training and Development* (April 2001), p. 60.
11. S. Begley, "I Can't Think," *Newsweek*, March 7, 2011, pp. 28–33; D. Dean and C. Webb, "Recovering from Information Overload," *McKinsey Quarterly*, Issue 1, 2011, pp. 80–88.
12. "Gobbledygook Begone," Workforce, February 2002, p. 12; and "Business Speak," *Training and Development* (January 2002), pp. 50–52.
13. See, for example, M. K. Kozan, "Subcultures and Conflict Management Styles," *Management International Review*, January 2002, pp. 89–106.
14. A. Mehrabian, "Communication Without Words," *Psychology Today*, September 1968, pp. 53–55.
15. See also W. L. Adair, T. Okumura, and J. M. Brett, "Negotiation Behavior When Cultures Collide: The United States and Japan, *Journal of Applied Psychology* (August 2001), p. 583.
16. See, for instance, S. P. Robbins and P. L. Hunsaker, *Training in Interpersonal Skills*, 4e (Upper Saddle River, NJ: Prentice-Hall, 2006); M. Young and J. E. Post, "Managing to Communicate, Communicating to Manage; How Leading Companies Communicate with Employees," *Organizational Dynamics*, Summer 1993, pp. 31–43; J. A. DeVito, *The Interpersonal Communication Book*, 6th ed. (New York: HarperCollins, 1992); and A. G. Athos and J. J. Cabarro, *Interpersonal Behavior* (Upper Saddle River, NJ: Prentice Hall, 1978).
17. From MindTools (www.mindtools.com), "Writing Skills: Getting Your Message Across Clearly," by James Manktelow & Amy Carlson.

Chapter 18

1. Taken from *Fundamentals of Management: Essential Concepts and Applications*, Sixth Ed., by Stephen P. Robbins and David A. DeCenzo.
2. Taken from *Fundamentals of Management: Essential Concepts and Applications*, Sixth Ed., by Stephen P. Robbins and David A. DeCenzo.

Chapter 20

* Answers: (1) Red Bull energy drink, (2) GEICO Insurance, (3) the Energizer Bunny, (4) "your way," "char," (5) Bounty paper towels.

1. Taken from Solomon, *Marketing: Real People, Real Choices,* 7th ed.
2. http://adage.com/digital/article?article_id=121406.
3. Schultz, Don E. and Heidi Schultz (2003), IMC. The next generation. Five steps for delivering value and measuring returns using marketing communication, New York: McGraw Hill, 20–21.
4. Barbara Lippert, "Windowns Debut: Almost 7th Heaven," *Adweek,* October 26, 2009, http://www.adweek.com/aw/content_display/creative/critique/e3i7a4f853fe47e-4cob5bf8e3a501635ead (accessed May 12, 2009).
5. Gert Assmus, "An Empirical Investigation into the Perception of Vehicle Source Effects," *Journal of Advertising* 7 (Winter 1978): 4-10; for a more thorough discussion of the pros and cons of different media, see Stephen Baker, *Systematic Approach to Advertising Creativity* (New York: McGraw Hill, 1979).
6. Taken from *Marketing: Defined, Explained, Applied,* Levens, 2d ed.
7. N. O'Leary and T. Wasserman, "Old Spice Campaign Smells Like a Sales Success, Too," July 25, 2010, www.brandweek.com/bw/content_display/news-and-features/direct/e3i45f1c709df0501927f56568a2acd5c7b?pn-2 (accessed September 1, 2010).
8. "Media Use Statistics," Media Literacy Clearinghouse, www.franwbaker.com/mediause.htm (accessed July 30, 2010).
9. S. Berg. Advertising in the World of New Media," in *Kellogg on Advertising & Media,* ed. B. Calder (Hoboken, NJ: John Wiley & Sons, 2008).
10. P. Kotler and G. Armstrong, *Principles of Marketing* (Upper Saddle River, NJ: Prentice Hall, 2008), 436.
11. *The Nielsen Company Issues Top Ten U.S. Lists for 2007,* Nielsen Media Research, December 11, 2007, www.nielsen.com (accessed September 14, 2008).
12. P. Farris, N. Bendle, P. Pfeifer, and D. Reibstein, *Marketing Metrics: 50+ Metrics Every Executive Should Master* (Upper Saddle River, NJ: Wharton School Publishing, 2007), 275.
13. S. Berg, "Advertising in the World of New Media," in *Kellogg on Advertising & Media,* ed. B. Calder (Hoboken, NJ: John Wiley & Sons, 2008).
14. L. Moses, "Best Use of Print," *Adweek,* June 16, 2008.
15. The Pew Research Center for the People & the Press, "Key News Audiences Now Blend Online and Traditional Sources," August 17, 2008, http://people-press.org/report/444/news-media (accessed September 15, 2008).
16. D. Oulette, "unfit to Print," September 24, 2007, www.mediaweek.com (accessed November 1, 2008).
17. J. Sissors and R. Baron, *Advertising Media Planning,* 6th ed. (New York: McGraw Hill, 2002), 342–343.
18. L. Miles, "Out of Sight," September 24, 2007, www.mediaweek.com (accessed November 1, 2008).
19. S. Berg, "Advertising in the World of New Media," In *Kellogg on Advertising & Media,* ed. B. Calder (Hoboken, NJ: John Wiley & Sons, 2008).
20. IAB, "Internet Ad Revenues Reach Record Quarterly High of $6.3 Billion in Q4 '09," www.iab.net/about_the_iab/recent_press_releases/press_release_archive/press_release/pr-040710 (accessed July 30, 2010).

21. M. Shields, "Digital Destiny," September 24, 2007, www.mediaweek.com (accessed November 1, 2008).
22. M. Shields, "Best Use of Mobile," *Adweek*, June 16, 2008.
23. J. M. Lehu, Branded Entertainment (London: Kogan, 2006), 254.
24. Ibid., 142–143.
25. J. Sissors and R. Baron, *Advertising Media Planning*, 6th ed. (New York: McGraw-Hill, 2006), 215.
26. R. Lane, K. King, and J. Rusell, *Kleppner's Advertising Procedure* (Upper Saddle River, NJ: Prentice Hall, 2008), 254.
27. Taken from *Marketing Defined, Explained, Applied*, 2d ed Levens.
28. D. Hayman and D. Schultz, "Measuring Returns on Marketing and Communications Investments," *Strategy & Leadership* 3, No. 27 (1999): 26.
29. Ibid.
30. "Loyalty Highest for Pet Food Shoppers," *Quirk's Marketing Research Review* 16, No. 11 (2002): 72–73.
31. www.millwardbrown.com/Sites/MillwardBrown/Content/Services/Link360.aspx (accessed April 2, 2010).
32. www.nytimes.com/2009/02/23/business/media/23adcol.html?_r=1 (accessed March 15, 2010).

Chapter 21

1. Taken from *Marketing: Real People, Real Choices* 7th ed., by Michael R. Solomon, Greg W. Marshall, Elnora W. Stuart.
2. Bradley Johnson, "Top 100 Outlays Plunge 10% But Defying Spend Trend Can Pay Off," *Advertising Age*, June 21, 2010, 1, 10–11.
3. Bradley Johnson, "Agency Report 2010," *Advertising Age*, April 26, 2010, 22-23.
4. Bradley Johnson, "Top 100 Outlays Plunge 10% But Defying Spend Trend Can Pay Off," *Advertising Age*, June 21, 2010, 1, 10–11.
5. "What Consumers Watch: Nielsen's Q1 2010 Three Screen Report," Nielsen Wire, June 11, 2010, http://blog.nielsen.com/nielsenwire/online_mobile/what-consumer-watch-nielsens-q1-2010-three-screen-report/ (accessed October 10, 2010).
6. William Wells, John Burnett, and Sandra Moriarty, *Advertising: Principles and Practice*, 5th ed. (Englewood Cliffs, NJ: Prentice Hall, 2000).
7. Rance Crain, "Dow's Corporate Ads Have Great Chemistry, But Will Respect Follow?" *Advertising Age*, August 6, 2007, http://adage.com/columns/article?article_id=119676 (accessed May 22, 2010).
8. John M. Broder, "Governors Join in Creating Regional Pacts on Climate Change," *New York Times*, November 15, 2007, http://www.nytimes.com/2007/11/15/washington/15climate.html?scp=1&sq=governors+join+in+creating+regaional&st=nyt (accessed June 8, 2008).
9. Bob Garfield, "PSA Won't Change Perennial Parental Bleacher Creatures," *Advertising Age*, April 14, 2008, http//adage.com/Garfield/post?article_id=126354&search_phrase=PSA (accessed April 19, 2008).
10. Bradley Johnson, "Agency Report 2010," *Advertising Age*, April 26, 2010, 22–33.
11. Stuart Elliott, "Do It Yourself Super Ads," *The New York Times*, February 9, 2010, B3.
12. Julie Bosman, "Chevy Tries a Write-Your-Own-Ad Approach, and the Potshots Fly," *New York Times*, April 4, 2006, Section C, 1.
13. "Customer Made," Trend-watching.com, www.trendwatching.com/briefing/; "Generation C," http://www.trendwatching.com/trends/GENERATION_C.htm
14. Karen E. Klein, "Should Your Customers Make Your Ads?" *Business Week Online*, January 3, 2008, p. 9.
15. Abe Sauer, "D.C. Lottery Gambles on New Logo," *Brandchannel*, February 23, 2010, http://www.brandchannel.com/hom/post/2010/02/23/DC-Lottery-Gambles_On-New-Logo.aspx (accessed March 15, 2010).

16. Emma Hall, "In Greece, Kraft Scores a Kit for Lacta Chocolate with Crowdsourced Film," *Advertising Age*, March 24, 2010, http://adage.com/globalnews/article?article_id=142950 (accessed march 25, 2010).
17. Federal Trade Commission, *FTC Policy Statement on Deception*, October 14, 1983, www.ftc.govbcp/policystmt/ad-decept.htm (accessed July 2, 2006); Dorothy Cohen, *Legal Issues in Marketing Decision Making* (Cincinnati: South-Western College Publishing, 1995).
18. Natasha Singer, "A Birth Control Pill That Promised Too Much," *The New York Times*, February 11, 2009, B1.
19. Leslie Kaufman, "Enough Talk," *Newsweek*, August 18, 1997, 48–49.
20. "Index to the 100 Leading National Advertisers," *Advertising Age*, June 20, 2007, http://adage.com/datacenter/article?article_id=118652&search_phrase=top+ad+spenders+2007 (accessed April 21, 2008).
21. Peter Cornish, personal communication, March 2010.
22. Kate Macarthur, "Why Big Brands Are Getting into the Ring," *Advertising Age*, May 22, 2007, http://adage.com/print?article+id=116722 (accessed April 21, 2008).
23. Jeremy Lee, "Ofcom Bans Follow-Up Renault Megane Spot," *Campaign*, August 6, 2004, 10.
24. Russ Johsephs, "I'd Like to Buy the World a (Virtual) Coke, and Keep It Company," *Brandchannel*, January 28, 2010, http://www.brandchannel.com/home/post/2010/01/29/le28099d-Like-To-Buy-The-World-A-%28Virtual%29-Coke-And-Keep-It-Company.aspx (accessed April 15, 2000).
25. Stephanie Kant, "magic of Clorox Sells for a Song," *Wall Street Journal*, March 28, 2008, http://online.wsj.com/article/AB120666813235770429;html (Accessed April 17, 2008).
26. James Berrinder, "Tech Box Meuromarketing: Ad Agency Bark Gets Emotional with Neuromarketing Technology," *Research-live.com*, 28 April 2010, http://www.research-live.com/news/new-business/ad-agency-bark-gets-emotional-with neuromarketing-technology/4001806 (accessed April 15, 2010).
27. Christopher Rocchio, "Report: Writers Strike Spikes 'American Idol' Ad Rates to $1 Million Plus," *Radio-TV World*, January 14, 2008, http://www.realitytvworld.com/news/report-writers-strike-spikes-american-idol-ad-rates-1-million-plus-6390.php (accessed April 21, 2008).
28. "TV Advertising Is Less Effective: Survey," *PROMO Magazine*, www.promomagazine.com/news/tvadvertising_survey_032406/index/html (accessed July 29, 2006).
29. "Who Owns What," *Columbia Journalism Review*, http://www.cjr.org/resources/ (accessed April 18, 2008).
30. Phil Hall, "Make Listeners Your Customers," *Nation's Business*, June 1994, 53R.
31. Jack Neff, "Viva Viva! K-C Boosts Brand's Marketing," *Advertising Age*, June 11, 2007, 4.
32. Sean Corcoran, "Defining Earned, Owned and Paid Media," Forrester Blogs, December 16, 2009, http://blogs.forrester.com/interactive_marketing/2009/12/defining-earned-owned-and-paid-media.html (accessed April 27, 2010).
33. "Internet Advertising Revenues Again Reach New Highs, Estimated to Pass $21 Billion in 2007 and Hit Nearly $6 Billion in Q4 2007, February 25, 2008," press release, Interactive Advertising Bureau, http://www.iab.net/about-the-iab/recent_press_releases/press_archive/pressPrelease/195115 (accessed April 21, 2008).
34. Kevin J. Delaney, "Once Wary Industry Giants Embrace Internet Advertising," *Wall Street Journal*, April 17, 2006, A1.
35. Michael McCarthy, "Companies Are Sold on Interactive Ad Strategy," *USA Today*, March 3, 2000, 1B.
36. Louise Story, "Online Pitches Made Just for You," *New York Times*, March 6, 2008, 7.
37. Ann M. Mack, "Got E-Mail," *Brandweek*, March 20, 2000, 84–88.
38. Mobile Marketing Association, "Mobile Marketing Industry Glossary," http://www.mobilemarketer.com/cms/news/messaging/3002.html (accessed April 27, 2010).
39. Kumar Patel, "How the iAd Gave mobile marketing needed Short in Arm," *Advertising Age*, September 13, 2010, M-2–M-3; Rich Karpinski, "Why Mobile Advertising

Networks Are on the Cusp of Real Change," *Advertising Age*, September 13, 2010, M-2–M-3.

40. Dan Butcher, "Kellogg Runes MMS Campaign for Cereal Recipes," *MobileMarketer .com*, April 9, 2009, http://www.mobilemarketer.com/cms/news/messaging/2002 .html (accessed April 27, 2010).
41. Giselle Tsirulnik, "Oprah Grows Mobile Media Empire," MobileMarketer.com, April 26, 2010, http://www.mobilemarketer.com/cms/news.media/6075.html (accessed April 27, 2010).
42. Claire Cain Miller, "Take a Step Closer for an Invitation to Shop," *The New York Times*, February 24, 2010, B4.
43. Lon Safko and David K. Brake, *The Social Media Bible* (Hoboken, NJ: John Wiley & Sons).
44. Bruce Schreiner and Emily Fredrix "KFC Pays Indiana Cities for 'Fiery' Ad Space" (January 6, 2010), Indystar.com, (accessed January 25, 2010).
45. Ethan Smith and Sabrina Shankman, "Fellow Graduates, Before We Greet the Future, a Word from My Sponsor," *Wall Street Journal* (July 28, 2009, wsj.com/.../ sb124873785621885167..., (accessed January 28, 2009).
46. Irina Slutsky, "Meet YouTube's Most In-Demand Brand Stars," *Advertising Age*, September 13, 2010, 8.
47. Sheila Shavonm "Adidas Steps into the World of Augmented Reality," Brandchannel.com, January 27, 2010, http://www.brandchannel.com/home/post/2010/01/27/ Adidas-Steps-Into-The-World-Of-Augmented-Reality.aspx (accessed April 15, 2010).
48. Amy-Mae Elliott, "10 Amazing Augmented Reality iPhone Apps," *Mashable*, http:// mashable.com/2009/12/05/augmented-reality-iphone/ (accessed April 15, 2010).
49. Karl Greenberg, "Audi Ties R8 to Promotion of 'Iron Man,' Due Out May 2," *Marketing Daily*, April 23, 2008, http://publications.mediapost.com/index .cfm?fuseaction=Articles.san&s=81185&Nid-41887&p=941737 (accessed April 23, 2008).
50. Andrew Hampp, "in This Year's Upfront, It's All About Branded Entertainment," *Advertising Age*, May 26, 2008, http://adage.com/print?article_id=127312 (accessed June 6, 2008).
51. "Interactive Advertising Revenues to Reach $147B Globally, $62.4B in US," The Kelsey Group, http://www.marketingcharts.com/direct/interactive-advertising-revenues-to-reach-147b-globally-624b-in-us-3567/ (accessed April 21, 2008).
52. www.adweek.com/aw/content_display/news/agency/e3i9ee4b481143e87d75b-75c7e38e0a3f84, (accessed March 25, 2010).
53. Louise Story, "Away from Home, TV Ads Are Inescapable," *New York Times*, March 2, 2007, 6.
54. Jeremy Wagstaff, "Loose Wire—Bootleg Backlash: Software Industry Groups Are Snooping for People Using Pirated Software; But Their Assumption about Who's a Pirate Seem Awfully Mixed Up," July 31, 2003, *Far Eastern Economic Review*, 31.
55. Bristol Voss, "Measuring the Effectiveness of Advertising and PR," *Sales & Marketing Management*, October 1992, 123–24.
56. This remark has also been credited to a British businessmen named Lord Leverhulme; see Charles Goodrum and Helen Dalrymple, *Advertising in America: The First 200 Years* (New York: Harry N. Abrams, 1990).
57. Stuart Elliott, "New Survey on Ad Effectiveness," April 14, 2004, http://qury.nytimes .com/search/query?frpw=0&n=10&srcht=s&query=new+survey+on+ad+effectivene ss&srcjst=nyt&submit.x=0&submit=sub&c
58. Kate Fitzgerald, "Homemade Bikini Contest Hits Bars, Beach for 10th Year," *Advertising Age*, April 13, 1998, 18.
59. Alan J. Liddle, "Guilty Pleas End Wendy's Finger-Pointing, But Will They Inspire Leniency in Sentencing," *Nation's Restaurant News*, September 19, 2005, 202; Johnathan Birchall, "Jail for Wendy's Finger Claim Couple," *Financial Times*, January 19, 2006, 25.

60. "Jail for Wendy's Finger Scam Couple," CBS News, January 18, 2006; http://www.cbsnews.com/stories/2006/11/18/national/main1218315.shtml (accessed June 9, 2008).
61. "Man Who Put Dead Mouse in Burrito at Taco Bell Given Prison Time," FoxNews.com, http://www.foxnews.com/story/0,2933,197993,00.html (accessed June 9, 2008).
62. The Star-Ledger Continuous News Deal," Apple iPad tablet is unveiled at live press conference," January 27, 2010, http://www.nj.com/business/index.ssf/2010/01/apple_ipad_tablet_is_unveiled.html (accessed March 15, 2010).
63. Andy Pasztor, "FAA Ruling on Long-Haul Routes Would Boost Boeing's Designs," *Wall Street Journal*, June 5, 2006, A.3.
64. Amy Chozick, "StarPower: The LPGA Is Counting on a New Marketing Push to Take Women's Golf to the Next Level," *Wall Street Journal*, June 12, 2006, R.6.
65. Michael R. Solomon, Greg W. Marshall and Elnora W. Start, *Marketing: Real People, Real Choices*, 6th ed. (2009).
66. Carol Driver, "Five-Minute YouTube apology from Toyota boss as first lawsuit filed over faulty pedal recall," *Daily Mail*, February 5, 2010, http://www.dailymail.co.uk/news/article-1248588/Five-minute-YouTube-apology-Toyota-boss-lawsuit-filed-faulty-pedal-recall.html (accessed March 15, 2010).
67. Quoted in Michelle Kessler, "IBM Graffiti Ads Gain Notoriety," *USA Today*, April 26, 2001, 3B.
68. Howard Stumpf and John M. Kawula, "Point of Purchase Advertising," in *Handbook of Sales Promotion*, ed. S. Ulanoff (New York: McGraw Hill, 1985); Karen A. Berger, *The Rising Importance of Point-of-Purchase Advertising in the Marketing Mix* (Englewood Cliffs, NJ: Point-of-Purchase Advertising Institute).
69. Gardiner Harris, "Drug Makers Offer Consumers Coupons for Free Prescription—But Patients Still Have to Get Their Physician's Approval, and Most Don't Pay for Pills," *Wall Street Journal*, March 13, 2002, B1.
70. "Virgin Atlantic Rolls Out Space Miles," *PROMO Magazine*, http://promomagazine.com/incentives/virgin_atlantic_miles_011106/index.html (accessed June 12, 2006).
71. Michael Fielding, "C'est Delicieux," *Marketing News*, September 15, 2010, 10.
72. This section based on material presented in Don E. Schultz, William A. Robinson, and Lisa A. Petrison, *Sales Promotion Essentials*, 2d ed. (Lincolnwood, IL: NTC Business Books, 1993).
73. "Ben and Jerry's Launches Ice Cream Flavor Contest," *PROMO Magazine*, http://promomagazine.com/news/benjerrycontest_031606/index.html (accessed March 16, 2006).
74. "Lengthy Research Leads Disney to Global 'Dreams' Theme," *PROMO Magazine*, http://promomagazine.com/research/disney_reseasrch_061206/index.html (accessed June 12, 2006).
75. "Consumers Vote for Oreo Idol," *PROMO Magazine*, http://promomagazine.com/contests/news/oreo_idol__contest_061206/index.html (accessed June 9, 2008).
76. Kerry J. Smith, "It's for You," *PROMO Magazine*, August 1994, 41(4); Sharon Moshavi, "Please Deposit No Cents," *Forbes*, August 16, 1993, 102.
77. Amanda Beeler, "Package-Goods Marketers Tune In Free-Sampling Sites," *Advertising Age*, June 12, 2000, 58.

Chapter 22

1. Taken from *Marketing: Defined, Explained, Applied*, 2e, by Michael Levens.
2. Woodstream Corp., Victor, www.victorpest.com (accessed March 27, 2010).
3. Microsoft Corp., "Communities," www.microsoft.com/communities/defalt.mspx (accessed March 27, 2010).
4. "The Story of Cotton," Cotton's Journey, www.cottonsjourney.com/Storyofcotton/page7.asp (accessed March 12, 2010).

Chapter 23

1. Taken from *Marketing: Defined, Explained, Applied, 2d* ed., Levens.
2. Inline footnote 5, p. 247, Levens.
3. Inline footnote 6, p. 247, Levens.
4. Inline footnote 8, p. 248, Levens.
5. Inline footnote 9, p. 248, Levens.
6. Inline footnote 10, p. 248, Levens.
7. Inline footnote 11, p. 248, Levens.
8. Inline footnote 12, p. 248, Levens.
9. Taken from Tuten & Solomon, *Social Media Marketing.*
10. Taken from Armstrong and Kotler, *Marketing: An Introduction,* 11ed.
11. Inline footnote 34, p. 437, Armstrong.
12. Inline footnote 35, p. 438, Armstrong.
13. Inline footnote 36, p. 438, Armstrong.
14. Inline footnote 37, p. 439, Armstrong.
15. Inline footnote 38, p. 439, Armstrong.
16. Inline footnote 39, p. 439, Armstrong.
17. Inline footnote 40, p. 440, Armstrong.
18. Inline footnote 41, p. 440, Armstrong.
19. Inline footnote 42, p. 440, Armstrong.
20. Inline footnote 43, p. 440, Armstrong.
21. Inline footnote 44, p. 440, Armstrong.
22. Inline footnote 45, p. 441, Armstrong.
23. Inline footnote 46, p. 441, Armstrong.
24. Inline footnote 47, p. 440, Armstrong.
25. Inline footnote 48, p. 440, Armstrong.
26. Inline footnote 49, p. 440, Armstrong.
27. Inline footnote 50, p. 443, Armstrong.
28. Taken from Tuten & Solomon, *Social Media Marketing,* pp. 14-18.
29. Inline footnote 10, p. 14, Tuten.
30. Inline footnote 11, p. 15, Tuten.
31. Inline footnote 12, p. 18, Tuten.
32. Taken from Tuten & Solomon, *Social Media Marketing,* p. 203-211.
33. J. Sterne, *Social Media Metrics* (Hoboken, NJ: Wiley & Sons, 2010). p. 4.
34. J. Sterne, *Social Media Metrics* (Hoboken, NJ: Wiley & Sons, 2010).
35. Zachary Sniderman, "5 Winning Social Media Campaigns to Learn From," September 14, 2010, http://mashable.com/2010/09/14/social-media-campaigns/, accessed December 27, 2010.
36. J. R. Roy, "Marketing Metrics and ROI: How to Set Up a Measurement System That Can Double Your Profitability," 2009, www.marketing-metrics-made-simple.com/index.html, accessed September 19, 2010.
37. Fraser Likely, David Rockland, and Mark Weiner, "Perspectives on the ROI of Media Relations Publicity Efforts, Institute for Public Relations," Institute for Public Relations, 2006, www.instituteforpr.org/research_single/perspectives_on_the_roi/, accessed December 26, 2010.

Chapter 24

1. Taken from *Marketing: An Introduction*, 11th Edition, by Gary Armstrong and Philip Kotler.
2. Adapted from material found in Jeff Heilman, "Rules of Engagement," *The Magazine of Branded Engagement*, Winter 2009, pp. 7-8; and "Mattel's The Playground Community Created by Communispace Helps Them Weather Recall," accessed at

www.communispace.com/uploadedFiles/Clients_section/Forrester_Groundswell/Groundswell_Mattel.pdf, August 2011.

3. See The World Bank, "The Costs of Corruption," April 8, 2004, accessed at http://tinyurl.com/ytavm; "Bribe Payers Index 2008," *Transparency International*, www.transparency.org/policy_research/surveys_indices/bpi; and "Global Corruption Barometer 2010," *Transparency International*, www.transparency.org/policy_research/survey_indices/gcb/2010. Also see Michael Montgomery, "The Cost of Corruption," *American RadioWorks*, http://americanradioworks.publicradio.org/features/corruption/, accessed June 2011.
4. See www.marketingpower.com/AboutAMA/Pages/Statement%20of%20Ethics.aspx, accessed November 2011.
5. See Samuel A. DiPiazza, Jr., "Ethics in Action," Executive Excellence, January 2002, pp. 15–16; "Interview: Why Have a Code?" accessed at www.pwc.com/gx/en/ethics-business-conduct/why-have-a-code-interview.jhtml, August 2011; Samuel A. DiPiazza Jr., "It's All Down to Personal Values," August 203, accessed at www.hollywoodreporter.com/hr/search/article_display.jsp?vnu_content_id=2000910; and "Ethics and Business Conduct," www.pwc.com/ethics, accessed November 2011.
6. DiPiazza, "Ethics in Action," p. 15.

Chapter 25

1. Taken from *Marketing: Defined, Expained, Applied*, 2d ed., by Michael Levens.
2. H. Italie, "Potter, At the Speed of Light," *Washington Post*, July 26, 2007, www.washingtonpost.com/wp-dyn/content/article/2007/07/26/AR2007072601339_of.html (accessed August 25, 2008); J. Trachenberg and J. DeAvila, "Mischief Unmanaged," *Wall Street Journal*, July 19, 2007; D. Foust, "Harry Potter and the Logistical Nightmare," *BusinessWeek*, August 6, 2007.
3. M. Hugos and C. Thomas, *Supply Chain Management in the Retail Industry* (Hoboken, NJ: John Wiley & Sons, 2006).
4. Ibid.
5. M. Solomon, G. Marshall, and E. Stuart, *Marketing* (Upper Saddle River, NJ: Prentice Hall, 2008).
6. Ibid.
7. U.S. Census Bureau, *Annual Retail Trade Report, 2008*, www.census.gov/retail/ accessed July 12, 2010).
8. U.S. Census Bureau, *2010 Statistical Abstract*, www.census.gov/compendia/statab/cats/income_expenditures_poverty_wealth/gross-domestic_product_gdp.html (accessed July 12, 2010).
9. Bureau of Labor Statistics, *US Expenditures*, 2008.
10. M. Solomon, G. Marshall, and E. Stuart, *Marketing* (Upper Saddle River, NJ: Prentice Hall, 2008).
11. Ibid.
12. P. Kotler and G. Armstrong, *Principles of Marketing*, 12th ed. (Upper Saddle River, NJ: Prentice Hall, 2008).
13. A. O'Connell, "Improve Your Return on Returns," *Harvard Business Review* (November 2007).
14. D. Blanchard, *Supply Chain Management—Best Practices* (Hoboken, NJ: John Wiley & Sons, 2007).
15. Inline footnote 9, p. 213, Levens.
16. D. Blanchard, *Supply Chain Management—Best Practices* (Hoboken, NJ: John Wiley & Sons, 2007).
17. U.S. Department of Transportation, *Maritime Administration, 2008 U.S. Water Transportation—Statistical Snapshot*, July 2009, www.marad.dot.gov/documents/US_Water_Transportation_Statistical-snapshot.pdf (accessed July 27, 2010).

18. www.alyeska-pipe.com/pipelinefacts.html (accessed June 27, 2010).
19. D. Blanchard, *Supply Chain Management—Best Practices* (Hoboken, NJ: John Wiley & Sons, 2007).
20. American Marketing Association, *Resource Library—Dictionary*, www.marketing-power.com/_layouts/Dictionary.aspxdLetter=W (accessed September 5, 2008).
21. R. Heinlein, *The Moon Is a Harsh Mistress* (New York: G.O. Putnam's Sons, 1966).
22. www.apple.com (accessed November 1, 2008);C. Sorrel, "Apple's iPod Strategy: Aggressive Prices, Overwhelming Feature," *Wired Magazine*, September 6, 2007, www.wired.com/gadgets/ortablemusic/news/2007/09/ipod_follow (accessed September 10, 2008); E. Hesseldahl, "Are There Problems with iPod Sales?" *BusinessWeek*, February 22, 2008, www.busioniessweek.com/teechnology/ButeOfTheAple/blog/archives/2008/02/is_there_troubl.html (accessed September 10, 2008; www.apple.com/itunes/ (accessed May 24, 2010).
23. Air Transport Association, *Quarterly Cost Index: US. Passenger Airlines*, September 9, 2008, www.airlines.org/economics/finance/Cost+Index.htm (accessed September 9, 2008).
24. P. Farris, N. Bendle, P. Pfeifer, and D. Reibsten, *Marketing Metrics* (Philadelphia: Wharton School Publishing, 2006).
25. S. Maxwell, *The Price Is Wrong* (Hoboken, NJ: John Wiley & Sons, 2008), 41–44.
26. www.amazon.com (accessed September 17, 2008).
27. R. Baker, *Pricing on Purpose* (Hoboken, NJ: John Wiley & Sons, 2006).
28. J. Cooper, "Prices and Price Dispersion in Online and Offline Markets for Contact Lenses" (Working paper, Bureau of Economics, April 2006).
29. I. Sinha, "Cost Transparency: the Net's Real Threat to Prices and Brands," *Harvard Business Review* (March–April 2008).
30. I. Peel, *The Rough Guide to eBay* (London: Penguin, 2006); 2007 *eBay Annual Report, 2008*, www.eBay.com (accessed September 10, 2008); www.shareholder.com/visitors/dynamicdoc.cfm?CompanyID=ebay&DocumentID=22868PIN=&Page=4&Zoom=1x (accessed September 10, 2008).
31. S. Coomes, "The Big Chase," *Nation's Restaurant News* 34 (January 28, 2008).

Appendix A

1. Taken from *Marketing, An Introduction, 11e*, Armstrong/Kotler, ISBN-13: 9780132744034.
2. This is derived by rearranging the following equation and solving for price: Percentage markup = (price – cost) ÷ price.
3. Again, using the basic profit equation, we set profit equal to ROI × I: ROI × I = (P × Q) – TFC – (Q × UVC). Solving for Q gives Q = (TFC + (ROI × I)) ÷ (P – UVC).
4. U.S. Census Bureau, available at www.census.gov/prod/1/pop/p25-1129.pdf, accessed October 26, 2009.
5. See Roger J. Best, *Market-Based Management,* 4th ed. (Upper Saddle River, NJ: Prentice Hall, 2005).
6. Total contribution can also be determined from the unit contribution and unit volume: Total contribution = unit contribution × unit sales. Total units sold in 2012 were 595,238 units, which can be determined by dividing total sales by price per unit ($100 million ÷ $168). Total contribution = $35.28 contribution per unit × 595,238 units = $20,999,996.64 (difference due to rounding).

7. Recall that the contribution margin of 21 percent was based on variable costs representing 79 percent of sales. Therefore, if we do not know price, we can set it equal to \$1.00. If price equals \$1.00, 79 cents represents variable costs and 21 cents represents unit contribution. If price is decreased by 10 percent, the new price is \$0.90. However, variable costs do not change just because price decreased, so the unit contribution and contribution margin decrease as follows:

	Old	**New (reduced 10 percent)**
Price	\$1.00	\$0.90
– Unit variable cost	\$0.79	\$0.79
= Unit contribution	\$0.21	\$0.11
Contribution margin	\$0.21/\$1.00 = 0.21 or 21%	\$0.11/\$0.90 = 0.12 or 12%

Index

Note: Page numbers followed by *f* and *t* indicate figures and tables, respectively.

D

T

U

V

W

Y

Z